A

GEOGRAPHICAL, STATISTICAL,

AND

HISTORICAL DESCRIPTION

OF

THE DISTRICT, OR ZILA,

OF

DINAJPUR,

IN

THE PROVINCE, OR SOUBAH,

OF

BENGAL

A

GEOGRAPHICAL, STATISTICAL,

AND

HISTORICAL DESCRIPTION

OF

THE DISTRICT, OR ZILA,

OF

DINAJPUR,

IN

THE PROVINCE, OR SOUBAH,

OF

BENGAL

FRANCIS BUCHANAN (HAMILTON)

GYAN

Published by

GYAN

Gyan Publishing House
5, Ansari Road
Daryaganj, New Delhi-110002
Phone: 011-47034999, 9811692060
E-mail: books@gyanbooks.com

Distribution Network
gyanbooks.com
India, USA, Canada, UK, Australia

ISBN: 978-93-6780-148-2 (PB)

First Published, 1833

2nd Impression 2024

Printed at: Gyan Press, Delhi.

A GEOGRAPHICAL, STATISTICAL, AND HISTORICAL DESCRIPTION OF THE DISTRICT, OR ZILA, OF DINAJPUR, IN THE PROVINCE, OR SOUBAH, OF BENGAL

Author: FRANCIS BUCHANAN (HAMILTON)

A

GEOGRAPHICAL, STATISTICAL,

AND

HISTORICAL DESCRIPTION

OF

THE DISTRICT, OR ZILA,

OF

DINAJPUR,

IN

THE PROVINCE, OR SOUBAH,

OF

BENGAL.

BY

DOCTOR FRANCIS BUCHANAN (HAMILTON).

PUBLISHED WITH THE MONTHLY NUMBERS

OF THE

GLEANINGS IN SCIENCE,

AND

THE JOURNAL OF THE ASIATIC SOCIETY.

Calcutta:

PRINTED AT THE BAPTIST MISSION PRESS, CIRCULAR ROAD.

1833.

PREFACE.

In 1807, the Directors of the East India Company having recommended that a full and accurate Statistical Survey of the territories under the immediate authority of the Presidency of Fort William should be executed, for the purpose of obtaining such information on the real state of the country as might be productive of future improvement and advantage, the Governor General Lord Minto resolved, that Dr. Francis Buchanan, whose abilities and experience were justly considered by the court to qualify him in a peculiar degree for such an investigation, should be appointed to this duty.

The extent and variety of the objects to which his attention was to be directed, will be understood from the following extract from the instructions drawn up by the Seeretary to Government for his guidance :

" Your inquiries are to extend throughout the whole of the territories subject to the immediate authority of the Presidency of Fort William.

" The Governor General in Council is of opinion, that these inquiries should commence in the district of Rungpúr, and that from thence you should proceed to the westward through each district on the north side of the Ganges, until you reach the western boundary of the Honorable Company's provinces. You will then proceed towards the south and east, until you have examined all the districts on the south side of the great river, and afterwards proceed to Dacca, and the other districts towards the eastern frontier.

" It is also desirable, that you should extend your inquiries to the adjacent countries, and to those petty states with which the British Government has no regular intercourse. In performing this duty, however, you are prohibited from quitting the Company's territories, and are directed to confine your inquiries to consulting such of the natives of those countries as you may meet with, or natives of the British territories who have visited the countries in question.

" Your inquiries should be particularly directed to the following subjects, which you are to examine with as much accuracy as local circumstances will admit.

" I. A *Topographical* account of each district, including the extent, soil, plains, mountains, rivers, harbours, towns, and subdivisions ; together with an account of the air and weather, and whatever you may discover worthy of remark concerning the *history* and *antiquities* of the country.

"II. *The Condition of the Inhabitants;* their number, the state of their food, clothing, and habitations; the peculiar diseases to which they are liable; together with the means that have been taken or may be proposed to remove them; the education of youth; and the provision or resources for the indigent.

"III. *Religion;* the number, progress, and most remarkable customs of each different sect or tribe of which the population consists; together with the emoluments and power which their priests and chiefs enjoy; and what circumstances exist or may probably arise that might attach them to Government, or render them disaffected.

"IV. The *Natural Productions of the Country,* animal, vegetable, and mineral; especially such as are made use of in diet, in medicine, in commerce, or in arts and manufactures. The following objects deserve your particular attention:

"1st. The *fisheries*, their extent, the manner in which they are conducted, and the obstacles that appear to exist against their improvement and extension.

"2nd. The *forests,* of which you will endeavour to ascertain the extent and situation, with respect to water-conveyance. You will investigate the kinds of trees which they contain, together with their comparative value, and you will point out such means, as occur to you, for increasing the number of the more valuable kinds, or for introducing new ones that may be still more useful.

"3rd. The *mines* and *quarries* are objects of particular concern. You will investigate their produce, the manner of working them, and the state of the people employed.

"V. *Agriculture*, under which head your inquiries are to be directed to the following points:

"1st. The different kinds of *vegetables* cultivated, whether for food, forage, medicine, or intoxication, or as raw materials for the arts: the modes of cultivation adopted for each kind; the seasons when they are sown and reaped; the value of the produce of a given extent of land cultivated with each kind; the profit arising to the cultivator from each, and the manner in which each is prepared and fitted for market. Should it appear that any new object of cultivation could be introduced with advantage, you will suggest the means by which its introduction may be encouraged.

"2nd. The *implements of husbandry* employed, with the defects and advantages of each, and suggestions for the introduction of new ones, that may be more effectual.

"3rd. The manure employed for the soil, especially the means used for irrigation.

"4th. The means used for excluding floods and inundations, with such remarks, as may occur to you, on the defects in their management, and the remedies that might be employed.

"5th. The different breeds of the *cattle, poultry, and other domestic animals* reared by the natives. The manner in which they are bred and kept; the profits derived from rearing and maintaining them; the kinds used in labour; whether the produce of the country be sufficient, without importation, to answer the demand, or to enable the farmer to export; and whether any kinds not now reared might be advantageously introduced.

"6th. *Fences*, the various kinds, that are used, or that might be introduced, with observations concerning the utility of this part of agriculture in the present state of the country.

"7th. The state of *farms*; their usual size, the stock required, with the manner in which it is procured; the expense of management; the rent, whether paid in specie, or in kind; the wages and condition of farming servants and labourers employed in husbandry; tenures by which farms are held, with their comparative advantages, and the means which, in your opinion, may be employed to extend and improve the cultivation of the country.

"8th. The *state of the landed property*, and of the *tenures* by which it is held, in so far as these seem to affect agriculture.

"VI. The progress made by the natives in the *fine arts*, in the *common arts*, and the state of the *manufactures*; you will describe their architecture, sculptures, and paintings, and inquire into the different processes and machinery used by their workmen, and procure an account of the various kinds and amount of goods manufactured in each district. It should also be an object of your attention to ascertain the ability of the country to produce the raw materials used in them; and what proportion, if any, is necessary to be imported from other countries, and under what advantages, or disadvantages, such importation now is, or might be made; you will also ascertain how the necessary capital is procured, the situation of the artists and manufactures, the mode of providing their goods, the usual rates of their labour; any particular advantages they may enjoy, their comparative affluence with respect to the cultivators of the land, their domestic usages, the nature of their sales, and the regulations respecting their markets. Should it appear to you that any new art or manufacture might be introduced with advantage into any district, you are to point out in what manner you think it may be accomplished.

"VII. *Commerce*; the quantity of goods exported and imported in each district; the manner of conducting sales, especially at fairs and markets; the regulation of money, weights, and measures; the nature of the conveyance of goods by land and water, and the means by which this may be facilitated, especially, by making or repairing roads.

"In addition to the foregoing objects of inquiry, you will take every opportunity of forwarding to the Company's Botanical Garden at this presidency, whatever useful or rare and curious plants and seeds you may be enabled to acquire in the progress of your researches, with such observations as may be necessary for their culture."

In pursuance with these instructions, Dr. Buchanan was occupied, during the years 1807, 8, 9, 10, and 11 in a minute survey of the districts of Dinájpur, Rangpur, Púraniya, Bhagelpúr, Behár, and the city of Patna, Sháhabád, and Gorakhpur. Upon each of these districts he submitted a voluminous report, accompanied with statistical tables, maps, and drawings, and where an opportunity was afforded him of collecting it, with collateral information illustrative of the people, or of the geography and natural history, of the neighbouring countries; thus the report on Púraniya embraces an account of Nipal, and of the Sikkim country; the report on Bhagulpúr contains vocabularies of the languages spoken by the hill tribes of that district, compared with the Hindí; and that of Behar exhibits a similar vocabulary of the Dhangar and Bengalí dialects.

The original records, occupying twenty-five folio volumes in manuscript, were transmitted by the Indian Government to the Honorable Court of Directors; a copy of the whole having been previously made, and deposited in the office of the Chief Secretary at Calcutta. Duplicates of the drawings and maps, however, were unfortunately not preserved with the rest, probably from the difficulty at that time of getting them executed in India.

It is matter of surprise and regret, that these valuable documents were not given to the public when stamped with the interest of originality and immediate applicability to the actual circumstances of the districts, and when they would have proved of great utility to the public officers of Government. Although, however, no immediate steps were taken for their publication in an entire form, we learn from the preface to Hamilton's Hindústan, that the Honorable Court allowed the author of that useful compilation the freest access to the manuscripts of Doctor BUCHANAN, and it must be confessed that much of the information they contain has been condensed into the body of that work, throughout the pages of which continual references will be seen to the *Buchanan manuscripts.*

The readers of the Journal of the Asiatic Society are aware of the manner in which the arrangement for their publication in the present form originated. Captain J. D. HERBERT, Editor of the GLEANINGS IN SCIENCE, being anxious to secure to his subscribers a privilege which should render the support of his journal less burdensome to the few and scattered cultivators of scientific knowledge in India, negociated with the Government for permission to circulate the work free of postage on condition of devoting monthly a certain number of pages (stipulated at not less than eight) to the publication "of valuable official documents, having reference to public utility." The privilege was accorded by the Government; and the first volume of the reports, being the statistic account of Dinájpur, was placed in his hands, by Mr. G. SWINTON, Chief Secretary to Government, who had been warmly interested in the promotion of the scheme. The Editor of the GLEANINGS, in fulfilling the conditions of his agreement, wisely determined to print the documents in a separate form, rather than incorporate detached portions of them as separate articles in the body of his journal. "On a full consideration of the subject," he says, in his notice to Subscribers, dated April, 1832, "we deemed the latter course the preferable one; particularly, considering the very full information contained in these journals, and that it related to the least known districts, as well as the great pains taken in the arrangement of all the particulars. It was thought that to break down and throw into detached pieces a work which the author had taken so much trouble to systematize, would be to lose one of the principal features of excellence which distinguish these records."

It has necessarily occupied many months to complete the present volume, under such circumstances; but the delay will not have caused much inconvenience, if the subscribers to the GLEANINGS and the JOURNAL have attended to the injunction, frequently repeated, that the scattered sheets should be reserved with care to be put together in the form of a separate volume.

It will be remarked, that many plates are referred to in the text: the drawings alluded to, as has already been stated, are in possession of the Honorable Court of Directors. It was thought better to preserve the references as they stood in the manuscript, in case the Honorable Court should hereafter be induced to publish them, either in a separate form, or of a size adapted to the present volume.

The interest which the work may command among the Subscribers to the Journal, and with the public at large, will determine how far it may be advisable to continue the publication of the remainder of the series, or whether they may for the present give way to other "official documents," of a more exclusively scientific nature.

ARRANGEMENT OF THE VOLUME.

ACCOUNT

OF THE

DISTRICT OR *ZILA* OF DINÁJPÚR.

BOOK I.

TOPOGRAPHY AND ANTIQUITIES.

CHAPTER I.

EXTENT, GENERAL APPEARANCE, AND SOIL.

§ 1.—*Extent and Boundaries.*

THE district or *zila* of Dinájpúr, which forms the extent of the jurisdiction of a Judge and Magistrate, and of a Collector, is situated in the northern part of Bengal. Its greatest length from its southern extremity, at the junction of the Punabhoba[1] with the Mohanonda, to its northern extremity, on the Nagor, is 105 B. miles. Its greatest breadth, near its southern, and between the Korotoya and Nagor, is 82 B. miles. It is somewhat of a triangular form, with its most acute angle to the north; its longest side to the N. E., and its shortest to the south. It extends from 24° 48′ to 26° 18′ N. Lat., and its southern extremity is exactly in the meridian of Calcutta.

The western boundary of this dictrict is very well defined. It is separated from that of the Puroniya by the rivers Nagor and Mohanonda, to the junction of the latter with the Punabhoba.

Its boundary on the south, with Rajshahi, is not only destitute of any natural marks, which indeed were not easily procurable; but winds about and intersects these districts in a manner that is very inconvenient, both in the administration of justice, and in the support of the police. This I suppose originally arose from an inclination to accommodate the different proprietors of estates, to whom it is inconvenient and expensive to possess lands in two different jurisdictions, as they must employ an agent at each: but as estates are frequently changing their boundaries, and as in the case in question, the estates have been entirely altered, it would perhaps occasion, on the whole, less inconvenience, were the boundary to be rendered somewhat straight, and were detached portions added to the district by which they are surrounded.

On the east this district is separated from Rangpur by a river, which owing to frequent changes, that will hereafter be explained, has different names in different

[1] These statements are given on the supposition that Major Rennell's Maps are exact. The subdivisions on these Maps are not adapted to the present state of the country, but to the zemindaries or estates that existed when they were constructed, and which are now entirely altered.

parts of its course, but which is usually called the Korotoya. Towards the north the boundary of these two districts is less clearly defined, but is not liable to any particular objection, as it is tolerably straight, and as there are no portions detached.

Dinajpur, as represented in Major Rennell's maps, consisted entirely of a large estate which belonged to a family that resided at the town of this name, and contained between three and four thousand square miles. The *sila* or present district, however, is much more extensive, and by tracing its boundaries, as nearly as I can, on Major Rennell's map, and estimating the extent, I find that it contains 5374 square B. miles. Such a manner of estimating the extent of the country, I am aware, is liable to several objections :—it is merely an approximation to the real situation and extent, founded on the best documents within my reach.

§ 2.—*Soil.*

The soil, when dry, is in general of a very light ash colour, often almost white, but becomes dark when moist. In a few places, however, chiefly near the Korotoya, the soil is a very red and stiff clay. Such soil, wherever found, seems to be called *Ranggamate*, and many places derive their name from this circumstance; for in Bengal this kind of soil is rather unusual. The common ash coloured soil, which occupies more than 99 per cent. of the whole district, is of two kinds.

The one, in dry weather, becomes exceedingly hard and impenetrable, and retains very little moisture, so that in the heats of spring it is entirely destitute of vegetation. In wet weather again, it changes into a soft sticky mud. This is called *Khyarand Matiyal.* The first expresses its parched state during the dry season. The latter is said to be a provincial corruption for *Athia*, which implies its sticky quality during the rainy season. Another derivation is given of the first appellation; it is said to signify saline or alkaline, and much land in Bengal is, no doubt, of that nature : but this is by no means the case in Dinajpur.

The other ash coloured soil contains a much larger proportion of sand, on which account, it is said to be mixed (*Doangsh*). This is much more retentive of moisture than the purer clay, and in the dry season produces more vegetation. Its tenacity also being diminished by the mixture of sand; even the wretched implements and cattle of the natives are able to penetrate it in the dry season, so that it produces a crop with the early rains of spring, while the hard clay is still impenetrable to the plough.

The greater part of the stiff land produces, therefore, only one crop of rice, which is sown in the middle of the rainy season; but with the occasional rains, that happen in winter and the early part of spring, some portion, often a considerable one, is ploughed, and then produces two crops of rice.

A great proportion of the mixed land produces either two crops of that grain, or a great *variety* of valuable articles, that grow in the dry season. On this account it is frequently called *Poli* or the nourishing soil.

Much confusion, however, prevails in the application of the terms *Khyar* and *Poli*. Mr. Hatch, when he made the settlement of the estate of Dinajpur family, assumed this distinction, as the foundation of his estimate. He considered as *Khyar* all such land as produced only one crop, and as *Poli* all such as was capable of producing two crops in the year. As, however, some of the former is really more valuable than much of the latter, many exceptions were made, and much land really of a stiff soil is reckoned *Poli,* while much of a mixed soil is only considered as *Khyar*. Among this last may especially be mentioned the sandy banks of many rivers, which do not contain clay enough to enable them to produce many rich crops, but which are very capable of producing certain articles with the early rains of spring. The soil is usually called *Chora* by the natives, as being situated on the bank of a river, or *Baliya* as consisting mostly of sand. The extent of this cannot exceed $\frac{3}{8}$ per cent. of the land in this district, while the red earth may occupy $\frac{1}{2}$ per cent. the real *Doangsh* 46, and the *Khyar* 73.

§ 3.—*Elevation and Appearance.*

Although there is nothing in the whole district, that approaches to the elevation of a mountain, yet the face of the country is by no means so level as that of Bengal. In general many parts are more entitled to the appellation of hill than the elevation in His Majesty's green park. In fact, some parts rise to a considerable height, especially a long ridge extending north from the town of Dinájpúr almost to Kantonogor, and a considerable elevation N. E. from Nalogola, on the banks of the Brohmani river, which at least rise 100 feet perpendicular height above the level of the inundated country. Although these can scarcely deserve a place in a map, yet as the various degrees of elevation occasion a most essential difference in the produce of the country, they deserve the most minute attention in this inquiry.

In the first place, near several of the rivers, especially the Nagor, Mahanonda, Tanggon, and lower part of the Punabhoba, a great deal of land is so low, that every rainy season it is inundated to a great depth, and owing to this circumstance is considered by the natives as almost unfit for cultivation. Many people have imagined, that in level alluvial countries, which are liable to inundation, the banks of the rivers, owing to a more copious deposition of sediment, are higher than the more remote parts. In many cases this may be true, but in this district the parts near rivers are generally not higher than those more remote, and in many places they are much lower. I should imagine that about 7 per cent. of the whole land in this district may be overflown in the rains, and considered, on that account, as nearly incapable of cultivation.

The inundated land of a stiffer soil is not all a perfect flat: its surface, in many places, rises into considerable swells; so that, while some portions are covered with 20 feet of water, others are covered with very little, and some project like islands. This is peculiarly the case near the Mahanonda and Nagor rivers, where the most extensive inundations take place, and where a considerable part of this inundated land is cultivated. The higher spots afford situations for villages, but it has often been necessary to assist nature by digging tanks, and to raise the foundations of the houses with the earth thrown out by this operation. It is much to be lamented that the cultivation of these lands could not be farther extended; for the soil, although in some places covered by the beds of sand, is in general remarkably rich; while in its present state the value of its produce is very small, being chiefly a wretched pasture, and long reeds, which are applied to several uses, as will hereafter be described. The advantage, however, arising from either the pasture or the reeds, is much more than counterbalanced by the destruction which is occasioned by the wild animals that such waste land harbours, especially deer, buffaloes, and hogs.

In this portion must be included the *Chora* land, or sandy banks of rivers, which does not readily produce rank vegetation, and therefore is better cultivated than the richer lands, in which reeds vegetate with an astonishing vigour. The *Chora* land can produce a plentiful but precarious crop of indigo, and a great many cucurbitaceous plants, and sometimes wheat and barley. It is seldom, however, regularly rented, and can only be included among the land, that is sometimes in fallow, sometimes cultivated, *(Uthit Polit.)*

No trees grow on this inundated land, and its appearance is as dismal as its produce is of small value. A considerable portion might be embanked to advantage, by the proprietors: and wherever the soil is good, I have no doubt that it might be cultivated as the lands of Nator are: or it might be cultivated for wheat, barley, mustard seed, and various kinds of pulse; for the inundation dries up in most places before the season for sowing these begins. At present, nothing is cultivated in it but some poor kinds of rice, that will hereafter be described. Farther, the long reeds might be destroyed, and nothing allowed to grow except short grass, which would feed a great many more cattle than this ground does at present, and would give no harbour to destructive animals: but the right of common pasturage is a complete bar to such an improvement. As this kind of land, however, is a common nuisance, by spreading disease, and harbouring wild beasts, the proprietors might, perhaps with justice, be compelled either to clear it, or to part with it to such as would undertake the cultivation, for in its present state it yields no profit to the owner. At present the only step taken to diminish the evil, is to burn the dried reeds during the heats of spring: this is not done with sufficient care, neither is it by any means effectual.

The *Doangsh* or mixed soil, which occupies about 46 per cent. of the whole ground in this district, that is exempt from inundation, differs very much in its manner of cultivation, according to its various degrees of elevation. I exclude from this the low sandy banks of rivers, called *Chora* by the natives, although these are a mixture of sand and clay; but they are in general inundated.

The proper *Doangsh* land is capable of producing almost every thing that agrees with the climate, and the vegetation on it is remarkably luxuriant. This, in fact, in the present circumstances of the country, is a nuisance. The great variety of lofty flower and fruit-bearing trees, and the luxuriant bamboos by which the cottages are shaded, would render their situation delightful, did not rank weeds and bushes shoot up with unceasing vigor in every corner that is not in constant cultivation; prevent all circulation of air; preserve a constant damp noisome vapour, and harbour a great variety of loathsome and pernicious animals. The poverty, shyness, and indolence of the natives, (especially the two former,) prevent them from removing those nuisances. They are fond of having their houses buried in a thicket, which skreens their women from view. These thickets serve them as a place of retreat on all their occasions, which adds very much to the noisome smells that they occasion. This is even the case in families of considerable wealth and distinction, as in this district women servants are scarcely procurable.

The lowest parts of the *Doangsh* land produce one crop of winter rice, which is amazingly rich; and pulse is often sown amongst the growing corn, and ripens among the stubble. This land is eagerly sought after by the farmers, and little of it waste.

The *Doangsh*, which is somewhat higher, produces, in general, two crops of rice, which little exceed in value the single crop on the lower lands, and require at least double the labour. In place of a summer and winter crop of rice on this land, are sometimes sown Pat and Son plants used for making cordage.

The parts of this soil, that are neither very high nor low, and that are sufficiently near the house of the cultivator, produce various rich crops, that occupy the soil during the whole year, such as mulberry, sugar cane, ginger, and turmeric; or they produce a crop of summer rice, followed by wheat, barley, mustard, and other seeds for yielding oil, and various kinds of pulse, all of which are collectively called *Robi* by the farmers of this district, as they grow in the season of sunshine. A considerable portion also is cultivated for plants raised for chewing or smoking, or as vegetables for the use of the kitchen.

Lands of this kind, that are too far from the farm yard, and on that account receive no manure, produce only one crop of summer rice, or different kinds of the plants called *Arum* by Botanists, and *Kochu* by the natives, the roots of which are esculent. This is land, that seems to me well fitted for the cultivation of cotton, which deserves encouragement.

The highest parts of the *Doangsh* soil afford situations for the houses and gardens of the cultivators, and for the plantations by which they are surrounded. In the gardens are generally some plants of the Ricinus, on the leaves of which the natives raise a species of moth, (Bombyx,) that spins a very coarse kind of silk. In a few places fishermen rear in their gardens a kind of nettle, which yields a sort of hemp. In many parts this description of land is too extensive for those purposes, and then it is, in general, much neglected. It is too stiff for the regular and constant cultivation of grain, unless it could be regularly manured. A large proportion is occupied by burying grounds, and as a common pasture, where the cattle are turned out, rather to take air than to procure food, as the grass, at least in the season when I saw it, is entirely burnt up. Where not occupied by graves, this poor land is usually cultivated once in from three to five years; and after giving one or two crops of rice, pulse, esculent roots, turmeric, ginger, cotton, or sesamum, is allowed again to remain fallow. This is also the kind of land that is most usually cultivated for indigo. The profit that accrues to the owner from this land is very inconsiderable, but the cultivation is of great use, as it prevents those parts of the country from running into long reeds or bushes, which would harbour destructive animals; some part, however, in several rich districts, is reserved for rearing long grass, which is used for thatch and fuel, is regularly cut once a year, and pays a considerable rent.

This diversity of elevation in some parts of the district, especially towards the N. E. where the whole soil is *Doangsh*, occasions a division into *Nina* and *Dangga*, or low and high, that has been adopted in the settlement of the revenue. Its origin is not, however, more regularly attended to than the distinction of *Khyar* and *Poli*; for all the land near the cultivator's hut, that produces valuable crops, is reckoned *Nina*, and is high rented, although it is, in general, the highest part of the country. The lands that are a little elevated, and produce two crops of rice, are called *Nina Dangga*, or neither low nor high; and the highest lands, that are only cultivated occasionally, are called *Uthit Polit*, that is cultivated and waste.

The stiff soil, *(Khyar,)* forms a large proportion of the parts of this district that are exempt from inundation; and extensive tracts of it, although sufficiently high to prevent floods from injuring crops, are yet so very flat, that they are covered with water for four or five months in the year, and form a mud that is almost impassible. Sometimes the rice plains of this nature are intersected by narrow rising grounds, distant a mile or less from each other, and affording a situation where the inhabitants can build their houses. In other places these plains are so extensive, that it has been necessary to dig tanks, so that the earth thrown out might afford room for the dwellings of the cultivators.

These tanks are also extremely useful, by supplying the inhabitants with water, not only for domestic purposes, but for the irrigation of the fields. The persons, therefore, by whom they have been constructed are justly entitled to much praise, wherever they have had the utility of the tanks in view; but ostentation, and the desire of fame, have increased the number and size of these works to a destructive extent, especially as no one is sufficiently interested in their repair, which is attended with no reputation. Almost every tank, therefore, is soon chocked with aquatic plants, and becomes a source of noisome smell, bad water, and disease;

while there are infinitely more tanks than the habitations of the people can occupy, and much land is for ever rendered useless. It were indeed very much to be wished, that in this district at least the digging new tanks should be altogether prohibited; at least none should be permitted without an investigation into the necessity for its construction, and without proper security being taken from the estate in which it is dug, for its being kept for ever in repair, and free of noisome weeds. The measure at present taken for this purpose is quite absurd. When the tank is formed, a quantity of mercury is put in the bottom. This is only done in great tanks; and although bottomless examples of its inefficacy are constantly before their eyes, the natives continue perfectly credulous. However desirable it might be either to have old ones cleaned or filled up, the means I confess are not obvious. The necessity for tanks in this part of the country, it ought to be observed, is much smaller than in many others; for in almost every part wells, constructed at very little expense, produce much better water for domestic purposes than tanks; and with the pains that are bestowed on machinery in the south of India, would answer much better for the irrigation of the fields. At the same time it must be confessed, that this soil is favourable for tanks, the water which it contains being remarkably good, and in a few instances, (Ram Sagor and Siddheswori Pushkorne,) no weeds grow in them.

The high lands and raised banks in this stiff land are not favourable to most kinds of vegetation, and where the declivity is considerable, are, in general, waste. Many kinds of trees, particularly the *jak*, will not grow in such situations, and bamboos do not thrive so well as in looser soil; still, however, the mango, banyan, pipol, tamarind, and some others are very thriving; bamboos grow to a useful, though not to a great size; and the *tál* and *khejúr* palms might, no doubt, be cultivated to great advantage, were their uses known to the inhabitants. Besides affording a dry situation and shelter for the habitations of the people, the elevated parts, where not too steep, produce the seedling rice, that is transplanted into the field. By means of artificial watering, in many parts of the country, this soil produces fine cotton, mulberry, and vegetables for the kitchen, especially onions and garlic. The banks of tanks also are favourable for betel leaf. In all such parts of the country, however, vegetables are scarce; and in many parts the cultivation of mulberry and of cotton, especially of a good quality, is altogether unknown. This last circumstance is particularly to be regretted, as much cotton-wool is imported from territories not subject to the Company.

In this kind of land almost nothing is reserved for pasture, and it is much better occupied than any other soil in this district; perhaps 3 per cent. of it is very poor, and is allowed a fallow between the crops.

Other parts of the district, where the soil is stiff *(Khyar)*, are more uneven, and are, in general, badly cultivated, but a considerable proportion has been levelled with great pains, for producing rice; and as the soil, in such situations, is not so hard as in the more level parts, and contains somewhat more sand, so the nature of the produce approaches nearer to that of the free soils, and most of the articles cultivated on the one are raised also on the other; but, in general, where the soil is stiff, every thing except rice is raised only in small quantities, for the immediate consumption of the cultivator.

Although the produce of a given extent of ground be small in value, when compared with that of some light soils, yet I must say, that I, in general, observed the condition of the people to be best in the districts which consisted almost entirely of this stiff soil. The hardness of the clay, which renders it a good material for the construction of walls, both of houses and for surrounding the farm yard, gives a comfort to the inhabitants, that is unknown to the cultivators of the friable soil; while its dryness, without any assistance, checks that rankness of vegetation, by which the villages, in a richer soil, are overrun with weeds and bushes, that render the vicinity of the houses disgusting and unwholesome, and which shelter serpents, hogs, and various noisome or disagreeable animals.

CHAPTER II.

RIVERS.

§ 1.—*Nomenclature.*

The rivers of this district are very numerous, and are but ill represented in Major Rennell's maps, in some measure, probably, owing to his want of sufficient materials, but chiefly, perhaps, in consequence of changes that have taken place since his time. In a country so level as this, and that consists almost entirely of loose materials, upon which running water has a powerful action, the rivers are not only gradually and constantly changing their place, by wearing away different portions of their banks, but very frequently a small obstacle placed in one of their channels, forces the water to form another; and as that gradually becomes wider, the former is left entirely empty in the dry season, or at least has no current, and forms a stagnant marsh. This generally retains its original name among the neighbouring people, who very naturally continue to perform their religious ceremonies in the same places that their ancestors did, and call a bank by the name that was given to it by their fathers. This has been a source of great trouble to European geographers, who endeavouring to trace a great river from where it joins the sea, to its most remote source, by its principal channel, are astonished to find that it sometimes loses its name altogether; or again another river, after having for some part lost its original name, if traced farther, is found with its former name restored. The geographers of Europe are apt to be enraged, when, in tracing a river, they find, that an inconsiderable stream falling into their grand channel changes its name, and that the source of this smaller stream is obstinately considered by the natives, as the source of the river, having either been the first to which thay had access, or having at one period been the largest. The geographers are, in general, very unwilling to admit of these absurdities, and, therefore, construct their maps according to their own plan, with the same name following the same river, from its most remote source to its mouth. It must however be confessed, that this improvement, until it shall have been adopted by the inhabitants of the country, is attended with considerable inconvenience to those who wish to use the maps on the spot, and often leads them into most troublesome mistakes. In the following account of the rivers of this district, I shall endeavour to trace them by the names known to the natives.

§ 2.—*Of the Mahanonda and its dependent Rivers.*

The Nagor, after running for some way through the district of Puroniya, forms the boundary between that and Dinájpúr, from the northern extremity of the latter until it joins the Mohanonda, for the space of about 90 B. miles, without reckoning its various windings, which are very numerous and large. During the dry season the upper part of this river is not navigable even for canoes, but during the inundation, boats of considerable burthen can go to the northern extremity of this district; and in this upper part of the river a little commerce is carried on at Mundomala.

About 26 miles below where it begins to form the boundary of this district, the Nagor receives a small river named Trinoyoni in the Songskrito, and Trini in the vulgar dialect; but in common pronunciation the Rand Jare usually transposed. Trinoyoni signifies three eyes, and is a name of the spouse of Sib; but Trini, the usual name, has no meaning in the Songskrito language. This little river runs for about 20 miles, and in the rainy season admits of boats carrying 100 mons of rice, by which a little commerce is conducted at Rupgunj. At all seasons it retains a small stream of good water. Below the mouth of this, the Nagor admits always of canoes, but the communications of commerce are of little importance. From the mouth of the Trini to that of the Kulik, in the space of about 34 miles, Jogodol is the only place in this district on the Nagor from whence any exports are made.

The Kulik takes its rise from a marsh in the S. W. part of the division of Thakurgram, and after running through the divisions of Ranisongkal, Pergunj and Hantabad, joins the Nagor in the latter, at about 36 B. miles from its source, and receives from Pergunj a small rivulet named Kalayi. No derivation of the Kulik from the Songskrito, that I have heard, is feasible; I conclude, therefore, that the original name has been preserved. The same may be said of the Kalayi. During the greater part of the year the Kulik is navigable in canoes as far as Songkol; and in the rainy season large boats can go to that place, where there is some trade; but it is at Raygunj that it becomes navigable throughout the year. At all seasons boats of 125 mons burthen can come to this great mart, and during the inundation it is frequented by those of a very large size. This is by far the greatest mart in the vicinity, and exports most of the produce of the N. W. parts of this district.

The lower part of the Kulik is very deep; but the Nagor, for some way below its junction, is filled with shallows and difficulties, and its banks being much inundated, and little cultivated, there are no towns near it, in the Dinájpúr district, except Churamon or Churamohon, until it joins the Mohanonda; but during this space there are several communications between the two rivers; formerly large islands that belong to the Puroniya district, and by which the size of the Nagor is much increased, so that boats of 200 mons burthen can, at all seasons, come to Churamon; and this place, accordingly, carries on a considerable trade, though much smaller than that of Raygung. In the Songskrito language, Nagor is said to mean amorous, and to have been adopted in that sense by the polite dialect of Bengal: and this is said to be the source of the name of this river, as connected with some fable concerning its origin. The fable being improbable, is, perhaps, of a much later date than the name, which I should rather suppose is derived from the original language of the country; its water is reckoned good.

From where the Mohanonda receives the Nagor, to where it is joined by the Punabhoba, it forms the boundary of this district. The name of this river is undoubtedly Songskrito, signifying great pleasure; for great happiness is procured in a future state to those who die with their feet immersed in its stream. The upper part of its course being in Puroniya, a district I shall say nothing of here; but in this district it is a large river, containing water that is reckoned wholesome; but its course is very much interrupted with sands; and in the dry season, boats carrying more than 200 mons cannot come up to Maldeh. At Ayiyargunj it receives the Tanggon, which increases the size so much, that at all seasons boats of 500 mons burthen frequent this Mart. The commerce on the Mohanonda is, therefore, very considerable; and Ayiyargunj, Manggolvari, Maldeh, and Nawabgunj, are marts of some importance.

§ 3.—*Of the Tanggon and its Branches.*

The Tanggon, which seems to have a barbarous name, enters this district near its southern extremity, and from thence to its junction with the Mohanonda, is 96 B.

miles in a direct line. In its passage it first crosses the division of Thakurgram, where is a small river, which however admits of canoes during the whole year, and of boats of considerable burthen in the rainy season. In this space is Govindo Nagor, a small mart; and the river is increased by three streams, the Rosiya, the Sok and the Ramdangra. The two former are small streams arising in the district, and joining the Tanggon from the west; their names signify, in the Songskrito language, sweet juice, and grief, but these explanations having no rational application, their derivation is probably to be sought for in the language that was spoken in this country previous to the Bengalese dialect having received a polish from the Songskrito. The Ramdangra is an artificial canal, with an elevated bank on one side, and was constructed by Rajah Ramnath of Dinajpur, as a road between Praw Nagor and Govindo Nagor, at both of which places the family had seats. The canal communicates between the Tanggon and Punabhoba, and conveys a portion of the latter into the former, at least at the season when I saw it.

The Tanggon then passes through the centre of the division of Pergunj, where it receives the Nachi, a small stream rising in two branches at no great distance. In this division the Tanggon is a fine little stream, like the Punabhoba at Dinajpur, and at all seasons admits of goods being transported on it by means of floats, which are supported by canoes. Little commerce, however, passes this way; and Sadamohol, Ranigunj, and Kornayi, three small marts, export only a small proportion of the produce of the country, which is chiefly carried by land to Raygunj.

After passing through a corner of the division of Kaliyagunj, without change, the Tanggon enters Bongsihari, and passing through it for some way, it afterwards separates that division from Gonggarampur. In this space also it undergoes little change. There are several small marts on its banks (Besatipara, Sihol, Berakuti, Chondipur, Kornayi), but most of the produce is carried to the neighbourhood of Maldeh.

The Tanggon then passes through a great part of the length of division Jogodol, and in this it first receives from the west a small river called the Beliya, that is joined by the Chhiramoti, both of which pass through the divisions of Kaliyagunj and Bongsihari, and contain perennial streams of water, but they are not navigable. Below the junction of the Beliya the Tanggon receives from the east a river called the Brohmani, which is, in fact, a considerable branch of the Punabhoba, and about the middle of its course is still farther augmented by an artificial canal made by a merchant many years ago; but the period cannot now be ascertained. This canal between the Punabhoba and its branch the Brohmani, increases the latter so much, that boats of 500 mons burthen can, at all seasons, ascend to Nalagola at the junction. Boats of 100 mons burthen can pass through this canal to the Punabhoba, at all times; and in the rainy season boats of any size (3,000 mons) can pass from Nalagola by this canal. The Brohmani separates from the Punabhoba about 12 miles below Dinajpur, and after a course of about 24 miles joins the Tanggon at Bamongola. Even from Nalagola upwards, before it is joined by the canal, it contains more water than the Punabhoba; but it is little navigated. During the rainy season indeed the passage through the canal is shorter. From about the middle of October until the 10th of February boats of 200 mons burthen can pass through the Brohmani; and even at the dryest season, floats capable of transporting goods could come within 12 miles of Dinajpur, were it not that towards the end of February a proprietor of land stops the navigation, for the purpose of cultivating a kind of rice to an extent that is very inconsiderable. Being an officer of the Court of Circuit he has much influence at Dinajpur, and his people are informed, whenever any gentleman is going that way, so that they may remove the dam, and avoid detection; but the merchant has suffered considerable inconvenience. From Nalagola downwards the Brohmani is navigable at all seasons, and communicates its size to the Tanggon. But it must be observed, that this part of its course is frequently called Kangkri. In the division of Jogodol, however, there is no mart of any consequence on these rivers; although during the dry season, Nalagola may be considered as the port of Dinajpur, and there is a little commerce at Bamongola, Ranigunj, and Rajnagor.

In passing the whole breadth of the division of Maldeh, the Tanggon continues nearly of the same width. It receives from the west a small rivulet called Dokhariya, from its consisting of two branches, and a small branch of the Mohanonda, which passes through the town of Maldeh, and is called the Beliya.

The Tanggon, in its whole course, does much injury by inundating its banks, which, in general, are very low; and in the lower part of its course, during the rainy season, it spreads out into a very large lake, which extends almost from Bamongola to Maldeh, and which may be 12 miles long, and five wide.

§ 4.—*Of the Punabhoba and its branches.*

The next river, and nearly of the same size, although not of so long a course, is the Punabhoba, which rises from a tank called Bamonpukhor in the N. part of Birgunj division, and joins the Mohanonda at the southern extremity of this district, about 72 miles from its source. For about the last 10 miles of its course it forms the boundary between the districts of Dinajpur and Rajshahi: at its source the Punabhoba is a small stream, and soon afterwards it has a communication with the Tanggon, as before mentioned. It continues, however, a pretty little stream, even in the dry season; but is quite unfit for navigation, (except for canoes in the floods,) until it reaches the town of Dinajpur, where it receives a river, now much larger than itself, and which is named the Dhepa.

The source of this is more remote than that of the Punabhoba, and is a tank called Sosela Peyala, in Thakurgram division, about 12 miles to the N. of the source of the Punabhoba. The Dhepa runs south from thence, and is a stream more inconsiderable than the Punabhoba, until it comes near the town of Birgunj, where it receives a very large addition of water from the Atreyi, through an artificial canal, which is called Panjra Kata, from being situated in a district of that name, and Malijol, from a small creek that entered the Atreyi, where the canal now separates. This canal was dug by orders of a Mahommedan chief, named Sadutali, and formerly contained a large quantity of water; but since the Bengal year 1194, (A. D. 1786-7) this has been diminished by an accident that happened in the Stishta river (Teesta,) which I shall afterwards have occasion to describe. At present, during 4 months of the rainy season, the Dhepa is navigable from Birgunj downwards in large boats, and these boats can then pass through the canal to the Stishta. The river continues open for canoes until about the end of October, but is quite unfit for navigation from thence until the beginning of June. The only mart upon the Dhepa is Birgunj, a place of little consideration, south from Kantonogor. The Dhepa communicates with the Gorbheswori or Gobura, a branch of the Atreyi, by means of a small channel called the Kachayi, which contains water in the rainy season only, and which sends to the south a branch of the same name, that separates the town of Dinajpur into two divisions, and immediately below joins the Punabhoba. Between the lower part of the Kachayi and the Gabura, Raja Ramnath, of Dinajpur, formed a canal named the Ghorghora, or Ghagra, which now also has become dry, except in the rainy season. These cuts and channels seem to have been of considerable importance when Mr. Rennell constructed his map, and then insulated the town of Dinajpur. They might be now altogether omitted in a map on a small scale.

The Punabhoba, from receiving the Dhepa until it reaches Ghughudangga, continues much of the same size as the Dhepa at Birgunj, and does not afford any greater facility to navigation; that is to say, boats of 500 mons burthen can ascend it for 4 months in the year. In this space the only mart is Dinajpur, or rather one of its suburbs, called Kangchonghat.

The Punabhoba below Ghughudangga does not receive any stream, but an inconsiderable rivulet, named the Lona, and sends off the Brohmani, as before mentioned; yet in the rainy season boats of 1000 mons burthen can ascend to Ghughudangga by both branches, which shows the extreme lowness of the country. In fact, from thence downwards much of the country is subject to inundation.

From the commencement of this low country to Noyabazar, about 14 miles distant, and including the two extreme places, are 4 considerable marts, and the navigation becomes easier; for boats of 1000 mons burthen can ascend from about the 12th of June until the middle of October; boats of 400 mons can ascend a month longer, and floats constructed on canoes, can ascend until about the 10th of February.

At Noyabazar, without any apparent addition, the river becomes more navigable, and floats can come to that mart at all seasons. About 6 miles below, near Kordaho, a considerable mart, the Punabhoba sends the canal, already mentioned, to join the Brohmani, and it sends to the east a branch named Bhangg'a Dighir Dangra, which seems to have been formed since Mr. Rennell's survey, and now is, in fact, the principal branch of the river; for during 5 months in the year, boats of any size can pass through it; and those of 200 mons burthen can continue to ascend until about the 10th of March. After receiving a rivulet from the east it rejoins the Punabhoba, about 10 miles below, where it separated from that river. In this space there are, on the branch, two small marts, Bhalukdoho and Teliyaghata; and on the old channel there is one named Jobayi.

From the rejunction of these two branches to where the Punabhoba unites with the Mohanonda, the river resembles the Tanggon at Bamongola, but is not quite so large. In the dry season it is a muddy, narrow channel, with scarcely any stream, and winds excessively through a low country covered with reeds, and with extreme difficulty admits of boats carrying 200 mons of rice. In the hot months of spring, even these cannot pass. In the rainy season it becomes a great lake, about 20 miles in length, and 3 miles in width, which leaves behind many marshes, that formerly were channels of the river. In the whole of this extent, at least in this district, there is only one mart, Nitpur or Nitgunj, but that is very considerable; a small rivulet enters from the east, but I did not learn its name.

A little beyond the Punabhoba, to the east, is Matindro Khari, a rivulet which rises with two branches from the Purusa and Potnitola divisions, and after a course of about 12 miles in this district enters Rajshahi.

§ 5.—*Of the Atreyi and its branches.*

I now come to the most considerable river of the district, the Atreyi, which, from the appearance in the maps, would seem to be the direct and principal channel of the Stishta. Where this last name is lost, and where the Atreyi begins, I have not yet been able to learn. It enters this district near its N. E. corner, and there receives from the N. W. a rivulet named the Pathraj, which for some way forms the boundary between Dinajpur and Rongpur. The Atreyi passes for about 84 miles through this district, in a straight line, and in the rainy season can be frequented by boats of 500 mons for the whole way; but at Jharvari, the mart nearest its upper end, no vessels carrying any load can ascend after the middle of November; before the alteration in the channel of the Stishta took place in the year 1787-8, boats carrying 100 mons of rice could trade to Jharvari during the whole year.

From the mouth of the Joyram to where the Atreyi sends off a branch, called Gabura, in the space of about 15 miles, are Jharvari, Harirghaterbazar, and Khansamagunj, all of which marts have declined much since the decrease of the river.

The Gabura or Gorbheswori rejoins the Atreyi, about 14 miles below where it separated. For 4 months in the year boats of 300 mons can pass through it. In the dry season it is a small stream of dirty water, full of weeds, and admits of no navigation. It has no marts on its banks, which seem to have been the favourite retreat of the chief servants of the Dinajpur family, some of whom had handsome houses there, and have now good estates, part of the spoil of their master.

About 5 miles below the separation of the Gabura, a branch called the Kakra separates from the east side of the Atreyi, and rejoins it about 5 miles below the rejunction of the Gabura. It resembles that stream, but is rather larger, as during the rainy season boats of 500 mons can pass through it. Towards the upper part of its course it sends off a branch, called the Ichhamoti, which after receiving a rivulet from the east, and a course of 24 miles, rejoins the Atreyi. This branch, in the rainy season, admits of canoes. There is no mart on the Kakra nor Ichhamoti.

The principal channel of the Atreyi seems little affected by these branches, and in this space are Bhushi, Pheringgir-hât, Sahebgunj, Somdiya, Fakirgunj, Kongyargunj, and Tara, marts where there is a considerable trade. In the rainy season boats of from 500 to a 1000 mons burthen, can ascend to Bhushi; small boats can go up until the end of January, and boats of 40 or 50 mons can, with some difficulty, reach Somdiya at all seasons.

In the remaining part of its course through this district, for about 38 miles, the Atreyi undergoes little change. Boats of 1000 mons frequent it from about the 12th of June to the 14th of October. Until the end of November it admits of boats of 500 mons, and of 100 mons until the middle of January. Until the 10th of February it admits of boats carrying 50 mons, and floats carrying that weight can navigate it until the floods return. In the cold season, when I saw this river, it was a gentle clear stream, in some places very deep, in others there were fine fords on a bed of beautiful hard sand. The channel may be about 300 yards wide, and has high banks of a rich soil, over which the floods do not rise, since the water of the Stishta altered its course. Formerly considerable damage was occasionally done to the crops; but the soil is said to have been the more fertile, and much less sugar-cane is now cultivated on its banks, than was formerly.

The only branch, that the Atreyi receives in this lower part of its course, is one called in different parts Mohanaj, and Asuri, and Kasiyari, which comes from the N. W. and contains a perennial stream. In the rainy season boats of 200 mons can ascend it for some way, but there is no mart on its banks.

The marts near this lower part of the Atreyi are Potiram, and its port Nawabbundur, Balurghat, Mahigunj, Ranggamati, Kangchonghat, Khatavari, and Sibgunj, where there is a considerable trade.

East from Atreyi are too small streams, that run into the Rajshahi district, after courses of 12 or 14 miles, but are not of any service to commerce. The first called Pherusa rises from a marsh of the same name, and is said to be artificial, having been dug by Dolet Ray, proprietor of Mosida, in order to drain the marsh or lake.

The other named Kungdona rises from a marsh called Kalna, and after receiving the Gorkha, a smaller rivulet, runs into Rajshahi.

§ 6.—*Of the Jomuna and its branches.*

I next come to a much finer river, the Yomuna or Jomuna, a name which is common to several Indian rivers, and which has been variously corrupted by Europeans into Emona, Jomuna and Jubuna. It is a small river, with a gentle clear stream of considerable depth. Its water is considered as remarkably pure and wholesome, and its banks are the richest part of the district, and are now little subject to injury from its floods. Its has diminished in size since the waters of the Stishta were turned to the eastward, and is now probably of the size just proper for fertilizing the soil, without injuring the crops. It reaches this district at its N. E. corner, separates it from Rongpur for about 3 or 4 miles, and runs through Dinajpur for 65 miles in a direct line.

It first passes through the divisions of Birgunj and Rajarampur, where in the rainy season it admits canoes for the transportation of goods; but there are no marts on this part of its course.

In passing through the next division Hawora, it receives two rivulets from the east. The uppermost, named Chita, admits of canoes carrying 100 mons of rice during the rainy season, but in the cold season it becomes dry, and has no mart.

The southern rivulet, named Tilayi, is more considerable. It contains a stream throughout the year; boats of 400 or 500 mons navigate it from about the 12th of June until the 14th of September; and boats of 200 mons can frequent it a month longer. Hawora, called also Ranigunj, a very considerable mart, is situated on its eastern side.

In this division the Jomuna itself is frequented by boats of 400 or 500 mons from about the middle of June until the middle of October, and canoes can ascend it until about the 12th of December; but there is no mart on its banks.

It then passes from about 15 miles through the whole length of Chintamon division. The boats, that usually frequent this part of its course in the rainy season, carry from 500 to 600 mons, and canoes can navigate it for 8 months in the year. Like all the rivers of Bengal, it is liable to have its channel interrupted, and the navigation injured by trees, which are undermined, and allowed to fall into the water. In passing through Chintamon the Jomuna receives no stream, but on its banks are Phulvari, Sujapur, Khoyervari, and Muhammedpur, all marts, but none of them considerable.

The Jomuna then passes through the division of Lalbazar, and at the town of that name separates into two branches. Before the separation it has two marts, Buksigunj and Belamla, both on the decline. The western branch is the most considerable, and preserves the name.

Immediately below the separation, it receives a stream named the Chiri, which arising in Chintamon division, has a course of 18 miles, but is not navigable.

On entering the division of Badolgachhi the Jomuna receives two other small rivers from Chintamon, which pass also through Lalbazar, and are nearly of the same size, having courses of from 25 to 30 miles, and during the rainy season both are navigable in canoes or small boats.

The first or eastern is called Podmawoti, and also Chiri, which occasions great confusion.

The western of these small rivers is called Ghashki, and during the rainy season inundates its banks to a considerable extent.

This branch of the Jomuna is navigable at all seasons for canoes, and very small boats, and in the rainy season admits of boats carrying 1000 mons as far as Kisorgunj. The marts on it are Kisorgunj, and opposite to it Syamgunj, and Badolgachhi.

The eastern branch of the Jomuna is called Kata Jomuna, and is said to be an artificial canal, which was made by a very rich merchant, ancestor of Baidyonath Mondol, at present the principal landholder in the vicinity. In the rainy season it admits of vessels carrying 400 or 500 mons, and possesses two small marts, Joypur, and Yamalgunj or Jamalgunj. At the former is the residence of the founder, Baidyonath Chaudhuri, which is more like the residence of a gentleman or man of rank, than any other place in the district.

About 9 miles from its separation from the principal branch, the Kata Jomuna joins the Tulosi, a small river which rises in the division of Lalbazar from a marsh called Roktodoho, and afterwards it forms the boundary between that and Khyetlal, between this again and Badolgachhi, and for a short way between Dinajpur and Rajshahi, and it then joins the western branch of the Jomuna. In the first part of its course the Tulosi is very inconsiderable, but it soon receives an addition from the Karawoti, which running through the adjacent angles of Ghoraghat, Khyetlal, and Lalbazar, admits of small boats during the rainy season, and has on its banks two small marts, Chrishti and Pirerhat.

It sends off a branch to the east which, from its name, Katahari, is probably artificial; connects the Harawoti with another small river, the Nagor, and in the rainy season is also navigable for canoes. The only spring of water that I observed in this district, was on the bank of the Katahari, and it is a very fine one; it has escaped the notice of the natives, who in other parts of India would not have failed to have made it a place of religious worship.

Below the junction of the Harawoti the Tulosi receives a small river from the east, it is named Itakhola, and during the rainy season is navigable in canoes.

Between the Jomuna and Korotoya, in the south-east part of this district, are the sources of three rivers belonging to Rajshahi, and all capable, during the rainy season, of conveying goods in canoes.

The most westerly is Degangpoleshto, and the next is Dinggaduba. Both of these join a river of Rajshahi, named Bakhora, of which I see no traces in Mr. Rennell's map.

The most easterly of these three rivers is the Nagor, which receives the Katahari from the Harawoti, as before mentioned. It joins the Korotoya at Sibgunj; but separating again immediately, forms one of the principal rivers of Rajshahi.

§ 7.—*Of the Korotoya and its branches.*

The Korotoya, which in general forms the boundary between Dinajpur and Rongpur, is very difficult to trace, owing, probably, to the many changes that have taken place in its course, and in those of the neighbouring rivers. Its upper part passes through the district of Rongpur to the frontier of Dinajpur, and, exclusive of windings, descends along that for about 22 miles, where it divides into two branches, the Kalonodi, and the Ghrinayi, and at the separation it looses its name. Previous to this it is a small river, that has suffered considerably by the change in the direction of the Stishta, but still it swells considerably in the rainy season, and then admits of boats which carry 100 mons of rice, and canoes and floats loaded with 50 mons, can pass until December. On this part of the river is a mart called Buksigunj.

Here also the Korotoya receives the Khor Khorya, which comes from the Rongpur district, and after running parallel to the Korotoya for some way, joins it from the west. Small boats can frequent it in the rainy season, and it has a small mart called Fakirgunj.

The Korotoya in this part also receives a small rivulet from Dinajpur, called the Sonarbangdh.

The western branch of the Korotoya, called Kalonodi, or the river of death, has one mart named Uttora, and seems to me to have been the original channel of the river; for it goes in the direction of Nawabgunj, where we again recover the name; and Mr. Rennell brings to this place a small branch of the Korotoya, which is now lost.

At present two small rivers, the Nolsisha and Asuli, join at Nawabgunj, and their united streams are called the Korotoya. During the rainy season both of these rivulets admit of small boats, but no marts have been established on their banks. The Asuli is a very large channel, and no doubt has at one time contained a larger river.

During the rainy season, the Korotoya for about 15 miles from Nawabgunj, to Ranigunj, both considerable marts, admits boats 700 or 800 mons burthen.

A little below Ranigunj the water of the Korotoya, in the dry season, turns suddenly towards the east, and joins the Stishta by a small channel called the Mauliya, while the proper channel of the river, extending from Ranigunj to Ghoraghat, is of great size, but in many places is dry, while in others it contains deep and large pools of water.

The eastern branch of the Korotoya, where that river loses its name, as I have before mentioned, is called the Ghrinayi, and is nearly of the same size with the upper part of the river, but has no mart. It forms the eastern boundary of Dinajpur for about 8 miles, when it joins the large river called Stishta.

The Stishta is called also Jomuneswori or Yomuneswori. The latter name seems to be the most proper, and the name Stishta seems to have been given to it, since the greater part of the water of that river has been diverted to this channel, which happened in the year 1787-8. I observe, however, that Mr. Rennell gives it this name in his survey, which was made long before the time to which I allude. The Stishta, since that time, has increased greatly in size, and its inundations have done considerable injury to agriculture. It is navigable at all seasons for boats of 200 mons, and in the rainy season admits those of the greatest burthen. Yet after forming the boundary of Dinajpur for 18 miles, exclusive of windings, it loses its name where it joins the dry channel of the Korotoya, at Ghoraghat. On the Dinajpur side there is no mart on its bank.

The Korotoya, after receiving the Stishta at Ghoraghat, forms the boundary of Dinajpur for 15 miles, and admits of the same kind of navigation; on the Dinajpur side are Ghoraghat, Sahebgunj, Kengiyagunj, Gumanigunj, and Gujiya, all marts where there is considerable trade.

§ 8.—*General Remarks.*

On the whole it must be evident, that changes in the course of the rivers are attended with great loss and inconvenience. The new channel is so much land lost, and the old one leaves behind it a marsh or kind of lake, which for ages is rather injurious than of use. While the vicinity of the new course is deluged with water from the smallness of the channel, and the banks of the old course are often deprived of fertility, and still more certainly of the means for conveying their produce to market. The towns must, therefore, disappear, and the uncertainty of their place of abode, seems to be one of the reasons which prevents the inhabitants of Bengal from building more substantial and comfortable houses. The forming new cuts for the purpose of commerce seems on this account very dangerous, and except near the sea should in general be avoided.

In a country however so level and of so loose a soil, such sudden changes cannot perhaps be altogether prevented. All, that I can propose for the purpose is, to remove in time the most usual cause of change, which is the trees that fall into the rivers, and which, collecting sand round them, form banks that obstruct the channel, and not only occasion great and sudden changes in the course of the rivers, but impede navigation. On the mouldering bank of every river may be observed trees growing close to the precipice, gradually undermining, and then falling in and lying to rot; for the proprietors will not allow them to be cut or removed while growing, and afterwards they are in general of no value, except for fuel; and the expense of cutting them for that purpose exceeds the means of the neighbouring poor. Some of the kinds are venerated by the Hindus, who consider it as sinful to cut them. I am persuaded, therefore, that it would be an useful regulation to direct, that every landholder should remove the trees, which are growing within 20 feet of a mouldering bank; and where he neglected or avoided doing it, that a proper officer of police should clear the bank, and charge the proprietor a reasonable price for the labour.

CHAPTER III.

LAKES AND MARSHES.

In this district there is no proper lake; although during the rainy season some of the rivers, especially the Tanggon and Punabhoba, swell out so as to resemble very fine ones. Many marshes (Bils) then also are enlarged into a kind of lakes, and even in the dry season retain a little water in their centres. I am persuaded, that in these marshes there are many fine springs, although I only observed one, and although the natives every where denied having noticed them; but in such inquiries they have little curiosity, and these marshes give rise to many little perennial streams, which can only be supported by springs. The edges of these marshes are often very fine land, and are called Kandor; indeed by the lower classes Bil and Kandor are often considered as synonymous.

The deserted channels of large rivers also contain large quantities of stagnant water, always in the rainy season, and sometimes even in the parching heats of spring, and have a resemblance to lakes. These are properly called Jhil by the natives; but it must be confessed, that they often use Jhil and Bil very indiscriminately, although the two kinds of places are of a very distinct nature.

CHAPTER IV.

ON THE CLIMATE OF DINAJPUR.

There have been no meterological observations of any accuracy made in this district; what I have been able to collect is chiefly from the reports of the natives, totally destitute of science, and of the means for making accurate observations.

When a country is intersected by very large rivers, I imagine, that the winds are much affected by their course. In the south of Bengal the prevailing winds are north and south. In Vihar or Bihar the winds are east and west, and the same is the case in Asam. In Dinajpur the course of the rivers is north and south; but the rivers are so small when compared with the Ganges and Brohmoputro, that their influence is much checked, and the winds here are more variable than in any part of India that I have visited. On the whole, however, the east winds are by far the most prevalent, and are very usual even at the seasons in which I have stated other winds to be the most common.

The rainy season, as at Calcutta, usually begins about the 12th of June, is accompanied by much thunder, and ends nearly about the 14th of October. The rain most commonly comes from the east; but towards the end of this season there are pretty often light southerly winds, which increase the heat, and the nights then are very close and suffocating.

In favourable seasons there ought to be one or two days heavy rain between the middle of October and the middle of November; and if these fail, the crop of rice is very scanty.

Again, from the 12th of March to the 12th of May, there are usually strong winds from the west, which are generally hot, but are often interrupted by squalls from the N. W; sometimes arising to storms, and usually accompanied by thunder, rain, and often by hail, of a very great size. The clerk of division Rajarampúr declares, that he saw one hail stone 6 inches in diameter; and that during the storm in which this fell, several people and cattle were killed; and that the hail broke through the roofs of several huts.

From the middle of May until the commencement of the proper rainy season, the winds are light, and come usually from the east; and the heat is great, but not so violent as at Calcutta. The heat continues strong, until about the middle of September, when the nights, at least, become somewhat moderate. From the middle of October until the middle of February, the winds are light, and there are very heavy fogs and dews. The east winds are most prevalent in the beginning of this period; and the north, towards its end. When the fogs and dews commence early, it is expected that there will be much rain early in the season, which I have found verified this year.

The west winds usually blow cool, pleasant, and dry, with a fine clear sky, from the middle of February until the middle of March, which is, no doubt, the finest time of the year. Two days' fog that happened early in February, during my journey, were considered as very remarkable. From the beginning of November, indeed, until the beginning of April, I experienced the weather to be delightful.

During November, December, January, and February, the cold is at times troublesome, and the Europeans use fires in their chambers, and woollen clothing. The natives enjoy neither luxury, and suffer exceedingly all night; they shiver and lament, and in the morning continue benumbed, both in body and mind, until the sun acquires some height, dispels the fogs, and invigorates them by his cheering beams.

Natives of Calcutta, who have lived here for some years, think, that, on the whole, the heats and thunder are more severe at Calcutta than at Dinajpur. Whenever the east winds prevail, are the people sickly, and health is restored by those from the west. The most violent and only hurricane remembered, was in November, 1787, (Kartick 1194), and came from the N. E.

CHAPTER V.

DIVISIONS, HISTORY, AND ANTIQUITIES.

Historical Introduction.

Before I proceed to give a more particular account of the different sub-divisions of this district, and of the towns and remarkable places which each contains, I shall, in order to render myself more readily understood, give such notices concerning its history, as I have been able to procure. These, however, as usual in India, are either mere traditions preserved amongst ignorant people, or legends mixed with the most monstrous fables; for I believe it may be safely asserted, that the Hindus have nothing which ought to be dignified with the name of history, nor which could even, with propriety, be denominated a chronicle. In this district tradition is remarkably obscure, owing to the Hindus having, at one time, been nearly eradicated.

PART 1.—*Hindu Government.*

The tradition belonging to this district, which is referred to the earliest period by the Hindus, is that it was under the Government of Porosuram*, a very powerful monarch, who had subject to him twenty-two princes, and who lived at Moha-thangor (Muhtangurs) in Rajshahi, near the frontier of this district. The Brahmons whom I have consulted, consider this personage as the same with the 6th incarnation of the God Vishnu, who appeared an immense number of years ago, and on this account I have placed this tradition first; but the common belief of the country is, that Porosuram, of Mohasthan, was destroyed by a Muhammedan saint, named Shah Sultan Hazrut Auleya. This does not appear remarkable to the Brahmons, as they consider, that Porosuram is still on earth, and that he now resides in the western parts of India. The ruins of Mohasthan are said to be very considerable.

The tradition referring to the next highest antiquity, is that of Ram, king of Oyodhya (Oude), and 7th incarnation of the God Vishnu. After his return from Longka, this hero could not avoid suspecting that his spouse Sita had granted favors to Ravon, while she was in the power of that prince. He therefore separated from her, and she retired to this province, which was the residence of Balmiki, a very holy person of these times. She was attended by Lokshmon, the brother of Ram, and during her abode here was delivered of a son named Nob, and the saint gave her another named Kus. These two sons attacked Ram, and he was induced to restore their mother to his bed.

At a great interval, but still in the most remote antiquity, a personage named Boli raja governed in this country. He was an Osur, or person who opposed the worship of the gods, and is now suffering the punishment of his heresy in a place under the earth, called Patal. The Pondit of the survey has no doubt, that this was the Boli raja, of whose house the ruins are shown; but some traditions place him only a few hundred years ago. Even this tradition, however, acknowledges him to have been the father of a still more distinguished personage, Ban raja, who appears to have governed this country with great distinction. He also was an Osur, that is to say, he was a worshipper of Sib, and opposed Krishno, king of Brindabon and of Mothura who was a follower of Vishno, and indeed is consi-

* Throughout this work it has been thought proper to preserve the Author's orthography: the frequent occurrence of the letter *o* shews that the names are derived from Bengali authorities; in Hindi they would all be expressed by the short *a*.

ED.

dered as the 8th incarnation of that god. Ban raja seems to have lived in much more splendour than his father, and to have been a very superstitious prince. He introduced that severe mode of worship, in which the votary is swung round, while suspended from a lever by iron hooks, which are passed through the skin of the back. As people formerly lived a long time, he employed a thousand years in this penance, and obtained the favour of Sib, who promised that no god should have power to kill him. He was a very great hero, having had no less than 1000 arms; and Sib bestowed on him two ponds, Omrito and Jivot; those who drank the water of the former, were invulnerable; and those who drank the water of the latter, when wounded, were immediately cured. While Ban raja was governing with great glory, Oniruddho, grandson of Krishno, came in disguise to his court, and corrupted his daughter Usha. Ban raja was naturally enraged, and being ignorant of the high rank of the young man, placed him in a horrid dungeon. In order to liberate his grandson, Krishno came with a great army, and attacked Ban raja, and a severe engagement took place near the palace of Usha. In this battle Ban raja lost 998 of his arms, which were burned in triumph at Kordaho, on the banks of the Punabhoba. It was during this war that fever first appeared; and in hopes of being saved in that disease, many persons labouring under it, read the history of the war, or the *Ban Juddho stob*. The protection of Sib, however, saved Ban raja, and the water of his ponds saved his troops, so that Krishno was unable to take the city; and peace, of course, was made, on condition that the young prince should be released, and marry the princess. Krishno, however, could not forget the injury, and sometime afterwards, a barbarous people, who devoured cows, and who were called Yovon or Jovon, having entered the country, and having procured the government of Hostinapur, were sent by the god to attack Ban raja. He instructed them to defile the water of the ponds by means of beef tied to the foot of a kite, which frequented them to drink; and this having been done, the city of Ban raja became an easy prey to the barbarians. Ban raja, although by nature immortal, was so enraged, that he deserted his body.

These wars between the princes, considered as incarnations of Vishnu, and the Osurs or princes who worshipped Sib, such as Ravon and Ban, no doubt, refer to the time when the worship of these gods was still in recent vigor, and each was contending for superiority. There is little doubt, but that the Yovons are the Macedonians of Bactria, who obtained large possessions in India; and if any reliance can be placed on this legend, the times of Krishno cannot be of very remote antiquity. The story, however, rests on the authority of one of the Purans attributed to Vyas, which probably are very modern compositions, although the foundation of the legends which they contain, may have been borrowed from books that have been since lost.

The next personage of this country, who is celebrated in tradition, is Virat Raja, king of Motsyodés, a name which is still retained by the whole of this district, except a small portion east from the proper Korotoya, for that river separated Motsyo from Kamrup, which was then governed by a prince named Bhogodotto. The boundaries of Motsyo, towards the south and west, I have not yet exactly learned, as they certainly included, at least, portions of Rajshahi and Puroniya, which I have not visited. In the war which took place between Yudhishthir and Duryodhon for the throne of Hostinapur, and the supremacy of India, Virat raja assisted the former or successful side, while his neighbour, as usual, joined with the opposite party. The mother of Virat raja happened to be impregnated by means of a fish. The circumstances being very indecent, shall not be mentioned; but it is on this account, that this vicinity has been called Motsyodés, or the country of the fish. The war between Yudhishthir and his competitor, is usually placed by the present Hindu chronologists about 3,200 years before the birth of Christ; but here a great difficulty occurs. Ban raja preceded the time of Yudhishthir, and yet his city is taken, and his government is destroyed by the Yovons, who, beyond doubt, were the Macedonians. I must, however, say, that the ruins alledged to have belonged to Virat, who was contemporary with Yudhishthir, every where betray a greater appearance of rude antiquity, than those which are considered as the works of Ban raja; and my Pondit has probably been mistaken in placing the latter prince earliest. Virat and his son were killed in the war.

The next princes, of whom any traces remain, had the common name of Pál, and of these many works are to be seen in this district. In the Ayeen Akbery, these princes are placed as a dynasty governing Bengal, between the dynasties of Adisur, and Bollalsen, which Abul Fazil considered as distinct. This, however, by no means accords with the common traditions of the country. These state, that on a certain occasion twelve persons of very high distinction, and mostly named Pál, came from the west country to perform a religious ceremony in the Korotoya river, but arrived too late; and as the next season for performing this ceremony was twelve years distant, they, in the interval, took up their abode here; built palaces and temples, dug tanks, and performed many other great works. They are said to have been of a tribe called Bhungiya, to which also the raja of Kasi (Benares) and Betiya belong. From inscriptions remaining, and which have been published in the Asiatic Researches, it is well known, that the Pála were powerful kings; and according to Captain Wilford, As. Res. vol. ix. p. 203, the first of them, Bhupál or Mohipál, was alive in the year of Christ 1017, when his country was disturbed by the invasion of Sultan Mahmud, who took Kasi, and penetrated far into Bengal. It was probably on this occasion, that Mohipál retired to this remote part of the country, with his family and principal officers; and it is probable, that according to tradition, they returned again to the west after a few years stay, and after the terror of the Muhammedan invaders had subsided.

The traditions given here concerning the next dynasty, differ also very much from the Ayeen Akbery. They make Bollalsen the immediate successor of Adisur, who was a person of the Baidyo, or medical tribe, that procured the government of Bengal, but still subject to the princes of the west. He lived partly at Gaur, in the immediate vicinity of this district, but chiefly at Vikrompur, about 8 miles south-east from Dhaka. Adisur's tribe being descended from a Brahmon and a Sudro woman, he probably had a reverence for the sacred order, and accordingly he introduced five families of them from Kanyokubjo (Kanoje). Whether there were any Brahmons in this district before that time, or whether they had been all destroyed by the Pál family who worshipped Buddha, I cannot take upon myself to say; but no traces of any ancient families remain, and all those who are now to be found in this district, are descended from these five families of Adisur, or from a still later colony called Baidik, who came from the same place a few centuries ago.

It has, indeed, been said, that one of the ten nations of Brahmons called Gaur, were the original Brahmons of Bengal, and derived their name from its capital. This supposition, however, seems to me attended with great difficulties. The present Gaur Brahmons occupy the country near Dilhi, and no account can trace their emigration from Bengal. Besides Gaur did not become the capital of Bengal, until immediately before the Muhammedan conquest, and it was the princes of the dynasty of Adisur, who first bestowed on it that supremacy; so that, if any Brahmons had derived a name from this city, it should have been those of the five tribes introduced by that family. I am, therefore, disposed to think, that Mr. Colebrooke's opinion was well founded when he supposed, that the country of the Gaur Brahmons is situated in the west of India. It must, however, be confessed, that the Brahmons, whom I have consulted, place the country (Dés), called Gaur, below Patna, in the vicinity of Janggira, one of the most holy places on the Ganges.

Adisur's wife had a son named Bollalsen, who was begotten by the Brohmoputro river, in the convenient form of a Brahmon. This son succeeded Adisur, and regulated the different castes as they now stand in Bengal. It seems to have been owing to this that the medical tribe, being that of the prince who regulated the precedence, has been placed next in rank to the Brahmons. Bollalsen was succeeded by Lokhymon Sen, who, according to the traditions here, had a son named Madhob Sen, and he a son named Su Sen. As in the Ayeen Akbery, the last king of the dynasty is named Lukminyah, the son of Lukmen; it is possible that Lokhymon the first, may have had a son of the same name, who succeeded his nephew Su Sen; although by the Hindus the latter is usually considered as their last king. Captain Wilford assigns good reasons for believing, that Lokhymon was expelled by the Muhammedans, A. D. 1207, (As. Res. ix. 203.)

During the government of this dynasty, a division of the country, which was subject to them, took place, and is still remembered. Gaur being the capital, formed the centre division, and was surrounded by five great provinces; 1st, Barondro, bounded by the Mohanonda on the west, by the Podma (Ganges R.) on the south, by the Koratoya on the east, and by neighbouring governments to the north: 2d, Bonggo, or the territory east from the Korotoya, towards the Brohmoputro. The capital of Bengal, both afterwards and before, having been long near Dhaka, in the province of Bonggo; this name is said to have been communicated to the whole: 3d, Bagri, or the Delta, called also Dwip, or the island; bounded on one side by the Podma, on another by the sea, and on the third by the Bhogirothi, (Hoogly R.) 4th, Karhi, bounded by the Bhogirothi (Ganges and Hoogly R.), on the north and east, and by the adjacent kingdoms, on the west and south: 5th, Maithilo, bounded by the Mohanonda and Gaur on the east, by the Bhagirothi on the south, and by adjacent countries on the west and north. The extent of these provinces, towards the W. E. and north, I have not been able to ascertain; but it certainly fell far short of the present limits of Bengal, especially towards the east and north. Barondro, which includes part of Rajshahi and Dinajpur, did not extend so far north as the town of this name; and ends at Dumdumah, about 18 miles south from it. Whether or not the whole of the northern parts of this district, beyond the limits of the kingdom of Gaur, were subject to one prince, at the time of the Muhammedan invasion, I cannot say; because there are many ruins in these parts, but little or nothing of the history of any of the founders remains on tradition, except that Mohes raja, one of these personages, seems, from the ruins of his house, to have been a prince of some consequence; and according to tradition, he was overthrown by the Muhammedans at a very late period.

This traditionary account of the native princes of the country differs so much from that given by Abul Fazil, that I have great doubt concerning its approach to accuracy, especially as the deplorable state of learning in this country has prevented me from finding any person versed in tracing the families of the Brahmons introduced by Adisur, and who are called Ghotok and Kulacharyo; none of whom are to be found in Dinajpur nor Ranggamati. It must, however, be observed, that the dates A. D. 1017 and 1207, ascertained in a manner not liable to any error of above 30 or 40 years, as the times of the 1st Pál king, and of the last native prince of Bengal, are totally irreconcilable with the 858 years assigned by the Ayeen Akbery, for the two dynasties. Indeed, the small number of princes, and great number of years, in Hindu chronology, have introduced innumerable difficulties; for instance, the Ayeen Akbery makes 10 Páls reign 698 years, or 70 years each.

According to the Ayeen Akbery, (Luckmeenyah) Lokhymon, was king of Bengal at the time of its conquest, and then resided at Nodiya, or more properly Nobodwip. On the approach of the Muhammedan army, the raja made his escape in a boat. This last circumstance agrees in part with the tradition of the country, which states, that the raja being afraid of the destruction of Brahmons and sacred animals, which resistance might occasion, deserted his body, a power which holy men are supposed to possess, and which is called Oprokot or Onudes. The Muhammedan account will, of course, appear most probable to a (Mlechho) barbarian, who will suppose, that the raja being afraid, retired to his more remote capital Vikrompur, and endeavoured to obtain the best terms which he could, especially as we now find a family, who pretend to be his descendants, and who still possess considerable estates in that vicinity. Rajbollobh, the grandfather of the present representative, was in very affluent circumstances, and purchased from the Brahmons, at a great expense, (it is said 10 lacks of Rupees,) the privilege for the medical cast, of wearing a thread like the sacred order, from whom the physicians of Bengal are descended. We shall also find, that Sonargang, near Vikrampur, continued to be a place of refuge for those who were discontented at Gaur, and was not finally reduced, until a long time after the overthrow of Lokhymon.

Part 2.—*Muhammedan Government.*

The Muhammedan general, Muhammed Bukhtyar Khulji, having destroyed Nodiya, rendered Gaur again the seat of government. This city is also called Luknowty (Lokhymonawoti), from the son of Bollal Sen, who added much to its greatness; and those parts of Bengal, which were subject to the throne of Dilhi, continued, according to the Ayeen Akbery, to be governed for about 150 years, by viceroys who resided at this capital. According to the same authority, three different persons, about the end of that time, usurped the government; but by the people here, and according to a manuscript account which I procured at Peruya, Shamsuddin, the last of these usurpers, is considered as the first Muhammedan king of Bengal.

According to this manuscript, Firuz Shah, king of Dilhi, was a dissolute prince, fond of hunting in company with his women, one of whom was corrupted by Shamsuddin, then a servant of Ali-uddin, a principal officer under the king. The culprit having secreted himself, the king was enraged with the master, and sent him to Azmut Khan, governor of Bengal, I suppose with a view of having him killed. On the road he met with a holy man, Shekh Jalaluddin, of Tabriz, who prophesied to him that he would be king, and requested that an endowment might then be bestowed on him. I suppose the holy man also discovered to the noble the design of his being sent to Bengal; as the manuscript states, that he immediately killed Azmut Khan, and seized on the government. He only, however, assumed the title of Muktagh, or governor, but retained his authority for 20 years. He probably neglected the saint, who according to the manuscript, seems to have assisted the fugitive servant Shamsuddin to seize on the government.

After having murdered Ali-uddin, under the disguise of a religious mendicant, by the advice of the saint Jalal, of Tabriz, usually called Mukhdum Shah, he fixed the seat of his government at Peruya, and assumed the title of king. The new monarch built a great palace, and made war on Ibrahim, governor of Behar, on the part of Firuz. Two saints being consulted on the occasion, one gave it as his opinion that Firuz would be successful, the other gave an opinion directly contrary. The royal party, however, repulsed the usurper. The emperor then invaded Bengal, and the usurper, being afraid, retired to Ghoraghat; but an agreement was made, and Firuz returned to Dilhi. Shamsuddin governed 12 years, and was succeeded by his son Sekandar, who built a very large mosque, named Adinah, as would appear from an inscription remaining on it, in the year of the Hegira 707. It must, however, be observed, that in this inscription, which ought to be indubitable authority, Sultan Sekandar is called son of Sultan Shah Jalal, contrary to both the Ayeen Akbery and the manuscript. The usurper, however, may have had several names, as usual among Muhammedans. I suspect, that this date is not reconcileable either with the supposition of Abul Fazil, that the kings of Dilhi governed Bengal 150 years before the rebellion, or with the supposition in the manuscript, that Ali-uddin rebelled in the reign of Firuz; but I have not at present the means of finding out the years of our era corresponding with those of the Hegira. It must also be observed, that this date is scarcely reconcilable with that on an inscription in Gongarampur, where, in the year of the Hegira 718, the governor of the province acknowledges the supremacy of Dilhi; and another inscription, dated 765, mentions Sekandar Shah, son of Majahud Shah, son of Ayes Shah, who, I have no doubt, was king of Bengal. The most celebrated person, in the reign of Sekandar, was a holy man named Mukhdum Alulhuk, whose son Azem Khan, was commander of the troops. The saint having taken disgust at some part of the king's conduct, retired to Sonargang, near Dhaka, where the Hindu princes probably still retained considerable authority, if not independence. The good man was, however, soon after induced to return; but the king's son, Ghyasuddin, having also taken disgust, retired to the same place, and afterwards made war against his father, who after a reign of 32 years, fell in battle at a place called Satra near Goalpara, (probably Chattera R.) which is situated between the Tanggon and Punabhoba, near a favorite country residence of the king.

Ghyasuddin, on succeeding to the government, put 17 brothers to death. The most holy man at his court was Mukhdum Shah Nur Kotub Alum, son of Alalhuk, who attempted to make a peace with a Saheb Khan, with whom Ghyasuddin had been carrying on an unsuccessful war. While the treaty was going forward, Ghyasuddin seized on his adversary. He governed 16 years, and was succeeded by his son Syafuddin, who governed 3 years, and was succeeded by his slave Sahabuddin, who also governed 3 years.

Then Gones, a Hindu and Hakim of Dynwaj, (perhaps a petty Hindu chief of Dinajpur,) seized the government. Enraged at Shekh Bodor Islam, and his son Fyezislam, who refused to give him the compliment due to the rank he had assumed, he put them to death. The saint Kotub Shah, who was still alive, disgusted at this action, wrote to a Sultan Ibrahim, who seems to have retained part of the kingdom, while the remainder fell to the share of Gones, and who, in compliance with the request, came from Rajmohal with an army, and encamped at Satra. The Raja of Dynwaj was then terrified, and applied, in great penitence, to Kotub Shah, and obtained his forgiveness, by making his son Goduson, a Muhammedan. This convert assumed the government, under the name of Jalaludin, having been reconciled to the saint, and attacked Ibrahim Shah, grandfather of Hoseyn Shah, and having put him to death, seized on his government. The old man Gones then confined his son, and seized on the whole kingdom. After having been four years in confinement, Jalaludin recovered the government, and compelled the Hindus to become Muhammedans; but many of them fled to Kamrup, that is to say, the country beyond the Korotoya, and which was then probably independent. He governed 7 years, and was succeeded by his son Ahmed Shah, who reigned 3 years. He was destroyed by two of his nobles, Sadikhan and Nazar Khan, the latter of whom was made king, and erected many buildings at Gaur, to which he seems to have transferred the royal residence. He governed 27 years, and was succeeded by Sultan Barbuk Shah, who governed 16 years. He was succeeded by Yosuf Shah, a very learned prince, who governed 6 years. His son, Futeh Shah, governed 7 years, when he was killed by a slave of Barbuk Shah, named Kewajeh Soray, who governed six months, and was put to death by an Abyssinian, named Firuz Shah, who governed 3 years. Mozofur Shah then governed 3 years.

Then Sultan Hoseyn Shah, son of Said Ashraf, son of Ibrahim Shah, became king, and seems to have been by far the most powerful of the sovereigns of Bengal. He is said to have conquered Kamrup, that is, the country to the east of the upper part of the Korotoya, and to have killed its king, Harup Narayon, son of Malkongyar, son of Lada Lokhymon. He also conquered Audysah (Orissa) and Kamchah, and governed 27 years. He was succeeded by Nusrut Shah, who was killed while asleep, by his servant Khwajeh Soray, after a reign of 13 years. His son Firuz Shah governed 9 months, when he was killed by his uncle Mahmud Shah. A person, named Alum Shah, (probably governor of Bihar,) was killed in war by Mahmud; and his successor Shershah, (who before his usurpation of Dilhi was governor of Behar,) sent troops to revenge his cause. Mahmud implored the assistance of Hamayun, king of Dilhi, who came to his assistance. The two sons of Shershah, Selim Shah and Khawas Khan, defeated both princes. Mahmud escaped to a strong fort, named Dorweyshpur, and Hamayun fled to Kalgang; where soon afterwards he was joined by Mahmud. This prince having learned that his fortress had been taken, and his two sons put to death, was seized with a mortal disease, and died after a government of five years. Hamayun now went to Gaur, where he lived for some months. In the mean time Sher Shah subdued Sonargang and Chatgam. The former was, no doubt, the remnant of the Hindu kingdom of Bengal, near Dhaka, and which seems to have included Bonggo proper; the latter is the country which we call Chittagong. He then attacked Hamayun's army at Mongger, and entirely defeated it. Sheer Shah governed nine years, and was succeeded by Islam or Selim, who governed 10 years. Then Sher Shah his son governed some days, and was killed by Muhammed Ali, who was an intolerable tyrant, and was dethroned by Muhammud Khan, who governed one year, when Muhammed Ali attacked him. The other Muhammed resigned his government to Bahadur Shah, who defeated Muhammed Ali in a battle at Surajgur, (or Surjyogor,) and then took the kingdom from a Shahabaz Khan, who seems to have stolen into it during the dispute. He governed 6 years. His brother, Jalaludin, governed 5 years. His son was king for 17 days, when he was deprived of his government by Ghyasuddin, who only retained it 15 days, and was killed by Tajkhan, of Kermani. He was able to retain the government 6 months. His brother Suleyman succeeded, and having plundered Gaur, removed the seat of government to Kosba Haveli Tandah. He was also king of Audisah, and governed 10 years. His son Baizid Kermani governed 13 days, and was killed by Hansu, who was married to his sister; but after the murder he ran away, and a certain Daud Kermani became king, caught Hansu, and put him to death. At Patna he fought with the Khan Khanas, who had been ordered by Muhammed Akber Shah, the king's son, to seize on him. The Mogul nobles (Khan Khanas) obtained the victory, and drove Daud into Rajmohal, and he was killed in another battle by Mozofur and Hoseyn Kuli, two of the Mogul officers, when the whole of Bengal returned again to the dominion of Dilhi.

I have detailed this chronology at full length, because it differs considerably from that in the Ayeen Akbery, and is probably more correct.

Hoseyn, certainly one of the most powerful kings of Gaur, is altogether omitted by Abul Fazel, unless he be the same with the Alaudin 2d of that name, who also succeeded a Mozofur. The chronology of the MSS. evidently ends with the last year of Hamayun (A. D. 1554-5), because Akber is mentioned as the king's son, and his father governed only part of two years after his return to India. This would place the commencement of the rebellion, allowing for the shortness of Muhammedan years, in the year 1315, a year even before the accession of Muhammed, the predecessor of Firuz III. The time, therefore, granted to the reigns in this manuscript, is perhaps too long, for it comprehends 240 solar years; but Firuz began to reign in 1351, and the Bengal kingdom was overthrown 1555, which allows 204 years only, or 36 years less than the chronology in the manuscript. This, indeed, seems to protract the time after Sheer Shah unreasonably, unless we suppose, that it is wrong in styling Akber the king's son, and that he had really been king for a considerable number of years, before he reduced Bengal. For from the retreat of Hamayun, to his death, were only 14 years; and the manuscript gives 41 years' government to Sheer Shah and his successors, or 27 years too much, unless they continued to govern Bengal until the 27th year of Akber, which is indeed very probable. This would reduce the difference between the manuscript and the Ayeen Akbery to 9 years.

The nature of the government of these Muhammedan kings is, I believe, little known; as usual, they seem to have enjoyed little security for their lives or government; and so far as I can learn, were in general furious bigots, much under the influence of men dedicated to a religious life, and called *Pirs* or saints. In every part of the Dinajpur district are to be found the tombs or monuments of these personages; and the most remarkable contain traces to show that they have been erected on the ruins of Hindu buildings, and, in all probability, of temples. The account in the manuscript concerning the total conversion or expulsion of the Hindus, by Jalaludin, is confirmed by the present state of religion in this province, as I shall afterwards have occasion to show.

§ 2.—*Account of the sub-divisions of the District.*

During the government of Akber, new divisions took place, and are still remembered, and continued in writings descriptive of lands, although more recent division have been adopted both in the administration of justice, and collection of revenue. Of the 24 Sircars, into which Bengal was then divided, this district contains part of 6, viz. Punjra, Tajpur, Jennutabad, Ghoraghat, Barbakabad, and Bazuha. The divisions of Akber seem, however, to have been but ill arranged; and the districts belonging to each were very much interspersed with those belonging to others. They were sub-divided into Mahals, analogous very nearly to the present Perganahs, which have been as ill arranged as the Sircars. Almost each Perganah has peculiar customs or regulations, which affect the tenures under which it is cultivated. It would, therefore, have been highly desirable for me to have followed this division in the more minute topographical account which

I am about to give; but the different small divisions of each perganah, called Mauzas, Dehas, Gangs, or Grams, are so intermixed with those of other Perganahs, that I found this impracticable. Nor could it be adopted, unless the country were surveyed on a scale sufficiently large to allow the boundaries of the Mauzas to be defined. In the following account, therefore, I shall detail whatever I observed remarkable in the division attached to each Thana, or office of Police, that is placed under the management of a native officer, usually called a Darogah or Thanadar. When I come to treat of the tenures of landed estates, I shall mention the perganahs that are contained in the district, with an account of the changes that have happened in their proprietors, and the peculiar customs relative to each.

PART 3.—*Town of Dinajpur.*

The first division comprehends the town of Dinajpur, and its immediate vicinity, extending about 2 miles from N. to S. and about the same from E. to W. It is bounded by the Dhepa and Punabhoba on the west; by the Ghorghora on the south; and by 2 large tanks, Sukhsagor and Onontosagor, on the east. On the north there is no well-defined boundary. The whole is placed in the centre of another division, named Rajarampur. The Police is under the care of a native officer, styled Kotwal, and small suits are determined by an officer of the judges' court, named Munsuf. It is intersected by the channel of the Kachayi, which is nearly dry in the spring, but contains much water in the rainy season. The soil is mostly of the sandy kind, called Chora, and has, at one time or other, been all worn away, and again thrown up by the rivers, by which it is on all sides surrounded. It is, however, very ill supplied with water. The streams are small, and swarm with insects, and the wells afford no water but what is considered as unwholesome. The district may contain 4 square miles, of which, perhaps, 160 acres are cultivated fields; 1600 acres are occupied by houses and gardens; 640 acres are common pasture; and 160 acres are useless, from roads, sands, rivers, and ponds.

The town may be divided into four portions.

1st.—Dinajpur proper, on the east side of the Kachayi, where the Raja's house is situated. This part consists chiefly of detached houses, surrounded by gardens; yet it contains many people.

2ndly.—Rajgunj, which, properly speaking, is the town, and occupies the centre of the district, on the west bank of the Kachayi. It is about a mile in diameter, and closely built, but consists almost entirely of thatched huts. Near the middle it has a square, surrounded somewhat like Covent Garden, (to compare small things with great,) with a row of tiled sheds, which occupy the inner side of the four streets, and serve as shops for retailing various articles. The other streets are quite irregular.

3rdly.—Kangchonghat, which may be considered as the port. It is situated on the Punabhoba, at some distance from Rajgunj, and is occupied by merchant's warehouses, aud the people who are required to attend on them. It is tolerably closely built, and may be about half a mile in diameter.

4thly.—Paharpur, which contains the houses of the European officers of Government, the public offices, the jail, and the houses and gardens belonging to those whose attendance is immediately required. Like Dinajpur proper, this consists chiefly of scattered houses and gardens, intermixed with common pasture. From what I could learn, the houses (Vari or Bari), or rather dwellings, are about 5000; but many dwellings contain 10 huts, and the greater part above two. In a terrible fire, which happened in the year 1807, and which destroyed the greater part of Rajgunj, the Kotwal reported 8000 houses burned, by which, I suppose, he meant huts, for from the dimensions of the town, as I have stated, there could not have been so many abodes. This officer of police is, besides, far from being an accurate man; he could not, for instance, inform me, whether his district extended one or two coses in length or width.

I estimate the population, from the number of houses, at between 25 and 30,000 persons. The roads are kept in excellent repair, by the labour of convicts; and the town, as far as outward view, is remarkably clean and well watched, owing to the great exertions of the magistrate, for he has had much trouble in bringing the former about. The town, as I have before stated, is badly supplied with water, and no attempt has been ever made to light it. Indeed, so far as I know, no such thing was ever attempted in India.

It contains no public building of the least consideration, and decent bridges are very much wanted. The Raja's house was of a great size, but since the decay of the family, has gone to ruin. It was mostly built about 30 years ago, and consists of a strange mixture of European, Moorish, and Hindu styles, all in the very worst taste: in other respects, it was very becoming the fortune of the proprietors, who, with ordinary management, might have lived more like princes than subjects. It contains several temples, but these being appropriated to the family, cannot properly be enumerated among the places of public worship. It has been surrounded by a ditch and rampart of earth, called a Ramdangra by the natives. These are now neglected, as neither necessary for safety, nor effectual for rebellion. The houses of the European gentlemen and public offices, are also abundantly large, but are built in the very worst style of Anglo-Indian architecture; that is to say, are entirely destitute of elegance and convenience. Exclusive of these, there are about 8 dwellings, built partly of brick, the best of which by far belongs to an old prostitute, formerly kept by a European gentleman, and called the *great lady*.

Dinajpur signifies the abode of beggars, and it still is a very poor place. Whether or not it is the same with Dynwaj, the governor (Hakim) of which, Gones, usurped the government of Gaur, I cannot say. I understood at the place that it entirely owed its consequence, first to the residence of the Raja, a very recent event, and afterwards to that of the officers of government; and that the decay of the Raja's family, and diminution of the river, since the year 1787, have hurt it considerably.

It is situated in perganah Vijoynogor, of which it contains 16 Mauzas, or subdivisions. It contains 4 places, where there is a daily market (Bazar), for provisions, and other small articles. And twice a week there is a larger assemblage of people in the square, where cloth chiefly is sold; besides, there is daily a small market at the Raja's gate.

The Hindus have no place of public worship of the least note. The Mohammedans have one small mosque, kept in good repair. The *great lady*, whom I mentioned before, is building a place of worship, but does not seem exactly to have determined, whether it shall belong to the Brahmens or Fakirs. She was originally a Hindu; but having lost caste, and several of the Moslem officers of government having solicited the honor of her hand, (for she is very rich,) she seems rather inclined at present towards the Korán: but she has still scruples, and is afraid of the gods.

There is no remarkable antiquity about the place, except an image of Ganés, of which I have directed a drawing to be made, (Drawing No. 1.) because the image was brought from the ruins of Bannogor, and is, therefore, of great antiquity; and also because the image is reckoned very handsome. To my judgment, the drawing is rather flattering; but it must be confessed, that the image represents a gay deity, dancing on a Lotus flower, although it is not suited to the fastidious taste of a Roman artist.

PART 4.—*Division of Rajarampur.*

The division of Rajarampur surrounds the town on all sides, and is of a very irregular semicircular shape. It may be about 33 miles from W. S. W. to E. N. E. and 17 miles from N. N. W. to E. S. E., and contains about 340 square miles. About 103 square miles may consist of a free, loose soil; and perhaps 20 miles are sandy banks of rivers, liable to be inundated, of which a half may be occasionally cultivated; 154 miles are of a stiff ash coloured clay. The country fully occupied, including houses, gardens, and fields, under regular cultivation, may be 212 miles; of which, perhaps, 85 are of a free soil, and 127 are stiff clay. The following estimate was given by those I consulted of the 128 miles of waste land; 42 miles in tanks, of which one-half are entirely useless, and choked with weeds; 21 in marshes, rivers, and water courses; 15 under woods and bamboos; 10 occupied by common pasture, roads, market places, and burial grounds; but the banks of tanks, woods, and waste land serve also for pasture, and 20 miles of deserted land. I imagine that the extent of the tanks is exaggerated; although the pernicious custom of digging them has been carried to an unusual length in this division. The extent of woods also, I suspect, is exaggerated. They consist mostly of the trees and bamboos which grow on lands that were formerly occupied by villages S. W. from Dinajpur; however, there is a small wood of Sal, (Shorea robusta,) which may contain about 4 square miles, and which seems to have sprung up within these 50 or 60 years, in land that was reserved for the Raja's hunting. The country is badly wooded; a great many villages having little or no shelter, except bamboos.

There are 29 market places, of which 3 are marts for exportation; 4 are held in villages of some note, and the remainder are held in the open fields, or have only a few houses round them. Bhusi on the Atreyi, and Ghughudangga, on the Punabhoba, are the only place that can claim the title of towns; the former contains about 250 dwellings, and the latter about 190. Neither of them have a single brick house, nor any buildings worth notice. The native officers of police and justice, (Darogah and Munsuf,) reside near Rajarampur, a small place, where there are two or three brick houses, belonging to Brahmons and servants, that formerly depended on the raja.

Five proprietors of estates reside in this division, although only one of them lives on his zemindary. He is brother and heir of the person who was manager of Raja Ramnath's estate; is of the Raja's family; and has a handsome house in the Anglo-Indian style. The abodes of the others are built on free lands, and are decent habitations, partly brick and partly thatched. The Raja's Purohit, or family priest, has a very respectable brick house. Altogether, about 15 houses are built wholly, or in part, of that material.

There is no remarkable ruin nor remain of antiquity in this division; but at Josonabad, on the Atreyi, a ghat, or descent into the river, has been dedicated by Vyas, and about 5,000 people assemble, annually, to bathe on a moveable holiday, (Varuni in spring.) At what period of his life this great personage sanctified the place, I cannot say; as it is commonly alleged, that he was born somewhat more than 5000 years ago, and that he is still alive at Bodorikasrom, near the source of th Ganges. Indeed, his whole history seems attended with very great difficulties, for the Brahmons claim him with eagerness, while it is in general allowed, that his mother was of an impure tribe.

The only Hindu building dedicated to worship, and of considerable size, is the temple of Gopal, at a little distance north from Dinajpur. It is fast hastening to ruin, having been begun by Prannath, and finished by Ramnath, in the year 1743; and as its crevices now shelter the Pipol tree, which no one would be so impious as to destroy. The most remarkable place of Muhammedan worship is the tomb of Chehel Gaji, who is supposed to have been a saint of the largest size, as the dimensions of his grave testify, for it is 60 feet in length, and 12 in breadth, and is supposed to have been suited to his remarkable stature. The buildings are situated just on the north side of the town of Dinajpur; and except the grave, are rather ruinous; but have never been very remarkable, either for size or elegance.

The only other public works, in this district, are 4 tanks, dug by the Raja's family. Three of them, however, Sukhsagor, Malasagor, and Onontosagor, are not very remarkable; but have been joined by a canal and rampart, running south from the first to the last, and including the other. It is called a Ramdangra, which is a name given to a fortification, and was dug by a Janoki Ram, who managed the affairs of the family during the minority of the last Raja. Whether or not from some idle view of greatness, he intended to complete the fortification on all sides, is not known, as in the middle of his career he was thrown into jail, for debt, by a native merchant of Calcutta. The 4th tank, called Ramsagor, is about 6 miles south from Dinajpur. The water is about 3,300 feet in length, by 850 in breath. The banks occupy 200 feet, and are very ugly, the soil being so hard, that little or no vegetation has taken place on them; and they are so steep, that they are entirely useless. The water, however, is remarkably good; and the soil is so stiff, that no weeds have, as yet, grown in it.

PART 5.—*The division of Birgunj.*

The division of Birgunj contains about 340 square miles, is somewhat of a square form, and is about 23 miles from north to south, and 19 from east to west. The Darogah resides at Birgunj, near its centre. About 32 miles are destroyed by rivers, water courses, tanks, and marshes. In the rainy season 12 are inundated, of which half may be low, sandy land, occasionally cultivated. Setting aside the 44 miles inundated, about 180 miles are of a free soil, and 116 of hard clay; 12 are occupied by woods, chiefly where former towns have stood. The largest of these is round Prannogor, on the Punabhoba, and consists of the kinds of trees that usually grow near villages. There is no proper forest in this district; but it is very well wooded, and adorned with many bamboos. The land fully occupied, may be 76 miles of hard soil, and 154 of free mould; 10 miles are occupied by roads, markets, burial grounds, and sterile places, and 44 have been deserted, or are only occasionally cultivated.

In the whole division, there is no dwelling house of brick, and very few have mud walls.

The only place of worship, of any considerable size, that belongs to the Hindus, is Kantonogor, built in the ruins of a fort that belonged to Virat Raja. This temple is by far the finest that I have seen in Bengal. It was begun to be built by Prannath, who brought the image of Kanto (Vishnu), from Delhi. In 1704 the first foundation was laid. In 1713 a larger building was commenced, and in 1722 the foundation of the finest part was begun. Although it received a complete repair from Mr. Hatch, a few years ago, and although until lately it was a favourite residence of the family, young trees are fast obtaining possession of the wall, and it will soon be a ruin. This the natives do not seem to regret, as the place, having been erected and dedicated by a mere man, is not considered as holy. The Muhammedans have no place of worship of any considerable size or note.

The principal antiquity in the division, is Uttor Gogriho, round Kantonogor. It is said to have been one of the places, where Virat Raja kept his herds of cattle, and extends at least a mile each way along the eastern side of the Dhepa, and both sides of the Kachayi. This space is surrounded and intersected by high ramparts of earth; but these are so overgrown with trees, bushes, and reeds, that I could not trace their form, which seems to have been very irregular. In one place I observed 4 ramparts, with three intermediate ditches. Within the fortifications are several mounds of earth, in all probability, artificial; and perhaps the ruins of large mud walled buildings, that may have been occupied by the watchmen of the prince. There are no bricks in either the ramparts or mounds. In fact, there is nothing about these ruins, that can contradict the tradition of their being of great antiquity, and of their having been applied to the purpose mentioned. Their extent is great; but in an age when, according to all accounts, the greater part of India was overgrown with forest, and when the chief wealth was probably cattle, the princes are likely to have possessed numerous herds, and large ramparts would be necessary to allow them room to subsist during the incursions of neighbours, who, in general, seem to have had predatory habits. The place, too, is very near the frontier of Bhogodotto, an enemy. The only other ruin of antiquity is at Sonka, about 4 miles east from Birgunj, on the Atreyi river. Here a merchant, named Chand Sadagor, very celebrated in the legends of Bengal, is said to have had a mud fort. I did not see the place, and having had no opportunity of learning any thing satisfactory concerning this remarkable personage, I shall defer stating the reports usually current.

Both at Kantonogor and Prannogor, the Dinajpur family had country seats, now entirely in ruins.

The only public works deserving notice, are the canals which join the Atreyi with the Dhepa, and the Punabhoba with the Tanggon, which have been already described.

The public markets in this division are 35; 4 of them are marts for the exportation and importation of goods; and about 6 others form small villages. The remaining 25 are in the open fields. There is no place that can properly be called a town; neither Khansama nor Jharvari, the two largest places, contain 100 houses.

PART 6.—*Division of Thakurgram.*

The division of Thakurgram is the largest in this district, of which it occupies the northern extremity. It contains about 400 square miles, and is 30 miles from east to west, and 25 from north to south.

The Darogah resides in a central situation, at a miserable village, from which the name of the division has been adopted; and the Munsuf resides at a small town on the southern extremity.

Almost the whole of this division consists of a sandy soil, of which, perhaps, one fourth is a poor thin mould. The country, indeed, is of so light a soil, that iron is seldom used in the plough. About 300 miles are cultivated. The low land, exclusive of rivers, marshes, and water courses, is very rich, is all cultivated, and amounts to about 150 miles. The high land that is fully and properly cultivated may be 75 miles. That which is deserted, or only cultivated occasionally, may be 50 miles. This is partly overgrown with trees and bushes. The land that is unfit for cultivation may be about 45 miles, of which 25 is destroyed by water, rivers, marshes, &c. and 20 miles are burial grounds, roads, market places, steep banks, or wretched soil. The villages are well sheltered with fruit trees and bamboos, and there are few or no tanks, and no woods nor forests.

Govindonogor was the favourite country residence of Raja Ramnath, of Dinajpur, and there he had a handsome house, surrounded by a mud fort, and by religious buildings. The whole is very ruinous. The best dwelling now in the district, belongs to a person who has purchased some lands, and resides at Govindonogor. It has one or two small brick apartments, but is not fit for a person of any rank. The whole habitations are huts, and none almost have mud walls, although many are neatly plastered with that material.

The only place of worship in the district, of any considerable size, is the temple of Govindo, (Vishnu,) near the late Raja Ramnath's house; but it is neither large, handsome, nor considered as holy. The most extraordinary thing near it, are some artificial caves, built of brick, round the roots of two large trees, and covered with earth. In these wretched hovels a number of persons, (Vaishnoos,) of both sexes, resided, who were dedicated to God, and received a daily subsistence from the Raja. These caves are about 6 feet long, and 3 wide and high, and no air nor light enters, but at the end most remote from the tree, which is open.

There are no remarkable remains of antiquity in the division, and the only public work of note, is part of the canal mentioned already, as connecting the Punabhoba and Tanggon, and this has become useless.

The market places are 20, of which 3 are small marts for exportation and importation, and three others have a few shops and houses; but most of the produce that is exported, goes by the way of Raygunj. Goyora, the largest place in the division, contains between 70 and 80 houses; and Govindonogor, the only other place that has any pretentions to be called a town, contains about 60 dwellings, most of which, however, are rather comfortable, and neatly plastered with clay.

Part 7.—*Division of Rani Songkol.*

The division of Rani Songkol, is situated immediately south from Thakurgram, on the banks of the Nagor, and is nearly of the same nature with the western part of that district. It derives its name from the Thana having been placed between two villages, named Songkol and Rani; but it is near to neither, and in fact, is in a plain at some distance from any house, and is by no means centrical, being situated towards the S. E. corner. The division is nearly of a square form, about 15 miles from north to south, and as much from east to west, and may contain about 210 square miles.

The whole almost is of a fine sandy soil; about 10 miles may be destroyed by rivers, marshes, and ponds; 16 miles may be sterile lands, burying grounds, roads, market places, or temples; 26 miles of high land are much neglected, either from the cultivators having run away, or only choosing to cultivate it occasionally; 53 miles may be high land, fully occupied and cultivated; and 105 may be rich lowland, of which none is allowed to be waste. There is no forest in this district, but the houses are well sheltered by fruit trees and bamboos.

Two families of zemindars, Kholora and Maldwar, who have possessed estates for some time, have brick houses suitable to their rank, and built after the Anglo-Indian style of architecture. A few houses have mud walls, and perhaps one-eighth of the whole huts are plastered neatly with clay. The remainder are mere hovels, with walls made of straw or grass hurdles.

The principal place of Hindu worship is Gorokhyonath, where there is a small temple of Sib, and another of Kali; but the principal holiness of the place is owing to a small spring or well, which is about 2 feet each way, and is surrounded by a stone. It is supposed, that no multitude, however great, could empty this well. The temple has a small endowment of land, and 10 or 12 thousand persons assemble here, on the festival of the god (Siboratri), to drink the water, and perform other ceremonies. The chief Muhammedan place of worship also owes more of its celebrity to the sanctity of the place, than to its magnificence; for it is only a large thatched hut, but it contains the remains of Saiud Nekmurdun, a person of the greatest holiness. His festival is celebrated at a great annual fair, that will be hereafter mentioned.

Several remains of antiquity are supposed to have belonged to a certain Ram Ray, and his brother Syam Ray, about whom many miraculous stories are current in the vicinity. Nothing certain is known concerning these persons, but the most probable opinion is, that they were zemindars, who managed this part of the country before the present families obtained possession. The remains of works attributed to the two brothers are,

1st. A considerable tank, named Ramdighi, and situated west from the Thana; at its north end has been a building of brick, probably a temple; and a stair of stone led down from this to the tank. Most of the stones have been removed by the proprietors of the land; about half a mile S. W. from the tank is a large heap of ruins, containing many bricks, and many more have been removed to build a neighbouring house. Among the ruins I observed some bricks, that had been carved, and the building, therefore, has been ornamented in the high style of the country fashion. It is said to have been the abode of Ram Ray, and has been of considerable size, becoming a person of rank. Both round the heap of ruins, and the tank, the ground is excavated by numerous small ponds, like the usual sources of abomination, that are commonly scattered through the cities of Bengal; but there is no tradition concerning this having ever been a city.

2d. A small square fort, near Nekmurdun's tomb, which is surrounded by a rampart of earth and ditch, and is called Dhum.

3d. A rather larger fort, of the same nature, situated on the west side of the Kulik, near Songkol, and called Ramgor. At neither of these forts are there any bricks, or vestiges of building.

4th. Another small fort, called Bangal, which I did not see. It is about 6 miles N. W. from the Thana.

The market places, in this division, are 17, of which by far the most considerable is the great fair at Bhowanipur, on the festival of Nekmurdun. It continues for ten days, from about the 7th to the 17th of April. A military guard and civil officers, (often the magistrate,) attend to preserve the peace, and protect the innocent; for the multitude is very great, and rogues, thieves, prostitutes, musicians, jugglers, showmen, and religious mendicants, as usual, on such occasions, form a considerable part of the multitude; idle lookers-on, and religious persons, come to honor the saint, and increase the multitude, which is filled up by traders from Bhotan, Puroniya, Nepal, Benares, Patna, Murshedabad, Rangpur, and all intermediate places. About 3,000 ponies, partly from Bhotan, and partly from the west country, and from one to two thousand carriage oxen, are usually sold at this fair; and there is exposed for sale almost every kind of commodity, for which there is any demand in the country, especially of a more valuable sort, such as broad cloths, silks, fine muslins, shawls, copper, hard-ware, trinkets, spices, musk, Thibet cow's tails, and gold dust. It is said that the sales amount to between 3 and 4 hundred thousand rupees, and that one hundred thousand people usually attend.

There are, besides, 2 marts for exportation and importation, and 4 other places, where there are a few shops; but most of the produce that is exported, is sent by the way of Raygunj. The other markets are held in the fields. Songkol, the only place entitled, in any degree, to be called a town, contains about 150 dwellings, none of them in the least remarkable.

PART 8.—*Division Pirgunj.*

The division of Pirgunj lies on both sides of the Tanggon, south from Thakurgram, east from Ranisongkol, and west from Birgunj. It contains about 220 square miles, and is of an oblong form, 20 miles from north to south, and 14 from east to west. The Thana is situated near the western side, in a small village, from whence it derives its name.

The whole is a light sandy soil, so that no iron is required in the plough; about 138 miles are fully occupied; about 13 miles are occupied by rivers and marshes; 7 miles are destroyed by inundation, and are quite waste; 14 miles may be occupied by woods, of which some consist almost entirely of Sal, (*Shorea robusta;*) 20 miles by poor high land, fit for very little, and chiefly producing bamboos and wretched pasture, and include burying grounds, roads, and market places; 28 miles are high land, little occupied, and either altogether deserted, or only cultivated occasionally; but a considerable portion is poor, and fit only for being cultivated after a fallow.

In this division there are few tanks, nor does it contain one dwelling house built of brick. The huts are well sheltered with trees and bamboos, and are almost entirely constructed of straw hurdles.

There is no place of worship that receives any dignity from its ornaments or buildings, but many persons frequent the tombs of three Muhammedan saints, (Pirs.) There is no remarkable public work.

On the west bank of the Tanggon, near the southern extremity of the district, are some ruins, which consist of bricks, in some places thickly scattered in the ground, in others rising into heaps. On the largest of these is a carved stone. The ruins extend about 200 yards along the steep bank of the river, which is said to have carried away a great part. Many bricks have also been removed, in order to build small temples, and deep excavations have been made, probably in order to discover treasure. This place is called the fort of Mohadev, who is supposed, by the people, to have been contemporary with Virat Raja. At a little distance farther west, is another ruin, containing bricks, which I did not see: it is called Mogulan kot, and is said to have been the residence of a Moslem chief and his daughter; who are also supposed to have been contemporary with Virat Raja; the people having not the smallest idea of chronology. The agent of the proprietor, a Brahmon of Maldeh, who told me this, had so little curiosity, that he could not tell whether or not there was any inscription over the door of a small temple, which was built from the ruins, and in which he daily performed worship.

There are 11 market places, of which 2 are small marts for exportation and importation; but most of the produce of the country that is exported, goes to Raygunj, and a part to Maldeh and its vicinity. Besides the two marts or Bundurs, 4 of the market places have some shops. The only place, which can be considered as a town, is Kornayi on the Tanggon, which contains about 100 dwellings, and has 3 small brick temples, which were built by a person, who has lately purchased an estate in the neighbourhood.

PART 9.—*Division of Hemtabad.*

The division of Hemtabad is situated south from Rani Songkol, on the east side of the Nagor, and is divided into nearly 2 equal portions by the Kulik. It is about 20 miles from north to south, and as much from east to west, and contains about 300 square miles. The Thana is very near the eastern boundary. The soil is almost entirely loose, and contains too much sand. A great deal of it is too high for retaining water, and is therefore barren; and a great deal is so low as to be rendered useless by floods. About 187 miles are fully cultivated; 37 miles are destroyed by marshes, rivers, floods, and water, of which 20 are only occasionally inundated; 38 are unfit for cultivation, being very poor, or occupied by burial-grounds, market places, roads, &c. and 38 are high grounds, either deserted, or only occasionally cultivated. Two marshes (*Bils*) retain much water during the whole year, and form lakes. The huts are well sheltered by trees and bamboos, and the only woods are the trees and bushes growing near houses that have been deserted, and which may, perhaps, occupy 8 miles of the land mentioned under that head. There are few tanks in the division, and none of remarkable size.

There is no dwelling constructed of brick, except one belonging to a mosque. No dwelling has mud walls; but many have walls of straw, plastered with clay. Few walls are constructed of mats; hurdles are the usual material.

By far the most celebrated Muhammedan place of worship, either here or in the vicinity, is near Hemtabad, and is a (*Durgah*) monument, dedicated to Mukhdum Dokorposh, where the saint's tomb is shown, and where there is a small rude mosque of stone adorned with pillars and carvings, which it is evident from their containing human figures, have been taken from Hindu buildings. In the market place at Hemtabad, the same saint has a monument, which is much frequented on the day appropriated for the commemoration of his name; and near his own mosque, which was adjacent to his house, he seems to have erected another in memory of Kotub Shah, who was the most holy personage in the reign of Ghyashudin, as Dokorposh seems to have been in the reign of Sultan Hoseyn. The mosque of Kotub Shah has also been ornamented with stone pillars, the spoil of infidels. Four fakirs attend the mosque of Dokorposh, which is in tolerable repair, as well as the tomb, but the other buildings are quite ruinous. They have 500 bigahs of land, free of rent, but it is of a wretched soil. This mosque, from an inscription over the gate, would appear to have been built in the year of the Hegira 996, by Sultan Hoseyn.

At Baliyadighi is a mosque near a tank, which has an endowment of 1000 bigahs of land; and the fakir, who has the hereditary charge, lives in a brick house, and in a decent manner. There is no Hindu place of worship of any note.

The antiquities of this district are rather interesting, and are situated immediately west from Hemtabad. It is said that formerly there governed, at this place, a Hindu Raja, named Mohes, to whom much of the neighbouring country was subject. During his government, a certain Muhammedan saint (*Pir*), named Buzerudin, came and sat down at his gate, where he seems to have been but coldly received. Soon after came a still more celebrated person, Mukhdum Ghuribal Hoseyn Dokorposh, and the Raja immediately fled to Dhaka, which he is said to have founded. The *Pir*, I should suppose, was accompanied by an army, but tradition by no means supports this conjecture. On the contrary, it is said, that the Raja fled merely because he was shocked at the destruction which the two barbarian saints, and their attendants, committed on innocent cattle and poultry; Mohes, therefore, was probably very different from the Hindu Rajas of the present day, as indeed all Rajas of former times are said to have been. A Muhammedan saint, in these days, who attempted to kill a cow in a Hindu country, would run great risk, unless he was protected by an army. In support of my opinion, I must mention, that soon after Mohes had been expelled by the saints, Sultan Hoseyn appears to have been at the place, and gave his daughter in marriage to Mukhdum Uzi-Udin, brother to Dokorposh. The son by this marriage, Mukhdum Shah Bazit, is said to have retired to Sondwip, and took up his abode there; but his son Jamaludin returned here, and was buried near his grand uncle. In the inscription on his tomb, it must be observed, that he is called Jamaludin, son of Sheykh Yahia. On the whole, I am inclined to believe, that Mohes Raja was sovereign of this part of the country, which, not being included in the provinces of Barondro or Maithilo, did not probably belong to the kingdom of Gaur, until the time of Hoseyn the conqueror; and this territory may have been the country called Kamchab, which he added to his dominions. Having premised so much on the history of the place, I shall now describe its present appearance.

Near a tank, a little way west from Hemtabad, there is a space of ground about half a mile in diameter, over every part of which bricks are thickly scattered, and in some places the foundations of walls may be traced. In some places, this is thickly covered with trees and bushes, and in others, it is clear; at the northern end is a small hill formed of bricks, and said to have been the public office (*Kuchery*), of Mohes Raja. On the surface are a good many large squared stones, of which material, probably, a considerable part of the building consisted. South from that, about 100 yards, is a still larger heap of ruins, and here also are several stones, one of which, apparently the lintel of a door, is a good deal ornamented. This ruin is said to have been the Raja's house. Immediately south from this heap, are shown the foundations of a small square apartment, made of brick, in the centre of which is a tomb, said to be that of *Pir* Buzerudin. The door of stone is still erect, and as will appear from the drawing, (No. 2.) has been handsome. From the figures on it, the workmanship is, no doubt, Hindu, and in all probability it has been a door in the Raja's house; at the south end of the ruins are the mosques and adjacent buildings, which I have no doubt, have also been built from the materials of the Raja's abode. A door in the outer wall has still more perfect figures, than that which has been drawn; and the figure on the lintel strongly resembles the image of Gautama and his two favourite disciples, as usually represented in the temples of Ava. The pillars are remarkably clumsy, quite in the Hindu style; and being all of different forms and lengths, could not have been originally intended for the places which they now occupy. Besides, on a stone lying near the mosque, is carved a human figure, quite entire. I have given a drawing of this building, (No. 3.) as being one of the most entire in the district.

About a mile and a half beyond this ruin, is another, which has been surrounded by a brick wall, and is usually called the *tukht*, or throne, of Hoseyn (*Padshah*) the king. The *tukht* consists of a quadrangular truncated pyramid, of about 20 feet in perpendicular height, and is composed of bricks heaped confusedly together. Intermixed with these are some large carved stones, evidently of the same style as these of Mohes Raja's house; but whether they have been brought from thence, or whether they are the ruins of a temple, that formerly may have been on the spot, I cannot say. On the summit of this pyramid is a considerable square area, in the centre of which a terrace has been raised about three feet high, and this has been regularly built with cement, and its sides have been ornamented with mouldings covered with plaster. It was here, it is said, that Hoseyn Shah sat, and beheld sports which were exhibited at the nuptials of his daughter. South from the pyramid are the ruins of a brick building, the roof of which has fallen in, but the walls are standing, and have been encrusted with carved bricks. The building is nearly square, with arched doors and windows, and is elevated on a brick terrace about five feet high. This is said to have been the house that was erected for the accommodation of the princess during the ceremony, after which the whole seems to have been given to religious men. The tombs of two saints (Weleat and Bahador Shahs), now occupy the throne of the king, and many tombs of saints and fakirs surround the pyramid. There is a small endowment of land for supporting the fakir, who supplies the lamps burned at the tombs of the most distinguished of these personages.

Between the two ruins many bricks are scattered on the fields, and a very wide road, with a ditch on each side, may be traced most part of the way.

In this division are sixteen market places, of which Raygunj is the only mart for exportation and importation; and it is indeed the most considerable mart in Dinajpur, and one of its principal towns. It is quite a new place, that has arisen within these thirty years. This is the mart from whence the produce of Thakurgram, Pirgunj, Songkol Hemtabad, and part of Kaliyagunj, is chiefly exported; and a great part of the produce of the N. W. part of Rongpur comes also this way. It is, in fact, the principal mart in a rich country, which extends about seventy miles in length, and twenty in breadth; and it is almost the only place in that extent that deserves to be called a town: yet the usual computation makes its inhabitants occupy only 400 houses, and on a minute inquiry at the place, I could not learn that it contained more than 273 dwellings (*Varis*), and probably about 700 huts, for it does not contain any building worthy to be called a house. The merchants have large yards, surrounded by rails of split bamboos, about eight feet high. Within these are many huts and storehouses, with walls constructed of straw hurdles, and very few have the walls plastered with clay, or formed of mats. The streets are narrow, dirty, and confused; but it is a place of great stir, and crowded with boatmen and drivers of cattle. The people allege, that on an average for eight months in the year, 5000 loaded oxen arrive each day, which is probably an exaggeration, although I saw nothing to contradict its accuracy. Two other places are provided with shops, and one of these, Tajpur, is rather a large place, as it contains 100 dwellings. The part of this town, which is on the west side of the river, and which Mr. Rennell has laid down as Tajpur, is by the natives called Bhogoleta. On the east side there are no remains of brick houses, nor of its ever having been a place of consequence, although one of the Sirkars into which Bengal was divided, by Akber, derives its name from the place.

PART 10.—*Division of Kaliyagunj.*

The division of Kaliyagunj is almost forty miles in length from S. S. W. to N. N. E., and about fourteen miles from W. N. W. to E. S. E., but contains only about 310 square miles. The Thana is placed at Akhanogor, near one extremity of the district, while the Munsuf resides near the other end at Churamoon. In fact, this and the adjacent division Bongsihari, have been very ill contrived, and are two long narrow districts running parallel, which might be rendered much more convenient and compact by removing one Thana to Begumgunj, and placing under this the southern parts of both divisions, while the northern parts should be placed under a Thana situated at Kusumvarir hat, or in that vicinity.

About 40 miles of this division are subject to inundation; but this portion is much better cultivated than such lands usually are in this district, and probably 25 miles of these are occupied; of the remainder probably 160 miles towards Hemtabad and Pirgunj, are of a loose, sandy soil, much neglected, and rather poor; and 95 miles towards Bongsihari, are of a stiff clay very fully occupied. I should suppose, that the whole land occupied may be 215 miles; 30 miles are deserted villages and lands, 10 of which are overgrown with trees and bamboos; 10 miles are occupied by poor waste soil, burial grounds, market places, and the like; and 15 are occupied by rivers, tanks, water courses, and marshes, which are not cultivated; for a considerable part of these in this division produce the kind of rice called *Boro*. There are no remarkable tanks.

The huts, except in the inundated parts, are well sheltered with trees and bamboos. Much of the waste land is overgrown with reeds. Two families of the proprietors have brick houses, which are becoming their rank and fortune; and one of them, belonging to Guruprosad, of Sorur, is a place very much becoming the residence of a gentleman. It is situated in a large piece of ground finely wooded, and has been surrounded with a ditch and rampart of earth, now considered as unnecessary, and allowed to go to ruin. The family of the present proprietor has enjoyed the estate for some time, and he seems very worthy of his fortune; as very unlike most of the proprietors of land in Bengal, he attends carefully to his affairs, and has the manners of a gentleman: another proprietor of land, and the acting *Kazi* have decent thatched habitations. All the others are huts; but towards the east side of the district these are more comfortable, as they have mud walls.

I heard of no Hindu place of worship deserving notice. It is true, that the Churamon family have erected several temples of brick, one of them being totally sunk in indolence and superstition; but they are poor buildings, and in the opinion of the people possessed of no peculiar sanctity. The Muhammedans are not more fortunate; for although the acting *Kazi* has lately built a neat, though small mosque, little reverence is shown for it; in this district the monuments of holy men being the favourite places of worship.

The only remains of antiquity that I saw or heard of, is at Borogang, in the southern part of the division. These are several mounds consisting of bricks, covered in a measure with soil, and extending about 300 yards in diameter. Near them are many small tanks, like those of a Bengal town. On one of the mounds is situated the tomb of a Muhammedan saint, surrounded by a brick wall. The *fakir* says, that it was built by one of the Bengal kings, which is very probable; but his authority is as nothing, for he was a poor illiterate creature, with a silly show of devotion. Even while I was speaking to him, he continued to mutter prayers, and to sob forth pious ejaculations. Around the monument (*Durgah*) are a good many stones, like those at Hemtabad, but less ornamented. There is no tradition concerning the founder of the ruin. I have no doubt of its having been a Hindu edifice, and that the monument has been built from its materials.

In this division are 19 market places. The only mart is Churamon, a tolerable town, which contains at least 300 dwellings, much larger, better built, and cleaner than Raygunj, but a place of infinitely less commerce. Three other small places have a few shops, the other market places are in the fields. The exports from the district are chiefly made through Raygunj and Maldeh.

PART 11.—*Division Bongsihari.*

The division of Bongsihari contains about 240 square miles, and is about 24 miles from S. S. W. to N. N. E. by 11 miles from E. S. E. to W. N. W. The Thana is placed on the side of a tank, and has no shops nor market place in its vicinity; but is in a central situation, and the *Munsuf* resides within half a mile of the Thana.

Little of this division is subject to inundation, but almost the whole consists of hard clay, which, in most places, is level, and in some so flat, that the inhabitants have dug tanks in order to procure situations for their houses. In others there is a large extent of uneven land, rather barren. I should suppose, that 180 miles are fully occupied, 16 are occupied by high barren land, burial grounds, market places, &c. more is really high and barren, but a great deal of this is occupied by houses and gardens; 30 miles are poor or deserted lands, cultivated occasionally, and 15 are spoiled by tanks, rivers, and inundations. This portion also is, in reality, more extensive, but the banks of most of the tanks are occupied by houses; there are no woods, unless the trees, growing about a few deserted villages, may be considered as such. The waste inundated land is covered with long reeds.

There is no dwelling house built of brick, but almost all the huts have mud walls, and many of their yards are surrounded by fences of the same material; within the premises, many of the more wealthy farmers have small brick mosques, that are well white-washed, and add much to the good appearance of the country.

In this division there is no place of worship of any note, but there are several antiquities near the Thana; at about half a mile south from this place, is a small Hindu temple, called a *Mondir*, a work apparently of considerable antiquity. Its base is a quadrangular prism, about 20 feet high, and 12 wide. Its summit is a pyramid of about the same height. This part of the building has been much ornamented with carved bricks, especially a kind of escutcheon on each face, that possesses some degree of good taste. The artists have been ignorant of the method of constructing an arch; for the door is contracted above, to a point, by the horizontal rows of bricks, gradually encroaching on its width; not the smallest tradition remains concerning its founder, and the image has been removed.

At a little distance west from this *Mondir* begins a narrow elevated ridge of land, perhaps half a mile wide, which extends west to the Beliya, about 2 miles, and seems to me entirely artificial. It is every where full of small tanks, inequalities, and heaps, many of which consist almost entirely of bricks. The largest of these has been lately opened, probably in part to look for hidden treasure, and in part to procure bricks for building an office *(Kuchery)*, for collecting the rents, and this later view has not been in vain. The building has probably been a temple, in form of a polygon. The outer wall is about 4 feet thick. At the western end of this elevated space are two tanks of considerable dimensions, which are almost filled up, and entirely choked with weeds. The place is called Brojobollobhopur, and I have no doubt has been a considerable town; but no tradition remains.

About 1¼ mile west from the Beliya, is a very large tank, called Melandighi, which is nearly choked with weeds. The only tradition concerning it is, that it was dug by a princess *(Rani)*, and that a miracle was necessary to procure water. About 1¼ mile further west is Gordighi, a tank, the water of which has extended about 600 yards N. and S. and 400 yards E. and W. and which of course is a Hindu work. A considerable portion of it has now so far filled up, that it is cultivated for rice. About 1,200 yards west from this tank is another, called Altadighi, which extends nearly to the same dimensions, but is placed with its greatest length from east to west, and therefore is a Muhammedan work. Between these two tanks are the ruins of Borohata, which are very large heaps or mounds, that consist in a great measure of bricks. In many places the foundations of walls may be traced, and even the dimensions of the chambers. All these chambers are of a small size, owing to which they may have resisted the attacks of time better than more spacious apartments. They are chiefly situated in the southern division of the town called Kutwari. In this part are some small tanks, that have evidently been entirely lined with brick. In the centre of the ruins are indubitable traces of a small square fort, which has been surrounded by a double wall of brick, and an intermediate ditch. The ruin to the north of this fort is almost entirely without the trace of regular form, but the quantity of bricks, which it contains, is great. At its northern extremity is the monument of a Muhammedan saint, *Pir* Budul Dewan, which is built of brick; in its gate are two stones, but there is nothing about them to determine, whether they have been brought by the founders, or taken from the ruins. There is no sort of tradition concerning the persons, who either founded or destroyed these works.

I observed also in this division, on the road towards the S. E. two places where there were small tanks, and heaps of earth and bricks, which may have been towns; but there was nothing about them, which indicated their ever having been places of considerable importance.

In the N. E. part of this division is a very large tank, supposed to have been dug by Mohipal Raja, and called after his name (Moybuldighi R.) The sheet of water extends 3800 feet from N. to S., and 1100 from E. to W. Its depth must be very considerable, as the banks are very large. On the bank are several small places of worship, both Hindu and Moslem, but none of any consequence; nothing remains to shew that Mohipal ever resided either at the tank, or at Mohipur near it; but there is a vast number of bricks, and some stones, that probably belonged to religious buildings, that have been erected by the person who constructed the tank. One of the stones is evidently the lintel of a door, and of the same style with those at Ban Nogor, and may have been brought from the ruins of that city. The people in the neighbourhood have an idea, that there has been a building in the centre of the tank; but this is probably devoid of truth, as there is no end to the idle stories, which they relate concerning the tank and Mohipal. Both are considered as venerable, or rather awful, and the Raja is frequently invoked in times of danger. A canal and road, formed from the earth, thrown out, leads south from the tank, about 4 miles, where they join others leading east and west, but to what distance I did not ascertain.

There are, in this division, 20 market places, of which 6 are marts for exportation, but all of small importance; for a great part of the produce goes for exportation to Maldeh or its vicinity. One market place, (Mukhdumpur,) besides, is provided with several shops, and is rather a large place, for it contains 100 habitations; but the chief place is Horirampur, one of the marts, which with the adjoining town called Betona, contain 300 houses, and in this country is reckoned a considerable town.

PART 12.—*Division Jagodol.*

The division of Jagodol is somewhat of a triangular form, with its shortest side to the north, measuring about 20 miles; from north to south it extends about 23 miles, and contains about 250 square miles. The Thana is situated at Bamongola, near the centre of the division. It is much intersected by rivers that have very low banks, over which they extend far in the inundations, so that during the rainy season probably 62 miles are entirely covered, and of this not above 12 miles are cultivated for indigo, or for the rice, called Boro. Except in the inundated lands the soil is a hard clay, but is not level; 15 miles are, at all seasons, occupied by rivers, water courses, tanks, and marshes, and are unfit for cultivation; 19 miles are high useless land, either covered with long harsh grass or bushes, or are occupied by burial grounds, market places, roads and other purposes, which render them totally unfit for being rented; 44 miles are deserted villages, which are capable of cultivation, and 22 miles of these are overgrown with woods, from the trees that formerly surrounded the houses, and 110 miles are fully occupied. The most remarkable tanks are Dhormo Sagor, near Rajnagor, and two at Chaknagor, which have the title of *Pushkorini;* but none of them are of great dimensions, nor of singular holiness.

In this district there are 5 or 6 houses of brick, which belong to the landholders. Most of the farmers live in huts, with mud walls; but the traders who live in towns or villages, as if on purpose to encourage fire, usually build their houses with hurdles. This is pretty universally the case throughout the district. The reason assigned is, that their stay in one place is so precarious, that it would be absurd to incur the expence of building a substantial house.

There is no Hindu place of worship remarkable either for its architecture or sanctity. Many Muhammedans resort to the monument of a saint, about a coss east from the Thana, which is the only place of worship at all remarkable, that they possess. The building is of little consequence.

There are considerable remains of antiquity: but the death of the Darogah, just before my arrival, and the ignorance of the people about the Thana, prevented me from hearing of them in time, so that I was unable to lay down a plan for visiting them.

The N. E. corner of the ruins of Peruya, or rather of its dependencies, extend into this division, and in that direction I observed several heaps of broken bricks.

Sekunder Shah had a favourite residence on the banks of the Tanggon, about 8 or 9 miles south form Bamongola. The ruins are said to be very extensive, and to contain many bricks and stones.

Hoseyn Shah formed a fine road through the country between the Tanggon and Punabhoba, and it is said to have extended to Ghoraghat; but I have not been able to trace it. The width is said to have been 348 cubits, with a large ditch, and many fine trees on each side, and bridges constructed of bricks. The whole is overgrown, and gone to ruin; from these dimensions, it must rather have been a work of ostentation than utility, and probably was rather an appendage to the country residence of the kings at Sekundura, than a military way to Ghoraghat.

Near the centre of the island formed by the Tanggon and Punabhoba, is a tank surrounded by a large wood, in which there are many heaps of bricks and stones, said to be the ruins of the abode of Moyu Rudro, a prince of the family of the sun, but nothing is known concerning the time when he governed; at Ghatnagor, however, I heard of the same personages, and it is said that he was contemporary with Virat.

In this division there are 16 market places, of which 6 are marts, where goods are exported and imported; but these are rather inconsiderable places. One market place, besides, is provided with a few shops.

PART 13.—*Division Maldeh.*

The division under the Thana of Maldeh extends from the Punabhoba along the Mohananda and Nagor, for above 30 miles, and in some places is 10 miles in width. It contains about 280 square miles. The Darogah resides at Maldeh exactly on the frontier of Puroniya, but nearly in the middle of his district, with respect to length, and no other place would be a more convenient residence.

The inundated land in this division is of great extent, and may occupy 70 square miles, of which perhaps 20 are cultivated with Boro rice, or are (Chora) of a sandy soil near the banks of rivers, and occasionally produce indigo, cucurbitaceous plants, wheat or barley. The remainder is overgrown with long reeds. The remaining

210 miles are clay with a very uneven surface and some mixture of sand, so that perhaps 40 miles may be reckoned of a mixed soil, of which perhaps 15 are occupied; 17 miles may be occupied by tanks, rivers, and marshes, or water courses; 18 miles by poor steep unimprovable soil, or by burial places, roads, markets, and the like; 35 miles are occupied by forests, which formerly were towns and gardens; 35 miles by lands that have been, and occasionally are cultivated after a fallow, but which are of a soil perfectly good for regular cultivation; and 105 are fully occupied, of which perhaps 15 are of a rich free soil.

The huts in this division are remarkably well shaded with trees, especially on the banks of the Mohanonda, which are peculiarly favorable for the mango and banyan tree. The latter indeed surpasses in grandeur and beauty any thing of the kind that I have ever seen, and hence perhaps Linnæus might have been justified in calling it the Ficus Bengalensis, as flourishing peculiarly near the ancient capital of that country, had not the denomination of Ficus Indica been consecrated by its use in the writers of antiquity. A great many houses in this division are constructed of brick, and contain stones as thresholds and stairs; more, I imagine from the ruins affording a superabundance of these materials at no expence and little trouble, than from its manufactures and commerce having introduced an extraordinary wealth, or an improved manner of living. This in fact is by far the poorest and worst cultivated division in the district.

The only Hindu place of worship, that deserves notice, is a small pond, (Kundo,) to which on a certain day the women of the vicinity resort to bathe. It is chiefly frequented by women who have lost their children, either by abortion or disease. If in bathing they find a living snail, they think, that their future children will live; but if they find an empty shell, they think that it forebodes a continuance of their misfortune.

The Muhammedan places of worship are of much more importance. In Maldeh are five mosques of some size, and in which worship is performed, although they are ruinous, and have no endowments. According to an inscription over the door of the largest, it was built 210 years ago by a merchant of the place. Part of it is of stone, evidently brought from the ruins of Gaur.

By far the most conspicuous places of worship, however, are the monuments at Pernya, of Mukhdum Shah Jelal and Kutub Shah, who were the two most distinguished religious persons during the early part of the kingly government of Bengal. Numerous pilgrims repair to these monuments, at all seasons, and from all parts of Bengal. That of Mukhdum is chiefly frequented at a very great annual assembly, (mela,) while the memory of Kutub is celebrated at four smaller meetings, (ulos,) but all religious mendicants (fakirs) who come at any time, are fed for three days, and this is called charity. Both places have considerable endowments, which are expended in keeping the buildings in repair, and in the support of these vagrants, and of a numerous establishment of servants, who form the population of Pernya. The lands in this district, which belong to the monument of Mukhdum, are called Bais-hazary, or twenty-two thousand, as containing that number of biggahs, and have always been managed by a person appointed by Government. The lands belonging to the monument of Kutub Shah are under the management of his descendants, and are called Chhye-hazary, as containing six thousand biggahs.

On going north from Maldeh, the monument of Mukhdum is the nearest, and the entrance to it is pointed out by a plain, but not inelegant gate of stone and brick. At some distance within this is a village containing about 100 huts, that are occupied by the servants. They are rather comfortable, and are surrounded by good gardens. Beyond these are some rude shades, in which pilgrims and other vagrants find shelter. Beyond these, is the monument, consisting of a small square area, the entrance into which is from the S. E. corner by a small door. On the right of the door is a small chamber, in which Kutub Shah performed his devotions. Beyond that is the kitchen. The north side of the area is a refectory for fakirs. On the west side is a small plain mosque without pillars or pulpit. The south side of the area is enclosed by a small tank, lined with stones towards the area, from which a stair descends to the bottom, that is very dirty, and the water is bad. The tomb of the saint is not here, and the buildings are neither large nor elegant. Although not neatly kept, they are in tolerable repair, and from carving on the stones they would evidently appear to have been brought from ruins, probably from Gaur. From three different inscriptions it would appear, that these buildings have been erected, improved, or repaired by Shah Neyamut-ullah, in A. H. 1075, by Chaund Khan, A. H. 1084, and by Sadullah, A. H. 1093.

About a quarter of a mile beyond the monument of Mukhdum is the village which belongs to the attendants on Kutub Shah, who are fully as numerous as those of Mukhdum, and the sheds are capable of accommodating more strangers. These are placed on both sides of the road, but chiefly on the east; for the monument occupies a large space on the west. In the centre are the remains of Kutub's dwelling house, with a large gate in front. These buildings, which formed the dwelling of the saint, have been extensive, and included several courts; but they are very ruinous. The greater part, according to the natives, is buried in the forest, and inaccessible. The gate-way and two outer courts are still in part occupied by travellers, and by the kitchens, where food is prepared for the mendicants, but they are ruinous, and slovenly to the last degree. Beyond these I penetrated into what are said to have been the women's apartments, one of which has been a small square chamber, lined with tiles that have been enamelled with various glaring colours. The gateway is by far the most entire part, owing probably to its sanctity, for Mukhdum Dokorposh having come here one day very hungry, and having gone into the kitchen, could procure nothing to eat, and therefore became very angry, and struck the gate with both hands and feet, leaving the impression of both on the solid granite. These miraculous marks are considered as holy, and not fit to be trodden on, by which means indeed I discovered them; for to say the truth they have not the most distant resemblance to the impressions of the human hand or foot. This however is a trifle to the sturdy faith of a pilgrim, who is seldom very critical. Over the gate is an inscription containing a passage from the Koran. South from the house or palace of Kutub is an irregular square space of about 100 yards in diameter, enclosed with a brick wall: the principal entrance is from the east, through a gateway of considerable dimensions. The middle space is occupied by a square tank lined with cut stone. The S. W. corner is occupied by a small ruinous mosque without columns or pulpit. The S. W. corner is occupied by the tomb of Kutub, which I saw only from a distance, as my near approach would have given offence. It is covered with a canopy of white cotton cloth, and a cloth of the same kind is laid over the grave. Near it are two small buildings of brick, on one of which is an inscription bearing date A. H. 886. Between it and the tank is the tomb of Alal Huk, father of Kutub, and also a saint of great celebrity. It is covered in the same manner as the tomb of his son. Great part of the remainder of the area is filled by the tombs of Moslems that wished to be buried near these illustrious personages, who by the people here are said to have been the real kings of the place, as it was only according to their pleasure that the temporal kings could reign, and I am inclined to think that there is some truth in the assertion. In fact, the ruins of Kutub's house or palace are nearly as respectable as those which are said to be the remains of the royal palace. Among the tombs is a very neat one in good preservation, which from an inscription on it, appears to be that of the infant son of Enaet-ullah, son of Taher Muhammed, son of Imadudin Hoseyn, son of Sultan Ali Subzoari, A. H. 1017.

On the north side of the saint's abode is a small mosque, called the golden swing, I suppose, from its sanctity; for neither its materials nor architecture can entitle it to so high an appellation. It is surrounded by a brick wall, in the east side of which is a large gate, which is faced with cut granite, and contains an inscription. The walls of the mosque are also of granite, but the roof, which consists of 10 miserable domes, is made of brick, as the artist probably could not construct them of the granite. The domes are supported by 4 columns and 10 pilasters, all of different lengths and forms, and all equally destitute of elegance. In each end are 2 windows, and in the front 5 doors, all arched. Over the centre door is an inscription. The pulpit is of stone and very rude. The whole is hastening to ruin, for no pains are taken to remove the pipul and banyan trees, that have sprung from crevices. From the inscriptions it would appear, that both the mosques and its gate were erected in honor of Kutub Shah, by Mukhdum Sheykh, son of Muhammed Khalidi, in A. H. 993. There can be little doubt, from appearances of broken columns and other carved stones irregularly placed, that the whole of the stones in these buildings have been brought from Gaur or some other Hindu city.

I shall now describe the remaining antiquities of Pernya, Panduya, or Pandoviya, which being unconnected with the two great saints, are not objects of religious veneration, although some of them have been places of worship. A road paved with brick, from 12 to 15 feet wide, and not very straight, seems to have passed through the whole length of the town; and from about ½ mile south from Mukhdum Shah's gate may extend five or six miles to the north. From heaps of bricks on both sides of this, it would appear to have been a regular street, with brick houses on each side, and the foundations of many of the buildings may be still traced. The monuments of the two saints, the large mosque of Adinah, and the monument of Sultan Ghyashudin, are on its sides; and near the centre is a bridge of 3 arches, partly of stones, which has been thrown over a rivulet. It is of no great size, and very rudely formed of materials, evidently taken from Hindu ruins, as they contain figures in rude imitation of the human and animal form.

At the northern end of the street are evident traces of a rampart, and the passage through it is called the gate of the fortress, (ghordwar.) At the south end are many foundations, which cross each other and the road, which have also probably belonged to a gate; but the forest is there so impenetrable, that the wall could not be traced. To the south of this are many scattered bricks, and beyond that is a rampart, probably an outwork, as the street cannot be traced farther than the foundations just now mentioned.

Near the street, and amidst the heaps of bricks, are many small tanks, and I am inclined to think, that in general, the town extended only a very little way, either east or west from the principal street. It is said indeed by the natives, that 2 miles east from Kutub Shah's monument, there is a large tank dug by a Pherat Khan, and another a little north from that, called after Nasser Shah, and that so far traces of buildings may be discovered. Towards the west they say the traces extend but a little way, and the wood is so difficult to penetrate, that I was contented with visiting the ruins of the king's palace, which is about a mile east from the main street; and I found, that there are no traces remaining to show that the town extended half so far. At the same time it must be observed, that there seem to have been many large suburbs, which extended from the immediate vicinity of the town of Maldeh, towards the east and north, for at least 12 miles. Next to Maldeh was Sujapur, then Fatehpur, then Mehemanpur, then Dandigal, then Belwari partly, and Bahadurpur entirely in the district of Jogodol. In each of these is a considerable extent excavated with small tanks, and containing heaps of bricks and some stones.

Immediately north from the golden mosque, on the same side of the principal street, is another called that of one hundred thousand, (eklaky,) as having cost 100,000 Rupees. It is constructed chiefly of brick, but is the handsomest building in the place. It is a square of 80 feet front, with a small turret at each corner, and roofed by one dome. The walls outwardly have been ornamented with carved tiles, and the dome within has been neatly plastered; but the design of the whole is clumsy, as will appear from the drawings (No. 4). It is lighted by 4 small doors, one in each side, and within forms an octagon, having 4 miserable chambers in the sides between the doors. These wretched places were probably intended for the abodes of the fakirs, who were to take care of lamps. They have no air nor light, but what comes through the small aperture, by which they communicate with the central hall. This seems to have been intended as the mausoleum of three royal personages, whose tombs occupy the middle of the floor. There is no inscription to serve as a guide, but it is said, that the tombs are those of Sultans Ghyashudin, Zaynulabdin, and Wahuzudin. The two latter were probably sons of the first, who was the 3d Muhammedan king of Bengal. The eastern door has evidently been taken from a Hindu ruin, as it contains representations of the human form.

About 2 miles beyond this monument of Ghyashudin is the tomb of his father Sekunder, forming part of a very large mosque called Adinah, which is by far the largest building of the place. Indeed it is considered by the people of the vicinity, as of almost miraculous grandeur. It is on the east side of the principal street, between that and a large tank, which is almost entirely choaked with weeds and bushes, and has become very ruinous. Enough only remains to enable us to judge of what it has been, and to form a ground plan (No. 5), which will faciliate the comprehension of the following account.

It is a quadrangular building, consisting chiefly of cloisters (A B C D) placed round a court or central area (H E F G) of the same form, and extends nearly 500 feet from N. to S. and 300 from east to west. The principal entrance for so large a building is very mean, and is a small arched door (*a*) in the middle of the east side. It seems to have had a wall on each side that conducted to the tank. The whole east side of the building is 500 feet long, and 38 feet wide within the walls. It has been supported by 2 brick walls (A D H F) and 2 rows of stone pillars (*bd ce*) dividing it into 3 longitudinal aisles, and each row contained 38 pillars, dividing it again into 127 squares, each of which was covered by a small dome. On each side of the door (*a*) are 19 transverse rows, containing 3 squares, and in each of the 35 transverse rows towards the north is a small window facing the tank. Each of the three rows nearest the south end open towards the tank with an arched gate, which probably served as entrances for the populace. The 33 central rows of squares communicated with the area, by an equal number of arched doors. The three transverse rows of arches at each end, communicated with the three longitudinal rows or aisles of the south and north side of the building. In each end of this side of the building towards the N. and S. are three windows opposite to the aisles.

The northern and southern sides of the building were exactly of the same structure with the eastern, consisting of two rows of pillars between the outer and inner walls, and covered by 3 longitudinal rows of small domes. At each transverse row of domes there is a window towards the town, and an arched door towards the central area of the building; but these sides being shorter, contained only 13 rows of domes each, or altogether 78 domes in the two sides.

These three sides are nearly alike, and including the cornice are about 20 feet high. Their inner fronts, towards the area, were divided by plain rude pilasters, which supported a broad tasteless cornice. The whole space almost between the pilasters was occupied by an arched door, and the general appearance was that of rude cloisters, with 33 arched doors on one side, and 13 on each of the two others. The outer front of these sides was more ornamented. Each window is placed in a portion of the wall, which projects about 6 inches, and serves as a kind of pilaster to support the cornice. The window itself is very small, and is secured by a very neat lattice of carved tiles. It is surrounded by ornaments of carved tiles disposed in form of an arch. The spaces between the projections which contain the windows, are also ornamented with carved tiles disposed in arches. There are only two division walls in the whole, and these, as will appear from the plan, are placed irregularly.

The western side of the building is rather more conspicuous, and consists of a centre (I) and two wings (K L M N O P Q R). The centre is an apartment about 64 feet from east to west, 32 feet from N. to S. and 62 feet from the floor to the centre of the arch by which it was covered. Its eastern end seems to have been entirely open, and its western end quite shut. In this are two niches (sejdagah), towards which those who prayed turned their faces *(f g)*; and on one side of the largest was a pulpit *(h)* (mimbar) of stone, to which the priest ascended by a small ill contrived stair. These niches and pulpit are much carved, and somewhat polished.

Each side of the central place of worship communicates with its contiguous wing by five arches, for each wing is supported by 4 longitudinal rows of pillars, each containing 17 pillars, in all 68 pillars, which together with the walls, supported 90 domes. The southern wing being the most simple, I shall describe it first. It opens towards the area by 15 large arches in the same manner as the other sides, and it communicates with the cloisters of the southern side by 3 arches. Its southern end contains 5 windows. It has no opening in its west side, but opposite to each arch is a niche highly ornamented, and towards which people might turn their faces when they prayed.

The northern wing is exactly of the same plan, but contains only 16 niches on the ground, for the places of the 1st and 14th from the centre, are occupied by two small doors *(k l)*. 21 of the pillars in 7 rows, at some distance from the centre, are much thicker and shorter than the others, and support a platform of stone *(m n o p)* called the king's throne (Padshah-ka tukht), and elevated about 8 feet from the ground. It is about 40 feet wide, and 80 feet long, and is probably the place where the king and royal family performed their worship, while the chief of religion performed his in the pulpit of the centre *(h)*, and the populace prayed in the southern wing. Above the 11 outer columns of the platform are clumsy, four sided abutments, about 2½ feet high, from whence spring the arches that support the domes, which are no higher above the platform than in other parts of the wing. Above the 10 central columns, which support the platform, are 10 smaller and more elegant pillars, about 6 feet high, which also supported domes of the same height as the others. The wall adjacent to the platform contains 4 niches *(qqqq)* and two doors *(rs)* that are minutely carved, and ornamented with passages of the Koran. The doors lead from the chamber in which Sekundur was buried, and through which only the access to the platform could have been.

The form of the columns, both supporting the platform and roof, will be best judged of from the drawing (No. 6). The common columns are 2 feet wide at the base, and are 10 feet 4½ inches high, and some consist of one piece of granite, which is their principal merit. The arches which spring from these pillars to support the domes, are very clumsy and ill-constructed. Their form is gothic, approaching, however, very near to circular, and they are constructed entirely of brick. Their centres are 16 feet 5½ inches from the floor, and the centres of the domes are 26 feet 7½ inches from the same. Behind this wing, as above-mentioned, is the apartment (S T V W) where Sekundur was buried. This building is of the same height with the wing; and the apartment within is 38 feet square, and has been covered by 9 domes, supported by 4 columns in the centre, and its floor is on a level with the royal platform that is within the wing. The grave is in the centre, and is without ornament. It is composed of brick, and covered with an arch. Even here this unhappy prince, killed fighting against his son, and buried amidst the murder of 17 children, has not been allowed to remain undisturbed. The grave has been opened, probably in a vain search for money, and it is now entirely empty. The western side of the apartment has fallen, but the southern contains three windows, and the northern two and a door, by which it communicated with another chamber or platform of the same size (S V X Y) and on the same level. There is no evidence to show that this ever had a roof, but on the west side it had a wall and door, to which probably the stair led, by which the royal family entered the place of worship. There was probably also a stair on the north side leading to a door *(t)* in the back of the northern wing.

The outer front of this west side, although quite irregular from the projection of the tomb, is the most entire part of the building, and has been the most ornamented. A kind of sketch (Drawing No. 7) of the west end of the centre building, and of part of the adjacent wing, and taken from the S. W. corner of Sekundur's tomb *(w)* will give some idea of the style. The centre building is about double the height of the wings, on its outer end, opposite to the great niche within is a small one *(t)*, over which is an inscription that gives the date (A. H. 707) for the erection of the building by Sekundur.

The stone work, both in the centre and wings, is only 11 feet high, and is quite plain. The brick work in the wings is 12 feet 5 inches high, and contains a double broad cornice, exceedingly carved and subdivided into minute portions, which would have been very costly to form in stone. Rude broad pilasters support both cornices, and in these, in the brick work, are little arches highly ornamented with carved tiles. In fact the natives use pressions in their walls, where we would use projections, so that their pilasters are broader than the intermediate spaces, as will be seen in the 7th drawing.

The doors and windows of stone in this side of the building, are the parts of the whole that have been executed in the best taste, although they are much too small; for the windows are in general only 5 feet 3 inches by 2 feet 6. They are of very different styles, having probably been taken from different buildings; for I may observe of them in general, that most of them have evidently been taken from Hindu buildings: as on narrow inspection some compartments will be discovered, from which human figures has been eradicated; yet a foot, a hand, or somewhat sufficient to ascertain the truth of what I state, has been left, probably with a design to show the triumph of the *Faith* over idolatry. Over many of them in particular, is an escutcheon containing of figure sitting cross-legged. Some of these, I believe, represent Gones; but others, having a small waist, cannot be intended for that divinity, and seem to me evidently to represent either Jain or Gowtom. Great pains, however, has been taken to place every stone in an appropriate situation, and to conceal the Hindu carvings, where it was not intended that these should enter into the plan of the Muhammedan architect; and I observed only one stone placed in the north end of the north wing, that contained carving evidently misplaced; but the stair of the pulpit having fallen, discovers on the parts of its stones that had been concealed much carving, among which are some fragments of the human figure.

The view of the western side of the building from the area, must have been that of a small high centre with almost its whole end open, and two long low wings of cloisters, like those forming the other sides.

On the parts of the carved work executed by the Muhammedans, it may be observed, that they are too minute to produce any general great effect: and that, although, from their size and general design, they might answer for the pattern of a curtain or sofa, yet they lose the effect of neatness from their having been executed without care. Although carved on a stone that admits easily of a marble polish, the cuttings are quite rough. The small niches, towards which the people turned when they prayed, are on the whole the best; as less frittered away by too great an anxiety after perfection. The drawing No. 8, which represents the niche (*u*) next to the royal platform, will give an idea of the style. The upper part is in plaster. The lower part is in stone, and shows the curious nature of the masonry.

There is no calcareous marble in the building. The rougher parts are granite, the more polished are indurated potstone, impregnated with hornblende.

Concerning the building in general, it may be observed, that although of great size, it is so frittered away into small portions, that it has no grandeur; and although laboured with vast pains, its parts are so heavy, so ill proportioned, and so dark, that it totally wants elegance; and finally, that the badness of the masonry, the weakness of the pillars, and weight of the roof rendered it of little stability.

About a mile east from Adinah, is a ruin called the Satasghur, or sixty towers, and which is said to have been the palace of the king. On penetrating the woods and reaching this place, I was much disappointed, as except the high name I could find nothing worthy of a royal residence. The remains consist of a tank about 120 yards in length and 80 in breadth. The bank formed by throwing out the earth, has been surrounded by a brick wall, in one place entire and 16 feet high. This wall seems to have included many buildings, which from the bulk of the ruins, seem to have been most considerable at the two ends. At the N. W. corner is a small building which contains an arched chamber in the centre, communicating with several smaller ones, by which it is surrounded. These communicate only with the central room, from whence there is a passage to an antichamber in front. Some appearance of pipes in the walls, and the general structure of the building, confirm the opinion of the natives, that this was a bath. The north end of the tank seems to have been lined through the whole of its length, by a narrow gallery supported by arches, from whence stairs led down to the water, and within the gallery there appears to have been a row of small chambers; but these are now almost entirely choaked with rubbish. At a little distance from the S. E. corner of the tank, and without the wall, is another ruin like that of the bath, and which probably served for the same purpose. A cylindrical cavity lined with brick, which descends from the top of the building to a considerable depth, and which is about 10 feet wide, served in all probability, to give a supply of water. Very few stones have been employed in these buildings, and such as have been used are quite plain. Two large blocks of uncut grey granite are lying on the surface of the ruins. Some of the bricks are coated with green enamel.

About half way between Adinah and Satasghur is an earthen rampart, with a ditch on its west side, which probably is part of a fortification, that may have surrounded the palace.

The tank at Satasghur has its greatest length extending from north to south, and therefore has undoubtedly been the work of a Hindu; and in fact both Hindus and Muhammedans agree in attributing its construction to a Pandu raja, who lived a long time ago, and communicated his name to the place. He is very remarkable as having been the father of Yudhisthir who, according to legend, was sovereign of India in the commencement of this age, about 5000 years ago. The country then belonged to Virat, one of the adherents of the family of Pandu; and according to tradition, this part was under the immediate management of a certain Kichok, to whose sister Virat was married. It is possible, that during some rebellion, or disputed succession, Pandu may have been compelled to retire from Hustinapur, and to take refuge in a friendly territory. Pernya, it must be observed, is a corrupt vulgar name, and the true appellation of the city is said to be Panduya, or Pandoviya.

In this division there are 11 market places, of which Maldeh is a large town, and Nawabgunj, Mongolvari, and Ayeyar are considerable marts for exportation and importation; and Shahpur or Sahatpur has some shops, with two weekly markets, where large quantities of silk are sold. Maldeh is said to be a Persian word, signifying, the place of wealth; and the town of this name probably derived its origin from being the port of Pernya, during the time that was the capital of Bengal, and became afterwards celebrated for its manufactures. It is now the 2d town in this district, and independent of Nawabgunj, which may be considered as a suburb occupied by boatmen and people employed in exporting goods, contains about 3000 houses, of which it is said ⅓ are built with brick and stones from the ruins of Gaur. One house contains 3 stories, and about 370 have two stories. Each of these has at least 6 apartments, which however are in general very small, especially those of the upper story that serve for bed rooms. About 750 brick houses of one story have several apartments, and the remainder, occupied in general by weavers and other artists, consist of one room about 7 cubits long by 5 wide, and which has one small aperture that serves for door, window, and chimney. At each end is usually a thatched shed. The whole are mean and slovenly built, without lime, or at least only coated with plaster. Folding hinges for the doors and windows are just beginning to be introduced. These are an innovation from Europe: hooks were formerly in use. The town is miserably huddled together along the side of the Mohanonda, on a narrow stripe, that seems to have been raised with the earth taken from three large hollows, into which the river penetrates in the rainy season, and then indeed the town is in a great measure insulated. Owing to this probably, the streets are remarkably narrow, seldom exceeding 6 feet, and they are very uneven. The improvements made in Europe, on the arts of weaving and dying, having of late occasioned a great diminution in the demands on this country, the people here have had less employment than usual, and many of the principal houses have failed and become ruinous, among which are the French and Dutch factories: and there never was an English factory at the place, for that commonly called Malda is not even in this district. The ruinous houses, which are overgrown with weeds, and shelter dirt of every kind, together with the narrowness and irregularity of the streets, give Maldeh an uncommonly miserable appearance. I think, that it looks worse than even the towns, which consist entirely of thatched huts. The want of usual employment has also introduced many objects in the most squalid appearance of poverty, especially distressing, as it is intermixed with a degree of wealth and luxury, that are unknown in the other parts of the district. The police is not only defective in want of roads, streets, bridges, light, and cleanliness, but the town swarms with villains, who have been educated in the jail at Dinajpûr. There are very few open shops, and the markets are inconceivably ill supplied, as usual indeed in India wherever a great many Europeans have not been settled ; and no tolerable animal food of any kind, no bread, and no butter, are procurable in the market : almost every person however is a trader, and will retail in his house. So far from the commerce or manufactures of Maldeh having improved the country, the whole for 12 miles north from this town, with an excellent soil, is almost a desert. The only public building, except the mosques, which Maldeh possessed, was a serai or public inn, containing a great many small unventilated dark chambers surrounding a square, in which travellers might lodge, and merchants might deposit their goods. This work was erected by a Muhammedan merchant, brother to the person who built the principal mosque.

Aying (Jyoe R.) at the junction of the Tanggon and Mohanonda, containing perhaps 200 dwellings, must be considered as a town, although it has no brick house. Its streets are wider, and it has more the appearance of comfort than Maldeh, and it is a place of considerable trade and manufactures.

PART 14.—*Division Purusa.*

The division of Purusa is very much intermixed with the district of Rajshahî, and is of a very irregular shape ; but may extend about 24 miles from N. to S. and 19 from E. to W. and may contain about 260 square miles. The Darogah resides at Ghatnagor, not near the centre of his division. There is only one Munsuf for this division, and that of Lolbazar; which are separated by the intervention of Potnitolah, and each of them is larger than that division : about 24 miles may be inundated land, covered mostly with long reeds, but perhaps 6 miles may be cultivated with Boro rice. Tanks, rivers, and marshes, may occupy 12 miles ; woods, 10 miles ; steep barren places, burial grounds, markets and roads, 16 miles ; deserted lands, or those cultivated occasionally, 8 miles, and about 190 are fully occupied. The soil, where not inundated, is a hard clay, in some places pretty high, in others very level. Three wealthy farmers have some brick buildings in their dwelling houses, and a good many have small brick mosques ; almost all the huts have mud walls, and some of the better kind have wooden rafters to support the roof.

The most remarkable Hindu place of worship is a small temple of Komol Dohewvori, which as usual, is supposed to be of great antiquity ; but as it has been endowed by the Jahanggirpûr Zemindars, and receives 200 Rupees a year from that family, it has probably been erected by some of them, and is therefore quite modern. There is no remarkable place of worship among the Moslems. There are many old tanks, and some of them rather large, but none very remarkable, nor is there any tradition concerning the persons by whom they were dug.

The road made by Hoseyn Shah passes though the northern end of the division, and is the only antiquity of which I heard.

This division has 8 markets, of which 2 are marts, and Nitpûr is a very considerable one : 3 other places have some shops ; the largest is Nischintapur, which contains about 800 houses.

PART 15.—*Division Gongarampúr.*

The division of Gongarampúr is of an exceeding irregular shape, extends about 26 miles from north to south by 16 from east to west, and may contain 320 square miles. The Darogah and Munsif reside at Dumdummah, towards the N. W. at a distance from the centre of the division.

Rivers, marshes, and tanks, may occupy 20 miles; inundated lands may amount to 30 miles, of which 8 may be cultivated as Chora land, or for Boro rice; 30 miles of the high land may have a free light soil, and 240 may consist of hard clay; besides the portion of inundated land that is cultivated, 20 miles of a loose soil, and 220 of a hard soil are said to be fully occupied; 16 have been deserted or are occasionally cultivated, 2 may be occupied by woods or bushes, and 12 are barren roads, market places, and the like.

About 10 habitations may have one or two chambers of brick within their premises. On the East side of the Punabhoba most of the huts have mud walls, and near their houses about 150 farmers have small brick mosques. On the west the huts are miserable, and consist of hurdles. This part occupies ¼ of the district, but is almost entirely destroyed by inundations, rivers and marshes, so that it contains not above $\frac{1}{16}$ of the lands that are in full cultivation.

The antiquities of this district are very numerous; and in giving an account of them I shall have occasion to mention most of the places of worship, and most of the public works of any note. I shall proceed in the order in which I saw them.

First, about 7 miles southerly from Dumdummah, is a very fine tank named Topon (Tubbone R.), and the largest in the district; for the water seems to have extended 4100 feet from N. to S. and 1150 from E. to W. and the space occupied by the bank is about 300 feet wide, making the total dimensions 4700 feet by 1750. On the east and west sides have been 3 *entrances* through the bank, and each had a descent to the water (ghat) lined with brick. On the south side have been two entrances, and on the N. side one: opposite to this is a small heap, probably the ruin of a temple, and beyond this an avenue between two small tanks, which, together with the avenue, occupy the width of the great one. To the north of these is a space of about half a mile in extent, broken with small tanks, like the situation of a town; and near the northern extremity of this is a large heap of bricks covered with soil, once probably a temple of considerable size. These tanks are said to have been made by Banraja, and to have been the place where he performed his religious ceremonies (Toposya), and where he swung before Shiva for 1000 years, suspended by hooks passed through the skin of his back. It is from this that the name of the place is derived.

East from Topon, on the banks of the Punabhoba, is Kordaho, now a place of some trade, but celebrated as having been the place where Krishno burned the 998 arms of Banraja, which he had cut off in battle.

The proper name of Dumdummah is Devi Koth. It received its present appellation (which signifies the place of war), from its having been a military station during the early Muhammedan government, as it probably was then on the frontier; for I have already mentioned, that the province called Barendo extended no farther north than this place. While the troops were stationed at Dumdummah, the chief officer, under the title of wazir, seems to have resided on the banks of a very noble tank, which is named Dahaldighi, and has evidently been formed by Muhammedans: its water being about 4000 feet from E. to W. and 1000 from N. to S. It is probably exceedingly deep, as the banks thrown out are very large. They have been a good deal spread, and form many irregular rising grounds finely planted; and surpass in beauty any thing of the kind that I have ever seen. On many different parts, especially towards the N. E. corner, are heaps of bricks, probably the ruins of the houses that were occupied by the Moslem officers. On the centre of the North side is the monument (Durgah) of a saint (Pir) named Mullah Ata-ud-din, contiguous to which is a small mosque. Both are very ruinous, but a canopy is still suspended over the tomb, which is much frequented as a place of worship, and the Faqir has an endowment of 200 Biggahs (about 100 acres) of land. The present occupant is a remarkably handsome man, and has a perfect formed Arabian countenance, although his ancestors have held the appointment for several generations. A descent paved with stone leads down from these buildings to the tank, and the materials have been evidently taken from a ruin, as broken columns, parts of doors, windows, and stone variously carved, are intermixed with such as are quite plain. Traces of the human form on the pedestal of a column, show that the ruins from whence they were taken have been those of a Hindu building, and confirm the tradition of the supply having come from Bannogor. The wazir, who is reported to have founded the mosque and to have dug the tank, is said to be buried between them, and a large cavity covered by long stones is shown as his grave. From an inscription over the gate of the mosque it appears, that it was built before the time of Ata-ud-din and of Shekh Mukbu (another saint), by wazir Shair Musaur of Mozofurabad, commander of the troops of Firuzabad, in the reign of Hoseyn Shah, Sultan of Hostina, son of Mozofur Shah, A. H. 718. From an inscription under the former it would appear, that a place for prayer (Gombuz), which has been erected behind the tomb, was built by the order of Sekunder Shah, son of Majahud Shah, son of Ayas Shah, A. H. 765. Also from an inscription in a wing of the mosque it would appear, that this was erected as a place of prayer for Ata-ud-din by Futeh Shah, son of Mahmud Shah, A. H. 845. A part of the mosque called Hamada, from an inscription in it, was built in the reign of Kykaos Shah, by the order of Sekundar Sani or the 2d; A. H. 872. Finally, from an inscription over the door of an apartment to the right of the mosque, and which was a kitchen for the use of Faqirs, it would appear, that it was built in the time of Mukhdum Mullah, when Mozofur Shah was king. The date is no longer legible.

At a little distance east from Dahal Dighi is another tank of very large dimensions, called Kala Dighi, and supposed to have been dug by Kala Rani, the spouse of Ban Raja. Exclusive of the banks it is about 4000 feet long from N. to S. by 800 feet wide.

North from the tanks called Dahal and Kala are many small ones, which formerly in all probability were in the suburbs of Bannogor, the residence of Ban Raja, of whom I have already given an account.

The ruins of Bannogor occupy the East bank of the Punabhoba, which here runs from N. E. to S. W. for about two miles, beginning a little about Dumdummah. I first examined the citadel, which is a quadrangle of about 1800 by 1500 feet, surrounded by a high rampart of bricks, and on the south and east by a ditch: the remainder of the ditch has been obliterated or destroyed by the Punabhoba, which in the time of Ban Raja is said to have passed to the north of the present course of the Brohmani; and many large water courses, which are to be seen in that direction, render the tradition probable. On the west face of the citadel is a large projecting part, probably the outworks before gate. In the centre is a large heap of bricks said to have been the Raja's house; and on the east face is a gate and a causeway, about 200 feet long, leading across the ditch into the city, which has been a square of above a mile in diameter, and has been also surrounded by a rampart of brick, and by a ditch. Towards its S. E. corner is the monument of Sultan Shah, which is ruinous; but a Faqir has a small endowment, and burns a lamp before the tomb. The monument is much frequented by the faithful, and contains many stones, which from their position have evidently been taken from ruins, and the pillars are of the same order with those at the mosque of Dahal Dighi. They are somewhat more elegant than those at Adinah, and I have procured a drawing of one (No. 9), and of a door (No. 10), which I have no doubt belonged to Bannogor.

Near the monument of the Muhammedan saint are the two celebrated pools Omrito and Jivot, which I mentioned in my account of Ban Raja. In their present state they are very different from the pools of life and immortality, which their names imply, as they are filled with abominably dirty water. They have never been large, but the size of the heaps of bricks round them shows, that they have been surrounded by large buildings; and probably they have been sacred ponds (Pushkorinis), which occupied the areas of two temples. The women of the vicinity who have been unfortunate in their children, and have lost many by death, frequent these pools, and carrying with them two living fish of the kind called Kamach Singgi, bathe in each pond, and make an offering of a fish.

In Omrito a projecting stone was pointed out as the dead cow, that had been thrown into the water by the infidel Yovons, in order to deprive it of its virtues. I proposed to take it out, which excited a smile of contempt in my guides, who assured me, that one of the Dinajpur rajas had tied ropes to it, and with three elephants had attempted in vain to procure this monument of antiquity. The Pondit attached to the survey, who is perhaps somewhat of a philosopher, went next day with a dozen men and some ropes, and pulled it out with some degree of exultation. He found it to be an image of the bull Vrisho, which is usually worshipped by the sect of Shiva, and which the infidels very probably threw into the pond. This and the image of Gonés now at Dinajpur, which I have already mentioned, together with the custom of swinging attributed to Ban Raja, pretty clearly show the religion of that tyrant (Osur) who opposed Krishno, as the temples of Shiva constructed by Ravon, which I have seen in the south of India, point out the worship of the opponent of Ram.

At the N. W. corner of the ruins of the town, near the Punabhoba, are the remains of the monument of another Muhammedan saint, Pir Havakhari, which also have some columns, and other stones; and the same Faqir who lights the lamp at the tomb of Sultan Shah, attends on this, which is also much frequented by the devout.

Near this the river has undermined part of the ruins, and is encroaching on a thick bed of bricks, in which stands a column of granite of the same order with those in the monuments of the Muhammedan saints.

At a very little distance from the N. E. corner of the city is a large heap of bricks, said to be the ruins of a temple dedicated to Virupakhyo (Shiva) by Ban Raja. In the time of Raja Ramnath of Dinajpur, two religious men were informed in a dream where the image was concealed, and hastened to inform the Raja of their discovery. He accordingly sent people with the two good men, who pointed out the place in the ruins, and on digging there was found a Lingo, for which the Raja built a small temple, and settled 360 biggahs (about 180 acres) of land, with a monthly pension of 30 Rupees on the two brahmuns, whose children now enjoy the fruits of their ancestors' virtue. It is said and believed in the neighbourhood, that this image, when discovered, was a cubit high. It has since gradually diminished, and is now reduced to a span. The new temple is very ruinous, and the brahmuns who have the endowment will probably wait for a repair, until another dreamer can procure another Raja, who will perform that work of piety. It is now, however, the chief place of Hindu worship in the division.

About half a mile west from the north end of the city, on the opposite side of the Punabhoba, is a considerable heap of bricks, overgrown with bushes, and placed on the side of a small tank. For any thing that appears to the contrary, this, as is related, may have been the house of the princess Usha, whose fondness for Oniruddho brought about the destruction of her father and native city.

About ¾ of a mile beyond this heap, and on the other side of the Brohmani, is a place called Narayonpur, where there are many small tanks and heaps of bricks like an old town. This is said to have been the field, where the great battle took place between Krishno and Ban Raja. Near one of the tanks, evidently of Hindu construction, is the monument of a Muhammedan saint Pir Bahauddin, from whence to the tank is a large pavement and stair constructed of stones, that have evidently been taken from ruins. Near it is a small building of brick, much ornamented with carving, and which from its resemblance to the Mausoleum of Ghyas-ud-din, at Peruya, probably contains the tomb of some person of rank.

The great number of stones in these ruins, and a vast many that have been removed by the Dinajpur Rajas to construct their works, show that Bannogor has been a place much ornamented; and its walls show that it was of considerable size and strength. The people here allege, that all the stones, which are to be found in the buildings of this district, have been carried from it, and that Gaur owed its most valuable materials to the ruins of Ban Raja's edifices.

The only other work that I shall have occasion to mention is Pran Sagor, a tank made by Raja Prannath, of Dinajpur. Its basin of water is 2600 feet by 800; but it sinks into insignificance, after mentioning the grander works of mighty heroes of antiquity.

In this division are 16 market places, eight of them are marts for exportation; and of these Dumdummah, Noyabazar, and Kordaho are small towns.

Part 16.—*Division of Potiram.*

The division of Potiram is about 22 miles from north to south, and 17 from east to west. It is divided into nearly two equal portions by the Atreyi river, and contains about 280 square miles. The residence of the Darogah and Munsif at Potiram, is near the centre of the division.

About 18 miles may be occupied by tanks, rivers, and marshes; 17 miles are inundated, of which perhaps 10 miles are sandy banks of river (Chora) that are cultivated; 60 miles are of a free soil, of which 35 are fully occupied; and 185 are of a hard clay, of which 158 are fully occupied; 17 miles are deserted, or only cultivated occasionally; and 35 miles are poor sterile land or burial-grounds, roads, market places, or the like.

Although three zemindars reside in the district, one of whom pays 20,000 Rs. a year revenue, there is no dwelling that consists entirely of brick; but about 12 families have one or two rooms of that material, and about an equal number have small brick temples or mosques within their premises. The greater part of the huts have mud walls.

There is no place of worship remarkable either for its buildings, or for its supposed holiness.

The only ruins are of little consequence. Near Potiram are the ruins of a house, which belonged to the proprietors of Sontosh, before that estate belonged to the Dinajpur family. At Mahigunj are said to be some bricks and stones, near the monument of a Muhammedan saint.

This division contains 19 market places. Five are marts for the exportation of goods, and 3 other places contain some shops. Potiram, on the east side of the Atreyi, including Nawabgunj, must in Bengal be reckoned a town, and contains above 100 houses, rather neat and comfortable. It has however no buildings of note. Kongyargunj on the west side of the same river is a more considerable place, and has above 150 houses, with a good many shops and artists.

Part 17.—*Division Potnitola.*

South from Potiram, and also occupying both sides of the Atreyi for about 20 miles, is the division of Potnitola, which extends about 13 miles from East to West, and is of an oval form. The Darogah resides at Potnitola, tolerably near the centre of the division, which may contain about 240 square miles.

Rivers, tanks, and marshes, may occupy 15 miles; free sandy soil on the banks of the Atreyi, 30 miles; and stiff clay, 195. Twenty miles of the former, and 182 of the latter may be fully occupied (for this is undoubtedly one of the best cultivated portions of the district), while perhaps 8 miles have been deserted, or are occasionally cultivated; 10 miles may be occupied by burial places, roads, markets, or steep banks, and five by woods, among which some are of Sal.

Although 4 branches of the oldest and most considerable family among the neighbouring proprietors reside in this division, only 2 dwelling-houses contain any chambers of brick. Most of the huts have mud walls. About 40 wealthy farmers have lately built small mosques of brick in their premises, but there is no remarkable place of worship.

The remains of antiquity are neither numerous nor extensive. Towards the N. W. extremity of the division is Dhivor Dighi, which was examined by the Pondit. He reports, that it may have contained 40 or 50 biggahs of land, and is said to have been dug by a Dhivor Raja, who lived about a thousand years ago. In its centre is a stone pillar of 8 sides, 22½ cubits in length, and 6½ cubits in diameter. On its top are traces of iron ornaments, but it has no carving nor inscription. Near it is a place sacred to Bhairov, and a small wood of the trees which usually grow on ruined towns; but no other indication of there having been a city.

At Mosida on the west side of the Atreyi, about 7 miles below Potnitola, is the monument and tomb of the Muhammedan saint Sudurdaha, which is a good deal visited; near it are the tombs of Budurdaha father of the holy man, and of several persons of the same family. The tombs are constructed of brick, and surrounded by a wall, in which are placed several stones that have evidently been taken from ruins, as they have been cut in various forms of which fragments only remain. Near them are some fragments of pillars, and besides many other stones, the lintels of two doors, on one of which is an escutcheon containing a figure of Gones. There can be no doubt, that the Muhammedan building has been erected from Hindu ruins. The *Ciceroni*, who was the chief of the village (Mondol) and a good Muhammedan, attributed the whole carving to the saint. He was however a good deal staggered by Gones, whom he had never before observed. He had no tradition concerning the place, from whence the holy man had come, when he lived, or who had been his benefactors, but said that his forest contained many small tanks and heaps of bricks. I walked with him the whole breadth of the wood, about half a mile, and what he said was one half of the length, which might be a mile, and found that his account was true. Near the monument I could trace the foundations of buildings of a considerable size. I have no doubt therefore, but that this has been a Hindu city of some consequence, although tradition is silent on the subject.

At Mahigunj, on the east side of the Atreyi, near the northern extremity of the division, is said to be such another place, with a monument of a Muhammedan saint named Mohi Sontosh, who has communicated his name to the district in which his monument is situated. The most remarkable thing is that his name is said to be Songskrito.

This division contains 20 market places, of which 4 are small marts for exportation and importation, and no other places have any shops. None of them is entitled to be called a town, except Shiva-gunj, which contains about 300 houses, and carries on a considerable commerce.

Part 18.—*Division of Badolgachi.*

The division of Badolgachi on the Jomuna river is about 17 miles from N. to S. and 15 from E. to W. but is drawn out into a kind of triangular form. The Darogah resides at the place from whence the division derives its name, which signifies the Jujub tree, with which the place abounds. It is situated conveniently enough for the district, but the Munsif resides at Shiva-gunj near one extremity. Under all circumstances, however, a more convenient place could not have been selected, as he is also Munsif for another division, and that not immediately adjacent. A detached portion of Rajshahi district is within 200 yards of the Thana.

This division may contain 270 square miles, and although very valuable by nature, is but indifferently cultivated. Rivers, marshes, and tanks may occupy 17 square miles: poor, sterile, steep land, roads, burying-grounds, market places, &c. 18 miles; inundated lands, 13 miles, of which probably 6 are occupied; rich free soil, 110 miles, of which not above 54 are properly occupied; good hard clay, 130 miles, of which about 100 are fully occupied; 60 miles have been deserted, or are only occasionally cultivated; and about 8 are overgrown with woods, being ruined towns or villages.

Only two very small proprietors reside in the district; but there are in it 5 brick houses belonging to sugar manufacturers. One of them, which I saw, is built in the Moorish style, and is a respectable looking place. The proprietor, I believe, has landed estates in other districts. A large proportion of the huts have mud walls.

The most remarkable place of worship is a small temple at a place called Yogighopa towards the north end of the district. The temple is dedicated to Shiva, and is served by priests from the west of India, who are called Yogis. The shrine, where the image is placed, resembles very much a tomb, and is sunk below the level of the ground, but is covered by a neat enough building, of which the native painters made a drawing, (No. 11.) The materials appear to me to have been taken from a ruin, as some stones appear from their ornaments not to have been intended for the place in which they stand; and near the temples are several fragments of stones, that have been much carved, and are lying as materials, for which there was no demand. The temple in fact stands upon a large space of ground, that is covered and raised above the level of the adjacent country by bricks, and which contains several tanks. The Yogis say, that these are the remains of the house of Devpal, a prince who lived five or six hundred years ago. About a mile to the west, they say, at a place called Amari, are similar ruins belonging to the house of Mohipal. In order that I might see the ruins of the abode of Chondro Pal, which are the most considerable, the Yogis directed me to proceed to Chondira, a village about a mile to the east; I was however under the necessity of taking a very circuitous route to avoid a marsh, and on my reaching the place could find no other guide than a Muhammedan Mondol, who never had heard of Chondro Pal, but conducted me to the tomb of a saint constructed of ruins. He said also, that at a neighbouring place called Kotok there are many bricks, and small tanks; but that without previously clearing the road it would be impossible for me to visit it. A little way east from this, at Dhorol, I found many old tanks and heaps of bricks, said to have been the abode of a Zemindar, who possessed the country before it was given to the Dinajpur family.

The most remarkable ruin in this division is situated about 8 miles N. E. from Badolgachhi on the frontier of Lalbazar, and is called Gopal Chitorpahar, and Paharpur. I found it an immense steep heap of bricks, from 100 to 150 feet in perpendicular height, covered with bushes, and crowned by a remarkably fine tree. On ascending about half way I found three large rough stones, on which I had been led to expect an inscription; but I found afterwards, that the person who gave me the information, although a Brahmun and a Zemindar, could not read. On the summit is a small chamber of brick, with a door facing the east, and a small niche towards the west. This is said to have been the residence of a Muhammedan hermit, which is very probable. The heap of bricks, or hill as it is called, has been surrounded by a square rampart, the ruins of which contain many bricks, and each side may be 400 yards in length. The rampart is overgrown with trees, but the space between it and the hill is clear, and contains some small tanks and indications of brick buildings, especially towards the corners of the rampart. The thickness of this would induce one to believe, that the place might have been a fortress; but no ditch can be traced, and the heap, which is by far the most remarkable part of the ruin, could not have answered for defence. I am therefore inclined to believe, that it has been a temple; and its great steepness and height induce me to suppose, that it has been solid, like many of the temples of Buddha in Ava and Nepal; for a hollow temple, of which the roof had fallen in, would be much flatter. My conjecture is confirmed by the vicinity of several places, which are said to have belonged to the Pal family, who were worshippers of Buddha.

In this division there are 16 market places, of which 3 are marts. One of them, Shiva-gunj, on the Atreyi, is pretty considerable, and contains 300 families, among whom are many shop-keepers and artists. Bodolgachhi contains about 100 houses, and is chiefly remarkable for the manufacture of sugar. Badol is a name that extends very far, and includes both the Company's factory at Syam-gunj (Saumgunj R.), and a place called Hengriyapathar, where an annual fair is held for 20 days. During this 200 shops are opened at the place, and many people assemble to celebrate a religious ceremony that was established by one of the Dinajpur family.

PART 18.—*Division of Lalbazar.*

The division of Lalbazar is an irregular pentagon, much intersected by the Yomuna and its branches. The Darogah resides at a distance from the centre of his division, but near the middle of what is well occupied, as the N. W. part is mostly overgrown with woods. The Munsif resides at Buksigunj, at the northern frontier of the division.

The division contains about 280 square miles; of these 12 miles may be occupied by rivers, tanks, and marshes; 12 by inundated land, of which 4 may be cultivated; 12 by steep, broken land, sterile ground, and burial and market places; 52 miles by deserted land, of which 34 may have grown into forests, and 18 may be cultivated occasionally, and are still clear; about 192 miles are fully occupied, of which perhaps 122 are of a light, free soil, uncommonly rich, and 70 are of a stiff hard clay. Setting aside the 24 miles occupied by rivers, marshes, and inundated land, 164 will be about the proportion of light, free soil, and 92 that of the stiff land.

Two of the zemindars, that reside in the district, have houses of brick, fit for gentlemen, especially that of Baidyonath Chaudri, who is the most intelligent person with whom I have conversed on Indian architecture, and who is carrying on buildings with great spirit, in which he naturally takes a pride, and is much gratified by having an opportunity of showing them to strangers, which he does with great urbanity: eight manufacturers of sugar also have brick houses, suitable to decent circumstances. One of them a Muhammedan, has lately purchased land.

The two principal zemindars have built very considerable temples; but being both of low birth, these are considered as of no value; and the only place of worship, that is esteemed by the natives, is a small temple of Horogauri, which is much frequented for 4 or 5 Tuesdays in spring. Imamdi, one of the sugar-manufacturers that I mentioned, has built a pretty large mosque, and 10 or 12 small ones: about 20 rich farmers have small mosques within their premises; but the only Muhammedan place of worship, that is much frequented, is the monument of Nimay Shah, on the banks of the Tulosi.

At the monument of Nimay, the channel of the Tulosi, as well as the adjacent bank, consists of bricks and stones, and a high space covered with trees, and about a quarter of a mile in diameter, contains large quantities of these materials. Among these I observed a stone, apparently the capital of a pillar, which was ornamented with four tygers' heads; a brick and a stone at the saint's monument, had each a human figure. The materials have therefore been taken from a Hindu building, and the tradition concerning the ruin is, that it belongs to the house or palace of Usho Pal, which is called Atapúr. At a little distance to the west from this is just such another ruin, said to have been a house of Mohi Pal. Between these places are two large tanks, and a high mound, like a road, leads from the one to the other. On digging into this mound, it has been found to consist of bricks and stones huddled together. Among the stones some are carved, and seem to have been parts of doors or windows. The buildings of the Pal family, therefore, have probably been constructed from the ruins of former times, and very probably according to tradition, from the ruins of Ban-nogor.

A little south from the ruins of Mohi Pal's abode, is a small square rampart and ditch; within which an Indigo work has been erected. The proprietor, Mr. Tucker, in removing a heap of earth in this old fort, came to a small building of brick 14 cubits square within the walls, and these are 6 feet thick. On removing the earth from the cavity, the workmen came to a small arched building, like a tomb, but it contained no bones. There is neither door nor window in the wall. The building is therefore, in all probability, a tomb, and belonged to a person of some sect that did not burn the dead.

Near the temple of Horogauri, as already mentioned, is the pillar containing an inscription, of which Mr. Wilkins has given a translation in the first volume of the Asiatick Researches, and which refers to the Pal family. The tradition of the vicinity mention Mohi, Chondro, Usho, Deu, Hudom, Kasi, and Ojoy Pals, but of the three last I have not seen any monument. The vicinity of Horogauri and of the pillar is entirely waste, and contains many little tanks like the situation of a town, but I could not observe, nor hear of any remains of buildings.

At Apaul and Sontosh, there have been small towns, with several inconsiderable temples and houses of zemindars, whose lands were seized on by the Dinajpúr family, and which, together with two houses built by Ramnath, and some later zemindars, now form ruins, for every thing in this climate hastens to decay.

In this division there are 25 markets. There is no place large enough to be called a town, but there are four small marts for the exportation of the produce, and 6 places besides have a few shops; at the saint's tomb, on the ruins of Usho Pal's house, is held an annual fair, where about 2,000 people assemble and trade, as well as pray.

Part 20.—*Division of Chintamon.*

The division of Chintamon is of an oblong form, 20 miles from north to south, and 13 from east to west. It may contain about 200 square miles, and extends from the Atreyi in one part to the east side of the Jomuna, which runs through it for about 15 miles. The Darogah and Munsif reside at some distance north from the centre of the division entrusted to their care.

About 12 miles may be occupied by rivers, water-courses, marshes, and tanks; 6 miles may be inundated land, mostly covered with reeds, but a little is under indigo; 74 miles may be of a free rich soil, and 108 miles of stiff clay; setting aside the 18 miles inundated and covered by water, 8 miles may be occupied by steep barren places, burial-grounds, market places, and roads; 15 miles are occupied by woods, mostly dwarf Sal; 34 miles are either only cultivated occasionally, or have been altogether deserted; and 125 are fully occupied, of which 50 are of a rich free soil, and 75 are of stiff clay.

Nine families have in their premises one or two rooms built of brick, but no dwelling consists entirely of that material. There are many small *mondirs*, Pagan temples of brick, which have been built by sugar-boilers and other merchants; but the only two objects of Hindu worship, that have the smallest celebrity, are the Jomuna river, in which the people of the vicinity bathe on a certain day in spring; and an image of Sib, which is called Yamoleswor, which is supposed to have arisen spontaneously from the earth, and which is worshipped by about 2,000 people assembled on the proper day. There is no Muhammedan place of worship remarkable for its buildings, but the monument of Mir Medni, at Phulvari, is the most frequented. About 100 small mosques of brick have been erected by wealthy farmers, and others within their premises, and are served by the master of the family, who lights a lamp every evening, and prays at the proper hours.

In six places some ruins are to be found, but they are small, and in all probability of little antiquity. The most considerable is Pukhoriya, about 6 miles S. W. from Chintamon. Here is an elevated space of ground, about a mile in diameter, which contains many small heaps of bricks, and about 10 or 12 tanks, one of which is said to have been dug by a Raja's mother, (Rajarmar Dighi,) on the surface of the ground are three stones, one of which contains an image. This town is said to have belonged to a Raja Gaurikanto, son of Vasudev, who will be soon mentioned.

At Madapara, 10 miles S. E. from Chintamon, are said to be the ruins of a small town, built by a servant of the Dinajpúr family.

Vasudev, a zemindar, whose daughter married the first of the Dinajpúr family that rose to any eminence, had two places of residence in this division. The first called Mohunpúr, is about 6 miles S. E. from Chintamon, and is said to have been a town. The other is called Vasudevpúr, and has been a fortress of inconsiderable size. It has had a double rampart, and has contained some bricks. A Pathan, named Morowot Khan, is also said to have resided in this fortress.

In a forest called Hira, which occupies the N. E. part of this district, and the N. W. of Nawabgunj, is a place named Kali Shokor, where there are remains of brick buildings; the founder is unknown.

Six miles N. E. from Chintamon, on the side of the Jomuna, is a small fort, which contains about 50 acres, and is called Gorgovindopúr: within is said to be a pillar of stone; but there is no inscription, nor is the founder known.

In this division are 25 market-places. Goods are exported and imported from 4 different places, none of them considerable. 'Five places besides contain shops; among these Chintamon is the most considerable, and contains about 200 families. Sujapúr and Khoyervari may also be considered as small towns, each containing about a hundred families.

PART 21.—*Division Hawra.*

The division of Hawra occupies both banks of the Jomuna river for about 11 miles, and extends from thence to the Korotaya. It is somewhat of a triangular form, and the residence of the Darogah and Munsif is conveniently situated. It may contain about 180 square miles, and extends about 20 miles from N. to S. and 18 from E. to W.

About 10 miles may be occupied by tanks, rivers, and marshes; 20 may be inundated, and are chiefly sandy low lands, *chora*, partly used for pasture, and partly cultivated for indigo, or cucurbitaceous fruits; 90 miles may be of a stiff clay, and 60 of a free soil. Setting aside 30 miles of land that are inundated, or altogether occupied by water, 4 miles may be occupied by markets, roads, burial-grounds, and steep barren places; 11 miles by woods; 22 by lands which have been deserted; and 113 are fully occupied, of which 45 are a free soil, and 68 stiff clay.

One proprietor of land of the Dinajpúr family has a handsome although small house, which is built of brick, after the Anglo-Indian fashion; but he does not reside in it. This is the only dwelling of brick that belongs to a native. The huts here, and in general on the eastern frontier towards Rongpúr, are worse than usual, being very flat and low in the roof.

This having been on the frontier of Motsyo, its sovereign, Virat Raja, is said to have had a considerable part of his army stationed here, and a ruinous fort called Viratpat is said to have been his usual residence, when he came to inspect the station. The pondit, who went to Viratpat, says, that the rampart has been of brick, and that within there have been some buildings of the same material; but the size has been inconsiderable. On the outside are two or three small tanks.

At Deyli, 8 or 10 miles N. and W. from the thana, and near Viratpúr, is said to have been the residence of Modon, the principal general *senapoti* of Virat Raja. The pondit, who examined the place, says, that he could trace the remains of a fort about a quarter of a mile square, with a brick rampart, and surrounded by a ditch. Within there is a large tank, and a heap of bricks, said to have been a temple of Vridheswori. There are no stones either in this, or in the fort of Virat Raja. On the north side of the fort are many small tanks, said to be 72 in number, and it is also said, that each was dug by a servant of the general.

About 4½ miles north from the thanna are the ruins of a fort and city, said to have belonged to Kichok, the brother-in-law of Virat, and which I visited. The fort has been about ½ mile square, and surrounded by a rampart and ditch. It is now overgrown by trees and bushes. I saw no bricks; but it is said, and I believe with truth, that there are many in the soil. At the N. W. angle of the fort is a Hindu tank of some size. North from this is a heap, called Draupodidhab, which is said to have been the house of a person of distinction in the family of Kichok. On the north side of the fort, is Roghunathpúr, a high space of ground, overgrown with trees and bushes, which has probably been a suburb, and which derives its name from a sthan, or abode of the god Roghunath. In its present state, this is a very simple place of worship, being a square terrace of earth, about 2 feet high, and 12 square. The pondit was informed, that the image was originally of brass, and was stolen; some time afterwards the present one was found in digging by accident, and a low sudro acts as pujéri. This person has spread a report, which as usual is believed, that several people, who have attempted to remove the image, had been afflicted by some dreadful sickness, or have been visited by horrible apparitions. The image is of course called Roghunath; but appears to me to be that of a Lama, or incarnation of Buddha, with a representation of different Buddhas sitting in heaven, and three females or angels flying between, while an angel sits on each hand of the incarnation. The images, as represented in the drawing No. 12, are carved on a stone, about 16 inches high and 10 broad, and so strongly resemble pictures from Thibet, which I saw in Nepal, and had there explained to me, that I have no doubt concerning what they are meant to represent. The stone is supported behind by the female part of a Lingo.

About 3 quarters of a mile beyond the fort on both sides of the great road between Dinajpúr and Rongpúr, and near the Korotoya, are the ruins of the city, which depended on Kichok. At this place are many bricks, and among other traces of buildings, are shown those which belonged to the house of Hiravesya, who was a female dancer that had very great influence over the soldiers. This house has been about 60 feet long by 20 broad from E. to W., and on its east side has had a yard, surrounded by a brick wall, about 60 feet square. A smaller building, probably a gate and porter's lodge, has been on the east side of the yard, on the west side of the house there are traces of a small tank. It is said, that the whole house was covered with enameled tiles, but of these I saw no remains.

In all parts near the Korotoya from Hawra down to Ghoraghat, traditions remain concerning a Gopichondro, his son or descendant Hovochondro, and the minister of the latter named Govochondro. The first lived at Gopinathpúr, and the second at Vagdwar, both in the Rongpúr district, where I shall have a better opportunity of tracing the accounts of these personages.

The principal Hindu place of worship in this division is a part of the Korotoya, near where the great road passes from Dinajpúr to Rongpúr, and which is called a Tirtho. On a certain day, which happened to be that on which we passed; from 20 to 25 thousand people assemble to bathe. The Muhammedans so far adopt the custom as to throw garlands into the river; but they do not bathe, and are considered by the Hindus as unworthy of that honor. This place is said to have been consecrated by the god Sib, when he created the Korotoya; and it is generally admitted by all persons, that the bathing at this place on the proper day is just as meritorious, as bathing in the Bhagirothi (Ganges) on a common occasion. The people here indeed contend, that this particular part of their river is just as good as any part of the Bhagirothi on any day of the year; but my people from the banks of the Ganges laugh at such pretentions.

At a place called Parbotipúr, six miles N. from the thanna, the pondit discovered a hole under a tree, in which are deposited a plough and other implements of agriculture. They are made of stone, are of a large size, and are said to have belonged to Bhim Raja, contemporary with Virat, and son of Pandu, the lawful sovereign of India. The neighbouring farmers offer a sacrifice to these implements on the day when they begin to plough. There are in the division 10 or 12 temples of brick; but those are not in any sort of reputation with the people, although one of them is of tolerable large dimensions, and has a Rath, or chariot, for carrying the image in procession; but there is nothing miraculous about any of them, and they are considered merely as the private marks of the piety or vanity of the individuals by whom they were built. The state of the Muhammedan places of worship is nearly the same; about ten wealthy men have built small mosques in their premises.

The market places in this division are 20; of these 3 are marts for exportation and importation. The only considerable one, however, is Hawra, or Ranigunj, which contains above 100 houses, and has a great deal of trade. About 8 other places have some shops. Of these Yosayi is the most considerable, and is a small town containing at least 100 families.

PART 22.—*Division of Nawábganj.*

The division of Nawábganj is situated on the east side of the district, and on the banks of the Korotoya. It is about 16 miles from N. to S. and 11 from E. to W. Its form is oblong, and the residence of the Darogha and Munsif are rather to the north of its centre.

It contains about 150 square miles, of which 6 may be occupied by tanks, rivers, and marshes; 10 may be inundated, and are mostly low sandy banks, of which 4 may be cultivated; 20 may be a red clay soil; 62 may be a light-coloured hard clay: and 52 of a friable mould. Setting aside the lands wholly or partially under water, and occupying about 16 square miles, there will be about 6 miles occupied by market places, steep sterile land roads, and burying grounds; 16 miles overgrown with woods; 18 miles deserted, or only cultivated occasionally; and 94 miles under cultivation, of which about one half is stiff clay, and the other friable soil.

Two sugar-boilers have some part of their habitations built of brick; all the other places of abode are mere huts.

The eastern part of this division belonged to Kamrup, the kingdom of Bhogodotto, contemporary with Virat; and at a place called Hatisala is a large tank, near which, it is said, the elephants of this prince were kept.

Before the time of Bhogodotto lived Ban Raja, and it is said, that he had a house in a large forest, 5 or 6 miles from the thana. It has been a habitation like a common zemindar's kachary, that is to say, a space of 30 or 40 yards square, inclosed with a high mud wall; has contained eight or 10 mud-walled huts, raised on platforms of mud two or three feet from the ground. Traces of these may be distinctly observed near a tank, which has been dug out of very red tenacious clay.

The place therefore might have served for the cowherds of Ban Raja, or it may have been the residence of some petty chief, who lived partly by his flocks, and partly by robbery; and who, from his skill in archery, may have been called Ban Raja. There is nothing in its appearance to determine whether it went to decay 50 or 5000 years ago.

About 2 miles south and west from the thanna is a ruin, which is said to be of very great antiquity, as it was for some time the abode of the goddess Sita, during her banishment from Ram. I have already mentioned the fables concerning this circumstance. The place is called Sita-kundo, and is a square mound of bricks, surrounding a cavity, which may have been a small tank or pond, and the mound may have been a considerable temple or dwelling, by which the tank was surrounded, being perhaps 150 or 200 feet in diameter. There is nothing in its appearance to contradict the general tenor of the legend.

On the banks of the Korotoya, east from this, lived the great poet and saint Balmík.

This celebrated person bathed at Torpon ghat, which has ever since been considered as a holy place, and is by far the most considerable resort of devout Hindus, that exists in the division. On two days in the year, people from 12 to 20 miles around, assemble to bathe at it. The only other place of religious worship belonging to the Hindus, that have any peculiar holiness, are : 1st. Bhowanipúr, 6 miles N. from the thana, where the head of a destructive female spirit (Sokti) is represented in stone. The temple is small, but much frequented. 2d. At the far end of the division towards the N. W. is an image of Sib. At Khamarbhumido, where annually 10 or 12 thousand people assemble for 10 days in spring, and offer sacrifices of sheep, hogs, goats, and pigeons, and many shop-keepers attend to supply their wants.

Near where Bhogodotto kept his elephants, a merchant of modern times has dug two tanks, and built a small temple, which is extremely carved both on its brick and wooden work, but it has no reputation. There is no Muhammedan place of worship constructed of brick, nor any of considerable celebrity.

In this division, there are 10 market places, and 2 of them are marts, from whence a considerable quantity of goods is exported. Only one other place contains a shop. Nawábganj is a small town of about 100 families, and is by far the largest place in the division.

PART 23.—*Division of Ghoraghat.*

The division of Ghoraghat is the smallest in the district. It is situated on the Korotoya and Stishta; is about 21 miles long by 12 wide, and is nearly of a triangular form. The Darogah and Munsif reside at Ghoraghat, on one of the long sides of the triangle, but in a situation abundantly convenient.

The division may contain about 140 square miles; of this, 5 miles may be occupied by rivers, tanks, and water-courses ; 4 may be inundated, mostly low sand-banks, *choras*, of which probably one half is occasionally cultivated ; 18 may be a red clay soil ; 42 a rich free mould, and 71 a stiff light-coloured clay. Setting aside the 9 miles occupied always or occasionally by water, 4 miles may be steep or barren, or burial places, roads, and markets ; 10 may have been deserted, and not overgrown with wood ; 12 may be in woods ; and 105 may be fully occupied, 35 of a light soil, and 70 of a hard clay.

Although there is a resident proprietor of land, who has a decent estate, there is no brick house in this division; the present landholder choosing to give all his means to religious mendicants ; many houses however are built with mud walls, and those formed of the red clay are comfortable. About 15 rich farmers have small brick mosques in their premises.

The ruin said to be of the greatest antiquity in this district is that of Virat Raja's house, situated about 9 miles south and west from Ghoraghat. It has evidently been a square fort. The ditch although now mostly cultivated with rice, may be clearly traced, and has been 50 or 60 feet wide. The space enclosed has been about 600 yards square, part has been cultivated ; but there are also many heaps of brick covered with trees and bushes, and very irregularly placed. Low narrow passages, like lanes, wind among these heaps, none of which is of a very considerable size. The bricks are small and rudely formed, and no stones have been observed in this ruin. On the west side of the fort, without the ditch, are some small heaps like the remains of an Indian gateway, at some distance are larger heaps, probably the ruins of small temples. In the whole there is nothing to show, that this work may not have belonged to some petty chief, who lived 2 or 3 centuries ago ; at the same time there is nothing either about it to show, that the work has not been of high and rude antiquity. Every Sunday, during the month Vaisakh, the Hindus assemble at Viratgor, where they pray and dine. There is no image at the place.

Ghoraghat is the place where Virat Raja kept his horses, from which circumstance its name is derived. In the time of Nazrat-khan, king of Gaur, it belonged to a certain Nilambor Raja, who resided at Kantadwar in the Rongpúr district, and had at it a fort surrounded by a forest. In the conquest of this infidel, Nazrat employed Ismael Ghazi, a very holy man, as well as a good officer. He reduced all the neighbouring country, and took up his residence in the fort of Ghoraghat, which had formerly been constructed by the Hindus, and changed the name of the place into Nazratabad after his master's title. He then cleared the adjacent woods, and a city arose, which was much increased by the addition of Arangabad to the north, and Narangabad to the south. The principal increase seems to have been owing to the military station (Fauzdari) of the N. E. frontier having been withdrawn from Rangamati, after the unsuccessful attempt on Asam, and to the army having been stationed at Ghoraghat, for the governor of this place in all late records is said to have been called Fauzdar of Rangamati. The person who brought the troops from Rangamati to Ghoraghat, is said to have been called Muhammed, and he was succeeded in his government, by his son Zaynulabdin. Now from an inscription over a mosque, near the ruins of the governor's house, it appears that Zaynulabdin the son of Muhammed Hoseyn, son of Muhammed Saleh, Izdanah was governor A. H. 1153. This mosque is now deserted, no worship having been performed in it for 40 years, and it never has been large. The governor's house near this mosque is quite ruinous, although the gateway is pretty entire, and many walls are standing. These show, that the size has been considerable, but no traces remain either of elegance or splendour. The city in the time of its greatness, extended eight or ten miles in length, and about two in the width, and bricks and ruins may be traced in different parts through that extent ; but there is no reason to suppose that it was a close built town of these dimensions. On the contrary there is every appearance of, by far the greater part having been cultivated fields, with houses and gardens scattered among them.

Besides the mosque already mentioned, there were several others, but all of very small dimensions ; nor are there any traces of any great public buildings. The place suffered no particular misfortune, and has gone to decay merely owing to the removal of the courts of justice, and of the army.

The fort seems to have always been a sorry place, and the only remains are a ditch, surrounding a space on the bank of the river, about a mile in length, and half a mile in width. Part has been carried away by the river.

The most celebrated place in the town, is the tomb of Ismael Gazi, placed on the S. E. corner of the fort. He is much respected, and feared both by Hindus and Muhammedans, and a small canopy is still hung over his tomb, which is very ruinous.

In the ruins of Nazratabad are very few stones, and I observe nothing to indicate that these have been taken from a former ruins.

On the bank of the Stishta, north from the thanna about 7 miles, is an old fortress called Satparagor, or the fort of seven sentinels. It includes a considerable space, but is open towards the river, owing probably to the incroachments which this has made within the fort; and on a high mouldering bank of the river is a heap of bricks covered with earth and bushes. It is called the king of Bengal's throne, and the river has opened the interior to view. There appears to have been a building of about 100 feet in diameter, which has been supported by small arches. The piers are very thick, are faced with brick, and contain within them many masses of stone, which have evidently been taken from more ancient ruins, as some of them have been ornamented with figures and carvings of various kinds, and which could not have been intended for the place that they now occupy. One of them contained traces of the human figure, and has therefore been taken from Hindu ruins. The natives at the place have no tradition concerning the fortress, except that it was a place where a Raja kept his flocks. I am inclined however to believe, that this place, as well as Ghoraghat, belonged to Raja Nilambor; for in some accounts that I received, I heard of a fort belonging to him near this place, and which was called Varo Paikergor or the fortress of 12 soldiers, which is probably the same.

About 6 miles easterly from the ruins of Virat Raja's house are said to be other ruins, which belonged to a Gokorno Raja, of whose history I could learn nothing.

Except Virat Raja's house, the only place that is considered as holy by the Hindus is Rishighat, on the Korotoya, a little below the Bengal king's throne. On a certain day in spring, a number of people assemble there to bathe.

Two small brick temples have been built by the two principal families, which lately possessed the adjacent lands; but they have never arisen to any celebrity.

The market places in this division are 11 in number, of which Ghoraghat, Sahebganj, Kengia-ganj, Gumani-ganj, and Rani-ganj are marts for exportation. Ghoraghat is now almost reduced to the state in which it may have been during the time of Raja Nilambor, being every where surrounded by woods, and tigers prowl in its streets every night. Still however, it is probably the 3d place in the district, may contain 500 families, and carries on a good deal of trade.

PART 24.—*Division of Khyetlal.*

The division of Khyetlal is of an irregular form, somewhat approaching to a semicircle, about 22 miles from east to west, and 13 from N. to S. Khyetlal, the residence of the Darogah, is conveniently situated.

The division contains about 160 square miles, and is the most fully occupied in the district. About 8 miles are occupied by tanks, rivers, and water-courses, the tanks being much more numerous than necessary; about 4 miles are inundated, and on that account are waste; 20 miles are of a fine loose soil; and 128 miles are of a hard clay. Setting aside the 12 miles occupied by water, and 3 miles occupied by roads, burial places, markets, and steep or sterile banks, and 5 miles that may be occasionally cultivated, the remainder, or ⅞ of the whole, are fully occupied; and of this 18 may be of a light soil; and 122 of a clay very stiff, and so hard, that the jack tree will not grow on it.

There is no dwelling-house of brick, nor any public edifice deserving notice.

The Muhammedan place of worship, that is of most note, is the tomb of Maksud Ghazi, and of his mother Moykamal, about 2 miles east from the thanna, where great numbers go on Mondays, Thursdays, and Fridays, to pray and make offerings. The attendant fakir has 100 bigahs of land, and the buildings are of brick and stone, but ruinous as usual. Ten or twelve wealthy farmers have small brick mosques within their premises.

The only Hindu place of worship, that is much attended, is that of Siddhéswori, where there are three small temples surrounded by a brick wall. One of them was dedicated to Sib, and covered with carved bricks. The image was stolen last year; and the only thing remarkable, although not unusual, is the extreme indecency used in the representation of a god and goddess. The place is endowed with 100 bigahs of land, which maintains four brahmins, one pujéri, two servants (sebayit), and one cook, with all their families. The goddess, as usual in Bengal, is worshipped by bloody sacrifices. A spot near the temple is considered as remarkably holy, and is called Siddha. It is supposed, that any person, who presumes to sit there while he performs his devotions, will be deprived of reason. About 24 years ago this punishment was inflicted on a religious person (mohonto), who imagined that by worshipping on the awful spot, he would be favoured with an actual vision of God. On the east side of the temple is a small tank, which contains excellent water, and in which no weeds grow. This is not attributed to the stiffness of the clay of its sides, nor to the sand containing springs at its bottom, but to the holiness of the place. The pujéri says, that the temple of Siddhéswori was built about 200 years ago by a Boli Raja, who took the image from the heart of a large tree now growing near the temple. In fact there are two wild fig trees (Ficus religiosa and bengalensis) growing near each other, and having bricks intermixed with their roots; and it is very probable, that these trees having grown from crevices in an old temple, had destroyed it, and surrounded the ruins and image with their roots, and from among these the image may have been taken by the founder of the present building, which however has no appearance of being so ancient as the pujéri pretends.

The ruins of Boli Raja's house, and of a large city, are a little to the east of the temple, and my pundit alleges, that the priest is, as usual, an ignorant creature, which indeed seems to be true, as he knew nothing of the history of Boli Raja, one of the most common legends in Indian fable. The pundit thinks it probable that the ruins belonged to Boli Raja, the father of Ban Raja, whose great works I have already described. In favor of the pujéri however I must state, that I heard it also reported in another part of the country, that one of the persons, who accompanied the Pál family in their stay here, was called Boli Raja. In the ruins I see nothing to decide the period, nor *which* Boli Raja occupied this country; for with regard to the time when he lived, the legends allow ample scope, as he flourished and had wars with Krishno many thousand years ago, and is generally allowed to be still alive.

At Boligram, about 8 miles N. and E. from Khyetlal, are shown the ruins of Boli Raja's abode, which consist of many heaps of bricks covered with earth and bushes; and traces of walls or roads, constructed of brick, and reaching from heap to heap, may be clearly distinguished. The bricks are of the usual size, and in some places the foundation of houses may be clearly traced. These heaps occupy a space of perhaps half a mile in diameter. East from this is a space of about a mile in diameter, which is raised very high by numerous tanks, and in some places contains bricks. This has in all probability been a town adjacent to the Raja's house.

There are only four market places in the district, and two shops. The largest place is Gujeya, which contains about 60 houses. Khyetlal, or the fair-field, was formerly a large town, and the residence of a zemindar, to whom the ancestor of the Dinajpúr family was a servant; but there are no remains of a town, except a quantity of bricks scattered about some tanks.

Near it are some images of stone, which I was desired to visit, as they were rendered remarkable by having been cut asunder by the sword of Kalapahar, who contrary to what one would have expected from such a violent action, was a very holy brahmin. A Muhammedan king, enraged at his sanctity, seized on him, and compelled him to eat beef, by which the good man lost caste, and was under the necessity of becoming a Muhammedan. This he regretted very much, and, as a punishment on the gods for permitting such a profanation, he went about cutting their images in pieces. As this is a story very generally told in Bengal, I expected to have found the images cut in a reasonable manner through the middle, or at least deprived of their heads, as I had indeed been told; but Kalapahar appears here to have moderated his wrath, and the images seemed to have suffered no more than might have been expected from the usual dilapidation of time, which carries off noses, fingers, or hands, that are made of brittle materials, and that project too far from support.

BOOK II.

CONCERNING THE PEOPLE OF THE DINAJPUR DISTRICT.

CHAPTER I.

ON THE POPULATION OF THE DISTRICT, AND THE CAUSES WHICH OPERATE ON ITS INCREASE OR DIMINUTION.

On the important subject of the number of inhabitants, I have little or nothing to offer that is satisfactory, for no enumeration has been made by the officers of police or revenue.

A list called Khaneh Shumari, containing a statement of the number of houses, families, tradesmen, castes, ploughs, looms, tanks, and other public works, religious and civil, that are under the care of the magistrate, is very commonly kept in native governments, and seems to be useful, where attention is paid to have it tolerably exact, which may in general be easily accomplished, and I have never heard that the people were alarmed by the execution. I cannot however take upon myself to assert, that such a measure would not occasion alarm in Bengal, because the people, for some time at least, have not been accustomed to it; but I was told that several of the proprietors of land had made such lists for their own estates, without which indeed I cannot imagine how they should be decently regulated, neither did I hear that this had given any alarm or disgust to their tenantry. I was promised a sight of one of these documents; but the promise, as usual in such cases, was not performed.

The only manner that I have of calculating the population is from the extent of cultivation, which is of course liable to great error. Two calculations may be founded on this basis.

First, it will appear in my account of the agriculture of this district, that about 480000 ploughs are required, and one man is the usual allowance for each plough. The men employed in actual agriculture cannot therefore be less than 480000, and these I imagine will be nearly one-fifth of their families, including old people and children, which will make the agricultural population 2400000. Now considering the very imperfect state of agriculture, and the rudeness of the arts in this district, I do not think that we can add more than one-fourth of this number for all the other classes of society, especially as a quantity of grain is exported. This will give 3000000 for the total population, being about 558 persons for each square mile.

Secondly. An estimate may be formed from the quantity of produce, and rice being the chief food of the people we may consider that alone. The total quantity of rough rice, after deducting seed, that I have calculated to be annually raised in this district, is about 36800000 mons, which according to the trials that I made, will give 27650000 mons of clean rice. Now I have supposed, that to the value of 3200000 Rs. of rice, or 4400000 mons are exported, and there will remain for consumption 23250000 mons Calcutta weight. Then allowing ½ seer of 96 Sa. Wt. for each person daily, which is the calculation usually made in this district, this quantity of rice will feed more than 4000000 of people ; considerable deductions however must be allowed for grain that is wasted, distilled, consumed by fire, eaten by cattle, and used in the arts ; but still this population seems to be exaggerated, and the calculation founded on the number of ploughs seems more suitable to reality.

The most remarkable circumstance is, that with this overwhelming population there is a general complaint of a scarcity of workmen. The waste lands are attributed to a want of farmers ; and common workmen or porters cannot be procured without the utmost difficulty.

The difficulty in procuring farmers for waste lands, I imagine, is owing to the extreme poverty of the generality of that class of men, who have no farther means than will just enable them to cultivate land that is in good condition, and from which they can receive an immediate and certain return ; while the immense profit, which those who have any capital make by lending out their money to necessitous neighbours, prevents them from laying out money on improving the soil.

The difficulty of procuring workmen and porters proceeds, in my opinion, chiefly from the want of skill and of proper implements to facilitate labour, so that the quantity which individuals can perform is exceedingly small, and almost every person is therefore engaged. It must, however, I am afraid, be allowed that a want of energy and activity in the people contribute also to the same end.

That the population should be enormous is not wonderful ; for there are not probably 1000 persons born in the district who are in the army, or who have left it for service of any kind, or indeed who have at all emigrated, except scoundrels who are under the power of justice, or who have absconded from a fear of the law. These are indeed very numerous.

The notions of both Hindus and Muhammedans inculcate in the strongest manner the duty of women to propagate the species, and I may venture to say that the injunction is complied with, as far nearly as human nature will admit. A maiden at the age of puberty would be looked upon by the natives with disgust and contempt ; but few indeed are left in this humiliating situation. Besides, the Muhammedan law, and that of three-fourths of the Hindus of this district, allows widows to live in a kind of left-hand marriage, which, although not so honourable as proper matrimony, is far from being considered as sinful, or as excluding them from society. Accordingly, except prostitutes, I may safely venture to say, that in the whole district there are not 1000 women capable of propagating the species, who are not in a situation of doing so, either as wives or concubines. Even among the pure Hindus, whose widows cannot marry, there are comparatively few persons of that description , for most of them are from other districts, and a large proportion of their widows, who do not burn nor become prostitutes, retire to their families.

The hardships imposed upon Hindu widows of rank will be seen from many circumstances in the following account. They are stript of the numerous ornaments which they enjoyed while children and wives, and are not even allowed to wear a red border to their dress ; while they are compelled to sleep on the ground exposed to insects and vermin, and to act as menial servants to the vain beauties who are decked out in the ornaments of which they have been deprived. Women of a high mind often prefer the funeral pile, while many others submit with patience, especially in the families of land-holders, when they have young sons totally incapable of managing their affairs; but it is not wonderful that many young women, conscious of their beauty, and thoughtless concerning its decay, scorn to submit to such harsh regulations, and seek for refuge in the house of a bawd.

In fact the rage for marriage is such, that a man, who has not money sufficient to defray the expense of the ceremony, is every where willing to borrow it at any interest; and this involves himself and offspring in difficulties, from which death alone can relieve them. In some divisions I found, that even common labourers sold their services for from 18 to 24 months, in order to raise at once a sum sufficient to enable them to marry; and during that time, the wife of course is left to provide for herself in the best manner she can. The master in such cases finds the servant in food and raiment.

It may seem surprising, in a country where procreation has such encouragement, and where perhaps there is less emigration than in any place whatever, that the species should not multiply so fast as to render famine common, or that a single inch of ground should remain unoccupied.

I have already endeavoured to account for part of the lands remaining waste, from poverty of the farmers, and the high profits on capital. With respect to the supply of food, I must state, that in the remembrance of man there have only been two famines; one in the Bengal year 1177, and one in the year 1194, the one 21 years, and the other 38 years ago. Both these were owing to very unfavorable seasons, when a great part of the crop failed; and in the latter it was only in some parts of this district, that any considerable number perished. In common years, or even in times of scarcity, such as the present year 1808, such excess of misery is unknown; and none, so far as I could learn, perish of hunger: on the contrary there is usually a great abundance of food.

There seem to be two principal means that keep the population within the bounds of subsistence; one is early marriage, and the other disease.

In all the larger animals nearly resembling man, with whose manners we are well acquainted, such as the horse, ass, cow, or sheep, it has been found, that where the sexes have been allowed to unite so soon as actuated by desire, the offspring was puny, and the operation uncertain; and I think we may safely extend the analogy to the human race. Some peculiar tribes of men in India, especially those in the western parts, and the bearers of palanquins, are no doubt strong men; but it is not within my reach at present to form a rational conjecture concerning the reason why these differ from their countrymen. It suffices to say, that the inhabitants of Dinajpûr are a puny weak race, and are far from having numerous families, notwithstanding their early marriages, which on the woman's side almost always are consummated before the age of 13 years, and on the man's very commonly before the age of 16. In the families of land-holders, it is very uncommon to trace three successive generations; and in order to preserve the succession recource must be had to adoption, more usually after one regular succession than after a longer interval. These land-holders are all married when children, and enjoy an abundant diet, comfortable dwellings, and plenty of warm clothing. It may indeed be with justice said, that the villages of Dinajpûr swarm with children. This, however, I believe, does not proceed from the prolificness of individuals, but is the natural consequence of the people being unhealthy and short lived, which of course requires a large proportion of children to the number of adults. The moralist, who with a view of checking vice, should succeed in introducing early marriages, would, I am persuaded, produce great injury. The breed of men would not only degenerate, but vice would become more predominant. Female beauty reaped too early almost instantly decays, disgust soon follows, and the husbands, like the land-holders of Dinajpúr, would soon abandon themselves to intrigue.

The grand check however to the excess of population is disease, which makes ample room, and fever annually sweeps away immense numbers; although I do not think that any means would ever render Dinajpúr a country remarkably salubrious, yet I am persuaded, that the excessive prevalence of fever is more owing to the want of stimulating diet, and of comfortable lodging and clothing, the consequence of poverty, than to any extraordinary degree of malignity in the air; and the great poverty of the natives is no doubt to be chiefly attributed to their improvidence, especially in forming early marriages, by which they have been involved in debt. The fevers are generally of the remitting kind, and terminate fatally in a few days; but more commonly they terminate in agues, or commence under that form, and are accompanied by enlargements of the spleen and dropsical swellings, which carry off the sufferer after long confinement. In fact, there are few who escape with less confinement than one month in the year, and the whole are a sickly poor looking people.

The fever makes such ample havoc, that little room seems to be left for other diseases, some of which however are objects of great curiosity. I was prevented from gaining a proper knowledge of them, partly by my constant travelling, and numerous other avocations, which were incompatible with an attendance on the sick, and partly from my having met with no native physician. The practitioners of medicine are confined to Dinajpúr and Maldeh, and were so much engaged, that I could not procure an interview of length enough to afford satisfactory information.

The small-pox on the whole does little injury, and the inoculation for that disease is pretty generally diffused. The inoculators are of both religions, and of all castes. One of them, a Hindu, gave me the following account of his plan. Every year, so soon as the natural disease appears, which it usually does between the 10th of February and 12th of March, he begins to inoculate, and the season for inoculation continues until the 12th of May. Some years the spontaneous disease does not appear, and then he cannot operate, having no means of procuring matter. The inoculator in the course of his practice remembers this having happened four times. When he has found a person under the natural disease, he opens the pustules with a rude iron bodkin, and collects the matter on some cotton wool. It will keep three days, and no longer. He uses it by moistening the cotton in water, and rubbing it on the skin, and then in that part he makes 8 or 10 punctures with a needle; afterwards he rubs the impregnated cotton upon the punctures. Children are not inoculated under three years of age, but generally before ten. Those, who are too young for inoculation, are carefully separated from those who undergo the operation, and are made to drink sugar and water, over which some incantations to Sitola have been performed by a brahmin. Previous to the operation, the child is washed, and afterwards is not allowed to eat fish; meat is nearly out of the question, but it seems to be allowed whatever else it chooses, except cakes or bread; and sugar, plantains, water-melons, cucumbers, and cold boiled rice are recommended as the most proper diet. Two or three times a day it is washed in cold water. Should a fever accompany the eruption, the inoculator repeats a spell (montor) over some water, which he gives to the child to drink. He knows of no other remedy, and his skill is supposed to consist in the knowledge of a proper spell, which is a secret Muhammedan inoculators, as well as

Hindus, pretend to a knowledge of. Very few indeed of those who are inoculated die, even in the worst seasons; for although the disease appears naturally almost every year, there are certain seasons, once in 10 or 12 years, when it attacks more generally than others, and it then proves uncommonly fatal. In such seasons, there dies perhaps one in a hundred of those who are inoculated. It is indeed chiefly in such seasons, that the spontaneous disease proves fatal to the natives of Dinajpúr.

The inoculators, when not employed in the line of their profession, cultivate the ground with their own hands. Their fee is from 1 anna to one rupee for each child, according to the circumstances of the parent; and they are by no means respected, nor considered as on a footing with the practitioner of medicine.

The vaccine inoculation is totally unknown to the natives, even by report.

Measles appear occasionally, but are seldom fatal. Fluxes and choleras are common in spring, and rheumatisms in the cold weather; but these seldom kill.

The pox is rather uncommon; and except near the town, married men are ashamed to infect their families. In and near Dinajpúr, indeed, it is supposed that one person in four has this disease. Neither can the itch nor ring-worm be considered as very common, and they do not affect more perhaps than one-fourth of the people, and these of the lowest ranks, which in India must be considered as a very moderate proportion. The ring-worm is the most prevalent.

These diseases are common to natives of Britain and India, but there are others peculiar in some measure to the latter, which deserve particular notice.

The kind of leprosy, called Kushtho, or Mohavyadhi, (that is, the great disease,) is common, although not quite so prevalent as in some parts of Bengal. Some estimate the number affected at one in the hundred, while in other districts not more than one in 500 are supposed to suffer. I am doubtful whether or not it has yet been described by Nosologists, or at least clearly distinguished from some diseases to which it has a strong resemblance; but not having it in my power to consult the work of Savauges, I cannot speak positively. In this terrible disease, the skin becomes wrinkled and discoloured, the joints of the hands and feet drop off, and the patient becomes a most loathsome object. It has no tendency to spontaneous cure; but continues to afflict the patient until death. I am certain that it is not infectious; so that in several points it seems to differ from the leprosy to which the Jews were subject, and which I believe is that called Lepra Arabum by Nosologists. I have known women, who had laboured under it for years, and who had healthy children, which they suckled, without communicating infection; and I am here assured, that men labouring under it have for years cohabited with their wives, who have continued exempt. It is reckoned however hereditary, and I believe with justice; but it seldom makes its appearance before the age of puberty. By the natives here, it is reckoned of two kinds: Papoj, which is inflicted on those who are great sinners, and which may be cured, if the gods please, by a pilgrimage to Baidyonath near Janggira on the Ganges; and Kormoj, which is inflicted on those who have been sinners in a former life. Were it not for the overbearing credulity of the natives, one might from thence infer, that the disease sometimes goes away spontaneously; but after much inquiry, I have not been able to learn of one case. It seems in Bengal to occupy the place of Scrofula, being nearly as common as that malady is in the colder parts of Europe. In a native of India, on the contrary, I have never seen a clearly marked case of Scrofula; and believe such have rarely, if ever, occurred. I know from repeated trials, that arsenic is no cure for this leprosy, as has been pretended; and I have also tried mercury in vain. Neither had a full and nourishing diet any better effect in a fair trial, which I made by order of Lord Teignmouth, when that nobleman was Governor General. Mr. Halliday, surgeon at Dinajpúr, informs me, that he has had some success with the mineral acids.

The leprosy, in which the skin of the natives becomes white (Switre), is but rare, although at all times there are several examples of it in the district; and a similar state often probably takes place in the skins of Europeans, without being observed or considered as a disease. At least I have seen the skins of some Europeans, that exactly resembled those of the Indians who are affected with this disorder.

The leprosy, accompanied by an enlargement of the leg, and which has been called elephantiasis by Nosologists, has been often considered as a mere symptom of the first mentioned disease. The natives, I believe, with great justice consider them as perfectly distinct; and the disease which consists in a swelled leg they call *godh*. In Dinajpúr it is not a rare disease, and in some divisions it was said that one person in 200 labours under it, but in others it is not so common. It generally commences in adults, and is accompanied by repeated attacks of pain and fever, which the natives say appear always either at the full or new moon. Each attack of fever is accompanied by an increase of swelling, but when this has enlarged to a certain extent, the attacks of fever gradually become less and less violent, and produce less and less effect on the swelling; so that afterwards the patient enjoys good health, lives to the usual age, and suffers no inconvenience, except from the size of the tumour. Both sexes are subject to the three diseases, that have been last mentioned.

The women, in a few parts of this district, chiefly near the Punabhoba and Atreyi rivers, are subject to the indolent swelling in the throat, which seems to be exactly the same with the goitre of the Alps. By the natives it is called *gologondo*, and its progress is nearly the same with that of the *godh;* but the fever and pain are never so considerable, and the former is often not perceptible; while it is increasing, however, there are always slight paroxysms of pain. No remedy is known for either of these diseases.

The male sex in this district, as well as in other parts of India, are subject to a swelling apparently of a similar nature, but which affects the testicles. Its paroxysms of increase are accompanied by fever and pain, which last three or four days, and are said always to appear at full or new moon. It seldom attacks persons under 20 years of age, and usually commences on only one side. In this stage, it is called *eksira*, and sometimes is cured; but when both sides are affected, especially after a few paroxysms, and after it has acquired the name of *korondo*, no remedy is known. After some time the paroxysms of pain and fever entirely cease, and the swelling becomes stationary; but it is extremely inconvenient from its size, and frequently destroys the powers of generation. It is not, however, liable to degenerate into cancer, nor to affect the general health. The usual size is, that of a man's head, but it is often much larger. The natives consider these three last diseases, as a species of the same genus, and I believe with perfect accuracy. This last species is not so common in Dinajpúr as in the southern parts of Bengal, but still many are affected.

Two febrile diseases, accompanied by local inflammation, are also exceedingly common, but are not epidemic. The one is, by the natives called *sannipatik*, and is a swelling and pain of the submaxillary glands, accompanied by fever. It frequently attacks the same person at different times, in the course of his life. This disease is very common in Dinajpúr, and Mr. Halliday considers it as the same with the mumps (angina parotidea) and treats it with emetics. I cannot say that I am entirely satisfied concerning the identity of the two diseases. Many of my followers suffered from it, and some more than once; but it was a mild complaint, without any symptom that required so active a medicine as an emetic, otherwise I should have tried the plan recommended by Mr. Halliday.

The other disease is very common in every part of India, and by the natives is called *nasa*, or *nakra*. It is a considerable fever, accompanied by much drowsiness, and by general pains, especially in the neck and shoulders. The inner membrane of the nose is considered by the natives as the seat of the disorder; but there is no considerable uneasiness in that member. The membrane is however turgid with blood. The cure applied by the natives is to draw blood from the part, by thrusting a sharp-edged grass into the nose. So far as I have had occasion to observe, th disease would readily terminate in health, without assistance; some persons however pretend to have great skill in knowing the proper time for introducing the grass, and say that then the disease is ripe.

CHAPTER II.

CONDITION AND MANNER OF LIVING.

In order to give the most correct view of the manner in which the people live, in respect to food, drink, clothing, and habitations, I have, by means of Ramjoy, my native assistant, made out an estimate of the usual expence incurred by six families of different ranks in the town of Dinajpúr, and I am persuaded, that this will prove more satisfactory than any desultory observations that could be made on the subject; but I shall now offer a few explanations and remarks. The estimate will be found in the Appendix to this book, and an Abstract in the 2nd statistical table.

Ramjoy has unfortunately made his choice entirely from among the Hindús, with whom as a Brahmin he was naturally most connected; but in this district, as I shall afterwards mention, they are of less importance than the Moslem. The difference however in the manner of living between the two people is not very considerable in this district, and shall be pointed out under each head.

From the first class of people, I have excluded the great land-holders, very few of whom reside in this district. These live in a much superior manner, and maintain from 50 to 150 domestics of various kinds, from which an estimate may be formed of their manner of living.

The first class consists of the principal native officers of government, of small land-holders, of the chief officers of the great land-holders, of the principal proprietors of free estates, and of a few merchants and principal manufacturers. The greater part of these are natives of other districts, and have not brought their families with them; it being considered as improper for a Hindú to take his wife from home. The whole almost are Hindús.

The second class are also almost entirely Hindús, and consist of the 2nd class of native officers of government, such as *Darogahs* and *Munsiffs*, (although many of these live like the first class,) and of the agents of smaller *Zemindars*, or the inferior agents of the great land-holders, of petty land-holders, and of a considerable number of merchants, especially sugar-manufacturers, who are almost the only persons belonging to this class that are natives of the district.

The third class consists of the petty officers of government and land-holders being chiefly the persons employed to keep accounts (*mohurer*), and to command the men who enforce the orders of the magistrate (*jamadar*), or land-holders (*mirdua*) of the agents of the great merchants in the south, of many petty traders and manufactures who are natives of this district, and of rich farmers, mostly Muhammedans, who are the only persons of the class that possess any real wealth.

The fourth class consists of easy farmers who have three or four ploughs, of artificers in easy circumstances, and of the principal domestics of rich people.

The fifth class contains farmers who have one or two ploughs; tradesmen in tolerable circumstances, (such as oil-men who have one or two mills, or weavers who have one or two looms,) and petty shop-keepers.

The sixth class contains those who cultivate for a share of the produce, common labourers, and low artificers, such as basket-makers, washermen, the greater part of fishers, carpenters, &c. &c.

In my account of the architecture of the natives, I shall give some further detail concerning their houses. In the mean time, I may state, that it is not the usual custom of Bengal to build one house with a number of different apartments sufficient for the purposes of the family; but, except the great, natives in general build a separate house or hut for each purpose. The huts collectively sufficient for the accommodation of a family, are usually surrounded by a common fence, and are called *vati* or *vari*, according to their structure : they are called *bunggola*, *chauyari*, or *dalan*, as will be afterwards explained. Their comfort depends much on the nature of their materials. Except in the few brick houses built after the Muhammedan or European fashion, thatched roofs are the only ones known in this district, and no doubt in respect of excluding both heat and cold, are more comfortable than those covered with tiles ; but they harbour vermin, especially snakes, and are more liable to fire. The general use of tiled roofs cannot, however, be proposed in the present state of capital, although such roofs, even under existing circumstances, might with great advantage be more numerous than they are at present. The granaries of this district, which are exceedingly extensive, and on which a great part of Mursbedabad, Calcutta, and the intermediate towns, depend for a daily supply of food, are exposed to the danger of fire in a manner with which I was often shocked, especially as when I visited the country, scarcity was severely felt, and famine was even to be apprehended. The merchants to whom these granaries belong, are abundantly able to defray the expense of tiled roofs, but I am persuaded will never employ them without compulsion. Their agents and other traders have a carelessness and indifference about fire, that is quite astonishing, and seem rather to court it ; for I observed in several marts, that not only the granaries, but even their houses were built entirely of straw or reeds, when the hut of every labourer within miles of them had mud walls. As these people not only endanger their own property, but the lives of those who may suffer famine by their negligence, I can perceive no injustice in compelling them to secure their granaries.

In many parts of the country, the meanest huts have walls of clay, which are very much superior in comfort to those made of hurdles, especially in cold weather ; but such are not attainable in the parts of the country where the soil is loose, and even the huts that have mud walls are very damp and unhealthy, from their earthen floors, in a climate of the most excessive moisture. It is only where the ruins of Gaur or Peruya afford bricks, that in the present state of things even the higher ranks can afford houses of that material. Until the people shall have procured more wealth, which may never happen, one of the greatest improvements on their condition would be to introduce huts raised on posts, like those of Eastern India, which are infinitely less liable to dampness and to vermin than those of Bengal.

Farmers have in general larger and better houses than people living in towns, their respective situations in life being taken into consideration. Thus a rich farmer whom I have placed in the 3rd rank, will have 12 or 14 huts on his premises or *vari*, for he has many servants, and in general several brothers with their wives and children live together; and if a Muhammedan, as most of the richer farmers are, he generally has in his premises a small brick mosque, which gives his abode a respectable appearance. His expense however under this head is very inconsiderable, as he has all the materials at hand; and he and his servants build and repair his dwelling at intervals of labour, which would otherwise be unemployed. The same may be said of the common labourer in the country, into an estimate of whose expense the cost of a house can scarcely enter.

I suspect that the hut for receiving company is a Muhammedan innovation, and has been introduced when the example or command of these haughty conquerors rendered it necessary to secrete the women. This practice is not common in the south of India, where the manners of the Hindús are less altered, and the name universally used for this apartment (*boitakhana*) is foreign.

The furniture of the Muhammedans and Hindús is nearly the same, only the former require no apparatus for their worship; and the lower classes require nothing except a knife, a mat, a bit of sackcloth, a *unga*, and some earthen pots and gourds for vessels; the whole not exceeding the value of one rupee. The sofa made of wood, the carpets, and quilts, seem to have been introduced by the Muhammedans, and chairs seem to have been introduced by Europeans. The Hindús of rank originally, I believe, covered their floor of ceremony with a plain white sheet, and sat on mats, some of them very fine. The low stools (*piri*), on which they sit on their heels, while at meals, are merely intended to keep them from the mud or dust. By far the greater part of the people sleep on the ground on sackcloth or mats, and cover themselves with sackcloth, or *megilee*. The most valuable part of their furniture consists of copper or brass vessels; for they have no plate. For eating any thing acid, such as most of their curries, in place of copper vessels, which would be dangerous, they use coarse plates and cups made of pot-stone, which absorb oil and grease, and cannot be cleaned. From a principle of what they call purity, China or Queen's-ware are rejected, as a Hindú considers it as impure to use any vessel of potter's-ware more than once.

The jewels and ornaments worn by Muhammedans are quite different from those used by the Hindús; but I decline enumerating them here, because there are very few Muhammedans of rank. In general the Muhammedans use fewer ornaments of gold and silver than the Hindús, and are fonder of pearls and precious stones. In place of the brass or shell ornaments used by the lower Hindús, the lower Muhammedan women use rings of tin or lac. Both people, like other nations, are subject to the influence of fashions; although these do not travel with the same velocity that they do in Europe; for instance, the fashionable lady of Dinajpúr cannot endure a *maduli* of that place, but procures her's from Calcutta. The former is made in the shape of the *mridonggo*, while the latter imitate the *dholona*, another instrument of noise. At Calcutta again, the *maduli* in form of a *dholona*, has been completely exploded for at least 20 years; and the sable belles of that city wear none but those made of pearls or jewels, after the fashion of Delhi. Here the fashion takes 20 years to crawl four or five hundred miles, whereas in Britain, it flies with the mail from Bond-street to the Lands-end in three or four days; and even in the midst of a most sanguinary war, our moralists have seldom been allowed more than a year to descant on the impropriety of a Parisian fashion, before our beaux or belles have been able to appear in it.

Both Hindú and Muhammedan women colour their eyelids with lamp-black. The dress of the Hindú men of rank has become nearly the same with that of the Muhammedans, who did not allow an officer employed by them to appear at their levees (*durbars*), except in proper dress. At home, however, the Hindú men, and on all occasions their women, retain almost entirely their native dress, which consists of various pieces of cloth wrapped round them, without having been sown together in any form, and only kept in their place by having their ends thrust under the folds. The needle seems indeed to have been totally unknown to the Hindús, and I have not been able to learn any Hindú word for sewing, except that used to express passing the shuttle in the act of weaving. The wealthy Muhammedan farmers dress very poorly, and on this article many of them do not expend 10 rupees a year for their whole family. The poorer Muhammedans here have adopted almost entirely the Hindú nakedness, more from necessity than inclination; in fact the lower classes are exceedingly ill-clothed, night and day, and suffer much from cold, both in the cold season and when it rains. On this account it would be very useful to introduce the manufacture of coarse blankets, common in many parts of India, especially if the breed of sheep could be somewhat increased. The dress in this country is of less value than that stated at Dinajpúr, and that of a common labourer does not exceed 9 anas a year, with as much for that of his wife. Many of the lower Hindú women, who are mostly of tribes from the eastern parts of Bengal, use a dress nearly resembling that of the Burmás, that is, a square piece of cloth placed round the back, and folded across the breast, where it is secured by thrusting the corners under the fold which comes over the bosom ; this dress is usually made of a coarse cloth called *megilee*. It is only the two higher classes that make a common use of bleached linen, the third uses it only on high occasions.

The food of the people is in general superior to their lodging, furniture, and clothing : few are distressed by hunger ; and although in general their food is not of a nature sufficiently nourishing, it is abundant. The higher classes have plenty of fish, vegetables, and milk, and might procure meat, for they are not restrained from eating the flesh of sacrifices ; yet in general they abstain from this indulgence, which is always considered as disgraceful.

The large allowance for oil, made in the estimate, includes what is used for anointing the skin. This practice here is confined to the higher ranks. The allowance of oil in the estimate, in all ranks, includes that for the lamp. The third class burn a light two or three hours, the fourth perhaps one hour, and the lowest only for a very short time, to enable them to eat, after the labours of the day are over, or early in the morning, when the female rises before dawn to the hard labour of beating rice.

The 3rd rank, being mostly Muhammedans, or Hindús of low caste, although their allowance of luxuries, such as sugar, spice, and butter be small, yet often enjoy poultry and meat, especially that of sheep and goats ; so far as I could learn, the country benefits little in respect to beef, from having few Hindús, and no beeves are killed, except at Dinajpúr under the protection of the magistrate, and at Peruya under the protection of the Muhammedan saints, who are its proprietors. By far the greatest part of the proprietors of land, of their agents, and of the officers of government are Hindús, who exert the whole of their influence to save the sacred beasts, and are completely successful.

The poorer farmers very seldom taste milk, and their supply of fish is very scanty ; but, if Muhammedans, they occasionally have a fowl, pigeon, kid, or lamb ; and, if Hindús, they have sometimes a kid or duck, and in some parts they can catch deer or wild hogs ; their supply of oil and salt is scanty, and foreign spices, even pepper, are totally unknown to them, nor can they in general procure sugar to smoke with tobacco, as is usually practised in this country.

The lowest class often want beetle and salt, and in place of the latter use the ashes of various plants. The nature of this saline substance (*khyar*) I have not examined; but suspect, that it contains many other salts besides the carbonate of potass. The plants most commonly used in this district are as follows: the root of the plantain tree or Musa; the stems of two species of Sinapis; the *turi*, and *sorisha*, of which no account has been published in Botanical systems; and several plants that float on water, and by the natives are called *pana*, such as the Pistia, Stratiotes, the Salvinia natans, and another species of the same genus, of which I find no account published. I have had no opportunity of ascertaining whether or not there exists any difference in the qualities of these ashes. Their supply of fish, oil, and vegetables, is very scanty. The only fish that they procure is what they can catch in ditches; and the vegetables that they use are either wild ones collected by their children, or a few beans and cucurbitaceous plants that cover the roofs of their huts. The greatest deprivation however which they suffer is the scarcity of tobacco.

Modest women do not smoke, but they chew this stinking weed with beetle, and men of all ranks seem to delight in nothing so much as in devouring its smoke. The lowest class are unable to purchase it; but those who employ them to work, knowing its invigorating effects, supply their wants, otherwise their work would advance slowly.

Some of the lowest Hindús find a valuable addition to their nourishment in pork, which they have sense enough to rear, notwithstanding the contempt of their neighbours; and which is secured to their enjoyment more by the silliness than by the moderation of their superiors.

On the whole half a seer of rice, weighing 48 Sa. Rs. or rather less than 1¼ pound, avoirdupois (1,231), is considered as sufficient for the daily sustenance of each person in a family, young and old; to which if there is plenty of salt and oil, with pulse or other vegetables, rather to convey down the latter, than to afford nourishment, the person is considered as living on a full diet. The only drink is water; milk is scarce even with the 3rd rank, and distilled or fermented liquors cannot be considered as entering into the diet of the natives, and whenever taken, are used for the purpose of the most beastly inebriation.

Many persons, I am aware, consider, that vegetable food highly seasoned with capsicum, and water for drink, is the diet best adapted for a warm climate; but I am persuaded that they are mistaken, and have been misled by observing the sickness of newly arrived troops or seamen, which is too often preceded by excess and intemperance. Whoever, I think, has travelled much with natives, and been witness to the weakness of their constitutions, in resisting the changes of air or water, will agree with me in saying, that those who enjoy a diet, which includes animal food and strong liquors in moderate quantities, are best able to resist the influence of unhealthy climates, and the sudden changes of air.

From some, Muhammed has received praise for his having prohibited strong liquors; while others, wishing to detract from this merit, have stated, that in warm climates the prohibition is absolutely necessary, as the natives by intoxication are thrown into an ungovernable fury. This seems to me to be one of the usual exaggerations of the effects of climate. Nothing can in general be quieter than a drunken native. He either retires with his wife or mistress to some private place, where both parties drink under the foolish notion of receiving vigor, or he takes at once as much as deprives him both of reason and of voluntary motion, and falls down a stupid block, and it is only in this state, that he is usually seen. It is seldom or never, that he indulges in that drunken conviviality, which is apt to degenerate into quarrels. The ferocity with which the Malay in certain cases commits assassination has been attributed to the effects of intoxication in a warm climate: but I believe unjustly; the action is premeditated, and arises from a savage principle of honor, and recourse is had to intoxication to give courage in the perpetration of a deed that is followed by the most dreadful punishment.

In different parts of India, the juice of various palms affords a fermented liquor, which enters largely into the diet of many of the inhabitants; and I am persuaded might in most parts become the common beverage in place of the very indifferent water that is now used. Although I dislike this liquor, yet I believe that by habit every one would acquire a fondness for it, just as almost every one acquires a liking to beer; and I have no doubt, but that its use would prove highly beneficial and comfortable to the people. Those called moralists, with their usual eagerness to appear uncommonly virtuous, are apt to extend their declamation from the abuse to the moderate enjoyment of good things; but the present state of morals in Dinajpúr, under a water regimen, seems very little favourable to the wisdom of those who wish to deprive the people of the use of strong drink. Distilled spirits, I confess, are dangerous, as they readily lead to excess; yet in climates that do not produce wine, their prohibition would, I have no doubt, prove injurious to the health and vigour of the people. At any rate, the palms of India produce a liquor not liable to this objection; and I think it is much to be regretted, that the inhabitants of Dinajpúr do not use it.

The most common fuel used for cooking is bambu. The poor, however, and many farmers collect cow-dung, and mix it with the husks of rice; but this kind of fuel is not much valued in this district. Except near Ghoraghát and Maldeb, where there are many bushes, wood is seldom used as fuel; for the cutting a tree to pieces for that purpose, is attended with too much trouble and expense. The bambu is considered by many as an unwholesome fuel, and part of the sickliness of the district is attributed to it's common use; but this is probably an error. Reeds in some parts constitute the fuel, especially that used in manufactures.

The persons mentioned as domestics are freemen, there being very few slaves in this district: they are hired from month to month, and as will be perceived have miserable wages, and are very poorly clothed. Their employments are as follows: they wash their masters' clothes by dipping them in cold water, beating them on a stone a little, and then dry them; (for the washerman cleans the clothes once only after eight or ten wearings;) they bring water, clean the house furniture, and cooking utensils; they bring provisions, firewood, and pots from the market; they assist their master to cook; (for in general a man of rank passes a considerable part of his time in this office;) they go messages, they dress the *hooka*, or instrument for smoking tobacco; they dig and weed the garden; they clean and feed the cattle; and, in fact, do almost every thing that they are desired. The rules which the servants of Europeans have established, and by which they pretend that they will lose caste by performing more than oue business, seem therefore to be a mere invention of their own.

Except great land-holders, very few keep running footmen, and the only travelling carriages in the district, belonging to natives, are ten or twelve covered carts drawn by oxen, which belong to Muhammedans at Dinajpúr. Many persons even of the 2nd class keep palanquins; but except land-holders, and their chief agents, few or none have regular sets of bearers, nor people to carry torches, but hire them when wanted. The horses most commonly kept by persons of rank are ponies from Bootan, which are commonly piebald, and are called *tanggens*. From the estimate of the expense bestowed on keeping them, (3 Rs. a month, or ⅛ of what a European would allow,) some notion may be formed of their condition. Much work is not however exacted from them, and many, who are afraid to ride, keep them from ostentation; the pony has fine trappings, and his master either walks or goes in a palanquin, while the horse is led after him. People of the 3rd rank usually have small ponies of the country breed, on which they either ride to market, or at least walk there before the horse. The people indeed are less addicted to horsemanship than almost any that I know.

The most striking circumstance in the domestic economy of the people of Dinajpúr is the want or scarcity of female servants, even in houses of distinction; this does not proceed from the want of female delicacy in the women of rank, but from the difficulty of procuring women that will serve, as the whole almost are married.

As there is no provision for the indigent, except casual charity, the number of poor, that is supported by begging, is not considerable, and does not from all I could learn, amount to more than three persons in 1000. The persons who beg on account of their poverty are in general very proper objects of charity, lame, blind, and infirm persons, old women who are destitute of friends or support, and it is chiefly near the capital that I heard complants of idle vagrants. In justice to the people, I must say that they are charitable, and that in general, objects of charity seem to receive a sufficiency to support nature. During the great famine, which happened in the Bengal year 1177, a merchant of this district, named Gopimondol, gave 50,000 Rs. to the poor. The beggars are certainly very ill-clothed, and suffer much from the weather, but so do the labouring poor, and to make the condition of the beggar better than that of the labourer, although sometimes practised in England, has not yet been sanctioned in India. The necessitous beggars of Dinajpúr go from house to house, where they procure a sufficient quantity of food, and some good-natured person generally erects a miserable hut for them near a market place, but many are under the necessity of seeking for shelter under trees, in temples, or in ruins. They are generally very well-behaved, and are never very clamorous, except when they find a person of some rank, whom they solicit for a piece of cloth; their usual resources seem to supply them abundantly with food, for I observed, that they often rejected two anas or two days hire of a labouring man; and they were seldom satisfied unless they obtained a piece of cloth to shelter them from the weather. I saw no considerable number any where, except at Maldeh, although the year was scarce, and rice had risen above the usual price, in the proportion of 45 to 35. Maldeh, like all other manufacturing places, is subject to occasional stagnations of trade, and these are always accompanied with a misery that is unknown in agricultural districts.

Among the beggars, I have not included the religious mendicants belonging to both sects, whose number, whose impudence, and whose inutility, surpass all reasonable bounds; of them I shall have further occasion to speak.

Considering that by far the greater part of the more affluent portion of the people in this district have come from other parts, and have no families, the number of prostitutes cannot be considered as very great, so far as I could learn; there may be about 500 in the capital, and an equal number dispersed through the district at the principal places for trade. They are chiefly employed by persons from a distance, who are residing here without families for a longer or shorter period, from the reasons I have mentioned before. A great many of them are Hindú widows of some rank; another source of supply is from young Hindú girls, whose fathers are too poor to procure husbands for them before the age of puberty; by a strange custom not only the parent is disgraced by this neglect, but the poor girl is considered as totally vile and degraded, and they have little other resource. Parents however make every exertion, and very few girls in Dinajpúr have this excuse for their wantonness. Every prostitute holds out her house as an asylum for the girls who choose to join her, adopts them as her daughters, gives them clothes and ornaments to the utmost of her ability, and expects in return to be supported in her old age; with this view they endeavour, if possible, to purchase children from their parents who are indigent, although this practice is contrary to law. It is however perhaps owing to this, that few children in a state of common mendicity are to be seen, but the number sold in Dinajpúr is very inconsiderable. When the unfortunate women grow somewhat old, without having been able to procure adopted daughters, who might enable them to live in their own houses, they endeavour to procure some Muhammedan who will receive them as concubines (*nekas*), or they endeavour to join themselves to the *fakirs or vaishnov*, the two ordinary sets of religious mendicants; and they seldom fail to find some vagrant that will receive them into his company; very few are reduced to common beggary. They seldom acquire that hardened impudence so common in the European women who have departed from the paths of innocence, probably owing to their not being held in such great contempt; for it can scarcely be attributed to a superior mildness in the disposition of the Indian females. Until the age of 32 indeed, they usually put some restraint on their tongues; but after that, they consider themselves as pretty much at liberty, and a large proportion become determined scolds and vixens.

The people, I have said, are charitable; they are remarkably sober, and affectionate and kind to their relations. They are also hospitable to people of their own caste, but to no others; their chief faults seem to be lying, an insatiable rapacity in the higher classes, and a total want of inclination to pay what they owe in the lower, with a strong inclination in all to theft and robbery; in the perpetration of which they are cruel and bloody. Their credulity being a prominent feature, will unavoidably present itself often in the course of my report, and with their other faults may be chiefly attributed to their ignorance, which will be apparent from a view of the state of education.

CHAPTER III.

EDUCATION.

---

§ 1.—*Schools and Languages.*

THE first rudiments of education are usually given both by Hindús and Muhammedans in small schools called *pathsals*, under the tuition of teachers called *Guru*, who may be of any caste or religion, who is poorly rewarded, who is little respected, and who is quite different from the proper *Guru* or teacher of religion. There is no public provision for these useful members of society, and they depend entirely on their scholars for a subsistence. In the towns of Dinajpúr and Maldeh, indeed, the average number of scholars to each master may be about 20, and the fees are from 4-8 anas a month, according to the progress the children have made: on an average the fees may be 6 anas each, or 7½ Rupees a month for 20 scholars, which in this district is a decent income; but in country places the average uumber of scholars does not exceed 12, and the fees are from 1-4 anas a month, or on an average 2½, so that the total average income is only 1 Rupee 14 annas.

Even these small fees are far beyond the reach of the bulk of the people, and the number of *Pathsals* is inconsiderable, as appears from the general statistical table No. 1. ; so that were not many parents at the pains to instruct their own children, very few would be able to read and write. Even with this assistance, I am persuaded, that not more than one-sixteenth of the men born in this district acquire these accomplishments. Women are totally out of the question. My inquiries on that subject were always answered in the negative, and generally produced a smile of contempt.

Children usually go to school at five years of age, and are instructed to read and write at the same time, which seems to be an excellent method. They begin with tracing the letters on the floor with a pencil of steatite (*Ram khori*), beginning with a consonant, and afterwards joining the vowels so as to form syllables. In five or six months they are thus able to read and write. They then begin to write cyphers on palmira or plantain leaves with a reed and ink, and at the same time they learn numeration, and the sub-divisions of weights and measures. The subdivisions of time belong to astronomy, or rather astrology. This occupies 18 months. They then begin to write on paper, to learn to keep accounts, and at the same time to multiply, divide, and subtract, with the rule of practice, in which the usual Indian arithmetic consists. Accounts and arithmetic are divided into two kinds, one for agricultural, and the other for commercial affairs: where both are to be learned, the former is the one usually taught first; but very few of the natives of this district ever acquire that knowledge, or are able to tell how many bigahs, or fractions, a rectangled parallelogram of a given length and width contains; for the Hindu geometry, so far as is known in ordinary practice, extends no farther. Practical surveyors have no means of ascertaining the extent of irregular figures, but by reducing them to rectangled parallelograms, in which they are guided merely by a rough estimation, or what is called the eye; while, even in measuring parallelograms, they are destitute of any instrument that can ascertain whether or not all the angles are equal. In general, the parents of this country are contented with instructing their children in mercantile accounts, that is in being able to calculate how much of any article may at a certain rate be procured for a certain number of rupees; and keeping a very full day or waste book, in which every transaction is carefully recorded, and to which is added a kind of ledger, in which the transactions with each person are separately detailed; but their books do not admit of a regular balance, like what is called the Italian method. It is only the arithmetic commercial and agricultural, that is taught at *Pathsals;* and the application to mensuration, and to the keeping of books, either of a merchant or land-holder, are acquired in some office or shop, into which the lad enters as an assistant, and where he also learns the style and manner of correspondence. Boys are fitted for entering into an office, as assistants, when from 8 or 10 years of age, according to their industry.

The use of the sharp iron style, for writing on bark or leaves, although the original manner of Hindú writing, has been entirely relinquished, and a pen made of reed or bambu, and ink, introduced by Muhammedans, are universally employed, even in writing on the palmira leaf, which is still often used in works of value, as being more durable than paper.

The education in common schools is not only defective from not being sufficiently diffused, but is liable to still greater objections. Nothing whatever is taught in these schools, except the mere reading and writing of the common language of the country, or *opobhasha* of Bengal, together with arithmetic. The youth read no book in which any moral doctrines or any liberal knowledge is contained, so that their education being confined entirely to accounts, tends rather to narrow the mind, to confine its attention to sordid gain, and low cunning, than to improve the heart, and enlarge the understanding. Indeed no fit books, so far as I can learn, exist in the language commonly spoken in Bengal; neither does it possess any grammar or dictionary. I cannot indeed learn, that any composition in the proper language of Bengal has ever been committed to writing, except some love songs, common accounts, and letters. The same may, I believe, be extended to all the spoken languages (*opobhashas*) of India, and is to be lamented as a great cause of ignorance and error.

The Prakrito, or polite language of Bengal, like those of other Indian nations, may be considered as a dead language, or in the same light as Latin was in Europe about 200 years ago. All persons of a liberal education are acquainted with it, and among them it is the usual means of correspondence, and the language of ordinary composition. According to the best information, which I can obtain, the Prakrito of Bengal, like those of other Indian nations, is composed almost entirely of Songskrito words, with the inflexion and syntax of the vulgar language. Indeed the best informed Brahmins of the south, with whom I conversed, considered the Prakrito rather as one of the styles of writing in the sacred language, than as a distinct tongue. It is however commonly called the language of women and children; but this can only be taken in the sense of the Brahmins of the south, namely, that in books written in the sacred tongue this style is used by the women and children, that are introduced; for in no part of India is the Prakrito the common language of the country. In every part however, all well educated men can speak it, and in some parts of Bengal, even the women of Pandits and other high personages are instructed in its oral use, for in these parts writing is a very rare female accomplishment. Indeed, its practice is severely reprobated in the sex. This language is not taught in schools, not so far as I can learn, does it possess a written grammar nor a dictionary, except those composed by Europeans; but people of a certain rank and education acquire it by conversation and reading. Of course it is both written and spoken with little exactitude, especially by those who have had no instruction in Songskrito grammar, such as merchants, religious mendicants, and the officers of revenue and police. It is to be much regretted, that even in this dialect there are scarcely any books that can communicate valuable instruction to youth. The usual compositions in Prakrito, are songs, hymns, and translations of some of the more celebrated poems;—the whole, especially the latter, although probably possessing considerable poetical merit, so filled with monstrous fables and marvellous stories, that those who read nothing else are disposed to believe every thing that is contrary to the usual laws by which the world is governed, and lose all taste for the plain dictates of common sense. There are however in the Prakrito of Bengal, as well as in that of other Indian nations, some few histories of the families of chiefs that have lived of late years, strongly however disfigured by the taste for the marvellous, which the usual reading of the people inspires. A system of arithmetic also, better than the common, and which facilitates the more difficult calculations in revenue accounts, has long ago been compiled in the Prakrito language of Bengal, by Subhongkor, a Kayostho of Podiya. This book is called the *Arya*, or *Arjya*, of Subhongkor, and is no doubt of great utility; but its tendency, like that of the common instruction given in the lower schools, is certainly not of a liberal nature. The knowledge however communicated through the medium of the Prakrito is better than none, and it is therefore to be lamented, that it has made little way into the district of Dinajpúr, and is chiefly confined to those who have been born in Maldeh or its vicinity, to the few Pandits that are thinly scattered through the country, and to some of the religious mendicants. Probably one in the thousand may understand it; but men qualified to hold any office superior to a common clerk (*mohurer*) cannot be found in the district, which is of course invaded by strangers, from the principal officers of law, to the agent of the Calcutta merchant, most of them rapacious as kites, and eager to accumulate a fortune, in order to be able to retire to their native country.

The Prakritos of India being the only dialects, except Songskrito, in which any books have been composed, many have been led to consider them as the proper dialects of the different nations, by which that country is occupied; and on this basis, has it probably been, that the Songskrito has been considered as the source, from which all Indian languages have been derived. Every *opobhasha* no doubt contains many Songskrito words, perhaps as many as English does words derived from the Latin; but still, so far as I can learn, each has a copious vocabulary of words peculiar to itself; nor can I hope for any considerable improvement in the education of Indian youth, until each popular language has obtained some books fitted to render the vulgar wiser and better. I have no doubt, but that they would be read with avidity, yet great difficulty would arise in the composition. The taste of both Hindús and Muhammedans is so pedantic so fond of learned ornaments and of the marvellous, that it would be difficult to find a person qualified to write plain common sense; besides the vulgar are held in such contempt by the Brahmins, that it would be difficult to find a man of any education, who would become their instructor. Translations from the European languages, or compositions by Europeans, would be attended with still greater difficulty; as it would be almost impossible to separate them from the idea of religious innovation, which both sects watch with anxious terror. The books wanted for this district should be composed by Muhammedans, as the bulk of the people, and those most in want of instruction are of that faith, and persons abundantly willing to compose them might readily be procured at Calcutta, (where the exuberance of their erudition and imagination might be curtailed according to the narrow measure of Eùropean criticism.)

Notwithstanding Muhammedans form the greater part of the population of this district, the Indian dialect, adopted by that people, although pretty generally understood, is not the native language of the vulgar, who have universally either adopted or never relinquished the *opobhasha* of Bengal; neither is the Hindústani dialect taught in any school, nor is the Persian character usually employed to write it in any of the *Pathsals*. The people of higher rank however commonly teach this to their children, who also learn to speak a higher style, which may be compared to the Prakrito of the Hindús, and consists almost as entirely of Arabic and Persian, as the other does of Songskrito.

The number of *Muktubkhanas* or schools, where Persian literature is taught, as will appear from the general statistical table, No. 1. is very small. They are nearly as much frequented by Hindús as by Muhammedans; for the Persian language is considered as a necessary accomplishment for every gentleman, and it is absolutely necessary for those who wish to acquire a fortune in the courts of law. The number of pupils however in this district is very small, and most of the people of any rank or wealth are instructed by private tutors, who are procurable on the most moderate terms. There is reason however to fear, that their learning is not extensive, nor their taste correct; and so far as I could learn, the studies usually pursued, are forms for correspondence, or processes of law, to which are added the most improbable legendary tales that can be procured. There is no school in which Arabic, or the sciences of the Muhammedans are taught; and although some of the priests (*Mollahs*) can read the portions of the *Koran*, that are appropriated for certain ceremonies, I heard a general complaint from the *Kazis*, that few understand a single word of that language; and that the greater part had merely learned the passages by rote, so as to enable them to perform the ceremonies.

I do not profess to be able to form a proper estimate of the value of the science, which is veiled in the Songskrito language; but there can be no doubt, that it far excels that which is divulged in the Prakrito. Owing however to the institutions by which it has been guarded and confined to the sacred tribe, its utility to the Hindú nations may not be only doubted, but it may perhaps be maintained, that on the whole it has tended to increase the darkness. There can be no doubt, however, that those who possess it enjoy very considerable advantages over their countrymen; and the Brahmins, generally speaking, have an intelligence and acuteness far beyond other Hindús. I am further inclined to think, that they are subject to many fewer vices, and that those persons will be found to approach nearest their good qualities, who are admitted even to the porch of science. The manner in which the Hindú youths of this district are instructed. in the higher parts of science is not judicious, and shall be now mentioned.

Among the Brahmins, who have kept themselves pure and uncontaminated by service, and who in this country are called Pandits, as in the south they are called Vaidiks, are some men of learning, called Odhyapoks, who undertake the instruction of from three to six pupils, not only without fee or reward, but who even in general supply their scholars with food and lodging, and often with clothing, during the whole course of their studies, which on such a system must be very long. Every Odhyapok must be a Pandit, but every Pandit is not an Odhyapok; a man may acquire every science without choosing to teach it, and this is necessary to obtain the title, which both from the utility and liberality of the professors is deservedly held in the highest respect. Most of the Odhyapoks possess lands, which enable them to provide for their own subsistence, as well as that of their pupils, and they receive charity from all Hindús of any distinction. There is however no necessity for a person, who holds these lands, to instruct youth; and when the celebrity of an Odhyapok has procured large grants of lands, his heirs, although they continue to enjoy the estate, are in no ways bound to teach, and may for ever continue to enjoy the high title of Pandit, without any trouble, or they may even betake themselves to the degrading affairs of the world without forfeiting this property. Very much, however, to the credit of the Brahmins, such a neglect is not usual, and one son of the family continues generally to profess the instruction of youth. If there are other sons, they follow their natural inclination. With such a system, however liberal it may be in appearance, and to whatever merit the individual professors are justly entitled, it must be evident, that the work of education will go on slowly. It is even to be feared, that it would altogether stop, were it not for the charity which usually follows considerable reputation as a teacher. I cannot however avoid mentioning the very liberal conduct of the Purohit of the Dinajpúr family, Gaur Chondro Bidya Nidhi. This person has, I believe, proceeded no farther in learning than a knowledge of Songskrito grammar (*Vyakoron*), but he not only teaches that himself, and enables two brothers, who have some knowledge of the law (*Smriti*), to instruct pupils in that science; but he has settled on a learned man an income sufficient to enable him to instruct several youths in the Indian philosophy (*Nyayo Sastro*), and enables another to teach astronomy.

I took every opportunity of communicating with the Odhyapoks. Some of them declined an interview, others who came were soon tired of my inquiries, which of course were directed chiefly to acquire a knowledge of their manner of teaching. These left me in disgust, probably in general from not being able to answer questions on subjects with which they ought to have been familiar. There were others however, who most liberally, and patiently informed me, to the utmost of their power, concerning whatever I asked. Among these were the Purohit, his brothers, and friend, and also Roghuprosad of Potiram, a metaphysician or philosopher, and Ramsundor and Madobram, of the same vicinity, persons esteemed for their knowledge in the law, as well as in literature. These persons, as well as all the possessors of religious endowments, complain of the rapacity of the new land-holders, that have purchased lots of the Raja's estate, and who are alleged, under various pretexts, to make encroachments on the lands that have been given to learned and pious persons of both religions. I am inclined however to believe, that these persons would not content themselves with idle clamour, were they really aggrieved; but, so far as I can understand, the truth is, that in the careless administration of the Dinajpúr Raja's estates, these persons actually enjoyed more land than their titles justified, and it is on these portions that the new land-holders have encroached. As however the encouragement for learning is evidently too small in this district, a remedy might perhaps be found in the free lands, which the land-holders have now seized, owing to the failure of heirs. The amount is not considerable, and the Government, was an attempt made to recover, would wade through a disgusting scene of corruption, and very likely after all be frustrated; but if the recovery were granted to individuals of learning on whom it might be wished to bestow encouragement, the matter might be more easily accomplished.

The defects attending the plan of education by the Odhyapoks are so great, that perhaps any addition to their endowments may be considered as ill bestowed, especially in a district where the Hindús do not form the mass of the people. I am persuaded, that enough might be recovered for the establishment of some good schools for the instruction of youth in Muhammedan science and literature, for which at present there is no establishment whatever, and the teachers of the higher schools have neither profit nor honour to encourage them in their useful employment.

The academy kept by an Odhyapok is called a *Chauvari*. Youths usually go there at about 12 years of age, after they have been instructed in the knowledge taught at *Pathsals* and in the Prakrito language, but the pupil is not permitted to read any book in that low tongue.

§ 2.—*The higher Sciences, Literature, Law, and Metaphysics.*

The course of study in a Hindú Academy begins with the *Vyakoron* or Songskrito grammar and literature. For the first 10 years some study a grammar called *Songkhyiptosar*, said to have been composed by a Brahmin named Kromodiswro, concerning whose history the Pandits could give me no information. The study of this grammar is sometimes facilitated by the commentary of Goyichondor. Others again study a grammar called *Kolap*, said to have been composed by Sorbo Borma, who was contemporary with Salivaha. This grammar seems to be nearly as obscure and unscientific as the former, for its study usually occupies 10 years, although persevering students sometimes are masters of it in eight. Others study a grammar called *Mugdhobodh*, written by Vopodev, a Brahmin of the five tribes introduced by Adisur into Bengal, and therefore a modern author. These who use this grammar study two commentaries, one called *Gon*, written also by Vopodev, and another written by a Brahmin Ram Torko Vagis. This system is probably much more rational than the others, as youths require only from three to five years for its study. Finally, other masters use a grammar equally easy, called *Saroswot*, and composed by Onobhyut Acharyo of Varanosi (Benares). These also use the commentary of Govindo called *Podochondrika*, and that of Ramkrishno, called *Podmokumari*.

The pupils hitherto have been employed in studying the grammar of an unknown tongue, written in that language; and probably, as usual, in the most unintelligible style, the irksome nature of which perhaps draws out the study to such a length. They then begin to learn the meaning of the words in an *Obhidhan*. So far as I can learn, an *Obhidhan* is rather a vocabulary than a dictionary; and the natives have not yet adopted the alphabetical arrangement of their words to facilitate the study of their language. The only vocabulary used in Dinajpúr is the *Omorkosh* of Omorsingho, whom the Pandits here, as usual, consider as a person belonging to the sect of Buddha, who flourished at the court of Vikrom. The study of this occupies only one year, and is sometimes assisted by the commentary of a physician named Bhorot Mollick, and at others by the commentary of Ray Mukut, which by its prolixity lengthens the time of study for 6 months.

The students now are qualified to begin the poets, and the work usually chosen to form their taste is that called *Bhotti*, which is said to consist of extracts from the *Ramayon* of Balmiki, made by Bhortrihori, brother of Vikrom. A year is employed in reading this work, which according to the Pandits who use it, is so excellent and sublime, that every other poem appears flat, and is unnecessary; but others, among whom is the Raja's Purohit, prefer two poems of Kalidas, named *Roghu* and *Kumar Sombhu*. The former treats of the actions of a prince named Bhogiroth, who brought the Ganges to water India, and its study occupies six months. The latter treats of the actions of the goddess Bhogowoti the spouse of Sib, and occupies nearly the same time. Sri Chondro, a brother of the Raja's Purohit, although a professor of law, seems to extend the study of the poets more than usual, and beside the common extracts from the work of Balmiki, he reads with his pupils another history of Ram called *Natok*. The account, which he gives of this work, will afford an idea of the present taste of Hindús for fable. Honuman, the faithful servant of Ram, had written an account of his master's wars. Now Balmiki, who had written his account of these events 60,000 years before they happened, was naturally enough afraid that his work might be injured by that of one of the principal actors. He therefore applied to Honuman, who with great good nature threw his book, which was written on stone, into the sea, where it lay for many ages, until it was discovered by Kalidas while he was bathing. This ingenious person covered himself with wax, and having thrown himself into the sea, rubbed his body on the stones, until he procured an impression of a considerable portion of this valuable work; which he published to the delight of mankind. Other professors of law are less indulgent, and proceed to that dry study immediately after their pupils have read the *Omorkosh*. The pupils are now considered as completely instructed in the *Vyakoron*, or Songskrito grammar, and may peruse whatever of the classical authors in that language they can venture to read. In Dinajpúr no person except Brahmins are instructed in the *Vyakoron*; but in some parts of Bengal, the Baidyos, or medical tribe, and even some rich Kayosthos are permitted to study such portions of this science, as have been composed by mere men: but whatever is supposed to have been delivered by Munis, or by gods, is concealed from their profane eyes. Some Kayosthos have, however, had the audacity to lay open the veil, and have even translated part of the works of Vyas into the Prakrito language; but this is held to have been highly unjustifiable. Some

Brahmins, however, justify the action; not from their alleging that a Kayostho should read the work of a Muni, but because the works that have been translated are not in reality the composition of Vyas.

Persons who are desirous of extending their knowledge to the study of the law (*Smriti*), after such a course of *Vyakoron*, are qualified to begin with the works of Roghunondon, a Brahmin of Nodiya, whose great-grandson is said to be still alive. His works are said to be very voluminous, and to consist of 28 books. Of those however 8 only are usually studied in this district, and these require five years of constant application. They are as follows:

1. *Tithi Tottwo*, which treats of the laws to be observed in the performance of ceremonies at new moons and eclipses.
2. *Prayoschitto Tottwo*, concerning the ceremonies which ought to be performed for the remission of sin.
3. *Dayo Tottwo*, concerning succession to property.
4. *Molomas Tottwo*, concerning what is to be done or omitted during the intercalary month of the lunar year.
5. *Suddhi Tottwo*, concerning what is to be eaten on certain days, especially those of mourning.
6. *Udbaho Tottwo*, concerning marriage.
7. *Ahnik Tottwo*, concerning the rules for prayer.
8. *Sraddho Tottwo*, concerning what is to be done in commemoration of deceased parents.

After this course of law one Pandit reads with his pupils one of the 18 *Purans* called *Sribhagvot*, as containing an useful illustration of the dry precepts of Roghunondon. He supposes that this work was written by Vyas in the end of the first Dwapor yugo age, and that it is prophetical, as it gives an account of the wars which followed soon after. He also supposes, that there have been a great many successions of these ages, in which the same personages and transactions that appeared in one appeared also in the others; and that the history of the wars which Vyas delivered at the end of the first Dwapor yugo, is just as applicable to the war which happened in the commencement of the present degenerate age, as it was to the war which immediately followed the first composition of the work, in which most people will be disposed to coincide with this learned man. This, however, is one of the works that have been translated into the profane tongue, and doubts are now raised concerning its authenticity. In this school men have usually finished their education in the law by the time that they are thirty years of age. Some of the Pandits however, in place of this flight to poetical regions, after having finished the usual 8 books of Roghunondon, teach the *Prachin Smriti*, composed by Sulpani, a Brahmin of Yosor (Jessore), which treats of the same subject with the 2nd book of Roghunondon. They then give their pupils the *Sraddho Chintamoni*, a work of Vachospoti Misro, a Maithilo Brahmin, which treats on the laws for performing funeral ceremonies.

Grammar (*Vyakoron*) is a necessary preliminary to all science, but many proceed to study metaphysics or philosophy without attending to law, and many on the contrary study law without a previous knowledge of that important branch of knowledge. Metaphysics of the *Nyayo Sastro* are the glory of the Pandits of Bengal, and are no where in India so much studied. The Pandits here say, that the science was first disclosed by the god Sib to Gautom, who wrote a treatise on the subject that has been lost. Although the Brahmins strenuously assert the contrary, I think there is great reason to believe, that this Gautom is the same with the 4th great legislator of the Buddhists, whose doctrines being now thought heterodox will readily account for his philosophy having disappeared. The most ancient work on this subject now remaining, according to the Pandits of this place, is a treatise called *Chintamoni*, said to have been written by a Maithilo Brahmin; but it is so obscure and difficult, that few are able to comprehend its meaning. The works most usually studied have been composed in modern times, and are as follows:

1. *Bhasha Porichhed*, by Viswonath Siddhanto, of whose history the Pandits know nothing. This seems to be a treatise on perception, and is divided into four, according to the number of senses as reckoned by the Hindús. This treatise seems to be short or easy, as students usually are masters of it in 2 months.

2. *Byapti Pongehok*, the author unknown. Its study requires one year.

3. *Singho Byaghro Lokhyon*, or the doctrine of two brother philosophers of Maithilo, who probably from the violence of their arguments, are called the Lion and Tiger. Their real names have been lost in these titles, not ill suited for doctors of the schools. Their work requires 6 months study.

4. *Vyodhikoron Dhorma Bochhinnabhab.*

5. *Purbo Pokhyo.*

6. *Siddhanto Lokhyon.* The study of these three books occupies one year, and they seem to be a refutation of the objections against religion.

The minds of many students become confused by the abstracted nature of these investigations, and many of them are considered by the vulgar as little better than fools. The greater part however pursue their studies for 12 or 14 years more, reading a great variety of books, which it would be tedious to mention. In the Appendix to this book, however, I add a list of them in the native character, should any person be desirous of inquiring after them.

These three sciences, Grammar, Law, and Metaphysics, are considered as the noblest; and are the only knowledge which the Odhyapoks of Bengal will condescend to teach in their *Chauvaris;* and of those the study of Metaphysics is considered as by far the most honourable, and next to that is the study of the law.

Part 2.—*The Lower Sciences, Theology, Worship, Astrology, and Magic.*

There seem to be three other sciences, that are studied and taught by Pandits; but which, in this country, do not entitle them to be considered as Odhyapoks, nor their schools to be called *Chauvaris.* These sciences are *Bedanto, Agom,* and *Jyotish,* to which may be added medicine or rather magic.

The first is an investigation into the doctrine of the *Beds* concerning the Divinity, on which subject Pandits are exceedingly divided in their opinion; and in the south of India this appears to be the favourite study. In Dinajpúr the Brahmins seem to give themselves very little concern about the meaning of these sacred books, and content themselves with reading certain portions of them on certain occasions. In this they probably act judiciously, as the doctrine is delivered with such obscurity, that the systems founded on it by the most learned doctors of the south differ so widely, that the person whom one sect worships as the Supreme Being is by another considered as the Devil. There is no *Bedanto* Pandit in Dinajpúr. It is indeed alleged that there was none in Bengal until of late, when some learned men were brought from Benares by a rich Kayostho of Calcutta (Novokrishno or Novokissen), who had acquired a large fortune in the service of Lord Clive.

The *Agom*, or science which teaches the proper manner of worshipping the gods so as to obtain power, is the favourite part of divinity in Bengal. Several of the Dinajpúr Pandits have studied this, but none of them teach it; and those who wish to obtain a profound knowledge go to other places, especially to the neighbourhood of Dhaka, where the *Tontros*, or books which explain this doctrine, are much studied. The mode of worship accompanied by intoxication, indecency, or horrible practices, which these books are said to inculcate, is either altogether neglected, or carefully concealed in this district, although indecent figures are common in the ornaments of the places of worship. Indeed, I am told, that this mode of worship has made little progress among the Brahmins of Bengal, who are mostly married; and is chiefly confined to holy men, who have relinquished the world, and can trust themselves with safety in the midst of temptation. No books however are in such request as the *Tontros*, which I believe may be considered as a system of magic. In this country all the Brahmins who are of the sects of Sib or Sokti, acknowledge the *Tontros* to have been revealed by the former, and to be the proper guide in religious matters. Now in these books, there are said to be forms of invocations for six kinds of witchcraft.

1. Maron, by which an enemy may be killed.
2. Uchchaton, by which an enemy becomes a vagrant like an idiot.
3. Vosikoron, by which a person may procure the friendship of his enemy.
4. Stombhon, by which an enemy becomes dumb.
5. Vidiveshon, by which an enemy is made to quarrel with his friend.
6. Santi, by which a person may be cured of sickness.

These are supposed to be effectual only when pronounced by a Brahmin, and accompanied by sacrifices. The Brahmins of Kamrup are considered as the greatest adepts in this science, which is contained in the *Tontro*, called *Sarodatilok*. This I have stated on the authority of the *Tontrosar* composed by Krishnanondo of Nodiya, who is supposed to have lived about 300 years ago, and to have been descended from Agom Vagis, the most learned person in the *Tontros* that has ever been known.

The lowest of all the sciences studied by Pandits, in their opinion, is the *Jyotish*, which comprehends astronomy and the knowledge of the past, the present, and the future, which is attained by means of the stars, and of the lines on the human hand or forehead. Many people have imagined, that the *Jyotish* were a sect of philosophers, who neglected fable, and followed reason as a guide, and who were numerous, and much respected in India. If there are any such philosophers, I have never met with them; all whom it has been my fortune to see, professed astrology, and most of them also practised chiromancy. Although all Hindús of high rank are addicted to this folly, the Pandits, who profess no other science, are considered as the lowest of all others; and indeed the science is often possessed and practised by Sudros, who are called Gonok, and who belong to the Daivoggno tribe, commonly called Daibok. In this district, however, the Daiboks procure a living chiefly by selling almanacks, and cannot make calculations. As the practice of astrology is profitable, a considerable number of Brahmins, even men very learned in other sciences, follow this art, and in this district almost every academician (Odhyapok) practises it more or less. No undertaking of any sort of consequence can commence in a Hindú family of rank, without a wise man having been consulted to find out the proper day. Whenever a child is born, the star of its nativity is calculated, by the art called Thikoji, which is not considered as difficult. Afterwards, the earliest opportunity is taken of procuring a man of profound science in the art called Koshthi, by which from the Thikoji he foretels the events of the child's future life. Every Hindú of rank has two names, one public and one private, which last is only known to the parents, Gúrú, Purohit, and astrologers, and is carefully concealed from all others, lest any person should use it in enchantment (Montra, Bhibhut, or Gún), which is of no efficacy where the common name only is used.

The number of high Hindús being small in this district, and Muhammedans and low Hindús being exempt from the folly, the number of *Jyotish* is comparatively inconsiderable; and only one Pandit instructs any pupils in the science. He also constructed almanacks, but those commonly in use among the astrologers are chiefly brought from Mauleyo, near Múrshedabad, and Keoya, near Dhaka. The astrologers of the district, who live entirely by the art, reside chiefly at Churamon; but the man of science lives near Dinajpúr, and is supported by the liberality of the Raja's Purohit. He is now blind with age; but he never possessed any astronomical instrument, and never attempted to take an observation. His pupils have studied under him the *Siddhanto, Rohosyo,* and the *Vosoli;* but are not acquainted with the history of these works.

No person teaches medicine in this district, and indeed proper physicians are very few in number. In all cases of sickness, trust is chiefly placed in prayers and sacrifices, and in certain magical incantations, that are considered as effectual, and called Jharon Montros. People of rank are unwilling to acknowledge that they are instructed in these incantations, but so far as I can learn, this arises from a fear, that they would be too often called upon by the poor for assistance, and they would consider it as disgraceful to refuse relief when asked. But all ranks of Hindús, and even the low Muhammedans, believe in the efficacy of these incantations; although it is generally only the lowest persons that profess to be acquainted with them. Persons of this rank can receive, even from the lowest, a reward which is an object worth their acceptance. Such is the account, that I received in some divisions. In others, the higher ranks denied a belief in the efficacy of these incantations, except in the bites of serpents, in casting out devils, and in small-pox; and alleged, that in fevers they procure a Brahmin to read certain extracts from the *Sribhagvat,* which are called *Ban Juddhostov.*

People who are deprived of reason, or who have the epilepsy, or strong hysteric fits, are supposed to be possessed by devils (Upodevta), which are the spirits of those who have been killed by violence, or who have committed suicide at certain unfortunate conjunctions of the stars, which are detailed in the books of the philosophers called *Jyotish.* Until certain ceremonies have been performed, these unfortunate spirits cannot obtain any proper body, into which they can migrate, and therefore molest other persons, chiefly women, in order that the proper ceremonies may be performed. The spirits are of various kinds, according to the bodies which they formerly occupied. Those of a Brahmin are called Brahmadaityo, and are exceedingly troublesome; those of Sudros are Bhuts; those of women are called Songkhini, or Sangkchurni; those of unmarried girls, or of very low women, are called Aloya, and Pretiní, or Petiní; and those of Muhammedans, are Mamudas; and all those who have been killed in war (except Khyetriyos, who go immediately to heaven), on those unfortunate conjunctions, become Nishkondho or Nikondos. Both Brahmins and Sudros, it is imagined, can acquire the knowledge, by which they can tell whether the afflicted person labours under a disease or a devil, and the ceremonies by which these devils are supposed to be cast out, and these are detailed in the *Tontros;* but many decline the office, as it is supposed that among those who practise this science few ever have children. It is not lawful for them to take money; but they are much courted, when any accident happens that requires their assistance. The unfortunate spirits procure rest by any of their relations going to the Bhagirothi or Goya, and performing some easy ceremonies: but the latter place is the securest; for if there is a hair on the bank of the river where the ceremony is performed, it will be of no effect. These ideas are very generally received in the Dinajpúr district, and several persons are supposed to be possessed of the science, and have frequent opportunities of putting their mummery in practice, as devils are thought to be common, and Goya is at a considerable distance.

Other incantations are used on many other occasions, sometimes innocent enough; such as when a girl employs a wise man (Aushodhokari), to secure the affection of her lover: but they are also used with criminal intentions, such as to procure the destruction of an enemy, or to remove a disease from one person to another. The belief in these is not only universal among the vulgar, but seems pretty general even among the higher rank; and a landholder of old family, a Brahmin by caste, had lately before my visit attempted to remove a mortal disease from his mother to some person that was indifferent. All these incantations and the whole of the mummery are part of the *Tontros*, and of the Hindú science called *Agom*.

CHAPTER IV.

RELIGIONS AND SECTS.

Introduction.

According to the opinion of the principal native officer of revenue, three-fourths of the whole people of this district are Muhammedan; but my native assistant estimates the Muhammedans at $\frac{10}{16}$ of the population. In each division, I consulted the most intelligent persons on this subject, and have placed the result of their opinions, concerning the proportion of Hindús and Muhammedans, in the general statistical table. If the extent of occupied land in each Thana be divided in these proportions, and the whole sums of each be added, to enable us to form an estimate of the population, the result will be, that the Moslems are to the Hindús in the proportion nearly of 70 to 30, somewhat more than the estimate of my assistant, and considerably less than that of the officer of revenue. Both are Brahmins. In the statistical table, No. 3, will be found an estimate of the numbers belonging to each class, into which I have divided the population.

§ 1.—*Of the Muhammedans.*

The Muhammedans seem to be on the decrease; for most of the landlords and their agents being Hindús give these encouragement to settle, and wherever a landholder's house has been for any length of time established, there is found a considerable number of the pure tribes, which is seldom the case in any other part. I think it indeed probable, that the persecution by Sultan Jalaluddin nearly exterminated the Hindús; for at least a half of those now in the district may be traced as having emigrated from other countries, especially from Kamrup, which was not subject to the Muhammedans until after the persecution. Although the two people have mutually adopted many of each other's religious practises, yet there is a considerable ill-will between them, which is only prevented from going to excess by the fear of an indifferent power, that is superior to both. Many of the inferior offices of government, and almost all the lands being in possession of Hindús, the Muhammedans are rather sufferers; not however to any very outrageous degree. They chiefly indeed suffer from not being allowed to kill oxen, and from the depredations of sacred bulls or other consecrated cattle: and it is alleged, by encroachments on their religious endowments; these indeed cannot well expect to escape, even the Brahmins complain of the landholders' rapacity.

The chiefs of the Muhammedan religion in this district are the Kazis, who have a jurisdiction in all things considered as more immediately connected with religion, such as marriage, circumcision, the eating of forbidden things, and the like, and who act in some measure as notaries public in giving authenticity to contracts. The establishment in this province seems to be very irregular, some persons having under their jurisdiction 11 pergunnahs, and others, only one; and the extent of their jurisdiction has no connection with that of the magistrate. Many of them are not resident, at least within the bounds of their jurisdiction, and act by deputy. I believe, that formerly their office was in general hereditary; although the confirmation of the magistrate is now necessary. Their profits arise from fees. Those of them that I saw were decent persons, who had much more the manners of gentlemen than any other natives that I met in the district.

Under the Kazis are a set of priests called Mollas, of whom there is one in general for every very populous subdivision (Mouza), or for every collection of smaller ones, that is called a Diyar. They are generally appointed by the Kazi, according to the wish of the heads of families. Although they are only a kind of deputies to the Kazi; yet as they are usually ignorant fanatics, they are more beloved by the populace. They read, or repeat, prayers or passages of the Koran at marriages, funerals, circumcision, and sacrifices; for no Muhammedan here will eat meat or fowl, over which prayers have not been repeated, before it has been killed; and the animals are frequently killed before the monument of some saint. According to the Kazis, many of these Mollas cannot read, and these only look at the book, while they repeat the passages. Indeed they are in little danger of detection, none of their audiences understanding a word of Arabic. Even these who are able to read very seldom understand this language.

The religious persons, however, who are most respected among the Moslems, are the mendicants called Faqirs. The number of reputed saints who have had monuments erected to their memory, generally over their tombs, is astonishing; and is a clear proof of the ignorance and bigotry that prevailed during the Muhammedan government. It may on an average be estimated, that there is at least one saint's (Pir's) monument in each subdivision, and the worship of these by offerings (Sirni) is the principal act of devotion in this district. Many of these monuments have no endowment, but the people of the village unite to keep it in repair, which is easily done, as it is usually a heap of earth, perhaps a little whitewashed; and in the evenings they also in turns light a lamp before it. But to many of the monuments, and at all those of any considerable reputation, there is an endowment in land to support one or more Faqirs, who repair the tomb, light the lamp, receive the offerings, and read or repeat the prayers (Fatya), that should accompany these donations. The mosques too, that have endowments, are usually placed under the charge of a Faqir, who should perform there the same duties; but the first is in general much neglected. He also calls the people to pray at the proper hour; but this part of worship, and the ablutions prescribed by Muhammed, are in general very much neglected by his followers in this district. Some of these Faqirs are no doubt very decent men in their manners; and some families, from their features and appearance, would seem to have preserved their blood free from mixture with the natives of this country: but in general they are very poor creatures, sunk in bigotry and ignorance, and affecting great sanctity and austerity of manners. Several whom I met would scarcely answer any question, but were continually sighing, groaning, and muttering prayers. The common conversation of the more rational among them is concerning the wonders performed by their saint; and while they very seldom can tell when he lived, from whence he came, or any circumstance relative to his history, they generally suppose, that the whole affairs of the neighbourhood, if not of the world, are conducted by his interposition. As serpents are the common agents of some of the most usually worshipped Hindú deities, so tigers seem, not unaptly, to have been chosen by the Muhammedan saints. Many of the woods in this district grow on ruins, and most ruins have been taken possession of by a saint, whose vicinity is of course the common haunt of a tiger: and as these animals seldom attack man in this district, the Pir is generally allowed by persons of both religions to have restrained the natural ferocity of the beast, or, as it is more usually said, has given the tiger no order to kill men. The tigers and Faqirs are therefore on a very good footing, and the latter denounces the vengeance of the saint on any person who molests the beast of prey, and assures the people, that he is perfectly harmless towards all such as respect the saint, and make him offerings.

Besides these Faqirs, who have a regular establishment, whose office is hereditary, and none of whose families have been known to contaminate themselves by labour, but have lived entirely on the charity that has been procured either by themselves or ancestors, and who are exceedingly respected, there are some who have degraded themselves by industry, and many, who tempted by their notions of religion, or by indolence and avarice, have assumed the life of a Faqir, have dedicated themselves to God, and who live by begging. Fortunately some expense attends the ceremony, which prevents the order from increasing too rapidly, and new Faqirs are also expected to observe the rules of the order, according to the strict manner of those called Muríds. Faqirs in general marry, and all their children belong to the order; but a family does not obtain full respect for some generations, nor until all memory of their adoption into the order has been obliterated.

Some old Faqirs also observe particular customs, and are considered as more peculiarly dedicated to God. These are called Muríds, and cannot shave the head nor beard, and must perform the prayers and ablutions, as prescribed by their prophet.

Besides the neglect of prayer and ablution, the Muhammedans of this district forget the rules of their law in many points. They are in particular accused of being too easy husbands; for they neither confine their wives with proper strictness, nor are they even much offended at occasional private intercourse with those, who can render the situation of the family somewhat more comfortable. The Mollas also allege, that many persons, in order to save expense and defraud them, live as man and wife without having had the advantage of a religious ceremony.

A still more flagrant breach of the law is, I know, exceedingly common. Offerings at the monuments of saints are generally made from rather interested motives. The votary is in fact generally hopeful to procure some favour from the saint of much more value then the offering, and should he be disappointed, he usually has recource to some Hindú deity, and tries what may be done by means of a sacrifice. The heathen priest makes a little stretch of conscience, receives the offering for the honour of the god, and is liberal in his assurances that his prayers will be effectual. These priests, it must be observed, are of the dregs of the Brahmins; a man of a proper way of thinking would scorn to pray for a Turk.

Another practice savouring of idolatry is also very common. Images of horses, made of clay, are sold by many potters, and are placed on the monument of saints as offerings to induce them to cure the sick, or in consequence of vows made by those who have been in any danger.

Many of the resident Faqirs have been concerned in thefts and robberies; and it was a number of adoptive Faqirs, that some years ago collected in great bodies, in this and the neighbouring district, which they plundered with the utmost barbarity, and when pursued were wont to retire to Morang, in the dominions of Nipal, where they found shelter, and a sale for their booty. While spending the produce of their illicit gains, the Faqirs residing in Dinajpúr were suspected of watching for a favourable opportunity of bringing down their accomplices. Many still reside in Morang; but their depredations have of late been on a small scale, nor have they ventured for some years to enter this district in hostile array. By some unaccountable mistake they have been called Sonyasis, who are a sect of Hindú mendicants; and the pilgrims going to bathe in the Brohmaputra have often been suspected as concerned. That among these there are spies of the Faqirs, as well as many idle and disorderly persons, I have no doubt; but I was assured, both by Hindús and Muhammedans, whom I consider as perfectly well informed, that the Morang gang are entirely of the latter religion.

Pilgrimages are very much in fashion among the Moslems, as well as among the Hindús; very few however of this district ever think of going to Mecca, but wisely content themselves with Peruya, which I believe is the most celebrated pilgrimage in Bengal.

The parts of their religion that are most strictly observed, are fasting through the days during the month Ramzán, and the commemoration of the death of the two Imáms Hasan and Haseyn, which is performed with as much show and noise as possible; and for this purpose a kind of musicians named Zari are employed. Another kind (Pirer Gayon) is employed to celebrate the praises of the different saints, for this sort of noise is extremely grateful to the ear of the natives.

§ 2.—*Of the Hindús.*

The Hindús, especially those of pure descent, being but a small proportion of the people in this district, I might pass them over until I came to places where they are more numerous, but this would render some parts of my account obscure. I shall therefore notice some of the most remarkable particulars concerning them, and give a general view, which I shall endeavour to render more complete, when I pass into other districts.

Part 1.—*Of the Brahmins.*

There is no trace remaining to show, that before the time of Adisur, any Brahmin had obtained a permanent settlement in this district. It contains no Brahmin families of the five southern nations, nor any of Saroswot, or Utkol. A very few from the neighbouring nation Maithilo are to be found, but tradition relates their settlement to have been very recent. About 50 years ago, the proprietor of Rajshahi introduced about 200 families of Gaur Brahmins from the west of India; and three of these, who have relinquished the world, and who have become Sonyasis, according to the rules of Songkor Acharjyo, have settled in a convent of Hawora division. These are the only persons of that nation which are to be found in the district. Almost the only families therefore of proper Brahmins to be found in this district are the Kanyokubjos, of whom, according to tradition, two colonies have been brought to Bengal.

Adisur Raja, a physician, who founded a dynasty that governed Bengal for some time before the Muhammedan conquest, is said to have introduced five Brahmins with their families from Kanyokubjo or Kanoj, a city in the west of India. These five men were of five different tribes (Gotros), viz. Bhorodwaj, Kasyop,

Sandilyo, Batsyo, and Savornyo, and on that account all their descendants, who now form by far the greatest portion of the sacred order in Bengal, are called Ponchogotros, or the five tribes. The wife of Adisur had a son named Bollalsen, whose father was supposed to be the Brohmaputra river, who, for the purpose of impregnating the queen, assumed the convenient form of a Brahmin. Whether o. not Adisur knew of this circumstance, and was of so easy a temper as to overlook the liberty of the Brohmaputra, or whether it was not divulged until the favourable time when Bollalsen became a lawgiver, even in the nice affairs of caste, and might wish for the authority of divine origin, I cannot take upon myself to say, both being probable; but it is generally allowed by the Brahmins here that Adisur left the quiet possession of his kingdom to Bollalsen. In his reign the five families of Brahmins had multiplied so fast, that they not only had become numerous, but had obtained settlements in two of the provinces, Rarhi and Barondro, which as usual among Hindús, who delight in subdivisions, had produced a complete separation of caste. It even became advisable to separate each division into different ranks, and to assign different customs for each. This I confess appears to me inexplicable. Were I allowed to suppose, that the original colony was more numerous, or that Bollalsen was not the immediate successor of Adisur, but followed after an interval of some hundred years, as Abul Fazil imagines, the difficulty would be removed; but the tradition is positive against both these suppositions.

However this may have been, the Rarhi Brahmins are divided into Kulin, Bongsoj, and Srotriyo; and the Barondros are divided into Kulin, Kap and Srotriyo. These divisions took place according to the merits of the persons, at the time when they were formed. The most virtuous Brahmins of each province were made Kulins, those next in merit were made Bongsoj or Kap, and the remainder were classed in the lowest rank called Srotriyo. The pre-eminence however is now hereditary, so far at least as the Brahmins of the same province are concerned; that is to say, a Barondro Brahmin must respect a Barondro Kulin, however ignorant or knavish, more than the most learned and virtuous Srotriyo of Barondro. This however by no means extends to the other province. A Barondro Brahmin estimates all the three kinds of Rarhis according to the respective personal merit that each individual possesses. The Rarhi in the same manner respect his own provincials by their birth, but he values Barondros and all other Brahmins according to their virtues. Although Dinajpúr be in Barondro land, yet Brahmins of Rarhi are also numerous in this district, probably in the proportion of 6 to 10 Barondros. I must therefore give some account of each.

A Kulin Brahmin of Barondro cannot marry above three or four wives, the fathers of Barondro not choosing to pay for unreasonable undertakings; for the husband always gets money with each wife, more and more in proportion to the lowness of her birth; and he seldom gives himself any trouble about maintaining his wives or children, but leaves these duties to the care of his father-in-law. If the family happens to consist of sons chiefly, the maternal grand-father has great profit, because he receives money for each at his marriage; but, if there are many daughters, he has made a bad speculation: and unless very rich, is ruined, as he must not only sell every thing, but even borrow and beg to the utmost of his power, in order to procure them husbands. They have, however, a greater indulgence than the lower orders, for a Kulin girl continues marriageable at all ages, although it is considered as very disgraceful for the father to keep her long waiting; and he is even very apt to incur still greater disgrace, by her forgetting the laws of chastity, which these girls, brought up in the full expectation of early marriage, are very apt to do. Husbands are however often difficult to procure, as a woman cannot marry a man younger than herself, and as a large proportion of the men are bought by the parents of low women. If a Barondro Kulin marries the daughter of a Kap, he is degraded to that rank; but his sons and grand-sons are more respected than usual, and are more marriageable. A Barondro Kulin may, however, marry the daughter of a Srotriyo, without any degradation, and all the children of this marriage are Kulins. A Kap also receives money, when his son marries the daughter of a Srotriyo; the children are elevated to the rank of Kap; but the husband must keep his wives and children at home, and provide for them. The Srotriyo men were thus very ill provided with women; and so long as the rules of caste were strictly regarded, a great many of them could not procure wives. But since the deaths of Rani Bhowani of Rajshahi, and of Raja Krishna Chandra of Nodiya, two very pious and powerful landholders, who supported the laws of caste, these men have been let loose, and are not ashamed to give money to procure wives, so that the higher ranks of Kulin and Kap are defrauded both of their due profit and pleasure, for the Srotriyo fathers are not able to resist the temptation of the money, especially as they also save what they must have given to their betters.

A Rarhi Kulin Brahmin may marry as many wives as he pleases, and some have 60, but in general they cannot procure above 8 or 10. They visit them alternately, and give themselves no sort of trouble about the maintenance of either the mothers or children. In other respects, there is little difference between their customs, and those of the Barondros. By a marriage with the daughter of the next rank they are reduced to that order, or at least they are considered as a lower order of Kulin, but their children by women of the lowest order are elevated to their full dignity.

The Brahmins of the five tribes are subject to many other divisions, but I shall at present confine myself to notice a few. Whatever his birth may be, a Brahmin may either become a Pandit, who adheres to the proper duties of his profession, or he may engage in worldly affairs, and take service, in which case he is called Vishoyi. These two terms are analogous to the words Baidek and Laukik of the south; but the distinction is not so widely drawn in the north; and changes from the one kind of life to the other are there less uncommon, which is probably owing to the high pre-eminence given to family rank. It must also be observed, that among the Kulins there are very few Pandits, and most of these learned persons belong to the 3rd rank, or Srotriyos, who having little rank by birth must study, if they are desirous of obtaining respect.

The difference of sect or religious tenet produces much less separation among the Brahmins of Bengal than it does among those of the south, owing probably to the doctrine of the *Bedantos* having little attracted the notice of the former; so that the greater part of the Brahmins of Bengal, although divided into five sects, have not placed themselves under the banners of any great doctor, such as Songkor Ramany, or Madhov; not but that the writings of several such personages are known, but they have not produced heat enough to generate controversy. Indeed it is not customary with most of the Brahmins of Bengal to declare the sect to which they belong, except to their Gúrú, or spiritual instructor; and it is not considered as civil to ask them the question: whereas those in the south glory in their sect, and take every opportunity of declaring their adherence to it and their aversion to all others.

Among the Barondro Brahmins, however, many of the third rank openly profess themselves of the sect of Vishnu, and are called Odwaito Bongso, or descendants of Odwaito, a learned and holy Brahmin of Santipúr, who declared himself a worshipper of Krishno, and established rules for the belief of his descendants, none of whom, whatever his private opinion may be, will venture to say, that he departs from the creed of his ancestor. In the same manner a Rarhi Brahmin of Nodiya, named Nityanondo, who lived about 300 years ago, openly professed himself a follower of Vishnu; and his descendants follow his tenets. Both the descendants of Odwaito and Nityanondo are called Goswami, or Gosaing, (vulgo Goseyn,) but must be carefully distinguished from those of the same title, who come from the western provinces, who are persons of all castes, and who say that they have forsaken the world, and have taken vows of poverty and chastity, although most of them are keen merchants, and pay very little other respect to their vows, except in abstaining from marriage. The Goswamis of Bengal, on the contrary, marry; but almost all of them adhere to the proper duties of their caste, and very rarely accept of service.

The other Pandits of the five tribes, who do not acknowledge the nature of their creed, call themselves simply Pandit Gurus. The Goswami form about a tenth part of the five tribes, having been able to multiply fast, as they are Gurus, or religious instructors for almost all the Sudros, and have considerable means of subsistence. Like other followers of Vishnú they chiefly study, as their guide in religion, the *Purans*, or works attributed to Vyas; while the Guru Pandits, although they occasionally read the *Purans*, study chiefly the books called *Tontros*, supposed to have been revealed by the god Sib. The science contained in the *Tontros*, and which is eagerly studied in most parts of Bengal, is called *Agom*, and the most learned doctor in this law is esteemed to have been *Agom Vagis*, who lived at Nodiya about the same time with Nityanondo. These differences of sect produce no sort of difference of caste, and every Goswami is anxious to procure a husband of the 1st or 2nd rank for his daughter; although none of these dignified persons profess the worship of Vishnú, and the wife is always expected to adopt the sect of her husband.

A most essential difference arises in the rank of the five tribes from that of the persons, whom they condescend to instruct in religious matters, or for whom they act as priests. The former, or teachers, are called Gurus; the priests, who read prayers on solemn occasions, are called Purohits, and in general are less respected than the former. Those who perform these offices for Brahmins alone are the highest in rank; but few of such respected persons belong to the five tribes. Next follow such as perform these offices for the two higher ranks of Sudros, the physicians, and scribes. Then follow those, who act for the nine pure castes of tradesmen, (Novosakh,) and for a few tribes that are admitted to be of a similar rank.

All these Brahmins continue to be tolerably respected, and may give their daughters in marriage to Kulins; but certain religious offices in some measure deprive a Brahmin of caste, and his daughter cannot intermarry with a person of any of the three pure ranks.

The highest of these impure Brahmins are the Ogrodani, who receive the first charity *(Dan)*, that a person offers in commemoration of his deceased parents. The charity offered on all future occasions is accepted by the highest, and is a considerable source of revenue. A tradesman of the nine pure castes will condescend to drink the water of an Ogrodani; but rejects that of all the inferior Brahmins, who are considered as inferior in rank even to a Sudro.

The Brahmins who condescend to act as Gurus and Purohits for any of the impure tribes are called Vorno; and occupy the next rank, but differences exist in their rank, according to the various degrees of their disciples' impurity.

Next to Vornos are the Moruiporas, who read the funeral service over any person lower than a Brahmin. These are the lowest persons that are descended from the five tribes which were introduced by Adisur.

The Pujaris, or priests who officiate in temples, are considered as blameable for undertaking so low an office; but the Brahmins of the third order (Srotriyos), who usually accept of the office, are not on that account degraded from their rank, provided the temple has been built and endowed by a person of pure birth, such as a tradesman of the nine pure castes, and are the usual Gurus of the lower castes. The Pujari is indeed generally selected from the family of the founder's Purohit. The temples founded by persons of low origin are served by Vorno Brahmins.

Brahmins of the five tribes, very unlike those of the south, not only act as Pujaris in temples where bloody sacrifices are made, but actually make the offering, and eat the meat. They are also permitted to eat fish and venison, with five other species of animals, namely, the rhinoceros, hare, porcupine, turtle, and a large kind of lizard (Sworno Gadhika). Few however avail themselves of any animal food except fish, and many abstain even from that indulgence.

Next in number to the five tribes are the Baidik Brahmins, a colony which also came from Kanyokubjo, but at a later period. I have not been able to ascertain the time; but they say, that they were introduced by Adityo Subuddhi Narayon Raja of Srihotto, which is north from Dhaka. I do not know what place is meant, unless it be Silhet. These Baidik Brahmins seem to have nearly the same customs with the five tribes, but are considered as higher, are not divided into three ranks, and none of them have betaken themselves to service, nor have any degraded themselves so as to become Vornos, nor scarcely any so much as to act as Gurus for Sudros of even the highest rank. By far the greater part of the Gurus of the five tribes are Baidiks, who excel in learning. From having settled in different parts of the country, they have separated into two tribes that do not intermarry, the one called Paschatyo, and the other Dakhyinatyo.

The Paschatyo, who are mostly settled in the N. E. parts of Bengal, are considered as rather the highest, and their hereditary chief and religious instructor (Guru) still resides at Srihotto. Among the Baidiks also there arose a person of great celebrity named Chaitonyo, who openly professed the worship of Vishnû, and who having no children, instructed his pupils in that doctrine, which their descendants now adopt, and are called Chaitonyo Bongso, and Goswamis. The others conceal their sect, assume the title of Pandit Gurus, study the *Tontros*, and are by far the most numerous. The Baidiks do not indulge themselves in numerous wives like the higher ranks of the five tribes, and seldom, if ever, taste even fish. They offer sacrifices, but do not eat the flesh. None of them are Pujaris nor priests in temples.

In Dinajpúr are many persons calling themselves Brahmins, but neither the five tribes nor the Baidiks acknowledge them as such, nor as descended from the sacred persons who proceeded from the mouth of Brahma. Some pretend that their ancestors were created by Vyas, and this seems to be their own opinion, as they call themselves Vyasokto. A circumstance, said to be related in the Sri Mohabharat, will perhaps throw some light on the subject. Porasor, the father of Vyas, was on a certain day near the river, and observed a fisherman (Kaiborto), who had a most beautiful girl in his boat. The Gymnosophist could not resist the violence of the desire with which he was seized, but went into the boat, and impregnated the beauty with Vyas, who cannot well be considered as a Brahmin, the maternal line being impure. We may therefore suppose, that the Vyasokto are the descendants of Vyas. The Pandit of the survey, however, will not allow of the illegitimacy of Vyas, and supposes, that Bollalsen, when he raised the Kaibortos to the rank of pure Hindús, allowed their Gurus or priests to assume the name of Brahmins. It must be observed, that many of the impure tribes of Hindús have Gurus of their own, totally independent of the Brahmins, and the Vyasoktos continue to be the Gurus and Purohits of that tribe alone, and have no sort of connection with the other Brahmins. I met with no person of any learning among them, which has prevented me from entering into a particular detail of their customs.

Except families which have evidently migrated lately into Bengal, there are none in that country who pretend to be Khyetriyos or Vaisyos, and the people may be divided into Brahmins and Sudros.

Between these, however, are in some measure suspended two tribes, the Daivoggnos, or astrologers, and the Bhat, or bards; but I procured no information concerning these, that is interesting. The Daivoggnos here have been nearly deprived of their profession by the Brahmins, and in the south entirely. There they (Daivoggnos) have become weavers, have refused obedience to the sacred order, and have adopted priests of their own. Whether this was in revenge for the encroachments of the Brahmins, or whether these were in consequence of the rebellion of the astrologers, I cannot take upon myself to say.

The highest of the Sudros are the Baidyos, or medical tribe, concerning whom I shall say nothing, as I met with no man of learning among them.

The Kayosthos or scribes follow next, and were once of more importance than they are now, as at one time they managed most of the revenue and commerce of the country; but the Brahmins of the five tribes having applied themselves more closely to business, chiefly since the English government, there can be no doubt, from their superior intelligence and education, that they will soon obtain the whole, as they have already a considerable part. The Kayosthos however are now enjoying the fruit of their former labours, and a great many of the landholders are of this tribe. The five Brahmins, who were introduced by Adisur, were accompanied by five Kayosthos, but all the Kayosthos of Bengal are not considered as sprung from them; and their descendants seem to have settled chiefly in the western districts, forming the two tribes called Uttor and Dokhyin Rarhi, while the Bonggoj and Sudro Kayosthos occupy the eastern districts towards Dhaka, and seem to be of a more ancient colony. Bollalsen arranged their ranks, and subdivided them variously. Those of Dokhyin Rarhi, who seem to have been introduced into Dinajpúr by one of them, who was ancestor of the Raja's family, were divided by Bollalsen into Kulin and Mollik; but both can intermarry. On the whole, this caste has been frittered into endless subdivisions, concerning which there are several treatises, but to follow them would be tedious and perhaps useless. Those of Dinajpúr chiefly follow the Pandit Gurus and the *Tontros* as their guides in religion, the Rajas however were of Vishnú's part.

Next to the Kayosthos are nine tribes (Novosakh) of tradesmen, who although greatly inferior to the scribes, are still considered as pure Sudros; for a Brahmin may drink their water without loss of caste, and a Brahmin who condescends on certain occasions to give them instruction is not altogether disgraced. In this country they are mostly followers of the Goswamis. The trades are,

1. Gondhobonik, druggists.
2. Songkhobonik or Sangkhari, workers in shell.
3. Kongsobonik or Kongsari, copper-smiths.
4. Baruyi, cultivators of betle-leaf.

5. Tontrovay, or Tangti, weavers.
6. Málakar, makers of garlands.
7. Kormokar, or Kamar, blacksmiths.
8. Kumbhokar, or Kumar, potters.
9. Napit, barbers.

The extreme variance, that is found in the arrangement of castes in different parts of India, appears to me a pretty convincing proof, that they did not proceed from any original general law; but were adapted to the prejudices of the various Indian nations respecting the ranks of different trades, when these nations were induced to receive the doctrine of caste from the Brahmins. In Bengal, for instance, the copper-smiths and blacksmiths are considered as distinct castes; whereas, in the south of India they are united, and conjoined with the carpenters, masons, and goldsmiths, who in Bengal are placed among the impure tribes, as the whole are in the south; probably because there they persisted in having Gurus of their own.

Nearly in the same rank with the nine most distinguished trades, and within the limits of pure Sudros, (Sot Sudro,) Bollalsen, according to tradition, has placed the following castes which are found in Dinajpúr.

1. Teli, retailers of grain, salt, &c.
2. Tamoli, of the same profession.
3. Moyra, preparers of sweetmeats.
4. Ahiri Gop, or Goyala, keepers of buffalos.
5. Pollob Gop, or Goyala, keepers of kine.
6. Kaiborto, cultivators.

This list of the professions, which were admitted into the limits of pure Sudros, by Bollalsen, seems to me curious; as it probably shows the degree of importance which each possessed in his time: and it is probably owing to the same circumstance, that the Kaibortos obtained a preference over the other tribes of cultivators in Bengal, all of which are reckoned impure. This I think will be confirmed, when it is considered, that the fishermen among the Kaibortos, who in Dinajpúr are called Jhalos, have been left among the impure tribes, as being of little importance; while the Vyasoktos, or priesthood common and peculiar to both Jhalos and Kaibortos, have been elevated to the title of Brahmin. Before the introduction of proper castes, the various tribes of India were probably like the ancient states of Greece and Italy; a Roman could only marry with a Roman, or an Athenian with an Athenian; for the same circumstance takes place among the rude tribes of India, although these have no proper distinction of castes. This circumstance no doubt greatly facilitated the introduction of proper caste, each tribe took its place among the pure or impure Sudros, according to its importance, and continued as before to confine its marriages within itself. I am persuaded, that the impure tribes, are not as commonly supposed the offspring of the four pure castes contaminated by illegitimate connection. The Baidyos, for instance, who are alledged to be descended of a Brahmin, by a Vaisyo woman, are placed at the very head of the pure tribes of Bengal. The same origin is assigned to the Daivoggnos, who hold a still higher station; but of this more hereafter.

The pure Sudros are distinguished from those below them by having pure Brahmins for their Gurus and Purohits; and by their abstaining from all food that is forbidden to Brahmins, from intoxicating drugs, from concubines, and from marrying widows. The Kulin Kayosthos are allowed to keep two wives, and can sell their daughters to the lower rank at a great price. The other pure Sudros can marry only one wife, unless the first proves barren. Whenever a man, whose birth is esteemed remarkably pure, gives his daughter to a lower person, he receives a present. It must however be observed, that the Pollob-Goyalas are only allowed Vorno Brahmins, and the Kaibortos have Brahmins who are not considered as descended from the persons, that sprung from the mouth of Brahma.

Of the 900,000 Hindús, which I estimate to be in this district, my assistant supposes that 90,000 are of pure descent, and that perhaps 15,000 of these have been born in other districts, and an equal number are of the two tribes Kaiborto and Khyan, which border on impurity.

The impure tribes are divided into two kinds, Nich and Antyoj : the former observe some rules of decency, and the others are altogether vile.

The Nich have peculiar Brahmins, who, on account of their instructing low persons, have been degraded even below the pure Sudros. These Brahmins are called in general Vorno ; but as the various castes dispute vehemently about pre-eminence, and each pretends to be unjustly considered as impure, no one will employ a Brahmin that officiates for those of any other Nich caste, so that each has its own appropriate race of Brahmins.

The first five ranks of Nich cannot lawfully keep concubines, marry widows, nor eat or drink what is fordidden to higher Hindús. But the lower orders openly keep concubines, and, except the distillers of liquor, openly intoxicate themselves. The castes of Nich that are found in Dinajpúr are as follows :

1. Suborno-bonik, or Sonarbenya, money-changers.
2. Swornokar or Sakra, goldsmiths.
3. Sutrodhor, or Chhutar, carpenters.
4. Barandro Sow, or Sungri, a kind of merchants who deal in grain and salt.
5. Gones, a kind of potters.
6. Kolu, oil-makers.
7. Jhalo, fishermen of the Kaiborto caste.
8. Malo, another kind of fishermen.
9. Teyor, another kind of fishermen.
10. Gungri, boatmen and fishermen ; called also Pungri and Pundole.
11. Nori, makers of lac ornaments.
12. Bayuri, sellers of prepared rice and sweetmeats.
13. Rarhi Sow, or Sungri, distillers of spirits.

These may amount on the whole to about 1,50,000 persons. Many of them are rich, which makes them bear their degradation with impatience, and the women of the money-changers are in general accused of holding their husbands in contempt, and of going astray with persons whose rank is more conformable to their fortune.

There is somewhat more reasonable in the higher castes abstaining from communication with the tribes included under the general appellation of Ontyoj. These eat many things that are forbidden to other Hindús, although there is a considerable difference in the degrees of indulgence, which these tribes allow to themselves. Some abstain from pork, others indulge themselves in this luxury ; while some will even eat the flesh of oxen, which is considered as the utmost degradation of which human nature is capable. They have never been permitted to kill the sacred animal; their repasts therefore of this nature have been confined to carrion. The whole, except the washermen, consider themselves as permitted to intoxicate themselves, whenever they have a convenient opportunity ; and they are not disgraced by openly keeping concubines, nor are their widows disgraced by entering into that state. The Dhobas, Kopali, Chondal, and some of the Muchis, have Vorno Brahmins for Gurus. The Patonies, Bhumi-malis, and part of the Muchis have only Vaishnobs for Gurus, but Brahmins act as their Purohits.

Those of them that belong to Dinajpúr, and who are considered as having had their rank ascertained by Bollalsen, are the following:

1. Dhoba, washermen.
2. Kopali, weavers of canvas and sackcloth.
3. Chondal, fishermen.
4. Dom, or Patoni, basket-makers.

Bhumi-mali, divided into two classes:—

5. Borobhaga, gardeners and farmers.
6. Chhotabhaga, sweepers and scavengers.
7. Muchi, tanners and shoe-makers.

These classes, especially the fifth, are very numerous, and about 2,25,000 of them are to be found in Dinajpúr.

The whole of these tribes, that I have as yet mentioned, are considered as having belonged to Bengal, when Bollalsen settled the rank of its castes. I cannot however find, that any book or written regulation was made by that prince; but each caste, which possesses wealth, has persons called Ghotoks, who keep registers of marriages, with the names of the parties and that of their parents, and thus can ascertain genealogies. These are the persons usually employed to make up marriages, as they are answerable for the purity of the parties' extraction. The whole of the tradition concerning the settlement by Bollalsen seems to rest on the authority of those Ghotoks, which perhaps may be doubted; but I have not been able to find one person of this description, with whom I might converse on the subject.

One-half of the Hindús in Dinajpúr belongs to tribes, which are supposed not to have been settled in Bengal in the time of Bollalsen; and at least 2,90,000 of these belong to a people, which appear to me to have a common origin, and whose features mark them clearly to be of a different race from other Hindús; indeed they are most strongly marked as belonging to the flat broad-faced people, which occupies the Eastern portions of Asia. I think it probable, that it is since the time of Bollalsen, that they have come from the Eastern side of the Korotoya river, or Kamrup, where they are still more numerous than in this district; but all remembrance of the emigration has ceased. It is very possible, however, that they may have been the original inhabitants of the northern parts of this district, which do not appear to have been within the limits of Bollalsen's dominion any more than Kamrup, which I suppose to have been their original country. This however I shall probably have hereafter an opportunity of determining. These three tribes are the Rajbongsi, Kongch, and Polya, and consider themselves as distinct; but it is contended by many, that they were originally the same, and have now separated in consequence of some of them having adopted, more than others, those manners which Hindús consider pure. This I shall have probably an opportunity of showing to have been the case, when in my next report I come to state the history of Kamrup. I shall only mention now, that the Rajbongsis seem merely to me to be the families of the Kongch, which are related to their princes, such as the Rajas of Vihar, and Vijni, and Dorong, whose history is tolerably clear; and there are still Kongch remaining, who retain a language totally different from that of Bengal, who retain the old simple worship, and have no dealings with the Brahmins. In Dinajpúr, even the highest of them, the Rajbongsis are reckoned a very impure tribe; but in the countries that are subject to their princes, an assertion of this nature would be very imprudent, and it has been discovered, that they are Khyetriyos, who escaped from the persecution of Porosuram, and thattheir princes, *Nor*, are descendants of the god Sib. The Rajbongsis and Kongch drink intoxicating liquors without disgrace, and openly keep concubines; but they abstain from swine and fowls, in which the Polyas are not ashamed to indulge themselves. The principal difference between the Rajbongsis and Kongch is, that the latter condescend to carry palanquins, which the others do not; all the three are cultivators and weavers.

The other tribes of Dinajpúr who are considered as not having belonged to Bengal, when Bollalsen settled its castes, are as follows:

1. Khyan, cultivators from Maithilo, who follow the Brahmins of that nation.
2. Yogis, or Jogis, who are weavers from the west of India.
3. Thataru, workers in tin from the west of India.
4. Bangsi, cultivators.
5. Changyi, grass-cutters.
6. Dhanuk, wood-cutters.
7. Betuya, workers in ratan.
8. Kurails, who make leathern bags.
9. Byadh, or Bede, snake-catchers, and gelders of animals.
10. Múrdah Furash, or Mritop, who remove dead bodies.

The whole do not exceed 10,000 persons. The first caste is pure; the two last castes exceedingly vile, and it may be doubted, whether they can be considered as either Hindús or Muhammedans.

PART 2.—*Customs of the Hindús.*

To give an account of the ceremonies of each or any one of these castes would be endless. In the 5th and 7th volumes of the Asiatic Researches, they have been most ably explained by Mr. Colebrooke; and whoever wishes to investigate how time may be altogether wasted, will there see to what lengths the Hindús have carried this science. In the observance of these ceremonies, every Hindú, who can possibly spare time, seems to place his chief glory, and he consumes in a most miserable manner the hours that were granted for nobler purposes.

In other matters, the Brahmans of Bengal are not near so strict as those of the south. They have allowed themselves a much greater liberty in point of food, and they have yielded much farther to the Sudros, not only in assisting at their ceremonies, but in complying with the common worship by bloody sacrifices. It is owing to this that their law seems to be much more universally observed in Bengal, than it is in the south; and that the customs of its different castes have a greater uniformity.

I have already mentioned the foods that are allowed to pure Hindús. The only meat which they commonly use is, that of sacrifices, and the only animals that they offer are buffalos and goats. The impure tribes offer ducks, swine, and fowls; but these two last are reserved for the very dregs of the people, especially the fowls. The ducks are more respectable, and even some pure Sudros are allowed to use them, although they are never confined, nor prevented from eating any impurity.

The extracts of poppy and hemp, and the leaves of the latter, are considered as much more innocent than spirituous liquors; yet they are more apt, than even distilled spirits, to lead to the most beastly private intoxication. A Brahmin, who intoxicates himself with these drugs, is considered as highly blamable, just as a drunkard is with us, but he does not lose caste; many of the lower tribes use them, whenever they can: but it is only the very lowest, that will drink spirituous liquors openly; of course these are never used, except for mere private intoxication. All women chew tobacco, but it is only those of the unclean tribes and prostitutes that smoke. No man, however pure, loses caste by smoking tobacco, and all practise it, except a few Pandits, who content themselves with snuffing, which is esteemed more honourable than smoking. Men seldom chew this weed.

Except the bodies of children, the dead of all castes are burned. The higher the caste, the younger are the children, that are entitled to this kind of funeral. The body of a dead Brahmin of 2 years of age receives this honour, while burial is considered as sufficient for a low child; until he has reached his fifth year. The funeral pile however being expensive, many of the poor cannot be redueed to ashes. A torch or bundle of straw is kindled, and put to the mouth of the corpse with the proper ceremonies; and afterwards, if near a large river, the body is thrown into the water, or if at a distance, it is buried. The first, when practicable, is always preferred, and renders many of the rivers exceedingly disgusting. The expense of the funeral itself is not very burthensome; but the mourning is followed by a ceremony called Sraddho, which is very grievous, and often ruinous. The poorest Brahmin of pure birth cannot perform it for less than 40 rupees, and must sell, beg, and borrow to the utmost of his power, to procure this sum. Even the very low and pure tribe, called Patoni, who are basket-makers, require to raise 10 rupees for this ceremony, which is the value of at least three months labour; nor can they be freed from the restraints of mourning, until it has been performed.

Men, or rather boys, are always married, so soon as they can procure money sufficient to defray the expenses; which, except to some of the highest ranks of the Brahmins, are very great, and very frequently involve the parties in ruin. The higher ranks of Brahmins receive a price from the father of their bride, when they marry, and no Brahmin lawfully takes a price for his daughter; although of late this practice, as I have mentioned, is gaining ground. The Sudros, on the contrary, in general, may lawfully take money for their daughters. This sum given by the father, either of the bride or bridegroom, according to the custom of the caste, is called *Pon*; but, except with the Kulin Brahmins and Kulin Kayosthos, is never sufficient to defray the expense of the party who receives, it, although it renders his outlay less burthensome. The charges attending the marriage of a Kulin Brahmin, who is poor, cannot, to both parties, amount to less than 300 rupees. A Kayostho's marriage must cost at least 150. A tradesman of pure birth cannot spend less than 80; and even a Bhumi-mali, the lowest of all castes, must expend 17 rupees, 12 of which come from the father of the boy, and 5 from the father of the girl. The daughters of all Brahmins ought to be married before they are 10 years of age; but some indulgence is shown to those of Kulins. Even among the lowest Sudros both father and daughter are considered as highly blamable, if a girl remains unmarried at the age of puberty; for it is scarcely expected, that the girl in that case should be able to preserve her chastity. Girls before marriage receive little or no education. Those who are rich see how their mothers manage their family. Those who are poor must labor, and are taught how to work. In this country, even the women of Brahmins spin cotton, which in the south would be reckoned an abomination. So long as the parents are alive, it is they alone who are consulted in making marriages. Not that a contumaceous couple would incur loss of caste, but the man would be disinherited, and both they and the priest, who married them, might be fined by their Guru. Before marriage it is not customary for the parties to see each other, nor for their mutual inclinations to be consulted. The Ghotok, or register of pedigrees, among the higher castes, and the Poramanick, or chief of the caste among the lower, act as agents, and generally settle all particulars, before the bride or bridegroom know any thing of the matter. In the selection of husbands birth seems to have in general a preference to riches, which indeed are little regarded, the urgency of procuring a match at any rate, leaving little room for choice on that point: the avoiding disgrace seems to be what is principally in view. It is lawful for Hindús to marry as many wives as they please; but in fact it is impossible for any, except the two highest rank of the five tribes, to procure more than one, unless where the first wife has no child, and then the expence becomes so grievous, that none except a few rich persons can procure a second; for in such a case no father will give his daughter without a bribe, and two houses must be kept, otherwise disputes run so high as to render life intolerable.

No pure Hindú in Bengal can lawfully keep a concubine of any sort, whether he is married or single. But some of the impure tribes allow men to form a kind of left-hand marriage, called *nika*, with widows of their own tribe. The contract is accompanied by religious ceremonies, and the same fidelity, both in the man and woman, is expected as in proper marriage (*vivaho*); but in general neither the *nika* nor her children are so much respected as the virgin spouse, especially if the caste approaches in any degree to purity; for in some very low castes there is little difference shown. This contract is made up by the consent of the parties, and may be dissolved at pleasure by either, but this is considered as blamable. In these low castes even adultresses may become *nikas*, provided they have only indulged men of their own, or of higher tribes. A virgin cannot become a *nika*. A common concubine, who is not united by some religious ceremony, is called *dhemni*, and no Hindú, except the very extremes of impurity, can live with such a creature, without being in danger of losing caste, should his fault be discovered; but common fornication, especially with a woman of the same caste, does not incur such a heavy punishment, and the lowest castes admit of *dhemnis* of the same tribe.

Widows, I have already mentioned, are subject to great harshness of treatment, and even the lowest caste can be married in no way, except by the contract called *nika*. The virgin spouses of all Hindús are permitted to burn themselves with the body of their deceased husband on his funeral pile; but the practice is chiefly confined to those of brahmins, physicians, and scribes. The women of these two last castes are allowed a farther indulgence. If their husband dies at a distance, they may dig a pit, fill it with combustibles, and throw themselves into it, provided they have any article that belonged to their husband, which they can carry with them into the flames. Both practices are exceedingly rare in Dinajpúr, and probably not above one or two sacrifices of this nature are made in a year. If a man leaves children, or brothers who lived with him in the same family with a common stock, his widow is entirely destitute, unless the husband has made a will or donation in her favour, before he died; but this is not commonly done, and the widow in general receives nothing more than food and mean apparel. But if her husband had separated his stock from his brothers, and has left no children, the widow is his heir; and at any rate, if he has children, she is her son's tutor during his minority, which renders her condition tolerable for some years. It is the interest of the wife therefore to create difference between her husband and his brothers.

Hindú virgins have seldom an opportunity of misbehaving, because none almost remain unmarried after the age when they are in danger; but widows of all ranks, especially in the higher castes, who cannot hope to become *nika*, are very frequently unable to resist temptation, and become with child. Either virgin or widow who has so far disgraced herself, whether she is high or low, ought to be excommunicated; but as the disgrace extends also to the whole family, every pains is taken to conceal the affair, and to procure abortion, for which very violent means are said to be employed; and the higher castes are said to be in general successful, but the lower can seldom procure the means, and excommunicate the woman, who either becomes a common prostitute, or a religious mendicant.

Poor parents, in times of scarcity, may give their children to persons of rank as slaves, and are sometimes induced to sell them to prostitutes. This however is quite contrary to Hindú law, although such parents are not liable to excommunication.

Divorces from a virgin spouse are only admitted in cases of adultery, and the wife cannot in any case divorce her husband. Pure Hindús must turn away their wives, if they are publicly known to have disgraced them; but many of the lower castes, provided their fickle wives confine their amours to the caste, rather pay a small fine than part with them, as the expense of marrying again would be intolerable, and it is considered as impossible to live single. In such castes a divorced woman may become a *Nika*. In cases of divorce the children belong to the father.

All proper Hindús regret, that in these days no caste adheres to its proper duties, but that many persons, in order to procure a subsistence, betake themselves to professions for which they were not originally intended. In fact, the compelling a person for ever to adhere to the profession of his father is so contrary to justice and human nature, that it has been found impracticable; and the Hindús, although with regret, have been compelled to relax the spirit of the law, and even to admit into their written code numerous exemptions: yet every deviation from the strict letter is considered more and more improper, in proportion to the rank of the person by whom it is made, and to the extent of the deviation. These exemptions, however regretted by well disposed, but over-zealous persons, have certainly in a great measure removed, or at least alleviated one strong objection to the institution. Enough of evil still however remains behind; for instance, the inconvenience which every Hindú of decent rank experience in travelling, and in procuring food which he considers as pure; so that there is scarcely any man of rank who does not waste much time in the disagreeable and degrading office of a cook, while the least irregularity in his motions, or any extraordinary exertion required, totally deprives him of 2 or 3 hours labour, that he has thrown away on that service, and deprives him of a meal of which he was perhaps in the utmost need.

The principal evil, however, that the Hindú doctrine of caste has imposed, is the confinement of science to a hereditary priesthood, elevated by birth above the governors of the country. The brahmins indeed may read some of their books to princes, and other great persons; but the explanation, not only of religion, but of civil law and ethics, was always confined to the sacred order, and supported by divine authority. Of late a considerable relaxation has taken place, although it is severely condemned by persons of strict notions, yet the works that have hitherto been translated into the Prakrito or polished language, so far as I can learn, are not of a nature to diminish the credulity of their readers, nor to increase either their wisdom or virtue; and there are still many books kept carefully from the profane, to which on all occasions a reference may be made as to a superior authority. The state of knowledge in this district, I have already detailed.

The better informed brahmins may in some measure be called worshippers of two deities, a male and a female; and this doctrine seems to have been pretty generally adopted by all the rude tribes scattered through India, or situated on its frontier, whose poverty had prevented them from receiving instruction. The male is generally considered as good-natured, but the female delights in the blood of sacrifices. This simple doctrine the brahmins have considerably enlarged and diversified. The sexes are considered as forming in some measure one body, which is explained by comparing them with the two lobes (cotyledon) of a pea; but all the brahmins, with whom I have conversed, consider, that many deities have proceeded from these two supreme spirits, and the division into sects arises from its being disputed, which of these inferior deities ought to be the sole or principal object of worship, or which of the deities, universally admitted to exist, is to be considered as the supreme. Some for instance contend that the sun ought to be the principal object of worship, others contend that Sib is the chief god, while others assert, that Vishnu is entitled to that dignity, and one sect gives pre-eminence to the female. In this country there are five sects:

1. Saibo, who consider Sib as the principal god, but always worship this deity in conjunction with the female power.
2. Sakto, who worship chiefly the female portion of the deity.
3. Saur, who worship the Sun.
4. Ganpotyo, who worship Gones.
5. Vaishnov, who worship Vishnu. This sect has branched into two; one worships Ram, the other Krishno.

The members of each of these sects, although they consider one deity as the principal object of worship, and as the chief of the gods, do not imagine, that the other gods have no existence, and occasionally address their prayers to several of them; the whole may therefore with propriety be considered as polytheists, and the whole are idolators. A large proportion of the brahmins, indeed, know nothing of the disputes from whence the differences of sect have arisen, nor of the more refined doctrines of their sects; and are most implicit believers in polytheism, and in the peculiar holiness of certain images, arising from the actual presence of the deity. Of course the Sudros are still more addicted to these errors; but still in general they adhere nominally to some sect. Three of the sects above-mentioned contain so few members, that they may be altogether neglected. The sects that are by far the most numerous are those who worship Sakto among the brahmins, and those who worship Vishnu under the form of Krishno, among the Sudros. These last, however, are in general addicted to worship whatever god comes in their way; and although their spiritual guides avoid the worship of Sakto, yet few of the Sudros are able to resist the temptation. The two principal reasons for this seem to be, 1st, that Vishnu is considered as a benevolent spirit, while Kali and Bishohori, two common forms of Sokti, are represented in terrible forms. 2ndly, the sacrifices offered to appease the Soktis are a temptation not to be resisted by those who could eat no flesh, unless they offered it in sacrifice, and Vishnu will accept of no offering of this kind.

It is not indeed to be wondered, that the followers of Vishnu should occasionally pray to the Soktis, in a district where even Muhammedans adopt this custom, and where every one in distress, who finds no relief from prayers to his saint, betakes himself to a sacrifice to Kali; accordingly in almost every village, even where there is not a Hindú, there is a place of worship for this deity. This is in general very simple, being a heap of earth, commonly under a tree, with a stake to which the head of the sacrifice is fastened, so that the neck may be stretched out for decapitation, which is the manner of making the offering. Others are somewhat more improved, and consist of a hut in which a terrible figure or painting of the deity is suspended, and a few have rude images. Bishohori is the goddess of serpents, and is a very common object of worship, as are also Sitola, Siddheswori, Vriddheswori, and especially Monggol Chondi, all destructive female spirits, considered by the brahmins as the same with the wife of Sib, but worshipped by the ignorant as the inflicters of various evils, which they wish to avoid. These are also called the Gram Devotas, or village gods. None of their temples have any considerable establishment; but by far the greater part have brahmins for Pujaris, or officiating priests. Some however of the small places dedicated to Kali are served by very low castes, such as Rajbongsis, or even Bhumimalis. The chief of the village is never Pujari to the village deity, as usual in the south; probably because most of them are Muhammedans. No music nor dancers are here attached to the temples; but there are many sets of musicians, who are of the lower castes, and who generally have a boy or two to dance and sing, that are employed in the worship of the gods. They are of three kinds: Bishohori and Monggol Chondi, that are employed in the worship of the goddesses whose names they bear, and Kritons, who sing the praises of Krishno. Several of the low castes have deities that they consider as having a peculiar care over them, and that probably were their only gods, before their instruction by the brahmins; but this belief is not near so common as in the south. The worship, which consists in the votary suspending himself from the end of a lever by hooks passed through the skin of his back, and in being whirled round before the god in that painful situation, was invented in this district, and is still much practised; but not having had an opportunity of seeing it, I shall only notice some particulars that differ from those in the south. 1st. It is performed by many of pure castes. 2ndly. It is performed before the images of Sib; both of which would be considered as abominations in the south: but the most remarkable thing is, that the brahmins, physicians, and scribes, who are almost all worshippers of Sib, abstain altogether from this practice, and the Sudros seem very fond of it, although they are almost all worshippers of Vishnú. The invention is attributed to Banraja, who was an Asur or infidel.

Well-informed people of the higher ranks believe in a future existence, and that it is a state of reward and punishment: but most of the lower tribes, and many even of the more ignorant brahmins seem to have no belief in this opinion, although in general they have heard of the doctrine; and their worship is performed merely in hope of temporal reward, or for fear of punishment in this life. The lower classes have very little respect for oaths, and the higher believe that no oath can be taken without sin.

There are few castes in Bengal that have not Purohits from among the Brahmins, unless we exclude from the sacred order, the Vyasokto, or priests of the Kuibortos; but among the low tribes, who have settled in this district, and form so large a portion of its Hindú population, the greater part have not Brahmin Purohits; and the impure tribes generally employ as Gurus, the religious mendicants, called Vishnúv, who from ignorance are often called Brahmins. In this however there are great differences. Some persons of these low tribes have proper Brahmins, both as Gurus and Purohits; and these observe the Hindú law with regularity, while other persons of the same caste, who addict themselves to impure practices, are not admitted to so high an honor. In these low castes, the persons who are appropriated to act as Purohits, hold their office by hereditary ranks, and are more respected than common. In this district, in fact, the person who is chief Guru for all those of the sect of Vishnú is a Goswami of the Rarhí division of the five tribes. He is named Otolvihari, and resides at Ghyaspur, in the district of Puroniya, near Gaur. He visits this district annually, performing his office of Guru to the Brahmins. He also employs Odhikaris, or brahmins who have been degraded by officiating as priests in temples, to act for him as Gurus for the pure Sudros; and in like manner he employs, as agents for instructing the impure tribes, certain Vishnovs, or other Sudros, who have separated themselves from their families, and have dedicated themselves entirely to God. His annual profits are said to be about 12,000 rupees, and his office and rank hereditary.

The Guru instructs the Hindú in a proper form of prayer, and this instruction is called *Upodes*. He also accepts of presents on various occasions. Some of the Goswamis have authority to punish low people, for transgressions against the rules of caste, by fine and excommunication; but this power is not general, and does not extend to the higher castes. The Guru however, in all ranks, receives the greater part of the fines that are levied on those who offend againt the rules of caste. The Gurus in Bengal do not seem to occupy so high a station as in the south, but they have very considerable emoluments. A man, unless he is of a narrow disposition, should give his Guru one-twentieth part of his income; but many give less, and many a great deal more. There is no written regulation for this, the whole contribution is voluntary.

The Purohit reads prayers on various occasions. If the prayers are portions of the Beds, the Sudro is not allowed to repeat after the priest; but there are parts of the service that the Sudros are allowed to utter. They understand no part. The usual proportion of the Purohit's emolument is about one-half of that which the Guru receives.

Both Gurus and Purohits, not only of the impure, but even of the pure Sudros, are in general so ignorant that they cannot read the ceremonies, which are in Sangskrito, and none of them understand a word of these writings. The prayers are commonly repeated from memory. Even among the Gurus and Purohits, who officiate for the Brahmins, there are many, who do not understand the obsolete language of the Beds, from whence a great part of the Hindú service is extracted.

Among the Brahmins of Bengal there are very few who forsake their families, and dedicate themselves entirely to what is called the service of God. Their law however admits of the practice, and allows them to be divided, in consequence, into four states or conditions *(Asrom)*. Between the age of nine and eleven years, when a boy is to receive the thread, which he is to wear as the badge of his dignity, he ought to pass some time in the most intense study, and severe practice of religious duties. In this state he is called Brohmochari. In general they content themselves with two or three hours of these exercises, and none protract them beyond 10 days. They then receive the thread with innumerable minute ceremonies, and enter into the state called *Grihi*, or persons living in a house with a family. When a man's father and mother have died, and if he has children, when these have grown up, or when he is fifty years of age, should he be desirous of acquiring more holiness, he may retire into woods or solitary places, and live with holy persons in the state of a *Banoprostho*, which may be translated hermit. The number of these among the Brahmins of Bengal is exceedingly small. They employ much of their time in pilgrimages, and in general have converted their effects into money, on which they live, although some trust to alms for a support: most persons indeed, who now betake themselves to this life, are men who have lost all their near relations. Those who wish to obtain greater favour from heaven, take upon themselves the state of *Dondi*. They throw their badge of honor into the fire, shave their heads, throw aside all their cloths, except what decency requires, and all their effects, except a staff and an earthen pot for drawing water. They no longer kindle a fire to prepare food, but take whatever a Brahmin gives them to eat. By the rules of the order, they are not allowed even to think of any thing that would give them pleasure, and in fact ought to be most egregious enthusiasts. The practice, owing perhaps to the good sense of the Brahmins of Bengal, is very rare; and the persons who adopt it, retiring to other districts, the fanatical multitude would be destitute of a supply sufficient for their silly admiration, had not several interlopers from the west made their way into the district. Of these I shall give some account, only previously observing, that among the natives of Bengal there are no gymnosophists; this extravagance seems to be confined to the west.

Among the followers of Vishnú there are two sects; the one worships Ram, the other Krishno; for the other incarnations (*Avotars*) of that deity are not worshipped by the Hindús. In Bengal the former conceal their sect, as much as the worshippers of Sib, Soktí, Gones, or the Sun; but near Oyodhya or Oude, the city of the hero, and in other parts of the west of India, the worship of Ram is openly professed. Many young brahmins are there dedicated to the service of the deity, relinquish the world, and take the name *Ramayet* or *Ramanondi*. Of these there are a considerable number in Dinajpúr. They live in small convents (*Akra*) of five or six persons, under the authority of a *Mohonto*, who appoints a successor before his death, giving him the proper secret instruction (*Upodes*). A description of one of these convents at Nimnogor, in the town of Dinajpúr, may serve to give an idea of the whole. It consists of six huts, like those occupied by wealthy farmers. One of them, which serves as a chapel (*Devaloy*), is rather larger than the others, and contains images of Ram or Roghunath, of his brother Lokhymon, of his wife Sita, of his servant Honuman, and of Gopal, another incarnation of Vishnú. The first and last are made of black stone, the others are of a composition called Oshtodhatu, from its containing eight metals. As objects of worship, there are besides 32 Salgrams or sacred stones, representing different gods of the side of Vishnú. Four of the other houses are appropriated for the accommodation of the persons belonging to the convent, and of any strangers (Hindú) of rank; and a small house is left empty for persons of low birth, or even for Muhammedans. The original endowment for this Akra was 45 bigahs (between 19 and 20 acres) of land, of which two contain the buildings, and are surrounded by a mud wall. Besides this the Raja allowed it a rupee daily; but on the decay of the family this has been stopped. Belonging to this Akra, there are five Ramayets, one of whom is Mohonto or chief; although they neither are of the five tribes, nor Baidiks, they are Brahmins of Kanyokubjo, and took the vows of celibacy when they were children, and are much venerated by the people. They possess little or no learning, but can read some *Montros* or forms of prayer; and they eat with no persons, but those of their own description. The Guru of the order, Janokidas, lives near Joypúr. Some two or three of them remain in the *Akra*, while the others travel about soliciting alms; but they obtain nothing that can enable them to live with any dignity. Five or six rupees are considered as a handsome offering from a rich man. While wandering about they generally sleep at some other Akra; but seldom receive any food. They have only one servant, who keeps their ground, and takes care of three cows that give them milk. Some part of their ground is waste, and a good deal is occupied by bamboos, mangoe, and jack trees, which give them considerable profit, as they sell the bamboos and the long-grass that grows on the waste land, which is used for thatch. They cultivate a small proportion of their ground by means of Adhiyars, who undertake all the expense and trouble of cultivation, and give the proprietors one-half of the grain produced, and the whole of the straw, which feeds their cows. Their servant's allowance is eight rupees a year and his food. This servant cultivates the garden, which produces vegetables (*torkari*) for the use of the Ramayets. Those that are present daily wash the gods, adorn them with oil, sandal, and flowers, offer them boiled rice and sweetmeats, and read *montros* or prayers. They also burn a lamp before the images, and offer incence (*dhup*). When they die they are burned, and their companions mourn (*Osauch*) for 13 days, in place of 11, which common Brahmins use. They never shave their heads.

The celebrated Songkor, when he came into the north of India, introduced the order of *Sonnyasi*, as he had done in the south. Many of these *Sonnyasis*, who are Brahmins of Konyokubjo, frequent this district, where they are usually called *Goswamis* or *Gosaing*; but as I observed before, they must be carefully distinguished from the Goswamis of Bengal, who are worshippers of Vishnú, and married; while those of the west are worshippers of Sib, have taken vows of celibacy, and are dedicated to the service of God when young. In general however they pay very little attention to the rules of their order. Most of them are rich merchants, and although they live in houses which they call *Akras*, are generally supposed to have female companions. Several have even entered into our military service, and are commonly alleged to be more than usually insolent and rapacious in the villages, which they enter without their officers. Except the few, who adhere more strictly to their rules, these are little respected. They have no sort of communion with the five tribes or Baidiks of Bengal, although these also are Kanyokubjo Brahmins. Among these Goswamis of the west, there are however many Rajputs, and others who pretend to be of the Khyetriyo caste.

The Sudros of Bengal are not excluded from dedicating themselves to the worship of God, and the very lowest of the impure tribes may attach both themselves and their children for ever to the king of priesthood, or order of mendicants called Vaishnú, or Vaishnúm. In Dinajpúr these are exceedingly numerous, and may be divided into three kinds. First, those who have assumed this order recently are very little respected, and cannot procure by begging more than a mere subsistence. A great part of them are persons who have lost all their relations, widows who have had children, and common prostitutes who repent of their profession, or are no longer able to procure a support by its means; but there are some also, no doubt, who are actuated by more worthy, although mistaken motives. In order to be received in the order, 14 rupees must be given to the Goswami who is Guru, and this is a considerable restraint. The whole of this class however can scarcely be considered as entering among the proper Vaishnovs; but their children, after one or two generations, arrive at the full dignity, and form the two remaining classes, called Grihi and Udasin. The former, like the Grihi Brahmins, marry and live settled lives in their own houses, although man, woman, and child among them are impudent beggars; and as they are much respected by the lower ranks, they procure a subsistence that is rather comfortable, and live like farmers who keep two or three ploughs. Besides begging they make beads from the stems of the Tulosi (Ocymum Sanctum) and common Flax, and of the wood of the Bilvo (Cratæva Marmelos), the Sriphol (Cratæva Religiosa), the Dude and Indrojov (Nerium Antidysentericum, W.) which they sell; for every Hindú, except a Brahmin, must have beads round his neck, otherwise he cannot lawfully drink water. Many of the Vaishnovs besides, are among the musicians (*kritoni*) who celebrate the praises of Krishno; for they are all worshippers of that incarnation of Vishnú. These professions are considered as lawful; but some have accumulated stock, have taken large farms, and degrade themselves by cultivation. Some of them can read and a few understand Prakrito, and peruse the book called Chaitonyo Choritumrito, which was composed by a pious physician named Krishno Das, who was contemporary with the two Brahmins, that introduced the worship of Krishno among the five tribes. The Udasin Vaishnov, like the Dondi among the Brahmins, dedicate themselves entirely to the service of God, and retire from their families to live in convents (Akras); but like their betters they seldom do this until time has considerably moderated the strength of appetite for pleasure. They are very much respected, and serve as Gurus for the impure tribes; but in general act merely as agents for the Goswami Brahmin, who of course has the lion's share of the profits. The Vaishnavom or Satananas of the south very much resemble the Vaishnov of Bengal; but they hold a higher rank, and are the garland-makers of that country, a profession which here forms one of the nine pure castes (Malakar) of tradesmen.

The number of Vaishnov is not however sufficient to consume the pious charity of the worshippers of Vishnu in Dinajpúr, and a considerable number (perhaps 500) of Vairagis come from the vicinity of Mothura, where Krishno reigned. They live in convents (Akras), and follow nearly the same rules with the Udasins of Bengal. The chief of a convent of Udasin is called Odhikari, but the Vairagi prior is named Mohonto. Neither have any endowments in land.

Except among the physicians and scribes in Bengal there is few or none of the Sudros, who worship Sib; and none of these two castes dedicate themselves to God, whether from superior understanding, or some other cause I cannot say. I can scarcely however attribute it to the first cause; for they venerate in the highest degree the Khyetriyos, Rajpúts, and Sudros, of the west, who have dedicated themselves to the service of God, who have separated themselves from their families, who worship Sib, and who are called Yogi or Jogi, to which the term Kanphata is usually prefixed, from their having their ears distended to a very great size by means of wooden rings. They trace their origin to the celebrated Songkor, and have their most numerous establishments in Lahor. In Dinajpúr they are not numerous. I saw only one convent, which they call a Ghopa. It had a neat small temple, (Drawing No. 11.) some comfortable houses although thatched, and the occupants were neither old nor austere in their manners. They were exceedingly respected; and a neighbouring Kayostho, in other respects a sensible man, declared to me, that he considered them as far superior to any Brahmin, and perfectly equal to Vishnu, Sib, and Bruhma.

The Hindús in Bengal, as elsewhere, in order to preserve the purity of caste by punishing such as transgress its rules, form themselves into companies, which in Bengal are called Dol. Very considerable differences however exist in the manner, in which these companies are formed. In Bengal a Hindú may enter into any Dol that he pleases, and which will admit him; and his rank is in some measure estimated by the company he frequents, as he would be expelled by the company should he do any thing contrary to its regulations. There is no necessity for all the persons being of the same caste. The Baidiks of Dinajpur will not enter into the same Dol with any Sudro. The two highest ranks of the five tribes, and those who are most esteemed among the third, admit only the physicians and scribes into their company; which requires, that on certain occasions they should visit in their houses, and then eat sweetmeats, curdled milk, and other things that do not require to be cooked. The lower part of the third rank of Brahmins admit the pure Sudros of the nine tribes, and also Telis, Tamolís, and Moyras.

At the head of each Dol is a chief (Dolpoti), whose office among the higher castes is hereditary, and whose duty it is to punish all transgressions, either by excommunication or fine, according to circumstances. The first operation is to turn the offender out of the company. He of course implores to be re-admitted;

and then the Dolpoti determines, whether or not this can be done, and on what terms; and the re-admission is always accompanied by an entertainment for the company. The power of the Dolpoti however is not arbitrary, as his decisions must be guided by the consent of the principal people of the company, which in Bengal is called a session *(baitok)*. His influence however is very considerable, as he expends much money in entertaining the company. Frequently indeed his profits are great in proportion, especially in large towns, where breaches of the law are common, and where the people are rich; and there he sometimes procures great wealth. Should the Dolpoti become poor, and unable to entertain, he is deprived of his office, and another is elected. No transaction of importance that can affect caste, such as a marriage or feast, should be undertaken without informing the Dolpoti, in order that he may know, whether any thing improper is going forward. The number of assessors does not seem to be fixed, nor is there any regular election. From 5 to 10 of the men, who are most esteemed for learning, wisdom, or riches, assemble to assist the Dolpoti. Among the higher castes they are called Visishtos; but among the lower castes they are called Prodans, or Raymaniks; and in many castes every head of a family obtains these titles.

In large places there are two or three principal Dolpotis, whose companies in general quarrel, and endeavour to do each other all the ill offices that they can. Each caste, when it is numerous in any place, has besides one or more Dols or companies, for enforcing the observance of its rules. Each kind of Brahmin, and each caste of Sudros, has its own, and most of those castes are subdivided into several branches, that dispute about precedence and purity, and that cannot intermarry, and each of these subdivisions has usually a separate chief. In the various castes the chiefs of companies are called by various names, the most common is Poramanik. His authority is similar to that of the Dolpoti. In some of the lower tribes, such as basket-makers (Patonis), the office of Poramanik is elective, and his power is restrained by that of the Guru, whose confirmation is necessary to render the election valid; nor can any person be excommunicated or fined without his consent. These two last rules are generally observed, wherever all the members of a company have the same Guru.

The faults usually punished by these sessions are eating forbidden things, or with forbidden persons, and cohabiting with those who are impure or forbidden: persons also, who have been convicted by the magistrate of theft or perjury, must pay, according to circumstances, before they are received into their company.

SECTION 3.—*Various small sects.*

The followers of Muhammed and of the Brahmins compose almost the whole population of Dinajpúr, so that I shall have little or no room to say any thing concerning other religious opinions.

Among the natives Christianity may be said to have made no progress. There are no native Portuguese, and no trace remains of the labours of Mr. Carey, although he resided for some years in this district, and his zeal and abilities are well known. His successor in the mission, Mr. Fernandez, a native of Portugal, who I believe was once intended for a popish priest, has had very little success, although he is a person of very good address, with some propensity to turn every thing into the wonderful, which cannot fail to be of use with such a people. His converts are five, and two are married and have families. One of them can read the Scriptures in the language of Bengal, and endeavours to instruct his countrymen; but the conduct of the converts is beheld with the utmost abhorrence by the other natives.

Many agents and persons belonging to a people called Oshoyal, frequent this district as traders, but have not taken up a permanent residence. They seem to form two tribes. At the head of one is the house of Jogot Seit, the chief banker in India, and these are commonly said to be Jain. At the head of the other tribe, who are usually called Kengiya, and who are extensive traders in grain, is a person named Bhoj Raja. One of his agents said, that he worshipped Gautom; but I met with no priest nor intelligent person, who could give me any satisfactory information.

A good many Sikhs frequent the district as merchants; but I have no information to offer concerning them, as I found no priest, nor well-informed person, to give me an account of their customs. They have however a meeting (Songgot or Dhormo-sala) at Dinajpur, where they assemble to worship morning and evening, and where travellers of the sect are received. At Maldeh was formerly another meeting; but it is now abandoned, and only one old woman remains in the place.

APPENDIX TO THE SECOND BOOK.

Estimate of the expence of a Hindú family of high rank and station in the town of Dinajpúr. It consists of the master, who is married and has one child; of a dependent relation, who is also married; of another male dependent relation who acts as steward, but his wife does not live in the family; of a widow, who acts as cook; of two men servants, and a boy or woman domestic; in all 10 persons.

LODGING.

To a small house, built of brick, 14 cubits by 7, usually divided into two apartments, with wooden doors and some small windows having wooden shutters. In this the master with his wife and child sleep and eat, ..	300	0	0			
To a hut, 8 cubits by 6, made of bamboo posts and beams, the walls of clay or of hurdles, the door a hurdle. In this the male relation and his wife sleep, ...	10	0	0			
To another hut of the same kind, 10 cubits by 7, which serves as a kitchen; and where the widow sleeps; if made of hurdles it is plastered with clay, ..	15	0	0			
To a hut like the last, which serves for a store-house, and in which the boy or woman servant usually sleeps,..	15	0	0			
To 3 huts of the same kind, but small, and their front only plastered; one serves for a temple, the other two for accommodating strangers, whether friends or religious mendicants, ...	25	0	0			
To a hut, 12 cubits by 8, placed near the gate for receiving company (Baitokkhana). It is usually made with a wooden door, with walls of mats, in which there are some openings by way of windows, that may be shut by hurdles which fall down (Jhangh). In this the steward and servants usually sleep, ...	30	0	0			
To a hut for the cattle, 8 cubits by 6. This is not plastered,	10	0	0			
To a house, 10 cubits by 7, for the watchman, and through which is the entrance, with a mud wall, which surrounds the premises, and which includes about 1½ bigah (½ acre) planted with trees and flowers, ...	35	0	0			
Total, ...				440	0	0
Interest, insurance, and repairs on the amount, at 36 per cent. a year, ...				158	6	5
Ground rent, ...				6	0	0
Total lodging in expensive families, . ..				164	6	5
Very few people however occupy such a house. In place of a brick apartment for the master and mistress, the usual accommodation is thatched, but the beams and posts are wooden, and the walls are plastered with mud. Many houses of this kind have two stories, but such are seldom inhabited by decent persons, and are chiefly appropriated to prostitutes. A house of this kind costs Rs. 60, which reduces the whole amount to, ...	200	0	0			
Interest, &c. on the amount, ..				72	0	0
Ground rent, ...				6	0	0
Total usual lodging, ...				78	0	0

FURNITURE of a durable nature, for the temple.

1 pair of copper cups, for pouring water on the gods, (*kosha kooshi,*)	3	0	0	
1 copper *kunsho*, another kind of cup used in prayer, ..	2	0	0	
1 copper *tat*, a kind of plate used in prayer, ..	1	8	0	
1 copper *pushpopatro*, a plate for holding flowers, used in prayer, ...	3	0	0	
1 brass *pudmason*, or salver, ...	2	0	0	
1 brass *tripodi*, or tripod, which supports a shell or sawcer (*Panisongkho*), containing holy-water, ...	6	0	0	
1 brass lamp with five lights (*Fonchoprodip*), ..	1	8	0	
1 bell-metal *kangsor*, or bell in form of a plate, ..	2	0	0	
1 bell-metal *ghonta*, or common bell, ...	2	8	0	
2 brass pots (*apkhora*), for holding the water that is to be offered, ...	2	0	0	
2 brass plates (*rikabi*), for holding fruit and sweetmeats as offerings, ...	3	0	0	
1 conch shell, for blowing to attract the deity's notice,	3	0	0	
1 *chotudola*, a wooden table or altar, on which the images are placed, ...	4	0	0	
1 *chondonpata*, or stone for rubbing Sandal-wood to dust,	0	8	0	
1 *ason*, or small woollen carpet, on which the person who prays sits, ...	0	8	0	
Total of furniture for the temple, ..				36 8 0

FOR THE HOUSE. Pots of various kinds for holding water; viz.

4 brass *kolos*, ...	21	0	0
3 ditto *garu*, ...	8	0	0
3 ditto *lota*, ...	5	0	0
3 bell-metal *apkhora*, ...	5	0	0
3 brass *omriti*, ...	3	0	0
6 brass and 4 bell-metal *thal*, or plates, ..	20	0	0
6 brass and 4 bell-metal *bati*, or large cups, ..	10	0	0
5 brass and 5 bell-metal *kotoras*, or small cups, ..	5	0	0
2 brass *bohuguna*, or pots for boiling rice, ..	4	0	0
2 brass *hanri*, pots for making curry, ...	4	0	0
1 brass *hata* or ladle, and 1 *bayuli* or hook for removing pots from the fire, ...	2	0	0
1 brass spitting pot (*dabor*), ...	2	0	0
1 brass lamp-stand (*pilsooj*), ...	5	0	0
1 brass mortar and pestle, ...	6	0	0
2 pair of betel salvers (*panbata*), one of brass, the other of bell-metal, ...	8	0	0
2 pair of betel-nut cutters, ...	0	8	0
1 brass implement for smoking tobacco through water (*hooka*), ...	8	0	0
1 *albala*, another instrument for the same purpose, with a long flexible tube such as is used by the Europeans in India; it is made partly of copper and partly of other metals, ...	21	0	0
2 iron (*khuli*) frying pots, used also for boiling milk,..	4	0	0
2 hoes and 2 hatchets (*kooral*), ...	3	0	0
1 *khonta*, or wooden stake pointed with iron, used as a spade and pickaxe, ...	0	4	0
3 *bothis* or kitchen knives, ...	0	12	0
3 sickles (*kastya*) for cutting grass for cattle, ..	0	6	0
1 iron rod for cleaning the *hooka*, ...	0	1	0
2 knives, ...	0	8	0
2 pair scissors, ...	0	4	0
2 bills for cutting bamboo or wood, ..	0	6	0
1 iron ladle and an iron hook for removing pots from the fire, ...	0	8	0
1 brass or iron pot for holding oil, and a handle for the same for a torch, ...	3	0	0

Item	Rs.	A.	P.	Rs.	A.	P.
1 hanging iron lamp, ...	0	4	0			
10 stone plates and 5 stone cups, ...	13	0	0			
1 stone for grinding curry-stuff, ...	1	0	0			
A palanquin (*Yan* or *Jan*), ...	20	0	0			
1 (*toktaposh*), a kind of large sofa, made entirely of wood, and more perhaps resembling the bench in a guardroom, where people can both sit and sleep. It stands in the place where company is received, ..	4	0	0			
2 bedsteads for master and mistress, (married people do not sleep in the same bed,) ..	12	0	0			
3 chairs, ...	3	0	0			
4 stools made of ratans (*mora*), ...	2	0	0			
2 large chests, ...	10	0	0			
2 small chests, ...	4	0	0			
2 bambu baskets covered with leather, and having lids (*petara*), ...	0	12	0			
1 instrument for beating rice (*dhenki*), and a wooden mortar, ...	1	0	0			
4 wooden stools for sitting on when they bathe (*jolchouk*),	2	0	0			
10 low wooden stools for sitting on when they eat (*piri*,)	4	0	0			
2 pair wooden slippers (*khoroms*), ...	0	8	0			
10 wooden platters (*barkosh*), ...	5	0	0			
2 plates for making cakes, ...	1	0	0			
1 large fan, ...	2	0	0			
Total durable household furniture, ..				238	2	0
Total durable furniture, ...				274	10	0
Interest and repairs, &c. on the above, at 24 per cent. ..				65	14	6¼
Household Furniture of a more perishable nature.						
For the floor or for sitting on, 3 *sutrunjis* or carpets made of cotton, or 3 *galichas* or carpets made of woollen: both kinds are of the usual fabric, and are long and narrow, ..	20	0	0			
2 *dulichas* or woollen carpets, with the nape thrown on one side, ..	12	0	0			
2 *sujoni*, or square pieces of cotton cloth flowered with silk and cotton thread, on which the master of the family sits, ..	4	0	0			
2 large calico sheets, which cover the floor of the sitting apartment, ..	6	0	0			
1 large pillow and two smaller, for leaning the back against, while sitting on the floor as usual, ..	4	0	0			
For sleeping in.						
5 sets of curtains, of muslin, for the master and mistress, male relation and wife, with one spare. The two latter persons sleep on the ground; but the curtains are hung from the roof of their hut, and are tucked under their bedding to keep off muskitos, snakes, and other vermin, ..	24	0	0			
5 mattrasses of cotton, ..	16	0	0			
4 blankets from Bootan or Patna, ...	8	0	0			
6 quilts, ...	24	0	0			
5 sheets for the beds of the master and mistress, ..	7	0	0			
8 sleeping pillows of *simul* cotton; no changeable covers,	8	0	0			
3 fine mats, made of the leaves of the (Thalia Palda, B. MSS.) *sitolpati*, on which the principal persons sleep in hot weather, ..	3	0	0			
2 pair of painted mats for the same purpose, ..	3	0	0			
4 coarse mats of leaves or stems of plants (*scirpi*,) for the widow, servants, or strangers to sleep on, ..	3	0	0			
5 fine sackcloth coverings (*megili*), for the same purpose,	2	0	0			
Total more perishable furniture, ..	144	0	0			
Interest for money, repairs, and replacing the above, at 36 per cent. per annum, ...				51	13	5¼
Umbrellas, ..				1	0	0
Total annual expense of furniture, ..				118	12	0

ORNAMENTS for the mistress of the family.

A gold ring for the nose (*noth*), ..	16	0	0			
A gold necklace, consisting of eight-sided beads (*dana*), small round beads (*mala*), and large beads of the same form (*motormala*), ..	96	0	0			
A golden ornament called *champholi*, which hangs from the necklace, ..	32	0	0			
A kind of gold ear-rings called *gengtha*, ..	24	0	0			
Another kind called *denri*, ..	32	0	0			
Another kind called *jhumka*, ..	12	0	0			
Another kind called *pipolpata*, ..	8	0	0			
A golden ornament for the forehead called *siti*, ..	32	0	0			
A golden ornament hung to the neck called *maduli*, ..	16	0	0			
A gold ring (*onggori*) for the finger, ..	8	0	0			
A gold ring (*noha*) for the left wrist, ..	32	0	0			
Silver bracelets or rings for the fore arms, several on each, called *boyuti*, ...	50	0	0			
A pair of silver ornaments tied round the arm above the elbow (*tar*), ..	30	0	0			
A pair of silver bracelets made of beads (*painchha*),	8	0	0			
A pair of silver ornaments tied round the middle of the arm (*tabij*), men wear a charm in this kind of ornament, the women are not guilty of this folly, ..	8	0	0			
8 rings of silver for the toes, (*chutki* or *pasuli*,) ..	8	0	0			
A pair of silver ornaments for the ankles, (*bankmol*,)	25	0	0			
Another silver ornament for the arm, (*rosuna*,) ..	8	0	0			
Another called *hatmaduli*, ...	10	0	0			
A ring or bracelet of shell, (*sankha*) which is worn by the women of rank, because it is reckoned lucky, ..	2	0	0			
Looking glass, comb, boxes for red-lead and other things for the toilet, kept in a small basket called *sindur chubri*, ..	0	8	0			
Total ornaments for the mistress of the family, ...				455	10	0

ORNAMENTS for the master of the family.

2 gold rings for the fingers, ..	16	0	0			
2 or 3 gold ornaments (*maduli*) hung round the neck,	16	0	0			
1 *tabij* or square ornament, which contains a charm, and is tied round the arm, ...	18	0	0			
1 looking glass, ...	1	8	0			
Total, ...				51	8	0

ORNAMENTS for child.

1 pair gold rings or bracelets for the wrists, (*bala*,) ..	30	0	0			
An ornament of gold to hang round the neck, (*podok*),	32	0	0			
A gold ring for the neck, (*hansuli*), ..	32	0	0			
A necklace of gold beads, (*dana* and *mala*), ..	48	0	0			
A pair of silver rings for the ancles, (*mol*), ..	16	0	0			
A square ornament, (*tabij*), for containing a charm, to be tied round the arm, ...	6	0	0			
Coral beads, ...	4	0	0			
Total, ...				168	0	0

The widow and dependent relations are allowed no ornament.

Total of ornaments, ...				675	2	0
Interest and new fashioning the above at 24 per cent. ..	162	0	5¼			

CLOTHING, for the master of the family.

His dress of ceremony adopted from the Muhammedans.

2 under coats or vests, (*nima*,) of white cotton cloth,	12	0	0
2 upper coats, (*jama*,) of the same, ...	24	0	0
2 turbans, ...	10	0	0
2 girdles, (*potko*,)	8	0	0

2 pair drawers, (*izar,*)	4 0 0		
2 handkerchiefs, ...	2 0 0		
A pair of shawls, Rs. 100, last 10 years, ..	10 0 0		
2 pair slippers, ...	2 0 0		
Total, ..	72 0 0		
His proper dress.			
2 pair of cotton sheets, 5 cubits by 3, which he wraps round his shoulders, and which are called *uranis* ..	8 0 0		
2 pair of cotton wrappers for the loins, (*dhuti,*) 8 cubits by 2, ...	8 0 0		
4 *angarkha* and *taj*, or jackets and caps of cotton cloth, a part of dress adopted from the Muhammedans, but now in general use among men of rank, *pondits* excepted, ...	6 0 0		
4 *phetas* or turbans of white muslin, ..	6 0 0		
3 *dolayi* or double cotton sheets, quilted together without stuffing for the cold season, 5 cubits by 3, ..	12 0 0		
2 *pachhuri* or *gelap* or double sheet, not stitched together, used also in the cold season, 10 cubits by 3,..	2 0 0		
1 piece of silk used at prayer. It is long enough both to serve for a wrapper round the loins, and to cover the shoulders, and is called *jor* or *dhuti dobja*..	5 0 0		
2 *jor* of fine cloth for receiving Hindu company, ..	4 0 0		
1 piece of European broad-cloth for the cold season, 5 cubits, costs 10 Rs. last 6 years, ..	3 0 0		
Total, ...		126 0 0	
For the mistress of the family.			
A silk cloth, 10 cubits by 2, which is called *sari*, and after having been wrapped round the loins is passed over the head and shoulders, ...	8 0 0		
6 cotton *saris* with red borders, ...	10 0 0		
A *chador*, or cotton sheet for the cold weather, ..	2 0 0		
2 *gamchhas*, or towels for bathing, ...	0 8 0		
Total, ...		20 8 0	
For the child.			
Common dress, ...	10 0 0		
Visiting dress, ..	10 0 0		
Total, ...		20 0 0	
For the two female relations.			
10 dhutis, ...	6 0 0		
2 *jor* for ceremony, ...	4 0 0		
2 *urani* or *chador*, ...	5 0 0		
2 turbans, ...	2 0 0		
4 *gelap* or sheets to throw round the shoulders in the cold weather, 10 cubits by 3, ..	8 0 0		
Total for two persons, ...		25 0 0	
For the female relation.			
6 *saris* of cotton cloth with red borders, ..	7 8 0		
1 *gelap* or sheet for cold weather, ..	1 0 0		
1 pair shell bracelets, ..	3 0 0		
Total, ...		11 8 0	
For the widow.			
6 plain coarse wrappers (*bhuni,*) of cotton cloth, ..	6 0 0		
1 *gelap*, ..	1 0 0		
Total, ..		7 0 0	
Total clothing, ..		210 0 0	

TABLE. Monthly expense.

Rice, 4 mds. fine old rice, at Rs. 1¼; ..		5 0 0	
2 mds. coarse at R. 1, (part is given away in charity,)		2 0 0	
Pulse, chiefly *oror* (Cytisus Cajan), and *hari mug*, md.		1 8 0	
Wheaten flour, 20 seers, ..		1 0 0	
Clarified butter, 6 seers, ..		2 8 0	
Mustard-seed oil, 16 seers, ..		2 0 0	
Spice and other seasoning, such as turmerics, capsicum, &c.		1 8 0	
Sugar and sweetmeats, ..		2 0 0	
Milk, 10 cows, prime cost 40 rupees, interest on which at 1 per cent.	0 6 5		
Food,	3 0 0	3 6 5	
Vegetables, ..		1 8 0	
Fish, used daily, ..		1 8 0	
Tobacco, ..		1 0 0	
Betel, ..		1 0 0	
Fuel and earthen pots, ..		2 0 0	
Total, per mensem, ..			27 14 5
Total for the year, ..			334 13 0

SERVANTS AND EQUIPAGE.

3 domestics, wages and clothes monthly, ..		3 12 0	
1 watchman, ..		3 0 0	
Barber, ..		0 4 0	
Washerman, ..		0 12 0	
Sweeper, ..		0 4 0	
Palanquin bearers employed occasionally, ..		1[illegible] 0 0	
Horse first cost 30 Rs. Interest and supplying a new one occasionally, at 3 per cent. ..	0 14 5		
Servant and food, ..	3 0 0		
		3 14 5	
Total servants and equipage per mensem,		23 14 5	
Total annually, ..			286 13 0
Celebration of Holidays, Guru, Purohit, and other expenses connected with religion, of which the Durga Puja alone consumes at least Rs. 200, (one man spent this year 10,000 rupees,) ..		300 0 0	
Stationary and master to teach the child to read and write,		6 0 0	
			306 0 0
Total, ..			592 13 0

II.—Estimate of the expense of a family of some consideration, consisting of a man, his wife, and two children, a widow who acts as cook, a dependent male relation, who is a kind of steward, and of two domestics, a man and a boy.

LODGING.

A house for the master and mistress, 15 cubits by 8, with beams and posts of wood, walls clay or plastered with clay, a wooden door, ..	40 0 0
A hut for the kitchen and where the widow sleeps, 10 cubits by 6, with bambu supporters, walls of clay, or of hurdles plastered near the fire-place with clay,	15 0 0
A store-house of the same kind, wher the boy sleeps, ..	15 0 0
A hut for the cattle, 8 cubits by 6, ..	8 0 0
A small hut for a temple, 8 cubits by 6, ..	8 0 0
Another for strangers, 10 cubits by 6, ..	10 0 0

A hut for receiving company, and where the steward and servant sleep, ..	30	0	0			
A house for the watch-man, through which the entrance is, with a high bambu railing round the premises, ..	24	0	0			
Total lodging,..	150	0	0			
Interest, insurance, and repairs, at 36 per cent. per mensem, ..				54	0	0
Ground rent, 1 bigah, ⅓ acre of land, ..				2	0	0
Total lodging,				56	0	0

FURNITURE for the temple.

1 pair copper cups (*kosha-kushi*), ..	2	8	0			
1 copper cup called *kundo*, ..	1	0	0			
1 copper plate called *tat*, ..	1	0	0			
1 brass salver, *podmason*, ..	1	0	0			
1 brass tripod or *tripodi*, with its shell, ..	3	0	0			
1 brass pot, *apkhora*, ..	1	0	0			
1 brass plate called *rikabi*, ..	1	0	0			
1 conch shell, ..	2	0	0			
1 stone for grinding sandal-wood, ..	6	8	0			
1 *kusason* or mat of grass, on which the master prays, ..	0	1	0			
1 bell-metal plate for ringing (*kangsor*), to call the attention of the god, ..	1	8	0			
1 brass lamp with five lights, ..	1	0	0			
1 wooden throne (*singhason*) for the gods, covered with cloth, ..	2	8	0			
Total, ...				18	1	0

HOUSEHOLD FURNITURE of lasting materials.

Pots or vessels of different kinds for holding water, viz.			
2 *kolos* of brass, ..	10	0	0
1 *garu* of ditto, ..	3	0	0
4 *lota* of ditto, ..	5	0	0
2 *omriti* of ditto, ..	2	8	0
2 *apkhora* of bell-metal, ..	3	0	0
2 betel salvers of brass (*panbata*), ..	4	0	0
2 pair betel-nut cutters, ..	0	8	0
4 brass or bell-metal plates (*thal*), ..	12	0	0
6 brass or bell-metal cups (*bati*), ..	6	0	0
2 brass lamp-stands (*pilsooj*), ..	3	0	0
2 brass pots for boiling rice, (*bohuguna*), ..	3	8	0
1 iron pot (*khuli*) for boiling milk and frying, ..	1	8	0
1 iron ladle, and hook for removing pots from the fire, (*hata* and *bayuli*,) ..	0	8	0
1 iron rod for cleaning the *hooka*, ..	0	1	0
1 hoe and one hatchet, ..	1	8	0
1 bill for cutting and cleaving bambus, ..	0	3	0
2 sickles, ..	0	8	0
2 kitchen knives (*boti*), ..	0	8	0
2 knives, ..	0	8	0
1 stake pointed with iron (*khonta*), ..	0	2	0
1 pair scissors, ..	0	2	0
3 plates and 2 cups of stones, ..	4	0	0
1 stone for rubbing curry-stuff, ..	0	12	0
2 bedsteads for the master and mistress of the family, ..	4	0	0
1 large and one small chest, ..	8	0	0
1 bamboo trunk (*petara*), ..	0	8	0
1 wooden stool, ..	0	12	0
6 low wooden stools for sitting on at meals, ..	2	4	0
1 instrument (*dhenki*) for beating rice, and a wooden mortar, ..	1	0	0
4 stools of ratans (*mora*), ..	1	0	0

2 wooden plates for making cakes,	..	0 1 0	
2 pair of wooden shoes,	..	0 6 0	
Total,	..		80 11 0
Total durable furniture, ...			98 12 0
Interest and repairs on the above, at 24 per cent,	..		23 11 2¼

FURNITURE of a less durable nature.

For the bed.

2 pair of curtains of cotton cloth,	..	6 0 0	
2 mattrasses filled with cotton,	..	6 0 0	
2 quilts,	..	8 0 0	
5 pillows stuffed with *simul* cotton,	..	2 8 0	
4 sheets,	..	3 0 0	
5 coverlets of fine sackcloth (*megili*),	..	1 8 0	
2 blankets from Bootan or Patna,	..	4 0 0	
Total,		31 0 0	

For the floor.

2 *sutrunjis*, or carpets made of cotton,	..	6 0 0	
1 *galicha*, or carpet of woollen with both sides alike,	..	3 0 0	
1 *dulicha* or woollen carpet with a rough nape on one side,	..	3 0 0	
These three are Muhammedan innovations.			
1 pair of large mats made of split reeds (*sop*), 10 cubits by 2,		2 8 0	
Total,	..	45 8 0	
Interest and repairs of the above at 36 per cent.	..	..	16 6 5½
Umbrellas,	..	..	0 12 0
Total furniture,	..	..	40 13 7¾

ORNAMENTS for the mistress of the family.

A gold ring for the nose (*noth*),	..	8 0 0	
A string of gold beads (*dana* and *mala*), for the neck,	..	32 0 0	
A pair of gold ear-rings called *gengtha*,	..	16 0 0	
A golden ornament for the forehead, called *tikili*,	..	1 0 0	
A golden ornament for hanging round the neck, called *mridonggo maduli*,	..	16 0 0	
Total,			73 0 0
Several silver rings for the arms, called *bayuti*,	..	40 0 0	
In place of this some wear a pair of silver bracelets, called *kanghon*,	..	20 0 0	
And a pair of shell bracelets,	..	5 0 0	
Silver ornament tied round the arm, and called *tar*,	..	20 0 0	
A pair of silver bracelets (*painchha*), made of beads,	..	8 0 0	
A pair of silver ornaments (*tabij*), tied round the arm,	..	6 0 0	
A silver ring (*loha*), for the left wrist,	..	4 0 0	
8 silver rings (*chutki* and *pasuli*), for the toes,	..	5 0 0	
Total,	..	..	108 0 0

For the master of the family.

2 gold rings for the fingers,	..	16 0 0	
1 or 2 gold ornaments (*maduli*), hung round the neck,	..	8 0 0	
			24 0 0

For the children.

2 gold ornaments (*madulis*) hung round the neck,	..	8 0 0	
4 gold ear-rings (*champa*),	..	24 0 0	
2 pair of silver rings or bracelets for the wrists,	..	16 0 0	
2 silver rings for the neck (*hansuli*),	..	10 0 0	
2 pair of silver rings for the ancles (*mol*),	..	24 0 0	
			76 0 0
Total ornaments,	..	..	281 0 0
Interest, and new fashioning at 24 per cent.		..	62 14 1

CLOTHING for the master of the family.						
2 pair of cotton wrappers for the loins (*dhuti*), 8 cubits by 2,	6	0	0			
4 (*phetas*) or turbans of white muslin, ..	4	0	0			
4 cotton sheets, 5 cubits by 3, which he wraps round his shoulders, and which are called *uranis*, ..	6	0	0			
4 *angrakha* and *taj*, or jackets and caps of cotton cloth, ..	4	0	0			
2 pair of slippers, ..	1	0	0			
6 common *dhutis* or wrappers, ..	3	0	0			
1 *jor* or pair, including wrapper and shoulder cloth, ..	1	8	0			
2 *dolayis* or double cotton cloth, 5 cubits by 3, ..	5	0	0			
2 *gelap* or sheets for cold weather, 10 cubits by 3, ..	3	0	0			
2 *gamchhas* or towels, ..	0	8	0			
Total, ..				34	0	0
For the male relation.						
4 *dhutis*, ..	2	0	0			
1 *jor*, ..	1	8	0			
1 *gelap*, ..	1	8	0			
Total, ..				5	0	0
For the mistress of the family.						
1 silk cloth, 10 cubits by 2, which is called *sari*, ..	6	0	0			
6 cotton *saris*, ..	8	0	0			
1 *gelap* or *chador*, for the cold weather, ..	1	8	0			
2 *gamchhas*, or towels, ..	0	8	0			
Total, ..				16	0	0
For the widow.						
5 coarse wrappers (*bhuni*) of cotton cloth, without red in borders, ..	4	0	0			
1 *gelap* or *chador*, ..	1	0	0			
Total, ..				5	0	0
For the children.						
2 pair of *jor*, ..	6	0	0			
6 *dhutis* of cotton, ..	3	0	0			
3 chintz coverings for the cold season (*dolayi*), ..	3	0	0			
Total, ...				12	0	0
Total clothing, ...				72	0	0
FOOD—8 people, 2 of them children, for one month.						
3 maunds of good rice, at 1 Rupee, ..	3	0	0			
1 maund of course ditto, ..	0	12	0			
20 seers pulse, commonly *thakuri* and *oror*, ..	0	8	0			
8 seers oil, mustard, ..	1	0	0			
1½ seers clarified butter, not of a good quality, ..	0	8	0			
8 seers salt, ..	1	0	0			
2 seers sugar, ..	0	6	0			
5 seers wheaten flour, ..	0	4	0			
Fish daily, ..	0	12	0			
Milk from 5 cows, ..	1	8	0			
Vegetables and pots, ..	1	0	0			
Black pepper and *musala* or seasoning, ..	0	8	0			
Chirra murki and *goor*, preparations of rice and sugar-cane, used without being cooked,	1	0	0			
Tobacco, ..	0	8	0			
Betel, ..	0	12	0			
Firewood, ..	1	2	0			
Total monthly, ..	14	8	0			
Total annually, ...				174	0	0

Servants' wages and clothing.

Man,	1	4	0			
Boy,	0	12	0			
Washerman,	0	8	0			
Barber,	0	4	0			
Sweeper,	0	4	0			
Watchman,	2	0	0			
Total monthly,	5	0	0			
Total annually,	60	0	0			
Expense of holidays, ceremonies, Guru, Purohit,	80	0	0			
Small expenses of various kinds, including stationery and the instruction of the children in reading and writing,	4	0	0			
Total,				144	0	0

III.—Estimate of the expense of a family in easy circumstances. It consists of one man, one woman, and two children, one dependant relation, one man servant; in all six persons.

LODGING.

1 hut for the master and mistress, with bamboo posts and beams, and mud walls, 14 cubits by 7,	20	0	0			
1 hut for kitchen, 8 cubits by 6,	10	0	0			
1 hut for cattle, 7 cubits by 5,	5	0	0			
1 hut for relation and servant,	10	0	0			
1 shop or one hut over the entrance, with the fence round the premises,	15	0	0			
	60	0	0			
Interest and insurance at 36 per cent.				21	9	7
Ground rent, 12 kathas, at 4 Rs. per bigah,				2	6	5
Total lodging,				24	0	0

FURNITURE for prayer.

1 copper cup (*kosha-kushi*),	1	8	0			
1 copper cup, called (*kundo*),	0	8	0			
1 copper plate (*tat*),	0	8	0			
1 stone for rubbing sandal,	0	3	0			
1 *kusason* or grass mat,	0	1	0			
Total furniture for prayer,				2	12	0

HOUSEHOLD FURNITURE of a durable nature.

1 brass pot (*kolos*),	4	0	0
1 brass pot (*lota*),	4	8	0
1 bell-metal pot (*apkhora*),	1	8	0
1 pair betel salvers (*panbata*),	2	0	0
1 betel-nut cutters,	0	4	0
2 brass plates (*thal*),	2	0	0
2 bell-metal plates (*thal*),	3	0	0
2 brass and bell-metal large cups (*bati*),	3	8	0
1 brass lamp-stand (*pilsoj*),	0	12	0
1 brass boiling pot (*bohuguna*),	1	8	0
1 iron ladle (*hata*) and a hook (*bayuli*), for removing pots from the fire,	0	8	0
1 iron pot for frying or boiling milk (*khuli*),	1	0	0
1 hoe (*kodal*),	0	12	0
1 hatchet (*kural*),	0	6	0

Item		Rs.	As.	P.	Rs.	As.	P.
1 bill for cleaving bamboos (*dah*,)	..	0	3	0			
1 sickle (*kastua*),	..	0	2	0			
1 kitchen knife (*boti*),	..	0	4	0			
1 iron rod for cleaning the *hooka*,	..	0	1	0			
1 knife,	..	0	3	0			
1 stake pointed with iron (*khonta*),	..	0	2	0			
3 stone plates and 3 stone cups,	..	3	0	0			
1 stone for rubbing curry-stuff,	..	0	8	0			
2 bedsteads,	..	2	8	0			
1 chest,	..	2	0	0			
4 low stools for meals (*piri*),	..	1	0	0			
2 wooden platters (*barkosh*). No pure Hindu can eat out of a wooden platter, although such are much cleanlier and better than the vessels of stone. These in use here are not turned, but dug out with chisels, and are used as washing-tubs, &c.		0	5	0			
1 instrument for beating rice (*dhenki*), and mortar,	..	1	0	0			
2 wooden instruments (*hooka*), for smoking tobacco,	..	0	4	0			
2 wooden lamp-stands,	..	0	1	0			
2 wooden cups for holding red-lead,	..	0	1	0			
Total of durable household furniture,	..			..	36	5	0
Total durable furniture,	..			..	39	1	0
Interest, and renewing the above at 24 per cent.	..			..	9	5	9

HOUSEHOLD FURNITURE of a more perishable nature.

For the bed.

Item		Rs.	As.	P.	Rs.	As.	P.
2 mattrasses,	..	4	0	0			
2 quilts,	..	5	0	0			
2 curtains,	..	3	0	0			
1 mat of leaves (*sitolpati*),	..	0	4	0			
4 pillows,	..	2	0	0			
4 coverlets of fine sackcloth (*megili*),	..	1	0	0			
					15	4	0

For the floor.

Item		Rs.	As.	P.	Rs.	As.	P.
2 mats of split reeds,	..	0	8	0			
1 blanket,	..	1	4	0			
1 carpet of cotton (*sutrunji*),	..	2	0	0			
1 mat of leaves (*sitolpati*),	..	0	4	0			
					3	8	0
The relation and servant sleep on these at night, covering themselves with the sackcloth.							
Total,	..				18	12	0
Interest on the above at 36 per cent.	..			..	6	9	6
Umbrellas,	..			..	0	8	0
Total,	..			..	24	13	6

ORNAMENTS for the mistress of the family.

Item		Rs.	As.	P.	Rs.	As.	P.
1 pair of shell ornaments for the wrist,	..	4	0	0			
1 pair silver bracelets (*painchha*),	..	6	0	0			
1 silver ring for the wrist (*loha*),	..	3	0	0			
1 silver ring for the neck (*hansuli*),	..	5	0	0			
1 silver *maduli* hung round the neck,	..	2	0	0			
1 pair silver rings (*gengtha*),	..	2	0	0			
6 silver rings for the toes (*pasuli*),	..	3	0	0			
1 gold ring for the nose (*noth*),	..	4	0	0			
Necklace of red stone or glass beads (*pot jampola*),	..	0	3	0			
1 comb, 1 glass, and some boxes for red lead (*sindur chupri*),	..	0	3	0			
Total,	..			..	29	6	0

For two children.			
2 pair silver rings for the arm (*bala*),		.. 12 0 0	
2 silver rings for the neck (*hansuli*),		.. 8 0 0	
2 silver ornaments for the neck (*maduli*),		.. 4 0 0	
Total,		..	24 0 0
Total ornaments,		..	.. 53 6 0
Interest on the above a 24 per cent.		..	.. 12 12 11¾
CLOTHES for the mistress.			
1 *sari* or wrapper of silk, 10 cubits by 2,		.. 4 0 0	
6 *saris* of cotton with red borders,		.. 5 0 0	
1 *gelap* or sheets for cold weather, 10 cubits by 3,		.. 1 0 0	
2 towels for bathing (*gamchha*),		.. 0 8 0	
Total,		..	.. 10 8 0
For the master.			
2 fine wrappers (*dhutis*) for ceremony,		.. 2 8 0	
2 *uronis* or shoulder cloths for ceremony,		.. 2 0 0	
2 turbans,		.. 1 8 0	
6 common *dhutis* for wrappers,		.. 3 0 0	
1 *jor* or pair, including wrapper and shoulder cloth,		.. 1 0 0	
2 *gelaps* or sheets for cold weather,		.. 3 0 0	
2 towels,		.. 0 8 0	
Total,		..	.. 13 8 0
For children.			
2 silk *jor* or pair of wrappers for shoulders and loins,		.. 4 0 0	
1 cotton *jor*,		.. 2 8 0	
2 chintz or white *dolayi* or quilted wrappers,		.. 2 0 0	
Total,		..	.. 8 8 0
For the relation.			
4 *dhutis*,		.. 3 0 0	
1 *uroni*,		.. 0 12 0	
1 *gelap*,		.. 1 4 0	
Total,		..	.. 5 0 0
Total clothing,		..	.. 37 8 0
FOOD.			
Rice, common, 2½ maunds a month, at 1 R.		.. 2 8 0	
Pulse (*thakuri* and *khesari*), 15 seers,		.. 0 7 0	
Oil of mustard seed, 6 seers,		.. 0 12 0	
Salt, 4 seers,		.. 0 8 0	
Fish occasionally,		.. 0 12 0	
Clarified butter, 1 seer,		.. 0 5 0	
Vegetable and seasoning,		.. 1 4 0	
Milk and its preparations; interest on the prime cost of 4 cows, (16 Rs.) at 1 per cent.	.. 0 2 6¾		
Food for ditto,	.. 1 0 0		
		1 2 6¾	
Sugar, sweetmeats, and prepared rice,		.. 1 0 0	
Betel and tobacco,		.. 1 0 0	
Fuel and potter's ware,		.. 1 0 0	
Part of the fuel used in cow-dung collected by the women.			
Total per month,		..	.. 10 10 6¾
Total for year,		..	.. 127 14 9
Baskets,		..	.. 0 4 0
Total,		..	.. 128 2 9

Servants' wages.

Domestics' wages and clothing, at 12 ans. per mensem,	..	9 0 0				
Barber,	..	1 8 0				
Washerman,	..	3 0 0				
Sweeper,	..	1 8 0				
Total,	..		..	15 0 0		
Holidays, ceremonies, Guru and Purohit,			..	48 0 0		
Total,	..		..	63 0 0		

IV.—Estimate of the expense of the family of an artist in easy circumstances, consisting of a man and wife, two children and one widow, or dependent relation.

HOUSE RENT.

1 hut, 10 cubits by 6, walls of hurdles,	..	10 0 0		
1 hut for cooking, 6 cubits by 5,	..	4 0 0		
1 hut for the cow,	..	4 0 0		
1 small hut for the widow or strangers, and a fence made of reeds,	..	6 0 0		
Total,	..	24 0 0		
Interest, 36 per cent.			..	8 10 3
Ground rent, 10 kathas at 2 Rs. a bigah, being in the suburbs,			..	1 0 0
Total lodging,	..		..	9 10 0

FURNITURE—Durable.

2 brass water pots (*lota*),	..	2 0 0		
1 brass water pot (*apkhora*),	..	1 0 0		
1 brass or bell-metal plate (*thal*),	..	3 0 0		
1 wooden mortar for beating rice,	..	0 4 0		
2 stone plates and 2 cups,	..	0 12 0		
1 stone for rubbing curry-stuff,	..	0 8 0		
2 wooden stools for eating (*piri*),	..	0 2 0		
2 brass cups (*bati*),	..	1 0 0		
1 instrument for smoking tobacco (*hooka*),	..	0 1 0		
Total,	..	8 11 0		
Interest and repairs, at 24 per cent.	..		..	2 1 3¼

More perishable furniture.

2 coarse coverlets of sackcloth (*chati*),	..	0 4 0		
1 finer *megili*,	..	0 4 0		
3 coarse mats of reeds (*patpati*) for sleeping,	..	0 3 0		
2 quilts made of old clothes,	..	1 0 0		
2 quilts made of new cloth,	..	2 0 0		
2 curtains,	..	2 0 0		
2 pillows,	..	0 8 0		
2 Mattrasses made of old clothes, quilted together, made by the people themselves. They sleep on these, usually placing them on straw or on a stage made of split bamboos.				
Total perishable furniture,	..	6 3 0		
Interest and repair, 50 per cent.	..		..	3 1 6
Total furniture,	..		..	5 2 9¼

ORNAMENTS for women.

1 pair shell bracelets, ..	2 0 0	
1 pair bell-metal bracelets (*painchha*), ..	0 8 0	
2 silver ornaments for the neck (*maduli*), ..	0 8 0	
1 string of beads (*jampola*), ..	0 2 0	
1 pair of silver ear-rings (*chaki*), ..	0 8 0	
1 pair of another kind (*gengtha*), ..	1 0 0	
1 silver ring for the nose, ..	1 0 0	
1 comb, glass, and red-lead, ..	0 2 0	
Total, ..	..	5 12 0

For the children.

2 pair silver rings for the wrists, ..	4 0 0	
2 silver ornaments for the neck (*maduli*), hung by a string of beads (*jampola*), ..	1 4 0	
For the man, a string of *tulosi*, or wooden beads, ..	0 1 0	
Total,	..	5 5 0
Total ornaments,	..	11 1 0
Interest and repairs, at 24 per cent.	..	2 10 $4\frac{7}{8}$

CLOTHING for the wife.

1 fine red-bordered cotton wrapper (*sari*), ..	1 8 0	
4 coarse ditto, ..	2 8 0	
In cold weather they wrap an old *sari* round them.		
Total, ..	..	4 0 0

For the man.

1 fine loin-wrapper (*dhuti*), ..	1 0 0	
1 turban, ..	0 12 0	
1 *gelap* or sheet for his shoulders, ..	1 4 0	
6 loin wrappers (*dhutis*), coarse, ..	2 0 0	
2 towels (*gamchhas*,) ..	0 4 0	
Total, ..	..	5 4 0

For the children.

2 red-bordered *jor* or cloths, which wrap round both loins and shoulders, ..	2 0 0	
3 loin wrappers (*dhutis*), ..	2 0 0	
2 old chintz quilts not stuffed (*dolayi*), ..	1 8 0	
Total, ..	..	5 8 0

For the widow.

Four plain wrappers, (*bhuni*), ..	..	3 0 0
Total clothing, ..	..	17 12 0

FOOD.

2 maunds coarse rice, at 14 ans. ..	1 12 0	
10 seers pulse (*khesari* or *mosur*), ..	0 3 0	
4 seers salt, ..	0 7 0	
5 seers oil, ..	0 8 0	
Fish, vegetables, and seasoning, ..	1 0 0	
Tobacco and betel, ..	0 8 0	
Sugar and rice prepared for eating, without being dressed,..	0 6 0	
Firewood, pots, and baskets, ..	0 12 0	
Total monthly, ..	..	5 8 0
Annually, ..	..	66 0 0

They keep a cow, but very seldom use any of the milk except for a young child on particular occasions. The cow is therefore a source of revenue.

SERVANT, &c.

Barber, ..	0 12 0	
Ceremonies, Guru, &c. ..	15 0 0	
Total, ..		15 12 0

V.—Estimate of the annual expense of the family of a poor artist, consisting of one man, one woman, and two children.

Item	Rs. a. p.	Rs. a. p.
HOUSE.		
1 hut, for sleeping, 7 cubits by 5, ..	3 0 0	
1 hut, one end for the cow, another for cooking, ..	2 0 0	
Total, ..	5 0 0	
Interest at 36 per cent. ..		1 12 9⅗
Ground rent of 5 kathas, ..		0 8 0
Total lodging, ...		2 4 9⅗
FURNITURE, durable.		
1 brass water-pot (*lota*), ..	1 0 0	
1 bell-metal plate (*thal*), ..	0 12 0	
1 kitchen knife (*bothi*), ..	0 3 0	
1 stone plate, ..	0 4 0	
1 stone for rubbing curry, ..	0 2 0	
1 sickle, ..	0 1 0	
1 hatchet (*kural*), ..	0 4 0	
1 instrument for smoking tobacco, ..	0 1 0	
Total, ..	2 11 0	
Interest at 24 per cent.		0 10 3⅘
PERISHABLE FURNITURE, renewed yearly.		
3 pieces sackcloth for bedding (*choti*), ..	0 6 0	
3 rugs made by themselves of old clothes,		
4 bamboo mats (*chatayis*), ..	0 2 0	
2 pillows of sackcloth, stuffed with grass, ..	0 1 0	
Total, ...		0 9 0
Total, ...		1 3 3⅘
ORNAMENTS for the women.		
8 brass rings for the wrists (*kharu*), ..	0 8 0	
1 fine brass ring for the nose, ..	0 1 0	
2 brass ear-rings, ..	0 1 0	
2 brass ornaments suspended from a necklace of wooden beads (*patimala*), ..	0 1 0	
Total, ...		0 11 0
For the man.		
A necklace of *tulosi* or wooden beads, ...		0 1 0
For the children.		
4 brass rings for the wrists, ..	0 4 0	
2 strings of beads (*jampola*), and brass *madulis*, ..	0 3 0	
Total, ...		0 7 0
Total, ...		1 3 0
Interest and repair, 24 per cent.		0 4 6¾
CLOTHING for the women.		
1 red bordered cotton wrapper, 10 cubits by 2, ..	0 12 0	
4 coarse white wrappers, 4 cubits by 2, for common use, ..	0 12 0	
A rug made of old clothes, stitched together for cold weather.		
Total, ...		1 8 0
For the man.		
1 loin wrapper (*dhuti*), ..	0 8 0	
4 *kappins*, clouts to hide their nakedness, ..	0 2 0	
1 sheet for cold weather, ..	0 4 0	
Total, ...		0 14 0

For the children.

4 *kappins*—these are made of old clothes, but are seldom used.		
3 *gelaps* for cold weather, ..		1 0 0
Total clothing, ...		3 6 0

FOOD.

1½ maunds of rice, at 14 as. ..	1 5 0	
12 seers of pulse (*khesari* or *mosur*), ..	0 4 0	
2 seers oil, ..	0 4 0	
2 seers salt, ..	0 4 0	
Seasoning and tobacco, ..	0 3 0	
Prepared rice, sugar, &c. ..	0 3 0	
Fuel they collect themselves.		
1 pot and basket, ..	0 1 0	
Total monthly, ..	2 8 0	
Total annually, ...		30 0 0
Barber once a month, ...		0 8 0
Ceremonies, Guru, &c. (The sacrifices are the only animal food they procure, except what fish they can catch in ditches.)		6 0 0
Total, ...		36 8 0

VI.—Estimate of the expense of a common labourer, his family, consisting of his wife and two children. If there are more children, as is often the case, the elder ones are supported by tending cattle.

HOUSE AND LODGING.

One hut, 8 cubits by 6—the man purchases bambus and cuts the roots of coarse rice straw for thatch and hurdles, which he puts on at leisure hours, ..	0 9 0	
One-third of annual expense, ...		0 3 0
Ground rent, ...		0 4 0
Total, ...		0 7 0

FURNITURE, durable.

2 stone plates, ..	0 4 0	
1 *dashtya* or sickle, ..	0 2 0	
1 *ka* or bill, ..	0 2 0	
Earthen or bambu pots for drinking water, ..	0 0 6	
1 *hooka* for smoking tobacco, ..	0 0 6	
Total, ..	0 9 0	
To one-third for annual charge, ..		0 3 0

Perishable, renewed yearly.

3 pieces of gunny or sackcloth for bedding, ..	0 6 0	
3 rags made by themselves of their old clothes. ..		
Mats and straw pillows for sleeping on, ..	0 1 0	
		0 7 0
Total, ...		0 10 0

ORNAMENTS.

Brass rings for the arms of the woman, ..	0 2 0	
1 ditto for the nose, 2 for the ears of ditto, ..	0 1 0	
1 string of wooden or stone beads for the man, ..	0 1 0	
2 string of stone beads for the children, ..	0 1 0	
..	0 5 0	
One-third of annual expense, ...		0 1 8

Clothing.

For the woman.

1 large red-bordered cotton wrapper (*sari*),	..	0	8	0			
3 small wrappers,	..	0	8	0			
					1	0	0

For the man.

1 cotton cloth wrapper (*dhuti*),	..	0	5	0			
2 *kappin*,	..	0	1	0			
1 sheet for his shoulders in cold weather,	..	0	4	0			
					0	10	0

For children.

4 waist cloth (*kappin*), and 2 sheets,	..			..	0	12	0
					2	6	0

Food.

1½ seer of 96 Sa. wt. of coarse rice daily is 13mds. 27½ seers a year, at 12 annas,	..	10	4	3			
1 seer oil a month at 2 annas,	..	1	8	0			
6 seers a month of pulse (*khesari*) or lentils, at 2 annas,	..	1	8	0			
1 seer salt 2 annas (many however use ashes),	..	1	8	0			
Pots, baskets, seasoning,	..	0	6	0			
They use no fuel, fish, nor vegetables, but what they collect.							
Tobacco and betle,	..	1	8	0			
	..	16	10	3			
Holidays, Guru, Purohit, and other religious expenses,	..	2	0	0			
Barber once a month,	..	0	8	0			
Total,	..				20	10	11

BOOK III.

NATURAL PRODUCTIONS.

CHAPTER I.

ANIMALS.

With the exception of fish, the animals that are found in this district, are of little importance.

I observed only one kind of monkey, which has a tail that reaches below the knee, but not to the heel, and is called *Morkot* by the natives. Its hands are black, and the calosities on the buttocks are brown. When old, the face and buttocks become red. It seems to be the *Simia Rhesus* of Andibert, and the Macaque *à queue courte* of Buffon. The younger animal, the face of which is not red, seems to be the *Patas à queue courte* of this great naturalist. In the district of Dinajpúr monkies are neither numerous nor very troublesome. Those that I saw, were in the woods near Peruya; but I was told, that the greatest number is to be found near Nawabgunj. They assemble there on the banks of the Korotoya, and collect the fruit of Singgur (*Trappà*). According to the natives, after having procured a quantity, the monkeys divide the spoil, and bathe; and then each eats his share. This is probably an idle story, such as are usually current concerning the manners of different animals.

The wild elephant and rhinoceros can scarcely be said to be known. Two wild elephants certainly made their appearance in the forests of Peruya in the year 1806, and remained there a rainy season. They were seen by many, and are said to have killed some people, who straggled near them. It was supposed, that they were accompanied by a rhinoceros, for what reason I cannot say; as this animal, so far as I could learn, was not seen, and does not usually frequent such company. The elephants had probably wandered from Morong. A thousand idle stories were immediately circulated. It was said, that they were actually elephants which had belonged to Bhim Raja, the son of Pandu, who lived about 5,000 years ago. Two elephants to a multitude of people, who chose to assemble and attack them, are not at all formidable: and these invaders ought to have fallen an easy prey, had the people been led to the attack; but no officer of police nor landholder took any pains, and what is every one's business is commonly neglected. They were allowed to ravage at pleasure, and occasioned great dismay, so that several villages were deserted. The only step taken was a grand sacrifice, to which even the Moslems contributed. Twenty or thirty brahmins received a sum of money, and performed a grand ceremony, which was effectual, as the dry season approached.

The jackal and Indian fox (*Canis Bengalensis*, Pennant,) are very common, but harmless. I heard of no wolves nor hyænas.

Tigers and leopards are not numerous; as they therefore have an abundant supply of food, from the cattle which feed in the woods, they very seldom attack men. Although they frequent the neighbouring forests, and even the streets of Ghoraghat, the people walk alone through both, even at night; and I heard of only one person in the whole district, who had been killed in the course of the year. It was in this district, that a white animal of this kind was killed some years ago, the skin of which having been sent to Europe by Lord Wellesley, occasioned a dispute, whether it was that of a lion or tiger. No such animal has been seen before nor since. Mr. Tucker, an Indigo Planter of this district, declares, that in a wood near Lalbazar, he saw an animal resembling a tiger in size and colour, but it had a mane like a lion. I offered a considerable reward for it, dead or alive, but without success; this however is no proof of its not existing, as I found the people totally unwilling to bring even fish, plants, or any other natural production. At Ghoraghat I heard of a small spotted animal of the cat kind, called Nakéswori, which is said to be common in the neighbouring woods, where it lives on trees. No offer of reward could induce the people to bring one. This perhaps may be the *Cerval*, an animal which I have never seen. I have not been able to learn that any where in India there is such an animal as the panther.

The Indian ichneumon is very common, but is seldom tamed. Otters are so numerous, that their fur might become an object of commerce; but there is no person here who understands the method of taking them: so far as I can learn, it is practised by the people of Dhaka alone. Bears (*Ursus labiosus*, B.) are not numerous nor destructive, and are found chiefly in the ruins of Peruya.

Where the soil is loose and sandy, the common porcupine is abundant, and even destructive; as it prevents the cultivation of turmeric and ginger. It may be eaten by Hindus of all ranks; and some that I had caught were disputed for with great eagerness by the people: yet these animals are seldom molested.

Rats and mice are by no means so troublesome as in Europe.

Hares are very numerous, and easily caught: yet although they are considered as pure food, they are seldom molested. When a man wishes to give a feast, he sends out some people with poles, who surround the long grass, and knock down as many as are required.

There are many deer in the vicinity of the Mohanunda, and of the lower parts of the Punabhoba and Tanggone; but scarcely any where else. They are so numerous among the long reeds and woods of these parts, that they are a nuisance by destroying the crops. I saw no kinds except the axis and porcine deer, and in this class of animals, the natives apply specific names so indefinitely, that I cannot follow them as guides. There are no hunters who make a profession of killing these deer, and of carrying the venison to market, although no one would hinder them. The neighbouring farmers keep nets, and occasionally hunt, partly to save their crops, and partly to procure animal food. I went twice with them, and on one occasion took two deer, and on the other had no sport. I was a good deal surprised at the method. The net is made of whip-cord, and may be about 6 feet wide, and each farmer brings a piece with him of 30 or 40 feet in length. All the pieces having been joined, they are set in a straight line, and are supported on one edge by poles, which incline towards the direction from whence the game is expected to come, and lean on forked sticks. Some persons then remain behind the poles with lances, to kill or seize the game, which comes into the net before it can disentangle itself. The others advance from the net in a line parallel to it, and beat the grass and bushes, and make a great noise. I expected, when they had set the net, that they would have gone in silence to a distance, and have roused the game as they advanced towards the net; but this they assured me, would not answer: for the game always runs backwards in the direction from whence the noise advanced upon it. The game taken in these nets consists of wild hogs, deer, and tigers.

I saw no antelopes, but there may be some; as by the natives they are confounded with deer.

The wild buffalo, exactly of the same kind with the tame, is very common, and exceedingly destructive; nor has any considerable exertion been ever made to free the people from this evil. The animal is too formidable for individual effort to produce any good, and the property of the landholders is so much intermixed, that the endeavours of any one of them would have little effect, provided his neighbours contributed nothing. Many indeed are said to levy money from their tenants, under pretence of hiring armed men to kill these animals, but very few hunters are employed. I inquired every where after such people, but could find none except in two or three places, some of whom were employed by the judge. Unless the destruction of these animals becomes an object of police, and unless the expenditure of the money raised, be carefully checked, no hope of success can be entertained. I have indeed great doubt how far any exertion will be entirely sufficient, unless the woods and reeds which give them shelter are removed. The wild buffalos usually go in small herds, and may be easily killed by means of musket or poisoned arrows. These are the only effectual means for destroying the breed altogether; but others are employed for procuring the animals; for the flesh is eaten both by the Múhammedans, and by the lowest tribes of Hindús. They are sometimes caught in pitfals, or by a noose suspended between two trees; but they are a shy, sagacious animal, not easily deceived. The natives near the lake at Bamongola, when they find a herd swiming, attack it with boats or canoes, and having seized on the hindmost buffalo by the tail despatch him with a large knife. In the same vicinity the keepers of tame herds are said to be sometimes able to secure wild males, by means of trained females, which surround the male until a keeper comes up, passes a rope through the septum of his nose, and then the females push him towards a tree, where he is fastened until tame. The bulls thus caught are reckoned more valuable than such as have been born in the domestic state; but I believe, the practice is very uncommon: I heard of it only at Bamongola.

The wild hog is by far the most destructive animal in the district, although never of a size to be formidable to the villagers, if armed with pikes. Near many woods they are almost innumerable, and in some places seem to be gaining ground. All that I have said concerning the destruction of the buffalo is applicable to that of these animals: and it seems an object worthy of the most serious attention from the police; circumstances should direct whether it would be most advantageous to make a general hunt, or to levy a contribution with which regular hunters may be hired. I should in general prefer the former, because at convenient seasons all persons may turn out, for a day or two, without inconvenience; and because it can never be the interest of the regular hunters to extirpate the animals. The wild hog is often hunted by the low Hindús for food. He is sometimes caught in nets like deer; at other times he is pursued with common curs of the country, which run round him barking, and thus keep him at bay, until their masters come up, and dispatch him with arrows or spears.

Porpoises are pretty numerous in the large rivers, but are not applied to any use.

No birds are caught for being trained to sport. At present indeed it may be said, that the natives have no turn for any of the amusements of the field. A late Raja spent vast sums upon it, but almost all the people, whom he employed, have disappeared.

There are no paroquets nor birds that are commonly caught to be tamed; and except about Maldeh and other places of much trade, few tame birds of this kind are kept, which must be considered as a comfort to those who have been annoyed, at day-break, by fellows bawling to a miserable paroquet, what they call the name of God, as is very common in Bengal.

Although the country swarms with water-fowl, both web-footed and waders, the natives derive from thence little or no resource for their tables. The common wild goose (*anas anser*) is exceedingly abundant in the cold season, and remarkably good, but is never used; and there is a great variety of ducks and teals, with abundance of snipes, that are equally neglected. When a very extravagant man, at Dinajpúr, wishes to give a feast, he hires some people to catch birds with a rod and bird-lime. Those that are preferred are three birds of the cormorant or shag kind, called by the natives *panikauri;* several small herons included by the natives under the general name of *vok;* several birds of the Jacana and Gallinule kinds, included under the native term *jolpipayi*, but above all the common house sparrow. This indeed being considered as possessed of aphrodisiac qualities, is in request at all times.

The peacock is very common in the woods, and in many places so numerous, as to be destructive to the crops; but on the whole, the people of this district have little to complain of the feathered tribes, and neglect the luxuries of that kind, which nature has poured forth in abundance.

Several kinds of tortoise are more eagerly sought after, but to European taste they are execrable. Frogs are not eaten by any of the natives, but some lizards are used in food, especially one of which I have sent a description to the India House, and which is called the *Swarne Soohika*. The crocodile is common both in rivers and tanks, but few accidents happen from his violence.

At the season when I visited the district, serpents had retired into holes in the earth, and were very rarely seen; but in the beginning of the rainy season they are driven from their lurking places, and fly for refuge into the huts and higher places near villages. At that time accidents are common, and a good many perish every year from the bite of these vile reptiles. They are supposed to be under the immediate direction of the goddess Bishohori. In the dangerous time many sacrifices are offered to her images, and people are employed to sing her praises to music. Many persons are supposed to know spells (*montros*), that will cure the bites of serpents; and I was gravely assured, by both Moslems and Hindús of the highest rank, that they had known these forms of prayer tried with perfect success. Dumdumah is one of the places most infested with serpents, especially with the different kinds whose necks swell, and have what is called a hood; and all of which are exceedingly venomous. There are a few of the people called Byadhs who catch snakes, which they tame, and who are supposed to be possessed of a charm, which prevents them from being bitten. This charm, I know, consists in a blunt rusty knife, with which they scrape out the animal's teeth; the fellows however possess great intrepidity in seizing these formidable reptiles, and great impudence and dexterity in deceiving the people.

Fish forming by far the greater part of the animal food consumed in the country, the fisheries deserve particular notice. The demand being very considerable, and the supply being rather scanty, there is none exported, and salt is too expensive to admit of its being used in curing fish. The whole fish caught are therefore consumed in the country, and none are imported. During four months of the year, when the rivers are much swollen, fish is very scarce; for the animals have then such an extensive range, that they are not easily caught; but as the inundation subsides, and when the fish are confined within narrow bounds, they are easily secured by various simple means which the natives employ: and a very large portion of those taken are secured, when they may be said to be almost left sticking in the mud, or by means, that in most countries would be quite ineffectual.

The most simple method, when a pond, ditch, or marsh has become nearly dry, and the fish of a large space have been collected into a small pool, is to divide it by dams of mud, and then, having thrown the water from each successively, to catch the fish as they are left dry. This is usually practised by all the poor labourers, especially in the ditches and pools near the rice-fields, which are not let to fishermen by the land-holders.

It must be observed, that in about six weeks after the rainy season commences, every rice-field, although quite dry and hard in spring, abounds with small fishes. They are certainly most numerous near rivers and marshes, from which they in general come; but I am inclined to think, as I observed in Mysore, that the eggs often continue dry in the field, and are hatched after they have been moistened by the rain. The natives account for their appearance in such places by supposing, that they fall from heaven with the rain. The clerk (*mohurrer*) of the division of Rajarampúr assured me, that he had often seen them leaping among the grass, as the shower fell. In fact, a person, who is well disposed, can see any thing: like a very good Danish naturalist, who imagined, that he saw a fish gravely walking up a tree, for he had been assured by the natives, that such was its common practice.

Where the water is deeper, and communicates with the large extent of low land, this method is improved by inclosing a square piece of shallow water, perhaps 15 feet in diameter, with a mound of earth, and leaving an opening of about three feet wide in the side next the deepest water. The space within the dam is then filled with branches of trees, which attract the fish. After the branches have remained for some days, the opening is shut with a dam, the branches and water are thrown out, and the fish are secured. This also is chiefly practised by those who are not regular fishermen; but when this plan is farther improved, it becomes one of the most effectual means of procuring fish, that are employed in this district.

In the old courses of rivers, called *bil*, or in the courses of such as have little current, a large quantity of branches and twigs of trees are tied together, and thrown into the water, so as to occupy a space of 20 or 30 feet square, from the bottom to the surface. After they have remained for from 10 to 30 days, and the fish have entered into all parts, the branches are surrounded by a kind of screen called *byana*, which is made of reeds (*ikiri*) tied parallel to each other, by means of twisted grass (*kese*), and placed so close that the smallest fish cannot escape. These screens are about four feet wide, and of length sufficient to surround the whole heap of bushes. When this has been done, the bushes are thrown out, and the fish are secured by small bag-nets (*chakoni*), the mouths of which are fastened to hoops.

The *byana* or screen is sometimes used, without having previously thrown in branches of trees. This is done in shallow water, where there are many weeds. A space is surrounded by the *byana*, and all the fishermen go in with bag-nets, and secure the fish.

This kind of fishing requires about seven men, who usually have 2 heaps of branches in the water, for nine months in the year, or from about the middle of October, until the middle of July, when the country becomes too much inundated. They draw one of these *byanas* once a week, and in the intervals of this labor surround spaces, as above-mentioned, where no branches have been placed.

These same fishermen employ a kind of traps called *onta*, which are made in form of a truncated cone, four feet high, and from 18 to 24 inches wide at the bottom. These traps are made of reeds in the same manner with the screen, and the edges are not fastened together, but are bent in towards the cavity, so as gradually to approach each other. The fish can readily force their way into the cavity, but their efforts to come out are vain. The fish are directed to the opening by a screen placed on each of its sides, and according to the situation of the fishery, these are disposed in two manners; the one is used during the dry season in shallow water-courses that are stagnant, or contain but little stream; and in such situations the screen extends the whole way across, and has traps at the distance of every 20 or 30 feet. In the one, at Akhanogor, from which the drawing No. 13 was made, and which was about 300 feet wide, a net was suspended over the screen, in order to prevent the fish from leaping over; for some of the carp kind, leap with an agility equal almost to that of the salmon. This apparatus, called a *band*, procures a great many small fish, and is usually rented for a certain sum.

The other situation chosen for this manner of fishing is much more common, as during the rainy reason it is the only way in which these fisherman can procure employment. The screen is placed on the shelving side of a river, with one end to the shore, and the other as far into the water as possible; but it cannot be placed, where there is a greater depth of water than four feet. Such a screen admits of one or two traps, according as the water deepens more or less suddenly; and one man manages two screens. The fish caught in this manner are much smaller than by the other method; but the quantity makes up for this defect. These fishings with the *byana* and *onta* are very productive, especially in the southern and western parts of the district, and require no boats.

Still more simple traps are used. One called *polo* and *trapa* (drawing No. 14) is a basket with a hole in the bottom. In shallow water the fisher puts the mouth on the mud, and then, passing his arm through the hole in the bottom, gropes for the fish which he may have secured. Another called *jakoyi* is a basket of an irregular three-sided form, open at one end, and has a bamboo shaft; see drawing No. 15. The fisher places the bottom flat on the mud, treads among the weeds before the opening, thus drives the fish into the trap, and then suddenly raising the handle, brings the opening above the surface. These two methods can only be practised in very muddy places covered with aquatic plants, and are commonly employed by labourers of the lowest rank to catch fish for their own use.

The most simple net in this country is the *besal* (drawing No. 16), which is stretched between two bambus, that meet behind at an acute angle, (about 75°;) by which the fisherman holds. The net is of a triangular form, so as to apply to the bambus, but is much bagged behind.—The fisherman, walking up to the middle in the water, pushes the points of the bambus along the bottom for a little way, and then raises them up to secure whatever fish may have come into his net. The bambus are from 12 to 15 feet in length.

The same form of net is inlarged, so as to have bambus 19 cubits long, and is then used in a boat. A rower at each end manages the canoe, which is kept broadside on to the stream, and allowed to descend with it; and a third man lowers the points of the bambus, which are fixed at right angles to the gunwale, and then occasionally raises them to secure the fish. This is one of the most common nets used by fishermen—its mesh is small. The boat is 16 or 17 cubits long, 2¼ wide, sharp at each end, and broadest abaft the middle. At the widest part of the boat two forked sticks project between three and four feet outwards and upwards from the gunwale, and a stick lashed between the forks serves as a lever, over which the bambus of the net are raised and lowered. On the gunwale opposite to the net is a small outrigger, which serves as a balance.—This kind of fishing may be carried on at all times, but the rainy season is the most favourable. Most of the fish caught in this manner are of the crustaceous kind. On the Mohanonda, a boat built of *sal* will cost 20 rupees, and will last 15 years; but it requires considerable repairs. The net is usually made of *son*, but sometimes of cotton, and were it sold, is worth 10 rupees; but the fishermen usually make it themselves, and it costs only the materials.

The same kind of net is still more enlarged, and is raised by a complicated machinery of bambus; see drawing No. 17. It is called a *chauri* or *khora*, and is fixed on the steep side of some river. A frame of four strong bambus (*a b*, *c d*, *e f*, *g h*), supports the net (*i k*, *l m*), placed with its descending edge (*l m*) towards the mouth of the river; and also supports two sloping bambus (*n o*, *p q*), on which a man walks, who has one end of a long rope (*r s*) round his middle. The other end passes over a bambu, for they have no pulley, and raises the net when the man walks down, and lowers it into the water when he walks up the sloping bambus. The moving power is increased by a lever of bambu (*t u*), the heel of which (*t*) rests on the bank, while the rope from the man's waist is fastened to the other end, and that again is connected with the bambus of the net. This is the most complicated machine that I have seen the natives employ, and seems to me very ill contrived. I regret that my draftsman's want of skill in perspective, will render the drawing scarcely intelligible. The net is quadrangular. Two corners (beyond *l m*) are stretched to the bambus; one of the other two corners (*i*) is fixed to the bambu lever, while the other (*k*) is fixed to the end of a bambu, that projects over the river, which is fastened to where the lever and the two lateral bambus (*r m*, *r l*) join, and which is suspended by a rope (*w x*) from the frame, so that this corner should always be high.—Ropes (*y z*) also pass from the bank to the two lateral bambus, which prevent them from yielding to the stream, while a small bambu (1, 2,) from one of the lateral ones, stretches out the lower edge of the net. Two men are employed at this net; one below, who is generally the proprietor, and who takes out the fish; the other walks backward and forward on the inclined bambus, and is usually hired, getting $\frac{1}{3}$ of the fish. These are generally small, and most are caught from about the middle of September until the middle of November, when the rivers are falling.

Another kind of net, somewhat of a similar nature, would appear to be better fitted for such a large machine. It is called *chak* or *jhati*, and is of a square form, a good deal bagged in the centre; see drawing No. 18. Its angles are fastened to the ends of two bambu bars that cross each other at right angles in the centre, which is suspended from the end of a bambu lever, the other end of which rests against the bank where the fisher sits. He lowers and raises his net by means of a rope that is fastened to the far-end of the lever. A large net of this kind, raised and lowered by a man on an inclined plane, with the assistance of a pulley, might be a good contrivance in muddy water. The *chak* is used chiefly by poor farmers and labourers.

The casting net is very much used. One from 9 to 11 cubits in diameter, and called *bhomore* and *khyepla* and *khyepujal*, is commonly thrown from the shoulder, either from the shore or from a boat. The mesh is small, and the sinkers are often merely earthen rings baked by the potters; but iron rings are also used for the purpose. If made of cotton, the net will last seven years; if of *son*, it will last only four, and will cost from 8 to 10 Rupees. If the net is thrown from a boat, two men are required to this fishery; one to throw the net, and another to manage the boat. This latter and the boat are usually hired by the man who fishes with the net, and who allows the boatman $\frac{4}{16}$ of the fish that are caught. The boat is only 13 or 14 cubits long, and 2½ broad, and costs on the Mohanonda about 14 rupees. Small fish, especially of the crustaceous kind, are chiefly caught in this manner, which is only used in the dry season.

A much larger kind, 38 cubits in diameter, and called *othar*, is frequently employed, and is thrown by means of a long narrow boat, which must be rather longer than the diameter of the net. This is gathered carefully into the boat, one edge being taken in first, and then one fold is placed above another. The boat is rowed into the stream, and by a rower at each end, is placed broad-side on. Two other men then throw over first one edge of the net, and, as the boat drives, they throw gradually the remainder. The whole sinks to the bottom, and the boat is allowed to drive, until the edges of the net have been dragged close to each other, when the net is drawn to the shore. Very large fish are caught in this manner.

The natives use the sein of several sizes, and different names.

The *pahiljal* of Ghoraghat is a sein composed of several pieces, about 11 cubits wide by 12 cubits long, which belong to different fishermen, six or seven of whom unite their stocks, and join their different pieces into one net. The centre pieces are the widest, the mesh is small, the floats are gourds, and the weights are rings of potter's ware. It is thrown out in the usual manner from the stern of a boat, and requires six or eight men to draw it. The fish are divided equally, the owner of the boat taking ½ share more than the others.

At Potnitola, on the Atreyi, the large sein is called *bed*, and is made in one piece 60 fathoms long and 10 or 11 cubits wide in the centre. It is floated by the spongy stems of the sola (Æschynomene diffusa, W.), and sunk partly by iron rings, and partly by those made of baked clay. The twine made of *son* would cost 10 rupees: but the plant is usually reared by the men, and spun by the women in intervals of labour, so that no estimate can be formed of its value. The boat is made of mangoe wood, costs about three rupees, but lasts only two years. Six men are required; the proprietor of the net and boat takes $\frac{6}{16}$ of the fish, the remainder is divided equally among the other five men; so that a capital of less than 16 rupees is reckoned adequate to the labour of two men for the rainy season, at which time only this net is used in the river. At all seasons it is used in tanks. The largest fish are caught by it, such as rohit, katol, chitol.

The *tana* is a smaller sein of fine twine, about 90 cubits long and 3 cubits wide. It is floated by cuttings of a spongy reed called *ulu khagra*, and sunk by rings of potter's ware. One man goes with the boat, and another holds the end that is left on shore. I should have supposed, that the man in the boat had most trouble, but his situation is considered as preferable. This net seems well fitted for clear water, a shallow river, and sandy bottom. Two or three nets of this kind are sometimes joined into one.

The *tune* is a small drag net, that is well fitted for fishing in shallow water among weeds. It is about 20 cubits long and 5½ cubits wide, and has neither floats nor sinkers. A row of sticks, about two feet long, and two feet from each other, unite the two side-ropes, so that the net bags behind. A man at each end goes into the water, until both are about three feet deep; they then immerse the net, and drag it towards the shore with one end of the sticks touching the ground.

In the Mohanonda, which is frequented in the rainy season by the fish called *ilish*, four other kinds of nets are used. They are called *khurki*, *sanggula*, *konayu*, and *ber*: but as I was there at another season, I had no opportunity of seeing them, and cannot describe them from the accounts of the natives. This fishery lasts from about the middle of June until the middle of October, and two very fine kinds of Cyprinus, the rohit and katol, are frequently caught in the same nets.

Wherever the fishery is of such importance as to employ regular fishermen, the landlord exacts a revenue, which seems judicious and proper; because the proprietors are interested to improve the fishery, and to take care of the people employed; for, I am persuaded, that a common property is in general neglected, and turns out of little or no advantage either to the public or to individuals. In this district the property in the fisheries (*jolkor*) has in many places been separated from that of the adjacent land, which seems to me to be a great loss; as it is the proprietor of the neighbouring land alone that can take care either of the fish or fishermen. Yet, probably some specious reason was held out for the separation, which I am told was made when the Raja's estates were sold for arrears of revenue, and the sales were of course conducted by the collector. I heard however no reason assigned for such a separation, and must confess, that I know of nothing rational which can be alledged in its defence. Even the fish in ponds do not always belong to the proprietor of the banks, who of course will never take care to stock them, and who is the only person that can prevent poaching, so that probably not ¼ of the fish is produced for use that might be by proper care. —The same may be said of *bils* or water-courses.

The duties, that are levied on the fishermen, are in general moderate enough, and do not amount to a considerable sum. The largest proprietor, of whom I heard, (Boloram Yoti,) receives only 2,000 Rupees a year, and I believe, that part of this arises from some duties which he levies on ferries. The proprietors generally let their fisheries from year to year, and the farmers (*Izaradars*) sometimes employ fishermen to catch the fish, either for wages or for a share; and sometimes levy so much money for each man or boat employed. Thus, a water-course in the Maldeh district pays to the proprietor 130 rupees a year. The farmer employs 14 men to fish with the *byana*, and these give him one-half of the fish. They fish for nine months in the year, and each can make about four Rupees a month, out of which, however, they have to deduct all expenses; but these are inconsiderable, as they require no boat and make the whole apparatus. The farmer therefore receives about 500 Rupees, out of which is only to be deducted the rent, and the charge of watching to prevent imposition. Small traders come and purchase the fish, which they retail at different markets.

These fishermen, when they fish with the trap (*onta*), pay two rupees a head for the season of three months. Their profit is then still greater, but they have remarkably good market in the manufacturing towns. Those who fish on the

Mohanonda pay 12 annas a head yearly for the dry season, and the same sum, with four rupees for each boat that is wrought by five men, if they are employed in the *ilish* fishery. In this case the more wealthy men furnish the boats and nets, and take one-half of the fish, while each man pays his share of the duty. The profits of those who fish with nets and boats is more considerable than of those who use the screen and the traps.

Near Maldeh, the traders who retail fish have some capital; in other parts they are in general very poor, and the fish are often retailed by the wives of those who catch them.

The rent in most parts is lower, and the fishermen poorer than near Maldeh. At Ghoraghat, for instance, on a noble river, each fisherman pays five annas a year, and fishes in whatever manner he pleases. His monthly gains are reckoned from two to three rupees. On the Atreyi at Potnitola, each fisherman pays six annas a year; but then except from the chief men, 10 annas more are said to be exacted as presents, making the whole duty one rupee a head, and they may fish in whatever manner they may please. At Potiram, each fisherman pays 1½ rupees a year. Fishermen in general are not so poor as the common labourers who are employed in agriculture, and many of them live like farmers who have two ploughs. The whole number in the district may be about 2,500 houses.

The kinds of fish taken are very various, and mostly very small. There is nothing like an extensive fishery of any one kind, except that of the *ilish* in the Mohanonda, which I have just now mentioned. On all other occasions, among 100 fish taken there will be 20 different species. Although the last system of this part of Natural History, published by M. Lacepede, is extremely valuable, very few of the fishes of Bengal are described in it. I must therefore content myself, for the present, with reducing them to his genera, although I have spared no pains in procuring descriptions and drawings of these interesting animals. The names vary a good deal in different rivers, even of the same district. I begin with a list of those I found in or near the Atreyi at Potnitola.

1—Tengpa, *Tetrodon*, a bad small fish, reckoned impure by the Brahmins.

2—Vam, *Macrognathe armé*.

3—Gongti, *Macrognathe aquillonné*.

4—Gongor Gangti, *Macrognathe*, good fish resembling eels in taste.

5—Baliya, *Gobie Eelotre?* a small but good fish.

6—Kholisha, *Trichopode*, a beautiful small fish.

7—Gojal, *Ophiocephale*.

8.—{Goroyi, Bhoroyi,} *Ophiocephale karawey*.

9.—Cheng, *Ophiocephale*.

Much used by the natives, but very indifferent eating.

The last, being extremely tenacious of life, is often found wriggling from one pool to another, when there has been a heavy rain. It is one of the kinds which are supposed to fall from heaven with showers of rain.

10.—Koyi, *Lutjan grimpeur*. This is a fish very much esteemed by the natives, and one of those supposed to fall from heaven. They also have a fable of its being able to climb a coconut tree. It is with the utmost astonishment, that I perceive M. Lacepede was carried into this error by a foolish account published in the Linnæan Transactions. I should rather have classed this fish with the Holocentres, and M. Lacepede has probably taken his account entirely from the before-mentioned source. The animal is remarkably tenacious of life, and I know can live a whole day without water. It is very well tasted, but full of bones; and is reckoned a restorative.

11.—Chanda, *Centropome.*

12.—Rangga Chanda, *Centropome.*

13.—Nam Chanda, *Centropome.*

These fish are very common; but are too small for being dressed in the European manner.

14.—Bheda, *Holocentre.* This fish has a strong resemblance to the Koyi, in its external appearance, tenacity of life, and dietetic qualities.

15.—Pongya, *Cobite,* a small fish, little esteemed.

16.—Magur, *Macropteronote grenouiller,* an ugly fish, but very much esteemed by the natives, who consider it as very strengthening. I think it is far from being pleasant to the taste.

17.—Kamachasinggi, *Silure Fossile,* a fish very much resembling the former in appearance and qualities. It is reckoned impure for Brahmins, who eat the other readily.

18.—Poba, *Silure,* a small pretty fish of an excellent flavour.

19.—{Boyali, Keyali,} *Silure,* a large ugly fish, which often grows to six feet in length. By the natives it is thought good; but does not suit my taste. The Brahmins consider it impure.

20.—Labhuy, *Silure.*

21.—Gagra, *Pimelode barbu ?*

22.—Rita, *Pimelode.*

23.—Ari, *Pimelode.*

24.—Vagari, *Pimelode.*

Large ugly fishes; but thought very good by most natives.

25.—Gagot, *Pimelode,* a small fish with many bones.

26.—Vacha, *Pimelode,* a fish about the size of a herring, and considered as very good by the natives.

27.—Banspatari, *Pimelode,* a beautiful small fish, which from its shining colours and shape is by the natives compared to a bambu leaf.

28.—Tengora, *Pimelode,* a pretty small fish, that the natives think very good.

29.—Kangkila, *Esoce,* an excellent small fish.

30.—Pangchok, *Esoce,* a very small fish.

31.—Ghobol, *Muge,* a fish about a foot long, which swims with its eyes above water. It is very good to eat,

32.—Telar, *Clupee,* a fish about the same size and value.

33.—Pholuyi, *Myste,* a fish about the same size and value.

34.—Chitol, *Myste.* This grows to a very large size, and is a rich fine tasted fish; but the natives do not like it, because it feeds on dead bodies.

35.—Koroti, *Clupanodon,* a small fish of little value.

36.—Chela, *Cyprin.* This is one of a numerous tribe of Indian fishes, which resemble the *Cyprin clupeoide.* It is very common in every part of Bengal, but is of little value.

37.—Elangga.

38.—Sangpuyi.

39.—Dangrika.

40.—Debori.

41.—Titpungti.

42.—Pungti.

These are all small species of the *Cyprin*, which are very common, and much used by the natives, but are very poor eating. Some of them are very beautiful, especially No. 39 and 40. No. 41 and 42 are the best for eating.

43.—Soron-pungti, *Cyprin Bulatmai?* a beautiful fish which grows two feet in length. It is not much valued.

44.—Kalbosu, *Cyprin*, an ugly black fish, strongly resembling the barbel. It grows often to a foot and a half in length, and sometimes to double that size. It is considered by the natives as a good fish, and is both light, and well tasted; but it has many small bones.

45.—Rohit, *Cyprin Rooee* of the English in Bengal. This is one of the most beautiful of fresh-water fishes, being finely shaped, and elegantly adorned with green, purple, gold, and silver, constantly varying one into the other. It thrives well in ponds, but is best when found in running streams. The fish is much and deservedly valued, being light and well-flavoured. It is only inferior to the following in not being so rich.—It grows to about three feet in length.

46.—Katol, *Cyprin*, when taken from rivers with a good stream, this is perhaps the best fresh-water fish in the world; the body is white, light, and firm, and the head and belly are remarkably fat without being luscious or heavy. It grows to a very large size, and weighs from 16 to 50 lbs. Though only a clumsy made fish, it is remarkably active and strong, and frequently springs over the net with great violence. Its colours are not remarkable for beauty.

47.—Kuchiya, *Unibranchaperture*, an eel, as good as the kind common in Europe. The natives reject it, from its near approach to a serpent.

Besides these I observed many other fishes in the district, especially the following:

48.—Khoskhosya, *Muge*, a small fish of little value.

49.—Dari, *Cobite*, a beautiful small fish.

50.—Korki-tengora, *Pimelode*.

51.—Kavasi-tengora, *Pimelode*.

52.—Ram-tengora, *Pimelode*.

53.—Changrarmara, *Pimelode*.

54.—Uruya, *Pimelode*, a small fish of little value.

55.—Silon, *Pimelode*, a large ugly fish, much used by the natives.

56.—Chakunda, *Clupanodon*, a small fish of little use.

57.—Ilish, *Clupanodan*. I have already mentioned the fishery of this species in the Mohanonda, which is almost the only river in the district that it frequents. This species is called Sable-fish by the English, and is the most important in Bengal. It has a strong resemblance to that called *la Fiente* by Lacepede, but has no teeth. During the floods it ascends in immense numbers to spawn in the Ganges and its larger branches, for 500 miles from the sea, and retires as the rivers decrease. It is usually about a foot and a half long, and is a rich, high-flavoured fish; in taste it resembles somewhat both the salmon and herring, to which last it has the strongest affinity. It is however rather heavy and difficult of digestion, and contains a vast number of small bones, so as to require much precaution in eating. These bones are destroyed, when it is cured with tamarinds, and the fish then becomes a very relishing morsel.

58.—Peyoli, *Cyprin*, a small fish of little value.

59.—Kursa, *Cyprin*. This sometimes grows to a foot and a half in length, but is little valued.

60.—Hayali, *Cyprin*.

61.—Tila, *Cyprin.*

Two small fishes of little value.

62.—Mirgal, *Cyprin*, a most beautiful fish like the Rohit, and almost as good; but it does not grow to quite so large a size, being seldom found more than two feet in length.

63.—Khorki.

64.—Bhanggona.

These are two beautiful fishes, somewhat between a carp and a mullet, as their lower jaw resembles that of the latter. They grow to about a foot in length, and are tolerably good to eat.

The crustaceous fishes are perhaps more valued by the natives of Bengal than the fish properly so called, and are excellent seasoning to eat with a food so insipid as rice. In some parts, especially near the sea, they are of many different kinds and sizes, from that of a shrimp to those which are larger than lobsters, for those that are mostly used are of the oblong kind, and are called by the generic name Chinggori. In almost every ditch near the sea they are found in myriads; but in Dinajpúr, except near the Mohanonda and the lower part of the Korotoya, they are very scarce. In the Mohanonda there are three kinds :

1.—Jhingga, a small prawn.

2.—Tengguya, a large prawn.

3.—Mauho, a crawfish, which is often 15 inches in length, and as much in circumference.

Crabs frequent the fresh waters of Bengal, and are distinguished from the oblong kinds of crustaceous fishes by the generic name Kangkora. They are reckoned much inferior to the long-shaped fishes of this kind, and are indeed considered as impure by the higher ranks, who eagerly devour the others. In this district there are many crabs, but few of them grow to a size that would fit them for a European table. They are chiefly found in the parts near the Nagore, Tanggon, and Punabhoba, that are entirely inundated in the rainy season. When the inundation retires, these parts may be observed covered with little heaps of earth, about a foot high, and eight inches in diameter, and in the top of each is a perforation. Under these are the lurking places of the crabs, which retire there for the dry season, and live in pairs. According to the report of the natives, these animals, as the water subsides, dig perpendicular shafts, about three inches in diameter and seven or eight cubits deep; and, when at that depth, they form a chamber about a foot in diameter, which contains water until the next inundation, and in which a male and a female crab take up their residence. I attempted to dig several; but being too early in the season, the water always rose upon me before I reached the chamber.

Insects are not very troublesome in this district; at least from November until April, the season when I was there, I scarcely observed any musquitos. although this is the season, when they are most troublesome in Calcutta. I was told, however, that in the parts of this district which are inundated these insects become almost intolerable in the rainy season.

The only wild insect which produces any thing of value is the bee, and it is the wax alone that is an object of commerce. Mr. Fernandez has rented the whole, except some portion of what is produced in Maldeh, and to each land-holder he pays a certain sum, which must be very inconsiderable, as the whole wax which he procures is said to be only 100 maunds, probably 70 or 80 per cent. Mr. Fernandez employs people in different parts to collect the wax ; and these, who are called sirdars, employ servants to cut the combs. At Nawabgunj, which is one of the most productive districts, and which gives ten or twelve maunds each of 3,840 sicca weight, the people told me, that he allowed them 25 Rupees for each maund, (about lb. 82) delivered at Dinajpúr, and they had all the honey ; but this is of little value. In other places, however, it was said, that the sirdars contract to give him a certain quantity of wax, and take the surplus and the honey for their trouble.

In this district there is only one kind of bee, which so strongly resembles the insect domesticated in Europe, that I should consider it as of the same species, were not its manners very different. The natives of India have no where tamed this industrious creature, and every kind, of which the honey is collected, is in Bengal usually called a honey-fly ; nor could I discover, that the people had any appropriate name for this species. It frequents the forests in the rainy season, and in some districts the people employed in collecting the wax suppose, that the bees do not then build, nor live in society, but that they take shelter from the rain under leaves, and that a great part of them perish from the severity of the weather. This is probably a mistake, and is believed only owing to these people having never frequented the woods to look for the bees ; for I found, that at Nawabgunj, a considerable part of the wax is procured in the woods, about the end of September, and must have been formed in the rainy season. Besides at Ghoraghát, that is the most productive district of which I heard, and yields near 30 maunds a year, most of the wax is gathered in the rainy season ; and the people say, that then the bees breed, and live in society just as at other times. In the dry season the bees frequent the vicinity of villages, and form their nest on the branches of the neighbouring trees. Each nest consists of a single semicircular comb attached to the lower side of a horizontal branch by its diameter. One, which I measured, and which was said to be of the usual size, extended about two feet in radius. On each face is a series of cells, and in some parts of the comb there are three rows, with passages conducting to those in the centre. The bees, when at rest, cover the whole surface of the comb. Near the villages they begin to build in November, when the cruciform plants, resembling mustard, that are cultivated for oil, begin to flower. In January, when they have brought up a brood of young, they eat the honey and desert their nest, which is collected for wax. In the middle of December, I examined a comb : the greater part of the cells were filled with young bees, a small portion was filled with honey, and a larger with a yellow powder, which the natives, I believe, justly consider as the food for the young bees, and as the pollen of various plants. The bees begin to build again in March, when most of the trees come into blossom ; and having bred in June, they consume the honey, and retire into the woods. The combs formed at this season are the most valuable, and contain most honey. In order to procure this, the people chase away the bees, which is easily done by a little smoke occasioned by some burning husks of rice held under the comb in a basket that is made of a green plantain leaf. I saw this practised with great success before a multitude, who imagined that the wax-gatherer was possessed of a spell or prayers, which saved him from being bitten. A comb, such as I have mentioned, is said usually to give about a pound of wax, when cleared and melted ; but those collected in spring are said to give 20 pounds of honey and wax.

There are several species of shells, chiefly snails (Helices), that are burned into lime, sufficient to supply the usual demand of the country, which is confined to the chewing with betel, to the white-washing of a few religious buildings, and to a small quantity used in manufactures. When any large building is to be constructed by a European, stone-lime is generally brought from Sylhet, but the natives prefer that made from shells. They of course must make advances long before the lime is wanted, to enable some poor people to collect shells in the dry season. Most are procured from marshes and old courses of rivers, where the water is stagnant.

CHAPTER II.

PLANTS.

A country so much cultivated as this district, is not favourable for the pursuits of a Botanist, neither was my journey through it performed at a favourable season. I have not much therefore to offer on the subject, especially as I found a great difficulty in procuring any satisfactory intelligence from the natives, who apply names so indefinitely even to the most common plants, that in order to avoid numerous mistakes great precaution is required.

Among the natural vegetable productions of most countries, forests constitute a valuable and most distinguished part. In this district, however, although not very extensive, the demand for their produce is so small, that forests may be considered as not only almost useless ; but from their harbouring destructive animals, they ought to be looked upon as injurious, and therefore should be eradicated as soon as possible. By some unaccountable caprice the property of the forest is often vested in a person different from the owner of the soil. This person, although he has no legal right to prevent the owner of the soil from cultivating it, will of course take all indirect means of securing or enlarging his property, and none is so effectual as the encouraging the breed of destructive animals. In one division, I accordingly heard it alleged, that the keepers of buffaloes turn loose all the young males, and allow them to become wild.

The wastes (*jongol* or *bonya*) of this district may be divided into two kinds, one containing trees called here *katal*, the other contains reeds of various kinds, and is denominated from the species which is most predominant with the term *bonya* annexed. The English call this kind of waste or forest by the appellation of grass-jungle. The proprietor, as I have said before, receives a very inconsiderable profit from both kinds. Those who want timber for building, or for the implements of agriculture, must pay a trifle for permission to cut a tree ; and where there is a demand for the produce of the forest, a *bonkor* is appointed, who levies a small duty on those who cut fire-wood, thatch reeds, bambûs, or the tree of which catechu is made. Other persons (*pholkor*) rent the wild fruits which are used as acids in cookery, for medicine, or for dying and tanning. Finally, other persons rent the duties (*kahachorayi*) that are levied on the buffalos which pasture in forests.

The only people who can be called wood-cutters in this district are those employed for supplying manufacturers, and especially the Company's factories, with fuel. At Maldeh the fire-wood is cut by farmers, who live near the woods of Peruya, at times when they would otherwise be idle. Fifteen times a month a man cuts as much wood, as when green, loads four oxen, and brings it for sale. For the 60 loads he receives four Rupees, and pays a small monthly duty for each ox ; the load does not exceed 1 maund of 100 sa. wt. the seer, or is about 103⅞ lbs. Avoirdupois. At Ghoraghát, each wood-cutter pays 12 annas a year.

The timber, which the woods contain, is little fit for building boats; and the poverty of the natives prevents them in general from using timber in their houses, or even for fuel: so that almost the only demand for the wood in this district is confined to the making of a few small implements of agriculture, a little coarse furniture, a few beams and posts for the houses of the more wealthy inhabitants, and to the supply of a little fire-wood for some of the Company's factories, Maldeh, Nichinta, and Shilboris, R. (Maldeh, Nichintapúr, and Selvorish). All the former of these purposes might be much better supplied from trees planted round villages; and the last would require only three small woods, provided these were properly managed, and regularly cut. A wood of a thousand acres would be fully adequate to supply the demand of any factory, if properly managed, and no encroachments were allowed. At present I have supposed, that about 220 square miles are under forests, woods or bushes.

Before this country was cultivated, I imagine that the lower parts were rendered almost impenetrable by thickets of reeds, while the high parts were covered with a forest consisting almost entirely of a tree, which is called here Sal or Gojal, and is well known by the former name to the carpenters of Calcutta. It has lately been described by Botanists under the name of Shorea robusta. In this district there remain several small forests of this tree, which indeed seems to spring up almost spontaneously wherever a dry soil has been left unoccupied: for the fruit, having wings, is carried far by the winds. In this district, however, the tree is not procurable of a size fit for sending to a distant market, and is chiefly of use for making ploughs and small posts and beams for the better kind of the native houses; and as it is a handsome tree, with very odorous flowers, it might be planted to great advantage round the villages, in the stiff clay soil, where it thrives. It is said, that in Morong, a resin called *dhuna*, is extracted by incision from this tree; but this is not practised in Dinajpúr.

In this district, however, by far the greater part of the forests owe their origin to deserted towns or villages. The trees which grew round these have gradually increased, and have given shelter to some others that are not usually found in such situations. I shall therefore give a list both of the trees that usually grow round villages in this district, and that have found shelter among these in the woods, which have sprung upon ruins. I shall add the Botanical names, so far as I know: but the list is far from exhausting the subject. In this place I shall also take an opportunity of mentioning the management of plantations; although, strictly speaking, that might be considered as a part of agriculture.

The bambú is the most common and useful woody plant in this district. The houses, furniture, boats, and implements of agriculture are entirely or in part made from this valuable reed, and it is the common fuel; so that it supplies all the purposes to which wood is applied in Europe; and is no doubt one of the principal articles of produce in the country; for, the annual value of the bambús that are cut cannot be estimated at less than 5,00,000 Rupees.

It grows from a creeping root, which extends from 12 to 20 feet in diameter, and sends up 40 or 50 stems. These form a clump that keeps separate from the others which are adjacent. Every year from 5 to 10 bambús of a clump are ripe and are cut, while young ones shoot up from the roots to supply their places. If the whole is cut at once, the plant is apt to die: and the stem perishes whenever it produces fruit, which very rarely happens in cultivated parts of the country. On this account, indeed, many of the natives believe, that the plant never produces either flower or fruit. When a new plantation is to be formed, a portion of the common root extending 2 or 3 feet in diameter, together with five or six stems, is separated from a clump. The tops having been cut away, this is planted in the situation where it is intended to rear a clump, and this begins to produce ripe bambús in about seven years. The plant requires to be exempted from inundation, and thrives best in a free soil. In this district, bambús, according to their size, sell at from 1 to 3 Rupees a hundred ; except at Dinajpúr and Maldeh, where they are about 50 per cent. dearer ; ground under bambús, therefore, in general gives a considerable return, and pays a high rent.

In this district the people have several specific names which, so far as I could judge, they apply with little or no accuracy. I could clearly however, distinguish four species, but there may be more ; and I apply to these the names, that seemed to me the best ascertained.

1.—The most valuable kind seems to be called indiscriminately Boro Bans and Jauta Bans. It grows to the largest size, and is used for posts, rafters, beams, scaffolding, and whatever requires large dimensions, and it is the one most usually cultivated.

2.—The next species is also much cultivated, being that used for making all sorts of basket-work and mats. It seems to be indiscriminately called Makla and Jaoya.

3.—The Korongji is a small bambu that is not much cultivated. It is strong, but is chiefly useful for making some small implements of agriculture, or fences. It is often found wild.

4.—The Beru Bans, or thorny bamboo, is only cultivated about the monuments of saints as an ornament ; for it grows very straight, and its branches are beautifully feathered, so that it has a very different aspect from the others. It is often found wild, especially in the woods near Maldeh and Ghoraghát. Its chief use is for making dry fences, or for the shafts of javelins or spears, for which it is remarkably well adapted ; but it is also employed in the roofs of huts.

No account of any of these kinds has yet been published in the writings of any Botanist, to which I have access. This genus has indeed been much neglected, and its study is attended with numerous difficulties, even to those who are on the spot where they grow.

The same may be said of the useful plants which I shall next mention, the ratans or canes, concerning which modern Botanists may be said to have published nothing that is useful in ascertaining the different sorts. In this district there are two kinds which grow spontaneously, both in woods and near villages, where the soil is moist and very rich, two circumstances that appear necessary for every kind of this plant. Both are of a very bad quality.

5.—The one is called simply Bet, and its leaves resemble those of a coconut (*Foliolis æquidistantibus bifaries.*) So far as I know, all the species, that have leaves of this structure, are proper ratans, and have slender stems fit for switches, or for being split to form baskets or wicker-work.

6.—The other called Gorol Bet has leaves like those of a date tree (*Foliolis subfasciculatis squarrosis*). All the species, that I know, having such leaves, should be called canes, as they have thick stems fit for forming walking sticks, and are not used for the purposes to which the others are applied. The stems of these are often of an immense length, so as sometimes to be twisted into cables.

7.—Nearly allied to those is the Gaya or Guvak of the Bengalis, the *Areca* of Botanists. The plant seems to thrive in this district, but it may be considered merely as ornamental; for it seldom, if ever, brings its fruit to maturity, so that great quantities are imported. The reason of this seems to be, that it is not planted in groves which are sheltered by trees and hedges, and watered so as to preserve a constant moisture, which seems necessary for this palm. In the same latitude towards the east, where parching winds do not prevail in the spring, the tree thrives remarkably; and the same is the case in Mysore, where pains are taken to preserve moisture. This therefore seems an article, the culture of which may be readily introduced, and may annually save a large sum to this district. At present a few are planted among other trees, near some rich men's houses, merely, as an ornament, for which they are happily selected.

8.—The cocoanut palm, *Narikel* of the Bengalis, is nearly in the same state. I imagine indeed that it could with great difficulty be made to ripen its fruit.

9.—The elegant palm called Caryota by Botanists, and *Ramguvah,* or *Bonkhejur* by the Bengalis, is found growing spontaneously, but rarely, in the woods of this district, neither does it seem to thrive. It is applied to no use. In Malabar its stems produces a kind of sago, and its flowering shoot (spadix) yields a saccharine juice.

10.—The *Khorjur* or *Khejur* of the Bengalis has been considered as the *Elat* of Linnæus, and is no doubt the Katoindel of Rheede, which Linnæus quotes as being the same with his *Elate;* but it is probable, that this great Botanist had some other plant in view, otherwise he would scarcely have separated it from the date tree (*Phœnix*). This valuable palm is not common in Dinajpúr, but grows spontaneously, and thrives remarkably, and, could the inhabitants be induced to use its wine, might become a most valuable addition to their diet, as I have before mentioned, especially as it thrives on dry elevated places, such as are at present almost useless. Its juice may also be inspissated into a kind of saccharine matter.

11.—The *Lontarus* of Botanists, called usually *Palmira* by Europeans, and Tal or Triniraj by the Bengalees, is a still more elegant and useful palm, now totally neglected by the people of this district, except as an ornament like the former. It might become highly useful from its juice, and its stem is both a very durable material for building, and may be converted into small canoes, which in the rainy season serve to go from house to house. It thrives in this district, although it never grows spontaneously; and is finely adapted for covering the naked sides of tanks, which are now almost entirely useless.

12.—The Badam of Bengal (*Terminalia Catapa,* L.) is found in this district, and is a very ornamental tree. Its nut is however almost the only useful part; but, although remarkably light and well-flavoured, it is so incased by a hard shell as to be of little value. It does not grow spontaneously, and seems to have been introduced by Europeans.

13.—Nearly allied to the above, and having a nut equally good, is the Boyara, Bohora, or Bauri, of Bengal, the *Myrobalanus Bellirica* of Gærtner. It is a fine tree, grows to a large size, and produces a timber that the natives reckon valuable. The fruit is used both in medicine and by dyers, and both the bark and fruit are used by tanners. Unfortunately, when in flower, the tree emits a most abominable stench, which perhaps should prevent it from being cultivated, as the demand for its produce is very small.

14.—The Horitoki of Bengal, or *Myrobalanus chebula* of Gærtner, is not liable to the same objection; but its wood is not so strong, nor is its kernel esculent.

Its myrobalan, or dried fruit, is however more used in the arts; and when the fruit is preserved green in syrup, it is a valuable laxative medicine, which is much employed by the natives. Men, who have made a vow of chastity, and who are inclined to adhere to their resolution, endeavour to assist their virtue by eating this preserve, which is supposed to diminish the desires of the flesh. Were its growth encouraged near villages, in place of useless trees, the dried fruit might be procured in great quantities, and might become a valuable article in commerce; as I have no doubt, but that it might be employed in the finer kinds of tanning to great advantage. At present there is a sufficient supply for the demand of the district; and those who collect the fruit pay a trifle to the land-holder.

15.—The *Tomex Japonica* of Botanists is found in this district, and is a timber tree. It was shown to me as the Bijolghota, a plant used in medicine; but I have little confidence in the skill of the person by whom it was brought.

16.—The Siyuli, or *Sephalika* of the Bengalis, is a pretty small tree, called *Nyctanthes arbor-tristis* by Botanists, from its flowers spreading at night and falling at sun-rise. The flowers that have dropt are gathered, and produce a beautiful though perishable purple dye; the bark and leaves are used in medicine, and the inner bark affords a red dye, when beaten with a little lime, or with ¼ of its own weight of that of No. 113.

17.—There is a species of *Gmelina*, of which no account published by modern Botanists has yet reached me; but Dr. Roxburgh in his manuscripts calls it *Gmelina Arborea*, and Rheede long ago described it under the name of Cumbulu. It is valuable on account of its wood, which although light is durable; is not readily attacked by insects, and is therefore peculiarly well fitted for making trunks, and is much employed by the natives in making their instruments of music. It is found in this district near Ghoraghát, but is rare, and is called Yoginichokro; while Gambhar, the name by which it is commonly known in the eastern parts of Bengal, is here applied to a very different tree, that will be hereafter mentioned, No. 92.

18.—A species of *Cordia* called Dhovoli, of which I have seen no account in Botanical books, is found in this district, where it grows to be a considerable tree.

19.—The *Ehretia lævis* of Wildenow is a small tree found in this district. It was called to me Jonggoli Guroak or Guya, that is wild *Areka*, a plant to which it has in no part the most distant resemblance. I therefore suspect, that this name is not the real one.

20.—Another *Ehretia*, which I have found in many parts of India, but of which no Botanical writer has yet taken notice, was here called Bijol. It grows to be a very considerable timber tree, but is not very common. It was sent to Dr. Roxburgh, as a tree which in Nipal produces a good fruit; but, although the tree is very common in that country, some other must have been meant, as the fruit of this could not be eaten any where.

21.—One of the most common ornamental trees in this district is the Gulongcho, or *Flos convolutus* of Rumphius. It is often 20 or 30 feet high, and is very ornamental near the monuments of the Moslem saints.

22.—The *Nerium Antidysentericum* of Linnæus, which ought to have been classed as an *Echites*, is very common in this district. It is not only a medicine, but its wood made into small beads, which the Hindús wear round their necks. At Peruya it was called to me the Dudé, and a plant of that name is no doubt applied to make similar beads; but in other places, I know, that this *Nerium* is called Indroyov, while the Dudé is considered as distinct. In fact, a very different plant was shown to me afterwards as the Dudé, as will be hereafter mentioned, No. 93.

23.—The *Echites Scholaris* of Botanists is known to the natives of this district by the names Chhatin and Soptoporlo. It is very common, and sometimes grows to a great size; one which I measured at Potiram was 12 feet in circumference, at five feet from the ground. Its bark is used as a medicine for cattle. Its wood is considered as useless.

24.—The *Bassia obovata*, if different from the Latifolia, is found, but very rarely in the woods of Dinajpúr, where it is called Muha, and is applied to no use.

25.—The *Mimusops Elengi*, L. called Bokul or Baul by the natives, is a common ornamental tree about villages. Its bark may be used as a tan, but the tree is of little value. The flowers are much valued by the natives, as they are convenient for forming chaplets. Their smell is too strong.

26.—In the woods of Peruya considerable quantities of a fruit called Khyrini are collected for sale. They are produced by the *Achras dissecta*, W. a very handsome tree nearly allied to the former.

27.—The *Diospyros cordifolia*, W. was shown to me in the woods, and called Sundor; but, as other people gave the same appellation to a quite different tree, there is no proper authority for this name. The other was of the order of rubiaceous plants.

28.—The Gab of the natives, and *Embryopteris glutenifera* of Botanists, is a beautiful tree common near the villages of Bengal: the fruit is eatable, but excessively sour. Its principal use is for paying the bottom of boats. It is beaten in a large mortar, and the juice expressed. This is boiled, mixed with powdered charcoal, and applied once a year to the outside of the planks. A good tree will give 4,000 fruit, worth two Rupees, and will be in full bearing in eight years from the time when it was planted. The number in Dinajpúr is small, but sufficient for the demand. The wood is of little value. Gærtner, who first described this family of plants, has either made a great error in his description, and mistaken the upper for the under end of the fruit; or else later botanists have been equally mistaken in considering the Gab as being a species of Embryopteris.

29.—The *Vangueria edulis* is one of the most common small trees about the villages of Dinajpúr. It varies in sometimes having spines, and sometimes wanting them, and is called Moyna. Its fruit, which is about the size of an apple, possesses an intoxicating or rather deleterious quality, when fresh plucked; but after being kept a few days, may be eaten without danger, and is said to be sweet and agreeable.

30.—The natives give the same name to a species of *Gardenia* or *Randia*, which shows the affinity of the two families of plants. In fact, these two species have a strong resemblance. So far as I know, no account of this species has yet been published.

31.—The Piralu of the natives is the *Gardenia uliginosa* of Botanists. It is a middling-sized ugly tree, and its fruit is sometimes used in the curries of the poor.

32.—The two following species of *Morinda* seem also hitherto to have escaped the notice of Botanists. The one is called Daree Horidra, or yellow wood. It grows spontaneously in the woods, and its root is used as a dye.

33. The other, from its containing about four berries united in its fruit, is called Charichoka. The bark of its root, beat up with a duck's egg and a little lime, is applied to the rude images made of potter's work, that are offered at the monuments of saints, or used by children as toys, and gives them a red colour.

34. The Kadombo or Kodom, called by Botanists *Nauclea Orientalis*, is a very ornamental tree, and is common in Dinajpûr. It is however inferior in size, and in the quality of its timber to the next species; but its beauty procures it a more common place near villages.

35. The *Nauclea parvifolia* is called here Kelikodombo or Talikodombo, and like several other species of this family is a good timber tree, but is very little used.

36. The *Crœteva Tapia*, called by the natives Vorna, is a common tree, especially in the Eastern parts of this district. It does not grow to a considerable size, and is of little use except as an ornament.

37. The name Dengphol (at Ghoraghat) is applied to a tree which cannot well be reduced to any family of plants established by Botanists, but which comes nearest to the *Harangana* of Lamarck; and has a great affinity to the Mangosteen. It is a very ornamental tree, and its fruit is about the size of an apple, but too acid. It is now growing in the Company's Botanical Garden, and it is to be hoped, that Dr. Roxburgh's description of it will be soon published.

38 The Jolpayi has usually been compared by Europeans to the Olive, on which account it has been called the Eleocarpus; but the affinity is very slight, consisting merely in the fruit being of the same shape and size. The opinions of Botanists concerning this tree are not very easily reconciled, which has probably arisen from the *Perinkara* of Rheede, and the *Ganitrus* of Rumphius, having been considered as the same. The tree of which I am now giving an account, and which is common in every part of Hindústan, is no doubt the *Perinkara* of Rheede, and is totally different from the *Ganitrus* of Rumphius and Gærtner. The fruit contains no oil, but is acid, and gives a good flavor to curries, which is its principal use. In some parts it is preserved in oil and salt, and then no doubt acquires a greater resemblance to the olive; but it is always a very inferior pickle. It is a very common tree in Dinajpûr, both in gardens and woods.

39. The tree called Kopittho, or Kotbel by the natives, has been classed by Botanists with the *Limonias*, and called *acidissima*, for what reason I do not know. Rumphius, who is remarkable among Botanists for having named plants with sagacity and good taste, calls it *Anisifolium*, the leaves having a strong and agreeable flavour of the Anise, and this name ought to be preserved. The fruit is eaten by the natives, but is very poor. In Dinajpûr the wood is not applied to any use. Retzius has been blamed for classing this plant with the *Crœtevas*, and it certainly has not the smallest affinity with the plants, which have been properly so called, such as No. 35, but then its affinity to the *Crœteva Marmelos* of Linnæus is striking, and they cannot be separated in any system, that pretends to follow nature. The natives indeed have had more accurate notions than many Botanists, and call the plant of which I am now writing the Kot or wild Bel, while the *Crœteva Marmelos* is called simply Bel.

40. This Bel is a very common tree, and thrives even in the hardest clays. The natives place a great value on the fruit, but it is miserably insipid. The tree is not so ornamental as the Kotbel.

41. Another tree, very much allied to the last, is by the natives named Billeŭ and Sriphol, or the venerable fruit; for it is considered as an emblem of the spouse

of Sib, and is a common offering to that God. The natives admire this fruit also; in fact, I have some doubt whether these two are not mere varieties of the same species. It is reckoned very sinful to cut this tree, except for the purpose of making a kind of carved stake, that is put in the ground on the consecration of a bull, (a ceremony which will hereafter be mentioned.)

42. The Nim, or *Melia Azadirachta*, is another sacred tree among the Hindûs, and one of the most common in every part of their country. The tree has a considerable resemblance to the Ash, and its leaves are intensely bitter, and much used in medicine, especially as a fomentation, and in assisting holy men to resist the allurements of beauty. Images are made of its wood, which is considered as pure; as it is seldom eaten by insects, it might probably serve more useful purposes. In some parts of India a medicinal oil is extracted from its seed.

43. Nearly allied to the former is a family of Bengal plants, of which no account has been given in the late Botanical systems. One of this family is a common tree in Dinajpûr, especially near Ghoraghat, where it is called Pithras. In other parts an oil is extracted from the seeds of the two last mentioned trees; but its use is not known in this district.

44. Allied to these also is the species of *Cedrella* called by the natives Tun or Jiya. It is pretty common near Ghoraghat, and is a valuable tree, both as affording flowers which give a dye, and as yielding a wood that makes tolerable furniture, and in Calcutta it is much used for that purpose. None is however exported from this district.

45. The Konok Changpa, called by Botanists *Pterospermum suberifolium*, is chiefly remarkable for its beauty, and certainly is one of the most elegant flowering trees that can be seen. The flowers are offered to the gods.

46. Nearly allied to the above is the Salmoli or Simul, called also Mondar, and when in flower it is one of the most gaudy ornaments of the forest or village, for it is every where common. It is the *Bombax heptaphyllum* of Botanists, at least the Moulelavou of Rheede, which is supposed to be of the the same kind with an American plant described by Jacquin; but this seems highly improbable. There is no reason to suppose that this is not a native of Hindûstan, and I believe that there are very few plants indeed that were originally natives of both Indies. Linnæus seemed to consider all regions within the tropics as India, and that they all produce nearly the same plants, and on this subject he has been the great source of error. In fact the cotton tree of the West Indies is much larger than our East India plant, and grows in a very different manner, with an immense tall stem, which sends out from its summit long horizontal arms. I have no doubt but that the trees are quite different, although having taken no notices concerning the West Indian kind, I cannot now point out the essential difference. I cannot account for Wildenow's stating that the stem has no prickles, as in Rheede's figure that circumstance is most accurately expressed. Our Indian plant is a valuable tree. Its wood is that commonly employed by the natives for making doors, and window-shutters; for it lasts well in such situations, and is very strong to resist the attacks of robbers. The cotton is that commonly used for stuffing pillows. It is neither used for quilts nor mattrasses, as it readily forms into lumps, and does not last. The fibre is much finer than that of common cotton, but is so straight that it cannot be spun.

47. One of the most favorite flowers with the natives is the Changpa or Chompak, called by Botanists Michelia. The flowers are no doubt very odorous, but

their smell is too strong and overpowering. The tree is common; but it is useful only as an ornament, and as affording flowers that are offered to the gods.

48. The Chalita of the Bengalees is no doubt the *Syalita* of Rheede, which is said to be the *Dillenia speciosa* of Botanists; but the definition given of the *Dellipsica* agrees better with our plant. Indeed this family is as yet but indifferently described. It is a superb tree, although of little value; the fruit however is an agreeable acid in curries. The flowers are white and very showy.

49. The *Anona squamosa*, called Ata by the natives, when cultivated with care is a tolerable fruit; but when it grows spontaneously about villages, it is exceedingly bad. It is called Custard Apple by the English; but whether it is the same with the West India plant of that name I cannot say. It is however probably an exotic in India, as I understand, that it has no name in the Songskrito language.

50. The same is the case with the *Lona* or *Anona reticulata*, which in all situations is a most wretched fruit.

51. The *Uvaria longifolia*, from its growing tall and straight, has been called Mast Tree by Europeans. The natives of Bengal call it Devdaru, a name that they also give to the Pine, and to several other trees which have not the smallest affinity to either. This is especially the case with the *Erythroxylon sideroxylloides* E. M. Devdaru is in fact a celebrated tree, and together with the Sara Asod and But, to be hereafter mentioned, is considered to be the usual residence of devils. The two latter are occupied by male devils, (Brohmodaityo and Bhut,) while female devils (Sengkhine and Petine) occupy the two former. This kind of Devdaru being very ornamental, and fit for forming shady walks, has been much spread since Europeans began to pay attention to the ornament of the country. In other respects it is a very useful tree.

52. One of the most common small trees in this district is the Panyala of the country, Panyamal or Phalsa, which by Botanists is named *Flacourtia*. I must however say, that I am very doubtful concerning the species, and although I doubt much whether there is more than one kind in this country, I have been inclined to refer it sometimes to one and sometimes to another of the species that have been described. The fruit is like a small bullace plum, and very poor, but is eaten by children. I have not observed here the kind that is common at Calcutta.

53. At Ghoraghat, the *Microcos paniculata* of Botanists was brought to me as a tree called Bunchuniya, and said to produce wood better fitted for making furniture than any other found at that place, although it grows to only a small size. The woodcutters there being remarkably stupid, I cannot place much reliance on what they said.

54. The Bixa, an American plant, is now rapidly spreading over Bengal, the inhabitants having found it a useful yellow dye, which they employ to give their clothes a temporary colour in the Dolyatra or festival of Krishno. With this also they colour the water, which on the same occasion they throw at each other with squirts. For these purposes it is well qualified, as the colour easily washes out, and the infusion has a pleasant smell. By them it is called Lotkan, and they say that before it grew commonly in the country, the dry fruit was brought from Patna. Probably some other fruit was then brought, and its use has been superceded by that of the Bixa, to which the natives have given the old name, as there can be no doubt of its being an American plant, and its fruit could scarcely have been brought here from the west of India. In many parts it is called European Turmeric.

55. There is little doubt, that America has also furnished us with the Goyava, which now is spread all over the country, and propagates itself without care. In the vulgar language it is called Peyara; but it has no name in the sacred tongue. When cultivated with care, I have sometimes known this fruit tolerable; but in general it is very bad. With the authors of the Encyclopedie, I am inclined to believe, that the *Psydium pyriferum* and *pomiferum* form only one species, and differ infinitely less than most kinds of the apple tree do.

56. The Jombi or Jom is a very common tree both in woods and near villages. The Indians indeed are said to have given its name to their portion of the world. Jombudwip, or the Island of the Jumbu tree. It would be difficult to assign any good reason for this, as the tree is neither very large nor ornamental, and the fruit is execrable. By the natives however it is reckoned wholesome, and the timber is strong, although it does not polish. This I take to be *Calyptranthes Jambulana* of Willdenow, although most of what has been written by Botanists concerning the *Myrti Eugeniæ* and *Calyptranthes* of India would require revision. In fact, every thing concerning most of these plants is obscure and incomplete, and the subject is extremely difficult.

57. From among these, Jussieu has with great propriety separated the *Eugenia acutangularis* of Linnæus, which is a common tree in this district, where it is called Ijjol or Hijol. It is very ornamental, and its wood is much used; but is neither strong nor handsome.

58. The Nichon is a large tree, called by Botanists *Lagerstræmia parviflora*. Its timber is reckoned good; but it seldom grows near villages.

59. The Babla or Gorsundor of Bengal has usually been referred to the *Mimosa farnesiana* of Linnæus, in which, I suspect, there is a mistake; and I am rather inclined to suppose, that it is the *Mimosa Indica* mentioned in the Encyclopedie Methodique, of which no proper account has yet been published, although it is one of the most common trees in India. It is rather rare in Dinajpúr, and is seldom applied to use, although it is valuable for many purposes. The wood is hard and strong, fit for the plough and the naves of wheels; the bark is an excellent tan, and the tree yields a gum equal to the Arabic. The flowers are remarkably odorous.

60. The Guye Babla is another very common species of Mimosa, not yet properly introduced into Botanical works; and it is to be regretted, that Dr. Roxburgh's accounts of these two trees should not yet have been published. In his manuscripts he calls this the *Mimosa Sepea;* for it makes excellent hedges, and serves equally well all the purposes to which the other is applied. Its flowers are not so odorous, and the bark, when recently cut, emits a most intolerable stench.

61. The Khodir or Khoyer is the *Mimosa Catechu* of Botanists, and the tree from whence the valuable drug called Terra Japonica is prepared. The tree is common in the woods of Peruya, Jogodol, and Ghoraghat; but it is only in the first that any of the drug is prepared. The number of people employed in this manufacture is small, and the following account was given by the agent of one of the landholders; for I could not find any of the manufacturers. According to the agent there are 25 furnaces, and each employs three men. Trees are selected, that are at least two feet in circumference, and these are old, for in this district the tree does not grow to a large size. The bark and white wood are removed, and then the heart is cut into small pieces, and beaten into a kind of stringy substance by

means of the instrument called *dhengki*. Equal quantities of this and of water are put into earthen pots, each holding from 10 to 20 seers, and are boiled for about six hours. Each fire contains two or three pots. The decoction is then decanted into a pot, and is formed into two kinds of Catechu, Khoyer and Papri Khoyer, the first dark and the second light coloured. The first is made by simply allowing the extract to dry in the pot without addition, the latter is made by putting some ashes of cow-dung in the bottom of the cooler. The ashes are covered with a fold of muslin, over which the warm extract is poured. It is sold to the merchants in these pots, and by them is formed into balls, and dried in the sun. The merchant makes about four seer of 100 sa. wt. from each pot, and pays a rupee for five pots, which should make about lb. 51¼ avoirdupois. None can be made in the rainy season. Each furnace could make 50 pots in the month; but the workmen seldom exert themselves, and always are in debt to the merchant, who has great difficulty to induce them to work. Each furnace pays four annas a year to the landholder. The merchants sell the dried balls at seven rupees for the maund of the same weight, which is almost 103¼ lb. avoird.

As I was not satisfied with this account, I sent a native into the woods, who gave me the following account: A manufacturer, of whom there are five or six in Maldeh, hires four men, and remains with them in the woods for seven months in the year. He pays 12 rupees a year to the landholder for the wood, and cuts as much as he can manufacture. 40 seers of chips give five seers of catechu, and each month the manufacturer with the assistance of four labourers can make four maunds, or 160 seers of 100 sa. wt., or about 413 lb. avoirdupois, which he sells immediately to the druggists for 28 rupees. The whole produce of seven months is therefore R. 196. From this deduct 12 rupees for rent, 84 rupees for workmen's wages, at three rupees each a month on account of their living in the woods, and four rupees for the expense of sending the drug to market, and there will remain 96 rupees for the manufacturer, who does not require, at the utmost, a capital of more than 30 rupees.

It is very likely, that both methods of conducting this manufacture may be employed. The rent stated by the agent is perfectly absurd. The Maldeh khoyer or catechu is not reckoned of the best quality. The tree is rather scarce; and if it were wished to increase the manufacture, it would be necessary to destroy all the useless trees in some parts of the forest, and to allow none to grow, except this kind of *Mimosa*. It is one of the nine sacred plants of which small branches are burned to the planets, and the Hindûs reckon nine of these bodies. This is sacred to the planet which presides over Tuesday (Mongol).

62. The Chorki is a very common tree near Ghoraghat, and is a species of *Mimosa* that has not yet found its way into the modern systems of Botany: but did not escape the industry of Rumphius, who seems to have described it under the name of *Cortex Saponarius*. It is reckoned a useful timber.

63. The *Mimosa Lebaeck*, as described in Encyclopedie Methodique, is a very common tree in most parts of India, and grows near several villages in this district, especially in low places. It was called to me Jonggolijot; but I suspect, that it was not accurately named, and that its proper name is Korai, which is also given to the following; for the two resemble each other so much, that in common language they might readily be included under the same name. Its timber is strong.

64. The *Mimosa marginata* E. M. is a tree that produces more valuable timber than the former, and is found in the woods of this district, where it is called Korai. Small boats are sometimes built of the Korai, which probably includes both kinds.

65. The Sangi or Somi, which Sir W. Jones makes a synonime of the Babla, is alleged by my people to be different, and they show me the *Prosopis aculeata*. It is one of the nine sacred plants, and is offered to Soni, the planet which presides over Saturday. It is common in Dinajpúr, but is applied to no use.

66. The Tamarind tree, by the natives called Tetul and Tinteri, is a most valuable and elegant plant. Besides producing a fruit, that is too well known to require being described, and which is much used by the natives as an acid in seasoning their food, its timber is excellent for many purposes, and makes handsome furniture. As it is hard and strong, it is commonly employed for making oil and sugar mills, and washermen's boards. The seeds are frequently employed by the India dyers, and by those who weave woollen cloths. A good tree will give about 350 lb. of fruit, worth from three to four rupees. The average value however may be two rupees a year, and is nearly of the same amount with that of a good mangoe tree. The wild tamarinds of Peruya are the only fruit exported from this district, except a few mangoes from the same vicinity.

67. The *Cassia Fistula*, called Songdhalu and Sonalu by the natives, is one of the greatest ornaments of India. The leaves bruised and mixed with lime-juice are used as a cure for the ring-worm, and are applied to reduce tumours in cattle. The natives here seem to be ignorant of the purgative quality of its fruit. It sometimes grows to a very considerable size.

68. The *Moringa* of Botanists is one of the most common trees about the villages of this district, where it is called Sogena and Sobhangjon. The flowers, unripe fruit, and leaves, are common ingredients in the dishes of the natives. The bark of the root is used by Europeans as a succedaneum for horse-radish, to which however it is very inferior; the seeds, which are said to be the Behen-nuts of the old shops, are applied to no use by the natives, who do not know that they contain oil.

69. The *Adenanthera pavonina*, called Roktochondon by the natives, is found about the village of Dinajpúr. The native name signifies Red Sandal Wood, and its wood is said to be odorous, and it may be used instead of Sandal in the worship of all the gods except Vishnú. It is probable, that the trees which grow near villages may have no scent, for that is often the case with the real Sandal. There seems however to be several different trees in India that are called Red Sandal, and my inquiries have not yet been sufficiently extended to enable me to treat the subject fully.

70. 71. The Sal Kangchon, a *Bauhinia* of which no mention is made in Botanical systems, and Swet Kangchon, or *Bauhinia candida*, are very common trees near the villages of Dinajpúr. They are small trees for little use except ornament, but they produce most elegant flowers. The young pods are used as a vegetable in curries.

72. 73. The Vokpushpo of the Songskrito is by the vulgar divided into two kinds, called from the colour of the flowers Lalvok and Sadavok; and in this they have been imitated by modern Botanists, contrary to all their professions of not regarding colour. Ever since the latter times of Linnæus they have been also very un-

fortunate in the different families of plants into which they have thrust these elegant trees. Linnæus, in his first attempt to class these plants with the *Robinias*, seem to have approached much nearer perfection than afterwards, when he classed them with the *Æschynomene*. Willdenow, who names them *Coronilla grandiflora* and *coccinea*, has been equally unfortunate. The tree is very common about villages, and its flowers are used as offerings to the gods. The calyx and pistillum are fried and eaten with rice. The unripe pods are also used as a vegetable in curries. The wood is of no use except for fuel.

74. The elegant tree, called *Erythrina Indica* in the Encyclopedie Methodique, is called by the natives Palitamadar. In this district, although it possesses several advantages, the tree is not very common. Any cutting, however large, immediately takes root, so that it is an excellent material for hedges, especially as it is prickly. Its wood is both light and strong, so that the carpenters of Calcutta prefer it to all others for the poles of palanquins. Its leaves are used in medicine, and its flowers are very ornamental. It does not however grow to a large size.

75. A much more common, and equally beautiful tree, and much resembling the former, is the Polas, or *Butea frondosa*. The flowers of this are not only offered to the gods, but in the festivals of spring serve to give a temporary yellow dye to the clothes of their votaries; on which account it is called Vosonti. The tree is of little use; and cannot be propagated by cuttings; but it is very common in most forests. It is sacred to the planet of Monday.

76. The *Dalbergia arborea*, W. is one of the most generally diffused trees in India; but is not very common in this district, where it is called Dorkorongjo or Dorkoromcha, and is applied to little or no use.

77. The plant consecrated to the memory of Sir William Jones, and called Osok, is not uncommon in this district. It is of no use except to afford elegant flowers that are offered to the Hindú gods.

78. The original *Onacardium* of the shops, a name properly restored by Jussieu to the *Semecarpus* of Linnæus, is the Bhela of the natives. The juice of its nut leaves an indelible stain on linen, and is used for marking it. The nuts are also used by tanners, especially in dressing the hide of the rhinoceros or buffalo to form targets. The timber is of little value. It is common in the woods.

79. The Mango (Amro or Am of the natives) is one of the most common trees, not only in the plantations of this country, but in the woods, where it has grown spontaneously from the seeds of those that have been planted about villages, which have been deserted. The mangos called Maldeh have a high reputation, and may be considered as one of the finest fruits in the world: but few of these grow at Maldeh; all the plantations of the most valuable kinds are on the opposite side of the Mohanonda, in the Puroniya district. Still however the mangos of the left bank of the Mohanonda are preferable to any others in Dinajpúr.

As the produce of the mango tree, even in its present state, is one of the most valuable in this district; for it cannot be of less annual value, on an average, than 4,50,000 Rupees, and as the management is better understood at Maldeh than any where else, I shall give some account of the manner in which this fine tree is cultivated by the people of that place. A bigah of ground, which there is rather more than ⅓ of an acre (3,644) is considered as a direct plantation. I shall now detail what the cultivators state as their expense and profit on such an orchard.

First Year's Expenses.						
To making a mud wall round the whole, Rs.	2	0	0			
To ploughing 10 or 12 times from the middle of September until the middle of November, ...	1	0	0			
To 25 seedlings, three years old, raised with much earth,	6	4	0			
To planting in deep pits, ...	2	0	0			
To watering and weeding, one man for eight months, ..	18	0	0			
Total, ...				29	4	0
Expense of each of the 2, 3, 4, and 5 years.						
To ten or twelve ploughings, ...	1	0	0			
To repairing the wall, ...	1	8	0			
Total, ...				2	8	0
Expense of the first year, ...	29	4	0			
Expense of the 4 following years, ...	10	0	0			
Rent for 5 years, at 14 Ans.	4	6	0			
Stock required, Rupees,				43	10	0

In the 6th year, or when the trees are from 8 to 9 years old, they begin to yield saleable fruit, partly green, partly ripe; and their produce is reckoned to be doubled every year for 5 years, in the following manner:

6th year each tree	160 M. totl	4,000, at 960 per R., Rs.	4	2	8
7th, ...	..320	8,000, at do.....	8	5	4
8th, ...	..640..	16,000, at do.....	16	10	8
9th, ...	....1,280..	32,000, at do......	33	5	4
10th,.. ..	....2,560..	64,000, at do......	56	10	8

The produce now becomes nearly stationary, for although the trees grow longer, and produce a greater number, the size and value of the fruit diminishes. The only expence after the first five years is to watch and collect the fruit, the rent, and a little ploughing or hoeing. The wall is allowed to go to ruin. In other places of this district the produce is of less value, and may be estimated at two rupees each tree; for a very large proportion of the mangoes, when allowed to become ripe on the tree, contain an insect *(Curculio)*, that renders them useless. They are therefore in general gathered when unripe. A plantation will last fifty or sixty years.

It might be supposed, that with such a large profit, the plantations would be extending fast, but this does not appear to be the case. Most even of the old plantations are neglected, and do not contain one-half of the trees which they might. Useless trees, especially wild figs, spring up, carelessness allows them to take root, and the prejudices of the landholders prevent them from being cut. Besides, there is no encouragement for plantations. If a tenant gives up his lease, he is allowed nothing for the trees that he leaves behind, although he may have been at the whole expense of rearing them. The great uncertainty of the crop is no doubt also a strong objection to these plantations. In many years the mango almost entirely fails, and in others it is so exceedingly abundant, that there is scarcely any sale for the produce. Heavy fogs or rains, when the flower has expanded, almost certainly prevent the fruit from forming. Besides, a capital of 40 or 50 rupees is rather uncommon.

The natives are entirely ignorant of the art of engrafting, which is the only means, by which good kinds can with certainty be reared; for the seed taken from one tree will produce 20 different kinds, not one of which perhaps may resemble the parent. The precautions, which the natives take, are no doubt entirely useless.

They will not plant a mango seed, the fruit of which has been bitten by the teeth, or cut with iron. The people of India usually attribute the abundance of the insect to the soil or to climate; but I am rather inclined to think, that the quality of the fruit has much more effect, because I observe some trees that always escape in the worst districts, and observe that the insect is peculiarly fond of the sour resinous kind. I confess, however, that this opinion is still liable to great uncertainty: but if well founded, it is a strong additional reason for the employment of engrafting.

In most parts of this district the fruit is chiefly used green or unripe; for when allowed to ripen, as I have said, it becomes full of insects. Those near Maldeh are not so subject to this loss. In Dinajpúr green mangoes come into season about the 12th of April, and continue until almost the end of May. During that season they enter largely into the dishes of the natives, and are preserved at Maldeh in sugar or honey. In other parts many are preserved in mustard seed oil. Some are cut into four parts and dried in the sun; but by far the greatest part is preserved by cutting the green pulp from the stone, and beating it with mustard seed (*sorisha*), salt, and turmeric, to which are occasionally added some of the carminative seeds, such as cummin. Those preparations keep throughout the year, and are a common seasoning for the food of the natives. The ripe mangoes continue common from the end of May until the middle of July. Their expressed juice is frequently inspissated by exposure to the sun: in this state it will keep throughout the year, and is eaten with milk.

The wood of the mangoe tree is much used, owing to its being plenty; for its quality is very inferior to that of many trees, which are little employed. Small boats built of it do not last above two years. Most of the package boxes are made of this wood. The inner bark contains a great quantity of a yellow colouring matter; but as yet no method has been devised for fixing it as a dye.

80. Nearly allied to the mangoe is a family of plants, which Sprengle, a learned German, has done me the honor of calling by my name. A species of this was shown in the woods of this district as the La or Lodh, which is used both by dyers and tanners; the former use the bark, the latter the leaves. I am far however from being certain that the person who showed it was sufficiently skilled.

81. The Jiyol of the natives is one of the most common trees in India, and is chiefly valuable for its being easily propagated by cuttings, no matter however large, so that a hedge or avenue may be formed very quickly, as has been done near Madras. In the dry season, the tree loses its leaves, and is never handsome. Its wood is of very little use, nor does it form a good fence, as it has no thorns. In this district, however, it is the hedge most commonly used. It produces a great quantity of gum; but the qualities of this have not yet been ascertained. In this district, many houses have been built with large branches of this tree, that have been placed in the ground for posts, and these have taken root, have pushed forth branches, and now produce a very picturesque appearance. I do not find this tree described in modern systems; but

in its Botanical affinities it comes very near to the *Rhus vernix*, W. although there are such differences that Dr. Roxburgh seems inclined to form it into a separate genus.

82. The *Spondias Amara*, E. M. is a much more elegant tree, of the resiniferous order. The French Botanists are justly to be praised for having preserved its native name, which is far from being barbarous. In this district it is called Amra or Amratok. The fruit, both green and ripe, is an excellent seasoning in cookery, which is the only thing of use that the tree affords.

83. The *Jujuba* of Botanists is by the natives called Koli, Kul, Boyer, and Bodori, usually pronounced Bodol, and is so common, that it communicates its name to several places, especially in the S. W. of the district. It is there however much more remarkable for quantity than quality; for I saw none, that could be reckoned good, and in some parts it is a tolerable fruit; the natives pick out the stones, and dry the ripe pulp mixed with salt and tamarinds, which forms a seasoning for their rice. It is a small tree, and its timber is of little use.

84. A larger species of the same genus, the *Zizyphus xylocarpus*, is common in the woods, and its timber is reckoned of some use. Some people called it the Jonggoli Boaer, or wild *Jujuba*; while others call it Pitalu, but this was also applied to a very different tree (No. 92), so that I cannot adopt it with certainty.

85. The Kamranga is a small tree very common near villages, and in the woods of this district, and is the *Averrhoa Carambola* of Botanists. The fruit, which is very acid, is often made into tarts by Europeans, who sometimes imagine, that it has a resemblance to the gooseberry. It is also used by the natives as an acid seasoning, but is not much valued.

86. Nearly allied to the above, and once joined with it in the same family by Linnæus, is the Horiphol, called also Loboni and Loyair. It is now called *Cicca* by Botanists, and probably both *disticha* and *nudiflora* may be referred to the same plant; at least I am unable to determine to which of the descriptions the plant of this district has the greatest resemblance. It is a handsome, although small tree, and grows pretty frequent near villages. The fruit is the only part used, and in its qualities very nearly resembles that of the last mentioned tree.

87. Still nearly allied to these is the *Emblica* of Botanists, who seem to have borrowed the native name Amlaki. It has been placed in one of those convenient tribes (*Phyllanthus*), into which European Botanists squeeze any thing with the structure of which they are little acquainted, and from which they have carefully excluded the only plants, *Xylophylla*, that deserved the name. The fruit preserved in either sugar or honey is much used by the natives as a sweetmeat, and dried as a medicine. The natives have an idea, that this fruit, and that of the *Chebula Myrobalans*, have never been found ripe, except by some very holy persons; and it is supposed, that such as have been favoured with eating such a rarity, have been ever afterwards exempted from hunger. The wood is little used.

88. A fruit called Lotko is mentioned in the Ayeen Akbery as peculiar to this district; but it is found in all the eastern parts of Bengal, and is common in the kingdom of Ava. It has strong affinities to the three last-mentioned plants, and the pulp, that surrounds its seeds, is rather agreeable, and might perhaps be improved by cultivation. It has not yet found its way into the systems of Botany.

89. The plant which I described in the account of the embassy to Ava by Colonel Symes, under the name of *Agyneia coccinea*, must be removed to a newly-formed

tribe called *Bradleya.* It was shown to me in the woods of this district by the name of Boro Amla, and is a small tree of no value.

90. The *Clutia stipularis,* L. was shown to me by the name of Bonkangthali, but I am uncertain concerning the accuracy of the information, as a very different tree (92) was called by the same name. The tree grows to a pretty considerable size, and has been very improperly classed with some African shrubs. Its fruit is a berry that contains much oil in its pulp, which is rather an uncommon circumstance. I have already seen seven or eight Indian plants of the same family; its bark is used as a yellow dye.

91. Among the other plants of this family is that called Kukurbichha, of which I have seen no account in the writings of Botanists. It is common near villages, and grows to be a small tree with very ornamental foliage.

92. One of the most common trees in the Dinajpúr district, both near villages and in woods, was called by so many different names, most of them applied also to other plants, that I am quite uncertain concerning its real appellation. It was called Bonkathali (a name given to No. 90), Bharul, Pitali, and Pitalu, (a name given to No. 84;) but its most common appellation is Gambhar. Now this name, I know, is given to No. 17 both in Chittagong and at Goalpara, where the wood is much esteemed, and the leaves of the two trees have such a strong resemblance, that inaccurate persons may be readily mistaken. The confusion renders me doubtful, whether or not the wood of this tree is really as useful as that of No. 17, which is undoubtedly the proper Gambhar. I find no account of this tree in the writings of modern Botanists; but it is either the Cansehi of Rheede, or approaches near to that plant. I am in a great measure induced to believe this from that valuable author's having placed it next to the Cumbulu, which is the tree No. 17, to which our plant has the strongest resemblance. According to the present plan, it might be thrust among the *Crotons,* a collection of plants, which seems to have been made from any specimens of exotics, that could not be otherwise arranged.

93. To this convenient family may also belong a tree that was shown to me as the Dudé, from the wood of which are made beads that are much worn by Hindús; but in this there is some doubt (see No. 22). The tree has not yet found its way into modern systems of Botany.

94. The Sindur derives its Botanical name from the worthy Dr. Rottler of Madras, and its Bengalee name from the powder which covers its fruit, and resembles red lead. The use of this as a dye is not known to the natives of this district. The tree is very common, but does not grow to a large size.

95. The *Ficus Indica* was celebrated among ancient writers, and under the name of Banyan tree came to be equally renowned among the modern English. Indeed no person who has visited India could avoid being struck with admiration at its great size, the picturesque appearance of its trunk, the fineness of its foliage, intermixed with thousands of golden coloured berries, and above all by its singular manner of sending down roots from its branches, and of forming new stems. Every thing concerning the history of this tree is clear, except among Botanists, and the editor of the Hortus Malabaricus seems to have led the way of error (Partis III. pagina 74, in notâ), in which he has been followed even by Linnæus. So far as can be judged, this great Botanist received specimens from the West Indies of a tree which resembled the Indian Fig in its remarkable manner of growth; and as he seems to have considered that the two Indies had nearly the

same vegetable productions, he immediately concluded, that his specimens belonged to the Indian Fig, and described them as such. He also had probably received specimens of the true Indian Fig from Bengal, without any account of its manner of growth, and described this under the name of *Ficus Bengalensis*, and I have already made an excuse for the appellation: but I believe on the whole, that the safest plan for Botanists to adopt on the occasion, would be to expunge whatever has been said concerning the *Ficus Bengalensis* and *Indica*, since the time of Rheede. The authors of the Encyclopedie, indeed, seem to have been aware of the Linnæan error, but even they are wrong in considering this tree as the Pipol, and the description which they give of the *Ficus Indica* is too nearly applicable to the *Ficus Bengalensis* or Bot. The leaves of this tree have no dots on their upper surface, which is said to be the case with the *F. Indica;* but I suspect, that the leaves of the *F. racemosa* has been taken for those of the Indian Fig, by the Botanists, who have given it that character.

This tree, probably from its beauty, for it is of little use, is in great esteem with the natives of Bengal, and is considered by them as the female of the Pipol. As they are supposed to represent a Brahmun and his wife, it is reckoned a sin to cut or destroy either, but especially the male; and it is considered as very meritorious to plant a young male tree close to a female, with some religious ceremonies approaching to those of marriage, but not so intolerably prolix nor expensive. In this union the natives have discovered great taste, the elegant lightness and bright foliage of the Pipol being well fitted to contrast with the rigid grandeur of the India Fig, although from these qualities it is difficult to account for their having appropriated the sexes of these trees in the manner that has been done. The branches and leaves of these two trees being a favourite food of elephants, the keepers, who are low people, make sad havoc on the emblematical Brahmuns; but this is submitted to with patience, provided they do not attempt the entire destruction of the plant. It is usual to place a piece of silver money under the Banyan tree, when it is planted, for it is supposed, that otherwise, it neither will grow to a large size, nor send down fine roots. In Bengal this tree is called Nyagrodh and Bot. Besides its being an ornament, and affording a wholesome and cool shade, and being a good fodder for the elephant, this noble tree contains a milky juice which coagulates into a kind of elastic gum, and makes admirable bird-lime. The milky juice is collected by making incisions in the branches, it is strained and mixed with ¾ of its weight of mustard-seed oil. It is then fit for use. The juice of the tree next to be mentioned possesses exactly the same qualities; their wood is of little value. In this district, the young roots, which this tree sends forth from its branches, are often used for ropes. Notwithstanding some good qualities of these trees, the prejudice in their favor is attended with many bad effects. Their fruit being a favourite food of monkies and birds, their seeds are constantly deposited on buildings, and on other more useful trees: and wherever they find a crevice, they take root. They send long filaments to the ground, and no sooner procure nourishment from thence, than they crush and overpower their original supporter, and thus lay waste all old buildings and plantations. This is not peculiar to these Figs; most other Indian trees of this family possess the same noxious faculty, but these may be eradicated, whereas the two holy trees can only be removed, when it can be done without danger to their lives, that is, when they may be transplanted, which is seldom the case.

96. The *Ficus Religiosa* of the Botanists is the Oswottho, Asod, or Pipol of the Bengalees. Although it wants the majestic size and numerous stems of the Banyan, it possesses great elegance. The various roots that it has sent down from a tree or building on which it first germinated, often form a trunk of the most picturesque form, while the beautiful shape of its leaves, and their tremulous motion like those of the aspen, give it a peculiar elegance. Its qualities have been detailed in the account of the Banyan tree. It is sacred to the planet of Thursday, (Vrihaspati, Jupiter.)

97. There are several trees, that have a great resemblance to the last mentioned Fig, and although they want some of its elegance, are still very fine, and nearly of the same use. They are reckoned, however, rather heating food for the elephant, although from this theory, their unfitness for the animal may be doubted. They are not considered holy, and a great many names are applied to them very indiscriminately, such as Porkoti or Pakur, Naksa, and Nakor. I think that in this district I have observed three very distinct species: the first I shall call Pakur. In the Encyclopedie it is considered as a variety only of the *Ficus Religiosa;* but for this I see no sort of reason.

98. The next Fig tree of this district I shall call Nakor. It may perhaps be the *Ficus pyrifolia* of the Encyclopedie; but this is doubtful. It is readily known by its berries, which are about the size of a pea, and are covered by long white hair.

99. The next Fig, which I shall call Naksa, differs from the former in having smooth berries. I cannot refer it to any species in the modern systems of Botany; but it is the *Tojela* of the Hortus Malabaricus (P. III. tab. 63); from whence it would appear, that the Brahmuns of the south give the same name to this tree, that those of the north give to the *Ficus Religiosa;* the leaves of these two last are much smaller and narrower than those of No. 97.

100. Among the Indian Figs that are esculent for man, there are two kinds in this district; they cannot be called fruit in the common acceptation of the word, as they are only used as vegetables in cookery: the first is one of the most common plants in India. Dr. Roxburgh, in his Plants of Coromandel, No. 124, calls it *oppositifolia,* which at once distinguishes it from every plant to which it has any considerable affinity. I should have supposed, that this was the *F. symphytifolia* of the Encyclopedie, had not the learned and accurate authors omitted this circumstance. It is not improbable, however, that they may have seen only imperfect specimens; for the plants of this kind are very difficult to preserve. In this district it is called Dumor, Dumbor, and Khoska, and its fruit is very much used.

101. The *Ficus glomerata* of Dr. Roxburgh, (Coromandel Plants, No. 123) is the Yogdumor, or Jogdumor, Yogingyo or Jogingyo Dumbor of the natives. Dr. Rottler, in a conversation which we lately had at Madras concerning the *Ficus Indica* of Linnæus, seemed inclined to think, that this may have been the plant which that celebrated Botanist meant; and it certainly comes nearer his definition than any common Indian Fig that we know: but I have no doubt that Linnæus had in view an American plant, which sends roots from its branches, and this is not the case with the Jogdumor. This tree is no doubt the *Ficus racemosa* of the Encyclopedie; nor do I know the reason, that has induced Dr. Roxburgh to consider it as different from the *Ficus racemosa* of Linnæus, unless it has been discovered, that the plant described by the celebrated Swede differs from the Atty Alu of Rheede, which no doubt is our plant. It is a very common tree near villages, and its trunk and larger branches produce bunches of large Figs, which make very good curry. In Songskrito it is called Orumbor, and it is sacred to the planet of Friday, (Shukra, Venus.)

102. Nearly related to the Figs, are the Bread Fruits, of which the Jak is the finest that we have in India. It is very common in this district wherever the soil is free, but does not thrive in a stiff clay. This tree, called *Artocarpus integrifolia* by Botanists, is the Ponos, Kontokiphol, and Kangtal of the higher and lower dialects of Bengal. It has a beautiful foliage, exhales a delightful odour in February, when in flower; produces a very useful fruit; is an excellent fodder for elephants, and produces a timber that is both useful and ornamental for the cabinet-maker. Unfortunately it warps much with heat, and therefore is not well fitted for this country; but would be useful where the climate is less severe. The wood is also used as a dye. The fruit has a nauseous smell, and its flavour is not agreeable to the generality of Europeans; but the natives are fond of the pulpy envelope, by which the seeds are surrounded, although they do not think it wholesome. The green fruit is much used as a vegetable in curries, and the ripe seeds are preserved for the same purpose. In some parts of India, indeed, they form the common food of the people for two or three months in the year, just as chesnuts do in the south of Europe; and in fact, when roasted, they have a strong resemblance to that fruit. In Dinajpúr, the Jak is rather neglected, and its produce does not sell so high as that of the Mangoe.

103. The species of *Artocarpus* called in this district Dohu, Duyo, and Borol, does not seem to be described by the systematic writers on Botany, and is the least useful plant of its family. The fruit is small and sour, and is very seldom used, except by the poor. The wood is of little or no value. The inner bark, when beaten with that of the tree No. 16, gives a red dye that is used by some artists of this district, and is employed by tanners to give their skins a dirty orange colour.

104. The Sakot or Sara is one of the most common trees in this district, and indeed in most parts of India. By Dr. Köenig it was considered as a species of *Trophis;* but has strong Botanical affinities with the Mulberry, and is no doubt the *Tinda Parua* of the Hortus Malabaricus, which Linnæus has called the *Morus Indica;* but most of what has been written concerning the *Morus Indica,* relates to a totally different plant, on which the silk-worm is fed. It is of very little use. The natives use a small branch of it in place of a tooth-brush, and suppose that it not only cleans but strengthens the teeth.

105. The Pangpiya of Bengal has had its name preserved in the *Papaya* of Botanists. In every part of India it is a common tree near villages, but is of very little use. The natives like the ripe fruit, and reckon it wholesome.

106. The *eltis orientalis* of Botanists is a very common tree in this district, where it is called Jig. It has an ornamental foliage, but I know of no use to which it is applied.

107. The Khagorbhela is one of the most common trees in this district, but as I never saw its fructification, I know not its Botanical history. By boiling its bark yields a gum or gluten, that is used by those who make artificial flowers.

108. Jibon.

109. Goneyari.

110. Parul.

111. Keng.

112. Chamkul.

113. Jamrul.

114. Borophedus.

I had no opportunity of seeing these trees, and have nothing to say concerning them; but that they are found growing in the woods, or near the villages of this district.

In the general Statistical Table (No. 1), I have mentioned, that in this district there are perhaps about 260 square miles which are overflooded in the rainy season; and great part of this extent is covered with long reeds, commonly called grass jungle by the English. Some part is no doubt bare sandy land, but as a small part of the land that is not inundated is overgrown with long reeds or harsh coarse grass, we may estimate the extent of this division of the wastes at 260 miles. Although several of these reeds are applied to use, this land in its present state, may be considered to be of as little value as that which is overgrown with woods, and it is equally pernicious by harbouring destructive animals. If the whole were equally diffused through the district, use might be perhaps procured for a considerable part of its produce; but it is generally disposed in such large masses, that the neighbouring cultivated country cannot consume a hundredth part, and the produce is too bulky, in proportion to its value, to admit of being carried to a distance.

The natives, whom I consulted, seemed to have only confused notions concerning the different kinds of reeds that are contained in these wastes, and sometimes they brought the same species under different names, while at other times two or three species were called by the same appellation. What I have to say on this subject, therefore, gives me very little satisfaction; and I may farther state, that in this district less use than common is made of these plants, and their place is supplied by the bambu, which indeed might probably serve every where much better, were it not somewhat more troublesome to work.

1. The Kus or *Poa cynosuroides* is a sacred plant among the Hindús, and is dedicated to the invisible planet Ketu, which occasions the eclipses of the sun. It is very common in the wastes of this district, and mats made of it are exported to Calcutta, where they are used in religious ceremonies.

2. The Kesé is another harsh grass, the leaves of which are used to form a coarse kind of rope. When exposed to the weather, in tying fences and hurdles, these ropes last about a year. The plant brought to me as the Kesé was the *Saccharum spontaneum*; but I suspect that a wrong plant was brought. It is also used as fuel.

3. The Ulukhoris, one of the reeds most used by the natives of this district, I have not seen in flower, and therefore cannot say what its botanical name may be; but the plant called by this name at Goalpara is the *Saccharum cylindricum.* Its leaves form an excellent thatch, and its stems are very frequently used in making the hurdles, which serve the natives for walls, both to their houses and to surround the yard. These hurdles (*tati*) are usually made of reeds laid parallel to each other, and confined between sticks or split bambus, which are tied together, and cross each other, at right angles. In the better sort of hurdles the reeds or bambus are first split and wrought into mats, and these are formed into walls in the same manner. In this district no mats of this kind are made from reeds, unless we include the bambu under that denomination. The Ulukhor is often used as fuel, and its stems, which are spongy, are employed to float nets. In some parts fields of it are preserved for thatch, and yield a good rent. These two last reeds are eaten by the buffalo; but they are extremely coarse.

4. The Nol or *Arundo Bengalensis* is a very large reed, not common in this district.

5. The Khagra is a reed with which the natives usually write; from its various sizes, I should judge, that there are several different kinds; but I have not seen the flower. In this district it is not common, and does not grow to a large size.

6. The Sor, from its white flowers which I have seen at a distance, must be either an *Arundo* or *Saccharum*. It is little used.

7. The Sorongjo is the *Saccharum spontaneum*; a fine large reed, pretty common, but little used.

8. The Ikir is one of the most common reeds of this district; but is chiefly used for fuel, by fishermen in making their traps, and by the cultivators of betel-leaf for sheltering the tender plant which they rear.

9. The Byana seems to be the *Andropogon schœnanthus* of the Encyclopedie; at least, the description applies tolerably well to our reed, which is very common, but is applied to little use.

10. The Gongdhayi is an *Andropogon*, of which no account is to be found in the botanical systems. At Calcutta its root is used for making hurdles, which are placed at the doors and windows of chambers in the hot season, and are watered to produce coolness. The natives here know nothing of this art, but the stems are much used for making hurdles. In the parts of this district, where much sugar is boiled, fields of it are kept for fuel, although wood might be had in abundance, but wood is troublesome to cut. This plant seems to vary much from the soil in which it grows: when it is produced in a dry place, it is largest, and its root is odorous; the stem is then called Birna, and the root is called Khoskhos, but its leaves are very harsh. In moist places, the elephant-keepers call it Kotra, and the young shoots are a useful fodder for this noble animal.

11. The Sokorkondo is a most elegant *Andropogon*, of which no description has been published in the Encyclopedie.

12. Nagormutha is a species of *Scirpus*, with a triangular stem, of which the mats that the natives sleep on are usually made. I have not seen the flower.

These are the vegetable productions, which nature, with little or no assistance, has chiefly provided this district; but numerous bushes and herbs are scattered in the fields, ponds, marshes, and other waste places, and many of them are applied to use. Of these I shall now take notice.

The poorer class of inhabitants, as I have before mentioned, are unable to procure from gardens the vegetable seasoning that would be requisite for their insipid diet; they have therefore recourse to the fields, to ponds, and thickets, from whence they obtain a scanty and coarse supply.

I. Plants of the kind called *Torkari*, which are insipid succulent fruits or roots that are fried with oil in curries, or are boiled with salt and capsicum.

1. Dumbor; Ficus—see trees No. 100.
2. Yogingyo or Jogingyo Dumbor—see trees No. 101.
3. Piralu—see trees No. 31.
4. Jonggoli Alu, Wild *Dioscoreas*, probably of several sorts.
5. Bangser Kongra, young shoots of the bambus.
6. Ram Baigon or Begun, *Solanum stramonifolium*, E. M.

II. Omboltos, or acids.

1. Jolpaye, *Eleocarpus serrata*—see trees No. 38.
2. Tetul, *Tamarindus Indica*—see trees No. 66.
3. Chalita, *Dillenia speciosa*—see trees No. 48.
4. Amra, *Spondias Amara*, E. M.—see trees No. 82.

5. Noyari, a tree nearly related to the *Hansium* of Rumphius.
6. Deuyo, *Artocarpus*—see trees No. 103.
7. Kamrangga, *Averrhœa Carambola*— see trees No. 85.
8. Boruyi or Kul, *Zizyphus Jujuba*—see trees No. 83.
9. Koromcha, *Carissa spinarum.*

III. Sak, or leaves, flowers, and stems, that may be fried or boiled to give a taste to rice.

1. Sojina, flowers of the *Hyperanthera Moringa*—see trees No. 68.
2. Kangta Notyia, Kangta Khoriya, } *Amaranthus spinosus.*
3. Notiya, *Amaranthus oleraceus.*
4. Kochu, the petioli of some wild *Arums.*
5. Helongcha, *Polymnia*, a species not published, *Jussieua repens.*
6. Jonaki, *Jussieua repens.*
7. Kalanunya, *Convolvulus repens* and *reptans*, which are of the same species.
8. Susoni, *Marsilia quadrifolia.*
9. Hela nali; the root is called here Baromutha, but its proper name is said to be Saluk. It is eaten raw by children. The stem, which supports the flower, is dressed in curries as a Sak. The fruit in this district is called Bhengyit, but its proper name is said to be Sovla. When unripe, it is dressed as a Torkari; when ripe, the seed is parched and eaten. The plant I believe is the *Nymphæa Lotus.*
10. Dima, Gima, } *Pharnaceum Mollugo.*
11. Putika, Soda Pungyi, } *Basella cordifolia.*
12. Lal Pungyi, *Basella rubra.*
13. Sangchya.
14. Dron, Dulobi, } *Phlomis Indica*, W.
15. Goyaliya, *Cissus quadrangularis.*
16. Dengke Sak, an *Asplenium*, of which I see no notice in books.
17. Siyal Bathuya, *Chenopodium album.*
18. Kalo Teporiya, *Solanum nigrum.*
19. Nuné.
20. Amrul, *Oxalis corniculata* vel *pusilla.*

IV. Vegetables used without being cooked.

1. Ata, *Anona squamosa*—see trees No. 49.
2. Lona, *Anona muricata*—see trees No. 50.
3. Kalo Jam, *Calypthranthes Jambulana*— trees No. 56.
4. Singgur, Paniphol, } *Trappa*, fruit.
5. Kesur, *Cyperus tuberosus*, roots.
6. Podmo bij, *Nelumbium* seeds. The flower-stem is also eaten raw. In China the plant is cultivated on account of these stems, which are a vegetable very commonly used in that country.

It was my earnest wish to have ascertained the officinal plants, or those used by the natives in medicine; but after much pains I have been able to obtain no information concerning the subject, on which reliances could be placed. Being unable to procure a physician to give me information, at Dinajpúr, I sent an intelligent man to the shop of a druggist, to make out a list of such plants as he sold, for I found that this class of men have no books containing a list of officinals. The man, after several days' labour, brought a list sufficiently long, but on examination it was found to want many of the most material articles. A collection of simples, usually employed by the druggist, was procured to bring the plants, but after some days' trial I found, that no trust could be placed on what he said. He repeatedly brought the same plant under different names, and applied the same name to various plants, which had not the smallest affinity. I have therefore been reluctantly compelled to wait, until I shall reside for some months near an intelligent physician or druggist, to whose knowledge of the plants I can trust.

A few other plants that are in common use remain to be mentioned:

1. The *Lawsonia inermis* or *spinosa*, Mehendi, are used by the Muhammedans of both sexes for colouring their hands and feet. The leaves beaten with a little Catechu are applied like a paste for a night, and the colour remains for about 15 days. These can scarcely be considered as different species.

2. The Panisiuli, or *Phyllanthus Rhamnoides*, W. is a very common shrub, which produces a black berry. The juice of this gives a dark purple colour, which is sometimes applied to turbans; but it does not last.

3. The *Mimosa saponaria*, or Amlokungche, is common in the district, and its fruit is sometimes used in tanning; but the natives are not acquainted with the saponaceous quality, which occasions it to be in much request with more cleanly Indian tribes.

4. The Gaukungchi, or Changmolloti, is a small shrubby species of *Guilandina*, of which, so far as I can discover, no account has yet been published. Its pods are much used by the dyers of this district, and the people who collect them pay a revenue to the proprietors of woods.

4. The Sola is a plant much used both by fishermen, who employ it for floating their nets in place of cork, and by the makers of artificial flowers, who are numerous in Bengal. Their work is indeed coarse, but the material is excellent, and seems to be the same with that of which the elegant artificial flowers of China are formed. In fact, nothing can more strongly resemble the structure of the petals of a flower than the pith of the plant, which I am persuaded would be a valuable acquisition to our artists in Europe. It might even be worth while to send some home as a trial. This plant grows in tanks and marshes. The trunk, which remains under water, is three or four feet in length, and three inches in diameter. It consists almost entirely of a fine grained very light white pith, which has a considerable coherence of parts even when cut in very thin slices, and which can be dyed of the brightest colours. For making ornaments, the plant must be cut between the middle of October and that of November; what is procured after the marshes become dry is fit only for floating nets. Some confusion seems to have taken place in the Hortus Malabaricus concerning this plant: the drawing (Part IV. tab. 18) seems to have been taken from the *Aschynomene Indica* of Wildenow, while the description, page 31, seems to refer to this plant, which is the *A. diffusa*, W.

6. The *Valisneria spiralis* is the plant used by those who refine sugar, in the same manner as clay is used for this purpose in Europe and America. The plant grows very copiously in the rivers that have a gentle stream, especially in the Jomuna. By the natives it is called Pat.

CHAPTER III.

MINERALS.

It is impossible to find a district less interesting to a mineralogist than Dinajpúr, as it consists entirely of soil, sand, and clay, and these in no great variety. The soil is seldom very deep. Under it is often a bed of clay; but sometimes even this is wanting, and the soil rests on sand.

The clay is of three kinds: first, a black moist smooth clay; second, a red hard clay, which contains black angular concretions that are sometimes indurated. This resembles entirely a porphyry in a state of decomposition. Third, a yellow hard clay, which contains much ochre, sometimes in a sort of veins. It also frequently contains small rounded pebbles, and seems to be a rock in a state of decay. All these are fit for the potter, and all of them become red in the kiln.

The sands are of two kinds: first, large-grained dark-coloured sand, mixed with black mud; when water is found in this, it is always bad; second, a fine light-coloured sand of quartz and mica. In digging wells, the water is usually found in this, and is generally very good.

The wells in the stiff-clay land are in general best, as that soil prevents the surface water from penetrating. In some places, such as between the Tanggon and Punabhoba, water has seldom been procured by digging; and when it has been found, the wells have been at least 60 feet deep. In other parts, such as Bongsihari, it is usually found at a depth of from 20 to 30 cubits: but in most places it is found at a still less depth.

It is said, that formerly, where Rajgunj now stands, the people used to dig out a clay called Khorimati, with which they white-washed their houses. Such earths are common in many parts of India, and are shistose mica or granite in a state of decay; the mica being the predominant and colouring matter. It is said, that Mr. Hatch, formerly magistrate, ordered the pit to be shut, which is not at all probable.

In some parts of the district, nitre was formerly made; but there seems to have been nothing peculiar in the soil, and it might be made equally well any where with the earth taken from the floor of cow-houses, as was practised here. The Company has of late withdrawn the manufacture to more favorable situations.

BOOK IV.

STATE OF AGRICULTURE.

CHAPTER I.

DIFFERENT PLANTS CULTIVATED.

In the Statistical Table, No. 1. I have supposed, that in the whole district there are fully occupied 3,585 square miles, that is 6,883,200 Calcutta bigahs. I have also supposed, that there are 649 square miles occasionally cultivated, of which perhaps a fourth part may be annually tilled; this increases the occupied land to 7,194,720 bigahs. Now the manner in which this is occupied, and the gross value of its produce, as coming for the cultivator, may be somewhat nearly similar to the estimate contained in the Statistical Table No. 4.

It is said, that when Mr. Hatch settled this district, it was estimated that $\frac{4}{5}$ of the whole were fully occupied. If that report is true, and the estimate as well founded, this country has been declining, and (according to my estimate) 643,840 bigahs have since been deserted.

Section 1.—*Plants cultivated for their grain.*

Part I.—Introduction.

In almost every civilized country, plants cultivated for their grain are a principal object of the farmer's care, and this is especially the case in Bengal, where these grains form almost the only sustenance of man. It is probable, that in this district about 6,400,000 bigahs are annually cultivated to produce grain, and the Statistical Table No. 5, will give a general notion of the proportion and value of each. Several other heads might have been introduced, as will be seen from the account of the particular objects of cultivation; but these are sufficient for such a table as can be formed by mere conjecture, and the average value would be little or nothing affected by greater minuteness. The grains which are cultivated in this district are as follows:

I.—Culmiferous Plants.

1. Rice, *Oryza Sativa*, W.
2. Wheat, *Triticum Sativum*, W.
3. Barley, *Hordeum Vulgare*, W.
4. Merua, *Cynosurus Corocanus*, L.
5. { Millet, Kanguni, } *Panicum Italicum*, L.

II.—Leguminous Grains.

6. Thakuri Kolayi. I did not see the plant, and cannot say what it is. In some parts the *Phaseolus Max* is called by this name.

7. { Khesari, Teyuri, } *Lathyrus Sativus*, W.

8. { Lentil, Mosur, } *Ervum lens*, L.

9. { Harimug, Kharimug. } a *Phaseolus*, of which no mention is made in Willdenow, nor in the Encyclopedie.

10. Oror, *Cytisus Cajan*, W.

11. { Field Pea, Kalomotor, } *Pisum arvense*, W.

12. { Chona, Chhola, Lalbut, } *Cicer arietinum*, flore purpureo.

13. { Kablibut, Sadabut, } *Cicer arietinum*, flore albo.

III.—Oily Seeds.

14. Sorisha, a species of *Sinapis*, not mentioned by Willdenow, nor in the Encyclopedie.

15. Turi.

16. Rayi. Two species of *Sinapis*, that however approach very near to the *Brassica*. Neither is mentioned by Wildenow, nor in the Encyclopedie. The latter is commonly called Mustard by the English, and its seed is hot and pungent.

17. Tora. This may be the *Raphanes sativus* of Willdenow, and no doubt belongs to that family. I see no reason, however, for supposing, that it is a variety of the radish.

18. Kasthotil, *Sesamum*.

19. { Flax or Linseed, Mosina, } *Linum usitatissimum*, W.

In the annexed Table, No. 6, many particulars relative to these will be seen. I shall now proced to give some farther explanation.

PART 2.—*Culmiferous Plants.*

Rice is by far the principal crop in this district, and some portion of the land produces annually two crops of this grain. That, however, as will be seen from the table, does not increase the general produce very much, as the two crops do not yield much more than a single crop would : as the trouble is nearly double, it may be thought wonderful, that this practice is generally diffused ; but it is not done without very strong reasons. The seasons are so uncertain, and the latter crop is so liable to fail, that it is of importance to seize the earliest opportunity of cultivating as much as possible for the first crop, so that should the latter fail, the effects of scarcity may be mitigated. But should the first crop succeed, why exhaust the soil by a second, that will be superfluous? The reason here is also urgent. The first crop is reaped in the rainy season, so that its straw cannot be preserved, and as rice-straw is almost the only food which the cattle have in this district, their is an absolute necessity for sowing the second crop for fodder. In inundated lands, such as near Churamon, the uncertainty of the crops, owing to the irregular swellings of the rivers, has introduced another singular mode of having two crops from the same field. The ground is ploughed in the usual manner as for summer rice; and in spring the seed of the summer and winter kinds intermixed are sown in the same field, so that if a season favorable for either happens, the people may not be altogether destitute of food. Although there is no difference in the management, the two kinds ripen one after the other at the appropriate seasons, which shows, that there is an essential difference in the kinds.

The kinds of rice are very numerous, and the first division among them arises from the seasons in which they ripen.

1. One kind, called Boro by the natives, ripens in the hot-weather of spring, and is cultivated only in small quantities, chiefly in inundated lands, where there are marshes and old water-courses, that preserve a small quantity of water throughout the year; sometimes a dam is made across the water-course at the end of the rainy season, and its upper part forms a reservoir filled with water, which is let gradually out to supply the rice that has been planted in the lower part, which has been drained in order to admit of cultivation. In other parts small quantities of this rice are cultivated on the sides of old tanks, that are partly filled up, and the water is thrown upon the rice by a simple machine. In times of scarcity, many poor people engage in this kind of cultivation, which gives them a temporary supply of food at the dearest season. In other years, less attention is bestowed on it, for the grain is very coarse, and the produce small, so that it would ill repay the labour. It is always transplanted, and its straw can seldom be saved. The grain is almost always consumed by those who have raised it.

2. Next follows the summer rice, called in this district Bhaduyi, and reckoned to be only of one kind. The grain is used almost entirely by the labourers on the farm, and is seldom sold. It is said, that it will not keep for more than a year. It is reckoned very heavy and indigestible for those who are not hardened by labour; very considerable quantities however are raised, as where two crops of rice are taken in the year, or where a crop of rice is to be followed by wheat, barley, oil-seeds, or most kinds of pulse, this is the only kind that can be cultivated. In some places the pulse called Thakuri is sown along with this rice, and ripens a month after it is cut. This does not prevent the field from giving a winter crop of any thing except rice. It is generally sown broad cast, and unless it is to be followed by a winter crop of rice, does not require that the field in which it is sown should be reduced to an absolute level. In a few places however it is transplanted, and is then a month later in coming to maturity, so that it cannot be followed by another crop of rice; but this does not prevent it from being followed by any other crop, and the quality of the grain is rather superior to that which has been sown broad cast. Its straw cannot be preserved, as I have before mentioned. The grain may be used in all the same ways that the coarse winter rices are.

3. The winter rice in this province are called Henguti, which is said to be a corruption of Haimontick. This implies rice that is cut in the season of dew, which is copious in the cold season. The words seem however to be radically different. The kinds are very various, nor can I pretend to give a full enumeration of them, but I shall reduce them to classes, and mention the principal kinds belonging to each.

1. The coarsest kinds are those which grow in very low land, that is deeply inundated. These are sown broad cast in spring, and require a long time to come to maturity. Sometimes they are sown intermixed with summer rice, as I have before mentioned; but this practice is confined to a small extent of ground in the vicinity of the Nagor river. These kinds are little better than summer rice, and their usual market value when clean may be 12 anas the maund at 96 sa. wt. the seer, which is at the rate of 64 Calcutta seers, or about 131 lbs. for the rupee. These coarse rices do not keep well, and are generally consumed in the course of the year by the labourers on the farm. If kept longer than two years, they do not absolutely spoil, but acquire a bad flavour. Except the tops, none of the straw is preserved for cattle. These rices are the common food of the poor, form better cakes (pitiya) than the finer sorts, and may be also prepared into *chira* and *muri*, which will afterwards be described; but a large proportion is used simply boiled.

The most common kinds are,

1. Pakra,	2. Pakor,	3. Keledongga.
4. Kalanunga,	5. Dholanunya,	6. Bagun bichi.

Much less of the land fit for producing these is waste, than of any other kind of land in the district, and that portion of it, which has a free soil, is high rented. We may therefore safely conclude, that this is the kind of cultivation, from which the farmer has the greatest profit.

2. Somewhat finer is a numerous tribe of rices, which are transplanted into land rather higher than the former, and are not preceded by a summer crop of rice, but in a free soil they are generally followed by a crop of pulse, which is sown among the growing corn and flowers soon after it has been cut: but when the rice is cut early, the field is ploughed afterwards, and sown with the pulse. This kind of cultivation is also very advantageous, and the land fit for it is eagerly sought after by the farmers. The straw is not very good for cattle, but is used. As it is very rank, about a foot only, near the top, is cut with the grain, and the stems are afterwards cut for fuel or thatch. The rice, like all the transplanted kinds, keeps well, even when cleared. It is reckoned better and lighter after the first year, and continues in perfection for three years. It then generally becomes worse, and in ten years it is almost useless. These kinds of rice are prepared in the same manner as the former, but do not yield meal so fit for making cakes, and are the kinds that are usually exported from Calcutta under the denomination of Cargo rice. In this district the usual price is 14 anas for the heavy mon, which is at the rate of nearly 55 Calcutta seers or 112 lbs. for the rupee. The most common kinds are,

1 Kangdisayee,	2 Panisali,	3 Dudkolma.
4 Bethupa,	5 Rajpal,	6 Kangsa.
7 Rajmoyil,	8 Horinpangjor,	9 Kocheedola.
10 Kangkuya,	11 Bajar,	12 Kengya.
13 Guti,	14 Gurjal.	

3. Next follow a great number of winter rices, which are of rather a fine quality, and are transplanted into high fields, generally as a second crop, especially where the soil is free. Sometimes however the summer crop is omitted, and at other times in a very rich soil, a third crop (generally of pease) is produced.

These kinds of rice are particularly valuable, as their straw is almost the only tolerable forage that is procurable. In ordinary years, these sell at one rupee for the heavy maund, which is at the rate of 48 Calcutta seers, or about 98½ lbs. for the rupee. They are used chiefly boiled, but some is made into *chira*, and a preparation called *khoyi*, is made from the two last-mentioned in the following list, and these are one-eighth dearer than the others.

1 Soni,	2 Varibanggola,	3 Chhoto Soruna,
4 Kautormoni,	5 Bohumali,	6 Duyini,
7 Bokori,	8 Dumora,	9 Boroputra,
10 Chaupor,	11 Morichdal,	12 Malisa,
13 Munggi Malisa,	14 Elayi,	15 Josa,
16 Karticksali,	17 Subondori,	18 Layudumo,
19 Kesorwotie,	20 Chengga,	21 Samrosh,

4. The very finest rices in this district are inferior to those of Patna, but in ordinary years they sell here at 30 seers for the rupee, or at the rate of 36 Calcutta seers, or 73¾ lbs. for the rupee. They are transplanted into high land, generally of a stiff clay, and this rarely admits of two crops. They are almost always used boiled, and are very seldom prepared in any other way. The straw is the best fodder for cattle. The kinds are only three:

1 Choudonchur. 2 Kalonelya. 3 Bernaphul.

The rice that is intended for seed must be well dried in the sun, and is preserved in a kind of straw bags, which inclose it on all sides, which contain about 82lbs. and which are preserved on a bambu stage at some distance from the earth. Except in a very few places, it is not the custom, in this district, to prepare the seed by moistening it so as to occasion it to sprout before it is sown. It was near Nawabgunj only that I heard of this practice.

The ground for rice is ploughed, until the surface is well broken, and after every double-ploughing (one lengthwise and one across) it is smoothed with an instrument called a *moyi*. These operations are performed, whenever there is no crop on the ground, and whenever the earth is soft enough to admit the plough. The number of ploughings depends much on the nature of the soil. In some three double ploughings are quite sufficient, in others more than double that number is required. The field, after having been ploughed once, and smoothed with the *moyi*, is sown broad-cast, then ploughed across, and smoothed. If the rice is intended to be transplanted, the seed is sown very thick, generally on poor high land. In some parts this pays no rent, because no crop is taken from it, and it serves only for pasture. Where the soil is a rich clay, although stiff, this land, after having produced the seedlings, gives a crop of cotton and sorisha, in which case it pays a high rent; but in other places this land produces a winter crop, and pays the usual rent. For every ten acres that are to be transplanted one should be sown for seedlings.

Rice that is sown broad-cast, and is not intended to be transplanted, ought to be harrowed with a kind of rake drawn by oxen, and called *bida*. The intention of this is to destroy weeds and superfluous plants of rice, so that the corn may come up in little clumps nearly as if it had been transplanted. The same effect in some places is produced by dribbling a few seeds into holes at every span's length from each other. This kind of rice also requires to be weeded with a spade (*khurpi*); but I do not think that the farmers of Dinajpúr are very careful in this operation.

The low lands require no manure, the higher lands receive very little; but all that can be procured is given to the summer rice, which is to be followed by winter crops, except where much sugar-cane, tobacco, or other valuable article is cultivated, in which case these are allowed almost the whole manure. When the rice is nearly ripe, it is a common practice in this district, to lay it quite flat on the ground, which is done by a man at each end pushing a bambu over the field. Various reasons are assigned for this. It is said, especially in the N. W. parts of the district, where the practice is most common, that it in some measure secures the field from the depredation of thieves, who according to the most moderate computation compose $\frac{6}{18}$ of the men in these parts. It is also said, that it prevents shaking; that it gives time for harvest, as the crop will receive no injury, is left on the ground for a month, after it is ripe; and finally that by this operation the reaping is facilitated, for the reaper when at work always sits on his heels. It is chiefly the second and third kinds of winter rices that are managed in this manner. In reaping the coarse kinds of rice, the straw of which are not used for fodder, nothing but the ears are cut; and where the fodder is coarse, only about a foot of the straw is cut with the grain. In the finer kinds, the straw is cut close by the ground.

The ears and corn are carried home by the reaper to the farmer's house, and is kept in small rude stacks, until it can be trodden out by oxen walking over it in a circle, which is always done in the course of a month after it has been reaped. The straw, where in any considerable quantity, is preserved in small stacks very ill fitted to resist the weather, and not thatched. Indeed, before the rainy season commences, the quantity is generally so much reduced, that there is room in the store-house or barn for the whole.

The grain is dried in the sun, and then preserved in the house. Poor people have one or two large cylindrical baskets which stand in an end of their house, and hold about six maunds, Calcutta weight, each, or a little more than 492 lbs. Large farmers have store-houses, in which the rice is deposited on a bambu stage, to keep it from the ground. Principal people have round store-houses, of which the walls are made of bambus interwoven together, and plastered with clay and cow-dung intermixed. The roof is conical and thatched, and the whole in size and shape resembles a common stack of corn. These are by far the best and safest granaries in the district, as in case of fire two or three active men with a long bambu may push off the roof, and the grain will suffer little injury. The quantity consumed every year in the other granaries is very considerable.

Farmers always keep their rice in the husk, until they want to use it, or to carry it to market. Sometimes indeed they load their cattle with the grain in the husk, and it is very seldom indeed that they carry clean rice to market; the common practice with them is to sell half-cleaned rice.

This may with some proceed from a want of sufficient skill in the economy of labour, but there is reason to apprehend, that sometimes it is employed with a view of passing their grain on the merchant as better cleaned than it is in reality.

The operation of cleaning is performed entirely by the women, is very laborious, and is generally done by an instrument called a *dhenki*. This is a wooden lever, usually about six feet long and six inches in diameter, that moves on a small bolt passing through it and two cheeks, which are driven into the ground, until the bolt is about 18 inches high. Under one end of the lever is fastened a cylindrical piece of wood, about 18 inches in length and six inches in diameter, the lower end of which is surrounded by an iron hoop. This serves as a pestle, that is raised by the lever, and falls down by its own weight; and the power is increased by the bolt, that serves as a fulcrum, being placed at ⅘ of the whole length of the lever from the pestle. Two women work this machine. One alternately presses down the end of the lever with her foot to raise the pestle, and then by removing her foot allows the pestle to fall. The other removes the beaten grain, and puts fresh into the mortar, which in this country is merely a circular hollow in the ground, with a piece of wood in the bottom to receive the blow. One woman usually relieves the other; but sometimes one performs the whole labor, and has a cocoanut with a long handle, by means of which she moves the grain. In place of the *dhenki*, some women, who cannot leave their own houses on account of a young child, and who cannot find a companion, beat the rice in a wooden mortar with a long wooden pestle, which they raise first with one hand and then with the other.

All the coarse kinds of rice, and all the winter rice that is to be exported, which forms a great part of the second class of winter rices, are cleaned by boiling. A quantity is put into an earthen pot with some cold water, and is boiled for one hour. It is then dried and beaten, and the facility with which this is done, and the little waste in cleaning, does more than compensate for the expence of fuel. It is not lawful for a Brahmin to use this kind of rice. When not boiled the rough rice is merely dried in the sun, then beaten, and the grain, bran, and husks, are separated by a fan (*kula*). The quantity cleaned in this manner is comparatively so small, that in general estimates it may be altogether omitted.

Concerning various important circumstances in the operation of cleaning rice, I found the accounts, given by both merchants and farmers, vary in a manner that I did not expect, and which I have no doubt arose from a general consciousness of fraud. I found no one who could or would tell me, how much clean rice he usually procured from a given qnantity of rough grain; and the accounts which I received of the rate of hire, varied considerably.

In other parts of India it is usually stated, that two measures of rice in the husk give one measure of clean grain: if therefore the average weight of a measure of each kind of grain is ascertained, it will be easy to know what proportion of clean rice, can on an average be procured from a given weight of grain in the husk. In order to ascertain this, I weighed ten different samples of rice, taken at different times and places, and each containing a cubical foot of rough and an equal quantity of clean rice, as usually exposed in markets. The following is the result in ounces avoirdupois.

	Rough	*Clean*
No. 1	536½	755
2	534½	764
3	543	731
4	541	764
5	528	754
6	540½	762¼
7	544	758
8	523	761
9	533	760
10	537	750¼
Average,	53,635	75,565

These differences are owing in some measure to different qualities of the grain, but chiefly to different degrees of moisture; and in several trials, that I have made, I have found the grain chiefly affected by moisture, which produces greater changes both in the bulk and weight of the grain, than in those of the husks and bran. This allows much room for fraud, especially in retailing; for I have known, that one seer weight of rice bought in the market has been reduced to $\frac{7}{8}$ of a seer, merely by having been dried in the sun.

On the usual estimate of rough rice, giving one-half by measure of cleaned grain, and on the average difference of weight, as taken from the experiment now related, every 40 seers weight of the former should give 28$\frac{17}{100}$ seers of the latter.

Not having been entirely satisfied with this average, I made a set of 10 experiments on 10 samples of rice of various kinds, each containing one cubical foot of rough grain, which I had carefully cleaned by boiling, and then carefully dried. The result will be found in the Table No. 7. From this it will appear, that in fact the clean rice amounts to considerably more by measure than one-half ($\frac{5623}{10000}$) of the rough grain, and that each maund of rough rice will give rather more than 30 seers (30,054668) of clean.

I tried only one experiment on rice beaten without having been boiled, as in this district that is of less importance. The following is the result:

A cubical foot of old winter rice of the second quality, when dried, weighed 551 ounces avoirdupois. On being beaten, it gave 796½ inches of entire clean rice, and 63½ inches of broken grains.

The entire clean rice weighed, ... oz.	354
The broken rice, ...	26½
The bran, ...	21
The husks, ...	150½
Ounces, ...	552

In this district the most usual manner of paying for cleaning rice thoroughly is for the owner to give the labourer 23 measures of rough rice, and to receive back nine measures of clean grain, if it has been cleaned by boiling, and eight measures if it has been cleaned without boiling. In other parts the woman takes 24 measures of rough grain and delivers 10 of clean. Now, on the usual estimate of one-half of the grain by measure being clean rice, the woman in cleaning rice by boiling would in the first case procure rather more than $\frac{1}{5}$ part of the grain, in the latter case she would receive $\frac{1}{6}$ part; but according to the experiments which have been detailed, when she received 23 measures and delivered nine, she would have about $\frac{1}{4}$ or $\frac{3}{10}$ parts of the clean grain for her trouble; and when she received 24 and delivered nine measures, she would have nearly $\frac{41}{138}$ parts of the grain, or about $\frac{1}{4}$. According to the experiment that I made on cleaning rice without boiling, the woman who receives 23 measures and delivers eight; would, for her trouble, have $\frac{13}{53}$ parts or nearly $\frac{1}{4}$ of the clean grain, besides a considerable quantity of broken grains, which are very good food. On the whole, I am persuaded, that the value paid for cleaning the rice in this district cannot be possibly estimated at less than $\frac{1}{5}$, and may more probably be taken at $\frac{1}{4}$ of the whole grain produced, after deducting the seed; for although some is exported in the rough state, this is made up by the additional hire, which the cleaners receive for beating the rice in various other ways that will be just now mentioned.

The most usual of these preparations is called *chira*, of which there are two kinds *siddho* and *alo*.

The first is the most common, and is made thus—some rice in the husk is boiled in water for about an hour. It is then dried and beaten to separate the husks. It is then put little by little into a wide-mouthed earthen pot over a fire, and heated a little; after which, it is again beaten while still hot. By this, it is rendered flat, and is sold in very great quantities, chiefly for consumption in the district, but some is also exported. The *dhenki* used in this operation is rather heavier than common. On an average of two experiments carefully made, one cubical foot of winter rice in husk, which when well cleaned weighed 580 ounces, gave 1379 cubical inches of *chira*, which weighed 402 ounces. The husks weighed 137 ounces, and there were 7 ounces of rice in the husk, which had not been broken in the operation, so that 34 ounces were lost, which, as I am told, is usual in this operation. *Chira* sells by weight considerably higher (19 per cent.) than rice of the same quantity. The ceremonies of cooking being very troublesome; many of the natives kindle a fire only once a day. This is generally done in the evening, when they make their principal meal. In the morning and at noon, they eat something that does not require to be cooked, and *chira* is one of the most common meals of that kind. Those who can afford the expense, mix it with the extract of sugar-cane (*gur*), or molasses, and form cakes or balls, which are eaten without addition. These balls are of two kinds, one in which the *chira* is previously parched, the other does not require this preparation; such people also mix the *chira* with milk and tamarind, or with sour curdled milk (*doyi*). The poor either eat the *chira* without addition, moistening it with a little water; and, if they can procure these luxuries, season it with a little salt and some acid fruit.

The *alo chira* is prepared by steeping the rough grain a whole night in cold water. It is then parched, and beaten in the husk, which finishes the operation. The *alo chira* is little used, is dearer than the other, and is eaten in the same manner.

The next, most common, of these preparations is *khoyi*. The rough rice, after being dried in the sun, is exposed a whole night to the dew; next morning, it is dried in the sun, and is afterwards parched in a wide-mouthed earthen pot, of which a part is broken from one side, in order to give readier access. A small quantity (¼ lb.) is parched at one time, and must be carefully watched to sweep it out when it is ready. The grains swell very much, burst the husks, and become white. The operation is sometimes performed in a pot without addition; at others sand is put in the bottom, in which case the grains become rounder. That prepared on sand is considered as best. Two *bisas* of the rough rice fit for this preparation usually sell for a rupee and a quarter, and give 10 *bisas* of *khoyi*, which will sell for about a rupee and a half. The labour is so intermixed with that of other kinds, that it is impossible to say how much a person can make in a day; for this preparation is made chiefly by those who prepare sweetmeats. This *khoyi* is seldom used by the poor. It is often eaten mixed with milk, fresh or curdled, but the usual manner of using it is to mix it with molasses or the extract of sugar-cane, so as to form what is called *murki*. This is eaten by all who can afford it, either by itself or with milk. The *khoyi* mixed with molasses is also made up into balls or cakes, that are sold by those who prepare sweetmeats.

The next preparation, called *muri*, is made by women. Coarse rough rice is boiled for about two hours, and then dried in the sun. It is then beaten with a heavy *dhenki*. The grain having been cleaned is then dried, and about five or six lbs. at a time are heated for half an hour in a flat earthen vessel, adding a little salt, and agitating the vessel well. The rice, after it has been heated, is then parched in the same manner as *khoyi*, but it does not swell so much. One measure of rough rice gives only three measures of *muri*. The poor people eat this sometimes with the addition of a little oil and salt, but more commonly by itself.

Rice that has been cleaned without any precaution is also frequently parched, and is used in the same manner, but it does not swell so much. In this district wheat is but a small crop, and is generally sown after a summer crop of rice has been taken from the ground, which in that case is manured, and gives two crops every year. The rice is a full crop, the wheat is scanty; along with the wheat, on rich soils, are often sown sorisha and lentils. On sandy banks of rivers, it is often sown mixed with barley and lentils. The wheat is ground in hand-mills, after having been washed and dried in the sun. The mill is so imperfect, that it reduces only a part to fine flour. In this district 40 measures of wheat give 15 of coarse flour (*ata*) and 15 of fine (*moyda*). The remainder is bran. Wheat commonly sells at 35 seers (96 sa. wt.) or 86¼ lbs. for the rupee. The fine flour sells at about 20 seers, 49¼ lbs. for the rupee. The coarse, which contains much bran, sells at 1½ rupee the maund, or rather more than 65⅔ lbs. for a rupee. Both men and women work at the mill. Two persons will require three days to grind and clean 1 maund, (98½ lbs.) The fine flour is used for making sweetmeats; the coarse is formed into unleavened cakes, that are commonly fried in butter. Neither the Hindus nor Moslems of this district possess the art of fermenting bread. The straw is considered as unfit for fodder.

The barley, cultivated in the same manner as wheat, is generally consumed by the farmers who raise it, and is almost always used immediately after it is cut. It is first washed, then dried in the sun, then parched in an earthen pot, then beaten with the *dhenki* or pestle, which reduces it to a coarse flour, that is eaten by the poor; who mix it with cold water, and, if they can, add tamarind, or sour curdled milk or molasses. The straw is considered as unfit for fodder.

The *meruya* is commonly raised by a curious manner of cultivation, and chiefly in the poor lands, of a loose soil, that are only cultivated once or twice after a fallow of two or three years. The field, from about the middle of October until the 12th of April, is allowed six double ploughings. It is then ploughed and sown with summer rice, and this is covered by the plough. Ten or fifteen days afterwards, seedlings of the *meruya* are transplanted into it, and at the same time furrows are drawn throughout, at two or three cubits from each other. In these are placed seeds of the *oror*. The rice is cut in the end of August or beginning of September, the *meruya* about 10 days after; the *oror* is not ripe until the following March. This kind of cultivation is confined almost entirely to the northern part of the district.

It is there also that the common millet is usually reared, and that in very small quantities; but as it ripens early, in general before the rivers swell, this crop seems very capable of being extended to all the lands that are inundated. In years, when the crop of rice has failed, or has been scanty, it is usual, in some parts of this district towards the N. W, to sow both *meruya* and millet on the rich lands that produce summer rice; and the practice is judicious, because they ripen much earlier, and procure an earlier relief. In ordinary seasons, indeed, the millet seems to be sown in very small quantities, just to keep the seed in case it should be necessary to use it.

PART 3.—*Leguminous Plants.*

The *Thakuri kolayi* is sown on high land, in a loose soil, and generally either on the land which has produced the seedlings of rice that have been transplanted, or on poor land that is only cultivated occasionally, or as a crop in the intervals between those of sugar-cane, when there is no time for any thing more valuable. It is also sown, after a single ploughing, among the stems of growing cotton, and sometimes is sown intermixed with summer rice. The entire grain of every kind of pulse in this district is called *kolayi;* when cleared from the integuments, like split pease, it is called *dall.* Before it is used, *thakuri* is always split, and freed in some measure from the husk. This is done in two manners—1st, most commonly it is dried in the sun, and then ground in a hand-mill. This splits it, but removes only a small portion of the integuments. In this state it is boiled by itself with capsicum, turmeric, salt, and oil, or butter, if these can be afforded, and is eaten with boiled rice. 2nd, the pulse is mixed with a little oil, then dried a whole day in the sun, then ground in the mill and fanned, which removes all the husks. This is used in the same manner by the rich. A little is parched before it is ground, but this is seldom used, being considered as heating. The straw is of no use except to burn. Its ashes are, sometimes, eaten in place of salt. The pods and bran are good forage for cattle. The pulse sells at 60 seers the rupee, which is at the rate of 72 Calcutta seers, or 147¾lbs.

The *khesari* is a coarser pulse, and is generally sown on low, moist land of a free soil, among the growing rice, and ripens after this is cut, so that the only trouble is the sowing and reaping. In other cases it is sown as a third crop after one of summer and other of winter rice. This requires a high rich soil, in which the winter rice ripens in November. The field is ploughed once. The seed is sown broad-cast, and it is reaped in the end of March. It is split after being dried in the sun, and the bran separates readily from the pea. It is dressed in the same manner as the *thakuri,* and is the common fare of the fourth rank of people. The fifth and sixth can seldom afford even this. The common price of the entire grain is 80 seers, or 96 seers Calcutta weight, or 197 lbs. for the rupee. Its straw is of no use.

The *mosur* or lentil is sometimes sown as a winter crop, after a summer crop of rice has been cut; in which case, it is usually accompanied by flax, but more commonly, especially in the south, it is sown mixed with the different kinds of mustard, or with wheat and barley. It is prepared in the same manner as the *khesari,* and is reckoned rather better in quality. It sells usually for 50 heavy seers, or 60 Calcutta weight, for a rupee. Its straw is not used.

The *harimug* is raised in very small quantities. It is sometimes sown by itself, as a winter crop after summer rice; but another crop of that grain cannot follow it in the ensuing year, for it is ripe in May and June. It is also sown among cotton. It is split like the *thakuri,* is still more valuable, and one heavy maund or 48 Calcutta seers sell for a rupee.

Oror is the next most common pulse, and is prepared in the same manner. It sells for about 35 heavy seers, or 42 Calcutta weight, for the rupee. I have already mentioned one manner in which it is cultivated; but in a few fields near the house, it is also reared by itself, and occupies the ground for the whole year. The greatest quantity however is raised in a hedge that surrounds almost every field of sugar-cane. It grows from 6 to 10 feet high, and its stems are woody, and serve for fuel.

The common field pea is the next most common pulse. It is prepared like the others, and is reckoned nearly of as bad a quality as *khesari*. It is raised on high rich land, as a winter crop, sometimes after a summer crop of rice; at others it is sown among the growing winter rice in October, and it is even sown after two crops of that grain. It sells for 50 heavy seers for the rupee. The straw is not used.

The *chona* is nearly as much cultivated as the pea. It sells usually for 35 heavy seers the rupee, and is reckoned an excellent food for both men and cattle. Its straw is not used. It is sown chiefly near the Nagor and Mohanonda, on land which has given a crop of rice.

The variety of the same plant with a white flower is more valuable, but very little indeed is raised in this district.

All the pulses are thrashed with a stick. The natives have no flail.

PART 4.—*Of plants which produce oil.*

Of the seeds which produce oil, by far the most common is that called *sorisha*, which is raised in all the southern and eastern parts of the district. It is the great winter crop raised on land that has given a summer crop of rice; but it is frequently intermixed with wheat, lentils, and some other pulses, and it is also sown with cotton, of which considerable quantities are raised in these parts of the district. It is trodden out by oxen, and sells usually at about 48 Calcutta seers for the rupee.

The *turi*, is that which is cultivated in the N. W. part of the district, mostly as a winter crop after summer rice, but sometimes also on poor land which gives no other crop. In these parts it is not the usual custom, to mix any thing with this plant. There is very little, if any, difference in the qualities of the oils; but the *turi* sells for about one or two seers less for a rupee, as it is reckoned to give a greater quantity of oil.

The *rayi* is raised only in very small quantities. The oil being very hot, is reckoned good for eating, but it does not answer for anointing the body. The seed is beaten with several acid fruits into a kind of pickle, as I have before mentioned. It is chiefly raised in the cotton fields of the S. E. part of the district. It does not sell higher than *sorisha*.

The *tora* is generally raised along with the *rayi* in cotton fields. The quantity is so small that I received no information concerning its peculiar qualities.

In Bengal there are two kinds of Sesamum cultivated. The seeds of both are black. The quantity raised in this district is so small, and confined to so few parts, towards the north chiefly, that I had no opportunity of examining its Botanical affinities. It is raised on the poor parts of a light soil, that require frequent fallows. The oil is used only for the lamp, but the seed is sometimes mixed with the coarse flour of rice to make cakes.

Linseed is raised in still smaller quantities, and is usually sown in rows, in cotton fields, or among lentils. The seed is expressed for oil, the stem is considered as useless. The oil is only used for the lamp.

The farmer sells all these seeds to those who express the oil, whose process will be detailed in the account of manufacturers. The oil-cake is partly used as food for cattle, and partly for manure.

PART 5.—*Profit on this kind of cultivation.*

From the foregoing account, it will be evident, that, as the crops are so much intermixed, it would be extremely difficult to form an estimate of the profit which attends each separately. Neither can any charge be ascertained for the different steps of each manner of cultivation; for it is not customary to perform these by job work; but a man who has a plough cultivates a certain extent of land, in which he has a proportion of many of the different grains above mentioned. What the actual cost of each therefore may be, it would be very difficult to ascertain, but we may make a near approximation to the cost of the whole. It is a common practice in this country to employ persons to cultivate the land for a share of the produce, and this share is usually one-half. Sometimes the land-holder receives the whole straw, but that is not common. Now the condition of the person who cultivates for a share is generally allowed to be better than that of a common labourer; and indeed it is evident that it must be so, otherwise no man would keep the stock that is necessary for carrying on the cultivation. We may therefore safely conclude, that the farmer's neat gain is more than the difference between the rent and the half of the produce. The lands that are most eagerly sought after by the farmers, are low rice-fields, which produce nothing except that grain, and in many parts where I had an opportunity of forming a tolerable opinion of the crop and rent, I found, that the produce of the grain might be about two rupees a bigah where the rent was 8 annas, so that, deducting one-half for the expense of cultivation of every kind, the farmer had a clear profit equal to the rent, or to one-fourth of the grain produced. He has besides a quantity of straw, with which in remote parts he keeps cows, from whence he derives a small profit. Near Maldeh and Dinajpúr the farmers sell the straw, and there their profit is somewhat more considerable; further, tradesmen who have farms generally employ the people who cultivate for a share, but in some places they hire labourers; and I procured the following estimate on two large bigahs, nearly equal to an acre, or to three bigahs Calcutta measure, of low, clay land, cultivated with rice alone.

To 11 ploughs for one day,	Rs. 1	0
To 10 men planting,	0	8
To 8 measures seed,	0	4
To reaping, 12 men,	0	9
To rent,	1	6
To various little expenses not included,	0	5
Total,	4	0

I have estimated the medium produce of such land in rice at two rupees a Calcutta bigah, or at six rupees for the quantity here stated, so that the profit, besides the straw, is to the rent as 32 to 22. If we estimate by the price charged for reaping, which is sometimes done by the job, at from $\frac{1}{10}$ to $\frac{1}{20}$ of the produce, according to the distance of the field, and take the medium of these two rates, the produce would be 7½ rupees; but this includes the straw, which may nearly make up the difference. According to the estimate founded on cultivation by share, the profit, exclusive of straw, equals the rent; according to the estimate founded on cultivation by jobbing, but including the straw, it is double the rent. This however is the land from whence most profit is derived, for it is most eagerly sought after by the farmers. We ought not therefore to allow, that upon the whole cultivation of grain the farmers have more profit than the amount of the rent, nor can we allow that they have less. Indeed, it will be afterwards seen, that the actual rental, in all probability, falls very far short of a fourth part of the produce; but this is probably owing to fraud and mismanagement.

SECTION 2.—*Plants cultivated as Vegetables for the table.*

In my general statement of the manner in which the rented land is occupied (Table No. 4), I mentioned, that about 5,00,000 bigahs are occupied by houses and gardens. Of these 1,40,000 may be occupied by plantations, of which I have already given some account in the part of this report which treats of the trees—see Bambu, No. 1; Tamarind, No. 63; Mango, No. 76; Jack, No. 108. Vegetables cultivated for the kitchen occupy 1,00,000 bigahs in the gardens, and perhaps, in justice, we ought to have added a great part of that which has been stated as the mere foundation of houses, for the roof of almost every hut is covered with gourds. Not however to enter too minutely into such matters, besides the 1,00,000 bigahs in gardens that are cultivated with vegetables for the kitchen, probably 1,50,000 bigahs in the fields are applied to the same purpose, making in all 2,50,000 bigahs; and this cultivation must be considered, next to that of grain, as the most important in the district, both in respect to extent and to the value of the produce, which cannot be less than 10,00,000 Rupees a year.

The plants, which I have included under this class, are reduced by the natives to four kinds:

1. Mosála, or hot seasoning.

2. Torkári, or succulent roots, stems, and fruits, that serve chiefly as a convenient receptacle for the salt, oil, and seasoning, with which they are dressed.

3. Ság, the leaves and tender stems of plants that are applied to the same purpose.

4. Omboltás, or acid plants used as seasoning.

I. MOSALAS. Although these do not occupy the largest extent of ground, they amount to the greatest value, and some part of them is exported. The different kinds are placed nearly in proportion to the value of each that is raised in this district.

1. *Ada*, Ginger. I have not seen the plant in a state fit for Botanical examination, but suppose, that it is the *Amomum zinziber*, W. It is cultivated chiefly in two or three of the northern divisions, where the soil is free, but it is surprising, that it should not also have been raised in the S. E. divisions, as their soil is excellently fitted for it, and the cultivation is profitable. The farmers, as an excuse for their neglect, allege that porcupines destroy the roots.

Poor high land, which is seldom regularly occupied, is most commonly chosen for the purpose. After a fallow, it is ploughed eight times in spring. In the hot season, from the middle of April until the middle of May, it is planted. The field is divided into beds about three feet wide, which are separated by trenches of half the width.

The beds having been dunged, the small roots reserved for seed are placed on them, and covered with a little straw, and then with earth from the trenches. In the end of August or beginning of September weeds are removed, and some more earth is thrown on the beds from the trenches. The roots are raised in the end of February or beginning of March. The smaller roots are preserved for seed, of which four maunds (lb. 394) are required for the bigah of 80 long cubits, about lb.900 an acre.) The produce of roots fit for sale in a good crop is three times the amount of the seed, besides small roots that serve for being planted. The merchants make advances for most of what is cultivated, and give one rupee for from three to four maunds, which in good crops is from three to four rupees for the bigah. The rent is from four to six annas. This account of the produce of poor land, which was given by an agent of a land-holder, seems to be under-rated. A farmer said, that on rich land, on which he cultivated it, he procured from a large bigah (½ acre) 80 heavy maunds (96 sa. wt. the seer), worth 20 rupees. The seed he stated at 20 maunds, at this rate an acre requires 3,942 lbs. for seed, and produces 15,768 lbs. worth 40 rupees, or about 394 lbs. for the rupee. The merchants dry it for exportation. In other parts of the district no more is raised than serves for the consumption of the country, and except as a medicine, it is always used raw. It is sometimes mixed with curries, and the natives, before they begin to eat, often take a slice of this root covered with salt, in order to increase the appetite, just as in Europe some persons are induced to take a glass of wine.

2. *Horidra*, Turmeric.—Not having seen this plant in flower, I cannot say whether it is the *Curcuma longa* or the *rotunda* of the Botanists, because both plants are cultivated under the same name. This plant requires a free soil, and being chiefly used in the district, its cultivation is more generally extended. In the richer fields, it is managed much in the same manner as the ginger, and produces according to the farmers about 1100 lbs. an acre, when dried, which operation is always performed by the cultivator, as the merchant makes no advances. The raw root is boiled a little, and then dried in the sun. In this operation it shrinks greatly, and loses much weight, and is sold by the farmers for a little more than 33¾ Calcutta seers, or 69½ lbs. for the rupee. Like turmeric in the northern divisions, it is cultivated on very poor high land after occasional fallows, and where it is allowed a richer soil, cotton is raised in the same field. From the beginning of January until the beginning of April, the field is ploughed eight times. In the course of the two following months, the small roots are planted in furrows that are drawn at a cubit's distance throughout the field, and they are covered by the plough. Seeds of cotton are placed between the rows. It is weeded occasionally with a spud, and is raised in the end of February. The cotton ripens in December, January, and February, and its capsules are gathered as they come to maturity. This cotton is of the black-seeded kind, and is reckoned of a very bad quality, so that it sells lower than even west country cotton. The produce stated to me on one bigah of 85¼ cubits of 20 inches was 1¼ maund,

(101 sicca weight the seer) of dry turmeric, ...	Rs. 2 4
10 seers of cotton wool, cleaned,..	1 2
	Rs. 3 6

which is at the rate of Rs. 7 4 6 an acre from poor land. Turmeric is used raw as a medicine; and dried, both as a dye and as a seasoning that enters into every curry (Byangjon) where it can possibly be afforded. Its powder is also occasionally added to the soil, that is employed as an unguent.

3. *Long ka morich, Capsicum annuum.*—Of this the consumption is very great, and it enters into every curry. Sometimes the poor eat it alone with rice, being unable to procure oil to make a curry. It is also used in medicine. The quantity required being great, and a loose soil being necessary, where there is a great extent of stiff clay, large fields of it are required on the adjacent lands that

have a free soil, but, where the whole country is of a loose soil, there are no fields of this plant, and a few bushes in each garden suffice for the consumption. The field is thoroughly ploughed between the 12th of May and the 14th of September, and then is smoothed with the instrument called *moyi.* In the following month, the seedlings, which have been raised in the garden, are transplanted at a span's distance from each other. The plants require three weedings, and produce ripe fruit between the 12th of January and 12th of March. The fruit is gathered as it ripens, is dried in the sun, and kept in baskets placed on a bambu stage at some distance from the ground. It will preserve for more than a year. It is neither sold by weight nor measure; but the farmer carries a basket full to market, divides into small heaps, and sells each of these for as much as he can. I cannot therefore state the quantity or value of the produce of a bigah, but it is a valuable crop.

4. *Kumoriya Piyaj,* Onion. An *Allium* not mentioned by Wildenow, nor in the Encyclopedie.

5. *Rosún*, Garlic, *Allium Sativum*, W.—Both these plants are cultivated in the same manner, and their use is confined to Muhammedans, for they are an abomination to the Hindús of Bengal, although no seasoning seems so well fitted for their insipid food. They are the only produce of the garden that is artificially watered; and as they will thrive on any soil where they can procure water, the greatest quantities are raised on the sides of tanks in the stiff clay land. The field or plot is divided into small beds, carefully levelled, and separated by little canals, that convey the water to each.

All the remaining articles are cultivated on a very small scale in gardens, and, except the last, are sown in the end of the rainy season, and ripen as the heats of spring commence.

6. *Methi, Trigonella Fœnum græcum*, W.—Its leaves are used as a green (*sag*). The ripe seed is put in curries as a seasoning, and its flower is mixed with the oil with which women anoint their skins, as it communicates a good smell. It is also considered as a medicine.

7. *Sulpha*, Fennel, *Anethum fœniculum*.—The leaves are used as a green. The ripe fruit is used as a seasoning in curries, and is employed as a medicine.

8. *Dhoniya*, Coriander, *Coriandrum Sativum*.—The ripe seed alone is used, and is employed both in curries, and to chew with betel, and is considered as a medicine. Rows of this plant are often sown in fields of the pulse called *chona*.

9. *Joyain*, a species of *Ammi* not yet described, unless the plant called *Athamantha Chinensis* may have been intended, which is not improbable.—It is very seldom used in curries, but is chewed along with betel, and is employed in medicine.

10. *Randhuni*. This and *methi* are much used in a particular sort of curries, which after having been half-dressed in one pot, are poured into another that contains hot oil and these two seeds. It is also used in pickles, and as a medicine. It is of the order of the *umbelliferæ*.

11. *Mauri*, Anise, *Anethum graveolens*.—Is rarely used in curries, but is chewed with betel, and employed as medicine.

12. *Choyi*, *Piper Sylvestre*, E. M.?—Small cuttings of this are planted in the shade, and allowed to climb upon any sort of tree. It continues to live for many years. The old stems possess considerable pungency, and after having been beaten, or cut into small pieces, are dressed with curry, to supply the place of black pepper, which in this district is an uncommon article of luxury.

II. Torkari.

1. *Bartoki, Begun, Solanum insanum, et melongina,* E. M.

The natives reckon many kinds, which differ in the size, shape, and colour of the fruit, but I am inclined to think with the authors of the Encyclopedie, that the whole are merely varieties of one species. The kind that is most commonly cultivated in this district has the fruit in shape of a pear, and very large quantities of it are used. The unripe fruit is a very common ingredient in curries, and it is cut in large pieces, fried in butter, and eaten with rice. It is also roasted in the ashes. By many Europeans it is supposed to generate lice in those who eat it, which is certainly a mere prejudice. The fruit is no doubt wholesome, and dressed in various manners is a very good vegetable. The seeds are sown in a small bed in the beginning of the rainy season, and the seedlings are transplanted into the fields about the middle of July, at about two feet from each other. The field requires to be high, and of a light but rich soil, and must be kept clear of weeds. Should ants attack the young plants, some ashes must be sprinkled on the field in the morning. Fruit fit for eating begins to be obtained about the end of September, and continue procurable until the hot season. The fruit is not sold by weight nor measure, but a bigah of 80 large cubits produces about six rupees worth, which is at the rate of almost 13½ rupees an acre.

2. *Sokorcondu Alu,* Sweet Potatoe, *Convolvulus Batatas,* W.—This root was the original potatoe known in Europe, and communicated its name to the more valuable plant from America, which is not yet cultivated by the natives of this district. The sweet potatoe is much cultivated wherever the soil is free, and is highly valued by the natives. Its root is a common ingredient in curries, and, after it has been boiled, and the stringy parts separated by the hand, it is mixed with a small proportion of rice-flour, and formed into balls, which are fried in oil. The kernel of cocoanut and extract of sugar-cane are sometimes enclosed in the middle of the balls. The roots are sometimes eaten raw, and the leaves are used as a green. It is propagated by planting the smaller, and otherwise useless, roots in the middle of the rainy season. The field must have been well ploughed and smoothed, and the roots are planted with the dibble. Weeds must be carefully removed. The roots come in season in October, and continue until March, and are dug as wanted for sale or use. The value of the produce is nearly the same with that of the last mentioned article.

3. *Mokhi kochu, Gungri kochu, Chaumok kochu, Teliposa kochu.*

These are all small arums, which are cultivated in the fields, as potatoes are in Europe. I did not see them in a state that could enable me to judge, whether they were mere varieties of the *Arum peltatum,* E. M. or different species, or whether they have been described by Botanists. To my taste these are superior vegetables to the sweet potatoe, but they are not so much liked by the natives, and are used only in curries. They are mostly cultivated in the poor high lands, of a free soil, that abound in the northern parts of the district. The *Gungri* and *Teliposa* are planted in the end of February or beginning of March. After four double ploughings, the small roots that have been preserved for seed are planted in furrows, about two feet from each other, and a little dung is put along with them. In about a month, the young plants are covered with earth thrown up in ridges by the hoe. In two months more they are fit for being dug. The Mukhi are planted in the commencement of the rainy season, begin to be dug in

September, and last all cold season. I received no estimate of the quantity raised on a bigah: the value may be about three rupees, or seven rupees an acre.

4. *Potol*, a species of *Trichosanthes* that is not mentioned by Willdenow, nor in the Encyclopedie.—The leaves are used as a green, and the fruit is a common ingredient in curries, or is fried in oil or butter, or roasted in the ashes. By the natives it is reckoned a very wholesome vegetable. It is cultivated on high sandy land, and is propagated by the root, which is perennial. It is often allowed to remain three years in the same field, but then the fruit is very inferior to what is produced the first year. The root is proliferous, and five or six small ones adhere to each old plant. One of these is planted after two or three ploughings in September. They are placed about a cubit from each other. Weeds are removed, and the fruit is fit for use from February until September.

5. *Mula*, Radish, *Raphanus Satives*.—These grow to a very large size, and are often about 15 inches in length and four in diameter, but they are rather spongy. They are however a favorite vegetable among the natives, and are eaten raw, and enter into curries. The leaves are used as greens (*sag*). The ground for them must be high, rich, and of a loose nature, and it must be very thoroughly laboured, which in this country requires 12 double ploughings. The seed is sown broad-cast in September, and weeds should be removed in October. The plants that are superfluous are then removed, and serve the poor for a green; about the middle of November, the roots begin to be in season, and continue for three months, but people of rank use them for two months only; as towards the end of the season they become coarse.

The produce is not above four rupees a bigah, or about nine rupees an acre.

6. *Kola*, Plantain, *Musa*.—I know only of one species that is cultivated in India, and it ought to be the *Musa paradisiaca* of Linnæus, as a bunch of flowers and red leaves always continues at the end of the fruit bearing stem, unless it has been removed by accident. In this district there are three classes or kinds:

1. *Kanch kola*, the fruit of which, when green, is used in curries, or is fried in oil or butter, or is boiled along with rice. It is never roasted in the ashes, as is done in the West Indies, which seems to be a loss, as the aliment is wholesome and much more agreeable, to my palate at least, than the common food of the natives. Young shoots with a part of the root are planted in June or July, and begin to produce fruit in about 14 months; after four years, the fruit begins to degenerate. The roots are then grubbed, and new shoots are set in other places, for they do not thrive in the old soil. No fields are employed in this cultivation, but every farmer has a few clusters in his gardens. The stems are given to cattle. A bunch of these plantains is worth about four annas.

2. *Tatiya kola*, called *Dawria* at Calcutta. This is cultivated exactly in the same manner. When the flowering stem (*spadix*) has formed, and just before the flowers begin to open, the tree is cut; the whole *spadix*, and the centre of the stem, about two inches in diameter, are used in curries, and are worth 1½ annas. The leaves are used for platters, and those of one tree are worth about an anna, so that the whole tree is worth 2½ annas. The leaves of the other kinds are too old before the fruit is ripe, and having been broken by the wind, will not answer for platters.

3. *Kantali kola*, called by the same name at Calcutta. This is what is commonly eaten at Calcutta under the name of plantain, and when ripe has a thin yellow skin, which easily separates from the pulp, and may in general be about six inches in length. The pulp is commonly too dry, and is but a very poor fruit.

In Dinajpúr it is worse than at Calcutta, and generally contains seed, which is always a bad sign. It is cultivated exactly in the same manner. The natives eat it sometimes by itself and sometimes mixed with fresh milk, or with that which has become sour and curdled.

The two finer kinds, the small Banana, or *Champa kola* of Calcutta, and the rich luscious thick-skinned *Omurtoman* of Dhaka, are not known in this district. It is said, indeed, that the plantain was first introduced by one of the Rajas, which therefore must be a recent circumstance.

7. *Urchha*, *Momordica muricata*, W.—This is raised in very considerable quantities on the sandy banks of rivers, that are capable of producing little else, and which are inundated in the rainy season. Little pits are made at five or six feet distance from each other, about a foot wide, and six inches deep. In each are placed two or three seeds in January, and they produce fruit fit for eating in the hot months of spring. The fruit, when green, is fried with oil, and is eaten with rice. It is often also dressed with fishes, especially that which is half rotten. These are made into a loathsome dish, which many of the natives eat with avidity. The produce of a bigah is less in value than that of radishes.

8. *Korola*, *Momordica Charantia*, W.—This is used exactly like the preceding, but is sown on high poor sandy land in July, and comes in season in October, lasting three or four months. Its produce may be nearly of the same value.

9. *Layu*, Gourd, *Cucurbita Lagenaria*, W.—I have already mentioned, that the roof of almost every hut in the district is covered with one or more gourds. They differ considerably in shape, which gives rise to different names ; but it is needless to enter into these distinctions, as all the kinds are nearly of the same use. The fruit, when green, makes an excellent curry, especially with prawns, or other crustaceous animals of that sort.

The shell of the ripe fruit is used by religious mendicants for carrying water, and poor labourers use them as vessels. A musical stringed instrument, named *Tombura*, is made of a round variety. In July, two or three seeds are planted near the hut, and the stems are allowed to cover the roof. The fruit begins to be fit for use about the beginning of November, and continues until the hot weather of spring. Another sort is sown in November, begins to be of use in March, and continues until the commencement of the rainy season.

10. *Kumra*, *Kushmando.*—I had not had an opportunity of examining this plant, which is said to resemble a pumpkin, and may be some variety of that vegetable. It is used green in curries. When ripe, its pulp is beaten with the pulse of the *Phaseolus Max*, and formed into balls, which are dried in the sun, and will keep six months. They are used in curries. It is used also in medicine. It grows upon the roofs of houses or hedges. The seed is sown in the heat of May, and transplanted when the rains commence. It begins to give green fruit in August, and continues until December. The ripe fruit hung up will keep a year.

11. *Mit'ha kumra*, Pumpkin, *Schakerie Schora*, Hort. M.—This plant also grows on houses, but is more commonly allowed to climb upon a small stage of bambus erected for the purpose. It is in season the whole year. The plant lasts five or six months, and a succession is constantly secured. In Dinajpúr it is not very much used, the principal demand for it is from boatmen, as the fruit keeps well on their voyages : it is used in curries, and is also fried.

12. *Dengguya*, the *Amaranthus oleraceus* of European Botanists, probably includes several species, and among others this, which grows to be a large bushy

plant with a thick succulent stem, which is the part that is eaten, and is used in curries, especially in those that contain little water and much oil (*chorchoree*), but its young leaves are also used as (*sag*) a green. In March, it is sown broadcast in large beds. For one or two months the young leaves are used, and the plants are then thinned, and allowed to grow large. The stems continue fit for use during the greater part of the rainy season.

13. *Sim, Dolichos lignosus*, W. and perhaps *Dolichos Bengalensis* ?—Of this plant, which is so common in India, I have seen no Botanical account that is satisfactory. A great many kinds are cultivated, but they run so into one another that they must be considered as mere varieties, although the extremes are often very different: they have all nearly the same qualities, although some are thought better than others. They are either allowed to climb over the roof of the hut, or have a small bambu stage erected to support them, and almost every house has two or three plants. It is an annual plant, although it has a woody stem, and the seeds are put in the ground in the end of April; after eight months, it begins to produce green pods. For three months the fruit continues fit for eating. It then ripens; and is seldom used in that state, being considered as too heating. In its green state it has a strong disagreeable smell of beans, but is much used in curries, or fried with oil, or boiled along with rice.

14. *Chupri Alu, Dioscorea alata*, E. M.—*The Dioscorea sativa* of Linnæus is a plant of which I know nothing, and I may venture to say, that at least 20 species in India carry small bulbs on their stems, which was considered as peculiar to the Linnæan plant. Indeed, I know no kind that does not occasionally propagate itself in this manner. All of them that I have seen cultivated may perhaps be included under the *Dioscorea alata* of the Encyclopedie, although I am persuaded that there are several distinct species to which the description in that valuable work will apply. This excellent root is not a favorite in Dinajpûr, and is only used in curries. The bulbs, that grow on the stem, are used as well as the roots that are under ground. In most gardens a few roots are planted near trees, on which the stems are allowed to climb, but there is never a field cultivated with this plant, which appears to me as both salubrious and agreeable nourishment.

15. *Mancochu, Arum mucronatum*, E. M.—This is the *Arum macrorhizon* of Willdenow; but his definition is so bad that I prefer the name of the Encyclopedie, although I strongly suspect that the American and Asiatic plants are not of the same species, as the authors suppose. This plant is preferred to the former on account of being considered as not so heating. To my taste it is a poor vegetable. Its common size is about 1½ foot in length and six inches in diameter; but it has been six feet in length, although it does not increase in thickness. Young shoots come up from the side of the parent plant, are separated in June, and planted in high dry land, generally near the house, where it receives ashes and other impurities as manure. It may be taken up in seven months, but continues to grow larger for three or four years. It is only good for eating in the dry season. It is used in curries, especially the upper end, and this part is sometimes cut in pieces and boiled with rice. The lower end is cut in slices, dried in the sun, beaten with the *dhenki* or mortar, and mixed with tamarinds. This is used as pickle.

16. *Sola Kochu.*—This and the two following are kinds of *arum* that I had not an opportunity of examining. The small roots, that spring from the large bulb of this arum, are separated, and planted on the sides of tanks or ponds, so that in the

rainy season the water may reach its roots. These are planted in April, and at first receive a little water. The root is not reckoned so good as the last mentioned, and is not half so thick, but it is almost as long, and is used in the rainy season. The plant continues in the ground, and propagates itself without trouble; some roots being taken from it as wanted; it is only used in curries.

17. *Anaji Kochu.*—The petiols or stems that support the leaves of this arum are used in curries, and are fit for use during the cold months. It is planted in high ground, during the rainy season. The plant requires to be renewed every year, and was new to my Calcutta people.

18. *Ol*, the *Schena* of Rheede.—At Calcutta the root of this arum is in great request, and to supply the market, it is cultivated on the great scale, in some neighbouring districts; but in Dinajpúr it is not a very common vegetable, and no person has more than a few, which are planted in high ground near his house. The root is generally round, is about the size of a man's head, and takes two or three years to grow to that size. Young roots are planted in the beginning of the rainy season, and are fit for use next year about the same time. It continues two months in season, and is used in curries, or fried in oil, or boiled along with rice.

19. *Dhondhul*, *Cucumis pentandrus*, R. MSS.—When this fruit is dressed, while tender, it is to my taste one of the best native vegetables, and is excellent in stews or curries. But the natives do not like it. A few seeds are sown in the end of the rainy season, and the plant is allowed to climb upon trees, hedges, railings, or any place that is convenient in the garden. It is fit for eating in the cold season, and is an annual plant.

20. *Chichingga*, *Trichosanthes anguina.*—This is not much more valued than the former, and is allowed to grow in the same manner; but it is sown in April, and in the rainy season produces green fruit fit for eating.

21. *Jhingga*, *Cucumis acutangulus*, R. MSS.—The same may be said of this plant, which, together with No. 19, should be included in the genus called *Luffa*, for the fruit of the two have the strongest resemblance to each other, and are totally different from that of a cucumber. This is the *Luffa fœtida*, W.

22. *Kankrol*, *Momordica dioica*, W.—This is cultivated exactly as the two preceding, and is very little valued.

23. *Dhenros*, *Hibiscus esculentus*, W.—This is much used by Europeans in both Indies, especially in soups; but is very little valued by the natives, and is seldom to be seen in this district.

III.—Sag.

1. *Lapha*, *Malva verticillata*, W.—For three months in the year this mallow is by far the most common green that is used by the natives of this district, and large plots of it are cultivated in many gardens. It is sown broad-cast, in the beginning of the dry season, and begins to be fit for use in December.

2. *Khoriya Notiya*, *Amaranthus oleraceus*, W.—Is of two kinds, red and green, and is in season the whole year. The red kind is sown broad-cast, in small beds, soon after the commencement of the rainy season; and the green kind is sown in April, after the first showers of spring. It will continue in the ground for two or three years, but degenerate after the first. The leaves and young shoots are collected when a few inches high, the stems being procumbent. The natives reckon it better than the mallow.

3. *Bastuk*—4. *Bethuya.*—There are two very distinct species of *Chenopodium* cultivated in this district, and one that grows wild, all of them are used as greens. The cultivated kinds are called *Lal Bethuya* and *Chondon Bethuya.* The wild one has already been mentioned. I cannot refer any of them with certainty to the species that are described in the Encyclopedie, or in Willdenow ; both the cultivated kinds are ornamental plants, and grow 5 or 6 feet high, but they are used when very young, and by the natives are reckoned equal to spinach. They are sown in small beds, in the beginning of the dry season, are used in December and January, and are annual plants.

5. *Kankhura.*—This is a species of *Urtica,* and perhaps the *Nivea* of Willdenow. I have seen it no where else except in this district. It is a woody plant, and its bark is frequently used by fishermen to make a kind of hemp, of which they form the ropes for their nets, and all the ropes used for tracking boats are made of this material. It is propagated by slips from the roots, which are planted out in the beginning of the rainy season. There are no fields of this plant, but many gardens have a few beds. The leaves are used as a green, but are very indifferent, and the fresh shoots are cut and steeped in water to procure the fibres of the bark. It is a perennial plant.

6. *Phlong, Spinach.*—A species of *Spinacica,* of which I see no account in the Botanical systems. It is probably as palatable as the European kind, and by the natives is considered as very good. It is sown in small beds towards the end of the rainy season, and is in use for three months from the middle of November.

7. *Pering, Trigonella corniculata,* W.—This sweet plant was brought to me as the *Pering,* but I suspect, that the person who brought it was careless. The *Pering* is reckoned a good green ; but not so good as spinach. It is cultivated in the same manner, and at the same season.

8. *Sorisha.*—A species of mustard that is much used for its grain, as before mentioned ; where it is sown too thick, the superfluous plants are removed while young, and used as a green, which is very coarse.

9. *Pungyi Putika, Bassella lucida,* W.—This is a common resource of poor people, who find young plants growing under the parent vine, and remove them to the place where they wish them to grow. They generally climb upon the fence which encloses the yard, or form a little arbour above the door they live, and produce leaves the whole year, and are perennial, but degenerate after the first 12 months. It is a very poor vegetable.

10. *Methi, Fenugreek, Trigonella fœnum Græcum.*—The young plants that are too thick, when this plant has been cultivated for its grain, are removed, and used as a green which the natives reckon good. They are used in December. This also is the case with the three following plants. Only the smaller kind of *Corchorus,* called *Olitorius* by Botanists, is sometimes cultivated merely for its leaves, and these are reckoned very good. The green produced by the *Corchorus capsularis,* and by the *Crotolaria juncea* is exceedingly coarse, but much used by the poor. Concerning the kinds that follow I have nothing to say, but that they are not much liked by the natives, and are reared in very small quantities.

11. *Sulpha,* Fennel, *Anethum fœniculum,* W.

12. *Nalita Fat, Corchorus olitorius,* W.—The leaves of the capsularis are also often used.

13. *Son, Crotolaria juncea,* L.

14. *Konkarangga, Amaranthus tricolor.*

15. *Babir, Chrysanthemum*, or rather *Balsamita*, of which I find no account in the modern systems of Botany.

16. *Rosuniya, Spilanthes oleracia.*

IV. OMBOLO-TAS, or acids used in cookery.

By far the greatest part of these are produced by trees that grow with little care near villages, of which an account has been already given among the natural productions of the country. A few remain that are cultivated in gardens.

1. *Kolombok Nimbu.*—This and the following kinds of the five family of *Citrus* can with difficulty be reduced to any of the species described by Botanists, who are always consulted with uncertainty concerning plants that are cultivated. It ought to be included with the *Citrus medica* of Willdenow; but its leaves are blunt. The fruit has not so fine an odour as the citron, is shaped like a pear, and ends in a point like a nipple. It is rough, with many longitudinal furrows, and has a thick skin. The juice is commonly squeezed among boiled rice.

2. *Gonra Nimbu.*—According to Willdenow's definition, this ought to belong to the *Citrus decumana;* but scarcely any two fruits can be more different. This is a round fruit about the size of an apple, with a very rough skin, not remarkably thick, and has a juicy acid pulp. It is used in the same manner as the former.

Kagji Nimbu, is the lime commonly used by the English, according to Willdenow's definition; this also should be a variety of the *Citrus decumana.* The fruit is oval, about the size of a fowl's egg, and smooth. The skin is thin, and adheres to the pulp, which is a most agreeable acid. This is used in the same manner, and is often eaten with sugar.

4. *Pati Nimbu.*—This also agrees with Willdenow's definition of the *Citrus decumana.* The fruit is about the size of a small apple, quite round, with a thick projection at the point like a nipple. This is used in the same manner, and the kind which is chiefly employed in medicine by the natives.

5. *Sontora Nimbu.*—This differs from the *Citrus medica*, just as much as the decumana does from the Aurantium; that is, it has obtuse indented leaves. The fruit has exactly the flavour of the citron, but its skin is thin, and the pulp very copious and juicy. It is shaped like a pear, has no point, and is about 6 inches long by 4 thick. It is used like the others.

6. *Koruna Nimbu.*—I have not seen. It is said not to be so acid as the others, and is often eaten by itself, or with a little sugar. The natives have no oranges, but are very fond of such as come from Silhet or Bhútan.

7. *Chuka Palong*, Sorrel.—A species of *Rumex*, of which I see no account in the Botanical systems. It is not so much cultivated here as in many districts, where large fields of it are reared. It is an annual, is sown in the end of the rainy season, and may be used during the cold weather. It is an agreeable acid, but is not used as a salad. The natives indeed use nothing of that kind.

8. *Mesta, Hibiscus cannabinus*, W.—In this district its bark is never used for making ropes. The leaves are used as an acid green, but very rarely.

The whole cultivation of these vegetables is carried on by farmers; gardeners indeed can scarcely be said to exist as a separate profession. For although there are many persons, who from the duties of cast, ought to act as gardeners, they have almost all betaken themselves to farming.

The greater part of European kitchen vegetables and salads thrive very well, and several even of the sweet potherbs, such as thyme, marjoram, and mint; but the natives seem to have acquired no relish for them, nor even for the potato, which I saw no where except in the gardens of Europeans. Having thus so far treated of gardens, I shall now mention what remains to be said on that subject. In my account of plantations I have already mentioned most of the fruits, which the natives possess, but a few others remain. I shall first give a list of the whole in the order of their respective plenty, together with the season in which they are ripe.

1. *Amro, Mangifera Indica*, 12th June—31st July.
2. *Kantal, Artocarpus integrifolia*, 12th June—14th August.
3. *Peyara, Psidium*, June—July.
4. *Anaros, Bromelia ananas*, June—July.
5. *Khira, Sosa, Cucumis sativus*, 12th March—12th June.
6. *Pala-sosa*, 14th July—14th October.
7. *Kangkur Phuti, Cucumis pepo*, 12th March—14th July.
8. *Tormuj, Cucurbita citrullus*, 11th February—12th June.
9. *Papya, Papaya*, the whole year.
10. *Golabjam, Eugenia Jambos*, 12th April—12th June.
11. *Batabi, Citrus decumana*, 15th September—17th November.
12. *Phut, Morus*, 12th April—12th June.
13. *Dalim, Punica granatum*, the whole year.
14. *Pich*, Peach, *Amygdalus Persica*, 12th May—12th June.

The 11th and 14th can scarcely yet be said to have made their way from the gardens of the Europeans. I saw however a few trees in those belonging to natives. The only kinds cultivated in any quantity, that deserve the name of fruit, are No. 1 and 4, and both are so much neglected in this district, that few good ones are procurable; although no doubt both would thrive admirably, were adequate pains bestowed on their cultivation. The English in India seem to have taken a dislike to the pine-apple, and imagine, that it is always a very inferior fruit to what is reared in Europe; and no doubt those raised by the natives are usually indifferent, but a very little pains indeed in every part of India, produces much finer pine-apples than those that I have seen in England.

The common cucumber, No. 5, the common melon, No. 7, and the water-melon, No. 8, are raised in great quantities on the sandy banks of rivers. In January, the field is ploughed two or three times. At every three feet a few seeds are planted, in a little pit, and are kept clear of weeds. One acre of sand produces about 16 or 18 rupees worth of fruit. The cucumbers and water-melons are tolerably good. The melons are insipid. The musk-melon is not known to the natives of this district.

I did not see the *Pala-sosa*, which grows in gardens during the rainy season, and is supported on a stage of bambú: the cultivation of course is carried to no great extent.

The mulberry is small and black, and is a very poor fruit.

Many additions have been made to this list in the gardens of Europeans. The Chinese peach and pear thrive very well, and produce good fruit. The loquat (*Mespillus Japonica*), litchi (*Euphoria*), and wampi (*Cookia punctata*), all produce fruits that are tolerable. A plum (*Prunus*) has been introduced from Rangpur, but does not thrive so well as at that place. The fruit of it is beautiful; but, except as bringing to recollection those of Europe, is very indifferent.

The Avocata pear (*Laurus Persica*) is growing with great vigor in the magistrate's gardens, but has not yet produced fruit. It is probable, that in a climate so favorable to vegetation, the whole of these will soon become common in the district, like the custard-apple and guava; but without more care, than the natives are likely to bestow, they will probably degenerate, and become altogether vile.

Flower gardens are equally neglected, and I saw nothing that deserved the name. In their yards however even the lower classes have often some pretty flowers, and many of the villages are surrounded by fine flowering trees and shrubs. Besides the trees which have already been mentioned, I shall give a list of the flowering shrubs and plants that are cultivated round the houses, as ornaments.

1. *Joba, Hibiscus Rosa Sinensis.*
2. *Oporajita, Clitorea ternatea.*
3. *Korovir, Nerium odorum.*
4. *Málika Bél, Jasminum Zambac,* W.
5. *Kashtho Málika.*
6. *Juti, Jungyi, Jasminum auriculatum,* W.
7. *Jati, Jasminum grandiflorum.*
8. *Seyuti, Rosa moschata,* E. M.
9. *Rojoni gondha, Polianthes tuberosa.*
10. *Kundo, Jasminum pubescens,* W.
11. *Torulota, Ipomea quamoclit.*
12. *Krishnochura, Cesalpinea pulcherrima,* W.
13. *Togor, Nerium coronarium,* W. which is a Tabernæmontana.
14. *Pudmo Togor, Idem, flore pleno.*
15. *Golab, Rosa.*
16. *Chondro Málika, Chrysanthemum Indicum.*
17. *Ganda, Tagetes erecta.*
18. *Suryomoni.*
19. *Boro Suryomoni.*
20. *Otosi, Crotolariæ retusa varietas,* W. probably a different species.
21. *Madhobilota, Gærtnera racemosa,* W.
22. *Krishnokeli, Sondhyamoni, Mirabilis Jalapa.*
23. *Rongon, Ixora coccinia,* W.
24. *Bhumi Chompok, Kæmpferia.*
25. *Dimukhi, Dopati, Impatiens Balsamina.*
26. *Dosobahuchondi, Moræa Chinensis,* W.
27. *Morga, Jotadhari, Celosia.*
28. *Swetmorga, Celosia.*

The characters given by Willdenow and in the Encyclopedie, of the kinds of *Celosia* called *cristata, comosa,* and *coccinea,* are insufficient to enable me to refer these plants to the species described in these Botanical systems; the account of all plants common in the gardens of Europe being usually very imperfect.

29. *Dapidhupi, Amaryllis latifolia,* W.

In gardens also a few plants are cultivated for medicine.

The most common is the cress, *Lepidium sativum,* called *halim* by the natives.

Next to that is the *Vech* or *Calamus aromaticus* of the shops. One plant of this and another of the Amaryllis generally stand near a well, and daily receive a supply of water from those who frequent it.

The *Keligira* is very seldom found in this country, but in other districts is an object of considerable importance.

SECTION 3.—*Plants cultivated for producing thread or cordage.*

IN this district, the class of plants that occupy the next greatest extent of cultivated land, are those employed to make cordage or thread. In the distribution of the cultivated lands (Table 4), I have supposed that 80,000 bigahs are employed for these. Of this extent, I suppose the following may be about the disposition:

1 *Pat, Corchorus capsularis*, W.	B. 40,000
2 Cotton,	25,000
3 *Son, Crotolaria juncea*,	14,000
4 *Kankhura, Urtica nivea*, W.	1,000
Total	80,000

The *Pat* is called *Gania* by Ramphius from some native name of this plant, and from the same source is derived our word *Gunny*, which is applied to the coarse sackcloth that is prepared from the fibres of its stem. In this district large quantities of this cloth (*tat* or *chotai*) are made, and many of the poorer people are clothed with a coarse linen (*megili*) prepared from the same material. Of this also all the cordage employed in agriculture and for rigging boats is formed, and it is the material of which all the paper is made, so that it must be considered as an article of great importance. It will grow on all land, whether of a free or dry soil, that can produce summer rice; so that its cultivation may be easily extended to any length, and it is probable, that it might be employed to advantage in many of our manufactures at home, especially in making paper, as the quantity of flax now used there is so small, that linen rags cannot be procured without great difficulty. The bags made of the sackcloth, which are sent home in packages, are now, I believe, employed for that purpose, but the quantity might perhaps be very much increased by using *megili* for wrappers in bale goods in place of cotton cloth. The *megili* is much cheaper, would be equally fit for the purpose, and perhaps would be more saleable. Whether or not this plant might be employed in Europe to make cordage or canvas, I cannot say; but I hope, that no circumstance will divert the attention of the public, until a fair trial has been made with the *son*, which I have no doubt will be found to answer just as well as European hemp.

The *Pat* is cultivated as follows. From about the 10th of February, until the 12th of April, the field is ploughed. If the soil is free, it receives 3 or 4 double ploughings; if it is stiff clay, it requires 5 or 6. The seed, in the course of the following month, is sown broad-cast, and covered with a ploughing; and the field is smoothed with the *moyi*. Where the soil is free, weeds must be removed twice with a spud. In the stiff soil this is not required, so that in the two soils the trouble is nearly the same. The plant is fit for cutting between the 14th of August and 14th of September, but the seed is not then ripe, and some plants must be preserved to bring it to maturity. The plant when fit for cutting is from 5 to 6 feet high. After it has been cut close by the root, it is put in water, covered with a little dung, and held down by a frame of bambús. It remains about 10 days in the water, when the fibres are so completely separated, that they are taken up in handfuls, and by mere washing, reduced to a substance like hemp. The fibres are then tied up into bundles, which are hung over bambús to dry, and are then fit for sale, and weigh about 30 ounces avoirdupois. A bigah of 87 large cubits, which is nearly half an acre, produces from 100 to 120 bundles. According to two statements which I received, the medium produce may be 3 Calcutta maunds from the bigah, or about 480 lb. from the acre; but there is reason to think, that by these statements the produce is diminished, and is in fact considerably more: for the usual rate at which the farmer sells is 14 annas for the heavy maund of 96 S. W. the seer, that is, his large bigah would only produce the value of Rs. 2. 3. or a Calcutta bigah Rs. 1. 7. 4. which is too small an allowance by at least one-half. I am indeed credibly informed, that the usual produce at Calcutta is about 740 lb. the acre: the fields here are at least equally productive. The harvest price here is at the rate of rather more than 12½ annas the hundred weight. After the *Pat* has been removed, the fields, where the soil and elevation are fit, give a winter crop of rice or of mustard seed (*sorisha*). The greater part is cultivated by those who use or manufacture it, for almost all the low Hindu farmers weave cloth of this material, and every farmer requires some for the use of his farm. About a fourth part is sold for exportation. The average value of the whole, according to the statements which I procured, may be about 58,000 Rs. but if I am right in supposing the land to be as productive as at Calcutta, of which I have no doubt, the value of the *Pat* raised in this district will be about 87,000 Rs. even at the harvest price.

The cotton, I have stated to occupy 25,000 bigahs. A little, as I have already mentioned, is raised in the northern divisions along with Turmeric; but it is of a very bad quality, and the quantity is inconsiderable. In some few places a small quantity of this bad kind of cotton, which is sown in the beginning of the rainy season, is cultivated by itself, in spots that produce as much as the farmer's wife can spin for family use. The field, which is of a light soil, and situated high, is ploughed with the first rains of spring. It is then manured with a little dung, and smoothed with the *moyi*. The seed is sown broad-cast in the end of May, is covered with the plough, and the field is again smoothed. It requires two or three weedings. The cotton is collected between the middle of August and the middle of October. This is a miserable kind of cultivation, which should give way to that of which I am now to treat, and in which the cotton is sown in the end of the rainy season.

This kind of cotton is raised in the South East parts of the district, and is finer than that which is imported from the West of India. It is therefore an article of cultivation that merits encouragement. It is cultivated on the best and highest land, both of a stiff and free soil, and is generally mixed with *sorisha*, and often with *rayi*, flax, and safflower. In the stiff soil the cotton is most productive, in the loose soil the value of the other crops increases.—I shall first give an account of the manner in which it is managed in loose soil.

The land is of the first quality, is cultivated in a succession of crops as follows: 16 months sugar-cane, 7 months summer rice, 9 months cotton and mustard (*sorisha*), 4 months pulse (*thakuri*), in all three years. The same succession is then repeated. Some variations occasionally take place, but this is the most common. The *sorisha* is sometimes left out, and the pulse is sown among the growing cotton when it receives the last weeding. In this case, the crop of cotton is more productive. The rice is cut between the middle of August and the middle of September, and the field is immediately ploughed, until it is very well broken on the surface, which may require six double ploughings; and after about one-half of these has been given, it is manured with a little dung, and with mud from ponds or ditches. Between the middle of October and that of November, the seed is sown broad-cast, 20 measures of cotton and one of mustard, and the field is smoothed with the *moyi*, which covers the seed. That of the cotton before it is sown, is put in water for ½ of an hour, and is then rubbed with some dry earth, so that the grains may separate when they are sown broad-cast. A month afterwards the field is weeded. In the end of January or beginning of February, the mustard is ripe, and is plucked, and the field is at the same time weeded. Between the 12th of April and 12th of June, the cotton is collected, as it ripens; the produce of a large bigah of land, nearly equal to half an acre, may be stated at 75 seers, Calcutta weight, of cotton in the seed, in which state it is always sold by the farmer. Its value at harvest is 5 Rs. or about 30½ lbs. for the rupee. The mustard-seed produced on this bigah is about 75 seers, worth 1½ rupee. The produce of an acre is therefore about 300 lbs. of cotton, worth ten rupees, and as much mustard-seed, worth three rupees.

From the preceding account, it will appear evident, that the profit to be derived from each article cannot be ascertained, neither could I even ascertain the profits which a farmer may have on a bigah of land cultivated in this succession, because no man has a whole farm of such land, but each man, for every plough he has, cultivates from one to three bigahs of it, and also from 12 to 14 bigahs of poorer kinds, on which even a great variety of produce is raised.

A still greater quantity of cotton is reared on the stiff clay land. This cultivation is confined to the east side of the Punabhoba, and southern part of the district, but might no doubt be extended to the northern and western parts with the greatest advantage. It is high land, generally near tanks, which are indeed very numerous, wherever the soil is of this kind. If the soil is rich, it gives a summer crop of rice in the same year, or at least produces the seedling rice, that is to be transplanted. In the beginning of October, the field is ploughed, and in the end of the month the cotton seed is sown, mingled with *sorisha* or *tora*, (mustard and radish,) and some rows of flax and safflower are generally intermixed. In the end of January, or beginning of February, the oil-seeds are plucked, the field is hoed and manured with cow-dung ashes, mud from tanks, and oil-cake. It is then watered, once in from 8 to 12 days, when there is no rain, and four men in a day will water fully an acre. The cotton is gathered between the middle of April and the middle of June, and its produce may be from 360 to 500 lbs. an acre; but the value of the oil-seeds is very small, and does not exceed one rupee.

The value of the whole cotton produced in this district may be about 100,000 rupees. The *son* is an article of the utmost consequence, as likely to be able to supply our shipping with an excellent material for both sails and cordage. In this district the Company have made some advance to encourage the cultivation, which is therefore on the increase; for among the natives its use was entirely confined to making fishing nets. It requires a rich free soil, tolerably high, and no part seems to be better calculated for it than the whole banks of the Atreyi river within this district. Formerly much sugar-cane was raised there, and the vast profit which arises from the cultivation of that article must prevent any thing else from being sown, where it will thrive; but since the diminution that has taken place in the waters of this river, which is already mentioned, the soil has become less fit for sugar-cane, and seems now to be in an excellent state for the cultivation of the *son*. I conjecture, that at present about 14,000 bigahs are employed in that way, but probably 100,000 might be found in the district on which nothing could be cultivated to so much advantage, should there be a demand for the article at the price now advanced by the Company, with which the people seem perfectly satisfied. Owing to the use to which alone this plant was formerly applied, its cultivation was entirely carried on by fishermen, who hired the ground from the farmers at a high rent, and generally received it ploughed, and fit for sowing, and this practice still continues. The field receives four or five double ploughings between the middle of September and the middle of October, and after each is smoothed. The seed is sown in the end of October, and covered with the *moyi*. It grows without farther trouble, and is pulled by the root in March, when the seed is ripe. It is then steeped in water, and the principal art in the whole business seems to be to ascertain the proper time, which it should remain in the water. Of this the natives can only judge by practice, and it is therefore of the utmost importance, that none should be employed to raise this plant, except those who have had proper experience, or at least that experienced persons should superintend the watering: an intelligent fisherman gave me the following account of his process. He forms the *son* into bundles or sheaves of about two feet in circumference. These he places on their roots in water, which is one foot deep. In this the sheaves stand five or six days. They are then laid on their sides, so as to be entirely under water, and are covered with straw and earth to prevent them from floating. In this situation they also remain five or six days. The roots are then cut off, with all the part that was under water when the sheaves stood upright, and each sheaf is then taken by the root end, and washed by shaking it in the water. In this operation most of the stems fall out, the remainder is separated by the hand. The fibres are then dried, and afterwards are washed by dipping them in water and beating them against a plank. The washed fibres are then dried, and are fit for sale. He says that he receives one rupee for 22½ seers, Calcutta weight, which is at the rate of rather more than R. 1¾ a maund. The Company's agent makes advances to petty dealers, who of course must have a profit, and I understood, that it is very considerable. It was said, that these dealers receive the *son* from the cultivators at the rate of 30 light seers for the rupee, and deliver it to the company at from 20 to 25 seers.

The fisherman above-mentioned said, that he paid from 2½ to 2 rupees a bigah for the land, and that the farmer was at the whole expense of cultivation. The produce, he says, is from 3 light maunds to 2½ from the bigah, or from Rs. 4 to Rs. 3. 5. 4. His profit is from Rs. 1-8 to Rs. 1. 5. 4. and he can steep and clean the produce of a bigah in 15 days. I am inclined to think, however, that he underrated the produce, as might indeed be naturally expected. Another statement gave 5½ rupees for the Calcutta bigah, which is only a small value for rich land, but the expense of cultivation is almost nothing. We may take the highest statement of the fisherman, as the average produce, giving 56,000 rupees for the whole raised in the district, as coming from the farmer. The crop is exhausting, and cannot be sown oftener on the same ground than once in three years; the material in the state it comes from the cultivator is very unfit for exportation, and is combed at the factory, an operation with which the natives were totally unacquainted.

The *Kankhura*, I have already mentioned (page 71) as a potherb that is a good deal used in this district. As it is employed for the ropes used in tracking boats, it is probably the strongest material that can be procured.

SECTION 4.—*Plants cultivated on account of their saccharine juice.*

IN India several plants are cultivated, in order to procure a saccharine matter from their inspissated juice, and are almost always articles of considerable importance. In this district several of these plants grow, but sugar-cane is the only one used. This however is cultivated with great success, and, although I have stated the extent of land occupied by it as small, yet the value of the produce is great, and perhaps exceeds that of any single article raised in the fields of this district,—rice and mustard-seed excepted. On an average the produce of a Calcutta bigah, or one-third of an acre, may be taken at 12 maunds of inspissated juice, or about 26 hundred weight the acre; and ¼ more may be allowed for the richer soils, and ¼ less for the poorer. The value varies very much; in some years, as the present, it falls to 1¼ rupee a maund; in others, as the last, it rises to 2¼; but the average may be 1½ rupee a maund, or a little more than 2 rupees a hundred weight. The usual value of the whole annual produce, as coming from the former, may therefore be estimated at 4,50,000 Rs.

Sugar-cane requires a rich free soil, sufficiently elevated, to be entirely exempt from inundation, but not so high as to be deprived of moisture, or as to encourage the production of white ants (*Termes*). Of such land there is in this district a considerable extent, and a great part of it is now cultivated with this valuable article; for it must be observed, that in a proper system of agriculture, the same field produces only one crop of sugar in three years, so that the 25 thousand bigahs, stated as sugar-cane land, supposes that there are 75 thousand bigahs, which are employed in the rotation; but it is only reckoned as sugar land in the year when the cane is cut, for in the two remaining years it gives other crops. It is probably owing to the selection of a soil so admirably fitted for the plant, that the produce is so high, for there is little to be commended in the manner of cultivation. I do not think, while the cultivation is confined to such a soil, that it could be much extended, in the present state of the country, although much land formerly cultivated for sugar-cane is now applied to other purposes, or is waste; but this is chiefly owing to the drying up of the rivers, which has encouraged the breed of hurtful insects; neither can it be considered, as advisable, to extend the cultivation to less profitable soils, with a view to speculation in foreign markets, which are already overloaded.

In my account of the cultivation of cotton, I have already given one of the best systems of rotation, that is employed on this admirable soil, especially in the south near the Jomuna; but there are some others, which require to be mentioned. In some parts, especially towards the north, near the Tanggon, the rotation occupies four years: sugar-cane, 17 months; rice, 7; mustard, pulse, or wheat, 5; rice, 7; mustard, pulse, or wheat, 5; rice, 7; in all 48 months. The reason of this seems to be that the soil near the Tanggon is poorer than that near the Jomuna, the average produce there being about nine maunds the bigah, whereas on much good land in the southern parts of the district 15 maunds may be taken as the average produce, and 12 maunds as that of ordinary land. Towards the Kulik, the produce equals at least that on the Jomuna. In other places the rotation is 17 months; sugar-cane, 7 months; rice, 5 months; mustard and lentils, or mustard alone, and 7 months rice; in all 36 months. Some again, who are necessitous, take a crop of cane every two years, with rice, tobacco, or pulse in the 8 months of interval between the crops; but this exhausts the ground. In every part of the country it is usual to plant a hedge of *oror* round the field of cane.

There are two kinds of sugar-cane, the *Khagra* and *Kajoli;* the former is a yellow, hard cane, not thicker than the finger, and is only used by a few farmers in the northern parts, who are too lazy to cultivate the *Kajoli,* which requires some more trouble. The *Kajoli* has a tolerably thick stem, deeply stained with purple, and often grows 12 and 14 feet high. I shall give the full account of its cultivation.

The field from about the middle of October, until above the 10th of January, receives 10 or 12 double ploughings, and after each is smoothed with the *moyi;* during the last three months of this time, it is manured with cow-dung and mud from ponds or ditches. On this account the land fit for sugar-cane is generally divided into fields by wide ditches, into which much mud is washed by the rains, and is again thrown on the fields, when the country dries, and leaves it enriched by innumerable aquatic vegetables and animals, that have died as the water left them. When the ploughing has been completed, the field is manured with ashes and oil-cake. In February and March, the field is planted with cuttings of about a foot in length, which are taken from the tops of the ripe canes, that are cutting at that season. Trenches, about 4 inches deep and a foot distant from each other, are made by the hoe throughout the field; the cuttings are laid horizontally in the trenches, and are immediately covered by the land. The field is then smoothed with the *moyi.* In about a month, the young plants are two or three inches high. The earth is then raised from the cuttings by means of a spud, and the dry leaves by which they are surrounded are removed. For a day or two they remain exposed to the air, and are then manured with ashes and oil-cake and covered with earth. Weeds must be removed as they spring, and when the plants are about a cubit and a half high, the field must be ploughed. When they have grown a cubit higher, which is between the 13th of June and 14th of July, they are tied together in bundles of three or four, by wrapping them round with their own leaves. This is done partly to prevent them from being laid down by the wind, and partly to prevent them from being eaten by jackals. During the next month, three or four of these bunches are tied together, and about the end of September, when the canes grow rank, they are supported by bambu stakes driven in the ground; they are cut between the middle of December and the end of March.

The *Khagra* is cultivated nearly in the same manner, but does not require to be bound with leaves, as it is too hard for the jackals, and does not grow so rank as to be in danger from the wind. On the same extent of ground it produces about one-fourth part less of extract than the *Kajoli* does.

It is only large farmers that cut an acre of cane in a year; one mill therefore and one set of implements used in inspissating the juice, although very rude and simple, serve for several farms; and generally belong to some wealthy man, who lets them out for hire to his poorer neighbours, and the whole unite to clear each other's fields by turns; so that although many people and cattle are employed at one of these miserable set of works, very few indeed are hired, and the greater part of the labour is performed by the common stock of the farms.

The juice of the sugar-cane is always inspissated before it is sold by the farmers. I shall now therefore give an account of the process. Sixteen men and 20 oxen assemble from the neighbourhood, and during the crop season, continue to work night and day. Two oxen are required for the mill at once, but are relieved 10 times a day. One man skilled in the operation is generally furnished by the owner of the works, and is usually the only person that is hired for the occasion. The canes freed from the leaves are brought to the works by each farmer in his turn. Some of the workmen cut them into pieces from an inch to half an inch long, others put these into the mill, and clear it of such as have been squeezed: another drives the oxen, another carries the pots of juice to the boilers, and others attend the fire. The boilers and mill will be described in the account of the implements of husbandry. The juice is passed through a number of boilers, until it is sufficiently inspissated, which, so far as I can learn, is when it has been reduced to ¼ part, and nothing is either added or taken from it, nor is it even scummed, and in fact it contains many impurities. The inspissated juice or extract of sugar-cane is by the natives called *Gur*, and is of two kinds, which among the natives are called by various names; but concerning these there is so much confusion, that I shall call the one cake-extract, and the other pot-extract, which term I prefer to the word *jagary* commonly used by the English, as several substances of a very different nature are included under that name. The cake-extract is more completely inspissated, so that when cool it becomes hard. An oblong square hole from 12 to 18 inches long, and from 12 to 9 inches wide, is dug in the earth; a bag of coarse sackcloth is placed in it, and the inspissated juice is poured into the bag. When the extract has cooled, the bag is pulled from the earth, and the cake is shaken out. This is a black disgusting mass, weighing about 40 lbs. but not so bad as the other, which is less inspissated, and is poured into earthen pots, which hold from one maund and a half to one Calcutta maund by weight or from about 124 to 82 lbs. It is of the consistence of a thin extract, or of the inspissated liquor that comes from the cooler, and is put into the hogsheads in a curing house of Jamaica. The natives are very fond of both kinds, mixed with milk in all its forms, or with grain prepared into various kinds of sweetmeats, all very obnoxious to an English eye. The pot-extract is not so easily transported by water, and spoils in the first rainy season, which seems to be the reason why a considerable quantity of the cake-extract is made; for the pot-extract is thought best for eating, as being less liable to be adulterated with clay, a practice common in making the other kind; and it is preferred by those who make sugar, as being most fit for their purpose. The cake-extract keeps tolerably well for 18 months, stows easily in a boat, and cannot be so readily embezzled, as any portion removed from a cake would be instantly detected in delivery. A great part of the extract, which is made in the northern parts of the district, where there are no manufacturers of sugar, is therefore formed into cakes, while the sugar boilers of the southern divisions require almost all that is made there to be of the pot kind.

A bigah or ⅓ of an acre of good land in the southern districts is reckoned by the farmers to produce 168 maunds or 13,891 lbs. of cane, and 14 maunds or 1159 lbs. of pot-extract. Its produce of cake-extract is about 11 maunds 24 seers, or 952 lbs. The value of the pot-extract, at 1½ Rs. a maund, is 21 rupees the bigah; of the cake-extract, at 1¼ rupee for 40 seers of 58 S. W., the value is 20 Rs. a bigah.

The leaves, that were employed to tie up the stems, serve for fuel to boil the juice. When the canes are cut, the fresh leaves and the squeezed canes are given to the cattle employed at the mill. In the northern parts, the culture is not so well understood. The farmers there informed me, after reducing their weights and measures to the Calcutta standard, that a bigah produced only nine maunds of cake-extract. The management of the plant differs somewhat: the cuttings are placed in furrows not quite a cubit from each other, and are covered by ridges, which are formed by drawing a furrow on each side of the row. The shoots, before they are planted, are sometimes soaked in water, until the eyes begin to grow. When a foot high, the plants are freed from weeds about the end of April, the field is ploughed, and in the end of May, the ridges are levelled with the hoe. The field is then ploughed five times. About the end of June the canes are three feet high, and are tied together. The mill requires only 12 oxen and 8 men, but works only from about half after 6 in the morning until about 7 at night. It clears about half an acre of cane in twelve days. In the northern parts of the district the fields are not manured with the earth from ditches, which will account perhaps for their being less productive, and the rents are very low, which will perhaps account for the neglect of manure.

On considering that the sugar-cane is only a portion of the rotation of crops taken from a field, and that this forms only a part of a farm, the whole wrought at a common expense by a common stock, it will appear difficult, if not altogether impossible to state the expense of cultivation or profits which accrue to the farmer, but these must be very considerable. The expense of cultivating sugar-cane is however considerably more than that of cultivating grain, and wherever sugar is reared the rent is high. In some parts this is laid openly, and the same field, which when cultivated with grain, pays one rupee, pays five when cultivated with sugar. In most places however even this circumstance cannot be ascertained, for the rent of the whole higher land, of a light, free soil, is raised, and the tenant may cultivate whatever he pleases. But as the rent is made high, in proportion to the quantity of sugar land in this district, each farmer must receive his proportion, and he could not pay this rent, should he neglect this valuable article. In such districts the whole land of this nature often rents for two rupees a Calcutta bigah, and more than one bigah out of ten is probably not cut in the year. On the whole the farmers in districts, where sugar-cane is cultivated, are by no means richer than where grain is the only produce.

SECTION 5.—*Plants cultivated for being chewed or smoked.*

IN every part of India, chewing and smoking various vegetable substances, some of them highly intoxicating, is a favourite article of luxury. In this district the people, however, are less than usually addicted to these practices, and raise only some of the articles, that are commonly employed.

The articles used for smoking, that are cultivated in this district, are tobacco and hemp *(Ganja)*.

The articles fit for chewing, that are produced in this district, are *pan*, *Piper betel*.

Tobacco, *Nicotiana*.

Khoyer, *Mimosa Catechu*.

Dhoniya, *Coriandrum sativum*.

Joyaine, *Ajwan*, *Athamantha Chinensis*, ? [*Ligusticum Ajwan*. Rox.]

Mauri, *Anethum graveolens*.

Of the four last, an account has already been given. The *Khoyer* raised at Maldeh is not sufficient for the demand of the district, but most of it is sent to Moorshedabad, from whence again almost the whole of this district is supplied. The three last articles are carminative seeds, of which little is used, and that is raised in the country. Of the three remaining articles, tobacco occupies by far the greatest extent, and the betel leaf is by far the most valuable. Tobacco raised in the country is not adequate for its supply, and most of the *ganja* is exported.

The tobacco may occupy about 15,000 bigahs. It requires a light soil, but is cultivated in three different situations. 1st. In rich spots of land, immediately contiguous to the farmer's house, which are cultivated with this plant alone, and receive a great quantity of manure. 2ndly. In rich, high land, fit for sugar-cane, and often as a crop alternating with that valuable plant. 3rdly. On banks of rivers that are inundated in the rainy season. On the first of these it is most productive, and on the last the crop is most scanty. In good land it may produce eight maunds the Calcutta bigah ; but except on the rich ground that is reserved for this alone, the average cannot be reckoned at more than 4 maunds, or 328½ lbs. from ⅓ of an acre. It sells usually by the farmers at 1¼ R. the Calcutta maund, or at very near Rs. 1-11-4 a hundred weight. It is of a worse quality than that of Rangpur. In the last half of September and first half of October the field is ploughed remarkably well, and strongly manured. The young plants, that have been sown in a bed in the end of August, are then planted at one cubit's distance from each other, and watered for three days. Weeds must be removed, wherever they arise. When the plant has seven or eight leaves, the young central shoot is pinched away. It is fit for cutting in March and April. Each stem contains from five to eight leaves, which in a good soil are 18 inches long, and in a poor are only half that length. The stem is cut, and the plants are allowed to lie three days on the ground. The leaves are then separated, and are tied in handfuls, which are hung in the open air until dry. The handfuls are made into balls, by laying them together in two rows, with their roots outwards. The parcels are surrounded with straw, are tied very tight, and the bale is then complete.

The betel leaf may occupy 700 bigahs ; but its value is very considerable, although the accounts, which I received on this subject, vary so much, that I cannot depend on any of them. The plant is cultivated in what is called a *voroj*, which signifies a fort, and great pains are bestowed to defend it from the sun and wind. The proper cultivators form one of the nine tribes of tradesmen that were admitted to be pure by Bollal-sen, which shows the importance that was then attached to this plant ; but the Muhammedan invasion has introduced considerable disorder, and those who cultivate it now are of many different castes, and it is reared even by Muhammedans. They are, however, the richest cultivators in the district, although half a bigah, or one rood, may be considered as a decent garden, or fort. I shall therefore detail the manner in which such a one is managed.

From the middle of October until the 10th of February, the garden is repeatedly hoed and smoothed with the *moyi*, which costs Rs. 3. Then two ridges are formed with the hoe, each about one foot wide, and between them is a little channel, six inches wide : at every four feet throughout the garden similar ridges are formed. Then in the middle of every interval is made a ridge, which on each side, between it and the adjacent double ridge, has a flat space of about 18 inches wide, on which the people walk, when they clean the garden or gather the leaves. In the double ridges are placed rows of sticks, about six cubits long, of which four and four are tied together by the middle. To the tops of these are fastened parallel rows of split bambus, which are crossed at right angles by others, so as to form a net-work. On this are laid two or three rows of the stems of a reed called *ulukhor*, and these are tied to the bambus. The sides of the garden are secured in the same manner, and only a small door is left for the workmen to enter. Then cuttings of the betel-vine are planted in two rows on each of the ridges. This operation costs, for forming the ridges, three rupees; for bambus, sticks, reeds, and rope, twelve rupees; and for workmen four rupees. During the latter half of April, and first half of May, the garden must be watered by pots, which costs two rupees. The water is given once every five or six days, and is poured into the channels between the ridges. Between the middle of August, and the middle of September, the garden must be manured with fresh earth and oil-cake, and this must be repeated once a month, for four times. At the first time, a strong reed (*ikiri*), or bambu, is stuck into the ground near each vine, which climbs upon this supporter. These operations cost 19 rupees. In the end of March, the garden must be completely weeded, which costs four rupees. The rent for one-half year is one rupee. The total expense is therefore 48 rupees, besides the maintenance of the cultivators' family, which cannot be estimated at less than five rupees a month; or rupees 120. The total stock before the garden becomes productive is therefore Rs. 168; a garden lasts from 12 to 30 years; according to which, the interest of the stock must be calculated, and 18 per cent. ought at least to be allowed, say rupees 15. Then the annual expense will be

Interest of capital,........................	Rs.	15	0	0
Repairing the walls and roof, ...	,,	8	0	0
Watering in the heats of spring,..................	,,	2	0	0
Manuring, ...	,,	10	0	0
Weeding,...............................	,,	2	10	0
Rent,.................................	,,	10	0	0
Collecting the leaves,..........................	,,	36	0	0
	Sa. Rs.	73	10	0

This may be about one-half of the produce; but I have already said, that I cannot speak with any confidence on this subject. It is certain, however, that no land in Bengal gives any return nearly equal to that cultivated with betel-leaf. The situation in general chosen is the sloping side of a tank, where the soil is commonly a stiff clay. Capital of 168 rupees being very rarely employed in agriculture by Bengal farmers, the trade is not likely to be overstocked.

The cultivation of hemp on account of its buds, that are used for intoxication, is confined almost entirely to the division of Jogodol, where it is raised on very rich clay land, which like that reserved for tobacco, is generally a small spot near the farmer's house, and is allowed a great quantity of manure. The whole extent may be about 300 bigahs. Its produce by the bigah may be equal in quantity to that of tobacco: but it is sold here at nearly five times the price, so that the returns are great; but the expense is also considerable.

The natives have two proper names for the hemp (*Cannabis sativa*), and call it *ganja* when young, and *siddhi* when the flowers have fully expanded. It is a common weed in many parts of the district, and the wild *siddhi* answers for a particular manner of intoxication. The dried leaves are beaten in a mortar with water, and this infusion is drunk. This is not so strong as the *ganja*, nor its intoxication attended with such violent effects, but it may be readily procured, whereas the wild plant in its young state has little effect; and in order to procure *ganja*, the plant must be cultivated with great pains.

The seed is sown in a small bed, about the end of June. The field must be very thoroughly wrought with the plough, hoe, and *moyi*. The seedlings are transplanted in August, are placed three or four feet from each other, and must be repeatedly manured and weeded. The plant grows from four to six feet high, and sends out many lateral branches. In February, when the leaves are tender, and before the flowers open, the buds and young leaves are pinched off, and spread on the ground, where they lie 10 or 12 days, exposed to the dew and sun, until they are dry, and fit for use. It is smoked like tobacco, and about 12 grains may be the usual dose.

SECTION 6.—*Plants cultivated for Dyeing.*

THE plants cultivated in the fields of this district for producing dyes are two, Indigo and Safflower. The last is of little or no importance, and a few drills of it are occasionally put amongst cotton, as I have already mentioned, or a small bed is sown in a garden chiefly on account of its leaves, which are used as a green. The safflower is chiefly used at Maldeh; and the greater part is imported from other districts. The natives here do not eat the seed.

In this district, therefore, Indigo is the only dying plant, of which the cultivation deserves notice, and unfortunately the cultivation does not seem to flourish.

The extent of land may be about 15,000 Calcutta bigahs, allowing on an average about 700 for each set of works, of which there are 21 in the district. The value of the plant produced may be taken at about 37,500 rupees, or 2½ rupees for Calcutta bigah. This is therefore an object of very little importance to either farmer or landlord, and both classes of men have great objections, not only to the extension, but to the continuance of the culture. As however the value of the Indigo manufactured is very considerable, and as it is one of the principal sources of foreign commerce which Bengal now possesses, it comes to be of importance to the country, especially as it gives employment to the poor labourers, and in the parts of the district where it is most prevalent, has almost doubled their wages.

In this place I shall confine myself entirely to the cultivation of the plant; and I cannot avoid mentioning, that, both on this subject, and concerning the nature and state of the manufacture, I have received much assistance from Mr. Halliday, Surgeon to the station, and from Mr. Tucker, a manufacturer of Indigo.

The soil chosen for Indigo, and the seasons for sowing it, are very various, and as it is a very uncertain crop, it would seem to be a desirable circumstance for every manufacturer to choose as great a variety as possible, so as to render the average less liable to variation: for if the whole Indigo belonging to a set of works be sown on one kind of land, the whole may one year be entirely destroyed, so that the works may be useless; while another year the crop may be so luxuriant, and ripen so nearly at one time, that the works may be unable to manufacture one-half of the produce.

The land that is most commonly employed is high, with a sandy soil, as is in general poor, such as would be cultivated only occasionally, were it not for the Indigo, unless it happened to be near the farmer's house, and was allowed much manure, in which case, it would produce a variety of valuable crops. This is well ploughed, and should be manured, which however is generally too much, if not altogether neglected. The seed is sown broad-cast in March, April, and May, the lowest lands being sown earliest. Much pains should be bestowed on weeding Indigo, but this also is in general much neglected. It is fit for cutting in four months after being sown, and after being cut shoots out again. Sometimes the shoots are reserved for seed, sometimes they are cut for a second crop, and sometimes the part not reserved for seed is ploughed for other purposes. The seed is ripe in February and March, so that the crop occupies the whole year. The Calcutta bigah in general may be estimated to produce 25 bundles, six feet in circumference, worth 2½ rupees. The seed may be worth 8 annas more; but it is only some situations that answer for it, and in general little more is raised than serves to supply the farm. The cultivation cannot be considered as so laborious or expensive as that of rice, especially in the slovenly and careless manner in which it is usually conducted. The price given by the different manufacturers varies from 8 to 12 bundles (six feet circumference) for the rupee, and the money which they advance, (two rupees, a large bigah, or about 1¼ rupee the Calcutta bigah,) is always fully adequate to defray every expense that the farmer can possibly incur. The manufacturer pays the carriage to the works when these are not in the immediate vicinity of the fields. If the rent were therefore moderate, such as this land would pay if cultivated for rice, the raising indigo weed would be abundantly profitable, as it ought indeed from its uncertainty, for too much sun, and either too much or too little rain, entirely ruin the crop. The fact however is, that the landlords, either wishing to share in the profits of the manufacture, or to prevent the cultivation altogether, usually exact a rent, which ends in the ruin of the farmer, who has been induced to receive advances.

The next most common land for Indigo is the flat sandy banks of rivers, which are inundated in the rainy season, and which are very low-rented, and seldom occupied. The crop on this is extremely uncertain, as it is cut just about the time when the rivers begin to rise, and if these swell a little earlier than usual, it is entirely lost. This may happen probably once in three years. No seed can be procured from this land; but, when not destroyed by the river, its produce is very great, and was estimated to me at 60 bundles, worth five rupees the Calcutta bigah; the expense is very trifling. Two or three double ploughings suffice for this light soil. The seed is a principal part of the expense, and is sown in January. It should be weeded twice, but this is done in a very negligent manner. It is cut between the middle of May and the middle of July.

The red clay lands towards the Korotoya answer well for indigo, and the high clay lands of a light-coloured soil, near the Tanggon, are equally favourable. The indigo on the red clay is sown after the first rains of spring have softened the ground. It is reaped between the middle of July and the middle of September. The produce on the red clay was estimated to me at 20 bundles, worth two rupees on the Calcutta bigah; but this land is remarkably favourable for seed, and supplies the lower land, on which seed cannot be raised. The seed on red clay is often worth as much as the plant. The produce of the light-coloured clay was estimated to me at 10 bundles, worth rupees 3. 5. 4. This also is favourable for seed, but the hardness of the soil renders the cultivation expensive.

It has been attempted to sow indigo on rich low rice ground, which in the rainy season is deeply covered with water. The seed is sown about the middle of February, and the plant is cut in June, after which, there is abundance of time for the rice crop, and I believe that this will be found to be rather improved by the indigo, which does not exhaust the land. The crop of indigo is, however, both uncertain and small. Mr. Tucker, who has tried it, estimated it at 25 bundles, worth 2½ rupees for a large bigah, which is at the rate of between 16 and 17 bundles for the bigah of Calcutta.

This gentleman has also sown indigo seed among cotton, which is done at the last weeding that the cotton receives about the end of April, and requires no additional expense of cultivation. The stems of the cotton are pulled after all the seed is ripe, and the indigo is cut about the 1st of August. Mr. Tucker estimates the produce of this to be about 20 bundles or 2 rupees the Calcutta bigah. This cultivation will, I am persuaded, be very valuable both in clay lands, where nothing is raised after the cotton, and in the free soils, where only a miserable crop of pulse is procured between the cotton and sugar, and which is not more in value than ¼ of the indigo. The people are however afraid to venture, lest their most valuable crop, the sugar, should be spoiled; and it is natural that they should be so, until convinced of the contrary by experience. On the clay soils the cotton ground is often that which is applied to raise the seedlings for transplanted rice, and where that is the custom it will prevent indigo from being raised.

In fact, I am persuaded, that indigo in one way or other may be raised on most soils, and it would be of great importance to the manufacturer to have the whole compact near his works, to have a lease of the whole from the landlord, and to let it out again to the farmers. At present it is customary to have from one to three bigahs from each farmer, and these spots are scattered over a district of perhaps five or six miles in diameter, owing to which great losses arise from fraud, notwithstanding that a great expense is incurred to prevent imposition.

SECTION 7.—*Plants used for feeding Silk-worms.*

THE plants cultivated for supporting silk-worms are those of least importance in this district, if we consider merely the extent of ground which they occupy; but they are of considerable importance, if we estimate the value of the produce, and consider, that it affords the raw material for a valuable manufacture. Two plants are cultivated, the mulberry and *ricinus*, and these support two different kinds of worm.

The mulberry cultivated in this district is a dwarf plant, which I have had no opportunity of examining in a state fit for ascertaining its Botanical affinities. Its fruit is said to be black, and very small. The cultivation is confined to the banks of the Mohanonda, where a high free soil is chosen, and to those of the lower parts of the Korotoya, where a clay soil, chiefly that of a red colour, is mostly used.

On the banks of the Mohanonda the mulberry may occupy about 4000 bigahs, Calcutta measure, all within a mile of the river, amidst noble groves of mango, banyan, and *pipol* trees, which shelter the houses of those who rear the worm, and which would be delightful were it not for their slovenly condition. The plantations are surrounded by ditches and high banks of mud that form good fences, and ought to be secured from inundation, as this entirely destroys the plant, which otherwise lasts about 20 years. The Company's commercial resident makes advances for a great part of the cocoons; but as these are not manufactured in this district, and as all that is manufactured on the left bank of the river is done by the farmers, who sell the raw silk, I shall proceed to give an account of the whole process. I begin with forming a new plantation of one bigah, for many do not exceed that size.

	Rs.	as.	ps.
To 12 double ploughings between the 12th of June and the 15th October, at 1½ anna,	1	2	0
To making a fence of earth,	2	0	0

	Rs.	A.	P.
Brought forward,	3	2	0
To planting cuttings of the mulberry at about 18 inches from each other, after having hoed the field thoroughly. This is done between the 15th October and the 14th of November,	4	0	0
To weeding in January,	1	0	0
Rent from 6 to 20 annas, average,	0	13	0
Rs.	8	15	0
The annual expense afterwards: Interest on the above at 18p. ct.	0	12	10
Repairing the fence,	1	0	0
Ploughings,	1	0	0
Weeding,	0	8	0
Rent,	0	13	0
Collecting the leaves and pruning,	3	6	0
Rs.	7	7	10

The allowance for collecting the leaves I state on the following grounds. Many persons who rear the worms employ people to cultivate the plantation, and these agree to deliver one-half of the produce, and to defray every expense. The sum of Rs. 3. 6. 0. is the difference between the expense and the average half of the produce.

There are annually six broods of worms, and the leaves are collected at six seasons; at three of these the plants, which grow about two or three feet high, are pruned, and the prunings are fit for feeding the worm. The leaves and prunings are sold by the load, which a man carries in a basket (*khungi*), that may contain about 80 lbs. weight, and according as the crop is plentiful or scarce, vary from one to 30 burthens for the rupee, which shows that the crops are extremely uncertain. The average price however throughout the year is four burthens for the rupee. The usual produce at each of the different crops is stated to be,

12th March, 11th April, ... burthens	8
11th April, 12th May,	6
13th June, 14th August,	16
14th August, 14th September,	8
15th October, 13th November,	12
14th November, 13th December,	10
Total	60 burthens,

worth about 15 rupees. The profit on such land is therefore very great, and many people content themselves with this—sell the leaves, and rear no worms; but many more employ the leaves to rear their own worms, and no breeder trusts entirely to the market for a supply of leaves.

I shall now proceed to give an account of the manner, in which cocoons are procured, a step of the process at which a great part of the cultivators stop. It is supposed, that a man and his family of the usual strength, that is a wife and an old woman, or child capable of assisting, can cultivate, collect the leaves, and feed as many worms as can be reared on four bigahs of land.

He must in the first place build a small hut with hurdle walls, and which has an aperture that serves for door and window. Every side except the door is surrounded by two or three rows of shelves that support the frames, lined with mats, on which the worms breed, feed, and spin. The whole value of the apparatus may be six rupees, and that of his house may be 10 rupees : allowing him to rebuild every four years, the annual expense will be four rupees, and his ground rent will be one rupee. The total expense therefore of his accommodation will be five rupees. The eggs are placed on frames (*dala*), where they are to be hatched and fed, and the 240 burthens produced by four bigahs of land are sufficient to feed 240 frames of worms ; when full grown, the worms are removed to other frames (*chondro*), where twigs are placed to facilitate their spinning. The worms of two *dalas* are placed on one *chondro*, so that there are 120 *chondros*, each of which should produce 2¼ seer (88 sicca weight) of cocoons. The whole therefore should produce 7½ maunds, the usual price of which is 12 rupees the maund, or 90 rupees from the four bigahs. Deduct the expense of cultivation at Rs. 4. 1. 10. a bigah, and there will remain Rs. 73. 8. 8. Deduct farther the house-rent, five rupees, and there will remain Rs. 68. 8. 8. or Rs. 5¾ a month, which is a decent support for a family. Should the family keep more worms, the land would be cultivated by another person for one-half of the produce.

The people are so necessitous, that wherever they can procure advances for the cocoons, they always sell the produce of their plantations in that state ; the profit however by spinning the silk is not inconsiderable. The cocoons that are intended for spinning are exposed to a strong heat, which kills the animal. The natives have almost entirely relinquished the original Hindú manner of winding the silk from the cocoons, by means of a small reel (*saya*), about 8 inches in diameter, which is fastened to a spindle, that the workman twirls round with his hands ; and a larger reel (*ghayi*) moved by a wench after the European fashion is generally employed. Several people in this district have huts, in which there is one or two reels, each provided with a small furnace and vessel for containing hot-water, in which the cocoons are kept when winding. The instrument is let, by the day, to those who wish to use it. The price paid here for winding 2¼ seers (at 88 sicca weight) is one anna for the implement, and two annas for two workmen that are employed, altogether three anas. On the 7½ maunds of cocoons produced by four bigahs of land, the expense of winding will be 22½ rupees. Every 2¼ seers of cocoons produce 15 sicca weight of silk, altogether 1,800 sa. wt. usually worth 180 Rs. The value of the cocoons was 90 Rs. the expense 22½ rupees, altogether 112½ rupees, leaving Rs. 87½ or 33 per cent. for profit at the above rates. An acre of land, or three bigahs should produce 508 lbs. of cocoons, worth 67½ Rs. 180 burthens of plant worth 45 rupees. The value of the whole produce may be 60,000 Rs. of leaves, 90,000 Rs. of cocoons, or 150,000 Rs. of silk, were it all wound in this district.

Near the Korotoya, the mulberry is cultivated in both clay and free soil, and I took the account of the cultivation in the former only. The people were uncommonly shy, and I have no great reliance on their statements.

The field is surrounded by a ditch and bank of earth as at Maldeh. The seasons differ considerably, although the expense of cultivation is nearly the same. The field is ploughed between the 12th of April and 12th of June, and the fence is made at the same time. The cuttings are planted in the following month, and weeds are removed about the end of August. Every year, with the early rains in spring, the field is ploughed and manured with dung and fresh earth. The plants are pruned close to the ground about the beginning of September, and the field is then ploughed, weeded, and manured. The young shoots push forth with great vigour, and about the middle of October are three feet high.

In the ensuing month the leaves of the best quality are produced. In spring the same stems shoot forth new leaves, and these are gathered between the 13th of May and the 14th of August. Those gathered in the middle of that period are reckoned of the second quality; those gathered at the beginning or end are of the worst kind.

The following estimate was given of the produce of one bigah in baskets, said to contain leaves weighing 25 seers of 96 sicca weight, or about 63 lbs.

Leaves of the first quality,	baskets	24
2nd,		24
3rd,		22
		70 burthens,

weighing Calcutta maunds 52½. The bigah at Maldeh of free soil gives 60 maunds, and is smaller, so that making allowance for this, the red clay would give only about 37 Calcutta maunds of leaves on the Calcutta bigah. The crop however seems to be more certain, as the price varies only from four to six bundles the rupee. The usual price is five bundles the rupee, or 14 rupees for the bigah of leaves, which is at the rate of nearly 10 Rs. the Calcutta bigah, or one-third less than the produce of the land at Maldeh. Ten baskets are required to feed two frames of worms, but the frames are much larger than those at Maldeh, for two frames of worms are placed into one, when they are about to spin, and this one produces four seers (96 sa. wt.) of cocoons, so that one frame on the Korotoya produces 384 sicca weight of cocoons from 300 Calcutta seers of leaves, while on the Mohanonda a frame produces 220 sicca weight of cocoons from 160 seers of leaves. The leaves therefore on the banks of the Mohanonda are not only in greater quantity, but are more nutritions than on the Korotoya; for 300 seers of them would have produced 412½ sicca weight of silk, or about ⅓ more than the produce near the Korotoya. The bigah produces therefore 28 seers of 96 sa. wt. of cocoons, which at the Calcutta weight and measure is rather more than 23⅓ seers for the bigah, or very little more than one-half of what was stated at Maldeh. It must however be observed, that the soil is of a different nature, and I had no opportunity of ascertaining what the free soil near the Korotoya can produce. It is also probable that the people under-rated very much every part of the produce; for although they stated the seer of cocoons to be 96 sa. wt. yet there is the strongest ground to suppose that in reality it weighs 160 sa. wt. I conclude this to be the case from the farmer's stating, that they sold their silk at eight rupees a seer of the same weight with the seer of cocoons, and I know from the commercial resident, that the seer of silk which sells at eight rupees contains 160 sa. wt. It is extremely probable therefore, that the calculation requires to be corrected by taking this rate of 160 sa. wt. for the seer, in place of 96 sa. wt. as stated by the farmers. This will make the produce, reduced to the Calcutta weight and measure, about 40 seers of cocoons from the bigah, which is nearly the same with the produce at Maldeh. The cultivators state, that 28 seers of cocoons give 2¼⅜ seers of Bengal silk, worth 21 rupees; the rent is two rupees, the expense of winding Rs. 2. 10. and of cultivation five rupees, leaving a net profit of Rupees 11. 6. 0. Mr. Monkton states, that cocoons give ⅛ of their weight of 'silk, which would make their profit considerably greater. The cultivators say, that they have refused thirteen rupees for the maund of cocoons at seventy-six sicca weight the seer. The price offered is higher than that usually given at Maldeh, where the maund of 88 sicca weight the seer sells only for 12 rupees.

The whole value of the leaves produced near the Korotoya may be about 30,000 rupees ; that of the cocoons has not yet been fixed.

The *Ricinus* (Erondo of the natives) is raised in many parts of this district for feeding a silk-worm, which I take to be the *Phalæna Penelope.* There are two kinds of the plant, the *Ricinus communis* and *viridis* of Willdenow. This excellent Botanist has with great propriety changed the name given by Linnæus to the first species ; but with regard to the last, he has been uncommonly unfortunate, as the stem of the plant is of a bright red, and the leaves are stained with brown, so that it may be considered a very remarkable exception to the vegetable colour. Being green, both plants seem to answer equally well, and those who rear the worm drop a few seeds round the fence that encloses their farm-yard, or sow a small spot adjacent to their house. The seed is put in the ground about the beginning of November, and again about the beginning of May.

Both plants are annual, although they have strong woody stems of ten and twelve feet high, and they live about eight months, so that leaves are procurable at all seasons. The seed is sometimes made into oil for medicine, but is never used for the lamp, as in many parts of India. The plant requires a mixed free soil. In some places one brood only of worms is reared ; in others 12 broods spin silk in the course of the year. The cocoons preserved for breeding having produced moths, which are very beautiful, the impregnated females cling to a small twig that is hung up near them, deposit their eggs round it in spiral rings, and there die clinging to the stick. These twigs are often sold at markets, and with the dead moths hanging round make a very curious appearance. A breeder, having procured one of these twigs, scrapes the eggs into a piece of cloth, which he lays on a wide-mouthed basket, which is supported at some distance from the floor in one end of his hut. The eggs are soon hatched, and the worms are daily supplied with fresh leaves, and kept clean. The worm grows rapidly, and when ready to spin, some twigs are put into the basket to assist its operation. The cocoons that are to be spun are thrown into boiling water, and the threads of from five to six are wound into one by means of the common silk reel of Bengal. This forms a coarse rough thread of a dirty white colour, and totally destitute of the silky lustre. A seer of 96 sa. wt. (lb. 2 $\frac{444}{1000}$) of this thread is worth from 12 annas to one rupee, but it is very seldom sold, and the people who keep the insect in general rear no more than is just sufficient to make clothes for their own family. The cloth lasts very long, owing to which quality, it is probable, that some use might be found for this material in our manufactures at home. It would perhaps answer as an ingredient for mixing with wool in the fabrication of many kinds of cloths, and I think it might be of use to send home a few hundred weights, which might be distributed among the principal manufacturers, in order to discover whether or not it could be applied to use. I have no doubt, if advances are made, that large quantities would be procured at 12 annas for the seer, or about five annas for the pound ; so that it might be sold at 18 or 20 pence a pound in England, with a reasonable profit.

At present about 1000 bigahs may be occupied with the Erondo plant.

CHAPTER II.

OF THE IMPLEMENTS OF AGRICULTURE.

The plough (drawing No. 20) is of the wretched construction usual in India, and has neither coulter to cut the soil, nor mould-board to turn it over. In some parts of the district it even wants the share, or small piece of iron that usually strengthens the point. Such a light machine is often managed by a boy 12 or 14 years of age, and two oxen or cows are reckoned sufficient to drag it. These are most wretched creatures, and until the breed of labouring cattle is improved, or at least until the cattle are better fed, they are entirely incapable of drawing any more powerful instrument. In this district, two oxen or cows and one man are kept for every plough, and usually work from about seven in the morning until noon, when the man goes to do other jobs about the farm, and the cattle are given to a boy, who drives them to pasture, if there is any, or gives them a little rice straw. The quantity cultivated by one plough in this district is pretty uniformly about five acres; but some deduction must be made where cows are employed; these cannot plough more than four acres. Although there is much more ploughing performed on five acres of a loose soil, a great part of which gives two, and some even three, crops in the year, than on five acres of clay which is only cultivated once, yet the difference in the quantity of the two kinds that one plough can cultivate is very small; but then the plough is employed almost the whole year, where the soil is free, and is idle for more than six months, where the soil is stiff clay. The value of a plough is usually about 12 annas, of which the iron forms a considerable part.

The *moyi* (drawing No. 21) is an instrument made of two bambús, about six feet in length, which are joined together by some cross bars like a ladder. It is used to cover the seed, and to smooth the field like a rolling stone, and is inferior to the plank used for the same purpose in the south of India; it is yoked to two oxen, and the driver usually stands on it to give it weight.

The *bida* or *nangol* (drawing No. 21) is a rake with wooden teeth, which is drawn by two oxen, and is employed only in free soils, where it thins the crops of rice that have been sown broad-cast, and have come up too thick. In some stiff soils, near Ghoraghat, this implement has iron teeth, which is a great improvement; and were it common, and the teeth sufficiently heavy, the implement might serve for a harrow, and be very useful in every kind of ground, both as more effectual than the plough for breaking the soil, and also as much fitter then the *moyi* for covering the seed. Iron teeth however are a great deal too expensive for the common state of farmers' capital.

The *kastya* or reaping-hook (drawing No. 22) is made of iron, but is a most wretched instrument, and its teeth more resemble those of a saw than those of a sickle. The reapers usually sit on their heels, and although they seldom cut more than from 18 to 24 inches of the straw with the ears, it usually occupies eight men a day to cut an acre. It is true, that they carry the rice and tops of the straw home to the farm-yard; but from this it may be judged how slowly and at what an expense of labour the operations of husbandry are conducted in this district.

I have already described the *dhenki*, by which the husks are separated from the grain, and have shown that this operation in general costs more than ¼ part of the whole grain that is used in the country. The natives have no flail, but tread out the grain by oxen, which is not only an expensive and tedious operation, but also leaves the grain mixed with impurities. The only means that they have of separating these is a fan (*kula*). Some baskets are necessary in the operation: a coarse sieve is used in separating the rice from the bran.

The iron of the hoe (*kodal*) is well-shaped (drawing No. 23), but the handle is greatly too short, being accommodated to allow the natives to sit while at work, a custom which always prevents great exertion. When sitting is not practicable, the use of this implement becomes very fatiguing, as in order to reach the ground the labourer must bend himself almost double. The natives have no spade, which is a great loss; as I am persuaded, that with an instrument of that kind a man could cultivate fully as much as he does with a plough and two oxen, and the cultivation would be much more effectual, while it would save a vast deal of useless animal suffering; no creature on earth being probably so miserable as the plough-ox of India: besides, the straw would support many more cows, and increase the quantity of milk, which is a very scarce article in Bengal, so that very few of the labourers can procure any part of this food so natural to man. Such an improvement, however, would imply, that the Hindús should consent to the male calves being destroyed, which would be vain to expect, and disgusting to prove. The only implement approaching to the spade, which the natives possess, is a stake with a flat sharp point of iron, somewhat like a large chisel, (*khonta*,) with which they dig holes for planting trees, or for fixing stakes or posts in the ground, (see drawing No. 24.)

The hatchet (*kural*) (drawing No. 25) must also be considered as an implement of agriculture, as no farmer can well want this useful instrument. The iron of the hatchet is a great deal too narrow, and is nearly of the shape and size of the wedge that is used in England for cleaving wood.

The weeding iron or spud, (drawing No. 26,) called in this district by a variety of names, is an instrument sufficiently fit for the purpose, and is also useful in transplanting. Its form is that which usually prevails in every part of India.

The only other instrument of husbandry commonly used in this district is the *da*, or bill, for cutting bushes or bambús, (drawing No. 27;) and although rudely formed, it is well enough adopted for the purpose.

To recapitulate then the implements proper for the cultivation of five acres of land, they are,

Item		Rs.	
1 Plough,	Rs.	0	12
1 *Moyi*,		0	1
1 *Bida*,		0	1
1 Reaping hook,		0	1
1 *Dhenki*,		0	8
Fan, sieve, and baskets,		0	1
1 Hoe,		0	14
1 Weeding iron,		0	1
1 Hatchet,		0	8
1 Bill,		0	3
Ropes,		0	2
	Rs.	3	4

There only remains for me to describe the mill and boiler used in preparing the extract of sugar-cane, and which are usually let by the day. The mill (drawing No. 28) is on the principle of a mortar and pestle. The pestle however does not beat the canes, but is rubbed against them, as happens in many chemical operations, and the moving force is two oxen. The mortar is generally a tamarind tree, one end of which is sunk deep in the ground to give it firmness. The part projecting (*a a a a*) may be about 2 feet high and 1½ foot in diameter. In the upper end of this is cut a hollow in form of the small segment of a sphere (*b b*). In the centre of this a canal (*c c*) descends a little way perpendicularly, and then obliquely to one side of the mortar, so that the juice, as squeezed from the cane, runs through this canal, and by means of a spout (*d*) is thrown upon a strainer (*e*), through which it runs into an earthen pot, that stands in a hole (*f*) under the spout. The pestle (*g g*) is a tree of about 18 feet in length, and one foot in diameter, rounded into a foot (*h*), which rubs against the mortar, and which is secured in its place by a button (*i*) that goes into the canal of the mortar. The moving force is applied to a horizontal beam (*kk*), about 16 feet in length, which turns round the mortar, and is fastened to it by a bent bambú (*l l*). It is suspended from the upper end of the pestle by a bambú (*m*), which has been cut with part of the root, in which is formed a pivot, that hangs on the upper point of the pestle. The cattle are yoked to the horizontal beam at about 10 feet from the mortar; they move round it in a circle, and are driven by a man, who sits on the beam to increase the weight of the rubbing power. Scarcely any machine can be more miserable, and it would be totally ineffectual, were not the cane cut into thin slices. This is an expensive part of the operation. A man sits on the ground, and has before him a bambú stake (*n*) which is driven into the ground, and has a deep notch formed in its upper end. He passes the cane gradually through this notch, and at the same time cuts off the slices with a kind of rude chopper (*o o*).

The boiling apparatus is better contrived. The mill is without shelter, but the boilers are placed under a shed. The fire-place is a considerable cavity dug into the ground, and covered by an iron boiler (*p*). At one side of this is an opening (*q*) for throwing in fuel, and opposite to this is an opening, which communicates with a horizontal chimney. This is formed by two parallel mud walls (*r r*, *s s*), about 20 feet long, two feet high, and 18 inches distant from each other. A row of 11 earthen boilers (*t*) is placed on these walls, and the interstices (*u*) are filled with clay, which completes the chimney, an opening (*v*) being left at the end, for allowing the smoke to escape. The juice, as it comes from the mill, is first put into the earthen boiler, that is most distant from the fire, and is gradually moved from one boiler to another, until it reaches the iron one, where the process is completed. The furnace is on an excellent principle, and might be adopted in many manufactures to great advantage. The execution of its parts indeed is very rude and imperfect. The inspissated juice, that can be prepared in twenty-four hours by such a mill, with 16 men and 20 oxen, amounts only to eight maunds of 58 sa. wt. the seer, or 476 lbs. It is only in the southern parts of this district, where the people work night and day, that this mill is so productive. In the northern divisions the people only work in the day time, and do not inspissate one-half so much juice.

CHAPTER III.

ON MANURES.

This part of good husbandry is more neglected than any other by the farmers of Dinajpur. Not that they are unacquainted with the utility of manure, but they neglect the means, by which it may be procured in plenty. The cattle are so scantily fed that the manure of the cow-house is in very small quantity, and is never increased by the use of litter, although the straw of every thing, except rice, is either altogether neglected or burnt; and the same is the case with the coarser kinds and parts of even the rice-straw. If all these were carefully employed as litter, and if all the leaves that could be collected were added, as is done in Canara, the quantity of manure might be very much increased. At present it is altogether trifling, and in the largest farm-yard of the district I certainly did not see any dunghill, that would load five single-horse carts. The quantity of manure is very much diminished by the pernicious custom of using cow-dung for fuel, although this is more prevalent in some other districts than in Dinajpur. It is true, that the dung is usually collected from the fields, and would never have entered the farm-yard; but even that deprives the fields of the manure that they would otherwise receive, and the evil is increased by mixing the cow-dung that is to be used for fuel with oil-cake. This is another substance, that necessity has compelled the farmers to use in rearing sugar-cane, the quantity of cow-dung being so small, that it is totally inadequate. They have therefore been under the necessity of using for manure the best food that they have for their cattle.

Ashes are used as a manure, but as there are no fires, except for cooking, the quantity is very small.

The farmers here are quite unacquainted with the valuable manner of manuring fields into which rice is to be transplanted, by treading into the mud, the branches and leaves of all kind of plants, which in a hot climate immediately rot. This is practised in the south of India with great advantage, and might be equally so in Bengal.

One of the most valuable manures used is this district is, earth from the bottom of tanks, marshes, and ditches, which is procured in the dry season, after it has been strongly impregnated with vegetable and animal substances by the rains. This is chiefly used for sugar-cane, but might be more generally employed.

Fortunately irrigation is not so necessary here as in the south, but still in many cases it is of great use, and is frequently employed, although not so often as it ought. The crops of rice might be much more certain in the stiff-clay soil, were there adequate means to give the fields one good watering in October, for it is generally owing to a want of rain in that month, that the crops of rice turn out scanty. The number of tanks that abound in every part of this district, wherever the soil is of that nature, facilitates the operation, and recourse is had to them, whenever the crops are suffering; and as most of the tanks contain springs, the supply of water is generally sufficient. When the rains of spring fail, recourse is also had to the tanks, in order to enable the farmer to raise seedlings for transplanting, and by means of a watering, given to the fields near tanks, many of them can be ploughed in the dry season, and produce two crops of rice, the importance of which I have already stated. Without watering these fields, it would be so hard, that the plough would have no effect.

The means for raising water are not very perfect. At the season, when irrigation is mostly wanted for the rice fields that are in danger, the water in the tanks is seldom more than one or two feet below the level of the field, and the implement usually employed answers tolerably well for the purpose. It is called *jant,* and is in form of a rude canoe, of which one end has been cut away (drawing No. 30). The length is about 13 feet, the width one foot, and the depth about the same. It is placed with the entire end (*a*) towards the canal (*b*), leading from the tank (*cc*), and moves upon a fulcrum (*d*), placed near its centre of equilibrium. The cut end (*e*) is placed over a canal (*ff*) that communicates with the field. The entire end is first pushed down into the water of the canal, that communicates with the tank. It is then raised until the trough is on a level, when the water flows into the field from the open end. The moving power is a lever (*gg*), supported by four bambús (*hhhh*), which stand over the trough, and are tied together at the upper end. The lever is a bambu about 20 feet in length. Its extremity towards the tank is fastened to the entire end of the trough by a bambu (*i*), which is of a length just sufficient to raise that end of the trough to the proper level, when the extremity of the lever next the field touches the ground, and this extremity of the lever is loaded with clay, fastened by means of straw (*k*), so that it is heavy enough to raise the entire end of the trough, when that is filled with water. The only other power wanted, is a man to sink the entire end of the trough into the water. He is placed very awkwardly on a bambu (*l*), which is supported by four others stuck into the side of the tank, and he keeps himself from falling by a pole which he holds in the hand. He places his foot on the end of the trough, and sinks it down until it is filled; he then removes his foot, and the lever raises the water. His position is tiresome, and to fill the trough requires a considerable exertion, which might be much diminished by a simple valve in its bottom. I am persuaded, that the instrument might be still farther improved, by making the entire end of the trough heavy enough to sink of itself, and by applying the man's force in place of the weight of clay, to depress the end of the lever next the field, where his situation would be commodious, and his power might be increased by lengthening that end of the lever. Although one man can work this machine, two men are generally employed, one to relieve the other. They only work the usual ploughing time of five hours a day. Whenever the water is to be raised more than 18 inches, the *jant* becomes a very imperfect instrument; but as it is at hand, it is the one commonly employed for raising water in the spring to rear seedlings, or to enable the farmer to plough some of the adjacent fields, and it is also employed in the cold season to water cotton, mulberry, and onions or garlic. In these cases, the water in tanks is often four or five feet below the level of the field, and three or four *jants* are necessary to raise the same water, by different stages, to the level required. This imperfection confines its use entirely to such tanks as dry up but little, and in all cases renders the operation very expensive. In the dry season, two *jants*, one above the other, can in one day water half an acre of cotton ground, and one watering suffices for from 8 to 12 days.

I am persuaded, indeed, that another implement in use, both in Dinajpur and in all the east, would in every case, where the water exceeds a cubit in depth, be employed to more advantage. This implement, called here *siyuni*, is merely a basket wrought by four ropes fastened to its edges, which two men hold in their hands and lower and raise alternately. Two brisk fellows can raise a vast deal of water with this to the height of three feet, or as high as two *jants;* and two or three sets could raise it as high as is ever wanted from a tank; but the labour is pretty severe, which seems to be the reason why the implement is seldom used in this district, for the expense of the machine is nothing; and in every operation to be carried on by the natives that is a principal consideration, for they have in general no capital. I am indeed afraid, that they are never likely to acquire a proper stock; otherwise numerous machines, far from being complex and very effectual, might be contrived, especially for watering the cotton, mulberry and seedlings, that are the articles to which it would be of most importance. One however seems very capable of being introduced to great advantage, I mean the *yatam* of the southern parts of India, which costs little or nothing, and may be removed from one field to another with little trouble. No situation is better fitted for this instrument than the clay lands of Dinajpur, where wells that never dry, may be in general dug for eight annas, and from which one man with a *yatam* could always raise as much water as a man with a *jant* can raise to the height of 18 inches, from a tank. In one part of this district I found such an implement in use. In division Porusa, it is called *dab*, but is more rude than those used in Mysore, and infinitely inferior to the improved *pokota* of Madras.

The reservoirs and canals, that are formed in the south of India, for irrigation, would here be in a great measure superfluous, and most of what seems requisite in that way has already been done. In many old water-courses, which are filled only in the rainy season, a part of the water is confined in the upper part of the channel, at the beginning of the dry season, and is allowed gradually to flow out, to water the spring rice, that is cultivated in the lower parts: some navigable streams have been dammed up for the same purpose; but the loss suffered by commerce seems in general to be greater than the advantage derived by agriculture.

CHAPTER IV.

OF FLOODS AND BANKS.

In the general Statistical Table I have mentioned, that about 380 square miles of this district are every year inundated, and that in the present state of agriculture, not above 120 of these are considered as fit for cultivation, and that a great part even of this is only occasionally tilled. It might be therefore supposed, that great advantage would be derived from banks, and under certain conditions, I admit, that such may be the case. I am however of opinion, that no expense should be incurred on this account by the public, and that for the following reasons:

1*st*. The land thus inundated, even without banks, may be made productive both of several crops and of good pasture; for instance, wherever the soil is tolerable, it would give two or three crops of millet (*Panicum Italicum*), or of barley, wheat, or mustard, and then for three or four years would produce a short soft grass fit for cattle to eat; and this mode of cultivation, I should consider, as by far the most advisable for such situations, were not the prejudices of the natives in favour of common pasturage so strong, as to leave little hope for expecting that this pasture could be appropriated to the cultivator. Wherever this land was near high ground and indigo works, a part might be employed for indigo to great advantage, without altering the plan which I have now suggested. 2*ndly*. The inundated spaces are generally narrow, and of great length, so that the expense of a general bank, in proportion to the extent recovered, would be great; and although in such cases it would be perfectly just to levy a tax on the proprietors of the land, there is great reason to suspect, that the profits which they would receive would not enable them to pay a tax equal to the expense, without which the undertaking would be altogether absurd. 3*rdly*. The distress, that arises from the breaking down of general banks, which is occasionally unavoidable, and which at once involves thousands in misery, should prevent this mode of securing land from being often employed. It is probably much better, that a country should maintain 100,000 people, living in security, than twice that number in constant danger of losing not only all their property, but their lives.

For these reasons, the banks, that I could wish to see, are those formed on a small scale by the proprietors of the land, so that, although a few of them should give way, no material injury would arise, and so that none should be attempted, where the advantage would not be evident. A few such have been formed, and I have no doubt will gradually extend; as there is much reason to suppose, that a great part of the inundated land might on this plan be secured with benefit to the proprietors: for, taking advantage of natural inequalities of the surface, considerable spaces might be nearly enclosed by banks not above two feet high, and almost the only expense would be to fill up the intervals between these banks. Even this expense would fall very easy on a landlord, who, watching the favorable times when his people had little or no employment, might procure their assistance at a very trifling expense, and probably merely by giving them the lands, for a few years, at a low rent.

CHAPTER V.

OF DOMESTIC ANIMALS.

By far the most important domestic animal in this district is the ox, which is of the kind called *Zebu* by naturalists, and of the variety which has the horns placed forward, so as to form a considerable angle with the face. It may be said, that in this district no care whatever is taken to prevent the degeneration of the breed, while the food is uncommonly scanty and bad, so that it would be difficult any where to find more wretched creatures. I have never seen a poorer breed, except on the coast of Malabar. Notwithstanding their being small, and wretched from a deficiency of food, the breed is not deformed, and those of which any care is taken are very handsome animals, but rather too finely shaped for labour. They are of many colours, but white is the most prevalent. By the natives they are usually divided into two kinds, one fit for the plough, the other for burthen, but this discrimination is not accurately observed. In the dry season, every ox in the clay country is employed in carrying rice to market, and, except a few belonging to merchants and manufacturers, almost every one in the rainy season is employed in the plough. The difference arises from those called burthen-oxen being rather larger and better fitted for the road, while the most miserable creatures are considered sufficient for the plough. Indeed not only many of the Moslems, but even many of the low tribes of Hindus employ the cow in the plough, which by the proper custom of Hindu notions would be punished with death. The common plough cattle cannot carry more than 60 seers of 96 sicca weight, or 147¾ lbs. and many are able to carry only ¾ of that weight. Those that can carry from 80 to 120 seers, or from 197 lbs. to 295½ lbs. are reckoned good burthen cattle. Some fine ones however are occasionally imported from the neighbouring district of Puroniya; but the number is quite inconsiderable, and in a general estimate may be altogether neglected. Indeed the people in general have no means of feeding such heavy cattle. The usual price of the common plough breed is about three rupees, that of the carriage breed amounts to five or six. The cow and ox of the same size are nearly of the same value.

I have estimated the number of ploughs at 4,80,000, and the allowance for each plough being two oxen or cows, would make 9,60,000 the number of labouring cattle employed; but perhaps 40,000 are wrought by cows, and 4,40,000 by oxen, which will reduce the number of the latter to 8,80,000: but as many are wanted for carriages, on the whole perhaps in the district there may be 9,80,000 adult oxen, 1,00,000 of which may be of the better breed.

It is said by the natives, that the male animals of this species that are born, greatly exceed in number the females; but I am uncertain how far this may be true. The usual estimate is that there are 35 breeding cows for every hundred head of labouring cattle. Besides therefore the 80,000 labouring cows, which do not breed, as there are 9,60,000 labouring cattle, we must allow 3,36,000 breeding cows. The 1,00,000 carriage cattle are partly supported by importation, but about 30,000 cows may be necessary to supply the deficiency, and about 20,000 are kept by people in villages, who have no farms, and 10,000 are kept in woods and wastes by the herdsmen of wealthy persons, who have large flocks of milch-cows. It is therefore probable, that the adult females may be about 4,46,000; of these 80,000 may be employed in the plough, and 3,16,000 more may belong to cultivators, and live on the farms. 20,000 may live about towns, and belong to Brahmins, rich people, and tradesmen, who do not cultivate land; and 10,000 are the property also of wealthy men, and are fed in woods and wastes under the care of herdsmen. The young cattle of this kind will be about equal in number to one-half of the adults, and there may be about 20,000 bulls, so that the total number may be about two millions.

In the clay countries, that are fully cultivated, the number of cattle bred is not adequate to the demand, but where there are large tracts overgrown with wood, such as near Maldeh, Ghoraghat, and Jogodol, the number is more than sufficient. On the whole, there is no occasion to purchase the common plough cattle from other districts; but perhaps a thousand head of the better kind of oxen are annually imported.

The cows that are kept about farms and villages, are turned out to feed on the pasture about seven in the morning, return home in the evening, and remain all night in a hut, where they are allowed a little rice-straw to eat, and in the rainy season some grass, which is cut from the little banks that divide the rice-fields. If the proprietor is rich, they receive also a little oil-cake or bran, which alone renders their condition tolerable, as the quantity of straw is very small, and at some seasons the food that can be procured on the pasture is next to nothing.

The oxen are treated much in the same manner, only their time for procuring food is abridged by the five or six hours, during which they are employed in labour, and it is very seldom that the mere plough cattle receive either bran or oil-cake. These are reserved for the cows of the wealthy, and the oxen employed to carry loads.

The pasture in this country consists of the following descriptions of land:

1st. Of 261 square miles of inundated land, which is totally inaccessible during the rainy season, and in the dry is mostly overgrown with harsh coarse grass, which no hunger can enable an ox to swallow. The only nourishment, which the ox kind can procure from this land, is some fine grass, that creeps among the reeds, and of this the quantity is so small, that one acre of meadow land in England may with safety be asserted to produce more grass fit for a cow, than 20 acres of the marsh land in Dinajpur: this land is also disposed in such large masses, that it is accessible to the cattle of only a small proportion of the country. *2ndly.* There are 221 square miles of woods and forests. In these the pasture is rather better, and they are accessible at all seasons of the year. In the dry season the bushes preserve the vegetation from being entirely burnt, so that perhaps 10 acres give as much pasture as an acre of meadow land in England, and being more equally interspersed than the inundated land, they are a much greater resource for the cattle of the farmers. *3rdly.* A greater resource, and in many parts almost the only one, is in burial grounds, roads, market-places, and in steep barren lands, such as the banks of tanks, sandy heights, and the like, of which I have estimated the extent at about 300 square miles. During the rainy season, or for about six months in the year, these produce a tolerable pasture, and I am told, that the cattle then are in decent condition. In the remainder of the year the herbage on these parts is quite burnt up, and though the cattle are turned out upon them, it may be considered chiefly as a means of giving them air. In the fine rice countries of a clay land, necessarily abounding with labouring cattle, this is almost the only resource. The cows, that are kept there are few in number, in proportion to the oxen, and it is there chiefly that they are yoked in the plough. The quantity of straw also is considerable, and the cattle are often sent to other parts, when not wanted for the plough. *4thly.* The lands that have been deserted, and are not overgrown with forests, or that are occasionally cultivated, amount to about 650 square miles, of which about 520 may be in pasture. This is chiefly in the parts where the free soil prevails, and in the rainy season it is a great resource for the cattle: except in some parts that are flooded, the pasture is then very good. In the dry season it is much parched, and then the part that was inundated becomes useful, as it always retains a little moisture.

In some parts strangers encroach very much on this land, and in the rainy season the cattle from all the low land near the Nagor fly to the heights of Hemtobad and Akhanogor.

It would thus appear, that it is only during the rainy season, that the pasture affords a tolerable nourishment to the cattle, and even that only in some parts of the district. At that season they are compelled to fly from the inundated lands, and in the best cultivated parts, where the soil is of a stiff clay, there is no extent of pasture for the cattle to enjoy. In the dry season, want is felt every where, except immediately after the rice harvest, when the cattle are turned into the stubble, and the eagerness, with which they devour the coarsest stems to the very ground, is a clear proof of the misery which they suffer.

The pasture lands are every where left to nature, and in this district she has not been bountiful in grass, that is fit for cattle to eat. It would be in vain to expect, that any attention should be paid to improvement, where there is a right of common pasturage, and this must continue so long as the property is vested in Hindús, at least so far as respects cows and oxen; and while these are allowed to roam at large, it is of no utility for any man to improve a field of grass. The inundated lands and woods of this district, which at present are of little or no value, would maintain a great many cattle. Were the land cleared, and they were granted to Mohammedans or others, who were authorized, and willing to exact money from every beast that fed in them, it might be worth their while to clear them, and to free the country from the nests of those destructive animals, that now ravage its crops. It might perhaps be just to seize upon these lands, from which the present proprietors receive no advantage, and which they are either unable or unwilling to prevent from being a nuisance.

Almost all the proprietors of land being Hindús, their customs regulate every thing respecting cattle, and no rent is demanded for the pasture of the ox kind, nor are they hindered from going on any field that they choose, which is not producing some crops. This wretched liberality is a complete bar to all improvement of the pasture, or indeed to the introduction of any good plan of agriculture in the parts where there is any considerable extent of pasture without cultivated fields intervening. A boy is hired to tend the cattle of the village while at pasture, and one boy can keep about 25 heads. His reward consists of food, and a rag to tie round his middle, which is estimated at eight annas a month, so that he receives about three annas a year for each head of cattle. Where there is no pasture except on roads, market-places, high broken corners, and the like, the cattle, when there is a crop on the ground, are usually confined on the pasture by a tether. When the crop has been cut, they are allowed to range on the stubble under the care of a boy.

The males that are kept for breeding are chosen with little pains or attention, and no higher price than usual is ever given for the sake of improving the breed. Among the Mohammedans the rich farmers keep bulls, and these are allowed to impregnate the cows of their poor neighbours without reward. Among the Hindús a very pernicious custom prevails. When a rich man dies, and where, after the mourning, the ceremony called *sraddho* has been performed, a young bull is consecrated with much ceremony to Sib, and is married to four young cows. At the same time, a post much carved, and containing an image of a bull, is planted in the ground near some public place. A mark is then put on the bull, and he is turned loose. He may go where he pleases, and it is not lawful to beat him, even if he is eating a man's crop, or enters a shop, and is devouring the grain that is exposed to sale. The sufferers shout, and make a noise to drive him away, but he soon becomes reconciled to this idle clamour, and eats very quietly until he is satisfied. These consecrated bulls (*sanr*) accordingly become very fat and are fine animals, but exceedingly destructive. The wives are given away to a Brahmon, are not treated with any uncommon respect, and their husband has no particular connection with them, but serves as a common town bull. In this district, fortunately, they are not numerous. This idle ceremony never costs less than 50 rupees, and often amounts to 500. The two last Rajas of Dinajpúr, among numerous other contrivances for ruining themselves, in which they had great success in a very short period, consecrated about 2,000 cows in the same manner, and dedicated them to four temples, at their four favourite places of residence. As no person presumed to molest any of these sacred animals, the places became immediately waste. Mr. Hatch sold all the cows, except 100, which an old lady of the family still retains, and is probably soothed in her misfortunes by this mark of respect; but her cows, although beautiful creatures, are a great nuisance.

The Hindús of Bengal, before the Muhammedan conquest, are said never to have castrated the bull. In fact, I found, that any questions on this subject were exceedingly disagreeable, and that, although the landlords and their agents tolerated the practice in the Muhammedans and impure tribes, yet they consider it as very illegal and disgraceful, and not fit to be mentioned. I suspect, therefore, that until the Muhammedan invasion, Bengal must have been either cultivated with the hoe, or very much neglected; for much cultivation could never have been carried on by the bull. Pliny indeed mentions the elephant as the common labouring cattle of India; yet it is difficult to suppose, that he has not been in an error. Castration is performed by the very lowest people, and is generally done by excision. The bull is not castrated until his third year, nor wrought until his fourth, and generally lives until about 12 years of age, when he is completely exhausted. He is wrought in the plough about five hours in the day, and draws by the shoulder, the yoke passing over his neck. As the yoke is never stuffed, and as the saddle on which he carries loads is seldom good, the poor animal is often miserably galled, and covered with sores. He is driven by a goad, and by twisting his tail, and very few old oxen have this member entire and unbroken. Fortunately for the cattle of this district, the wise men are not fond of cautery, as in the south of India.

The cow usually has her first calf in her fifth year, and being better treated lives for 15 years. Some have a calf every year, others only one in two years, but the farmer's cattle are reckoned to be only one-half of their time in milk. The calf is allowed to suck all day, but is tied up in the evening, and the cow is milked in the morning, before her calf is turned loose. The common farm cattle, on an average, give to their master ½ seer a day for one-half of their time, or six months in the year. Those of the better breed, when fed by a Brahmin, give double that quantity.

The advantages, therefore, which a farmer receives from his cows are as follows:

1st.—They keep up his stock of labouring cattle, so that in stating the expense of a farm nothing should be allowed on that head.

2nd.—The cattle produce manure.

3rd.—They give a small quantity of milk. Of the 33,60,000 cows in this district, which belong to farmers, perhaps ⅕ or 67,200 are of a larger breed; and give one seer a day, or 180 seers a year, worth six rupees, and the remaining 26,88,000 give one-half of that produce. So that the total value of the cows' milk, that the farmers of the district obtain, may be 12,09,600 rupees. The expense of boys to tend these cows may be rupees 69,600 a year, leaving a neat profit of rupees 11,40,000, or Rs. 2. 6. 0. a plough. It would be unfair however to state the whole of this to the profit of the cattle, for if the farmer put a value on the straw, which he gave to each cow, the profits would in a great measure disappear, and those arising from the cultivation of rice would be greater than I have stated, for I have valued only the grain.

In fact, where there is a demand, the poorer farmers in general prefer selling their straw, and wherever there are many people in easy circumstances, who are not formers, there is a demand, for rich people wish to have cows of their own, in order to avoid the adulteration and inferiority of the milk that can be purchased.

Although a large proportion of the farmers are Muhammedans, they derive little or no profit from the meat of their oxen; for they are so strictly watched by the Hindú landlords and their agents, that it is almost impossible for them to kill a beast without detection, and every means in these people's power would be employed to ruin a culprit. It is chiefly under the immediate protection of the European magistrate, and of the two Muhammedan saints at Peruya, that the luxury of beef can be enjoyed; and, from all that I could learn, less than 100 head of cattle are killed in the course of a year.

On the whole, the farmers of this district would suffer little, were the breed of oxen exterminated, for the value of the milk is not considerable, and the same number of people might cultivate the ground to much more advantage by the spade or hoe, as is done in China and Nipal. Were that the case, the little loss, that would be suffered by the loss of the milk, would be amply made up by the saving of herdsmen, by the preventing depredations on the growing crops, which are very considerable, and by the saving on stock.

People in easy circumstances in towns and villages, as I have already said, are very desirous of keeping cows, in order to procure milk free from adulteration, and somewhat clean; and accordingly, so far as I have been able to learn, about 20,000 head are kept, and are comparatively in excellent condition, not that they are fed like the cattle of England, but they may receive as much nourishment as those in the Highlands of Scotland. In the town of Dinajpúr, a cow of this kind often gives two seers of milk to her master, but one seer or 180 seers a year may be the usual rate, and as milk is dear in towns, it is valued at 20 seers for the rupee, altogether nine rupees during the six months. When the cow is in milk, she is fed with straw, bran, and oil-cake, and her food may cost eight annas a month. During the other six months she is allowed only a little straw, and the wretched pasture in which she is allowed to range; this may cost four annas a month, or altogether 4½ rupees. The gross produce will be 180,000 rupees; the gain, besides procuring good clean milk in place of bad and dirty, is 90,000 rupees on a capital of 1,20,000. Brahmins or Hindús of pure birth, who are the people that usually keep these cows, ought not to sell the calves, but should give away in charity such as are superfluous; a great many however are forgetful, and make a little profit by disobeying a rule in which there is neither policy nor virtue. I have mentioned, that about 10,000 cows are kept entirely in the woods and wastes of this district, and never enter the villages. It has probably been the immense profit which arises from this description of cattle, that has led to an opinion of cattle being the principal wealth of an Indian farmer. In this district, there are not 500 of these cattle that belong to farmers. Some are the property of landlords, of their agents, and of merchants; but by far the greater part belong to *goalas* or milkmen, and by far the greater part belong to the people of Maldeh. A few from the banks of the Nagor and Kulik go every year to Morong; but I shall defer saying any thing on that subject, until I have access to the frontier of that country, and shall here confine myself to the manner in which the *goalas* of Maldeh and its vicinity manage their cattle. Each herd consists of from 100 to 500 adult cows, which in the rainy season are fed in the woods of Peruya, or in those between the Tanggon and Punabhoba, and in the dry season pasture on the inundated lands that are near the former river; during the latter season they never enter the house, but in the nights of the rainy season they are sheltered under long sheds. In the inundated lands a fence of dry thorns secures them at night from the beasts of prey.

The following estimate was given, by a *goala*, of the profit and loss of a herd of 100 cows, kept in this manner.

Charge—prime cost, 100 cows from 3 to 9 rupees, ...	600	0	0
Five bulls, at 4 rupees, ...	20	0	0
Rs.	620	0	0
Annual charge, interest of stock, at 12 per cent.................	74	6	4
One chief herdsman, at three rupees a month, ...	36	0	0
Three inferior herdsmen, at 2½ rupees, ...	90	0	0
Rope, at 2 rupees a month, ...	24	0	0
One blanket to each herdsman, ...	4	0	0
Sacrifices, ...	10	0	0
Petty charges of various kinds, ...	15	0	0
Total charges, ... Rs.	253	6	4

There are 70 cows in milk; for in this state, the cattle seem to retain their milk longer than when confined about villages. Each cow gives from ¼ to ⅛ seer, but the daily average produce is about 50 seers, which at Maldeh is worth 20 seers for the rupee. The total annual produce is Rs. 912. 8. 0. The milkmen of the town go to the herd, and purchase the milk on the spot, at the rate above-mentioned. The number of female calves keep up the herd. There is no rent. The avowed profit, besides full interest, is therefore Rs. 659. 1. 8. on a stock of 620 rupees. The *goala* was evidently concealing the value of the young oxen sold, this being a disgraceful action. But a capital of 620 rupees is so large a sum that the trade is not overstocked, and the pasture is capable of supporting many more cattle than now feed on it. The gross produce of these cattle may be reckoned at 90,000 rupees a year.

These two last methods of keeping cattle are highly advantageous, and might not only be continued, but greatly extended, were the farmers to adopt the cultivation by the hoe. The cows would supply milk for the luxurious, and the oxen that were bred would be sufficient for the road, and might be kept in tolerable condition.

With the immense population that overpours this country, even were the opinions of the people compatible with eating butcher's meat, the means of procuring it are totally inadequate; and there is no possible way of finding food for such a multitude, except by the cultivation of grain. The means that this affords are indeed ample, and there is besides sufficient room for the cultivation of many valuable articles, such as opium, cotton, silk, and indigo, that will enable the country amply to repay whatever it wants from foreigners. The resources, therefore, which cattle give to the country are so trifling that on all occasions they should give way to whatever may promote cultivation, that is, so long as the population continues at its present enormous standard. If the people could be contented to avoid breeding children so fast, and the population were reduced two-thirds, the condition of the cattle might enter into the system of agriculture, and all ranks might share in the comforts to be derived from the skins, milk, and meat, and their condition might in many other respects be improved: but this would require the introduction of so many new customs, directly in opposition to those which now prevail, that the hope of such improvements being realized may be looked upon as a dream.

Provided it were practicable, the principal objection against introducing the hoe husbandry in place of the plough, would be the loss of manure. This is the essence of good husbandry, and the cow is at present the only animal from whence the farmer of Dinajpúr receives a supply. This supply is however so scanty, that I am persuaded more advantage might be procured from collecting the straw in pits, where mixed with ashes, and whatever soil could be obtained, it would rot, and give a much greater supply than what is now procured. But the custom of ploughing with cattle is so habitual, that no means exist to eradicate it, were the measure advisable; at least it must be a work of great time and difficulty.

In this district, the buffalo (Bos bubalus) is of little importance. The number does not exceed five thousand adult females. Perhaps a thousand may frequent the banks of the Nagor and Kulik in the rainy season, and in the dry are sent to Morong. For the present, I shall pass over these, and content myself with noticing the manner in which the people manage about 4,000, that are fed chiefly on the banks of the Tanggon and Punabhoba. The Dinajpúr Raja, however, possesses a considerable herd, that feeds partly near Nawabgunj, and partly in the Rungpúr district; but an account of these also, as common to two districts, may be at present omitted. The management of a herd of buffaloes and a herd of cows is nearly the same. In the dry season, they frequent the inundated lands and marshes, and in the rainy season they are led to the woods; but the buffaloes require no precaution to keep them from wild beasts. Both kinds of cattle are subject to a disease called *bosonto*, or small-pox, which comes once in 9 or 10 years, and kills a great many; but the young females being added to the flock, the number increases greatly before the next occurrence of the disease, and the average number of the herd should be reckoned on the 4th or 5th year after the calamity has happened. This disorder has not the smallest affinity to the vaccine.

The tame buffalo of this district is a very fine animal, nearly resembling the wild one. Indeed, the breeds are very much intermixed; for many people keep no males, and allow the wild bulls to impregnate their tame females. Some persons also endeavour to seize upon wild males, and after taming them, keep them for breeding. On the contrary, others allow their young male calves to run wild, as the demand here for them as sacrifices is small; as they are never employed either for carriage or in agriculture, and in the wild state their depredations tend to prevent the encroachments of agriculture on the pasture.

Why the males are not employed in labour, it would be difficult to say, as they are very much fitted for the low lands of this district. The great demand for sacrifices has probably prevented their being used in the districts which lead the fashion, and that is blindly followed, where the same cause does not exist.

The following is a statement of the expense and profit of a herd of buffaloes, consisting of 100 adult females.

Charge—

Prime cost of 100 females, at 8 Rs.	800	0	0
4 males,	32	0	0
Rs.	832	0	0
Annual expense—			
One chief herdsman, at 2½ Rs. per month,	30	0	0
Four under-herdsmen, at 2 Rs. do.	96	0	0
Clothing for the herdsmen,	18	0	0
One blanket for each,	5	0	0
Rent for pasturage,	5	0	0
Sacrifices,	5	0	0
Interest of stock, at 12 per cent.	99	13	5
Rs.	258	13	5
Profit—			
60 female buffaloes in milk give on an average 120 seers a day, worth three rupees,	1,095	0	0
6 male calves, at three rupees each,	18	0	0
Rs.	1,113	0	0

The neat profit, besides interest, is therefore Rupees 854. 2. 7. on a capital of 832 Rupees.

The milk is bought, in the same manner as that of the cows, by people who reside in villages, and who prepare it in the various ways used by the natives. The annual value of the whole milk produced by the 5000 buffaloes will be about 54,750 Rupees. The annual value of the whole milk produced in the district may be estimated thus,

Cows belonging to farmers,	12,09,600
To villagers,	1,80,000
To *goalas*,	90,000
Total, cows' milk,	14,79,600
Buffaloes' milk,	54,750
Total	15,31,350

The milk has been valued partly at the highest prices of Maldeh and Dinajpúr, and partly at the low price of country places. This compared with the produce of the arable lands is about $\frac{1}{13}$ part of the whole. I must also observe, that, although these estimates were given by people interested, who seldom in this country exaggerate their gains, I suspect, that the actual produce of the dairy is not near so much.

Goats are very generally kept by both Muhammedans and Hindús of impure birth, and are very numerous, probably not less than 8,00,000. They are of the common short-legged smooth-haired breed, and have degenerated as much as possible. Their milk is never used, indeed they are so poorly fed, that none could be taken without the utmost danger to the kid. They are, however, a great source of comfort to the people, for the males about 6 or 7 months old, after having been offered to the gods or saints, afford the votary a nourishing food.

Perhaps three hundred thousand may be sacrificed in the year, worth on an average six annas, or on the whole, Rs. 1,25,000.

Sheep are of much less consequence. They are nearly of the same breed with those called *kurambar*, which I have described in the account of my travels into the south of India, but both their wool and milk are entirely neglected. The number is very inconsiderable, and the only useful produce is the skin, and the young males that are offered in the same way as goats. The natives prefer the goat's flesh, although to Europeans nothing can be worse, and no meat can be finer than that of the Bengal sheep.

Notwithstanding the prevalence of the Moslems, swine are more numerous in this district than sheep, which according to different views of the subject, is reckoned by some to be owing to the want of shame in the low Hindús, while by others it is attributed to their good sense. The animals are very much neglected, are never fattened, and are allowed to eat and wallow in every kind of impurity; but in this respect they are little inferior to the sacred animal of the Hindús, which in its distressed state in India is a very impure feeder. The meat of the hog, however bad, is a great resource for the poor, who rear the animals at little or no expense, and is offered by them to the gods. In some parts, they even procure money by selling them to people who come from Bútan; and it is rather remarkable, that the chief agent in this commerce should be a Muhammedan, a merchant of Rangpúr. In this district the condition of horses is exceedingly low, perhaps there may be 2000 poneys, of a most wretched breed, which never receive any nourishment, except what they can glean in the fields, and which are totally unacquainted with comb, brush, scissar or shoe. Their value is from 2 to 5 rupees each. The greater part belong to faqirs, who retain some faint tincture of the love for the noble animal, which was so eminent among their progenitors. A rather better breed of poney is brought from Bútan, and is called *tangon*. From the Ayeen Akberry, it would appear that Ghoraghat, in this district, was formerly celebrated for that breed of horses. I do not however think it probable, that any considerable number was ever bred in the plains of Bengal; but I suppose that many were brought to Ghoraghat as the most convenient market, just as they are now brought to Rangpúr. The number in this district may be about 400, and they are of the very worst quality: 20 rupees being considered as a high price. Except the horses belonging to Europeans, there is not one in the district fit to mount a trooper.

The only asses in the district are two or three, belonging to washermen from the southern parts of Bengal, who have come to Dinajpúr in the service of Europeans.

Dogs, that have such a familiarity with man in Europe, are not admitted to that honor in India, and no employment can be more disgraceful than the taking care of this fine animal; yet the breed is very numerous, and every village swarms with half-starved curs. They eat all manner of carcasses and impurities, and are not reckoned the property of any individual. The natives seldom enter into any sort of familiarity with them, nor are the children ever seen either caressing or tormenting them; but they are tolerated, and one or two, according to the wealth of the family, are permitted to eat the scraps. In return they sleep in the yard, and make a noise when any stranger approaches, especially at night. The bitches are few in number, and generally more starved than the dogs, as they are weaker, and no one interests himself in their quarrels; but they are so prolific, that the number of dogs always exceeds that of the houses which give them shelter, and a large proportion have no resource, but to live like jackals; upon whatever comes in their way, and numbers are hanging about the villages in the utmost misery. Their nature however is very different from the suspicious temper of the jackal, and the least attention shown to one of these dogs is repaid with gratitude. The most moderate feeding attaches him instantly, and he stands on the defence against all strangers not only of the canine species, but against men of every description, different from those that feed him. I often observed that the dogs, which followed my party from the villages, on account of the offals, became quite enraged when a villager approached; and no sooner were their most pressing wants supplied than they began to look out for distinction. At first they were satisfied with attending the servants, and other people at meals, and gratefully took whatever was left; but after they were a little fattened, their principal delight was to follow me, when I either walked or rode on the journey, and although I never fed them, the least attention on my part seemed to fill them with joy; for they very soon discovered, that I was the chief person in the company.

Cats are much in the same predicament with dogs. They are just tolerated, and live in a half-domestic half-wild state. They are not numerous.

Owing to the number of Muhammedans fowls are abundant; by the Hindús of Bengal they are reckoned impure. Every Muhammedan family has some, which receive shelter in its huts, and sometimes a little grain. They are never fat, and few are sold, but they are no doubt the best animal food that the natives enjoy, and there is scarcely any Muhammedan family so poor but that can occasionally offer a fowl to a saint and eat the meat.

Both low Hindús and Muhammedans keep ducks; but they are not so numerous as fowls, and although they are never confined, nor kept from impure feeding, are higher priced than pullets.

Pigeons also are very plentiful and cheap; many people keep them merely as pets, but at all times they are procurable in abundance.

Geese are chiefly kept by rich men as pets; as swans are now in England, or as geese were by our ancestors when invaded by Cæsar. They can seldom be procured for purchase, and are never fattened.

In many parts no person has even heard of a turkey; in others, people who have gone to Dinajpúr on business have seen the animal in the judge's farm-yard, and have told their countrymen of its wonderful appearance.

CHAPTER VI.

OF FENCES.

Very little of this district can be said to be fenced, and in many parts the fences include merely the yard and kitchen garden.

The houses of the natives, as I have before mentioned, consist of several huts, occupying a yard, that is almost always enclosed. By the natives the whole collectively is called *simana*, and it has been called compound by the English, for what reason I do not know. The yard, or the space within the fence that is not occupied by houses, is by the natives called *uthan*. The fence seems intended for two purposes, to conceal the family, and especially the women, from view or intrusion, and to keep out thieves and robbers.—Where the soil is a stiff clay, the fence is generally a mud wall, between five and six feet high, the top of which is thatched, to prevent the rain from washing it away; for there is no clay in this district, like that of Mysore, which with a very moderate repair will resist the rain for ages. This is a great loss, as the thatch is both expensive, and facilitates the communication of fire, and is besides ugly. It is probable, that a few broken bricks or pots, mixed with the upper layer of clay, might enable the wall to stand a rainy season. The expense of annual repairs would be a mere trifle. These mud walls are by far the best fences for every purpose required; but although they often exclude thieves, they are no security against robbers, who in this district are said to be very numerous and cruel. The houses are too much scattered, to enable the natives to secure themselves and their cattle from robbers, by means of a common mud wall, or fence of thorny plants, as is done in Mysore. Indeed their eagerness for concealment and privacy would not allow them to live huddled together in the small spaces that the villages of Mysore occupy. In the parts where the soil is loose, and will not form walls, the fences are not so good. Very poor people generally throw up a bank of earth from a ditch, and plant a row of reeds on the top of the bank, which gives them privacy; from thieves, they are in no danger, having nothing that can be stolen. More wealthy people surround their yards by hurdles made of straw or reeds, and the wealthy make neat bambú railings, often eight feet high, and line them with mats of bambús, which gives privacy, while the railings exclude ordinary thieves. The robbers of this district go in too great numbers, and are too bold to be excluded by any fence that is not defended from within; and their cruelty has struck such a terror, that flight is the only thing thought of on their approach.

The gardens in which vegetables for the kitchen are reared, and a small spot contiguous to the house for some rich crop, such as tobacco, are also generally fenced, to exclude cattle. In parts where the soil is stiff, this is done very effectually by a ditch and bank of clay, which is repaired every year at a very trifling expense; and indeed in many places every part of this soil, except the rice-fields, is enclosed in this manner. In loose soils the banks, unless made large, have little effect, and this is in general too expensive. The natives therefore endeavour to fortify the bank with a hedge; but owing to carelessness, it is seldom of much effect, and the plants commonly chosen for the purpose are very injudiciously selected; they are as follows:

The *Jiyol*, mentioned among the trees of the district, No. 81, is that most usually selected, merely I believe on account of the readiness with which it takes root, so that it is at once a kind of fence; but it wants thorns, and any animal that chooses to make a little exertion may force its way through the hedge.

The only other hedge, in such situations, that is at all common, is the *Bherondo*, or *Jatropha Curcas*, which is equally ineffectual and equally easy to raise. The seed is never used for making oil, but the juice is reckoned a good application for sores. This juice seems very different from the milk that flows from most plants allied to the *Bherondo*, and which is in general acrid. The clear juice of the *Bherondo* possesses little of that quality, but is very viscid, and boys blow it into bubbles as an amusement, just as in Europe they blow soap suds.

Two other plants, still less effectual, but very ornamental, are used in the fences of this district, and are raised from seed. The one is the *Joyonti*, or *Sesban Egyptiacus* of the Encyclopedie. It is very ornamental, and grows very fast. Its wood is useful for fuel and for constructing the roofs of huts.

The other I have seen only in this district, where it is called *Boro Jhinga*. It is perhaps still more ornamental than the Sesban, and is applied to the same uses. In the writings of Botanists, I have not been able to trace any account of this plant, which is a species of *Robinia*.

There are four thorny plants that are occasionally found in the hedges of this country, which would make good fences, and which do not harbour vermine nor stop ventilation, but the natives seem to have some aversion to them. The thorns are probably inconvenient to people with naked feet.

The first is the *Phonimonsa*, a species of *Cactus*, of which I can trace no account in Botanical systems, and which has been found to be a proper food for a kind of *Cochineal*, as I have detailed in my account of Mysore. (*C. indicus.*)

The next is the *Monsa*, or noble kind of *Euphorbia*, called *Nereifolia* by Botanists, and which is sacred to Bishohori, the goddess of serpents.

The third is the *Patasij*, an *Euphorbia* not yet described, but resembling the former a good deal, although not so fine a plant.

The fourth is the *Narasij*, or *Euphorbia antiquorum*, a very fine plant, which with a little care makes an excellent fence in any soil.

Except the houses and gardens, nearly the whole country is open; some little care however is bestowed on rich crops, especially on the mulberry every where, and on the cotton in clay lands, which are always surrounded by a bank of earth that is a sufficient fence even in lands of a loose soil. If this were extended to all the higher lands, the expense would not be great, were the fields of considerable dimensions; but where most farms do not exceed five acres, and where 20 things are cultivated in that extent, subdivisions would be intolerable. A cultivator of mulberry near Maldeh estimated the forming such a fence in loose soil at two rupees for 480 feet. The annual expense is one-half of the prime cost. This however is a man's wages for 40 days; and I am persuaded is over-rated. The common estimate in cotton lands of a stiff clay, which are all enclosed in the same manner, is 12 days' work for a man, to enclose ½ acre, or 600 feet, and six days to keep it in repair.

When a spot is cultivated with capsicum, or any other rich crop, it is generally surrounded by a hedge of dry bushes, and the fields of sugar-cane are surrounded by a row of *oror*, (*Cytisus cajan.*) The seed is sown; when the field is planted, and by the time that the canes become a temptation to cattle, the *oror* has grown and keeps off slight attempts at intrusion, besides producing a considerable quantity of an excellent pulse. It is however totally incapable of turning the wild hog, which is the most dangerous enemy to the cane.

I have already mentioned the great expense that is required to tend the kine of this district, to which must be added the trouble of tending the horses, goats, sheep, and hogs, and the still greater trouble and expense which attends the watching of the growing crops by night, to keep off wild hogs and buffaloes, and with which a great many of the labourers are constantly harassed.

The whole expense however thus bestowed is very ineffectual, and a very great loss is suffered both from tame and wild animals. It may indeed be safely said, that the natives in this respect are very bad neighbours, and too often seize an opportunity of allowing their cattle to satiate their ravenous appetites at their neighbour's cost. Fences, which would in a great measure prevent these expenses and losses, are therefore much wanted, but in the present state of things I know not how they could be made. The farmers are too poor, and the landlords too careless to lay out money to any great extent. Perhaps the introduction of the *Euphorbia Tirucalli (Lanka sij)* might assist. It grows very readily, makes a fine close hedge, and having no prickles, would be perhaps more acceptable to the natives than the prickly plants of the same kind. Besides its cuttings trodden into the mud of low rice-lands, form an excellent manure, and it grows on any soil that is not inundated. The finest fences that I have seen in India are formed of this plant, which preserves a freshness and moisture in the most scorching winds.

CHAPTER VII.

OF FARMS.

It is said, that in most parts of this district Mr. Hatch introduced a regulation, by which the size of farms is restricted not to exceed 50 bigahs. At any rate, the people every where almost said, that there is such a regulation, and therefore often concealed the real extent of their farms. I have not heard the reasons that were assigned for this restriction, although it was probably with a view either of doing away the manner of cultivation by sharing the crop, or from some scheme of equalizing property. It may have also been made in consequence of representations from the landlords, who pretend, that large farmers neglect their lands. Neither do I know certainly, whether or not such a regulation exists; for the landholders may hold out a pretence of that nature, in order to render the large farmers more dependent on them, by granting them leases, that they imagine are not strictly legal.

With whatever view it was framed, or alledged to be framed, I have no doubt in stating, that the observance of such a regulation would be highly injurious both to agriculture and to the labourer. These people, who cultivate land for a share of the produce, are in a better state than common labourers, and must fall to that level, unless they are employed as at present, for they have not stock sufficient to enable them to cultivate without assistance. Besides the reducing farms to 50 bigahs would compel every rich man to give up agriculture, and to remove his stock to some other employment, which of all other circumstances would be that most destructive. Indeed, the quantity of stock, belonging to actual farmers, is already a great deal too small, and the observance of this regulation would go near to banish it altogether. Like other useless or pernicious regulations, however, this is constantly evaded, and leases for 50 bigahs each are granted to five or six persons of the same family; it being understood, that the whole belongs to the principal person.

The actual size of the farms is very various. I have already stated, that the usual extent, which can be cultivated by one plough, is 10 large bigahs, or 15 Calcutta bigahs, or five acres; but many persons rent a much smaller extent. These are chiefly tradesmen, who wish to have as much rice as will maintain their families for some time before harvest, when traders take advantage of the demand, and usually raise their grain to an immoderate price. These tradesmen do not cultivate the fields themselves, but employ people to do it for a share. The people also who engage in this cultivation for a share have in general two or three bigahs, for which they pay rent, and employ their leisure time in cultivating land for their neighbours for one-half of the produce, on which account they are called *adhiyars*, or half people.

About a half of the farmers, or those who rent lands and follow no trade, have one or two ploughs, and seldom employ servants. The head of the family and a son or brother hold the ploughs ; only if there is no boy in the family, one must be hired to tend the cattle. If the farm is not quite large enough to employ their ploughs the whole year, they cultivate somewhat additional for a share of the produce ; and, if it is of a clay soil, which occupies the farmer only six months in the year, they hire themselves out as day-labourers, to those who cultivate free soils, or act as porters or labourers to merchants and manufacturers of sugar and indigo.

Middling farmers, who have three, or four, or five ploughs, form perhaps $\frac{7}{16}$ of the whole ; these are not exempt from holding the plough, but hire servants to make up the deficiency in the number of labourers, that may be in their families ; that is to say, always one man for each plough, with a number of boys sufficient to take care of the cattle. Where the soil is free, and produces a variety of crops, especially sugar-cane, more men are required at some seasons of the year, particularly in the cold season, when there is nothing to do in the clay lands. Persons of this kind never hire themselves as labourers ; but those who live on a clay soil employ the six idle months in purchasing rice, and carrying it to the marts, by which they have considerable profit. Those who live on a free soil have neither leisure nor cattle to spare for the purpose, and must sell their grain to their neighbours. The profits on this kind of traffic seem to be considerable, and it is owing partly to this, in all probability, that the farmers are richer on clay lands, that produce nothing except rice, than those who occupy the richest lands in the district.

About one farmer in 16 may rent from 30 to 100 acres. These seldom labour with their own hands, but keep as many ploughs as they have dependent relations, or hire two or three additional men. The remainder of their lands they give to people who cultivate it for a share. These men have in general large capitals, and advance money or grain both to those who cultivate for a share, and to their other necessitous neighbours, to enable them to live, while the cultivation is going forward. It may indeed be said, that their stock carries on at least one-half of the whole cultivation of the country. Most of the *adhiyars* and small farmers are more indebted to them than the whole value of their stock, and for six months in the year would starve, did not the wealthy farmers advance them grain to eat. It is they who even furnish the seed ; so that, whenever one of them is discontented, he gives up his farm, and retires with all his dependents to some other estate, where there are waste lands, which his stock enables him to clear. The village which he left is then for some years unoccupied, until the landlord can find a fugitive of the same kind, and in general must use a good deal of solicitation before he can induce the farmer with his dependents to settle. On this account, the landlords do not like this class of men ; but it is evident that they are absolutely necessary, unless the landlords themselves would advance money to their necessitous tenantry. In a few places I heard that this is done, but it is only practicable to advantage on very small estates ; and the having large farmers, who are able to supply the stock, is a vast advantage to all persons that have estate of a respectable size. It is true, that these large farmers exact enormous profits for whatever they advance to their necessitous dependents, but still they are of infinite use to these people, who without their assistance would be instantly reduced to the state of common labourers, and often, to beggary. It must also be considered, that the risk of advancing is great, where there is very little inclination among the people to discharge their fair debts. A clamour, however, as usual, has gone abroad against the wealthy farmers, who are considered as mere flayers of the poor, and no people privately join more earnestly in the cry than the landlords. In public, however, they court the wealthy farmers, and it is alledged often, purchase their assistance, to enable them to fleece the poorer tenantry. A landlord or his agent assembles his people, and states, that he is in want of money to build a house, to perform a pilgrimage, to celebrate some holiday, to marry a son or a daughter, or to alleviate the pecuniary distress in which he is involved, and solicits the assistance of his tenantry. The rich farmers have been previously gained, and give their consent to a general assessment, and the others follow their example, rather than quarrel with people on whom they depend, but it is the poor only who pay. By this mean rapacity, the landlord always renders himself more dependent on these farmers, as he squeezes from his other tenantry what might enable them in time to cultivate with their own stock.

It must be observed, that the wants of the smaller farmers, and of those who cultivate for a share, does not originate from the large farmers. It may perhaps have sometimes been owing to the exactions made by landlords, but in most cases it has arisen from their own imprudence in spending on marriages, or other ceremonies, the means that were absolutely necessary for their independent existence; and in this country the rate of interest is so high, that when once a person is involved, nothing but some very fortunate accident can possibly retrieve him. He receives the rice that is necessary for seed, or for his maintenance, at the high rate which prevails for six months before harvest, and he must pay it back at the low rate which is put upon it, when the market is glutted by every necessitous creature bringing his corn for sale, the moment that it has been beaten from the straw. He lives in tolerable plenty for six or seven months, and then is reduced to the same straits as before, and is again necessitated to borrow rice on as disadvantageous terms as formerly. The interest often therefore appears moderate enough, but the manner of payment renders the loss enormous.

I have already stated, that the lands now occupied in the district, exclusive of houses and gardens, amount to somewhat above 71,94,000 bigahs. Of these perhaps 1,94,000 may be reserved in the occupation of the proprietors, who cultivate them by their servants, or by those who take a share. The lands thus occupied chiefly belong to petty zemindars, or to the proprietors of small estates that are not taxed. Of the 70,00,000 remaining bigahs perhaps 4,00,000 are occupied by tradesmen and poor people, who have not a sufficient quantity of land to employ one plough; the remaining 66,00,000 may be occupied as follows:

6,600	principal farmers, at 165 bigahs, on an average....	10,89,000
8,800	great farmers, at 75 bigahs,....	6,60,000
11,000	comfortable farmers, at 60 bigahs,....	6,60,000
19,800	easy farmers, at 45 bigahs,....	8,91,000
55,000	poor farmers, at 30 ditto,....	16,50,000
1,10,000	needy farmers, at 15 ditto,....	16,50,000
2,11,200	....	66,00,000

I have already mentioned the stock of implements that is proper for a farm of one plough, to be 3¼ Rs. but in farms of one plough, or when a man cultivates for a share, the hatchet is generally omitted, and in larger farms one *dhengki* and one hatchet is sufficient for the whole, so that the average rate cannot be reckoned at more than 2¾ rupees. Then two oxen for the plough are 6 rupees, one cow, three rupees, seed, on an average 20 seers of rice for a bigah. This is furnished to the necessitous at double the harvest price, but this exaction ought not to be charged to the expense of stock. I therefore take it at the proper price, or suppose that the farmer brings it with him. At this rate, the seed for each plough, reckoning the average price of rice at 90 seers for the rupee, will be Rs. 3. 5. 4.

Thus then a farmer on each plough ought to have at least

Implements,	2	12
Cattle,	9	0
Seed,	3	6
House,	5	0
Furniture,	3	4
Clothing and ornaments,	4	0
Food for six months, until his first crops are for use at 2½ Rs.	15	0
Rent for six months, at 10 annas a year,	4	11
Rs.	47	1

Rich farmers generally have higher priced cattle, but their expences for houses, food, &c. do not increase in proportion. Thus a farmer having four ploughs cannot expend 10 rupees a month for food.

The quantity of stock required for rich land, of a free soil, differs very little from what is required for a stiff clay; but this does not render the situation of the farmer on the loose soil more comfortable; for he must labour or keep servants the whole year, while the farmer in the clay lands keeps servants six months in the year only, and in the other six may employ himself and cattle to great advantage; if poor, as a labourer, and if rich, as a trader; and in fact, as I have frequently mentioned, the richest farmers are those on clay lands, who rear little or nothing except rice. This however does not proceed entirely from their farms being of a more profitable nature, but in some measure also from necessity. The merchants are not so eager to purchase their produce, as they are the sugar and silk raised on the richer lands, and therefore they do not so readily receive advances; consequently the inconsiderate have not the same facility in anticipating the returns of their farms, which is the general source of the wretched poverty that prevails in this country.

I have already mentioned, that the greater part of this stock is borrowed, and on grain farms is advanced chiefly by the principal farmers before mentioned, many of whom have capitals of from 5,000 to 20,000 rupees, but perhaps 5,000 may be about the average. Much also is advanced by merchants who reside between Moorshedabad and Calcutta, both included, who annually purchase about 40,00,000 rupees worth of rice in this district, and make advance for a part.

The agents of zemindars in general allege, that small tenants, who cultivate with their own hands, have their farms in best order. This however may be doubted, as the agents have an interest in employing such people alone, for these are the men with whom agents can take the greatest liberty.

When the settlement of the Company's revenue was made, Mr. Hatch, who valued the greater part of this district, seems to have proceeded on a general estimate of the lands of each pergunnah ; and for that purpose he seems to have divided them into two kinds, one that produced two crops, and the other, which produced only one, and the rent of the one was usually considered as double that of the other. This may have answered his purpose sufficiently well, both in forming an estimate of the whole value of the district, and in fixing a maximum of rent beyond which the persons who then occupied the land could not be desired to pay ; but his mode of valuing estates by a general average has usually been followed by the proprietors, and both they and the farmers pretend, that they are bound to let their estates at no higher rate. This, I am told, is not strictly true, and would be a great absurdity. Every one must be sensible, that much land which gives one crop only is more valuable than a great deal that gives two ; and the only rational way, in which land can be let, is by valuing each farm. The zemindars, however, have probably adopted Mr. Hatch's plan, as a means of checking fraud in their servants and agents, for few of them manage their own estates. The usual plan, therefore, employed by the agents, is to state a certain portion of each farm as land producing two crops (*poli*), and a certain part as land producing one crop (*khyar*), so as to make the amount, at the valuation which Mr. Hatch took, equal to the rent which the farmer is to pay. This indeed seems to be best mode which could have been adopted, as there are very numerous objections to the only other way that I have seen used in such cases, which is to give each man a share of all the different soils in the estate in proportion to the extent of his farm. This manner of checking their agents in letting farms, by means that were intended for other purposes, has been in some instances attended with considerable loss to the proprietors. Where there is a great extent of poor land, it cannot be brought into the neighbouring farms, even at the lowest rate of average rent, and is therefore unavoidably out of lease, and is only occupied occasionally ; in which case the landlord, who resides at a distance, seldom receives any rent.

The avowed rent, so far as I could judge, seemed to be in general less than one-fourth part of the produce, except on lands that produce rich crops, especially sugar-cane. On the whole, however, one-fourth of the produce ought not greatly to exceed the actual rent ; for the houses and yards are always rented at the highest rate of arable land, and sometimes even at more, and yet produce nothing. The rent is always paid in money.

The usual time of entry is in the two months of spring, from the 12th of March to the 12th of May ; during these months no rent is paid, but in the month that precedes, and in that which follows, the term of entry, $\frac{1}{8}$ of the rent, is paid, and in each of the other eight months $\frac{1}{12}$ is due.

In almost every part of the district the leases are granted in perpetuity, and the tenants will not accept of any other. In some places, they even pretend to a right of perpetual possession at the usual rate of rent, if they have occupied a farm for ten years. This is probably one of the greatest bars to industry and improvement that can take place in any country, as the landlord has no inducement to lay out money in improvement, or indeed to attend to the condition of his estate, farther than to get his rent as easily as possible. It may indeed be safely said, that a gradual and moderate rise of rent is the grand source of wealth and prosperity to every country ; and the additional exertions which are required from the tenant, always, I believe, have turned out still more for his benefit than for that of the landlord. The proprietors of small free estates, who neither pay rent nor tax, are a proof, that the condition of the peasant is improved by paying rent. These lands are miserably neglected, and the wretched owners would just exert themselves so much as to prevent themselves from perishing of hunger, were they not religious mendicants, who find an additional resource, that keeps them in about as good a condition as those who cultivate a similar extent of land that pays rent.

But this perpetual possession, which is so eagerly sought after, is almost nominal; for, so far as I could learn, not one tenant in four resides seven years on the same spot, and the bulk of them are constantly changing from one estate to another.

The only advantage attending leases in perpetuity is the encouragement, which it gives to the tenant in forming plantations; but these are formed to much more advantage either by the landlord himself, or by his engaging to pay the value at the expiration of the lease, as is usually practised in Malabar, where the plantations are of much more importance than they are here. Still farther, a particular exemption may be made in favour of plantations, as is done in Mysore, where lands occupied in this manner are the only ones which can be said to be private property. Poor lands, that are only cultivated occasionally after a fallow, are let for the time that they are to be occupied, upon whatever terms the parties can agree; and the usual terms are one-half of the produce, although the proprietor is sometimes satisfied with a low rent in money.

The whole expense of cultivation, of every kind, cannot be reckoned at more than one-half of the produce, even on lands that produce only ordinary crops; as men can be procured who will cultivate it on these terms, and who live better than common labourers. These persons seldom cultivate the lands that produce the richer crops, which are generally reserved by the farmers for their own use. For the sake of round numbers, I shall take the rent at one-fourth of the produce. The farmers therefore have at least one-fourth of the gross produce of the lands as clear profit, besides the profit which they have from the milk of their cattle, and from their plantations. Now the gross produce of the cultivated lands being 2,00,00,000 rupees, their profit from the lands is 50,00,000, while the whole value of the milk procured from farmers' cows has been estimated at 12,00,000, and in all probability this is exaggerated. The greater part of this, however, should be considered as the value of the rice straw and bran, on which the cattle feed, and which have not been brought into the account. But, in fact, so far as I could find on investigation, the avowed rent does not amount to one-fourth of the produce, even excluding milk, bambus, and mangos, all articles of considerable value. Although, therefore, imprudence, or too great a compliance with custom, may have involved the farmers in debt, the interest of which consumes a great part of the above sum, the profits of the occupation are no less certain.

It is indeed alleged by the farmers, that their poverty is not owing to an imprudent anticipation of their produce, but has arisen from the rapacity of their landlords, who exact much more from them than the rent mentioned in their leases. I have already explained the manner in which, I believe, almost every landholder, and almost every individual employed under them, as far as the extent of their jurisdiction goes, beg money from the poor farmers, and, so far as it is voluntarily given, there can be no right in indifferent persons to check the practice, farther than by reprehending it as a mean custom, of which every landholder should be ashamed. The landlord, however, were he not tied down by perpetual leases, would have the most evident interest, and most indubitable right to prevent his dependents from taking a farthing; for the richer his tenants were, the more rent they would be able to pay. At present it is totally indifferent to him what their condition is, so long as they do not run away. The poorer farmers indeed very universally complain, that they pay a great deal more than their rent, partly from fear of giving offence, and partly from mere force or fraud. They allege, that unfair receipts for their payments are given, few of them being able to read; and in order to defray every kind of extraordinary expense, which the landlord or his agents can incur, that money is levied from them by confinement, and even sometimes by blows. The apparent expenses of the agents being much greater than their avowed allowances, leaves no room to doubt of their being in general rogues; but whether their profits arise from oppressing the farmers, or from joining them to cheat their masters, can be determined by those only who have judicial authority to investigate the matter. I am however inclined to believe, that the landlords suffer more than the farmers, because when I recommended an application to the courts of justice, to most of those from whom I heard complaints, the universal answer was, that there was no justice for a poor man against a rich, and that the rich farmers were never molested. A complaint of such a general nature being certainly false, makes me doubt of the truth of a great part of the others. It must however be stated, that the vast number of men employed in the collecting the rent, which far exceeds any thing that can be supposed necessary for the mere conveyance of messages, leads to a suspicion of force being sometimes employed; and in one place I had sufficient evidence, that the agent of a landlord had stocks in his office, which could only be employed for illicit purposes. Besides the general manner in which the agents spoke of the farmers convinced me, that they considered them as subjects, to whom they had a right to dictate law, and that this right was an excuse for whatever hardships they might choose to inflict.

The most common means of injuring the farmers however is, I believe, by giving them receipts for less money than they pay, which ignorance prevents them from detecting. When the time for a final settlement comes, they find, that they are in arrears two or three rupees more than they expected, and must either pay this balance or allow their effects to be sold.

The process for the recovery of rent is so easy and expeditious, that the landlord or his agents have no excuse for the employment of arbitrary power, which can only be considered in the light of robbery; and the frauds committed in granting improper receipts, or in suing farmers for more than is actually due, in confidence of their not being able to procure redress, can be considered as no less culpable; and fine, which is, I believe, the only punishment that can be inflicted for such offences, seems inadequate to the atrocity of their nature. As the detection of the crime is difficult, transportation beyond the seas for seven years, accompanied of course by loss of caste, could not be considered as too severe, and would probably be effectual.

If what the farmers allege has any foundation in truth, it would be also necessary to secure them in their proffers of payment being valid. If, when they offered payment, a receipt for the sum was refused, without an enormous deduction for light money, they should have a right to deposit the money in the hands of the *munsif*, whose receipt for it should be good to them, and whose commission and fees should of course come entirely from the person who refused the payment. At present, a farmer who does not agree to the terms proposed may be refused a receipt, and his rent being unpaid, a complaint may be made, and all the expense will come on him. This is so heavy, that in general it is better for him to comply with the original demand. Such at least is what they allege.

The principal means, that occur to me as likely to improve the agriculture of the country, so far as relates to the tenure of farms, are the following:

1st. To encourage, as far as possible, large farmers, from whom a landlord may collect his rent without the assistance of an army, and whom his agents cannot pretend to fleece.

2ndly. To enforce the regulation, that prohibits the granting leases in perpetuity, which is now almost universally adopted, and which is not only injurious to agriculture, but might in a great measure annihilate the landed revenue.

3rdly. To secure the farmers from every kind of demand, except those contained in their leases.

4thly. To introduce a greater spirit of independence among the farmers, by discouraging, as far as possible, the system of advances. This it is evident must be a work of time, as the present cultivators have no stock, and must borrow it. All that can therefore be done is, if possible, to check gradually the profits on such loans, by which means the money advanced will be gradually applied to other purposes, and necessity will gradually compel the farmers to save stock until they procure a sufficiency.

I am aware, that some able economists condemn all restraint on the rate of interest, and contend that no one will borrow or lend except when it is for his advantage. I cannot here enter into a discussion of this matter, the determination of which must, in a great measure, depend upon the definition that is given of the word advantage. The state of capital in this district will, I imagine, show, that where the usual rate of interest is higher than the ordinary gains of commerce or agriculture, the common prudence of mankind is not sufficient to prevent the rich from being tempted to lend upon very bad security, nor to hinder the poor from indulging their propensities, by borrowing money on terms which nothing but mere accident can ever enable them to repay. The consequence is, that the rich man, in place of a capital which can be realized, acquires a number of necessitous dependants, to whose wants he must administer, in order to procure a share of their labour in place of interest, and these dependants are reduced to perhaps one of the worst kinds of slavery, that of insolvent debtors.

5thly. Each Munsif should have a properly qualified land-measurer, liable to severe punishment, if detected in fraud. On application from either landlord or tenant, this man should measure the field, and be paid by the person at whose request the measurement is made, and no other measurement should be admitted, except by order of the magistrate, on complaint of fraud or corruption in the public measure.

I shall now give a few of the many statements of their profit and loss, which I received from actual farmers. I have selected one from each kind of land.

In pergunnah Devikoth, a grain farm was cultivated by five ploughs, and contained 55 bigahs of land of a free soil. The bigah contains 84 large cubits, the farm therefore contained about 79½ Calcutta bigahs, or 26½ acres. Two persons of the tenant's family managed two of the ploughs, and three servants were hired for the others: besides, 10 rupees were expended in procuring occasional labourers.

31 bigahs of this farm were called *poli*, as follows:

		Rs.		
1	bigah for house and garden, no produce.			
2	bigahs for raising seedlings, no produce.			
28	ditto sown with summer rice, at 12 maunds, Calcutta weight, the bigah, at three maunds the rupee, ...	112	0	0
20	of these bigahs produced *sorisha*, at 2¼ maund the bigah, ...	40	0	0
7	bigahs produced pulse (*khesari* or lentils), at 2¼ maunds the bigah, value 60 seers the rupee, ...	10	8	0
1	bigah tobacco, ...	5	0	0
24	bigahs were reckoned *khar*, each gave 15 maunds of winter rice,	120	0	0
55	bigahs.	Rs. 287	8	0

This produce of what was cultivated with grain is nearly 3¾ rupee a Calcutta bigah, which is one rupee more than my general estimate; but then the land is a rich free soil. The farmer said, that he paid 70 rupees rent, and 8¾ Rs. for extra demands. This is almost 16 annas for the bigah, while I allow only 10, but then the land is richer than the average. Deducting one-half of the produce for expense of cultivation, there will remain Rs. 144 4 0, and the rent exceeds the half of this by Rs. 6. 6. but the man puts no value on his garden, nor on the crop which he has from the land reserved for seedlings, and which in such soils always gives a good crop. This will nearly make up the difference. Deduct rent and half of the produce, there remains 55 rupees, or 11 Rs. neat on each plough.

A farmer of pergunnah Kordaho cultivates 40 bigahs, of a stiff clay, and keeps four ploughs; he has two men in the family, and hires two servants for six months. The bigah is nearly equal to ½ acre or 1½ Calcutta bigah; in all 60 Calcutta bigahs.

		Rs.		
4	bigahs reserved for house, garden, and seedlings—no produce.			
10	bigahs produce 18 maunds of winter rice, Calcutta measure, at 120 seers the rupee, ...	60	0	0
10	bigahs produce 15 maunds each, ...	60	0	0
10	bigahs produce 9 maunds each, ...	30	0	0
6	bigahs produce 12 maunds of summer rice each, ...	24	0	0
	144 seers of *sorisha*, at 48 seers, ...	18	0	0
	300 seers of *khesari*, at 60 seers, ...	5	0	0
40	bigahs.	Rs. 187	0	0

The produce of the 54 Calcutta bigahs of arable land is therefore Rs. 3. 10. also above my estimate, deducting one-half of the produce for the expense of cultivation. The rent, which appeared on the face of the lease to be one rupee for each bigah, without any deduction for seedlings, did not amount to one-half of the neat proceeds by Rs. 13. 8. 0. out of Rs. 93. 8. 0. But the farmer alleged, that the exactions amounted to ⅕ of the rent, in which case, it would exceed the half of the neat produce by Rs. 13. 4. I have, however, already stated my doubts concerning the reality of such exactions, at least to so great an amount. The man ought also to have allowed some produce for his garden, and probably a little for seedling-land, as the soil was rather rich. The rent, making a reasonable allowance for seedlings, is at the rate of nearly 10 annas for the whole, or about 11⅓ annas a bigah for what is actually cultivate. Deducting one-half for cultivation and the rent, with a moderate allowance for extra charges, the gain on each plough will be nearly the same as in the former case.

A sugar-cane farmer of Lalvari Pergunnah, who has three ploughs, cultivates 30 bigahs of land, the bigah consisting of 56 yards (*gas*), but about four are deducted from each bigah, by the measurers tying the rope round their middle: the farm may therefore be about 45 Calcutta bigahs, or 15 acres.

3 bigahs sugar-cane land.	
1 bigah of cane cut, at 18 maunds (of 96 sa. wt. the seer, Calcutta maunds 21. 24) of extract of sugar-cane, at 2 Rs. the md.	36 0 0
2 bigahs of summer rice, at 15 maunds, ...	10 0 0
108 seers *sorisha*, ...	2 0 0
60 seers *khesari*, ...	1 0 0
17 bigahs corn land.	
17 bigahs summer rice, at 15 maunds, value ⅓ R.	75 0 0
5 of it only produce a 2nd crop of *sorisha*, ...	10 0 0
2 bigahs for house, garden, and seedlings, produce of tobacco, ..	5 0 0
22 called *poli*.	
8 called *khyar*, produce each 10½ maunds of winter rice, ...	24 8 0
30 bigahs.	Rs. 163 8 0
The rent for *poli* lands, at 2 Rs.	44 0 0
For *khyar*, at 1 R.	8 0 0
	52 0 0

This is almost one-third of the produce, but in such rich land one-half of the produce is too much to allow for the expense of cultivation. Deduct however one-half, and the rent, and the remainder will be 29 Rs. 12 as. 0 p. or Rs. 9. 14. 0. neat on each plough. On sugar farms the statements which I have procured from the farmers generally make the avowed rent about ⅓ of the produce, on corn farms ¼. The alleged exactions would generally reduce both to nearly one-half.

Having now stated what I observed concerning farm and farmers, I shall give an account of those who have no lands, but cultivate on account of others. These people may be divided into two classes, the *adhiyars*, who cultivate with their own stock, and the *krishan*, who are servants hired by the month.

To those who have visited parts of India, where the soil belongs to the sovereign, and is cultivated on his account by persons who give one-half of the produce to the estate, it may seem wonderful, that the persons in Bengal, who cultivate on the same tenure, should be exceedingly poor. In these other countries the cultivators are at least as wealthy as the farmers of Bengal, and no one can pretend, that their soil is more productive, or requires less trouble and expense in the cultivation. Their wealth is to be accounted for in two ways. In the first place they have more prudence, industry, and skill, owing probably to advances being less frequent; but this difference is not very great. The second circumstance, which chiefly contributes to their gain, is that in these parts the produce of the cultivator's labour is divided between him and the state, which is always grossly cheated; and in Bengal the produce is divided between the farmer and cultivator, and each takes his fair share. The condition of an *adhiyar* however was every where represented as better than that of a common labourer. We may state his profit and loss as follows, allowing that each family has one plough.

Profit—

15 bigahs cultivated with grain produce on an average Rs. 41. 4. of which one-half is his share, ...	20	10	0
His farm occupies him six months; holidays and sickness, two months; he works four months for hire, at 1½ rupee, ...	6	0	0
His wife works about the same time as he does, only much harder, by cleaning rice as I have mentioned, ...	7	12	0
By spinning, 4 annas a month, ...	2	8	0
	36	14	0

Charge—

A boy to tend his cattle, ...	0	4	0
Seed, ...	3	6	0
Interest on 36 rupees stock (he has no cow), at 24 per cent. including all advantages taken of his distress, ...	10	0	0
	13	10	0

So that he has remaining Rs. 23. 2. a very little more than the expense of the lowest class mentioned in my account of the manner in which the people live. A considerable part of this poverty is however owing to their having anticipated their returns, and a man who had the small stock of 36 rupees might live in this manner without being in absolute want. That is, he and his wife might clear 30 rupees a year. The number of *adhiyars* is very considerable, but varies much in different parts of the country. It is probable, however, that there are above 1,50,000 families employed entirely in this manner.

The *krishan*, or servants commonly employed in agriculture, are by no means numerous, and do not amount to above eighty thousand families; for the families of the greater farmers are generally numerous, and all the sons and brothers hold the plough, while hired servants are only engaged to make up the number, and those who have large farms, often prefer the people who cultivate for a share. It is only the heads of the families belonging to the 16,500 large farms that are exempted from personal labour. The *krishan*, in lands that produce a constant succession of crops, are hired for the whole year; but in clay farms they are engaged for six months only. This, however, makes little difference, as in the months, when agriculture is at a stop there, the demand for workmen is great, and they can make rather more than in the season of cultivation. The usual wages are eight annas a month, with food and clothing, which the farmers estimate at one rupee a month, but in fact does not exceed 12 annas. The eight annas go to maintain his wife and family, who are very poorly supported, but the servant is tolerably well provided, as the farmer is interested, to enable him to work. He usually works about five hours in the forenoon at the plough, and two or three in the afternoon, weeding or hoeing, so that his labour is moderate; but at his spare hours he repairs his hut, and brings fuel. The gains and expense of his family may be as follows :

Gains—		
To the man's wages		6 0 0
To the woman's beating rice, ...		7 12 0
To ditto spinning, ...		2 8 0
		Rs. 16 4 0
Expense of a family of the lowest order, ...		22 11 0
Deduct man's clothing,.....................................	0 10 0	
Food ⅓ of the whole, ...	5 8 9	
		6 2 9
		Rs. 16 8 3

In the expense of these two kinds of labourers, I have only supposed two small children in each family, because the women are so hardly wrought that they do not breed fast, and before a woman has more than two children, the eldest is usually eight years old. At that age the boys of these two classes begin to tend cattle, and each can take care of 25 heads, for each of which they get three annas a year, with a meal from every proprietor in turns. The girls can then assist their mothers in beating rice, but are generally very soon married. This class of people live not only very miserably, but at the celebration of marriages and other ceremonies are generally so inconsiderate, as to run in debt, as much as possible. The only means, which they have of extricating themselves, is by running away or stealing ; and it is alleged, that they are much addicted to both practices. It must however be observed, that many of those who have been convicted of the last mentioned offence have been men who had not the excuse of want to plead in their behalf.

The inconsiderate manner, in which the natives of this district anticipate their revenue, may be well exemplified by a common custom of the *krishans* in the divisions of Howra and Rajarampúr. A young labourer, usually in order to defray the expense of his marriage, bound himself to a master for from 16 to 24 months, and received in advance the whole of his wages, which was immediately spent on the ceremony. For the first 16 or 24 months the wife provided for herself, in the best manner she could: but if she happened to be sick, or to have a child, her misery became extreme, and recourse was had to still farther anticipations of the wages, which were always made at an enormous interest, and of course the family always continued in debt, and the extremity of wretchedness. Some indigo manufacturers having settled in the vicinity, wanted labourers, and gave two rupees a month for wages, which has relieved the poor *krishans* from much of their distress, and compelled the farmer to allow them one rupee a month besides their food, and this, it is evident, if they are prudent, will render their situations very comfortable.

From the present state of husbandry requiring such a number of people to cultivate the ground, it must be observed, notwithstanding the immense population, that labourers or servants of any kind are difficult to procure in this district ; and in travelling through it, except with the assistance of the landholders, who obtained men from their dependents, I could not in any place hire 40 porters to go to the next stage, although double the highest wages were offered before they set out.

The number of slaves is very small: some rich Mahommedan farmers said, that in the last famines, some children had been purchased, in order rather to keep them from starving than with a view to profit. These had turned out very ill, and were so idle and careless, that their labour became much more costly than that of hired servants. Some landholders have a few slaves as domestics. The slaves that are employed in agriculture, and I believe the others, are allowed to marry free women; but as all the children are slaves, the master must pay a high price (five or six rupees) to the girl's parents: the ceremony costs three or four rupees more.

CHAPTER VIII.

OF ESTATES.

THE lands of this district, as usual, are divided into two kinds, free and assessed (*base* and *juma zemin*).

The free lands, which pay no tax to Government, have been granted by various sovereigns, either to different persons who were considered as deserving reward, or in order to maintain establishments that were considered as useful. How far the opinion of their utility is well founded, it is not perhaps necessary to discuss; but there is no doubt, that in the opinion of the people the utility is great, and therefore it is to be regretted, that there is no legal control over the proprietor of the land, for the performance of the duty, for which the grant was made. Whether there is no law for the purpose, or whether it has become obsolete, I cannot say; but the practice is to consider these lands as entirely the property of the possessor, who gives whatever part of it he pleases to the establishment, or even sells it altogether.

In this district the extent of these lands is not very considerable, as I was informed by the collector's *dewan*, that the whole amounted to about 1,20,000 bigahs of the country, or probably about 1,80,000 bigahs of the Calcutta measure. It is probable, however, that a considerable extent may have been granted privately, and of course could not appear on the collector's books; and the violent complaints, which I heard from the possessors of free estates, against the new landholders for encroachments on their estates, probably in a great measure originated from the landholder's depriving them of all the land which they held without right; and it is probable, that they still hold much land, to which they have no title, as it is natural to suppose, that the sacred character, which most of them enjoy, renders people unwilling to disturb them. There is however reason to think, that many of the families entitled to these estates, have become extinct, and that the landholders have seized on these and retain them under false names. At least I heard assertions of that nature frequently repeated; but their truth can only be investigated by those possessed of judicial authority. Of right, such estates should no doubt revert to the estate.

The free estates are in general very small, and the only two of any note are those belonging to the two Mahommedan establishments at Peruya, that have been already mentioned. These are managed much in the same way as the estates of zemindars, but are much worse cultivated; and the farmers who occupy them, although their rent is rather lower, are at least as poor as their neighbours. The other free estates, which are very numerous and small, are in general in a still more wretched state, and on an average probably one-half of each is waste. This however is not entirely owing to mismanagement, as in general the land is of the very worst quality.

The proprietors usually keep a house, garden, and plantation, and give as much of the remainder to be cultivated for one-half of the produce as they can : but those who cultivate in that manner cannot clear wastes, and the proprietors are two necessitous to undertake improvement. The greater part therefore, where the soil is not too poor to produce trees, is overgrown with woods. From viewing the state of this kind of property, I am fully convinced, that, if the landed revenue were removed, the country in a hundred years would not be half so well cultivated as at present, and the people would be still poorer.

The assessed lands, as is well known, are in possession of the zemindars or landholders, who enjoy them by hereditary right, and who pay a certain tax, which is considered as fixed for a perpetuity. In fact, they have been placed exactly on the footing of the landlords of England, except that the land-tax is higher; but then they are exempt from almost all others. At the time, when the settlement was made, it was supposed that they were only to receive $\frac{1}{11}$ part of the neat proceeds of their estates ; and the *dewan* of the collector stated, as his opinion, that no zemindar cleared less than 10 per cent., and none of the larger zemindars more than 25 per cent. of the neat proceeds. Some smaller ones, who could attend to the whole detail of collection, cleared 30 per cent. The few statements in detail, which I was able to procure, agree with this opinion. The following was given as an estimate of the expense and profit of the Raja of Dinajpúr's estate, in its now fallen condition. He is a boy of about 11 years of age, and lives with his mother by adoption, who has purchased eight lots of her husband's estate. He retains only one pergunnah of the immense estate that formerly belonged to the family, and I have reason to believe, that it is the worst managed in the district.

The eight lots requires the following establishment :

		Bigahs.	Rupees.
1	Dewan, who superintends the whole, ...		1,200
8	Thesildars or assistants, at 25 per month, ...		2,400
40	Writers (*mohurrers*), at 8 per month, ...		3,840
24	Sirdars or officers of the old militia, at 50 bigahs.. ..	1,200	
16	Mirdhas or inferior officers of the same, at 30 bigahs,	480	
200	Payiks or soldiers of the same, at 20 bigahs,..	4,000	
8	Dufadars or officers of a more recent militia,..		384
24	Burkundajes, the soldiers under these,..		864
16	Dufturies or keepers of papers, ...	192	
200	Kutwals or messengers, ...	2,000	
		7,872	8,688
	Bigahs of land 7,872, at 10 annas, ...		4,924
	The whole is let to *izaradars* or renters, who receive 4 per cent. commission on the rental, which is 1,10,000, besides the unrented land, which I cannot estimate,...........		4,400
	Land tax,..		79,000
			97,012

Rental,	1,10,000
Lands given to servants,	4,924
Gross amount,	1,14,924
Charges,	97,012
Clear income,	17,912

The gain here is about 15½ per cent. on the gross rental. The expense of collection is not quite 16 per cent. besides the lands not rented.

Now with regard to the pergunnah that has not been sold, the following is the account which I received :

	Bigahs.	Rupees.
1 Deputy of the dewan,		280
1 Accountant (*jama navis*),		360
7 Writers,		840
1 Officer of the more recent militia,		48
7 Armed men of the same,		252
3 Dufturies or keepers of papers,	36	
4 Officers of the old militia,	200	
100 Soldiers of the same,	2,000	
150 Messengers,	1,500	
	3,736	1,780
3,736 bigahs of land given to persons employed in the collections, at 10 annas,		2,335
Farmed at 4 per cent. on the rental of 96,582 Rs.		3,863¼
		7,978¼
Land tax,		81,591
		89,569¼

Rental of the lands,		96,584
Lands granted to persons employed in collection,		2,335
Lands granted to domestics, 1,210 bigahs, at 10 annas,		756
Gross rental,		99,675
Deduct Charges,		89,569¼
Neat profit,	Rs.	10,105¾

The gain here is about 10 per cent. ; the expense of collection not quite so much.

I shall now give an account of the management of a small estate, belonging to Odwait Chaudharí, a merchant, who has purchased a lot in the division of Thakúrgram, and Pergunnah Dehotto, the gross rental 6,300 rupees a year. He does not reside, and has the following establishment :

	Bigahs.	Rupees.
1 Tehsildar, or agent,		120
1 Jama Navis, or head accountant,		84

1 Moharrir or writer,		36 0 0
1 Potdár or Money-changer,		24 0 0
2 armed men, Barkandaz,		51 0 0
1 Sirdar or chief payik,	20	
10 Payiks,	120	
7 Messengers, Kutwal,	56	
		196 0 0
		315 0 0
196 bigahs, at 10 annas,		112 8 0
Commission on 6,300 Rupees, at 4 per cent.		252 0 0
		679 8 0
Revenue,		4,500 0 0
Total charges,		5,179 8 0
Gross rental,	Rs.	6,300 0 0
Neat profit,		1,120 8 0

Here the profit is about 18 per cent. and the expense of collection about 10 per cent. of the gross amount, which is the proper allowance.

From the statements that I have already made, I cannot see how such small profits only are gained, without supposing the most gross mis-management. I have stated the produce of the cultivated lands at rupees 199,60,000, and I have every where endeavoured to make my calculations rather moderate. I will deduct $\frac{1}{40}$ part for free lands, which is a very full allowance, even supposing that the possessors occupy more than what is their right—there will remain 194,61,000 rupees. Now, I think, it cannot be well doubted, that the farmers could, without just cause of complaint, pay a fourth part of the gross produce; and it is indeed in general alleged by them, that they pay more. The gross rental therefore of assessed estates ought not to be much less than Rs. 48,45,000.

Although I have no doubt, that with proper care the land-holders, without extending or improving the cultivation, and without the least hardship on their tenants, might realize this sum, yet I do not believe that their rental is so great. From the most minute inquiry at every division, I think, that the usual customary rent, on an average, may be taken at 10 annas for the Calcutta biggah. I avoid entering at all into the consideration of irregular exactions, the reality or extent of which I had not the means of ascertaining. Now, leaving out the lands which are only cultivated occasionally, and which do not enter into the (*Jama*) rental, there are 68,83,200 bigahs fully occupied: deduct 2,15,000 for seedlings on clay lands, which pay no rent, and there remain 66,68,200, from which deduct $\frac{1}{46}$ for free lands, and there remain 65,23,505, which, at 10 annas, is rupees 40,77,190. 10. To this must be added all rents for fisheries, pasturage of buffalos, &c. but these are small, and probably do not exceed 50,000 rupees a year. Call it only 25,000, to make up the odd number, and the very smallest rental, that ought to be admitted, should be 41,00,000 rupees; always, however, on the supposition, that the proprietor is not cheated, farther than by having his lands let too low, or under $\frac{1}{4}$ of the gross produce. At this rate, the tenants, exclusive of the milk, bambus, and mangoes, which are a fair part of the produce of their farms, do not pay one-fourth of the produce by 7,45,000 rupees, or by 13 per cent. The land-holders, therefore, after deducting 10 per cent. for the expense of collection, and paying the land tax of 17,50,000 rupees, should have to themselves 19,40,000 rupees, which is considerably more than 50 per cent. of the neat proceeds. I have no doubt, that an active man, with a moderate estate, would realize that sum, without raising the rents above 10 annas a biggah, and without taking a single farthing from any tenant, more than his due; and I have no doubt, provided he secured them from the frauds of his agents, that he might take one-fourth of the produce from his tenants, not only without oppressing them, but by giving a stimulus to their exertions, so as greatly to improve their condition. As the estates however are in general managed, it would be difficult to say what the real profits are. I can scarcely however think, that any of them produces so little as $\frac{1}{3}$ of the neat proceeds, and some I have no doubt amount fully to one-half, or even exceed this proportion. It is indeed said, that, when the large semindary of Dinajpúr was sold, the assessment was divided very unequally on the lots by the native assistant of the collector, who had thus an opportunity of informing their friends, where a valuable bargain was to be found; and that now, while the profits of some purchases are great, others make little more than what discharges the revenue. Such allegations however must be received with great caution; for in general each landlord pretends that he has no profit, and invents stories of this kind to account for his own situation; for it is perfectly evident, that the general amount of the assessment cannot consume near $\frac{9}{10}$ of the clear proceeds, as was supposed at the time when the settlement was made. A view of the manner in which the estates are managed will throw some light on the subject.

The greater part of the landholders are new men, who have purchased their estates within these few years, and who formerly were either merchants, manufacturers, agents of landholders, or officers of government. These last are not numerous. By those natives, who are not afraid of them, they are called *lotdars*, or fellows who have purchased lots, and are held in great contempt, while there is a general clamour against their rapacity and injustice. I must however say, that their lands are in general better cultivated, and the appearance of the people not so miserable as on some of the estates that have belonged to one family for several generations. Of these there are still some in the district, and indeed the Dinajpúr family still retains the largest possession, which seem of all others to be the worst managed, and their tenants appear to be the poorest. Still, however, they are much respected; for people submit with patience to many things, from a power, to which they are accustomed, that would grieve them to endure from a person, of whom they know nothing, or whom they once remember as their equal. The odium and ridicule thus thrown on the new landholders, probably, prevent most of them from being on their estates; and their merchants, traders, and officers of government, knowing nothing of country affairs, almost the whole estates of the purchasers of lots are managed by agents, and the check which the proprietors have adopted, to prevent fraud, seems in general, as I have before mentioned, to be taken from the settlement made by Mr. Hatch. They know, that they ought to have a certain number of bigahs in such and such pergunnahs, and that these were valued by that gentleman at such a rate, and the agent is expected to account for the amount. I know nothing of the grounds upon which Mr. Hatch went. It is said, that there is no account of them to be found in the collector's office; but, it is said, that he estimated $\frac{3}{4}$ of the whole district to be cultivated, and the rents have not been since raised, so that I am totally at a loss to account for the assessment having been made so low, especially as the country is said to have been then better cultivated than it now is.

The agents manage every thing in their own way; but are under the necessity of being very cautious, as their masters are in general men of business, and those who were formerly agents themselves understand country affairs, so that their estates are improving, and are comparatively well managed.

The estates of more ancient families are on another footing. The proprietors are possessed of documents concerning their management for a number of years, and being respected, live among the people, to whom they have been known from their infancy. They have, therefore, great advantages, were they disposed to attend to their affairs; but very few of them are men of business. A great part of them never pass the threshold of their doors, except to assist at some religious ceremony, and are either sunk in a miserable superstition, a prey to religious mendicants, and other idle persons, or are totally abandoned to dissipation; and some are addicted to both vices. Those are reckoned men of activity and business who sit in their office a few hours a day, and look a little into the accounts, and once a year go round their estates, to receive presents and homage from their tenantry. There are however some honourable exceptions, especially Guruprosad of Surahor Mankoyi, who not only investigates his accounts with care, but, when he suspects fraud, takes the measuring rope in his own hand, and examines on the spot the veracity of his agents. Every thing about him is decent and respectable, and the estate is like a garden.

On large estates, there is a dewan or chief agent, who resides at the principal office, and has under him a sufficient number of accountants (moharrirs), the chief of whom (jamanavis) keeps the rental. There are besides a keeper (baksí) and valuer (potdár) of money, people who take care of the papers (daftarí), and a number of messengers (kutwál). In order to protect the money, and convey it from place to place, and also, as is alleged, to enforce orders, two kinds of guards are kept—one called barkandaz, commanded by dufadars and jamadars, seems to be a more recent establishment. The other called payiks, commanded by mirdhas and sirdars, are the remains of the militia of the Bengal kingdom. Both seem to have constituted the foot soldiers, whose number makes such a formidable appearance in the Ayeen Akbery. At each large division of the estate (perhaps 20,000 rupees rental) is a deputy (nayeb or tesildar), with a similar but smaller establishment. Now, so far as we have come, the heads of these offices are considered as persons of consequence, who are not to travel through the country to examine into the affairs of the estate; but to sit quietly in the office, to keep the accounts, to receive money, and to manage affairs with the officers of government.

These principal agents manage the estate in two different manners.—They either collect the rent immediately from the tenants, or farm them out for a certain number of years to a kind of middle men, called izaradars.

If the rents are to be levied immediately from the tenants, the head officers employ men to cultivate the unrented land, either for a share of the produce, or for a certain sum from year to year. The rent of the land that is let on lease is actually received from the tenants by two persons, a patwari and mondol, of which there should be one mondol for each *mouza*, and one patwari for every two or three, unless these be very large. These two officers are in fact the only men employed, who are usually well versed in country affairs. Many landlords have of late discharged the mondols, and employ only patoyaris, and this seems to be a judicious saving, and a sign of approaching economy. The patwari is a penman, and keeps the accounts, for which he in general receives three per cent. on the rental, and the mondol, who in some places is called prodhan, is the chief farmer of the village, who manages the others, and usually receives one per cent. commission. This commission given to the patwáris and mondols is called *saramjáni*, and sometimes instead of 4 per cent. arises to 6. The payiks, and their officers, and the messengers, are paid in land. The other establishments is paid in money; but most of the domestic servants receive land in place of wages, and this land is not included in the rental, every means possible being taken to make that appear small.

On smaller estates, a nayeb or tehsildar, with his usual establishment, are sufficient; but there are very few indeed, in which the landlord manages his own affairs without assistance.

If the rents are to be farmed, an agreement is made with the person, named izaradar, who undertakes to collect the rent, as stated in the rent-roll, and to defray all the expenses of delivering it into the agent's office. For his reward, he takes the commission of from 4 to 6 per cent. above stated, and the whole profit that he can derive from the lands which are not rented. He receives also the assistance of all the militia and messengers who continue to receive their lands, and are directed to obey his orders. From three to five years is the usual period that the lands are rented, and the contract has in no instance been extended beyond nine years. When the commission is high, or the quantity of unrented lands is great, the renter often pays a sum of money in advance. The renters are in general perfectly conversant in country affairs, and make the most of the lands, being totally unconcerned whether the tenants are ruined or not. Indeed, where they are rich men, who have much influence, the tenants are uncommonly dissatified and clamorous; but, where they rent only small portions of an estate, the tenants complain no more of their condition than usual. Even with this security, and where a landholder receives the whole of his rent from a few izaradars, who have very good credit, it is not usual for him to diminish his establishment.

These unwieldy establishments seem to have been originally formed, when the government collected the rent immediately from the farmer or cultivator, and when the same persons managed not only the collections, but the police, and a great part of the judicial department. The vast number of armed men, barkandaz and payik, especially the latter, formed the infantry of the Mogul government. The whole was continued under the zemindars, until the perpetual settlement, because they not only collected the revenue, but managed the subordinate parts of the police, and of the administration of justice; and they were anxious to have as many armed men as possible, because these supported them in their enormities, and were no charge, as they lived on lands which the zemindars did not bring to account. Custom and the artifice of agents keep up the establishment; for I have great reason to think, that most of these people who are paid in lands are mere cultivators, and pay a low rent to agents, although on paper they are represented to the landlords as having each from 10 to 50 bigahs free of rent, and to be absolutely necessary to procure the money. Some landlords are now curtailing very much, and every man, that can be saved, will enable the zemindars to raise more money from his tenants, as the lowest messenger expects at least subsistence, when he goes on a message to a farmer, and all the others expect presents, and usually obtain them in proportion to their rank. These are avowed, but it is alleged, that they exact much more by violence. The greatest detriment, however, that the landlords suffer, is by the collusions between their agents and the farmers, who are allowed to occupy much more land than their leases bear, and pay a bribe rather smaller than the usual rent to the agents, who whenever the tenants are refractory, threaten a measurement. The perpetual leases at a low fixed rent are also very favourable to the agents. The people in possession of such more readily submit to impositions than those would who rented land at its full value for a short term of years; for such tenants would always go away, if any addition was required; but a man, who has a valuable farm in perpetuity, submits to much, in hopes, that hereafter he may have a more just agent.

It is not usual for the zemindars to make advances to the tenants, to enable them to cultivate, although, of late some have given assistance to those who were bringing in waste ground. This is in some measure excusable; but the practice is commonly very destructive, and encourages the tenantry in the anticipation of their means, which is the fault to which they are most addicted.

Although it appears evident from the Ayeen Akbery, that in the time of Akber, there were no hereditary proprietors of land in this part of the country, all the natives allege, that the office of zemindar has always been hereditary, which may have in some measure been the case. They then merely accounted to government for their receipts, and they pretend to say, that they have been injured by the new settlement. They allege, that formerly they were allowed great authority, both in criminal and civil causes, over the people whom they managed, which was a great source of emolument, being of course venally administered; and, although they were often squeezed by the Mogul officers, and on all occasions were treated with the utmost contempt, they preferred suffering these evils to the mode that has been adopted of selling their lands when they fall in arrears, which is a practice that they cannot endure: besides, bribery went a great way on most occasions; and they allege, that, bribes included, they did not actually pay one-half of what they do now, although nothing can be more moderate than the present assessment, which I am convinced does not amount to a tithe of the produce.

The principal things that ought to be inculcated on the landlords, for the improvement of their estates, is activity and industry in the management, and the utility of a suitable education, to enable them to perceive, that their estates cannot be improved by beggarly and irregular demands, made on the tenantry, but by encouraging those who are frugal and industrious, and by banishing those who are idle and thoughtless. The most bitter enemies of the landlords are idle religious mendicants, who represent all attention to worldly affairs as unworthy of a man; and dissipated flatterers, who represent moderation in expense as unworthy of a great prince, a title that is bestowed, by such persons, on landholders who have not 1000 rupees a year.

One of the principal causes that appear to me to prevent the landholders from acquiring proper habits of activity, and a proper education, is the subdivision of estates into equal shares among all the sons of a family. Where the estates are monstrous, like that of Dinajpúr, and exceed the usual capacity of men to manage, there may be no loss in the sub-division; the inevitable consequences indeed of mismanagement will always in a short time bring them to sale, and render any precaution unnecessary: but when the estate is moderate, it may be considered as a national loss, when it is broken into portions, none of which can enable the proprietor to bestow a decent education on his children, nor to encourage any thing that is ornamental or advantageous to the country. This however is not the greatest evil of the practice. The sons of the family, who know that they all will have a certain provision, naturally give themselves up to sloth, and make no exertion to acquire useful knowledge, even when their parents are willing to bestow it; but the parents even are in general sparing, knowing that their sons can exist without trouble. Now, where the custom is to leave the family estate to one son, the parent knows, that the only provision he has for the others is a good and useful education, by which they may be fitted to gain a living suitable to their rank, while the young men must exert themselves, knowing that they have no other resource. Even the son, who is to receive the estate, unless he choses to be the laughing stock of his brothers, must make an exertion sufficient to acquire a knowledge that will enable him at least to superintend his affairs. It is only among young men educated in this manner, that people fit for discharging offices in the police law or revenue can be procured. And the manner in which these offices are now in general filled, so far as I can learn, shows, that the education of those who hold them has been miserably neglected. Although the Hindú law directs, that property should descend to sons equally, or at least nearly so, there is nothing, so far as I know, to prevent assessed lands from being considered in a different light, and from being viewed as a trust vested hereditarily in the zemindar, for the security of government, which will be destroyed, if the lands are frittered away among the ramifications of a numerous family; and owing to the custom of adoption, these portions never re-unite. I am aware, that some of the ablest jurists and writers on political economy are strenuous advocates for the subdivision of landed estates. The speculations of these persons nearly resemble the plan that has been adopted in the colony of the Cape of Good Hope, and I will venture to assert, that this plan has hitherto repressed the progress of agriculture in that colony, and so long as it is in force, will keep that delightful country in a state of beggary. In fact, it has only been the money spent among the colonists, by the Dutch and British fleets and armies, that has prevented them from being clothed in sheep's skins like the Hottentots.

Although, as I have said before, the natives are persuaded, that the office of zemindar has always been hereditary, which is not absolutely incompatible with the idea of its having been merely an office, and totally unconnected with the property of the land; yet, from all that I could learn, there is no good reason to think, that any families of this district have had very ancient possessions; and it must be observed, that from the total want of history among the Hindús, any custom which has obtained for 100 years, comes to them with its origin as obscure, as if it had obtained for a thousand. A review of the (pergunnahs) estates will show the succession of families, so far as I could learn. I have however totally neglected the *lotdárs*, as they have all lately purchased. Some other particulars relative to these estates will be seen in the accompanying table, No. 8.

It must be observed, that the word pergunnah is not used in the Ayeen Akbery, but the serkers, into which each subah was divided, and which are somewhat analogous to our zilas, are subdivided into mahals, which are nearly the same with the present pergunnahs; several new ones however have been erected. In order to point out these, I have given the name in Mr. Gladwin's translation, whenever it could be traced.

The first six pergunnahs of Dinajpúr seem early to have been under the management of a man named Kási, who was reputed very holy, and passed most of his time in prayer at a temple in Dinajpúr. After some time, he was lost (oundes), and left a wife, who procured the zemindary for a slave, through the influence of Serimonto Dotto, who was deputy of the Kanungoe, or register general of Bengal. On the death of this lady and her favorite, Srimonto Dotto procured the zemindary for himself. He left one son and one daughter, who married Horirám Ghos, a Kulin Kayostho of Kuloyi Gram, in Bordhoman. This person, on marrying into a family that had some property, gave his paternal house to his brother Horinarayon, and lived with his father-in-law, who settled one-half of his estate on his own son, and the other on his grandson Sukdev, the son of Horirám. On the death of his uncle without heirs, Sukder obtained the whole. He seems to have obtained the first half of his grandfather's estate, in consideration of his rank; the Ghoses being much higher than the Dottos, although both are Sudras.

Horirám, or his son Sukdev, it is not certain which, but probably the former, was an officer under the zemindar of Khyetlál; and on his master's death without heirs, received a part of his zemindary, but the greater share was given to the principal officer, ancestor of the Bordhonkuthi family, which will hereafter be mentioned. Sukdev, having great influence, had obtained the title of Raja, and may be considered as the founder of the Dinajpúr family. He had three sons, Ramdev, Joydev, and Praunnáth. The two former died young, and he was succeeded in his whole zemindary by the youngest, Praunnáth, who lived in great splendor, and was a very great oppressor in the neighbourhood, seizing on all the small zemindaries near him, partly by force, and partly by corruption. Four inscriptions on stone remain to ascertain the time in which he was Raja, and are dated in the years of Sakadityo 1626, 1635, 1644, 1655, or A. D. 1704, 1713, 1722, 1733. He had no legitimate son, but adopted a male relation, named Rámnáth, who continued the same course and had such a number of followers, that the Mahommedan governors treated him with great leniency, and gave him the title of Maharaj Bahadur. There are two inscriptions on stone to attest the time in which this Raja governed. They are dated in the years of Sakadityo or Salivahon 1665, and 1675, or A. D. 1745 and 1754. It must be particularly observed, that by four wives he had only five sons, although two of them were men at their father's death; the eldest succeeded to the whole zemindary. This person, named Baidyonáth, seems to have been a quiet man, and lived much respected. He was married to a lady named Rání Soroswotí, who is still alive, and has a considerable estate, but she had no children. Baidyonáth therefore, although he had a brother alive, adopted a relation named Rádhanáth Roy, and died in the Bengal year 1187, A. D. 1780. His brother Rámkanto Roy seems to have acted a kind part to his adopted nephew; and, although he was a boy, made no attempts to obtain the management of the estate, which was left with Raní Soroswotí and her brother Jánokirám, who conducted every thing as he chose, until the arrival of Mr. Hatch in the Bengal year 1193, A. D. 1786. I have already expressed some surprise at the lowness of the assessment, which that gentleman fixed for this estate, which was only 14,60,000 rupees, and from this he deducted 1,85,000 for the expense of collection. My surprise is greatly increased, when I find, that the family complain of the most violent injustice on his part, and pretend to say, that he was their bitter enemy. In an account, which I received from the present manager, they first stated, that without the least reason, he imprisoned Jánokirám, who by his wise and just conduct had gained the love of all the subjects (for they speak in the royal style). The fact, so far as I can learn, is that Jánoki was thrown into jail for debt, at the instance of Varánosi Ghos, a merchant of Calcutta. Mr. Hatch then, of his own authority, and without consulting the widow (Hinc illæ lachrymæ), appointed as dewan and tutor for the minor, a certain Rámkanto, who was a descendant of Horirám, the first zemindar of the family. This man made the settlement with Mr. Hatch, and is accused by the family of the most gross corruption and mismanagement. In fact, he purchased large lots of the estate, which now belong to his brother. Whether it was owing to this person's conduct, or to the dissipation of Rádhánáth, or to both, and to the unmanageable size of the property, the family affairs went to ruin, and the whole estates, except pergunnah Vijoynogor, have been sold. Rádhánáth had no son by his wife Tripurá Sundorí, but adopted Govindonáth, who is the present representative of the family, and is about 11 years of age.

The 22 pergunnahs, from No. 7 to 28 inclusive, had been acquired at different times by the Dinajpúr family, but when, or from whom, I did not learn. I shall now mention the pergunnahs, of which they have obtained the sole possession, and concerning the history of which somewhat is known.

Rájánogor, No. 29, according to tradition, belonged to a Muhammedan family, which resided at Habinagor, near the Tangon, where ruins of the house are to be seen. The estate was then probably free, as it is not mentioned in the Ayeen Akbery. It was acquired by the Dinajpúr family so late as the time of Baidyonáth.

Sontosh, No. 30, was the zemindary of Durgarám, a Kulin Brahmin. He had a son named Sodasiv, who was father of Krishnochondro, but this person possessed only $\frac{4}{18}$ of the zemindary—the other $\frac{14}{18}$ had descended to Raja Roy, of the same family. The former lived at Badol, the latter at Dhoral, where the ruins of their houses and temples are still to be seen. Raja Rámnáth of Dinajpúr, on the death of Krishnochondro, seized the property, it is said, by force. A sister of the late zemindar had been married to a Brahmin named Horogovindo, from whose son I had the information. He said, that his father wished to have complained to the subadar, but he and his whole family were confined for 15 years by the Raja, when they agreed to give up their claims, for a pension of 360 rupees a year, which has not been paid for these 15 years. The man has a small free estate.

Sultánpúr Panjra, No. 31, and Gilávarí, No. 32, belonged to Vasudeb and Gourikanto, father and son, of the Kayostho caste, who lived partly at Mohunpúr, and partly at Pokair, at both of which places there are considerable ruins. They are said to have been related by marriage to Srimonto Dotto, whose daughter's son was the first Dinajpúr Raja, and it is said, were forcibly deprived of the zemindary by his adopted grandson Rámnáth.

Apaul, No. 33, belonging to four families—1st, the Dinajpúr family, who in the time of Rámnáth seized on the whole. 2nd, Ekhlás Khán, a Moslem, some of whose descendants remain, and have a small free estate. 3rd, Indrojit Chaudhurí of the Goyala tribe, whose descendants have 300 bigahs of free land, and a pension of 360 rupees a year; which is paid by those who purchased the pergunnah from the Dinajpúr family. 4th, Lokhymon Bollobh, a Kayostho, whose family has become extinct.

Sorohotto, No. 34, came to the Dinajpúr family, in what manner is not known. It was given by them to Rajbollobh, who was Company's dewan in the early part of the British government. He afterwards sold it to them, and it has shared the fate of their other estates. The following pergunnahs belonged in part to the Dinajpúr family.

Khatta, No. 35, at one time belonged to an Eladut Khan, upon whom the Rajas of Nator and Dinajpúr made war; the former took 13 parts, and Rámnáth took three; both divisions have been sold.

Koroyivarí, No. 36, formerly belonged entirely to a family of Brahmins, who sold $\frac{4}{8}$ of their estate to the Dinajpúr family. This was again sold, but has been purchased by the Raní of Tripura. The $\frac{10}{16}$ belong to two brothers, Rám and Brojo dalals, whose ancestors are reported to have been *zemindars* for 14 generations. They reside in the Rongpúr district, where I shall be able to ascertain how far this is probable.

The former zemindar of Chalun, No. 37, dying without heirs, his dewan Lokhy-kanto, a Rarhi Brahmon, obtained possession, but yielded up $\frac{6}{16}$ to Raja Pránnáth of Dinajpúr; these six annas have been sold. The ten annas are in possession of Kaliprosad and Kasinath, great-grandsons of Lokhy-kanto.

Shikarpúr, No. 38, was divided between two families. The Dinajpúr family had, $\frac{9}{16}$, which has been sold. The Jahanggirpúr family had $\frac{7}{16}$, which they still retain as will be hereafter mentioned.

Sogúna, No. 39, belonged partly to Dinajpúr, who had $\frac{10}{16}$. which have been sold. $\frac{6}{16}$ belonged to the family of Jahanggirpúr.

Khanggor, originally belonged to a *zemindar* named Rajendro, whose property the Dinajpúr and Bordonkúthi families divided between them; the former receiving $\frac{7}{16}$ths, the latter $\frac{9}{16}$ths. The Bordhonkuthi family still retain two *mouzas*.

No. 41, is said formerly to have belonged to a Mritunjoy, whose house, like that of Rajendro, stood on the banks of the Jomuna. His property was divided in the same manner.

The pergunnahs, from No. 42 to No. 60, both included, seem to have formed the estate of Raghovendo, Krishnonáth, and Onontoram, who were persons of the Kshetri casts and lived at Khyetal. Traditions are not exactly concordant on the subject, concerning which of them was first and which last; but they all were probably of the same family. On the failure of issue, their *zemindary*, consisting of the above pergunnahs, was divided in the proportions of 9 and 7 parts between their two principal officers. The one who obtained 9 parts was ancestor of the Bordhonkuthi family, which resides in the Rongpúr district, and still retains a part. The one who obtained the 7 parts was either Horiram or his son Sukdev, the ancestor of the Dinajpúr family. Some of the above pergunnahs belong entirely to the one division, and some entirely to the other, while others again are divided between the two.

Poladosi, No. 61, was divided between the Dinájpúr and the Bordhonkuthí families in the same proportions as the others, but is said to have been acquired in a different manner. It once belonged to a Kondorpo Roy, who having been thrown into prison for arrears of revenue, in the Muhammedan government, applied for assistance to his neighbours, who became security for him, and having paid the money took his estates.

These are the estates of this district in which the Dinajpúr family had any concern.

Except what they received in part with the Dinajpúr family, the Bordhonkuthi *zemindars* seem to have had no other property in this district, except the pergunnah Lavarikalisa, No. 62. There is no tradition concerning its former proprietors. It was lately sold to pay the family debts, but 16 *mouzas* have been repurchased. I shall defer saying any thing further of this family until I visit their residence in Rongpúr.

Two brothers, Ram Roy and Syam Roy, were men of consideration in Serkar Tajpúr, where several ruins and forts attest their former consequence. Their estate seems to have gone to two other families. One portion consisted of the pergunnah of Maldwar, No. 63. The first *zemindar* after Ram and Syam was Umapoti, a Maithili Brahmin: he was succeeded by his son Pran Narayon, he by his son Krishno Narayon, he by his wife Gonggawoti, she by her brother's grandson Komollochun, he by his wife Buddhimoti, she by her son Ram Lochun, the present *zemindar*, whose education has been much neglected. A relation equally ill informed is his *dewan*, and they are in the hands of kites, who in a few years will probably ruin their affairs.

The remainder of the estate of Syam and Ram Roys went to a family of considerable note, which has many possessions in the Eastern part of the district and in Puroniya, but has subdivided into many branches. The first of this family, that is known, was Ghonosyam an oil-man, who acquired a *zemindary*, containing Kholora, Mothurapúr, Delaworpúr, and Haveli Tajpúr, No. 64 to No. 67 inclusive, and dwelt at Churamon. He had a son Jogotbollobh, who succeeded. By one wife he had two sons, named (1) Hiramon, and (2) Udoymon, and by another wife he had also two sons, (3) Lokmon, and (4) Lalmon, the last of whom left no son. (1) Hiramon obtained Heveli Tajpúr and Mothurapúr, and had two sons, Sib and Kaliprosad: the former had no issue; the latter adopted a son Mohendro Narayon, who lately sold Mothurapúr, but retains Tajpúr. (2) Udoymon the son of Jogotbollobh obtained the *zemindary* of Kholora; he had two sons Dhir and Kritichondros, who divided the property equally. Dhir had two sons, Syamsundor and Bhorotchondro. These have not divided their half of Kholora, and Bhorot manages for his nephew Nornarayon, for his brother is dead. He is a very prudent man, and although he lives in a very respectable manner, and has a house (Sodabroto), where all travellers are entertained one day, he is improving his estate; and has purchased several lots that belonged to the Dinajpúr family. He resides at Horipúr, and takes his title from that place. His uncle Kritichondro, who received one-half of Kholora, left it to his 4 sons Durga, Gauri, Gongga, and Janokíprosad, who live together, and have also purchased some lots of Dinajpúr. (3) Lokmon, son of Jogotbollobh, retained the family seat of Churamon, and possessed pergunnah Delaworpúr. He adopted a son Bhowaniprosad, whose sons Chondi and Guruprosads are now in possession, and have divided their estates, which are partly in this district and partly in Puroniya. One is a clever man who has purchased several lots of Dinajpúr, the other is entirely given up to superstition and is hastening to ruin. His *dewan*, an old dependent of the family, did not altogether deny that he was cheating him; and defended himself on the plea, that if he did not, another would. He indeed observed, that his own father would take advantage of such a simpleton.

Bhuyihara, No. 68, belonged to Viswonath, succeeded by Sukdev, Loknath, and Krishnochondro, who sold the pergunnah about the beginning of this century.

Surahor Monkoyí, No. 69, belongs to Guruprosad, a Kayostho. I have already mentioned this *zemindar* as a very deserving person. The first landholder of his family, was Krishno-kanto, succeeded by Kasinath, by Rongolal, and by the present possessor.

Kasimpúr, No. 70, has belonged for some generations to a Muhammedan family, which has divided into four branches.

Nos. 71, 72, 73, 74, for 60 or 70 years, belonged to the Qanungoe or Register-general of Bengal. The two former and the last have been sold, but the third is still retained by the family, which resides near Murshedabad.

No. 75, called Baishazári, or 22 thousand, from the number of bigahs it is supposed to contain, is the estate belonging to the monument of Mukhdum Saheb at Peruya. It is not assessed, and is managed by a person appointed by Government.

No. 76, called Chyehazarí, or six thousand, is the estate belonging to the tomb of Kotub Saheb of Peruya, and is managed by the descendants of the saint.

Radhabollobhpúr, No. 77, seems to have been acquired from the Dinajpúr family by Gonggagovind Singho, who in the Government of Mr. Hastings held the then important office of Company's *dewan*. It is said, that it was given as a bribe; but that may be an idle report. The *dewan*, however, was a remarkably well-informed man, and the Rajas had many secrets which they might be very unwilling to reach the ears of Government. The villages formed part of various pergunnahs, which were erected into a new one by the *dewan*, and now belong to his grandson.

Kantonogor, No. 78, is an estate, which like the former, was made up by Kanto Babú, who was the private *dewan* of Mr. Hastings, and almost every *zemindar* in the district seems to have contributed. The new pergunnah contains 240 *mouzas*, and its managers appear to have a peculiar aversion to Europeans, and are uncommonly inhospitable. It is the property of a boy, grandson to the *dewan*.

Kakjal, No. 79, for about a century has belonged to a Muhammedan family, that has divided into two branches.

Mosida, No. 80, is said to have belonged to a Dinonath, whose ancestors have possessed it for 96 generations; but I can learn nothing to support this farther than vague report. About the year 1775, it was sold to Doleb Roy, an officer of revenue in the district, to which it then belonged. He was succeeded by his son Syam Singho, who was succeeded by Nilkontho, a son of his uncle. He was succeeded by his son Deviprosad, who has left it to an adopted son, that is now in possession.

I have already mentioned the Jahangirpúr family, as joint proprietor of Nos. 38 and 39, but it also possessed entirely the pergunnahs, No. 81 and 83, and a portion of No. 84, which were it not divided, would be a handsome estate. The first *zemindar* was a Brahmon who obtained a waste from Shah Jahangir (1605-1627), on condition of clearing it; for it was then entirely overgrown with woods. This constituted pergunnah Jahangirpúr. The others are later acquisitions. It is said, that the estate continued undivided for the first four generations, which must have been uncommonly long, for in the 5th generation, there being seven brothers, Kanto Babú, the *dewan* of Mr. Hastings, procured the undivided transmission of the estate to one of them; and is said to have received ⅛ part of the whole for his services, and this now forms a part of Kantonogor: but the natives are so fond of these scandalous reports, that little reliance can be placed on what they say. The estate has now subdivided into four distinct branches, each containing several members. These Brahmons have never been educated at a school, and can just read and write the vulgar language, so that they would have been totally destitute of any appearance of literature, had not they been taught by rote a few verses of Songskrito, and informed of their meaning, so that they may be occasionally repeated without absurdity. They seem to pass their time chiefly in sleeping, eating, picking their teeth, and other such recreations, and in listening to singers and story-tellers, and very rarely go out of the house.

The Jahangirpúr family has also procured $\frac{11}{16}$ of Chura pergunnah, No. 84, and the remainder is divided among six petty *zemindars.*

Barbukpúr, No. 85, was formerly divided into 12 small *zemindaries.* The occupants were deprived of their office by Jafer Ali Khan, Subadar of Bengal, who gave it to eight families that now retain possession.

Khorida Selvorish, No. 86, belonged for some generations to the ancestors of Budiojuma Chaudhurí. This family resides at Bogura in Rajshahi, and although part of the estate has been sold, the family is still very rich.

Khorida Barbukpúr, No. 87, and Khorida Chhirabazee, No. 88, formed part of an immense estate, which was given by Jafer Khan, a Subadar of Bengal, to a Brahmon who, at the expense of an act of treachery to his master, rendered the prince a most essential service. He was employed by the Register-general of the province to keep his seal, and the Register had refused to affix to the accounts this necessary sign of his approbation of the Subadar's conduct, who was in the utmost perplexity, until the keeper privately brought him the seals. The Nator *zemindary,* probably the largest private estate in the world, was the reward of this act, and these pergunnahs formed a part. One of the rogue's successors made a present of these pergunnahs to a very holy Kulin Brahmon, and they are now in the possession of Kalikanto and Rajendro, his grandsons. The greater part of the Nator estate has lately been sold to pay the debts of the family; such unwieldy possessions leading to certain destruction.

Soruppúr, No. 89, Amvarí, No. 90, and Sabek Soruppúr, No. 91, formerly belonged to a Raní Sotyowoti, widow of Roghunath, who possessed 8 pergunnahs in the neighbourhood. This lady falling in arrears of revenue, Ramjibon, the brother and successor of the knave who founded the Nator family, paid the money, and took the two first mentioned pergunnahs. They have lately been sold to pay the debts of the adopted grandson of Ramjiwon. The remainder of her estates, in which was included Sabek Suruppúr, was left by Raní Sotyowoti to Ram Roy Sandel, a Barondro Brahmin, and a relation of her husband; and his great-grandsons Kalikanto and Rajendro are now in possession of this pergunnah, and reside in the Rongpúr district.

Bobenpúr, No. 92, has belonged to the ancestors of Ramanondo, a Rarhí Brahmon, for eight generations; Ramanondo possessed it and several other estates in common with three other relations. They are of a very saving disposition, and made several purchases.

Joytaluk, No. 93, belonged to a Rarhí Brahmin who left two sons, the eldest received $\frac{9}{16}$, and left part to his son Krishnochondro now alive, and sold part to pay debt. The younger son, Moní Chaudhurí, received $\frac{7}{16}$ of his father's property. He became a notorious house-breaker, and has lately been liberated from confinement, having been a convict for 7 years.

Sultanpúr Ghoraghat, No. 94, for seven or eight generations has belonged to a Mahommedan family. The present representative is Chamalí Bibí, who lives in a part of the pergunnah that is situated in Rongpúr. She is a widow of the late *zemindar.*

Ghagra, No. 95, belongs to a family of whom I received no account.

Baror, No. 96, and the two last pergunnahs, I believe, form part of the estate which belongs to the Krishnogunj Raja, who resides in the district of Puroniya.

I am by no means satisfied with the accuracy of this list, as one furnished by the *dewan* of the Collector contained eight pergunnahs, of which I heard nothing during my journey. These are as follows: Amdohor, Alihat, Siksohas, Taherpúr, Khupie, Doyanogor, Bhitorbondo, and Rukminipúr. It is more extraordinary, that I found 16 pergunnahs, Nos. 6, 27, 37, 39, 41, 47, 50, 51, 52, 55, 56, 61, 74, which are not mentioned in the *dewan's* list, and some of these are of considerable size. It can scarcely be supposed, that the official list is imperfect, and it is probable, that the *dewan* was not at the pains to take an accurate copy; for such people are extremely neglectful towards every person of whom they are not afraid.

BOOK VI.

OF THE STATE OF ARTS AND COMMERCE IN DINAJPUR.

CHAPTER I.

FINE ARTS.

THE style of private edifices, that is proper and peculiar to Bengal, consists of a hut with a pent-roof, constructed of two sloping sides, which meet in a ridge forming the segment of a circle, so that it has a resemblance to a boat when overturned, and is probably of the same shape with the Mapalia of the Numidians. This kind of hut, it is said, from being peculiar to Bengal, is called by the natives Bangola; a name which has been somewhat altered by Europeans, and applied by them to all their buildings in the cottage style, although none of them have the proper shape, and many of them are excellent brick-houses, adorned with the forms of Grecian architecture.

Among the natives, the poor man has one hut for himself and cattle, and richer men increase the number without altering the plan of the building, and there is no contrivance by which a person can go from one apartment to the other, without being exposed to the sun and rain.

Where the materials admit, the walls of the hut are made of mud, and the floor is always raised a foot or two above the level of the plain, but not always so high as to be above water in the rainy season; so that a platform of bambus is then constructed at one end of the hut, and upon this the family sit and sleep, while they must wade through the mud to reach the door. Where the soil is too loose for making walls, the sides of the hut are formed of hurdles, which are usually made of straw, grass or reeds, confined between sticks or split bambus that are tied together. In the better kind of houses, in place of straw, hurdles made of mats are used, or those of straw are plastered with dung and clay; and in doing this the natives display the only neatness, that is to be observed in their buildings. The frame of the house usually consists entirely of bambus tied together. It is only in the houses of very wealthy persons, that wooden posts and beams are used; and these are never either polished or painted, and seldom fastened by nails.

Sometimes the beams support a floor made of clay laid upon bambus, and in general this is merely intended to lessen the danger from fire, as the floor will give some little time for the people to remove their children and effects. In a very few houses a trap-stair leads up to the apartment or garret above, and it is then inhabited.

The door is in general the only aperture in the hut, crevices excepted, and is usually shut by a hurdle (*Jhanp*), which is tied to the upper part of the door, and falls down like a valve. Wooden doors that fold from the side, are only used by the great. There are very few houses, that have any openings like windows to admit air or light.

If the house is intended for a shop, one side of the roof is extended four or five feet beyond the wall, is supported by a row of bambus, and forms a gallery (*Hatina* or *Osara*) which serves as a shop.

Another kind of hut, called Chauyari, has been introduced, and this is the form which Europeans have adopted in their cottages, when they use a thatched roof. It consists of four plain sides, which, if the building is square, are triangular, and meet in a point; but if the cottage is long, the two ends of the roof only are triangular, and the two sides (which are triangles truncated at the apex) form a straight ridge. Europeans have made great improvements on this kind of buildings, have surrounded it with a gallery to exclude the heat, have introduced windows, have divided it into convenient apartments, and have suspended cloth ceilings to free them from the vermin that occupy the thatch. These luxuries seem totally unknown to the natives of this district. Their Chauyaries are built of the same materials with their Bangolas, but being used chiefly among the rich, have usually wooden posts, and many of them have garrets that are inhabited, and have openings by way of windows.

The wealthy, such as great landholders and principal manufacturers, have in general brick-houses, and are fast imitating the European fashion of building, such as has been introduced into Bengal. It is alleged in the Ayeen Akbery, that in the time of Akber, even the houses of the great in Bengal were built entirely of bambus. I am inclined, however, to doubt the authority of Abul Fazil in many things, and among others in this. That the great in Bengal may have then built Bangolas entirely of bambus, with great neatness and very commodious, is highly probable; but that they had not also brick houses is not likely. In fact, tradition points out the ruins of brick edifices, that belonged to the natives of this district before the Muhammedan invasion; and the appearance of some of these ruins clearly indicates that they were dwelling houses, and neither temples nor forts. In the older brick-houses, the Moorish style, with wretched narrow steps rather than stairs, low roofs, small apartments, much minute carving, and small windows has been adopted. In some new houses a rude imitation of the Grecian architecture makes its appearance; the rooms are larger and better aired, and more furniture has been introduced.

Among public edifices, those dedicated to religion are by far the most conspicuous. In my account of Peruya and its antiquities, I have mentioned nearly all that occurs to me concerning the religious buildings of the Mohammedans: small mosques are numerous in the district, and consist of a cube covered with one dome, or of a parallelopid covered with several. The minaret, which is the greatest ornament in this kind of building, has not been introduced, and the whole style may be considered as in the most rude state.

The most numerous and simple Hindú places of worship are called the st'hans or abodes of such or such a deity, and are merely heaps of earth or square terraces, which are generally placed under trees. Sometimes as an object of worship, there is an uncut stone, at others there is an image cut in relief; but very often the only representation of the Deity is a small mass of clay, a little painted.

Most of these places being dedicated to the Soktis, or female destructive spirits, a stake is placed before the heap, for fastening the head of the animals, that are to be sacrificed.

A more improved place of worship consists of a thatched hut, called a Mondop. In the greater part even of these there are no images, except a lump of clay, and at holidays a rude image is made of the same material, and is thrown into the river, when the festival is at an end. The walls of these huts, when made of clay, are often painted with rude and horrible figures of the gods, and equally distorted representations are formed of the *sola* by the makers of garlands and artificial flowers; but both are considered as merely ornamental, and are not objects of worship. I have seen one building of this kind, which was said to have cost 16,000 rupees. The size was inconsiderable, but the walls were made of wood, carved with a most patient minuteness, in which however neither taste nor decency had been at all consulted.

Near many of these Mondops, and even near many houses, for the worship of the family gods, are erected the most rude form of the *mongchos*, or stages on which the images are placed on the (Yatras) days of procession, while the people sport before them. These simple *mongchos* consist of a small square terrace of earth divided into stages each less than the one below.

The next step at improvement is to construct a Mondop of brick for the usual residence of the deity. This is commonly a small square building with a flat roof. A temple of this kind has seldom any other *mongcho* than one of earth; but it has usually an image that is the object of worship, and commonly a house for the Pujari or officiating priest. The most elegant in the district, that I saw, is at Yogighopa, of which a drawing has been given No. 11. This is open above; the image is placed on the small altar seen through the door, and is covered by a dome.

The next step is to add a kind of pyramid to the roof of the temple, which then becomes a Mondir. The Mondirs are often cased with carved tiles, and at any rate are plastered on the outside, and the ornaments on the plaster in general possess some taste. Many Mondirs built of late, instead of the pyramid, have adopted the dome of the mosque, probably because workmen skilled to construct the pyramid could not be readily procured.

Advancing still further, the temple for the usual residence of the image is enlarged, and in addition to the central pyramid one is added at each corner, and the building is then said to be a Pongchorotno, or to have five ornaments: or, if enlarged a little more, the roof is divided into two stages, each having a pyramid at each of its corners. It then becomes a Novorotno, or building of nine ornaments. Such buildings are very expensive, as in this district they are almost always incased with carved tiles. The accompanying drawing (No. 36) of a Pongchorotno at Gopalganj near Dinajpur, built 75 years ago, by the mother of Raja Ramnath, will give a better idea of the style than any description. Only it must be observed, that, in buildings so frittered away into minute ornaments and parts, the drawing looks much better than the building itself, especially as no Hindu temple, that I have seen, is kept tolerably neat. The interior of the building is to the last degree wretched; there is no light, except what comes through the door, and the masses of brick, that are necessary to support such a roof, leave scarcely any cavity.

The first step towards improving the *mongcho* is to build it of brick, in several decreasing stages, nearly of the same form with that made of earth. A stair leads up to the highest stage, in which a small apartment is made for receiving the image at processions.

The next improvement is in each stage to have a chamber surrounded by a gallery, in which there are several doors or windows. Then at each corner of each stage a *rotno* or pyramidical ornament is added. The most finished kind consists of 12 sides with 24 *rotnos*, disposed in two rows, and one in the centre over the apartment in which the image is placed. The drawing of the one at Gopalganj (No. 37) will give a proper idea of this kind of building. Although it is of a considerable size, and cost an immense sum (it is said £20,000), there is no apartment in it above 12 feet in its greatest dimensions, and the stair is steep, perfectly dark, and will not admit a man to walk with both shoulders equally advanced.

The temples here and in the south differ entirely in structure, the latter approaching much nearer to the Grecian or rather Egyptian style. This is probably in a great measure owing to the nature of the material; for the long masses of granite, so easily procured in the south, lead naturally to columns, flat roofs and entablatures, while bricks lead to arches and pointed roofs. The style of ornament, however, is nearly the same in both parts of India. Some neat foliages possess considerable merit; the rest consists of numerous small mouldings, and monstrous distorted representations of the deities and their adventures, among which obscene figures are often a conspicuous part.

The number of public edifices of a civil nature seems never to have been considerable. One inn (*serai*) at Maldeh now in ruins, and a few small bridges form the whole. The bridges have very small arches, and none are employed on any thing like a river, they have been merely made over rivulets.

The fortresses seem to have been equally rude, and to have consisted in a straight rampart and ditch with a few outworks at the gate. The only one that appears to have been more strongly defended is Uttor Gegriho, as I have already mentioned. The number has always been inconsiderable.

The accompanying plan (drawing, No. 36), drawn by the chief architect in the district, of the house and buildings of Baidyonath Chaudhuri, who took a pleasure in shewing me all his works with the utmost politeness, will show the progress made in this branch of science.

Wishing to know, what skill he might have in geometry, I requested him to show me how he laid down the foundation of an octagon building, such as are in common use. He had a pair of ruinous European compasses, and a square, but no rule nor scale; and I soon found, that the others might as well have been omitted in his apparatus, and were designed merely for shew. His only scale was his arm, his only instruments a line and some pegs. He began by measuring off four equal portions of the line, fixing a peg at each; he then placed these in the ground so as to distend his four portions of rope into a parallelogram. He then moved the pegs backwards and forwards, until his diagonals were equal, he then had formed a square. He then divided each side into four equal parts, which he found by doubling one of the sides twice. He then truncated each angle by passing a line between the division next it on each side. He thus had an octagon, but four of the sides were shorter than the others. This objection having been made, he said, that the four alternate sides having doors in them ought to be larger, otherwise the building would not look well;

but being desired to make all the sides equal, he went round, adding small equal portions to each alternate short side, until he found by experiment, that he had succeeded. He looked upon it as impossible to lay down an octagon, that should have all its sides equal, and each side of a given size; all he attempted was to lay down an octagon within a given square. He said, that he could also lay down any figure of an even number of sides,—figures of an uneven number of sides, such as pentagons, he considered as far beyond human skill.

Sculpture and statuary are in a still more rude state than architecture. The figure of Gonès, which accompanies this account (No. 1) will serve to give an idea of their stone images, and this is reckoned very handsome. There are however many stones, on which images of the gods of small dimensions have been carved in high relievo, and these are a good deal superior to Gonès, although they are still very rude imitations of the human form, and are said to have been brought from the west of India many ages ago. One of them is represented in No. 12. The carvings on tiles, with which many of the religious buildings are incrusted, are still more imperfect. The images of brass and the metals are as bad as those of stones, and some which are made of potters-ware, much more rude than I could have conceived, that any grown person could have formed.

Painting is still at a lower ebb than sculpture.

To the ear of an European the native music appears in general harsh and disagreeable, and to men of science it is altogether intolerable. Although I am not at all nice, I confess, that I was much satisfied in travelling through the district to find, that the people had less turn for this pleasure than is usual among the natives, and I cannot say, that in any other part of the country I was ever so little disturbed by its noise. The performers notwithstanding are pretty numerous, and the variety of noises, which they can make, is considerable.

The highest description of musicians consists of bands of instrumental music, which accompany the voice of girls who sing and dance. In this district there are very few persons of this kind, and they do not exceed 20 sets. The two Hindu castes who follow the profession, the *rumjani* and *kangchoni*, have not found their way from the west of India to this district; and those who follow it at present are common prostitutes, that have learned to sing, and employ musicians to accompany their voice. As usual, their motions in dancing are slow, lifeless, and without grace; their greatest art is to jingle in time to the music, some chains *(ghungru)*, which are tied round their ancles. The girls are called *bayi*, and there are usually two or three in a set. The musicians, called *somaji*, are three or four in number; one performs on a small drum *(tubla)*, the others on a kind of fiddle *(sarangi)*.

Boys taught to dance and sing, and dressed in an effeminate manner, are in great request among the Hindus, and about 20 sets are employed in Maldeh and its vicinity, where the people are most luxurious. In other parts of the district there are no such persons. These boys, called *(bhottiyas,)* are usually suspected of very disgraceful practices; when they grow up, they perform on the musical instruments that belong to the set, which are the same as when girls dance or sing, only another kind of fiddle called *(sarinda)*, is sometimes used.

Most of the other musicians belong to sets, that are employed in religious ceremonies.

The sets of muscians who sing the praises of Bishohori, the goddess of snakes, or who are called Monggol Chondi, or who sing the praises of Mohummedan saints *(Pirer Gayon)*, usually consists of seven or eight persons; chief or sirdar, who has a Thibet cow's tail *(chamor)* in one hand, and a pair of small cymbal (*mondira*) in the other; six *pail* or assistants have small cymbals in their hands, and tie round their ancles, rings of bell metal, which make a noise as they dance. One boy is often kept to sing and dance; but not always. All these persons sing and dance; but two others *(bayen)* beat on large drums called *mridongs*. In this district there may be 350 of these sets.

There are probably about 150 sets, which sing the praises of Krishno (*songkirton.*) Each consists of a chief, who has a small drum (*khonjuri*), or a pair of cymbals (*korotal*), and of three or four *(pail)* assistants who use cymbals, and of one or two (*bayen*) drummers, who beat the *mridongs*.

Some persons (*zari*) during the Moharram, are employed to sing the praises of Fatima, the daughter of Mohammed, and of her unfortunate sons Hoseyn and Hassan. They are not accompanied by music.

It is however at marriages, religious processions, and such great solemnities, that the full din of music arises, and that a herd of the lowest dregs of the people are employed to rend the ear with these formidable implements of noise.

1 Dhol,
2 Tikera,
3 Dhak,
4 Madol,
5 Dogor,
6 Kara,
7 Jorghayi,
8 Nagara,
} Drums.

9 Kangsi or gongs.
10 Sanayi, a kind of hautboy.
11 Singga, or buffaloe's horns.
12 Turi, or brass trumpets.

Every man makes the most of his instrument, and pays little or no attention to his comrade's.

Men often amuse themselves by singing hymns or love songs, accompanied by small drums (*dholok*, and *pakhoyaj*); but it is considered as very disgraceful for a modest woman to sing, or play on any musical instrument. The only time when such a practice is admitted, is among the Mohammedans at the Moharram, when women are allowed to join in the praises of Fatima and of her sons.

A kind of men called *akras* are strolling musicians, and sing hymns and love songs to the rich, and accompany their voice with a pair of small cymbals (*mondira*), with the small drums called (*dholok* and *pakhoyaj*), or with two kinds of guitar (*tombura* and *setar*). Many young men, for amusement, play on these instruments, and accompany them with the voice.

CHAPTER II.

OF THE COMMON ARTS.

I SHALL in the first place give an account of the artists, that may be considered as employed about the persons of the natives, in cleaning, clothing, ornamenting, amusing, and feeding them. I shall then proceed to those who work in the metals, in timber, and in the earths. I shall in the third place treat of all those employed in making cloths of various kinds, and shall conclude with the two important manufactures of sugar and indigo.

SECTION 1.—*Personal Artists.*

1. Washermen are not so numerous in this district as in many others. The people are in general either too poor or too slovenly to employ them, and it is only persons in easy circumstances, that use bleached linen. The common people occasionally go into a tank or river, and wash the clothes in which they are dressed; for in general they have little change of linen. In this district the washermen use chiefly ashes, and they have no contrivance, such as a hot iron or a mangle, for making the linen smooth. The only bleachers in the district are those employed by the Company at Maldeh. The common washermen are almost all Hindus of a very low tribe. They have no capital. In the whole district there may be about 650 houses, of which 250, including the Company's bleachers, reside in Maldeh. All are paid by the piece. The bleachers make high wages, five or six rupees a month; but the common washermen do not earn above 1½ rupee.

2. Almost all the tailors are Moslems, for the needle seems to have been totally unknown to the Hindús. In this district, although the Mohammedans are numerous, the tailors are few in number and little employed, for the lower Mohammedans have entirely adopted the Hindú dress, and wrap their clothes round them as made by the weaver. The higher Hindús, on the contrary, have in a great measure adapted the Mohammedan fashions, especially those who are employed in office, or when they visit European gentlemen; and the tailors are chiefly confined to the towns af Dinajpur and Maldeh, in which there may be rather more than 100 families, and perhaps an equal number is scattered through the district. They have no capital, and usually work by the piece. A family, for the women also sew, may however earn four rupees a month, which is a decent subsistence.

3. All the barbers are Hindús, and are a pure tribe, and pretty numerous, for in this district there are between 1000 and 1,200 families. They attend at all markets, where they shave and cut the nails of those who employ them. The usual hire is 10 *gandahs*, or about the eighth part of an anna. Farmers and labourers shave only once a month, and generally pay the barber in grain. Rich men often keep barbers as servants, both as they are pure, and as they can shave them, pick their ears, cut their nails, knead their bodies, and crack their joints, of which operations the natives are very fond. A servant of this kind is allowed one rupee a month, and food and clothing. Those who work by the job make tolerable wages, and live easily. They shave without soap. Persons after mourning are shaved and pay liberally; so do also bridegrooms on the day of their marriage, as on that important occasion particular pains must be taken. Ten days after a woman has been delivered, the nails of both her and the child are cut by the barber. No native woman in Bengal, except a shameless prostitute, will allow her hair to be cut, such care of her person being deemed incompatible with modesty.

4. In Dinajpúr a few people are employed in making a tooth powder called *misi*, this is composed of the *Myrobalans* called *Bellirica* and *Chebula* by Gærtner (*boyera* and *horitoki*), of two other fruits called *majuphol* and *toi*, of green vitriol, sulphate of iron, and of iron filings. It is reckoned to strengthen the gums, and when applied in a certain manner with beetle, and some other substances, it renders the teeth entirely black, which is considered as an ornament. The persons who make this powder are usually poor old women.

5. The married Hindu women use red-lead as an ornament; but instead of painting their cheeks, like our belles, they rub it on their foreheads. This piece of vanity is not permitted to widows. The destructive female deities however, con-

sume a considerable quantity, as a present of this kind is supposed to be agreeable. In this district there are two persons who manufacture this pigment *(sindur)*, but I had no opportunity of examining their process. I understood, however, that they were poor and unskilled in their art. Their capital was supposed not to exceed ten rupees.

6. Female ornament gives employment to a great many other artists. Among these are the persons called Lahari or Luri, who make rings of shell-lac, which the Mohammedan women wear round their arms, and which are called *churi*. They are of various colours, and are in fact a hard sealing wax. The sealing wax indeed that is used in Bengal, is commonly made by the Lahari, for in a warm climate the European kind is useless. The people employed in this way may occupy 100 houses. Four or five rupees are a sufficient capital. They can make about two annas a day, or four rupees a month.

7. The Hindu females use bracelets made of shells, and this gives employment to many people, who are called Songkhobonick or Sangkhari. Of these there may be almost 200 houses in the district. The shells are brought from Calcutta by a merchant of Kumarkhali, and are cut, polished, and painted by the artists of this district. These require a capital of at least 50 rupees ; and a few are rich, as they have a stock of four or five hundred rupees, with which they purchase many shells and employ labourers to work by the piece. The shell is cut with a semicircular saw, and polished by rubbing it on sand-stone. The workmen are very inferior to those of Calcutta ; but no tradesmen in the district make better wages, nor have larger capitals. They make their goods chiefly without being commissioned, and retail them for ready money in their shops, or give them to petty traders, who retail them at markets. A pair of bracelets costs from one to seven rupees.

8. All Hindus must wear beads, and those of Vishnu's side ought to wear such as are made of wood, or of various seeds. The people who make them are religious mendicants, so that it would be difficult to separate the profits of their two professions. The number in the district may be about 100 houses.

9. The makers of garlands, of artificial flowers, and of ornaments prepared from the *sola*, (Malakar,) are a numerous class ; but very poor. In this district there are probably near 300 houses. They form garlands of flowers, which they collect partly in the fields, and partly from gardens. These are sold, and are used by the wealthy both for pleasure, and as offerings to the gods. The *sola* I have already described. The ornaments made of this plant are very gaudy, being stained with glaring colours, and mixed with tinsel; but the workmanship is very rude. The same artists make numerous ornaments, that are used as toys by children, and at all processions, and that are suspended in places of worship. Some are very large, such as the biers which the Mohammedans carry about on the Moharram, and the stages on which the Hindus place their images at the *pújahs* of Durga, Kali and Kartik. All these are committed to the waters, when the ceremony is over, so that on each occasion the artists find new employment.

The colours which these people employ are orpiment, vermilion, white-lead, red-lead, verdigris, and a white talcose earth called *Kori*, which is brought from the west of India, and is similar to that which is prepared at Moilcotay, of which I have given an account in my travels into Mysore.

The garland-makers use also ink, such as is employed by the natives, and the best kind is prepared as follows :—Take twenty sicca weight of rice, parch it in a pot, until it becomes quite black ; put it into 60 sicca weight of cold water, and allow it to remain a quarter of an hour. Then pour off the water, and mix it with lamp-black, by rubbing it in an earthen pot with a stick or wooden pestle. One sicca weight (179½ grains) of lampblack is sufficient. For fine writings a little gum of the *Mimosa Indica* (trees No. 59) is added. What is commonly sold in shops, however, is made of soot in place of lamp-black.

The garland-makers use also some vegetable dyes. The inner bark of the *Nyctanthes arbor-tristis* (trees No. 16), is beaten in a mortar. Its juice is expressed, mixed with lime, and by means of a brush is applied to the *sola*, to which it imparts a red colour.

Another red is prepared by 12 parts of the same bark, with 16 parts of the inner bark of the *Artocarpus* (trees, No. 103), and eight parts of water. These are well beaten, and then the water is expressed, and used as a dye.

The glue which these artists employ is made by boiling the inner bark of the tree, No. 107, then beating it, and expressing the water, which has a glutinous quality.

The tinsel which these artists use is partly tin-foil of various colours, and partly plates of Mica.

10. In many districts those who make the mats, on which the natives sit and sleep, and who make umbrellas, form a class that contains a considerable number of artists. In this district, however, I heard only of five houses at Dinajpur, who could be considered as belonging to this profession, and their work is very coarse.

The art of making an umbrella, that can be folded, is here quite unknown, and indeed seems to have been equally so in every part of Bengal, until introduced by Europeans at Calcutta. In this district almost the only mats that are made are composed of a species of *Scirpus* called Nagormatta (see reeds, No. 13.) The stems are split and interwoven, and form a mat which is soft, but destitute of neatness. Poor people make them at their leisure hours. The umbrellas that are most commonly used, are made by the next class of artists.

11. The Patoni, basket-makers, or workers in bambu and ratan, are a very low tribe of Hindus, who are however both useful and numerous. In this district there may be from 1000 to 1,200 families. They are miserably poor, and do not require any capital; for two or three annas will buy more materials, than a family can work between one market and another. Both men and women are equally capable of working the baskets, and both carry them to market, where in general they sell them for ready money; the women however, take the greatest share of this trouble. Their poverty is chiefly owing to their lavishness; for they are much addicted to intoxication. It is however a good deal alleviated by their keeping swine, which afford them a wholesome nourishment.

The goods which they usually make, are as follows:

1. *Chupri*, baskets for carrying provisions.
2. *Jhuri*, baskets for carrying earth or manure.
3. *Dhuchuni*, baskets for washing rice.
4. *Dala*, flat baskets used in shops for holding cowries or goods, and for carrying fruit and vegetables.
5. *Dál*, large close wrought baskets for preserving grain.
6. *Kula*, fans for winnowing corn.
7. *Chaloni*, serves for cleaning grain or flour.
8. *Don*, hemispherical baskets wrought very close, which serve for measuring grain, and among the poor as vessels, for eating and drinking.
9. *Petera*, baskets with lids, which serve for trunks.

10. *Jakoyi*, fish traps.
11. *Pinjora* or *Khancha*, bird-cages.
12. *Jharu*, brooms.
13. *Chatayi*, mats, made of bambus which are split on one side, and then laid open into a kind of thin planks, which are interwoven so as to form the mats. These are the principal article in demand, and the only one that is exported. In all good huts these mats are placed over the frame of the roof under the thatch, and, where there is not a clay soil, they form the side walls. They also are used in the fences, which enclose the yards of those who are in easy circumstances, and in all boats they form the roof to exclude rain, the cover of the platform on which the people work, and the donage by which the goods are kept dry. The demand is therefore very great. These mats are of two kinds; one four cubits by three, which at Dinajpúr cost four rupees a hundred ; the others are two cubits by one and a half, and sell for two rupees the hundred.—These people make also the umbrellas, of which almost every family in the rainy season has one or two. The top consists of a double net work of split bambus, which confines leaves of the *sal* or of the banyan tree for turning the rain. This head is fastened to a bambu handle, the upper end of which is split, and the divisions separated so as to render it more easily fixed. The whole is extremely rude.

These goods are always prepared by the Patonis for sale ; but if required, they can make many others: such as fine and coarse skreens (*chiek* and *chali*), chairs (*chauki*), and stools (*moras*). In some parts they are employed to make the bambu frames of houses, but in most parts this operation is performed by the common farmers, and by their servants. In some parts also they thatch, which art in many districts is considered as a separate profession (*ghorami*) ; but in the greater part of Dinajpúr every man thatches and builds his own house, either with his own hands or by means of his servants. The (*chatiya*) or mats are the only articles, in which the artists of Dinajpúr excel, and that seems to be chiefly owing to the goodness of the material. The mats made in most parts of Bengal consist of reeds ; but in Dinajpur they are made of bambus.—The demand for them is often so considerable, that merchants are under the necessity of making advances, for in this country no considerable quantity of any one thing can be procured to purchase for ready money.

12. Paper is made entirely by Mohammedans, who seem to have introduced the art. Before their arrival the natives in their writings appear to have used only the leaves or bark of trees. In this district there are between 80 and 100 families employed in making paper, and they are nearly adequate to supply the demand. The quality is very inferior even to that made near Calcutta. It is brown, rough, uneven, spotted, fibrous, full of holes and brittle, ink sinks into it, and insects devour it with avidity. The people who make it are in decent circumstances, and require little or no capital. They usually carry it to the markets just as made, and petty traders buy it from the manufacturers by wholesale, and afterwards retail it. The sheets are usually 24 inches long by 16 wide, and are doubled twice ; 24 sheets form a quire, and the manufacturers usually sell 10 or 12 quires for a rupee.

The material is the *pat* in its rough state. A sufficient number of bundles is thrown into a large jar, that is sunk in the ground, and they are covered with a mixture of lime and water in which they are allowed to soak for from two to nine days, according to the heat of the weather ; the hotter that is, the less time being required. The bundles are then dried, and the lime that adheres is separated from them by beating and shaking. They are then moistened with water, and beaten with a *dhenki*, which has a cap of iron, and falls upon a stone slab. While it is beating, the *pát* is occasionally moistened, until it is reduced to a kind of pulp. This part of the operation, which is the only one attended with labour, is performed entirely by the women. The pulp after coming from the mortar is thoroughly washed, and a portion of it is thrown into a wide-mouthed vat made of potter's-ware, that is sunk to the level of the yard. A large proportion of water is added, and they are stirred until the pulp is properly diffused; but little pains is bestowed on this, which seems to be the chief cause of several of the imperfections that are in the manufacture. In fact the pulp, with a very little stirring, is allowed to soak four or five hours, and is then wrought into paper. The workman's mould is made of bambus split fine, and tied together parallel to each other, and this is extended by a moveable frame, made also of bambu, which serves as a ledge to confine the pulp. The workman holding his mould with one hand stirs up the pulp with the other, then immerses his mould, and takes up a quantity sufficient to make a sheet. When he has allowed the water to escape, he lays aside the frame, and turning over the mould places his new sheet of paper above those that he had previously made, and he repeats the operation, until the pulp in the vat is exhausted. In this heap the paper is allowed to dry. It is then taken sheet by sheet, and immersed in a decoction of starch made of rice, and having been dried is placed on a smooth plank, and rubbed with a round stone. This is to serve instead of hot pressing, and in some measure effaces the marks of the mould, and renders the side of the paper that is next the plank tolerably smooth. The stone that I saw was a water worn piece of granite, far from being polished.

13. In one division I found three men who lived by binding books, such as are used by the natives for keeping accounts; these books are usually about 16 inches long, 6 inches wide, and 1 inch thick, and are stitched together at one end like some old books of music. The cover is usually made of coarse red cotton cloth. The learned still adhere in general to stringing the leaves of their books on two threads, which pass through the middle of each sheet; and through two boards that serve for a cover. This mode, which was fit for books made of leaves, is exceedingly awkward and destructive with paper; but old habits are difficult to eradicate, and proper binding is making daily advances.

14. The manufacture of leather is by no means so thriving, as it might be made, probably owing to the very low rank of the artists. These are of three kinds: the first, and by far the most numerous, are called *muchi* and *chamar*, and are tanners and saddlers, and make shoes and trunks. In the whole of this district there may be about 200 houses of these artists.

The hides which they dress are those of oxen or kine that have died a natural death, and those of goats and sheep. The Hindus here use the skin of the ox without scruple, although strictly speaking, this is contrary to law. Buffalo hides, and the skins of deer and of the wild hog, are unaccountably neglected.

Neat's hides are first put into lime and water to separate the hair, they are then washed. Take a pot, put into it five seers (96 sa. wt.=lb. 12 ⅓) of powdered leaves of Lodh (trees, No. 80), and an equal quantity of water; then put in two washed skins, and let them remain two days. Then in two other pots repeat this process on the same skins. The skins having been thus tanned are dried, and are beaten twice in a wooden mortar, each time having been previously moistened with water

The skin is of the usual brown colour of tanned leather, and may be made black by rubbing it with green vitriol. It serves for the soles of shoes, and for covering the baskets with lids, which are called *petaras*, and which are used in place of trunks. Raw neat's hides cost $\frac{1}{8}$ of a rupee ; the artists cannot tell the weight, but they are small and thin. When dressed they sell for $\frac{1}{4}$ of a rupee.

Goats' skins are those mostly used. Each costs $\frac{1}{16}$ of a rupee, and when prepared sells for $\frac{1}{4}$ of a rupee, if dyed red, white, or yellow; and for $\frac{1}{8}$ of a rupee, if stained black or brown. In order to separate the hair ten of them are put in a pot with some lime and water, and allowed to remain there from 25 to 30 days; each skin requires above a pound of lime. The ten skins, when freed from hair, are washed, and put in a pot with about ten seers (lb. $24\frac{5}{8}$) of the unripe pods of the *Guilandina* called *gaukungchi*, which have been beaten in a wooden mortar with about 20 seers ($49\frac{1}{4}$ lb.) of water. After standing two days they are put into an equal quantity of fresh tan of the same kind, and then they are dried. They are afterwards twice beaten in a wooden mortar, having been previously moistened with water. The skins are then fit for the upper leathers of shoes, and are of the common tanned colour, which may be changed into black by a little green vitriol. If red skins are wanted, they must be dyed with lac, before they are put into the tan. Skins may be made of a dirty orange or reddish yellow by rubbing them, when newly taken out of the lime, with the inner bark of the *deuyo*, (Trees, No. 103,) beaten into pulp with a little water. White skins are prepared, without tan, by rubbing them with salt, after they have been taken out of the lime, and then beating them. The only good colours are the black and red.

Sheep skins are treated exactly in the same manner. The whole of these operations is usually conducted by the women, as being the most laborious; but the hides are very badly dressed, as may be readily imagined from the account that I have given.

The shoes, trunks, and saddles are made by the men. A man and his wife can prepare eight pairs of shoes in a month, and these sell from $\frac{3}{8}$ to $\frac{1}{4}$ of a rupee a pair. The shoe-makers have little or no capital, but make tolerable wages or about 3 rupees a month, which would enable them to live decently, were they not violently addicted to intoxication. Every native, that can afford it, wears leather shoes.

15. A class of people called Kurrail make leathern bags, (*kupo*,) in which boiled butter, oil and molasses are kept. They live chiefly in the divisions where sugar is made, as the demand for their bags is principally to contain molasses. There are between thirty and forty families of this kind. They use the hides of buffalos, and are nearly in the same condition with the shoe-makers. I did not learn their process.

16. The great variety and number of drums, used in this district, would employ a considerable number of people to make them, did not most of the performers construct their own instruments. I heard only of 15 houses, of the low caste called Bede, who lived by this art, and I received no information concerning the manner in which it is conducted.

17. Although almost every man among the natives who has dedicated himself to the art of war, and uses a musket, knows how to make gunpowder, there are some artists who prepare this substance, and construct fire-works. In this district I heard of 12 families of this kind, and saw some of them perform. They are far from being dexterous, but require little apparatus, and are easily satisfied.

18. A Portuguese trader at Dinajpúr makes wax candles, a few of which are consumed by the natives at holidays, the remainder is exported. I have already mentioned, that he has a lease of the wax; part of this also is exported without being manufactured.

19. In Dinajpúr five families are supported by making matches of bits of wood covered with sulphur; these are called *diyoodais.*

20. Forty or fifty families of poor people are supported by making balls of charcoal dust, united by means of starch, which are used for burning the tobacco, that is smoked in the *hooqa*, or in other similar instruments.

21. Those who prepare the tobacco for being put into the pipe, are a much more important set of artists, and in this district they occupy between 7 and 8 hundred houses. They require very little stock, 4 or 5 rupees being sufficient. They take between 20 and 30 pounds of tobacco, dry it in the sun, and beat it in a wooden mortar, or with the *dhenki*. Then they dry it, and beat it with three-fourths of its weight of treacle (*kotra*). It forms a kind of cake or ball, and is sold by retail at all the neighbouring markets, as well as in the shop of the manufacturer. These balls keep for 10 or 12 days. Rich people use some other ingredients, but none is prepared in this manner for sale; it is done by the servants of those who use it. The artists are rather poor.

22. The people who distil spirituous liquors (*modwaleh*) are of a very low caset, and the profession is opprobrious; but they seem to live easily, and require some capital. The demand is very inconsiderable, and of course the number of stills is small, and may be from one to two in each division. These stills are extremely rude, and are only employed to distil rice. The body (see drawing, No. 32, *a*) consists of an earthen jar, which is placed over a hole in the floor (*b*) that serves for a fire place. An earthern pot (*c*) is luted to this by way of a head, a straight wooden tube (*d*) conducts from the head to the cooler (*e*) which is an earthen pot, that is placed in a pan filled with cold water (*f*); a man sits by the pan, and constantly pours water on the cooler with a coconut shell: another man supplies the fire. The whole apparatus is luted together, before the operation begins, and the distillation is continued until it is conjectured, that all the spirit has risen. The distiller then removes the lute, and takes away the cooler, which contains the spirituous liquor. It is scarcely possible to conceive any chemical operations so rude and imperfect. The liquor is never rectified nor re-distilled.

A manufacturer at Chintamon informed me, that he took 40 seers of rice (60 sicca weight or lb. $1\frac{4}{10}\frac{3}{8}$ the seer) and boiled it, just as rice is usually prepared for the table; he then added $\frac{1}{8}$ of a seer of *bakor*, which is a mixture of dried herbs, that is prepared by a kind of people called *Jogis*, who collect the plants in the woods. It is said, that this contains 300 different plants. I had no opportunity of verifying this, but know, that a few plants are sufficient. The boiled rice and *bakor* mixed remain in a heap for six days, are then very mouldy, and in this state are called *bichon* or seed. This seed is put into a jar with 40 seers of fresh boiled rice, and 160 seers of water, and are allowed to ferment two days. The fermented liquor is then distilled by 10 seers at a time, and about $\frac{1}{4}$ part is drawn over:—that is, the 80 seers of rice, give about 40 seers of spirit. This man said, that the grains are not saleable. People will not give them to their cattle, and the only persons that will carry them away are basket-makers, who give them to their hogs. Each still pays a rupee a day as duty, I suppose chiefly with a view of discouraging the manufacture. The spirituous liquor thus Prepared is execrable, but is not sufficiently strong to be inflammable. It is retailed by the distiller, and can be sold by no other person.

23. The oil-makers are a much more numerous and respectable class of tradesmen, and as they require nearly the same stock for each mill, that a farmer does for each plough, it is generally supposed that the profits of the two classes are nearly the same, mill for plough. The mill is indeed moved by one ox, but two must be kept for each, one to relieve the other, and the mill is much more expensive than the plough. This and the quantity of grain, that must be purchased, makes the oilman's capital rather heavier than the farmers; but there being no pretence for exactions on the part of the landlords, the returns being equally diffused throughout every week in the year, and above all there being no advances made for oil, the situation of the oilmen is, in general, preferable to that of the farmer. The mill is exceedingly imperfect, as will be seen from the drawing, No. 33. It is on the same principle with the oil-mill of Mysore, but much ruder. The principle is the same also with that of the sugar-mill; but is much better fitted for the purpose of expressing oil.

In some divisions the oilmen are wealthy, and make advances to the cultivators for their mustard seed. In others they are more needy, and buy no more at once than will last them from one market-day to another. Others again receive the grain from the farmer, deliver a certain proportion of oil, and for their trouble keep whatever more they can express from it, together with the cake.

In Ramisongkol, where the oilmen are richest and most numerous, and where they export a considerable quantity, I obtained the following account from one of them, a wealthy and respectable man. The mill receives at one time one *don* of seed (*turi*), which measures 421 cubical inches, and weighs 162$\frac{3}{5}$ ounces avoirdupois. A little water is added, and the mill grinds three hours, at first some seed comes from the spout, but afterwards, as this is thrown back, and as the cake forms, the oil comes away pure. It should amount to $\frac{4}{13}$ in weight of the seed, or to rather more than 47$\frac{1}{2}$ ounces. The oil at present sells at 206 ounces for the rupee, and the seed at 2$\frac{1}{2}$ annas for the quantity that is put at once in the mill. The value of the oil is almost 3$\frac{3}{4}$ annas, so that he has 1$\frac{1}{4}$ anna profit on each grinding, and the mill grinds twice each day. The cake is half the measure of the seed, and may be worth the 6th part of an anna.

At Dumdumah and Rajarampúr it is reckoned, that the oil of *sorisha* should amount to $\frac{4}{13}$ of the seed, and the oilman are contented to grind, and return in oil $\frac{4}{13}$ of the weight of the seed which they received. A mill there grinds daily 12 seers of 96 sicca weight, or about 29$\frac{3}{8}$ lbs. and produces very near 9$\frac{1}{4}$ lbs. of oil, of which the oil-man gets $\frac{1}{5}$ part and the cake. Sometimes he grinds for pay, and for his mill receives 2 annas a day with about 2$\frac{1}{2}$ ounces of oil.

At Potiram it is said, that 30 seers of *sorisha* give only seven seers of oil, and that a mill in one day can grind 30 seers of 60 sicca weight, or about 46$\frac{1}{4}$ lbs. The mills are usually employed by the day, and receive one anna in money, all the cake, and rather more than $\frac{3}{4}$ lb. of oil: worth in all about 2$\frac{1}{2}$ annas a day, or Rs. 4. 11. a month.

At Lalbazar, where there are a great many oil-mills, it is reckoned, that the capital required for each is double of that required for one plough. It is said that each seer of *sorisha* or *turi* gives $\frac{1}{4}$ seer of oil. Each mill can grind 15 seers of 58 sicca weight a day (or lbs. 22$\frac{1}{2}$), and obtain rather more than 5$\frac{2}{3}$ lbs. of oil. The usual price of seed is 75 seers or five days grinding for the rupee, which produces $27\frac{9}{16}$ lbs. of oil; and this selling at 10 seers the rupee, is worth R. 1. 14. The gain is therefore 14 annas in 5 days, or R. $5\frac{1}{4}$ a month, besides the oil cake.

It must appear very remarkable, that these accounts should vary so much; some alleging that *turi* produces $\frac{5}{16}$ and *sorisha* $\frac{4}{16}$ or even less of its weight of oil; while others allege, that the latter gives $\frac{5}{16}$, and there is no doubt that the *turi* gives more than the *sorisha*.

In the only experiment, which I made, I procured $\frac{1}{4}$ of the oil from *sorisha* seed. I suspect, however, that the oilmen often cheat; pretend that the seed gives much less than it actually does, and keep the remainder to themselves; for Mr. Tucker informed me, that an oilman had offered to express *sorisha* seed for the cake alone. This cake no doubt would contain abundance of oil, which must have been afterwards expressed, otherwise the man could not have lived.

The number of families which follow this profession amounts to above 2,000, many of whom have more than one mill, and several, as many as five.

24. In this district most of the persons who prepare milk (*goyalas*) have no cattle; but live in towns, and keep only two or three cows like other persons in easy circumstances. They purchase the milk partly from poor farmers, and partly from those who have large herds of milch cattle. Their number may be between 6 and 7 hundred houses, and a man who has 25 rupees capital is considered as in a thriving way. In many places they have shops, and they attend at all markets to dispose of their commodities, which are boiled butter (*ghi*, or *ghrito*), curdled sour milk (*doyi* or *doohi*), butter-milk (*mat'ha* or *ghol*), inspissated milk (*khyir*), and curd (*chhana*). The two last are made only when commissioned by the makers of sweetmeats, by whom alone they are used.

The first thing in general done with milk is to boil it, and the boiling is sometimes continued until the milk is reduced to a kind of extract called *khyir*, which is used in sweetmeats. The natives use only boiled milk: the taste of this fluid, as it comes from the cow, is considered as unpalatable.

In a few parts of this district the milk, as it comes from the cow, is churned, and the butter is separated; after which the remainder is boiled, and made into *doyi* as usual: but in general the boiled milk is put into a pot, and there is added a little old *doyi*, which occasions it to curdle and become sour. This is a favourite article of luxury with the natives, and butter is usually prepared by churning these sour curds or *doyi*. What remains, after the butter has been separated, is a kind of acid liquor (called *mat'ha* or *ghol*), which is analogous to our butter-milk, and is only used by the poor. The butter is never used without having been boiled, which converts it into an oil, that preserves much better than butter. Even in this climate it undergoes little change for one month, and may be used after having been kept a year. It is often adulterated by boiling *doyi* or sour curds along with the butter. This preparation of butter answers very well in cookery, and might perhaps be used in Europe to great advantage. The quantity consumed in the district is exceedingly small, and except in the largest towns none is ever made without being commissioned, so that it is not an article of common sale.

The *chhana* or curd is prepared by boiling the milk, and by adding to it, while hot, some acid milk, which coagulates the whole into one mass. This is put into a cloth, and the whey is expressed, so that it is a kind of cheese.

25. The people who prepare sweetmeats from curds are called Moyras among the Bengalee, and Halwáikors in western India. The artists of the two countries

however keep totally distinct, and those of Bengal use most milk, while those orginally from western India use more flour in their sweetmeats. In this district there may be about 100 houses of Halwáikors, and 120 of Moyras. They have capitals of from 15 to 20 rupees, and usually make four or five rupees a month. They all keep shops, and also expose their goods for sale at the common markets.

The Moyra prepare from sugar, curds and inspissated milk several kinds of sweetmeats (*mishtanno* vulgo *mitayi*), called *monda, pengra, tokti,* and *khyirpuli.* They prepare others, called *roskora* and *monohora*, from coconut-kernels and sugar; others made of sesamum seed and sugar are called *tilakhojd* and *kodma*, and finally a kind called *batasa* is made of sugar alone.

The Halwáikor prepare sweetmeats, called *chhanabora,* from curds and sugar; those called *paintaoya* are made of flour and curds; those called *motichur, jialapi, goja, khaja* and *monbhog,* are made of flour and sugar; and the *elaichdana* is made of sugar and cardamum seeds.

These sweetmeats please neither the eye nor palate of Europeans, especially those made by the Halwáikor, all of which are fried in oil or butter. The rich natives use large quantities.

26. Maldeh was formerly celebrated for its *morobba* or vegetables preserved in sugar or honey. The art seems to have been introduced by the Muhammedans from the west of India, and the fall of the Moslem power has reduced it to one practitioner. He preserves

Amloki, Phyllanthus Emblica, W.

Horitoki, Myrobalanus Chebula, Gærtn.

Amra, Mangifera indica.

Anaros, Bromelia ananas.

Sriphol, Cratæva religiosa.

Kushmando.

Sotomuli.

Tetul, Tamarindus indica. The sight of these conserves perfectly satisfied my appetite. I cannot therefore speak of their flavour.

27. In Dinajpur three or four families, from the west of India, make sweetmeats called *puya* and *phulari.* The former is composed of the flour of rice mixed with molasses (*kotra*), the latter is composed of the flour of pulse mixed with the same sweet substance. The art has now become common in the district, and in country places each family prepares for its own use.

28 Bhujaris are a class of people originally belonging to Bengal, as well as to the west of India, and about 600 houses are employed in this district. Seven or eight rupees are considered as a sufficient capital, and a family can make from two and half to three rupees a month. In large towns they keep shops, but in country places sell their goods in the open markets. These people make the preparations of rice called *khoyi* and *muri*, that have been already described; and they parch field pease and the pulse called *chona*, which form *motorbhaja* and *chonabhaja.* All these, and also the preparation of rice already described under the name of *chira,* are mixed with extract of sugar-cane (*gur*), and sometimes with treacle (*kotra*), and are either formed into balls (*moya*), or into cakes (*chakti*), that are much used by the natives. The same persons also sell a mere mixture of *khoyi* with the extract of sugar-cane, which is called *murki.* Cakes made of sesamum seed and extract of sugar-cane are called *tila-khaja.* These

same people take the cake extract of sugar-cane, and diluting it with water, boil it, and form two kinds of cakes, *patali* and *pheni*. The former is very heavy, and the latter is light, but I have not learned the difference in the operation, only that some milk is added to the *pheni*, when it is boiling, which must in some degree purify the extract.

29. Some persons (Dailhari) in Maldeh and Dinajpur live by grinding wheat and by making *dail* from *kolai*, that is, by separating the integuments from the grain of pulse. This is an art introduced from the west of India, but it has now become common, and except in large towns, is performed by the women of all families.

SECTION 2nd.—*Artists employed in working durable materials, Wood, Earth, or Metal.*

30. Under the synonymous names Chhutor, Sutrodhor, and Barai we must include joiners, cabinet-makers, carvers, and carpenters of all kinds. In this district there may be between six and seven hundred houses occupied by such persons. The greater part are merely employed to make the miserable instruments of agriculture, and occasionally a coarse stool or chest, and are among the poorest set of artists in the district. About towns, where a little furniture is used, and where some houses have wooden doors, window shutters, posts and beams, and where some palanquins are required, they live more comfortably, and make from four to eight rupees a month. A man who makes eight rupees must have 40 or 50 rupees capital, and employs some workmen. The following articles are those usually made at Dinajpúr, with the usual extent of price from lowest to highest.

Meyana, or palanquin,	10 Rs.	20 Rs.
Chests,	2 Rs.	10 Rs.
Toktoposh, a bedstead with plank bottoms,	2 Rs.	4 Rs.
Khat, bedsteads with ratan bottoms,	½ R.	3 Rs.
Jolchauki, bathing stools,	0	12 As.
Piri, stools on which the natives sit when eating,	1 A.	8 As.
Kursi, a kind of chair,	4 As.	8 As.
Mechia, a kind of seat,	1 A.	2 As.
Singhason, a throne for the images of the gods,	8 As.	3 Rs.
Sepaya, a wooden stand for a lamp or candle with three feet,	1 A.	2 As.
Mortar and pestle,	4 As.	5 As.
Spinning wheels,	0	2 As.
Wooden-shoes, *khorom*,	2 As.	4 As.
Plough without the iron,	4 As.	6 As.

The palanquin approaches to that of a Calcutta beau, about as much as a market cart does to my Lord Mayor's state coach, and the other articles are rude in proportion. Even this is not the greatest imperfection. The joinings are so badly fitted, that the furniture is very rickety and unfirm, a fault that extends even to the very neat workmanship, that is now made at Calcutta, Mongher, Patna, and other places, where European improvements have been introduced.

Oil and sugar-mills, *dhenkis*, and many other articles are made, when commissioned.

In this district the number of carpenters employed in building boats is very small; for although *sál* timber, fit for the purpose, may be readily procured from Nepaul and Bootan by the Mohanonda, Atreyi, and the Korotoya, yet few traders keep large boats, as they could not be used during a great part of the year. A few trading boats however are built of *sal;* but until I reach some place, where the business is carried on to a considerable extent, I shall decline saying any thing on the subject, farther than that all the materials are furnished by the merchant, who builds the boat, and the carpenters are hired by the month. The head workman is allowed seven rupees a month, inferior workman six rupees, and the lowest class three rupees. On the Jomuna river some boats are constructed of mango-wood. They are clinker built, and the fibrous roots of some aquatic plants, that grow in marshes, are used as caulking, being placed between the edges of the planks before these are nailed together. When moist these plants swell, and effectually prevent leakage. The boats last scarcely longer than two years.

One of the landlords, Baidyonath Chaudhuri, employs a few skilful men in carving figures of the gods on wood; but they have been brought from other districts. Their work is very rude, owing probably to the want of a good design, for they are capable of considerable neatness in execution.

The implements, which the carpenters have in this district, are the *bayis,* a narrow hatchet; the *basúli,* a very good adze; *batáli,* chisels of several kinds; the *randa,* a very imperfect plane, which is designed merely for smoothing, and not for forming grooves of mouldings; the *korat,* a small wretched saw: the *turpon,* a drill moved by a bow and string: and the *munggur,* a mallet. The natives have neither auger, gimblet, rule, square, compass, nor bench, instead of which one man holds the timber, and another plains it, while it is placed on the ground, and both workmen sit on their heels. A few European tools have found their way to the town of Dinajpúr, such as planes of various kinds, and the hand-saw, compass, rule and square.

31. Sawyers may occupy about 100 houses, and are in about the same circumstances with the carpenters. They are mostly Mahommedans, and generally work by the piece. At Dinajpúr the sawing a log, about seven or eight cubits in length, into plank, about 1¼ inch thick, was estimated at eight annas for every cubit of its circumference, which is the usual manner with these people of estimating the labour that a log will cost in sawing. This it is evident has no necessary connection with its solid contents, which the people of this district have no means of calculating. Sawyers are sometimes paid by the month, two men being allowed five rupees. The saw is about four feet in length, and its shape is an irregular curve. The handles are both fixed, so that the saw cannot be taken out without moving the wedges, which prevent the planks from impeding its motion. The teeth are very rudely formed, and are not bent alternately to the different sides, so as to make a cut sufficiently wide to admit of free motion; but the cutting edge of the saw is considerably thicker than the back, which answers the same purpose. The log is not laid horizontally; one end rests on the ground, the other ir raised on a wooden horse, so as to form about half a right angle with the earth. This enables the man below to sit during a considerable part of the operation. The log is first marked with lines, and then one end having been cut, the other end is turned up for the saw.

32. Turners, Kundkor, are very few in number; I heard of only seven houses, and it is probable, that not above three or four could escape my notice. They

work only in wood, and two men are always employed together; one who pulls a rope, first with one hand and then with the other, to turn the lathe, and one who applies the chisels. The two cheeks are fixed in the ground, and one must be dug out, every time that a new piece of wood is to be put into the lathe. The articles turned are:

1. Part of the spinning wheel.
2. Wooden platters, (*burkosh.*)
3. Wooden cups, (*kotuya* and *bati.*)
4. Wooden basons, (*belon.*)
5. Parts of the instruments used for smoking tobacco, (*nolicha, nol, boitok.*)
6. Rods carried by messengers, (*horkora chhori.*)
7. The feet of bedsteads.

Their wages and situation in life are like those of common carpenters. All those who work in wood have irregular employment, and are often very poor, although they have good wages when employed.

33. Potters, on the contrary, have a regular employment, and are as easy in their circumstances as any artists in the district. They require little or no capital; for whenever a kiln has been burned, the pots are sold for ready money to the petty traders, who retail them in markets. At Dumdumah, where there are many potters, and these reckoned as good as any in the district, I took the following account.

There are two kinds of ware made; the one red, the other black: I shall first describe the red, as that is in most common use.

The clay used for this pottery ware is called *kabal*, is of a dirty livid colour, and is purchased from people who dig it, and bring it to the house of the potter, who, for liberty to dig the earth, supplies the officers of Government and the landlords with pots. This clay is watered, kneaded with the hands and feet, and beaten with a mallet. It is then made up into a mass, cut into thin slices, watered, and kneaded again. It is then fit for being placed on the wheel.

The wheels are of three kinds, one is about 1½ cubit in diameter, and consists of four spokes and a rim of bambu, that are coated with clay, mixed with the fibres of *pát*, (*Corchorus capsularis.*) Another is about 1¼ cubits in diameter, and is composed of a solid mass of clay, mixed with *pát*. It is about four inches thick at the centre, and two inches at the circumference. Neither of these kinds is baked. In the centre of each is a stone, in which a small cavity has been formed; and this rests on a pivot of tamarind-wood, that rises a few inches above the floor. A little clay is added, wherever wanted, in order to bring the wheel to an equilibrium. The third kind of wheel is but rarely used, and is made of the transverse cutting of a *sál* or jack tree, two cubits in diameter. Its motion continues longer, but the expense of even this is considered as a serious objection. The workman sits on his heels as usual, and gives his wheel a circular motion by means of a stick, one end of which he places in a hole that is near the circumference. The motion communicated to the smaller wheels lasts only a short time, and requires to be repeated two or three times for each vessel. Except the wheel, the only implements required are a long knife, with a handle at each end, to cut the clay, a mallet to beat it, a few sticks, and moulds and mallets of baked clay to shape the pots, and a string, or wire, to cut them from the wheel.

A great part of the ware, however, is not made on the wheel. The mouths only of the most common vessels used in cooking (*hanri* or *patil*) are made in this manner; the bottoms are merely kneaded, and then joined to the circular mouth. This part of the operation, and the drying of the pots in the sun, after they come from the wheel, is performed by the women; who also apply to the most conspicuous parts of their pots, a kind of pigment made of *rangn mati*. This is clay much impregnated with red ochre of iron, which is found in a great many places of the district by digging to a little depth, and contains small pebbles. Overnight, some of this is put into a pot, with much water. Next morning the water and finer parts of the clay are drawn off, and evaporated in the sun, until somewhat thick, like a pigment, which is applied with a brush before the pots are quite dry, and when they are burnt, the parts that were so covered acquire a kind of metallic lustre. The pots having been dried six hours are fit for the kiln.

The manner of constructing the kiln is as follows: An oval cavity, see drawing No. 34, *a*, *b*, *c*, is made in the earth, which slopes gradually down to the centre, where a hemispherical cavity (*f*) about 2½ cubits in diameter, is dug to serve as a fire-place—at one side of this is erected a semicircular wall of mud, (*d*, *e*,) which crosses the longest diameter of the oval at right angles, and is ten cubits long and six cubits high. Its bottom is perforated with a square aperture (*g*) through which the fuel is thrown. An arch of clay, (*i*, *k*, *l*,) is thrown over the fire-place, and is perforated in several places, to allow the flame and heat to reach the pots. This kiln lasts, with a few repairs, for a long time, and its construction does not cost a rupee.

The following is the manner of burning. The whole space of the larger segment of the kiln over the fire-place, and as high as the wall (ground plan *b*, *c*, *d*, *e*, longitudinal section *d*, *m*, *c*, *l*, *i*, transverse section *d*, *b*, *k*, *c*, *e*,) is filled with all the kinds of unbaked potters ware, that are in demand, after they have been well dried in the sun. The pots are covered with three inches of reeds (*ulee*), over which is placed earth two inches in thickness. The fuel is then thrown into the fire-place, and consists of small sticks and reeds (*birna*). The fire is kept up from sunset until midnight. The pots are taken out in the morning.

These pots are well burned, and are of a bright brick colour, but they are very imperfect. They are brittle; and, having no glazing, imbibe so much grease in cooking, and are so rough, that they cannot be kept clean: although they imbibe a good deal of every liquor that is put into them, they are not sufficiently porous to admit of such an evaporation as will cool water.

The clay used for making the black earthen-ware is called *kassa*, and is of a yellowish colour. It is prepared and formed into vessels, exactly as the livid clay is: the difference of colour in the two kinds of ware arises chiefly from the manner of burning. The kiln for the black-ware is smaller, the wall being only six cubits long by three high. The fire-place is of the same size. The pots, when placed in the kiln, are covered with three inches of straw; above which the ashes of straw are laid three inches thick, and are watered, which makes them cohere. The fire is applied, at first slowly, and is then raised very high from sunset until midnight; when some dry cow dung is thrown into the fire-place, and the aperture is shut to confine the smoke, of which a great quantity issues from the dung. The pots are not taken out until the following afternoon. In fact, the colour seems to proceed entirely from the smoke, which enters the pores of the ware, and never can be entirely removed; but these black vessels are unfit for cooking, as boiling water always extracts some of the colour. They are more porous, and not so brittle as the red pottery, and their colour hides dirt. They are chiefly used as platters, and vessels for holding cold liquors; and sell about ⅛th dearer than the common red-ware.

It must be observed, that the want of glazing or enamel must always render the Indian earthen-ware a dirty kind of vessel; and accordingly no pure Hindu will use the same earthen vessel twice: but this custom, in itself proper, has been extended to the pottery of China and Europe, than which no vessels can be cleaner. This, it must be farther observed, is a complete bar to improvement. From a view of the drawings, (No. 35,) the various articles commonly made will be seen, and it will be perceived, that the potters of this district are not destitute of taste in the forms of their vessels; but the execution must necessarily continue wretched, so long as the prejudice against old vessels continues.

A potter, whose family consists of four men and two women, says that in each month he can burn five kilns of red-ware. Each kiln is worth about four rupees.

The expense is fuel, at 1 rupee a kiln,	Rs.	5	0	0
Clay 32 loads of about 98 lbs. for each kiln, at 10 annas,	,,	3	2	0
	Rs.	8	2	0

Leaving between 11 and 12 rupees a month for profit: this is probably somewhat underrated, as in such cases may be usually expected. Less cannot be allowed than four rupees for a man and woman, who live as these people did; or three rupees for a man's labour, and one for a woman's; which would make the profit 14 Rupees, or about ¼th part more than the potter stated. The number of potters in the district may be about 1400 houses. Besides making pots, a part of their profession, in several places of this district, is to dig wells.

This is the case, whenever the soil is light; as in such parts, in order to prevent sides from crumbling, recourse is had to rings made of potter's-ware. These rings are about six inches deep, and from 1¼ to 1½ cubits in diameter. The sides are about an inch or 1¼ inch thick. The well is first dug about two cubits in diameter until water is found. The rings are then laid one above the other; and, as they are laid, the space between them and the sides is crammed with earth. A well of this kind lasts about five years without repair. Where the soil is stiff, the rings are not necessary, and potters are not employed to dig.

34. The worship of *Durga*, *Kali*, *Kartikeya*, and *Soroswoti*, as performed by the Hindus of Bengal, and by these alone, requires a number of images made of unbaked clay, which, after the celebration of the religious ceremonies, are thrown into the river. In different parts of Bengal some other deities are worshipped in the same manner, but the custom does not extend to this district. This worship has given rise to a profession. Some who practise it are potters, and others are the makers of artificial flowers, who are at any rate employed in ornamenting the images, and the stages on which they are carried in procession. In some districts the artists of this kind possess very considerable merit, and mould in clay, with great neatness, whatever model is shown to them; and this might be employed as an excellent means of introducing a good taste among the natives. The images

it is true, that are used in worship, require little attention, except to make them gaudy, as they cannot be baked, and are thrown into the river; but good models might be given to these artists, and very handsome moulds might be formed and baked, which would come very cheap, and be an excellent ornament for the houses and domestic chapels of the natives, so as, by shewing them correct images, to wean them from the deformed objects which they now possess. The Mahommedans of this district are not behind hand in giving employment to those who make images; for rude clay images of horses are offered at the tomb of every saint, and these are baked. It would, however, be difficult to find out any workmen so rude as the image-makers of this district; nor did I conceive it possible, that any grown person could have failed so much in the imitation of nature. I shall therefore defer giving any account of the art, until I reach some place where it has arrived at some tolerable degree of perfection. The profession gives employment to about 80 families. They stain the earthen images of a red colour with the bark of the root of a wild species of *Morinda*, called *choy-choka*. This, beaten with a duck's egg and some quicklime, forms a kind of red varnish, that is not easily removed.

35. Brick-makers did not constitute a trade of such importance, as to obtain a place in the establishment of Bollal-sen, and still are not numerous. About 120 families are acquainted with the process, and when bricks are wanted, engage to furnish any quantity, for which advances are made.—On receiving the money they buy wood and hire labourers, whom they superintend and direct. Very often the fuel is furnished by the person who wants the bricks. The bricks are made in the open air, and of course can only be formed in the dry season; and if a heavy day's rain happens, very great losses are sustained. The earth chosen is the common free soil, which contains a large proportion of sand mixed with the clay. This is thrown into a pot with some water, where it is allowed to soak for two or three days. It is then taken out, lumps are separated, and it is well beaten. It is then spread on a piece of ground that has been cleared and smoothed, and is laid on this of the thickness which it is intended that the bricks should have, which is usually about 1½ inch. When it has dried a little, a man takes a long bambu, which has the blade of a reaping-hook fastened to its end at right angles, and he draws this through the clay, keeping it straight by means of a traveller or noose which runs along a line stretched in the direction that is to be cut. He thus cuts the whole into bricks about 7½ inches long, by 6½ broad. Some days afterwards these are raised, and placed on their edges: after a few days more they are formed into walls, until a quantity sufficient for a kiln is ready. In one kiln one hundred thousand bricks are usually built, with alternate layers of wood and straw; and these being burnt, the operation is completed; 20 men take six weeks to prepare 100,000 bricks, and 14 days to burn them. I found that per each kiln the landlord paid 30 rupees in advance. He also furnished the fuel, and when the bricks were delivered he gave 40 rupees more. He did not however receive 100,000 bricks for 70 rupees and the fuel, for the bricks were numbered before they were placed in the kiln, and many are spoiled in the burning. The usual wages in the dry season being 1½ rupee a month for each labourer, the contractor had 10 rupees profit, besides his monthly hire.

The use of the mould was totally unknown to the native brick-makers, until introduced by Europeans. I have not learned, what difference it makes in the expense; but even the bricks made for a gentleman of Dinajpur with a mould, I observed, were very rough, and could not be employed to advantage for building a wall that was not covered with plaster. Those made after the native fashion are exceedingly rude, although well burned; and in all their finer buildings are either coated with plaster, or incrusted with tiles, which are cut smooth, and are in general carved. The first plan is by far the cheapest, admits of all the ornaments of Grecian architecture, and looks fully as well as stone. It has accordingly been adopted in all European buildings.

The incrusting with cut tiles is exceedingly expensive, and never could be employed in any work of good taste; but it suits the native fondness for minute ornament and grotesque carving, and is employed in all the finer buildings of this district: I shall therefore give an account of it, which was taken from the best workman of the place.

The earth is of the same kind, and is prepared and cut in the same manner as for common bricks; only the pieces are larger, being usually four inches thick, 14 inches long, and nine inches broad. Some cow-dung is added to the fuel to increase the heat. The bricks, when taken out of the kiln, are soaked a whole day in water, after which they are cut exactly square, and smoothed on five sides by means of a small adze, with a short handle, and of chisels, which operation it is evident must be very expensive, and after all the bricks would not make such a smooth neat wall as those used in the south of England. The expense is however enormously enhanced by the carving on the flat side of the brick, which is often made to represent the fables of the Hindoo mythology; and gods, goddesses, princes, Europeans, animals, coaches, carts, ships, &c. &c. &c. are also represented, and most miserably caricatured. Some Europeans imagine, that this is done with a view of rendering them ridiculous; but I am persuaded, that this is not the case, the god being no better treated than the sailor. It proceeds merely from want of skill and taste in the designer. Obscene figures make in general a conspicuous part. The bricks are carved with small chisels. After the operation is completed, the brick is first soaked in an infusion of tamarinds, and then a number is put into an iron vessel with about a pound of oil for each, and they are roasted over a fire until the oil disappears. The workmen are employed by the month, so that it is difficult to state the expense. Each brick goes through the hands of three artists; one cuts it square with an adze, his wages is five rupees; a second smoothes the surface with a chisel, and receives six rupees a month; the third carves the figures, and is allowed seven or eight rupees wages.

36. Brick-layers are about twice as numerous as professional brick-makers, and from being often unemployed make but poor wages, for they receive five or six rupees a month, when they work. Neither their walls, nor arches are neat, and their principal merit is in the application of plaster, either as a coating for walls to form a roof or floor, or as a cement to retain the carved tiles with which the walls are incrusted. The most approved composition used in this district is as follows:

5 parts of slaked lime in paste, (*koli-chún.*)

10 parts of pounded bricks.

1¼ part of *Fenugreek* flour, (*Trigonella.*)

¼ part of *thackuri* flour, (*Phaseolus Max.*)

½ part of treacle, (*kotra.*)

5 parts of water, these are to be mixed with a trowel, and applied immediately.

37. There are several cutters of stones or masons, in the employment of Boidyonath Chaudhuri, whom I have several times mentioned as the chief encourager of the arts in the district; but all these tradesmen have been brought from a distance, and even from Benares, and of course have high wages. One man in Dinajpur lives by forming weights of stone.

38. About 80 families live by collecting shells, and burning them for lime. I had no opportunity of ascertaining the kinds of shells; for the people have a peculiar aversion to collecting the objects of natural history, probably looking on the study as idle or absurd, and the employment as ridiculous. The shells are collected in marshes and rivers during the dry season, and if any considerable quantity is wanted, such as for building a house, advances must be made in due time; for in common the people gather no more, than serves the usual demand for chewing with bettle, for dying and tanning, and for white-washing a few place of religious worship. Europeans in general procure stone lime from Silhet; but the landlords prefer the shell lime, as they can make the advances with little risk and trouble, and as they consider the lime better. I did not see the furnace. The lime is sold in three states by those who make it; 1st, slaked lime in powder, called simply *chún* or *gungrochún*, sells usually at Dinajpúr for three mons, (96 sa. wt. the seer, or $290\frac{1}{4}$ lb.) for the rupee. This is used for mortar, and is made of shells that are not cleaned. 2d, *Kolichún*, which is slaked lime mixed with a great deal of water, and is that used for white-washing, and for making plaster. The shells for this are carefully cleaned before they are burned. 3d, *Leya* or *kádáchún*, is reduced to a very white fine paste, and is used for chewing the beetle. This is made of some peculiar kinds of shells very carefully cleared.

39. In this district the working of the precious metals is at a very low ebb with regard to skill. The artists are sufficiently numerous, there being between four or five hundred houses inhabited by those who follow this trade. They are remarkably poor, and have no capital, except a few wretched tools, which they carry to the person's house, who wants any thing made, and who furnishes the materials. Their character for dishonesty is such, that a person must always watch to prevent them adulterating the bullion, after having secreted a part. In the account of the ornaments that are used by the people, will be seen the articles which these tradesmen make. All persons however who wish to be thought fashionable, bring their ornaments from Murshedabad or Calcutta, when they can procure a trusty friend at these cities to superintend the making. The charge for workmanship, both of gold and silver, is from $\frac{1}{12}$th to $\frac{1}{8}$th of the metal, so that, when they work in gold, they should have vast profit, or very little when they work in silver: but there is probably some secret in this which those who employ them do not understand; for those who are sent to watch can only judge whether any silver is absolutely taken away in a metallic state. The natives seldom, if ever, use plate at their tables.

40. Among the natives of Dinajpur the various preparations and alloys of copper are in great demand, as must have been perceived in reading the lists of furniture and ornaments; yet the number of copper-smiths does not exceed one-half of the goldsmiths, for most of the ware is imported ready made, and artists are chiefly required to keep it in repair, whereas no one can trust to the purity of the gold or silver ornaments that could be purchased; and it is only people of fashion, who occasionally go to capital towns, that can procure gold ornaments from thence.

In the base metals there is less danger. The imperfection of the workmen prevented me from taking an account of the manner, in which the alloys of copper are formed; a most interesting subject, to which I shall pay the most minute attention on the first favorable opportunity. The copper-smiths work in copper, brass, bell-metal, lead and tin; but there is a separate set of artists, who work in these two last alone. The copper-smiths almost always furnish the metals, and keep shops, where they retail their goods, and they also retail them in open markets. They therefore require a capital; from 50 to 100 rupees, however, are sufficient, as they purchase the metals in small quantities at a time, from the merchants who import them. In some parts of the country all the vessels are cast, in others they are all hammered. There are many persons, who retail the goods imported chiefly from Kangtoya, (Cutwa, R.) and Murshedabad, who are mere shop-keepers, and know nothing of the art. A copper-smith can clear between four and five rupees a month. Wrought brass costs from R. 1-8 to R. 1-14 the seer, according to the fashion. That which is cast is cheapest. Wrought bell-metal costs from 2-4 to Rs. 3. Wrought copper costs from 2-12 to Rs. 3; the seer is of 80 sa. wt. lb. $2\frac{51}{1000}$ avoirdupois.

41. In this district about 120 families of *thatéra* are employed in making tin bracelets, which are worn by Mahommedan women of all ranks. They are nearly as easy in circumstances as the copper-smiths, and require less capital; as they need no more metal at once, than will suffice from one market-day to another. Petty traders often purchase their goods, and retail them at markets.

42. One man from Puroniya makes *hooka* bottoms of a mixture of metals called *bidri.* I was very desirous of learning the art, because the alloy is said to consist of iron and lead, and is unknown to European chemists; but the man declined giving me any information on the subject.

43. Blacksmiths (*kámár*) occupy between six and seven hundred houses, and are about in similar circumstances with the copper-smiths. When not otherwise engaged, they prepare with iron of their own, and retail at markets, the common implements of agriculture, such as the ploughshare, sickle, bill, hoe (*kodal*), hatchet (*kurál*), *khonta*, and weeding iron. They also prepare in the same manner some household furniture, such as ladles, pothooks, kitchen knives, and lamps, both standing and hanging, and some coarse cutlery, such as knives, scissors, and beetle-nut-cutters; when ordered by the barber, they make his razors and nail-cutters; the former is an instrument very terrific to the patient. The European cutlery has made little way into this district. The blacksmith can also prepare an instrument called *kajollota,* which is placed over the lamp for collecting the smoke used as a paint; he also makes locks and padlocks, possessed of every imaginable defect, and can make such tools as the carpenters use. A few tradesmen, at Ghoraghát, chiefly the remains of a number who were formerly at that place, can make arms, such as matchlocks, swords and spears; but most of the arms now in the district are imported. The black-smiths also make nails and clamps for boat-builders; but the quantity required being small, and the demand irregular, no such thing as a nail can be procured ready made. If one is wanted, it must be commissioned. The hoes made near Nawábganj are reckoned good, and the manufacture employs several people, that receive advances from traders, who send the hoes to neighbouring markets. The greatest labour, however, which the black-smiths of this district undertake, is to make boilers for those who prepare the extract of sugar-cane, or for the manufacturers of sugar: an estimate of one of these latter

boilers of the smallest kind weighing six maunds of 60 sa. wt. the seer, lb. $369\frac{3}{5}$ will give some idea of the state of the art. The sugar-manufacturer furnishes 12 maunds of Birbhûm iron, one half of which is consumed in working. This costs from 36 to 39 rupees, according to the rate of the market. Six men working constantly can make a boiler of this size in a month, and receive 24 rupees or four rupees a month each. But such expedition is not usual; they more commonly require two months, and work only a part of each day at this heavy labour. The remainder is employed at small jobs for their usual customers, or in making some of the small articles which are sold at markets; thus $269\frac{3}{5}$lb. of iron, very rudely wrought, cost from 60 to 63 rupees, of which $\frac{2}{5}$ths are the price of labour.

In this district one black-smith cannot work by himself, he must have a man to blow the bellows, and he has usually an assistant to work with a large hammer; the man who manages the forceps and small hammer is the chief. The proportion of their pay is eight annas for the forceps, five annas for the large hammer, and three annas for the bellows. The two former sit on their heels, and cannot be said to display great activity; but the creature who manages the bellows may be considered as the quintessence of indolence. The bellows, except in being too small, are not badly contrived, and are made somewhat like too common pair of kitchen-bellows, joined by the muzzles, and far separated at the other extremity. These bellows are placed vertically, and on the back board of each is a button, which the workman takes between his toes, and lying quietly down on his back, moves the boards backwards and forwards with his feet.

44. In Dinajpur and Maldeh are five or six men, who may be called cutlers. They clean arms, especially swords; and two or three of them have wheels for sharpening knives and razors.

SECTION 3.—*Manufacture of Cloths.*

As Government are no doubt already sufficiently acquainted with the state of the manufactures carried on by the Company, I shall avoid saying any thing on that subject, further than to state the effects, that have been produced on the manufacturers by the diminution of the capital, which the Company employ in that way. I shall in the first place begin with those who prepare the raw materials, as brought from the merchant, or farmer. I have already given an account of the preparation of the silk and *pât* until fitted for coming into the weaver's or dyer's hands, and shall therefore here confine myself to cotton.

45. There is a description of people called *dhanâra*, who clean cotton, after it has been freed from the seeds, by beating it with the string of an instrument like a bow, which separates all the fibres, as is done in the operation called teazing. In this district there are only seven or eight persons of this profession, and they are employed only when cotton is wanted for stuffing quilts, matrasses, or pillows; and the operation of removing the seed, and of picking and cleaning the wool is performed by the women that spin it, who use a smaller bow (*dhankâra.*)

46. The preparation of cotton thread, therefore, is a principal manufacture, and occupies the leisure hours of all the women of higher rank, and of the greater part of the farmer's wives. Even the women of the Brahmins here employ themselves in this useful industry, and in fact every woman is employed in it, more and less, except those belonging to traders, in which both men and women are engag-

ed, such as weavers, tanners, and the like. The farmers' wives are however the greatest spinners, and are usually thus employed during the whole afternoon. The raw material chiefly used in about $\frac{3}{4}$ of the district, is imported from the west of India, by the way of Bhogowangola; but many of the people in these parts wear cloth made of *put*, and a little cotton is raised in some parts of that extent, while most of the cotton raised in the district is the highest priced, so that probably not above $\frac{1}{3}$ in value of the whole raw material may be imported. To the east of the Atreyi and south of Dinajpur the cotton produced in the country is sufficient for the demand, and, as I have said, is of a much superior quality to that which comes from the west; but this is so much cheaper, that it is more fitted for the coarse goods, that are the great manufacture of this district.

The cotton that is imported is already clear from the seed. It is brought by large dealers, who deliver it in small quantities, such as a C. weight, to petty traders for about eighteen rupees a maund (82lb.) and these retail it about 4 lb. the rupee, to the women who spin, and who again sell their thread to the weavers, unless they wish to have it wrought for family use, so that in the whole business scarcely any capital is required, except in the merchant who imports. In the part of the district, where the cotton is reared, a great part is spun by the wives of the cultivators, and the remainder is retailed by the farmers at the weekly markets; so that almost the whole business is carried on without capital, or at least with one so much subdivided, that its value can scarcely be perceived. In a few places, where the company makes advances for fine cloth, such as is not commonly used in the district, the weavers are under the necessity of bespeaking the thread, and generally pay the price before hand.

The women free the cotton from the seed by the usual hand-mill employed in India, then beat it with the bow, and spin it with a small miserable wheel that is turned by the hand: all implements extremely imperfect. In the district of Badolgachhi, where the cotton manufacture is the most flourishing, a woman buys one seer of 60 sa. wt. (lb. 1 888) of cotton with the seed, which in one month she cleans and spins. She obtains about $\frac{3}{16}$ of cotton wool fit for spinning, and her thread, when of the finest quality, weighs $\frac{1}{8}$ of the rough cotton, and sells at 12 sa. wt. or very near five ounces (4928) for the rupee. This is on the supposition of a woman's doing no other work. The price of her thread is $13\frac{1}{3}$ annas, the cotton costs two annas, she therefore has $11\frac{1}{3}$ annas for her trouble. Four annas a month may however be the usual rate of gain by spinning in the afternoon. There is no regulation for the length of the reel, and neither spinners nor weavers can form an estimate of the length of any given weight of thread. Very few of them indeed can either read or perform any arithmetical computation, and they judge merely by the eye or experience of the quality and fineness of the thread. They divide thread into four rates. The first sells at from 8 to 12 sa. wt. for the rupee. The 2d, at from 13 to 18 do. The 3rd, from 19 to 26 do. The 4th, from 27 to 50. The 1st and 2d qualities are chiefly spun from the fine cotton of this district, or from what grows at Gour in the immediate vicinity. The coarser kinds are made from imported cotton, and form the greater part of the thread spun in the district.—This coarse cotton looses from one $\frac{1}{12}$ to $\frac{1}{8}$ in spinning and cleaning, so that 75 sa. wt. intended for the coarsest kind of yarn costs eight annas, and at 50 sa. wt. of thread for the rupee produces $1\frac{1}{2}$ rupee. Intended for the finer quality of yarn 70 sa. wt. costs eight annas, and sells at about three rupees;

eight annas worth of cotton wool is therefore, on the average, converted into 36 annas worth of thread. The raw cotton produced in this district, as coming from the farmer, I have estimated at one lack of rupees in value, of which 80 thousand may be fine. Some of this is exported; but some fine is imported at Maldeh, so that 80,000 rupees worth of fine cotton wool may be spun in the district: when spun its value will be raised to about 400,000 rupees. About 1,50,000 rupees worth of coarse cotton wool is imported, and 20,000 grows in this district, and the value of this, when spun, may amount to 765,000 rupees; the total value of the raw material, as sold to the spinner, is about 2,50,000 rupees. The value of the yarn, as sold or applied to use by the spinner, may be 11,65,000 rupees, and the profit therefore will be 9,15,000 rupees.

The *pat* is spun by two kinds of spindles, the *takur* and *dhara*. A bunch of the raw material is hung up in every farmer's house; and every one who has leisure forms, with one or other of these spindles, some coarse pack-thread *(sutoli)* of which ropes are twisted for the use of the farm; but it is only the low Hindu castes called *rajbonkgsi kongeh* and *polya*, that form this pack-thread for being woven into sackcloth, or spin a finer thread from whence the cloth called *megili* is woven. As these people usually rear the plant, spin the thread, and weave it, no estimate can be formed of the different stages of the manufacture.

47. By far the greatest part of the cloth, that is used dyed in this district, receives the colour in the state of thread, and the operation is most commonly performed by the weavers; but there are a few houses of professed dyers, chiefly in Maldeh, who dye thread, and a few others in different parts, especially Dinajpur, who dye turbans and girdles.

The dyers of Maldeh have about 25 houses, and confine their operations to indigo and lac. The seer weight, by which all the operations are conducted, contains 92 sa. wt. or is nearly 2 $\frac{36}{100}$ lb. avoirdupois (16,522 gr.)

The indigo vat is made thus: take five seers of indigo, break it into small bits, put it into an earthern tub or vat with five pots (about 60 seers) of alkaline ley, and stir them about for three hours, then put this mixture into two pots, and add to each ¾ seer of *chakunda* seed (Cassia tora, W.) boiled in 2½ seers of water, and boil the mixture all night, that is to say a fire is kindled under the pots, and burns under them until the fuel is consumed, the people having gone to sleep at their usual time. In the morning, the fire having gone out, stir the decoction with a stick for 1½ hour, this boiling and stirring must be performed four nights and mornings. The vat is then ready for dying, the thread either silk or cotton is kept 40 minutes in the pot. It is then wrung, dried in the sun, and washed. If the colour is not deep enough, it must get another dip in the other pot. The remaining colour is applied to other thread, the dye of which is completed by other vats.

The alkaline ley is prepared as follows: take 20 seers of fresh burned roots and stems of the plantain tree, put them into a large earthen pot, that has a hole in the bottom, over which a quantity of grass is laid, through this filter slowly 60 seers of water, which forms the ley fit for use.

Five seers of indigo should give a good full colour to six seers of cotton thread, or to 2½ seers of silk. It costs two rupees, being a kind very inferior to that prepared by Europeans, and is made in the form of balls by the natives of Rongpur and is generally much adulterated with clay. The good indigo, prepared by

Europeans, is never employed by the tradesmen of Maldeh. The colour is very good.

The same people often dye green with indigo; but generally the weavers give them thread which has previously been dyed yellow, either with turmeric or with the bark of the jack tree, as will hereafter be described. The latter green is fixed. That dyed with turmeric is perishable.

For dying one seer of cotton thread blue, the dyer receives 12 annas, or 4½ rupees for each vat. The materials may cost 2½ rupees, the labour occupies five days, in which the workman gains two rupees. If he dyes the cotton green, and performs the whole steps of the operation, he receives 1½ rupee for each seer. The dying silk costs 1½ rupee a seer, so that the artist when he dyes silk has only a profit of 1¼ rupee on his vat, but probably some circumstance was concealed, which renders both equally advantageous.

It is to silk alone, that the dyers give a colour with lac, the manner, in which this is done, is as follows: Take 11 seers and two rupees weight (1/48 part of a seer) of stick lac. Having removed the sticks, it will weigh 10 seers, grind this in a hand-mill, and sift it, grinding the larger pieces repeatedly, until the whole is reduced to powder. It is then put into a boiler, which is a strong vessel of earthen-ware, coated on the inside, with melted shell-lac mixed with sand. To the powdered lac add 10 seers of water, in which 1/32 part of a seer of *sajimati* (carbonate of soda) has been dissolved, tread the lac and water with the feet, and then boil them for three hours. The lac must then be put into a basket and the water allowed to drain from it into the pot, and the infusion is then to be poured into another vessel. Five other similar infusions are to be made from the same lac, so that in all there are 60 seers of infusion. The lac exhausted of its colour is reserved for sale and the infusion must be boiled down to 55 seers. To this add ⅛ of a seer of *lodh* bark (see trees, No. 80), powdered, and stir about the mixture. Next day the infusion is decanted, and there are 50 seers of clear dye fit for use. In the mean time an infusion of 4½ seers of bruised tamarinds in 20 seers of water has been prepared, and decanted. Boil three seers of silk in one half of the dye, and in one half of the infusion of tamarinds for 1½ hour. Then wash it, and boil it for an equal length of time in the remainder, when the colour will be complete. The stick lac is brought from Asam by the way of Murshedabad, and costs 11 or 12 rupees a maund. The 11 seers of stick lac give seven seers of the lac separated from the colour, which sells at nine rupees a maund. The lac therefore costs in all three rupees, and the seed lac sold brings 1-9 rupee so that the dye for three seers of silk costs rupees 1-7, besides tamarinds *lodh* and soda; but these are trifles. The *lodh* is brought from Rajmohol, the soda from Patna. I did not learn the price of dying a seer of silk, but this branch is more profitable than the dying with indigo, and is in fact the chief employment of the Maldeh dyers, who make high wages. One man and his wife can clear at least 12 rupees a month, besides a house they require 100 rupees capital, if they dye with lac, 10 rupees are sufficient, if they dye only with indigo. They never buy thread to dye, and then sell it; but content themselves with dying, what is brought, at so much the seer. Whatever more remains to be said on the art of dying in this district, will be found in the next article.

48. The cloth manufacture, that seems most peculiar to this district, is that woven of a mixture of silk and cotton, and from the chief place where it is made,

this cloth is called Maldehi, as the thread is dyed before it is woven. I shall continue to detail the process of dying, as that is performed by the weavers and their wives, and then proceed to give an account of the other parts of their art.

And first I shall treat of the method used with silk. The first operation is to bleach it, and this is done in three ways, the operation is performed each time on from ½ to 2 seers (80 sa. wt.) or from about 1 to 4 lbs. of silk; but I shall suppose the quantity to be one Calcutta seer or $2\frac{81}{1000}$lb. and all the other weights to be in proportion. For the first kind of bleaching, the silk is steeped the whole night in water. In the morning it is wrung, and dried in the sun. It is then boiled with one seer of soap in a sufficient quantity of water, for about 48 minutes, then it is washed in clean cold water, and dried in the sun, the silk is of only a dingy white, but it is better than the others. The 2nd quality of bleaching requires 10 or 12-sixteenths of a seer of soap, the process in other respects is the same. The 3rd quality is not allowed soap; but is boiled with two seers of the fresh made ashes of the root and stem of the plantain tree. In each of these operations ¼ of the silk, by weight, is lost, all the kinds are used as whites in cloth, and all may be dyed of every colour, but the colours dyed on the 1st are clearer and higher priced, than those dyed on the 2nd, and these on the 2nd, are again superior to the colours dyed on the third.

In the following manner a fine bright but perishable yellow is given to silk by turmeric. For one skein of bleached silk, weighing two sicca weight (359 grains nearly) take 5 sicca weight of well cleared turmeric, and grind it upon a stone, adding a little water during the operation, until it is reduced to a pulp. Then add to this 20 sicca weight of water, and filter the infusion, soak the silk two or three days in this water. Then wash it, and put it into a solution of ½ sicca weight of alum in 20 sicca weight of water. Then dry it, and the operation is finished.

A good fixed yellow, although not so bright as that given by turmeric, is communicated to silk by the wood of the jack tree (Artocarpus integrifolia, trees, No. 102), a skein of silk, as before, is soaked a whole day in a solution of alum, and is then dried. It is then put into a decoction of jack-wood prepared in the following manner. Take 40 sicca weight of chips of jack-wood; boil them all day, adding occasionally water so as to make a strong decoction, which is strained. In this the silk remains two days, it is then washed, and dried in the sun.

Two colours are given with safflower (Carthamus Tinctorius) and are called *kusom* and *golabi*.

The *golabi* is a fine rose-red, but is not a fixed colour. For one skein of silk take 10 sicca weight of safflower, dry it, and reduce it to powder, then add one sa. wt. of impure carbonate of soda (*sajimati*), and rub them with the hands for about 12 minutes, then put them on a cloth strainer, and allow 40 sa. wt. of water to drain through them. In this water steep the silk a whole day, and wash it, then put it into an infusion of tamarinds, which is prepared thus. Take five sa. wt. of ripe tamarinds freed from the shell; and, having rubbed them well with 20 sa. wt. of water, strain this for use. In this infusion the silk is kept between 48 and 72 minutes, and is then dried in the shade.

The *kusom* colour is better fixed, but is not such a fine red, still however it is a beautiful colour. The only differences in the process are, that 30 sa. wt. of safflower are used, and that ¼ sa. wt. of alum, and 1 sa. wt. of lime juice are added to the infusion of tamarinds.

Silk is dyed of a fixed red colour with *monjista* (Rubia cordifolia?) soak a skein in water for four or five hours, then keep it as long in a solution of alum, then put it for an hour into a decoction of *monjista*, which is thus prepared. Take 10 sa. wt. of *monjista*, beat it to powder; and boil it for about five hours in 80 sa. wt. of water. Pour off the water; boil the *monjista* in similar quantities of water three times, and keep all the four decoctions. The silk remains an hour in each. It is then washed, and dried in the sun. The red of *monjista* by jack-wood is changed into what the natives call golden (*sonala*); but in fact into a colour which much resembles that of new copper. After the first immersion in alum the silk is soaked in the decoction of jack-wood for 120 minutes. It is then again soaked in an infusion of alum, and then is dyed with the *monjista*; but 5 sa. wt. of this is sufficient.

There are a great many colours given, in which a preparation of iron called *moski* is employed. This is a Persian word signifying black, and all these dyes have probably been introduced by the Mahommedans. I shall first give an account of the manner, in which *moski* is prepared, and then detail the various colours, in dying which it is used. Take 20 sa. wt. of wheat flour, 5 sa. wt. of extract of sugar cane (*gur*), 1 sa. wt. of boiled butter (*ghi*), 240 sa. wt. of old iron, 400 sa. wt. of water. Let them stand in a pot ten days in hot weather, and 16 days in cool. After being strained the liquor is fit for use, if not strained it will keep four or five months without spoiling. The *moski* contains an oxacetate of iron, but it would require very accurate experiments fully to develope its other ingredients, and how far these may have any share in the operations of the dyer.

There are three colours called *uda*, one given by the *horitoki* (Mirobalanus Chebula Gært. trees, No. 14), another by the *chamolloti* (a Cæsalpinia, not described by Willdenow, nor in the Encyclopedia), and the third by alum.

The first kind is dyed thus: take 10 or 12 myrobalans; beat them, and infuse them in 20 sa. wt. of water for four or five hours. Then put a skein of silk, that has previously been dyed with lac, into this infusion of myrobalans for from 120 to 144 minutes. Then wring it, and put it into 20 sa. wt. of *moski* for a similar length of time. Then wash it in cold water, and dry it in the sun. This is a fixed dark-red like Russian leather.

The second kind of *uda* is equally well fixed, and is darker than the former. I shall first describe the manner in which the infusion of *chamolloti* is made.—Take ½ sicca weight of the dry pods separated from the seeds; powder them, and beat them well in a mortar with 20 sa. wt. of water, and strain the infusion for use. The pods of this plant, when green, contain a quantity of clear viscid liquor, that surrounds the seeds, that in the ripe fruit becomes dry, and that probably is the part in which its dying qualities reside. In order to dye *uda* with this plant put a skein of silk, that has previously been dyed with lac, into the above-mentioned infusion for two hours. Then wring it, and put it into 20 sa. wt. of water mixed with 10 sa. wt. of *moski*. Dry it in the sun, and in two hours, if the colour is not good, put it again into 20 sa. wt. of water, and 10 sa. wt. of *moski*. Then wash the silk in cold water, and dry it in the sun.

The third kind of *uda* is equally well fixed, and is a clearer colour. Take a skein of silk that has been dyed with lac, put it for one hour into solution of ¼ sa. wt. of alum in 20 sa. wt. of water. Then put it into *moski* as in the last mentioned process.

Moski gives silk that has been dyed with *monjista* a fixed colour called *tamroj-yoti*, or copper colour. The process is rather tedious. First the silk is put into the infusion of turmeric for 24 hours, then washed, and put into the solution of alum 24 hours, then into a decoction of jack-wood, which is changed two or three times in the course of the third day. After this the silk is soaked for half a day in a solution of alum. In the remainder of the 4th day it is soaked in the decoction of *monjista*. It is then washed, and kept for two or three hours in a mixed infusion of myrobalans and *chamolloti*. It is then wrung, and put into *moski* for six hours.

The dye called *filtun*, from a Persian word signifying elephant-colour, is a dirty black, but is well fixed; a skein of bleached silk is soaked six hours in a solution of alum, and is then wrung. Two decoctions, one of jack-wood, the other of *monjista*, are then prepared as before described, 10 sa. wt. of each is mixed, and the silk is soaked in the mixture for an hour and a half. It is then washed, and put for an hour into the infusion of *chamolloti*. It is then wrung, and put for two hours into *moski*. Finally it is washed, and dried in the sun.

Silk is dyed a lead colour (*sisa*) by *moski*. The skein must have been bleached in the best manner, and soaked for an hour in a solution of alum. It is then wrung, put into the *moski*, washed, and dried in the sun.

The *polas-kungri*, or bud of the Butea frondosa, is a colour that I have not seen. The object, from whence its name is derived, is black with a tinge of green. The skein of silk is soaked for 24 hours in the infusion of turmeric, and wrung. It is then put for two hours into a solution of alum, wrung again, and soaked a day in the decoction of jack-wood. It is then washed in cold water, wrung, and put for three hours in the infusion of *chamolloti*. It is then wrung, and having been put into 40 sa. wt. of *moski*, the pot is placed in the sun the whole day. It is finally washed and dried in the sun. The colour is said to be fixed.

The dye called *lobonggo-kornophuli*, or clove colour; it is a fixed brown, the skein of silk is soaked three hours in the solution of alum, then wrung, and soaked for a whole day in the decoction of jack-wood. It is then wrung, and again soaked for three hours in the solution of alum. After being wrung, it is soaked for a whole day in a decoction of *monjista*, and during the course of the operation this is changed four times. It is then wrung, and put for two hours in the infusion of *chamolloti*. Finally it is wrung, kept for a day in a pot of *moski*, exposed to the sun, washed, and dried in the sun.

The colour called *panduki*, from the name of a flower, is a well fixed lilac. The skein of silk must have been bleached in the best manner. Take 2½ sa. wt. of the infusion of lac bought from the dyers, add to this 10 sa. wt. of water in which 1 sa. wt. of tamarinds had been infused for a short time. In this mixture soak the silk for three hours, wring it, wash it, and keep it for two hours in the infusion of *chamolloti*. Then wring it, put it for half an hour in 2½ sa. wt. of *moski*, diluted with 30 sa. wt. of water, wash and dry it in the sun.

These are the colours given to silk thread, I shall now detail those, which the weavers give to cotton, and which are three in number.

The first called *salu* by the natives, is a well fixed light pomegranate colour. Take 20 sa. wt. of cotton thread, soak it three days in cold water, wash it merely by rubbing it with hands without beating, and dry it in the sun. Then take of dried *chamolloti* pods freed from seeds 5 sa. wt.; powder them well in a mortar, and rub them for an hour with a little water. Then add two seers of cold water, mix them, put the cotton into the mixture in the mortar and knead it with the hand for an hour. Throw away the water, and dry the cotton, as impregnated with *chamolloti*, in the sun. Dissolve 3½ sa. wt. of alum in 40 sa. wt. of water, and add 1 sa. wt. of impure carbonate of soda, which has been dissolved in 10 sa. wt. of water, and then strained. In this solution put the thread, and rub it with the hands for an hour. Then wring, dry it in the sun, wash it well, and dry it again in the sun. Take 40 sa. wt. of dry *monjista*, powder it with the *dhengki*, and boil it in five seers of water to four seers. Then boil the thread in the decoction for half an hour, wring and dry it. Then keep it half a day in one seer of water holding in solution 3 sa. wt. of alum, and wring, and dry again. Then boil 20 sa. wt. of powdered *monjista* in four seers of water to 30 seers, and in this boil the cotton for a quarter of an hour. Finally wash and dry the thread.

Thread thus dyed may be changed into what is called *uda* by the following operation. Take 20 sa. wt. of the dyed thread put it in 7½ sa. wt. of the infusion of *chamolloti*, stir them with the hand for 24 minutes, then wring the thread, and put it for an hour into one seer of *moski* mixed with half a seer of water. Finally wash the thread in cold water and dry it in the sun. This makes a deep colour, and lighter shades may be obtained by using ¾ or ½ seer of *moski*.

The third colour called *kusem*, is not well fixed, but is a bright beautiful light-red, like the pomegranate flower. For 20 sa. wt. of cotton thread take 1½ seer of dry safflower, powder it, put it on a cloth, and wash it, until the yellow colour is entirely separated. Then add by degrees 15 sa. wt. of impure carbonate of soda (*sagimati*,) and rub them together for an hour until they become scarlet. Then put them on the strainer, and filter water slowly through them, until all the colour is carried away, and keep the infusion of safflower. At the same time put 60 sa. wt. of tamarinds, freed from the pod, into two seers of water, rub them and strain the infusion. Mix the infusions, and divide them into two equal parts, put the thread into one part for an hour, then wring it, and put it in the remaining half of the infusions for three hours. Then wash, and dry in the shade.

The whole apparatus required in this manufacture consists of a loom, a few sticks for warping, and some earthen pots for dying. The loom is exceedingly imperfect, especially the reed and shuttle, the warping is performed by the women, who taking a spindle in each hand lay two threads of the length required round some sticks placed upright in the ground, and repeat this by two and two threads a time until the warp is completed.

The Maldehi cloths, consisting of silk warp and cotton woof woven very thin, are manufactured entirely in Maldeh, and the towns on the banks of the Mohanonda for 12 miles below; but some of these are in the Puroniya district. The warp is generally disposed in stripes, and the woof is of one colour, the fabric is of two kinds; one called *elachi*, where both sides of the cloth are alike, the other called *mosru* is like satin, one side being different from the other. Both kinds are of a great variety of patterns, which it would be needless to enumerate, the only general distinction in the patterns of both kinds are; 1st, when one stripe is very narrow, and the other very broad, the cloth is called *goolbudun*; 2nd, when the spots and stripes are waved, the cloth is called *katar*. There is very little taste displayed in the patterns, and the weavers are very inferior to those of Bangalore.

Both have probably been introduced from the N. W. of India by the Mahommedan conquerors. The pieces wrought for the company, or for exportation by sea, are 30 cubits long, and two cubits wide; those made for common sale are 18 cubits long, and from 1¾ to 2 cubits wide; but the pieces rejected by the company, as unfit for their commerce, are readily bought up by all other merchants, the large pieces sell from 18 to 30 rupees, the *katar* being about five rupees dearer than the others, the small pieces cost from 3 to 12 rupees.

The persons in this district who follow this profession are said to occupy 2000 houses, and to possess 4000 looms. Every estimate that I received stated, the cloth wrought on one loom to be worth about 20 rupees a month, which would make the annual amount 9,60,000 rupees; but this is certainly too much, and from the apparent poverty in the place, it is probable, that a very great number of weavers are without employment. Besides almost the whole of the cloth is exported from this district, and the cloth of this kind, that is exported, I heard no where estimated at more than 2,50,000 rupees a year.

About 800 looms are said to be employed in weaving the larger pieces, chiefly in the form of *elachis*, and receive advances either from the Company's Factory, or from the agents of merchants residing at Calcutta and Moorshedabad. These advances are to the full value of the goods, that are to be wrought, and the manufacturers are eager for them, partly no doubt from being secured in employment, but also from the strong bias to anticipate their profits, which universally prevails. The Company's advances are always preferred; the remaining looms are employed in weaving the short pieces, generally from five to eight rupees value, and mostly of the kind called *mosru*, at least in the country towns. At Maldeh the *elachi* is chiefly in demand. The short pieces are sold at open markets for ready money, or very often to petty dealers, who go round the weavers' houses, and purchase whatever goods are ready; and the Goswamis or merchants from the west of India, purchase a large proportion, it is said to the amount 100,000 rupees.

The raw materials, except some of the drugs used in dying, are either the produce of the division of Maldeh, or of the adjacent banks of the Mohanonda, so that nothing further can be wished on that head, for the encouragement of the manufacture. This however is on the decline, and it is said that 7000 looms were once employed. The decline is chiefly owing to the demand having lessened, but partly also to the attention of the manufacturers having been turned to the weaving of cloth consisting entirely of silk.

Twenty rupees for each loom is reckoned an adequate stock. This will build a house and purchase a loom, pots, silk, cotton and dyes, sufficient for making one piece. A man and his wife, in one month, can generally weave and dye a piece of cloth worth 20 rupees, and may have about 5 rupees profit. If a man is rich, and keeps several looms, he and his wife warp and dye, and persons are hired to weave at the following rates: A long piece of *elachi* worth 18 rupees, costs for weaving from 3 to 3½ rupees, and is made in from 20 to 30 days, so that the wages are about 3½ rupees a month.

A large piece of *mosru* worth twenty rupees costs 4 rupees, and takes a month to weave it.

Short pieces of *elachi* worth from three to six rupees, occupy from five to ten days, and the weaver receives 2½ annas on each rupee of the value, so that he makes cloth to the value of 18 rupees a month, and receives about 2½ rupees profit.

The manufacture of cloth made entirely of silk is confined to the vicinity of Maldeh, and seems to have been introduced by a Mr. Henchman, who was Commercial Resident for the Company at English Bazar. This manufacture injured that of mixed cloth, and this has not recovered since the newly introduced one began to decay, which it seems to have been doing ever since Mr. Henchman left the place. It is remarkable, that the natives have no names to distinguish the cloths made of pure silk, and of silk mixed with cotton; both are divided into *elachis* and *masrus*, which when of pure silk we call *taffetas* and satins; of both there are patterns of the kinds called *golbudun* and *katar*, which I have already explained. The size of the pieces, and the manner of dyeing, bleaching, weaving, and selling the goods of pure silk, and of mixed materials, are exactly the same. The value of those made of pure silk is rather higher; but not a great deal, perhaps two or three annas on the rupee. The persons employed in this manufacture may occupy 200 houses. From 20 to 25 good tradesmen make long pieces, at from 18 to 30 rupees, generally commissioned by the Company's agent, and could make goods of higher value, if required. The workmen of about 100 houses are usually employed by private traders, chiefly the Armenians of Calcutta, to make cloths from 10 to 16 rupees a piece; but if required, could make cloths worth 25 rupees; and when there is much demand, these are sometimes employed by the Company's factory. The remaining 75 houses are occupied by poor workmen, who chiefly make goods worth from 8 to 12 rupees a piece, which they sell at the markets for ready money. The whole looms may be about 500, which should be able to manufacture goods to the amount of 12,000 rupees.

The people hired to weave this cloth have rather higher wages than those employed in weaving mixed goods, but are paid in the same manner; that is, fine goods are paid by the piece, and coarse goods, by a percentage on the value. Some good workmen make five rupees a month, and the usual wages are 3¼: the master's profit must be proportionably great; for instance, a piece of silk cloth, 18 cubits long by 2 broad, which is worth eight rupees, will cost the weaver, for silk, four rupees, for dyeing drugs, ¾ rupee, altogether 4¾ rupees; so that he has 3¼ profit for his own labour, and that of his wife, and he can easily make one piece in 12 days; so that his profits are at least eight rupees a month.

The cotton manufacture is of more importance, is more thriving, and is less liable to fluctuation, because by far the greater part of the commodity is consumed in the district, and the weavers would not suffer very materially were the exportation altogether to cease; because at present their is some imported, and it is probable, that, were the exportation to cease, the weavers would apply themselves to work in goods, that would suit the demand of the neighbourhood.

At Maldeh, and in its vicinity, are about 120 houses occupied by weavers, who make thin muslin *(molmol)* and turbans, and are the only persons in the district who weave these kinds of cloth. They have from one to seven looms in each house, and the whole looms may be about 360; most of them are said to receive advances for the *molmols*, either from the Company's factory, or from private merchants at Calcutta and Múrshedabad. About one-half of the goods, however, including all the turbans, is made for ready-money sale. The whole amount may be about 50,000 rupees. The goods made on commission are 40 cubits in length by 2 in the breadth, contain from 12 to 15 hundred threads in the warp, and sell from 12 to 16 rupees. Many, which are rejected by the factory, are sold for ready-money, at nearly the same rate. The common goods intended for ready-money sale are about a cubit shorter, about three inches narrower, and contain in the warp from 800 to 1000 threads; they usually sell at from four to six rupees a piece.

The following capital is required for this business—a loom, 2½ rupees; sticks for warping, and a wheel for winding, 2 annas; a shop, 4 rupees; thread for two ready-money pieces, worth 6 rupees each, 5 rupees; total, rupees 11. 10., to which must be added a month's subsistence. The man and his wife warp, wind, and weave two pieces of this kind in a month, and he has seven rupees profit, deducting however the tear and wear of his apparatus, which is a trifle. A person, hired to weave, can in a month make three pieces of this kind, and is allowed two annas in the rupee of their value, which is 2¼ rupees a month. The finest goods cost two rupees a piece for weaving.

At Maldeh is one person who weaves cloth, that is flowered in the loom, (*Jamdany,*) and two men who weave cotton carpets, (*sutrunji*); but these may be passed over as of no importance.

On asking the weavers of Maldeh, concerning the profits of the respective classes, each pretended to be the poorest, but on comparing the whole, it would appear, that at Maldeh and its vicinity, the silk-weavers had the highest profits; next to these, the weavers of mixed goods; next to these the weavers of muslin, and lastly, plough for loom, the farmers, whose usual profits on each plough may be about 40 rupees a year. This is on the supposition, that both looms and ploughs are wrought by persons of the family; a large deduction indeed must be made where servants or journeymen are employed, or where an imprudent anticipation of their resources have induced them to borrow money at an exorbitant rate. Silk-weavers, who have four or five looms, and hire journeymen, spend 12 or 15 rupees a month. In these calculations, it is taken for granted, that the weaver has regular employment. At present many near Maldeh are destitute, and this is an evil inseparable from the condition of a manufacturer, especially where he works for a foreign market. Indeed, this is a kind of employment that deserves less encouragement from Government than it usually receives: at one time the manufacturer is wallowing in riches and luxury, and claims every indulgence that he can imagine, on account of the supposed wealth that he brings to the country; next year, he is starving, and expects that all other considerations should give way to his interest.

Out of Maldeh the number of professional weavers is inadequate to supply clothing for the inhabitants. The whole number may be about 6,000 families, who may have 8,000 looms. A few of these are employed by different subordinate agents, belonging to the Company's factories, at English Bazar (Maldeh) and Rongpúr; but the number has decreased of late, and although the weavers suffer from not receiving the advances to which they had been accustomed, and which had enabled many to involve themselves in debt, there seems to be no want of full employment; and on an average each loom can clear four rupees a month for weaving, winding, and warping, whether they purchase the thread, and sell the cloth, after it is made, or receive the thread from the good women of the country, and weave it at so much a cubit. Both practices are common, and, except by the Company, no advances are made; but several native traders buy up the pieces that are rejected by the Company's agents, and export them. Each family generally keeps a loom for every man, where the caste is that of a proper weaver; but as many persons of other castes have adopted the profession, some brothers of such families cultivate the ground, and others weave. No person, however, that I have included in the list of weavers does both. The value of the thread, which each man may weave in a month, will be about eight rupees, making the whole value of the cloth 144 rupees a year for each loom, which on 8,500 looms, including those in Maldeh, amounts to rupees 12,24,000.

The cloths chiefly made for exportation, by means of the Company's factory near Maldeh, are *tongjebs*, or plain white muslin, about 40 cubits long by 2 cubits or 2¼ broad, and containing from 1100 to 1300 threads in the warp, and which sell at from six to nine rupees a piece. A few thicker cloths, called *báftas*, are made for the factory at Rongpúr.

The cloths which the weavers make for the natives are dresses of thin muslin, generally with red, blue, or white borders, and which sell at low prices, being very short. Pieces of 10 cubits by 2 sell for from 1½ to 2 rupees.

A great number both of the low Hindú and Muhammedan farmers have a loom in their house, and both men and women work at it when they have leisure, and make coarse thick cloths, such as *gosls* and *goras*, of which the total value may be 4,50,000 rupees.

The whole cotton cloth, therefore, woven in the district, may amount to 16,74,000 rupees, of which 140 or 150 thousand are exported, leaving about 15,13,000 for consumption. The cotton thread spun in the district has been estimated at 11,65,000 rupees; allow 65,000 to enter into mixed cloth, the profit of the weavers of cotton will be about 5,74,000 rupees.

The next most important manufacture of cloth is that which is made from the *pat*, or *Corchorus capsularis*, and is almost entirely wrought and spun by the women of the low Hindú castes, called Kongch, Polya, and Rajbongsi.

The very coarse kind of linen called *megili* is the common dress of these poor people, and it is woven in the same way with the coarse cotton cloths which I have lately mentioned. Most families have a loom, and the people, especially the women, in the afternoons, work a little, occasionally, and this serves to clothe the family, so that it is seldom sold. The pieces consist of three or four narrow cloths, sewed together, are 4 or 5 cubits long, and from 2 to 3 cubits wide, and are worth from 2 to 8 annas each; some have red or black borders. It is said to be much more durable than cloth made of cotton, and strongly resembles the coarse linen that is made of flax. The annual value of the *megili* that is woven in this district may be about 1,00,000 rupees.

The coarse sackcloth, called *choti*, is a more valuable manufacture, from the same material: this sackcloth is made of three kinds, and is always woven in pieces from ¾ to one cubit wide, of which two or three are sown together into one piece, before it is sold.

The first kind, intended for bedding, is 4 or 5 cubits long, and from 2½ to 3 cubits wide, and sells at about eight rupees for a hundred pieces.

2nd. That intended for covering bales of cloth, is of the same dimensions, but is thicker than the former kind. The hundred pieces cost from 6 to 10 rupees.

3rd. That intended for making rice and sugar bags, is 4 cubits long and 1½ or 1¾ cubits wide, and 100 bags cost four or five rupees. Some of the second kind are purchased for the Company's factory at Maldeh, but these form an inconsiderable part of the whole. The great demand is for rice and sugar bags, but of these 50,000 rupees worth are brought from the Rongpúr district, and perhaps 1,00,000 rupees worth are made here. Those for bedding may be worth 50,000 rupees, and those for packages 10,000 rupees, making the value of all manufactured in this district amount to 1,60,000 rupees.

The manufacture of *pat* is carried on entirely by females: a woman in the course of the month, besides beating some rice, or preparing *chiri* in the morning, and taking care of the family, can make two or three pieces of *megili*, each worth three annas, of which the material will be one-half, and her gain will be three or four annas. The materials produced in the country are not sufficient for the demand, and large quantities are imported from the N. E.

The cloth made of *arindi*, or the silk of *ricinus*, is of little importance, and is seldom brought to sale: the people who rear the worms have the cloth wrought for their own use. The pieces are from three to five cubits long, and from two to three cubits wide, but have a seam in the middle, and are worth from 8 to 12 annas. About ten thousand families may rear worms, and make each from one to three pieces in a year, so that the total value made annually may be about 10,000 rupees.

The flowering of cotton cloth with the needle has given a good deal of employment to the Muhammedan women of Maldeh, but the needle has never been used by the Hindús; women who work at this employment are called *butadars*, and the patterns are divided into two kinds, *kasida* and *chikon*. The former have running patterns; the latter are in detached flowers or spots, and are the kind most commonly made at Maldeh.

One of the women says, that in the town there are about 500 families who work at this business; they only flower the cloth that is given to them by manufacturers, and never stand the chance of purchasing cloth, flowering it, and then offering it for sale. Before the women receive the cloth, it is stamped with the pattern, which is done by men, and the stamps are cut and designed at the place. The Company's factory formerly employed many women, and gave from three to four rupees for flowering a piece, 20 cubits long by 2 broad; a woman could flower a piece in two months; so that she could gain from 1½ to 2 rupees, in that time; and they are anxious for the factory's work, as the employment is regular. The merchants, indeed, who now employ the women to flower coarse muslin, worth from four to eight rupees a piece, give good wages; but their demand being irregular, the women do not make above one rupee a month: if indeed the employment were constant, a clever woman could every month flower one piece, and the rate is from 2 to 2½ rupees a piece. On the whole, the value of this manufacture may at present be estimated at 500 rupees a month, or 6,000 rupees a year.

At Dinajpúr, about 31 families of Muhammedans *(patoyar)* are employed in making silk strings, which are used for tying trowsers, or for necklaces and bracelets—some of these consist of net work, others are plaited, and all are adorned with tassels. The work is not so neat as in most places of India; for in general it is very beautiful.

At Dinajpúr are 17 families who make chintz; but I had no opportunity of seeing their operation: their capitals may be from 5 to 10 rupees for materials, besides their house, and they live like dyers: the cloth that they print is chiefly brought to them, and printed at so much a piece, and is in general half worn, before it comes into their hands. None is exported.

Among all these artists, expect some of the weavers, who make coarse cloth, for their own use, there are few or no persons, who cultivate the ground at one season, and work at their profession during the remainder of the year. Many, it is true, rent lands, but they cultivate these chiefly by means of persons who labour for a share of the crop; although sometimes also servants are hired for the purpose.

I have already explained the reason why this practice is common, (B. iv. p. 235.) On the whole, the artists in general live as comfortably as small farmers, and their condition will finally improve, if advances are gradually discontinued. In the mean time, from the too sudden withdrawing of the capital formerly employed in that way, they have suffered great inconvenience, and sometimes even distress; but there can be no doubt, that the system of advances is in itself ruinous to both farmers and artists; as conjoined with the usual imprudence of mankind, it is an effectual means of preventing the accumulation of capital in their hands, and without this accumulation, it is utterly impossible that they should possess any independence or ease.

SECTION 4.—*Manufacture of Sugar.*

The manufacture of sugar is one of the most important in this district, and some of its productions have not yet been fully examined by chemists, being somewhat different from those procured in Europe. I shall therefore give a detail of the different processes, at considerable length, and leave the properties of the different articles for future investigation.

The manufacturers of sugar purchase the extract, or inspissated juice of sugar-cane *(gúr)* from the farmers, and in general prefer that which is little inspissated, and which is called *royadár* or *dánadár*, from being of a granular consistence, and *motki, kundo, hangru,* from its being brought for sale in pots. As this however cannot be conveniently brought from a distance, some of the extract *(gúr)* called *dhima,* from being formed in cakes, or *chaki,* from being formed in square masses is also employed.

I shall first mention the buildings necessary for the operation. The boilers are of two sizes, one adapted for making at each operation about 540 Calcutta seers, of 1105 lbs.; the other boils 464 seers, or 950 lbs. The former weighs about 600 lbs. and the latter 490 lbs. This will contain about 2672 lbs. of water, or about 42¾ cubical feet, reckoning 1000 oz. to the cubical foot. It is in shape of the segment of a sphere, nine feet in diameter at the mouth—the other is larger in proportion. The boiler is sunk into a cylindrical cavity in the ground, which serves as a fire place, so that its edge is just above the floor of the boiling house. The fuel is thrown in by an aperture close to one side of the boiler, and the smoke escapes by a horizontal chimney, that passes out on the opposite side of the hut, and has a small round aperture, about 10 feet distant from the wall, in order to lessen the danger from fire. Some manufacturers have only one boiler, others as many as four; but each boiler has a separate hut, in one end of which is some spare fuel, and in the other some bambú stages, which support cloth strainers, that are of use in the operation. This hut is about 24 cubits long and 10 broad, has mud walls six cubit high, and is raised about one cubit above the ground. For each boiler are required two other houses—one, in which the extract of sugar-cane is separated from the molasses by being strained, is about 20 cubits long by 10 wide; the other, that is about 30 cubits long by 8 wide, is that in which, after the extract has been strained, boiled, and clarified, the treacle is separated from the sugar by an operation analogous to claying. Each sugar manufacturer has besides a ware-house, the size of which is in proportion to the number of boilers. The walls of these three last huts are clay, and under the thatch, in order to diminish the risk from fire, they have a roof terraced with the same material. The floor of the ware-house is raised two cubits above the soil—the whole premises are surrounded by a high wall of mud.

I shall now detail the most simple process by which the sugar is procured from the pot-extract, as performed in a small boiler at Badolgachhi, and by which the sugar, called *badol* in the neighbouring markets, is procured.

Take 640 seers (58 sa. wt. or lb. $1\frac{488}{1000}$ the seer) of pot-extract, divide it into four parts; put each into a bag of coarse sack-cloth *(choti)*, hang these over an equal number of wide-mouthed earthen vessels, and sprinkle a little water on them, there will drain from these bags 160 seers of a substance called *math* by the natives, and which I consider as analogous to the molasses that flow from the hogsheads in a curing house of Jamaica: the remainder in the bags is called *ser*, and is a kind of coarse Muscovado sugar; but is far from being so well drained and freed from molasses, as that which comes from the W. Indies. Put the 480 seers of this substance into the boiler, with 180 seers of water, and boil them briskly for 144 minutes—then add 120 seers of water, and boil 48 minutes more. In the mean time, strain 60 seers of water through an earthen pot with some holes in its bottom, which is covered with straw, and over this the pot is filled with ashes of the plantain tree. Four seers of this clear alkaline solution are added to the boiling sugar, and occasion a thick scum, and this is removed. After 24 minutes, three seers of alkaline solution and a quarter seer of raw milk are added, and the boiling and scumming are continued 24 minutes. This must be repeated from five to seven times, until no more scum appears—then add 160 seers of water, take out the liquor, and put it into a number of strainers. These are bags of coarse cotton cloth, in form of inverted quadrangular pyramids, each of which is suspended from a frame of wood about two feet square. The operation of straining occupies about 96 minutes. The strained liquor is divided into three parts, one of these is put into the boiler, with from a quarter to one seer of alkaline solution, $\frac{1}{8}$ seer of milk, and nine seers of water. After having boiled for between 48 and 72 minutes, half a seer of milk is added, and the liquor is poured in equal proportions into four refining pots. These are wide at the mouth, and pointed at the bottom, but are not conical, for the sides are curves: the bottom is perforated, and the stem of a plaintain leaf forms a plug for closing the aperture. The two remaining portions of the strained liquor are managed in exactly the same manner, so that each refining pot has its share of each portion, When they have cooled a little, the refining pots are removed to the curing house, and placed on the ground for 24 hours; next day, they are placed on a frame, which supports them at some distance from the ground: a wide mouthed vessel is placed under each, to receive the viscid liquor that drains from them, which seems to be analogous to the treacle of the European sugar houses, and which is called *kotra, chite*, and *rab* by the natives. In order to render the separation of this more complete, moist leaves of the Valisneria spiralis *(pata)* are placed over the mouth of the pot, to the thickness of two inches—after remaining 10 or 12 days, these are removed, and a crust of sugar, about half inch in thickness, is found on the surface of the boiled liquor—the crust is broken and removed, and fresh leaves are repeatedly added, until the whole sugar has formed, which requires from 75 to 90 days. The sugar procured is usually 144 seers of 72 sa. wt., or $178\frac{44}{58}$ seers of 58 sa. wt., and the treacle is about 300 seers; so that in scumming and straining the boiled liquor very little is lost, or at least the loss is compensated by the water in the molasses and treacle; for the 160 seers of molasses strained from the extract, before it was boiled, must be also considered as part of the produce.

When cake-extract is used, it does not require to be strained before it is put into the boiler; but 480 seers of it are broken to pieces, and put at once into the boiler, with 80 seers of water, and are then treated exactly in the same manner as the *sár* or strained pot-extract. The produce is reckoned to be usually 96 seers of sugar, at 72 sa. wt. the seer, or 119[illegible] seers, at 58 sa. wt., 300 seers of treacle, and near 61 seers of scummings and strainings.

At Badolgachhi, and some other places, it is not usual to carry the manufacture any further. All sugar is considered as equally good, and the molasses and treacle are sold in that state. The former is used in several kinds of sweetmeats that are consumed by the poor. The treacle is used in preparing tobacco for being smoked; but the poor often use it in sweetmeats. Both may undergo farther operations from the boiler; but at Badolgachhi these are not usually performed. I shall now therefore state the account, which I received from a manufacturer, of the profit and charge of the operation conducted in the manner which I have just now described.

CHARGE.

To building	the boiling house,.............................. Rs.	50	0
	the claying house,..............................	50	0
	the straining house,..............................	30	0
	the ware-house,..............................	45	0
	the fence, by which these are surrounded,..............	25	0
	the iron boiler,..............................	96	0
		296	0

To pots of various kinds,.............................. Rs.	38	0
To sackcloth for strainers,..............................	3	0
To cotton cloth for ditto,..............................	1	8
To bambús,..............................	1	8
To ashes of the plantain tree,..............................	8	0
To milk,..............................	9	0
To mats on which the sugar is dried,..............................	5	0
To plants, ladles, &c...............................	1	0
To ropes and flax *(pat)*,..............................	2	0
To fuel, (reed called *birna*,)..............................	125	0

TO SERVANTS.

One Gomashta or agent, who also receives a commission on the extract, from the cultivators, at four rupees per maund, for 12 months,.. Rs.	48	0
One watchman and messengers, for 12 months,..............	24	0
To one head boiler, for five months,..............................	25	0
To four under boilers, for ditto,..............................	30	0
To one weigher and strainer, for ditto,..............................	10	0
To four workmen, for ditto,..............................	32	0
To 700 maunds of cake-extract, at 1¼ rupees,..............................	875	0
To 500 maunds of pot-extract, at 1½ rupees,..............................	750	0
	2284	0
Deduct the value of the buildings and apparatus at the end of the year,	100	0
	2184	0

PRODUCE.

By 700 maunds (lb. 41,663) of cake-extract, (the seer 58 sa. wt.,) 140 maunds (72 sa. wt. the seer or lb. 10,344) of sugar, at 6 rupees a maund,	840	0
By 500 maunds (or lb. 29,082) of pot-extract, 112½ maunds (or lb. 8,312) of sugar, at 6½ rupees....	731	4
By 800 maunds (or lb. 47,615) of molasses and treacle, at ¾ rupee, ...	600	0
	2171	4
Loss....................	12	12
	2184	0

The apparent loss here arises from the estimate having been formed on what happened last year, when the crop was unfavourable, and the price of extract high. In usual years, no cake extract is made into sugar, and the price of the pot-jagry by the maund of 58 sa. wt. the seer is seldom so high as 1¼ rupees. Then the charges will be,

To sundries,.................... Rs.	659	0
To 1200 maunds of pot-extract, at 1¼,..	1500	0
	2159	0
Deduct apparatus.....	100	0
	2059	0

RETURNS.

270 maunds sugar, at 6½,.................... Rs.	1755	0
800 maunds molasses and treacle,....................	600	0
	2355	0
Profit,....	296	0
	2059	0

This profit is probably somewhat under-rated, and would be a return totally inadequate in this country for a capital of 2,000 rupees; but it will be seen in what manner this is made up to the manufacturer. The sugar made in this part of the country is called *badol*, and is reckoned the best in the district.

I shall now detail another account and fuller process. It was given by a manufacturer of Chintamon, who, owing to the failure of the crop last year, had given up business, as his capital was small, and he could not make advances, until he recovers what has already been advanced, which probably may never be the case, at least so he seemed to think. He was on this account less liable to depart from truth in his account. All his weights are of the Calcutta standard, or 80 sa. wt. to the seer. The extract is all of the pot kind, and in straining it through the sackcloth, one-half comes away in molasses or *math*, whereas at Badolgachhi, a quarter only drains through the bags. To what circumstance this difference is owing, I could not ascertain; whether to the juice having been less evaporated than at Badolgachhi, or whether the manufacturer of Chintamon applies more water than is done at the last-mentioned place. The operation is nearly the same; only the sugar that is obtained by the two first applications of the leaves is kept separate from that procured by the third application, which is considered as of an inferior quality. Every maund, or 40 seers, therefore, gives 20 seers of molasses, 7½ seers of sugar of the 1st quality, 2½ seers of the second quality, and five seers only of treacle, while five seers are lost in scumming. The quantity of treacle is diminished in proportion to the increase of molasses. The custom near Chintamon is, to prepare the molasses by boiling them three days from morning until night. The quantity of this inspissation is reduced in the proportion of three to five. When this has been accomplished, the inspissated molasses are poured into pots, each containing 1½ maund, or lb. 123¼; a small quantity of sugar, $\frac{1}{18}$ part of a seer, and an equal quantity of potash, are put into each pot, and the contents are stirred about diligently with a stick, until they become cool. It then forms a substance called *khungr*, which sells at from rupees 5 to 5½ the pot. Every year one furnace could boil 1500 maunds of pot-extract, although many manufactureres do not boil more than 1000 maunds, not being able to procure a greater quantity. The following estimate will shew the produce of 1000 maunds, or a little more than 82,000 lbs.

To 187½ maunds of fine sugar, at 7½ rupees	1406	4
To 62½ maunds of coarse sugar, at 4¼ rupees	265	10
To 200 pots of inspissated molasses, at five rupees a pot,	1000	0
To 125 maunds of treacle, at one rupee	125	0
Rs.	2796	14

The expense, as stated by the same person.

1 agent or accountant, 12 months	Rs.	42	0	0
1 weigher and messenger, 12 months		15	0	0
1 head boiler, four months		16	0	0
2 scummers, ditto		10	0	0
2 men to supply fuel		8	0	0
2 strainers		10	0	0
2 curers		12	0	0
Wages	Rs.	113	0	0

Potash	Rs.	8	0	0
Milk		15	0	0
Fuel		120	0	0
Pots		24	0	0
Cotton cloth		2	0	0
Sackcloth		2	0	0
Bambú and ropes		4	0	0
Porters		12	0	0
	Rs.	187	0	0

The houses and boiler cost about 400 rupees, of which one-half should be deducted for interest, tear and wear, and insurance. The total expense will be

Servants	Rs.	113	0	0
Sundries		187	0	0
Buildings and repairs		200	0	0
1000 maunds of extract		1500	0	0
	Rs.	2000	0	0

The profit therefore is 796 rupees upon a capital of 2000; but owing to the very great fluctuations in the market, this is liable to great variations. The price of the sugar, January 1808, is very high.—The merchants refuse to take advances at 5¼ rupees for the maund of 72 sa. wt. the seer (lb. 73$\frac{985}{1000}$), and stand out for six rupees, although the extract is very cheap, being below what I have stated as the common price. Indeed if the estimate above given be accurate, they could not afford to sell it for less. The sugar of this division, called Phulvari, from the name of a pergunnah, is reckoned to be of the second quality in the district.

There is another method practised, although I have not been able to procure any satisfactory account of the quantity of each article produced. The manufacturer follows the same method as usual, and applies the weed three times, at each time from 20 to 25 days. All the sugar procured by this manner, is of the same quality, if the weed is allowed to remain a sufficient length of time. It is only when a short time is allowed, that the third cake is of an inferior quality to the two first. After three applications, what remains in four pots, is collected into one, and treated a fourth time with leaves, and then produces some sugar of the best quality. This process goes on, until the rainy season puts a stop to making sugar of the first quality. Then the kotra or treacle is boiled down to the thickness of pot-extract, and is mixed with an equal quantity of that substance, and is treated just as the pot-extract was by itself, this gives sugar of a second quality. The treacle from this is again treated in the same manner, and, with the addition of an equal quantity of pot-extract, yields sugar of a third quality. The treacle from this is inspissated, and then treated as extract without receiving addition, and gives a coarse kind of sugar called *buti*.

The following was given as the produce of 1000 maunds at 90 sa. wt. the seer, or of 1250 maunds of 72 sa. wt. the seer.

To 125 maunds of 1st sugar, at six rupees.	750	0	0
To 75 ditto of 2nd do. at 5½ do.....	412	0	0
To 50 ditto of 3rd do. at five do......	250	0	0
To 25 ditto of 4th do. at four do..	100	0	0
To 833$\frac{1}{3}$ maunds of molasses, at one rupee per maund of 60 sa. wt. the seer, or 1000 maunds......	1000	0	0
Rs.	2512	0	0
The price of the extract, at 1¾ rupees the maund of 90 sa. wt. the seer, should be	1750	0	0
	762	0	0
Deduct expense...	500	0	0
Profit	262	0	0

Near the Korotoya, the sugar is chiefly manufactured in this manner, and is called Ghoraghat sugar. It is reckoned the worst in the district.

The number of sugar manufacturers amounts to 141, and the boilers which they employ was stated to be 225. These on an average boil each 1000 maunds, Calcutta weight, or altogether 2,25,000 maunds. The sugar may amount to about ¼ of this weight, or 41,219 cwt. and may be worth 3,37,500 rupees, or a little more than eight rupees a cwt. The molasses and treacle may be about ⅜ of the weight and may be worth about 1,50,000 rupees. The raw material is produced in much greater quantity than the manufacturers consume, and by far the greater part of the sugar, and a large proportion of the molasses and treacle are exported.

All the manufacturers *(goldars)* are natives, and most of them are men of considerable wealth. Three or four thousand rupees for each boiler is the smallest capital that can carry on the business, and very few have borrowed money. Some live in a very decent manner, like landholders, and some indeed have purchased considerable landed estates. A principal part of their profit arises from advancing money to the cultivators, from whom they procure the extract. The farmers who want advances, in the end of June or beginning of July, apply to a manufacturer, who sends a person to inspect the cane. The terms having been then settled, a *kundokhalasi* or release is procured from the landlord, who accepts of the manufacturer's security for the rent, in place of his hypothee on the crop, and the manufacturer becomes bound to pay the whole money, that is to be advanced by four instalments, into the hands of the landlord. In general this is sufficient to pay the whole rent of the farm. It is usual to advance from 12 to 15 rupees on the *bigah*, that is equal to half an acre. The extract is received in payment at $\frac{1}{16}$ below the harvest market price, which the manufacturers keep low, as no one bids until this has been arranged. The manufacturer besides receives the value of half an anna in extract for every rupee advanced, and when the account is closed, from 1¼ to 1¾ anna on the rupee by way of interest. He therefore on the whole receives from 2¾ to 3¼ annas on each rupee that he has advanced, or from 17 to 20 per cent. Both landlords and farmers are desirous of dealing with sugar manufacturers.

The Company occasionally takes some of the sugar, and a little is bought by petty traders, for the purpose of retailing in the country; but by far the greater part of the sugar, and much of the molasses and treacle, are exported to Murshedabad and Calcutta, on account of the manufacturers, who dispose of them by their agents.

SECTION 5.—*Manufacture of Indigo.*

This manufacture has been entirely introduced by Europeans; for although a dye has long been prepared by the natives of India from the Indigo plant, yet no sooner had the plant been carried to America, than the dye manufactured by European skill totally supplanted the Indian kind in our markets, and it is only the same skill that has restored this manufacture to its original country. Whether or not the European dyers have used judgment in rejecting the original and cheap manufacture of India, I cannot say; for a great many considerations, which at present I have no means of investigating, must be previously weighed; but there is no doubt, that the dye produced by the Indian kind is perfectly good. The process, which is used by the Indian dyers with success, in extracting the dye from their own kind, would according to them produce no effect with the drug prepared after the European method; the Indian drug is therefore equally effectual, and probably easier wrought than the European; but the quantity of it required for a given quantity of thread is much greater, the freight on the same value would be much higher, and therefore it may be doubted, whether on the whole it would be a cheaper dye. It may be also doubted, whether it would keep so well in long voyages. The difficulties that are in the way of the manufacture, while carried on by Europeans, are so great, that if the Indian kind would answer equally well, great advantage would arise from diverting European enterprize and capital to other pursuits, for which they are better fitted.

Until however the experiment has been fairly tried, and it has been shewn to the satisfaction of the English dyers, that the drug prepared after the Indian fashion is equally advantageous with that prepared after the European method, which may never be the case, this manufacture is of great importance, and deserves encouragement so far as to supply the British market. How far the manufacturing for exportation to foreign markets may be advantageous, either for the public or for individuals, is doubtful. The state of markets becomes in that case so uncertain that many are ruined, and in fact there is reason to think, that upon the whole, more has been lost in this manufacture than has been gained, especially in this district, where it never has thriven.

The machinery at first was expensive and ill-adapted for the purpose; but considerable improvements have been made, both in reducing the expense, and in perfecting the operation. The following is an account of the works necessary in a small factory consisting of two vats.

First, a well, tank, or canal, for supplying water. In some parts of this district the water is found abundantly in wells at a very little depth from the surface, and in such cases, this seems to be by far the best method of procuring water, because the supply is more certain. Many situations, however, do not admit of wells, and recourse must be had either to tanks or to canals from rivers. The supply from the former, unless the tank is very large, or contains numerous springs, is very uncertain, and sometimes fails; so that the whole crop is lost. The supply from rivers is more regular, but at times the water sinks so low beneath the level of the works, that the raising it is attended with great expense. In a level country, raising water is always attended with a considerable expense. Pumps answer very well in point of effect, but they are very liable to require repair, and native artists want skill, so that the works in which pumps have been employed, have often been at a stand, and more simple machines are therefore in general preferred. The best that I have seen, is a wheel moved by people walking on its inner circumference, like the wheel of a crane. The water is raised by buckets fixed to the circumference of the wheel, which empty their contents as each arrives at the summit. One constructed by Mr. Tucker has cost only 60 rupees, can be easily repaired, and raises a great deal of water. It however requires the water to be always nearly on the same level, and cannot raise it to more than the diameter of the wheel. It is also occasionally liable to go wrong, and in such cases, may stop the works for a day or two. Some people, therefore, prefer raising the water by buckets with ropes passing over a pulley. On the whole, I am persuaded, that the introduction of the lever *(yatam* or *pacota)* of Madras, or the leathern bag wrought by oxen on an inclined plain, as used in the west and south of India, would be a great improvement.

From the well, the water should pass along a channel into a reservoir. Both channel and reservoir should be built of brick, and covered with plaister. The channel, like all the others in the works, should be of considerable length, to allow sufficient room for all operations. The reservoir should have walls about two or three feet high, and should be large and shallow, so that impurities may quickly subside, and that as much of the water as possible may be exposed to the sun and air, which Mr. Tucker has found to be of great advantage. The reservoir should be of a size sufficient to contain as much water as will at once fill the vats, by which means the operation goes on more equally and quickly, and this last circumstance, in every part of the operation, is a principal means of rendering it perfect, the drug *cæteris paribus* being always better in proportion to the quick ness with which it has been made. The cock, by which the water is drawn from the reservoir, should be at some distance from the bottom, in order to allow the heavy impurities to be entirely separated.

The steeping vat or vats are constructed like the reservoir, being built of brick, lined with plaster, open above, and having walls about three feet high. The dimensions now most usually employed are 20 feet by 30. They are filled with water by means of a brick and mortar channel, which communicates with the reservoir, the cock of the reservoir must of course be above the level of their upper edge. In these vats, the Indigo weed is infused, and the infusion is assisted by a fermentation, and much of the success of the operation, no doubt, depends on this being properly conducted. The vats which Mr. Tucker employs are very shallow, and are not covered above. The first circumstance may be of use, by giving a greater exposure to air, but I suspect that the latter is an ill-judged economy. A heavy fall of rain would no doubt in some measure check the fermentation, and the difference between a clear sun-shine day and cloudy weather would have strong effects, and although the fermentation might not be altogether stopped, the uncertainty of the time, from the difference of circumstances, will no doubt render the whole operation more uncertain. A simple shed therefore, to exclude sun and rain, I have no doubt, should be added to the steeping or fermenting vats, but a very free circulation of air is necessary.

It is of great importance that the plant should be brought to the steeping vats as fresh from the field as possible; for whatever has heated becomes totally unfit for use, and this is a strong additional reason, why the whole land cultivated with Indigo ought to be compact and contiguous to the works. The vat having been filled with weed, bambûs are laid over it, and across those are laid beams, in order to prevent it from floating. The reservoir is then opened, and the water is allowed to run into the vat until the wood is just covered. The infusion and fermentation is completed in from 12 to 16 hours, and the skill of the manufacturer is required to determine when this has been accomplished. When the superintendent judges fit, the infusion is drawn from the weed by a plug near the bottom of the vat, and is allowed to flow into the beating vat.

The beating vats are made exactly like those used for steeping the weed, and should be nearly of the same size; for according to the present system, the shallower the infusion is in them the better. The object to be attained in these vats is to impregnate the colouring particles, that are suspended in the water, with oxygen, by which it becomes insoluble in water, and unites into a solid substance called fecula by the artists. The means of attaining this is to mix the air and infusion together as much as possible, and the larger the surface is, this is so much the easier performed by the method now employed. Formerly a complex machinery, called beaters, was used for agitating the infusion, and thus mixing it with air; but a much simpler method is now followed. A number of naked men or boys go into the vat, and run backwards and forwards, beating the infusion with a wooden implement called *phauri*—see drawing No. 35.

The following rule is observed by Mr. Tucker, for judging when the vat has been sufficiently beaten. Dip a bit of cloth in it, and after the clear water has run off, a thicker liquid of a brown colour will begin to drop; receive some of this on a white plate, and add a little lime-water. If the colour changes in the least to green, the beating must be continued; but, if there is no tinge of green, then the beating has been sufficient, no injury however arises from a little too much.

Pure indigo is a substance as light or even rather lighter than water, and could not therefore be separated, from that in which it is suspended, by any means so readily, as by adding some heavy substance for which it has an attraction. The substance used is lime, dissolved in water, of which a quantity is put into the vat, after its contents have been properly beaten, that is, after the dying material has become a proper oxoid. The quantity of lime-water must be left to the judgment of the operator, no rule having been yet discovered for ascertaining what is proper. This is mixed by a few turns of the people through the vat, and the fecula or indigo is allowed to subside, which it will do in about an hour. The beating vat should have three cocks, one above the other, by which the water, as it becomes clear or pellucid, from the subsiding of the indigo, is to be drawn. The lowest, it is evident, must be at some distance from the bottom, in order to prevent the indigo from escaping. When the indigo has in this manner been drained as much as possible, it is collected by means of coarse towels into a well on the outside of the vat, and is from thence put into a boiler.

The boiling and pressing house must be covered ; but a thatched shed is well suited for the purpose. The boiler is a square furnace of brick, which in the centre contains a large cauldron of iron. In this the indigo is inspissated by a little boiling, which also probably contributes to give the particles a stronger tendency to cohere.

After having been boiled for a sufficient length of time, the moist indigo is poured on a draining table, which consists of transverse bars surrounded by a ledge. The table is covered with a cloth, on which the boiled indigo is poured, and the greater part of the water drains through the cloth. The indigo is then put in boxes, that are perforated with holes, and which are lined with a cloth that is brought over the indigo, so as cover it on all sides. These boxes are placed under presses, and the water is squeezed out as completely as possible, so that the indigo is left in a mass like a square cheese. The presses used, as in making cheese, are of two kinds, screws and levers. The screws are more convenient, as occupying less room, and being easily employed, but the pressure by them is constantly diminished, as the water runs off ; so that the levers ought to have the undoubted preference, as the pressure by them is uniform, which is a matter of the utmost consequence for completing the coherence of the particles.

The masses of indigo having been taken from the press, are cut into cubes of three inches, and for the convenience of packing, it is of importance that the size should be as uniform as possible. The cubes should be sprinkled with wood-ashes, which prevent flies from laying their eggs ; and, until perfectly dry, they should be exposed to the free air, in single rows, placed on bambú stages. The pieces are then brushed, and packed in boxes for market. The house in which the indigo is dried, or the curing house, as a security against fire, should be of brick, with numerous doors, to admit the air ; but many manufacturers content themselves with a thatched building.

Mr. Tucker was so good as to favour me with the following estimate of the expense of an indigo work, capable on the above plan of making 100 maunds of indigo in one year.

To buildings and utensils, ...	Rs. 2500
To 20,000 bundles of weed (six feet in circumference) at 10 per rupee,..	2000
Manufacturing charges, such as cloth, boxes, fuel, labourer, at two annas a bundle,..	2500
Servants employed the whole year,..................................	600

Loss by bad debts,.. 500

Sa. Rs. 8100

To which I must add the remuneration due to the superintendent,.. .. 3600

Rs. 11700

This is the least stock required ; but in calculating the profit, we must deduct from this charge the value of the buildings and utensils at the end of the year, which may be 1700 rupees ; there will remain 10,000 rupees ; add interest at 12 per cent. on the stock, and the charge will be 11,404. Now indigo at Calcutta may usually sell at 140 rupees a maund. The profit therefore will be rupees 2696. But this is the appearance of affairs in good years. When the crops fail, a great part of the charge is incurred, and the return is next to nothing. I know, that a higher value than what I have stated is generally put on the indigo at Calcutta ; but this high price is merely nominal. The whole indigo cannot be sold at this rate, and the manufacturer is tempted to send his indigo to London, on his own account, and borrows money on the credit of what he sends ; when all accounts are settled, I believe, it will in general be found, that what I have stated is rather above the true price.

The manufacturing and selling the indigo are however the easy, and, comparatively, agreeable parts of the business. It is the procuring the plant or raw material that is attended with a trouble, vexation, and disappointment, so great and incessant, that I am astonished how any person can labour through the employment. The manufacturers have in general given up cultivating the plant ; the frauds, indeed, and extortions, to which every man, cultivating on a large scale, must be exposed in this country, seem to render this plan unadvisable. They therefore have had recourse to purchasing the weed from the farmers ; but the difficulties in this way also are numerous. In the first place, each farmer will only cultivate to a very small extent, so that the space, in which weed sufficient for making even 100 maunds of indigo is raised, will extend for some miles. In the next place, the farmers will not undertake the cultivation without receiving, in advance, nearly the expected value of the whole crop, and after having received the money, they are very careless in the cultivation, or in the payment of what dificiencies arise, either from their want of care, or from the uncertainty of season. The ploughing, sowing, weeding, and watching the crops are, in fact, very generally neglected, unless the manufacturer employs people to watch over the farmers, and disputes naturally occur between these two classes of people, so that there is no end to the squabbles and petty suits that arise, unless where the manufacturer takes the law into his own hands, and quashes all dispute by force, which it is alleged is sometimes done. Yet, at looking into the nature of the agreements, every thing would appear easy.

When a factory is first established, the manufacturer usually assembles the *(mondols)*, most wealthy farmers of the neighbouring lands, and from the accounts, which they give of the population and nature of the soil in their respective subdivisions *(mauzas)*, a conjecture is formed how many bigahs of cultivation may be obtained in each, and upon this calculation, money is advanced to these principal farmers, who give a duly attested receipt, promising to divide the amount among the smaller farmers in such a manner as to procure the greatest quantity of properly cultivated land. A few days, commonly, after this transaction, each principal farmer, that has received advances, delivers in a formal written agreement, called a *satta*, by which he binds himself under a specific, penalty to distribute the money, to procure the cultivation of the number of bigahs for which he has received advances, and to give every facility and assistance to the manufacturer, in endeavouring to have the cultivation properly conducted. The *satta* also specifies all the labour which the farmer is to perform, such as plouging, sowing, and weeding, and the price which he is to obtain for his plant and seed. This agreement is sometimes not executed, until the contracting farmers have distributed as much of the advances as the other farmers will receive, and then it is accompanied with a paper, called *tayedad* or rule, which specifies the sum of money received in advance by each farmer, and the quantity of land which he has agreed to cultivate. It is generally understood, although not expressly mentioned, that the contracting farmer is to receive $\frac{1}{16}$ of the produce. This commission is paid sometimes entirely by the farmer in produce, sometimes entirely by the manufacturer, and sometimes each pays a half, but this is always previously settled. In fact, nothing is left undetermined, and there is written evidence for almost every part of the contract.

So far in general every thing goes on smoothly, but now the agents of the manufacturer must see, that the quantity of land agreed for has been ploughed, sown, weeded, and watched, otherwise the want of faith, that too much prevails in this country, would occasion a general neglect of these duties, the advances having removed the farmer from immediate danger of starving, the only adequate inducement for labour.

If the cultivators have not seed, this is sent from the factory to the contracting farmer, by whom it is distributed, to be repaid at harvest, at a rate fixed by the agreement. When the crop is ripe, it is cut by the cultivator, and usually carried to the factory, at the expense of the manufacturer, and the cultivators attend to see it measured, and the amount regularly entered in the books of the factory. When the crop season is over, the farmers assemble, and settle their accounts. If the season has been favourable, they receive a balance; but if it has been unfavorable, or if they have taken too large a sum in advance, they owe a balance, and it is generally alleged, that almost every farmer sooner or later falls into arrears. When any balance is due by the manufacturer, it is always paid immediately, together with new advances for the next season; the balances due by the cultivator, accumulated of course with interest, are considered as a part of the advances for the next year; and in old established factories, eight or ten neighbours are commonly required to be mutual security for each other, as each individual would no sooner be involved in difficulty, from his imprudent use of the money received in advance, than he would abscond, but eight or ten men cannot readily go at once, and those who stay behind would be instantly seized, they therefore watch each other's conduct, and give notice, if they suspect, that a neighbour is about to absent himself.

At the first commencement of a factory, the advances can only be made through the agency of contracting farmers; but as great evils arise from their conduct, the manufacturers endeavour to shake them off, as soon as possible, and to enter into a specific agreement with each cultivator.

The principal defect in this contract is, that a constant superintendence on the part of the manufacturer is necessary, and this gives rise to endless disputes and complaints, especially where the lands are so much scattered, that the greater part of the superintendence must be entrusted to persons of a description in whom very little reliance can be placed. In fact, the most violent complaints exist on all sides; and both farmers and landholders are very unwilling that the manufacture should be extended, or even continued.

Before I enter into any discussion on the causes of this dissatisfaction, it is necessary to premise, that were credit due to the universal clamour in this district, its inhabitants would be unfit for society. According to the querulous assertions of the people, every officer of justice and police is venal, every landholder, or in deed person in power, is a rapacious oppressor, every trader is a cheat, every one is a liar, the greater part are thieves, and many are robbers and murderers. At first the assertions which I heard were so confidently advanced, and from quarters so apparently disinterested, that I was inclined to believe a considerable part of what was asserted respecting the character of individuals; but I soon found, that the accusations were so universal, that society could not exist among such scoundrels, as the people represented each other to be. I therefore consider by far the greater part of such assertions to be unfounded ebullitions of no import, and intended merely as an excuse for the necessitous state, into which imprudent indulgence has placed the greater part of the inhabitants.

The reasons assigned by different classes of people for the dislike of the farmers and landholders to the indigo manufacture are so contradictory, that a judicial investigation would be required to ascertain their truth. I shall therefore simply mention them.

The reasons assigned by the farmers are—

1st. After they have taken advances from a manufacturer, he considers them as his slaves, beats and confines them whenever he is dissatisfied, and always refuses to allow them to pay their balances, and to relinquish the cultivation.

2nd. That they are cheated, both in the measure of their land, and in the measure of the weed. This does not imply, that the manufacturer is considered by the natives as a cheat, the fault, even by them, is usually attributed to his servant,

3rd. That the whole produce of the field does not exceed the rent which the land-holders heighten, so as to render the cultivation ruinous, and, as most of the land cultivated for indigo was out of lease, the owners may no doubt demand whatever rent they please.

The reasons assigned by the land-holders or *zemindars* are—

4th. That several of the manufacturers are so insolent and violent, that no person of any sort of rank can live near them with comfort.

5th. That the manufacturers intermeddle between them and their tenantry, so that it is impossible to collect the rent, especially from the farmers who accept of advances for indigo, who are encouraged and supported in refusing payment.

The reasons assigned by the planters are as follows—

6th. The *zemindars* are unwilling that Europeans should settle near them, for the lower natives look on every European as belonging to the governing caste, and thereby the consequence of the landlord is diminished in the eyes of the neighbourhood.

7th. That the landlords are afraid to make any of their usual illegal extortions in the vicinity of an European, lest the people, especially the farmers who raise indigo, should be able to lay their complaints before the judge.

8th. That the farmers are deterred from the cultivation by the threats of the landlords, and the increase of rent.

That the behaviour of the Europeans in general is so improper as to be the real cause of the unwillingness in the farmer, I think is highly improbable; but that occasional instances of blamable conduct towards the farmers have happened, there is little doubt, and so long as private Europeans are not perfectly subject, like other people, to the courts of law established in their neighbourhood, it is impossible altogether to prevent this inconvenience. It is indeed very much to the credit of the manufacturers, that, under such circumstances, their general behaviour must be allowed to have been correct. The only remedy, that can with propriety be employed, is to prevent in future every one from settling in the country parts of Bengal, who is not subject to the same laws and jurisdiction with the natives, and British subjects, probably should never be put on that footing. Gentlemen who have already engaged in trade or manufactures must of course remain, until they choose to retire; but, unless a colony is meant to be formed, infinite advantage would arise from altogether refusing new licenses, and restricting Europeans, who are not responsible to the Company for their conduct, to a residence in the principal towns and seaports. The manufacture might be carried on to a sufficient extent by native Portuguese, Armenians, or other persons who are in every respect amenable to the common law of the country.

The cause of dissatisfaction, that seems best founded, is the difference between the manufacturers and land-holders, for there is little doubt, that it is the influence of the latter chiefly, and the idle stories propagated by them, that have rendered the farmers discontented, whether or not, the manufacturers have protected the farmers from oppression, or whether they have been induced, by false represention to support those who were unwilling to pay the just demands of the landlords, it is evident, must be beyond my power to determine, but so far as I can judge,this is the chief point at issue. I am inclined, perhaps from national prejudice, to assign the former cause, yet even in this case, it must be confessed, that the manufacturer is interfering in a dispute with which he has no concern. The sugar manufacturers, who aid the land-holders in collecting their revenue, meet in return with every assistance, and among the natives I heard no complaints against this class of men.

CHAPTER III.

COMMERCE.

SECTION 1.—*Exports and Imports.*

As there is no public account of the goods exported and imported from this district, the amount which I can state is merely conjectural. In the accompanying Table No. 9, will be found the result of my inquiries on this subject, but it must be observed, that some articles are not included ; of these the most important are, 1st, cattle, of which an account has been already given under the head of agriculture. 2nd, foreign goods and articles of luxury, that are imported by different persons, for their own use ; and finally, numerous articles, which are sold at fairs, especially that of Nekmurdun ; for most of the dealers who meet at that mart are strangers, and the goods pass from one hand to another, so as merely to have a transit through this district.

With regard to the quantity allotted to each division, I have considered only the situation of the marts where the goods are landed or shipped, and not the places where they have been produced or consumed, except in the great manufactures of cloth, sugar, and indigo, the produce of which may be considered as exported from the workshops or factories.

The rice, and its preparation, *chira*, are sent chiefly to Múrshedabad, Calcutta, and the intermediate towns. A small portion also is sent to Bhagolpúr.

Along with the rice, I might to both exports and imports have added a small quantity of pulse, but this branch of commerce is very inconsiderable and fluctuating. The quantity produced is very nearly equal to the consumption, and the export and import usually arises from some season's being favorable, or the contrary, to certain kinds of pulse more than others. When any kind has thriven remarkably, a part is exported, and a little is imported of any kind the crop of which has been scanty.

The mustard seed is imported from Rongpúr, the oil is sent to Múrshedabad and Narayungunj, near Dhaka.

The *ghi* imported is the produce of herds of cattle belonging to this district, which in the dry season are sent to Morung, and bring back the produce of their milk in *ghi*. The exports are made to Múrshedabad.

Most of the betelnut comes from the neighbourhood of Dhaka, and is of the kind called dry, but a large proportion also comes from the Rongpúr district, and is of the kind called wet, the husk remaining on the nut in a humid putrescent state.

The cocoanut comes from Dhaka and Nodiya.

Tobacco is not raised in a quantity sufficient to supply the demand of the country, yet a little is exported. The reason of this is, that the commodity is very cheap in the northern parts of Rongpúr, and comes to this district in such quantities as to admit of exportation: some is sent to Calcutta and Múrshedabad, but the greater part goes to Narayungunj.

The *ganja* goes mostly to Calcutta, I believe for exportation.

The ginger and other seasonings are sent to Múrshedabad and Calcutta. These seasonings, which are sold by people called *jhalwálehs*, and which are exported, are turmeric, capsicum, onions, and garlic. The first is the only one of consequence.

The goods sold by *possaris* or druggists, that are objects of exportation and importation, are as follows:

1st.	Black pepper,	from Calcutta.
2d.	Spices,	from Calcutta.
3d.	Sandal-wood,	from Calcutta.
4th.	Paints,	from Calcutta.

5th. Lac from Asam, which comes chiefly by the way of Kumérkhálí. Except a little that is imported for the use of shoe-makers, almost the whole is used by the dyers of Maldeh, who after they have extracted the dye, sell the remainder to Múrshedabad, from whence a part is again sent into the district, to supply those who make bracelets and sealing-wax.

6th. *Monjista*, from Butan, is imported by the merchants of Dinajpúr and Raygunj, in a greater quantity than supplies the dyers of Maldeh, and part is sent to Múrshedabad.

7th. *Lodh* and a few other dying drugs are brought from Rajmohol and other neighbouring countries; but among these the only one of the least importance is the coarse Rongpúr indigo used at Maldeh.

The black pepper and lac are the two most important articles.

The wax imported is from Morung, that exported from Hemtabad and Dinajpúr goes to Calcutta, that from Maldeh is chiefly, I believe, used at the Company's factory on the opposite side of the river.

Most of the Bengal salt that is used in this district comes from Narayungunj, near Dhaka, which is the chief mart for the Chittagong and Bulwa salt. The coast salt from Calcutta. Both are always very much adulterated by the petty traders, before they are retailed, in so much indeed, that the retail price is often lower than that which is here stated.

All the metals, except the iron, are imported from Calcutta. The iron comes from Birbhúm by the way of Múrshedabad. The brass vessels are chiefly made at Kangtoya (Cutwa R.), a town between Múrshedabad and Calcutta, that is very famous for this manufacture. The *dosta*, or metal which I have called zinc, seems to be a kind of pewter, or alloy that contains a very large proportion of the zinc.

The goods sold by *monikaris* are beads, coral, mockcoral, rubies, and pearls, European cutlery, looking glasses, chiefly made at Múrshedabad, brass and wooden cups, silk strings, and wooden combs. They are imported from Calcutta and Múrshedabad.

The shells or *changk*, I believe, are the produce of the Maldive Islands, and are imported from Calcutta by the way of Kumarkhalí.

The stone plates and cups are imported from the west of India, by the way of Múrshedabad.

Sal and *sisu* timbers are brought down the rivers from Morung, and from the low lands subject to Bútan. I have not included in the estimate, those which merely float through the district. A little fire-wood is exported from Maldeh and Ghoraghat by the Company, in whose accounts the exact amount will be seen, I have not therefore included it in the estimate.

The bambús and bambú mats are chiefly exported in the boats that carry away rice and sugar, and are employed to keep the goods from injury by leaking and rain.

The sackcloth also is chiefly used for the package of these articles of commerce, and of piece goods, and a good deal is imported from the northern parts of Rongpúr, where it is very cheap. The *pat* is exported chiefly by the boatmen, who come for the above-mentioned goods, and is used in their vessels for cordage.

The *son* is mostly exported by the Company.

Cotton-wool, of a coarse quality, from the western parts of India, is imported into almost every division of the district, especially towards the N. and W. All this comes by the way of Múrshedabad, or of its port, Bhogowangola. A little of this fine cotton, which grows in the south-east part of this district, is sent into Natore, and about an equal value comes from English Bazar to Maldeh.

The raw silk, which I have mentioned as exported, is entirely the produce of the S. E. parts of the district, and is sold at Rongpúr and Lalvorish, chiefly to the Company's factories. I have made no allowance in the tables for the silk produced on the banks of Mohanonda, as the two sides of the river are so intimately blended in commercial concerns, that a great part of the silk passes more than once from one district to the other, before it is finally fitted for sale, and so far as I could learn, the left bank produces nearly about as much as is woven in this district.

The chintz is brought from Patna.

The shawls are brought from Múrshedabad.

The English woollen cloths from Calcutta.

The carpets are brought from Patna.

The *gur* or extract of sugar-cane, the sugar, molasses, and treacle are sent mostly to Múrshedabad. A little is also sent to Narayungunj. These three last are mostly exported by the manufacturers.

The indigo is sent entirely to Calcutta by the manufacturers.

From all this, it will appear, that the chief intercourse, which this district has in commerce, is with Calcutta, with Múrshedabad, or its port, Bhogowangola, with Narayungunj, which in some measure is the port of Dhaka, with Kushte, which is the port of Kumérkhálí, and with Patna.

SECTION 2.—*Of the persons by whom trade or commerce is conducted.*

Although some native houses deal in this district to perhaps a greater extent, the Honourable Company in every view must be considered as infinitely the most conspicuous among the merchants. Every native is desirous of dealing with the Company to the utmost extent possible, while it is notorious, that the goods procured by the Company are both better and cheaper than what individuals can obtain. These circumstances are no doubt owing to the fair manner in which the purchases have been conducted.

Merchants, that is to say persons who export and import goods, which they buy and sell without taking any share in their preparation, are by the natives divided into two kinds *sayodagur* and *mohajon*, which differ merely in the extent of their dealings, the *sayodagur* having a very large capital, and possessing many vessels; while the *mohajon's* capital is moderate, and he in general hires the vessels on which he loads his goods. *Sayodagur* is said to be a Persian word, and *mohajon* is said to be Songskrito, and both are said to be in fact synonymous, although the above distinction has been now adopted. Both words seem to have been introduced from the western parts of India, and probably by the Mahommedans; for in the time of Bollal Sen, these persons had not obtained a station or importance sufficient to procure a rank or caste appropriate to themselves.

Among the natives, in fact, their is now no person who resides in the district that is considered as a *sayodagur*. One family indeed has acquired immense wealth in that line, and for nine generations the forefathers of Baidyonath Mondol carried on an extensive commerce with great reputation and propriety. The present head of the family, who has given up trade, and made large purchases of land, is just as much despised as his forefathers were respected, and the different branches of the family, having no occupation for which they are qualified, have fallen into the most violent disputes. The greatest houses who trade with this district are Bhojraj of Bhojpúr, near Patna, and Thakurdas Nondi of Kalna, near Calcutta, who with several others send here for large cargoes of rice for the Calcutta and Múrshedabad markets, and have agents that reside constantly on the spot. The European manufacturers of indigo by the natives are generally complimented with the title of *sayodagur*, and one or two of them deal so largely as to be entitled to the appellation. Some of them are so ignorant as to consider the appellation as an affront, and their servants call them *boru saheb*, or great lord.

Many smaller merchants (*mohajons*) who have capitals from 2000 to 25,000 rupees, reside in the district, and trade to the same places. They export rice, sugar, molasses, extract of sugar-cane, oil, and tobacco, and import salt, cotton, the metals, and spices. Persons of the same description from Narayungunj bring salt, cocoanuts, and betlenuts, and take away sugar, extract of sugar-cane, and tobacco. Another class of small merchants, who mostly profess themselves to be persons that have dedicated themselves entirely to religion, and who are called *gosaing* or *goswamis*, purchase large quantities of silk and cotton cloths, and import chintz, carpets, and Patna blankets. Some small merchants from Patna and Bhogolpúr bring the same articles, and catechu, a few drugs, and stone cups and plates. These take away some rice and silk cloth.

The cloth merchants of Santipúr and Múrshedabad send agents who purchase cloths, especially such pieces as have been rejected by the Company. A house from Kumérkhálí supplies shells, and the lac used at Maldeh comes from the same place. The manufacturers of sugar, who also export a great part of it, are considered as *mohajons*.

The bankers, of whom mention will hereafter be made, import European woollens, pepper, spices, cotton shawls, metals, and hard-ware ; and export ginger and turmeric. These confine their speculations entirely to the vicinity of the capital, and are not classed among *mohajons*.

I shall now consider the persons with whom the agents *(gomastahs)* of the great merchants, or the smaller merchants, deal.

In the first place, in large towns, there is a class of men called *amdawaleh*, who purchase the investment brought in a boat by wholesale, and sell the articles in small lots to the different tradesmen, or petty dealers, as these require them. In this district, salt is the principal article of importation sold in this manner, and the number of such persons is very small. The name is Persian, and until the arrival of the Mahommedans, there were probably no such persons in Bengal.

The merchants therefore dispose of the greater part of the imports, in small lots, either to the different manufacturers who require them as raw materials, or to shop-keepers *(dokání* or *dokándár)* or finally to a class of petty dealers, who are called *paikárs*. I have already given an accouut of the tradesmen, manufacturers, or artificers, and shall now therefore proceed to the other two classes.

Dokán a shop and *dokándar*, a shop-keeper, are Persian words, and until the arrival of the Mahommedans, there were probably no such things in Bengal, unless we choose to call by this name the part of an open market, where a vender sits surrounded by his goods, and exposes them for sale. This I imagine, is the original native manner of disposing of all goods in Bengal, and in this district the number of shops continues wonderfully small. I shall give a list of the different kinds, that I observed.

1. Many of the *amdawalehs* above-mentioned have shops contiguous to their ware-house, where they retail the same articles that are sold by the next class, and have capitals of about 500 rupees.

2. *Mudis*, who retail rice, pulse, salt, oil, sugar, extract of sugar-cane, prepared rice, *(muri, chira, murki,)* boiled butter, *(ghi,)* seasoning, tobacco, betlenut, and in fact all sorts of provisions. Their capitals are about 40 rupees.

3. *Chauler phorya*, a retailer of rice, who sells nothing else, and requires a capital of about 20 rupees.

4. *Loboner phorya*, who retail only salt, and have capitals of about 10 rupees.

5. *Posari*, or druggists, called also *gondho-bonik*, retail spices, sandal-wood, dyes, paints, medicines, seasonings (such as pepper, dry ginger, and carminitive seeds), betelnut, sugar, paper, and ink. They require capitals of about 100 rupees.

6. *Jhalwáleh* retail raw ginger, turmeric, onions, garlic, and capsicum, and have capitals of two or three rupees.

7. *Gúrwáleh*, who retail only extract of sugar-cane. Their capitals are about 10 or 12 rupees.

8. *Pan-supariwálehs*, who retail betel-leaf and nut. Their capitals may be three or four rupees.

9. *Ganjawáleh*, who retail the prepared buds of hemp, which are used for intoxication, and require 50 or 60 rupees as capitals.

10. *Kosyi*, or butchers; these are confined to four or five shops in Dinajpúr, and sell chiefly goat's meat. Their capital may be about 10 rupees.

11. *Katra*, shop-keepers, who purchase wooden furniture, such as chests and stools, from the carpenters, and expose them for sale. They have capitals of about 25 rupees.

12. *Basonwáleh*, who retail brass vessels, and have capitals of from 200 to 1000 rupees.

13. *Monihari*. In treating of the exports and imports, I have already given on account of the articles which these persons retail. They have capitals of from 10 to 50 rupees.

14. *Sangkhwáleh*, who retail shells and bracelets, and have capitals of from 100 to 2000 rupees.

15. *Tulawálch*, who retail cotton wool. They have capitals of from 20 to 100 rupees.

16. *Sutli* and *chotiwálehs*, who retail the twine and sackcloth that is made of the Corchorus capsularis or *pát*. They have capitals of from five to 50 rupees.

17. *Kaporya* or retailers of cloth, who have capitals of from 50 to 1000 rupees.

Besides these shop-keepers, various artists, which I have already mentioned, retail in shops the produce of their labours. These are called by the general name of *bebosadar*. For the sake of method, I shall here recapitulate the names, and refer to the head of trades, where a fuller account of them will be found.

18.	Lahérí or Luri,....	No. 6.	19.	Sangkhari,..........	No. 7.
20.	Chamar,..........	No. 14.	21.	Tamakuwaleh,........	No. 21.
22.	Modwaleh	No. 22.	23.	Goyala,.............	No. 24.
24.	Moyra,...........	No. 25.	25.	Haluyikor,..........	No. 25.
26.	Morobbawaleh,....	No. 26.	27.	Puya and Phulariwáleh,	No. 27.
28.	Bhujari,..........	No. 28.	29.	Dailhari,...........	No. 29.
30.	Kungkor,..........	No. 32.	31.	Kumar,..............	No. 33.
32.	Stone-cutter,......	No. 37.	33.	Kangsari,...........	No. 40.
34.	Bidriwaleh,........	No. 42.			

The whole number of fixed shops in the district does not amount to 2000, but at open markets (*hats*) numerous petty traders expose for sale the same, and a few other articles.

The employment of all these shop-keepers, it is evident, is much more the sale of the produce and manufactures of the district, than of goods imported, the amount of which is very small.

The business of the *paikars* remains to be discussed. They are men who possess small capitals of from 100 to 500 rupees, and generally have a small ware-house, where they deposite their purchases, until they can again dispose of them. Their whole occupation is to buy and sell, and they deal in almost every thing; but do not retail. It is through their means, in a great measure, that the capital traders both dispose of their investments, and procure new ones. They more especially, however, deal in grain, cloth, cotton, silk, and salt. The *paikárs* take a small quantity of goods at a time, and go to all the neighbouring markets, where they make their sales, and purchase the articles, which they know the great dealers will take off their hands. It is through them chiefly that the great dealers make advances for cloth or grain, because the *paikárs* are acquainted with the characters of the individuals, for whom they become security. They have from five to 6¼ per cent. commission, including the premium for security.

The greater part of the investment of rice, which is the principal commerce of the district, is however, laid in by persons who are called *bepáris*, and who in fact are chiefly the farmers that occupy lands where the soil is stiff clay. These deal in cattle, poultry, and grain, and not only bring the produce of their own farms for sale, but in the dry season, when the labour of their fields is at a stop, they make large purchases from the farmers who occupy loose soils, and carry the grain to whatever ware-house (*gola*) gives the best price. The rich farmers make large advances, and can afford to keep the grain for a favourable market. The poor chiefly assist the rich in carrying their grain to market, and receive daily wages for themselves and cattle. The advances are usually made between the middle of June and the middle of November. The bargain must be confirmed by the landlord, in order to procure his consent to wave his right of hypothic, and the money is in fact generally paid to him for rent. The usual interest is half anna or $\frac{1}{32}$ part a month, until the delivery of the grain, and this is received at what is called the market price, with an addition of $\frac{1}{16}$ th part for profit to the person who advances the money.

An inferior kind of *bepáris*, are called *phiriwálehs*, and may be compared to pedlars. They go from house to house, to make their sales and purchases, and seldom possess cattle as a consequeuce.

A class of men called *dalál* are common in many districts, but here they are confined to Roygunj, to Maldeh, and to the Company's factories. They are brokers, who are employed to find out goods for those that wish to purchase, and receive a small commission.

In the time of Bollal Sen bankers or dealers in money were called *sonar-bonik*, and were probably of little consequence, as their rank is very low; but on the Mahommedan conquest, commerce seems to have increased, and to facilitate its operations, bankers were introduced from the west of India. These bankers are divided into two kinds. *Kut'hiwálehs*, or proper bankers, and *potdárs*, or money-changers. Both are commonly called *saráf*, which is a Persian word.

The proper bankers in this district are confined entirely to the capital, where there are seven houses. The principals live generally at Múrshedabad; but some of them occasionally visit Dinajpúr, and are all of the Osho-yal sect. I have already mentioned, that some of them import certain goods, and they export dry ginger; but their principal business is granting bills of exchange for money. In the Muhammedan government, the revenue was remitted to Múrshedabad through these bankers. This branch of profit they have now lost, and are chiefly employed by the landlords in keeping their rents, in paying their revenue, and in remitting the surplus to such as reside at a distance, which is the case with the greater part. The money also, which is necessary for purchasing the exports, is chiefly sent to the district through these houses.

Bills are never discounted by these bankers, except by the house of Jogotseit, and even by that very rarely: but they occasionally lend money in advance to landholders, who are in arrear of revenue. They take one rupee per cent. a month as legal interest; but exact as much more under the name of *munafa*, which is deducted from the principal at the time when it is advanced. Bills of a short date, granted by bankers on Múrshedabad, for cash paid at Dinajpúr, besides the stamp, cost from half to one per cent. and bills on Calcutta, from one to 1½ per cent. The capital of several of these houses is supposed to be very great, and their credit is considered as indubitable.

The *potdars* or money-changers are a very numerous class, and many of them have no shop; but attend at markets, and set with their *cowries* placed in heaps before them. Except indeed at Dinajpúr and a few other places, this is the universal practice. Their principal business is to exchange *cowries* and silver. Except in towns, it would be very difficult to obtain silver for gold, and could only be procured through the favor of private persons: none of the common money-changers having a capital of 16 rupees. Even in Dinajpúr, silver for 100 rupees worth of gold can only be procured from a principal bank or *kut'hi*. A *potdar* goes in the morning to a market place, with a bag of *cowries* on his head, or if a very rich man, with a loaded ox, which if good may carry to the value of 15 rupees. All the early part of the market he sells cowries for silver to the people who wish to purchase goods, and in the evening the various huxters bring their *cowries*, and exchange them for silver. In the morning, the *potdar* usually gives 5760 *cowries*, or 72 *pon*, for a rupee, and in the evening he gives a rupee for 5920 *cowries*, or 74 *pon*, which is a profit of two *pon*, or $\frac{1}{12}$ part on every rupee that they exchange. This is on the supposition that the rupee is a new *kaldár*, such as is now struck at the mint in Calcutta. All old rupees, and every kind of rupee but the *kaldár*, pay various rates of exchange *(batta)*, according to the will of the money-changers, who it is supposed always gain more by every kind of money than by the *kaldár*. As *kaldárs* are the only legal proffer of payment, their use has become very general, notwithstanding the efforts of the bankers and money-changers to the contrary, and the money-changers would therefore have suffered a loss, had they not fallen upon a plan of marking the *kuldars* with a stamp, under pretext of ascertaining, whether they are true or false; after which, the rupee is not exchangable, without paying an additional *batta*, that seems to be entirely arbitrary, and it becomes of course a circulating medium as valuable to the money-changer as if it were foreign coin. In order to render this more agreeable to the people, they pretend, that the marks will enable those who have received the rupees to have them changed, should any other dealer refuse them as bad. The loss that is sustained by the public is very considerable, especially by the poor, who are so necessitous, that they submit to take any rupee, either in loan or payment, rather than suffer delay, and they always must pay the full *batta* or loss on exchange. If therefore a banker chooses to put a mark on the money, he should ever afterwards be compelled to change it at full value, and the use of false stamps should be considered as equally criminal with coining false money. In Dinajpúr, where the money-changers have capitals of perhaps 100 rupees, it is usual for them to advance *cowries* to all servants who have monthly wages, and at the end of the month, when the servants' wages are due, he repays them in silver; for almost every man, if possible, anticipates his income. The money-changer gives these improvident persons 70 *pon* of *cowries* for the rupee, so that he has $\frac{1}{14}$ a month for his money; but he very often loses the principal.

SECTION 3.—*Of the Places where Trade is carried on.*

THE original manner in which all commerce seems to have been carried on in Bengal, and perhaps in every part of India, and which in this district is still by far the most common, is at markets called here *háts*, where once or twice a week all those, from the neighbourhood, who wish to buy or sell, assemble, and dispose of their commodities by retail. The farmer brings the produce of his lands, the artist that of his work-shop, and the fisherman that of his snares.

Numerous small traders, among whom may be included all the shop-keepers, also attend to buy up goods for exportation, to sell those which have been imported, or to act as intermediate agents between the producer and consumer, especially in the sale of betel-leaf and fish.

For this purpose is reserved a space of ground, divided by narrow paths into plots, like the parterres of an old garden, and each plot is occupied by two or three venders, while the buyers walk about in the paths. In general, the whole is conducted in the open air. In some places, however, sheds have been erected by the zemindars, for the accommodation of dealers, and are rented out to the principal persons that attend. In Dinajpúr, under the eye of the Magistrate, this has been found to be a great convenience; but many persons alleged to me, that in remote parts the proprietors made these sheds a pretext for levying a certain sum from every vender, whether they used the sheds or not.

Duties were formerly levied at each *hát* by the proprietor of the land, who was thus interested to preserve peace and justice, that their *hát* might be fully attended; but there is great reason to believe, that in general the proprietors and their agents studied more their immediate gain, than any regular profit, and were often so rapacious, that the market was deserted. The utmost advantage has therefore arisen from the removal of this tax, which was done by Lord Cornwallis, soon after his first arrival in Bengal. The *háts* are now free, and are placed under the immediate protection of the *darogah* of the division in which they are held. It must however be confessed, that some inconvenience attends this plan. The *háts* are so numerous, that even the principal ones cannot possibly be attended by the *darogah*, nor even by the *mohurer* or *jumadár*, the only persons of the least respectability that he can detach. It may therefore be said, that there is no legal adequate superintendence either to settle disputes or to prevent fraudulent measures and weights, and violent complaints exist concerning exactions made both by the landholder and by the native officers of police.

On the festivals of Hindú gods, and of persons reputed saints by the Moslems large assemblies of people *(mela)* take place, and traders embrace this opportunity of disposing of their goods, and of supplying the wants of the assembled multitude.

In this district, there are annually several such assemblies, which both in their origin and nature very much resemble the fairs of Europe. This is an original Hindú custom, although, as might be expected from the Muhammedan predominance, the most distinguished meeting is that held at Bhowanipúr, in the Ranisongkol division, in celebration of Nekmurdan, a Moslem *pír* or saint. In my account of that division I have already mentioned the nature of the assembly.

All the other places in this district, where sales are made, have names introduced by the Muhammedans, owing either to these conquerors having changed the names, or to there having been no such places until they came.

A *bázár* ought to imply a place where things in common use are regularly sold, but in this district there is no such place of any consequence except in Dinajpúr, where there are two or three streets of shops, and at Ghorághát, where there is one. At several villages there are two or three shops where provisions are sold, and these with some propriety may be called *bázárs*, although this name is not given to them, and is usually applied to places where every evening there is a meeting of people in the open air, to buy and sell fish, vegetables, and other such necessaries; and where there are no houses near, as is often the case, this meeting is called a *tahabázári-hát*.

Ganj and *bander* are indiscriminately applied to every place, from whence goods are exported and imported by whole sale dealers. Several such places have not a single shop, and do not afford to the travellers any means of purchasing the most common necessary of life, and merely contain a few ware-houses *(golas)*, where the goods can be deposited, together with the houses of the agents by whom they are bought and sold by wholesale. The name, it must be observed, is often very much misapplied, and many places are now called *ganj* or *bander*, where no merchant resides. The name is naturally enough continued, even after the place has lost its importance; and it seems frequently to have been employed in anticipation of hopes of greatness, which were never realized. *Nogor* is said to be a proper Hindú name for a mart; but this is liable to some doubt, and in this district, at any rate, has gone entirely into disuse in that meaning.

In the map will be seen the situation of every place where goods are bought and sold. The scale only admits of the insertion of numbers referring to the names in the Index, and no great reliance can be placed on the exactitude with which they have been placed, as in general I could only assign their situation from the report of the natives, few of them having been laid down by Mr. Rennell.

SECTION 4.— *Of Weights, Measures, and Coins.*

IN the account which I have given of money-changers, I have anticipated much of what I had to offer on the subject of coins.

The usual currency consists of silver and *cowries:* gold seldom appears, and copper has never been introduced. Some years ago gold was abundant; but has since become very scarce. This is a fortunate circumstance for the poor, and a loss to the bankers, who had an immense profit on the gold. The most common silver currency is the *kaldár*, or the new milled coinage of Calcutta, of which however a considerable proportion has been depreciated by marks. There are however still current a good many of the old unmilled coinage, and of French rupees, which pay a heavy exchange. Most transactions however are settled by *cowries*, which for some years have been very cheap. I have already mentioned the rate of exchange that has of late been usual.

There is no uniformity in the weights and measures of any kind, and there is every reason to think the most gross frauds are very frequently practised.

The weights not only vary in almost every market, and are different in the same market for different kinds of goods, but the same species; rice, for instance, is sometimes sold by one weight, and bought by another, and what is still more injurious, there is no stamp on the weights, which are in general bits of stone, and admit of the most gross deception. All these circumstances render it almost impossible for the officers of police to detect false weights. The various seers in use are of 100 sa. wt. 96 sa. wt. 82$\frac{4}{8}$ sa. wt. 80 sa. wt. 76 sa. wt. 60 sa. wt. and 58 sa. wt. Should it not be judged advisable to introduce one general standard, all dealers might be compelled to use weights formed of brass, with strong distinguishing marks for each denomination, so that the common people might at once distinguish them. This no doubt would be a great step towards preventing fraud; but still the scales that are used in weighing are so rudely formed, that a dexterous man can readily impose on the unwary. The scales are never suspended from any fixture, and being held in the hand, and being very loose and imperfect, a little twist prevents their free motion. Owing also to their being held in the hand, no scales of a considerable size can be used, so that the delivery of a large quantity of grain occupies a most intolerable length of time.

Whatever may be the weight of the *sir*, it is divided into 16 *chhatáks*, and five *seers* form one *posiri*, and eight *posiris* one maund. There is no higher denomination of weight, nor indeed in general is there any scale that can weigh more than one *posiri* at one time. The only exception is, that the sugar manufacturers have large scales suspended from a beam, and can weigh at once one or two maunds of extract or molasses, but even this is attended with vast trouble. A pot like that containing the commodity is placed in the opposite scale, and filled with sand, until the balance is equal. The sand is then weighed with the common small scale.

The grain measures are still a great deal more defective than the weights. The most ignorant and low people of the district make them of basket work, in form of a hemisphere, and they are supposed, when heaped, to contain a certain weight of rice in the husk. From hence we may judge of their imperfections. In the first place, the workmen have neither means nor skill to make them of an uniform size, and judge in general merely by the eye; secondly, even if the workmen could make a basket, that when heaped would hold a certain weight of rice, this would be a standard liable to great variation, as will be seen by looking at the table which I have made of the different weights of that kind of grain; thirdly, a basket approaching to a hemispherical form, by such enlargements or constructions of the mouth, as even from accident are altogether unavoidable, will when heaped contain very different quantities of the same grain; fourthly, the same basket when heaped with rough rice will contain more cubical inches of that grain than it will of clean rice, pulse, or mustard seed, as the rounder and smoother the grain is, the less can be heaped on a given space. Finally, all the imperfections of the weights are accumulated on the measures formed from them as a standard. The uncertainty attending all these circumstances would frustrate all attempts to prove intentional fraud, and the people may in fact be said to have no use of grain measures, although the farmers nominally sell their whole produce by this denomination; but in delivering and receiving the grain, each party measures by his own basket, and then they come to an agreement about the quantity. In small purchases, persons generally judge by the eye.

The integer measure is called a *don* or *kata*, and is divided into halves and quarters, which are always taken by guess. 20 *dons* form a *vis*, 4 *vis* one *dam*, and 4 *dams* one *pauli;* but the *don* is the only measure actually used. This varies in different places from two to five seers of all the various kinds that I have mentioned.

Liquids are always sold by the seer or maund, that is by measures supposed to contain such weights. These are not so bad as the grain measures, because they cannot be heaped; but are liable to all the variations in the weights, that served as the standards by which they were made.

In order to prevent imposition, both grain and liquid measures should be made of metal or wood, and stamped by the magistrate, and those for grain should be made very narrow, to render the heaping less precarious; for I suspect, that for some time at least, it would be found a very difficult task to induce the natives to purchase by streaked measures. The joint of a bambú, examined and sealed by the officer of police, answers very well for liquids, and might also answer for grain, were it streaked; but when heaped, the various proportions between the diameter and length would affect the contents; metal or wooden grain measures are therefore necessary.

It is probable, that much good might be done by establishing, at every considerable market place, a police officer, provided with proper standards for all the kinds of weights and measures that the custom of the market requires, and with an apparatus for measuring and weighing considerable quantities of goods at one time. Should it not be found proper to attempt the introduction of regular weights and measures, this would also serve as a great check to imposition, as there would be on the spot means for ascertaining, whether or not the weights and measures used by dealers were fair. The expense might be paid by small fees. I have already mentioned the want of public land measures, which office might be connected with the one above-mentioned; as the markets are held only once or twice a week. The present plan of sending a surveyor from the capital, in case of disputes, is totally inapplicable to common practice, such as measuring a field or farm; for the expense far exceeds any advantage that the party who pays can derive from the measurement.

The land measure in use here is the *bigah*, divided into 20 *katas*, and seems from the name to have been introduced by the Muhammedans, but the Hindûs of this district had a measure called *kura*, which has now gone into disuse. Regular standards of the measure customary in each *pergunnah* are kept in the collector's office, and furnished to all who are interested, at a moderate rate. The standard however is only the yard *(gaz)*, or cubit *(hâth)*, and the rope that is used for surveying, is measured with this standard. The rope is made of very loose twine, and being measured when dry, shortens very much when wet in the field, by which means a great imposition is suffered; when the two people, who carry it, usually tie the ends to their girdles, or sometimes round their waists, or sometimes to their shoulder, and when they measure, allow the rope to hang down, so as only to touch the ground in the middle. The loss thus sustained is very indefinite, and is called *guljinda*. Whether or not, the zemindars and their agents are aware, that the extent of different *bigahs* are in the proportion of the squares of the whole length of the ropes employed, I cannot say; but the people in general have no adequate notion of this, and seem to consider the loss by *guljinda* merely as in the ratio of the square of the length taken from the rope. To judge from what the agents say, they are of the same opinion, and may therefore be ignorant of the injustice they commit in taking the *guljinda.* In the account of the customary *bigah* of each *pergunnah,* I have deducted what is said to be the usual *guljinda,* and have calculated the number of square feet accordingly, as will be found in the table of *pergunnahs* or estates.

The natives of this district have scarcely any manner of measuring time. I heard of neither the sand-glass nor clypsedra, except one belonging to the judge. The art of dialing was, and is, totally unknown to the natives, and scarcely any have procured watches. The day and night is divided by them into eight *pohors,* and 60 *dondos,* and their almanack states in a general manner the number of *dondos* contained in the days of each month, but descends no further into particulars, which indeed would be useless, where the only means for measuring time is conjecture.

Section 5.—*Conveyance of Goods.*

In the topographical account of this district, I have already explained, that it is every where intersected by rivers, which in the rainy season, and when travelling by land is nearly suspended, admit of large boats to every division, and of small ones to most villages. In the dry season, the navigation is confined within very narrow limits, and the country, being every where dry, plain, and open, almost every part is accessible for loaded cattle, and few or no roads exist, at least for the conveyance of goods. The manner in which these are transported is of course adapted to such circumstances. Very little is exported or imported in the dry season, during which the produce of the country is collected in ware-houses, that are situated on the banks of rivers; and when these swell, is loaded on boats, and sent to the places of its destination. The imports are made in the rainy season, and during the dry weather, are distributed from the marts to the various market places. This is attended with so much inconvenience, from the slow returns of capital, that the smaller traders, who deal chiefly in the articles of import, use canoes and floats *(mars),* which consist of two or three canoes connected by a platform of bambus. Even in the dry season these can penetrate a considerable way into the country, from the Mohanondo, Atreyi, and Korotoya, which at all seasons are navigable into this district for boats of 500 maunds burthen. For rice, the great article of export, this would be too expensive a mode of conveyance, and indeed of little consequence, as the merchants would in general avoid, taking it to the Calcutta or Múrshedabad market, until the rice produced in the vicinity of these cities is consumed, which is not until after the commencement of the rainy season; and besides the Bhagirothi, which is the channel of conveyance between this and Múrshedabad and Calcutta, is not navigable in the dry season. At that period, the supply of goods, such as cotton, salt, betelnut, shells, and other articles of consumption, can only be procured from Bhogawangola, Kumèrkhálí, or Naráyanganj, which of course become the marts for these articles.

Very few of the boats employed in trade belong to this district, because during the dry season they could have no employment, except at a great distance from the inspection of the owner. Some merchants however keep a few large boats, which lie idle all the dry season; but are loaded, and ready to depart so soon as the season admits. These in general can annually take two loads of rice to Calcutta, and bring back two loads of salt; but the practice does not seem judicious. The hulls of the boats employed are almost all of the same construction. When open above, they are called *dingis;* when they have a thatched roof in the after part only, which is usually the case when their burthen is under 200 maunds of rice, they are called *pansuí;* when thatched from nearly one end to the other, and when under 700 maunds burthen, they are called *uláks*. Boats from 700 to 5000 maunds burthen, the largest used in this district, over the thatch have a platform of bambús, on which the people can walk, to pole the vessel along, or to manage the sail. A vessel of this kind is called a *chhapar beri*.

The burthen of the boat is calculated by the quantity of rice which she could carry, and not by the quantity of any other kind of goods with which she may be actually laden; and in all valuable cargoes, the boat takes much less weight than her estimated rate of burthen, because it would not be safe to load her so deep, as is usually done with rice.

In the dry season, a boat carrying goods from Naiagola, the port of Dinajpúr, to Bhogowangola, the port of Múrshedabad, or to Kushte, near Kumèrkhálí, is allowed from 3½ to 4½ rupees for the 100 maunds burthen, at 96 sicca weight the seer, or for about 88 hundred weight.

A large boat from the towns near Dinajpúr on the Punabhoba, such as Damdamah, or from the marts on the Atreyi, such as Potiram, is paid at the rate of 13 rupees for the 100 maunds, for carrying rice to Calcutta.

From the towns on the Korotoya, the freight to Calcutta, in the rainy season, is usually only 10 rupees for the 100 maunds.

For the purpose of commerce (as I have already said), there are scarcely any roads. Where the soil is light, an empty space is left in the fields that are cultivated in the dry season; but this is in general too narrow, and too much broken to admit of carts. In the rice grounds, there is seldom any trace of a road, because cattle cannot travel when the crops are on the ground, and when the crops are removed, loaded cattle find a good road in every direction. The little banks by which the water is confined on the rice fields prevent even then the use of carts, unless accompanied by pioneers to remove these, and to slope the banks of water-courses. Great inconvenience arises to commerce from this want of roads; for whenever there are any such, as in the vicinity of the capital, carts are constantly employed. Roads adequate to admit carts, in the dry season, from the principal *háts* to the chief marts, would therefore be of great advantage; and as the idea, in the present state of things, of making them suited for post-chaises at all seasons, would be absurd, the expense might be extremely moderate, and might be defrayed by a trifling composition for each plough, one-half to be paid by the landlord, and one-half by the tenant, and which of course should be levied on all lands free and assessed. The principal difficulty would be to prevent misapplication or embezzlement; and I confess, that this difficulty appears to me exceedingly great. Considering the duties that a magistrate has to perform, I look upon any expectation of advantage to be derived from his superintendency as totally chimerical, and little confidence can be placed in that of his native assistants. If the landholders were empowered to act as commissioners for high-ways, in the present state of their education, and as most of them would act by deputy, I am afraid, that each would endeavour to take as much of the money levied as possible, and that the roads would remain much as they are at present. Yet, upon the whole, this seems to be the plan most likely to succeed, especially if the collector, who is not so much oppressed with business as the magistrate, should be directed to prosecute all neglects of duty in the commissioners.

The usual mode of conveyance for goods by land is on oxen in back loads, and the common rate for 12 miles carriage may be reckoned 2$\frac{2}{3}$ *pon* of *cowries* (Rs. $\frac{1}{18}$) for each maund (96 sicca weight the seer), or lb. 98$\frac{1}{2}$.

Porters are seldom employed, and indeed can carry very little. Their load is divided into two equal portions, that are suspended from the two ends of a pole; which they carry on their shoulders. They are said to take about lb. 74 weight 12 miles a day; but I found it impossible to procure people who would perform any such labour for more than double the usual hire, which is $\frac{1}{12}$ (four *pon* of *cowries)* of a rupee each day. They are seldom employed for carrying goods, and are chiefly hired to carry parcels for travellers.

At the town of Dinajpúr, carts may be hired for six annas a day, and for this a cart conveys goods for *(six kos)* 12 miles. The cart is drawn by two oxen. These are poor creatures, which is perhaps owing to the rate of hire being fixed on the cart, and not on the weight of the load: each cart takes from 7 to 10 maunds of 96 sicca weight the seer, or from lb. 690 to lb. 985. This rate is apparently higher than the carriage on back loads; but the cart is always preferred, when it can be procured; the merchant probably pays less than the rate established for travellers. Except at the capital neither carts, oxen, nor porters can be usually procured for hire, no persons making the carriage of goods a profession, and the supply even at the capital is extremely scanty. Many of the *paikars*, or petty traders, keep oxen for conveying their goods to and from their warehouses; but the great means of conveyance depends on the cattle of those who cultivate clay-lands, and who in this manner find a source of profit, when nothing can be done on their farms. In general, however, they do not work for hire; but purchase the goods at the markets, and carry them to the marts for sale. There is no such thing as a regular carrier.

The roads of communication between the capital of the district, and the *thánas*, or chief places of the subordinate divisions, are equally neglected with those intended for commerce, and so far as I could judge, could only be farmed and repaired by similar means. It is the landholders who are chiefly interested in their repair, as their communications with the capital are very numerous.

The general roads of communication between the capital of this district and those of the adjacent jurisdictions are in a tolerable state, and the magistrates who have formed them, and kept them in repair, seem to be entitled to great praise, especially as one of them, conducting towards Múrshedabad, has been carried, at the expense of this district, through the whole breadth of Rajshahi. No employment can be fitter for the convicts, than making and repairing these roads; and the magistrate has it always in his power to obtain sufficient information concerning their state, to enable him to superintend the conduct of the overseers with proper effect. All that appears to be wanted in this district, with respect to these roads, seems to be some fund for erecting bridges over small water-courses, for these roads should be practicable at all seasons. In the present state of things, bridges over large rivers cannot be attempted. A little more attention to ferries is all that would be required.

In the Muhammedan government, these roads of communication between stations seem to have been numerous and well formed; but the roads which these conquerors made have become in a great measure useless from the change of stations, and have gone to ruin. It would not appear, that the natives ever had roads for facilitating the exportation and importation of goods. Those laid down in Major

Rennell's map are probably such as have been once intended to be made, and have never appeared except on paper.

The ferry boats here, as in every part of Bengal, are bad, and generally are so overloaded, that frequent accidents occur. They are also in general totally unfit for the conveyance of cattle. The land-holders, so far as I learned, admit, that they are bound to provide ferries; but the obligation, I am informed, in a strict interpretation of their engagements, is very doubtful. It is however so evidently their interest in many cases, that to a certain extent they will usually comply, but they can never be expected to furnish good boats. In general, the ferryman receives a small quantity of land, free of rent, and binds himself to find a proper boat, and to transport all persons free of hire; and it is the duty of the *darogah* to see that the boats are proper, and the people attentive. This I suspect is a duty to which very little attention is paid, and indeed its execution would be difficult. Heavy complaints exist on this subject, as on most others. Many of the ferrymen complain, that they are compelled to pay rent for their lands; and others allege, where the ferry is much frequented, that they are compelled to give the landlord a share of the profits, which arise from the usual and voluntary contributions, that are made by passengers. It would probably be found on investigation, that the lands assigned for the support of ferries were not included in the rental by which the revenue was fixed, and should therefore be considered as exempted from all claims of the land-holder; and I am inclined to suspect, that their ready acknowledgment of the obligation to find boats arises from a consciousness of this circumstance. I have no doubt but that great advantage would accrue from taking these lands into the management of the police, and granting them, and a right to certain fees from passengers to ferrymen, on condition of their keeping proper boats. A written copy of the agreement should be suspended at each ferry-house, so that any passenger might apply for redress, should any extraordinary demand be made, or should any stipulated conviction of attendance, care, or accommodation be neglected, and all interference of the zemindars, further than as other passengers, should be most strictly prohibited. The boats most proper to be used in the rivers of this district are the *mars* or floats consisting of two or more canoes joined by a platform of bambús. These are capable of conveying cattle or even carts, and where there are no waves, transport a number of persons with much safety. They are less fit for the large rivers of other districts, that have considerable waves, and that are too deep or wide to admit of the floats being pushed across by poles, or drawn by ropes.

There may be said to be no accommodation for travellers. In this district, one land-holder, as I have already mentioned, entertains all travellers who choose to apply; and natives in general find people of their own caste, who will give them room in their house to sleep on the ground, and the absolute necessaries may commonly be procured, when there are few persons in company. Unless Europeans are travelling post from station to station, which requires relays of carriages to be placed on purpose, and is attended with an enormous expense, they must travel in tents, and carry with them almost every person or thing that they require.

GENERAL STATISTICAL TABLE I.—*Of the District or Zillah of Dinajpúr.*

Nos.	Head and Total Division or Thanas.	Extent in square miles.	Rivers, tanks, marshes, water-courses.	Soil.				Waste.		Woods and bushes.	Steep barren places, roads, burial-grounds.	Manner of occupation.				Mauzas.	Market places.	Higher Hindú Schools.	Common Hindú Schools.	Persian Schools.	Proportion between number of		Value of Exports.	Value of Imports.
				Inundated in the rainy season.	Red clay.	Light-coloured clay.	Free soil.	Rivers, &c.	Inundated.			Clear land not let on lease but occasionally cultivated. Inundated.	Clear land not let on lease but occasionally cultivated. Not inundtd.	Lands let on lease. Stiff clay.	Lands let on lease. Free soil.						Hindus.	Moslems.		
1	Rajarampúr, ..	340	63	20	..	154	103	63	10	15	10	10	20	127	85	851 0 0	29	4	..	..	8	8	3,25,500	1,10,250
2	Birganj,......	340	32	12	..	116	180	32	6	12	10	6	44	76	154	477 0 0	35	..	2	..	4	12	85,300	29,300
3	Thakurgram, ..	400	25	5	..	..	370	25	5	..	20	..	50	..	300	268 0 0	20	..	1	..	4	12	28,450	11,800
4	Ranisongkol, ..	210	10	..	..	..	200	10	..	..	16	..	26	..	158	213 8 0	16	..	..	..	1	15	15,630	8,100
5	Pírganj, ...	220	13	7	..	..	200	13	7	14	20	..	28	..	138	373 14 0	11	..	..	..	4	12	7,030	8,200
6	Hemtabad, ...	300	17	20	..	..	263	17	20	..	38	..	38	..	187	355 0 0	16	..	..	1	9	7	6,27,620	1,28,200
7	Kaliyaganj, ...	310	15	40	..	95	160	15	15	10	10	25	20	85	130	566 12 0	19	2	2	..	8	8	40,830	7,400
8	Bongsiharí, ...	240	10	5	..	225	..	10	5	..	15	..	30	180	..	853 0 0	16	..	..	..	4	12	1,38,100	9,200
9	Jogodol, ...	250	15	62	..	173	..	15	50	22	19	12	22	110	..	628 15 0	11	..	2	..	8	8	1,85,700	21,050
10	Maldeb, ...	280	17	70	..	153	40	17	50	35	18	20	35	90	15	341 0 0	11	1	10	2	10	6	6,78,100	1,07,850
11	Purusa, ...	260	12	24	..	224	..	12	18	10	16	6	8	190	..	577 12 2½	10	..	..	..	2	14	1,16,700	24,250
12	Gonggarampúr,	320	20	30	..	240	30	20	22	2	12	8	16	220	20	615 0 0	16	1	10	..	6	10	1,76,900	74,800
13	Potiram, ...	280	18	17	..	185	60	18	7	..	35	10	17	158	35	983 0 0	19	3	40	3	12	4	4,72,290	85,800
14	Potnitola, ...	240	15	..	..	195	30	15	..	5	10	..	8	182	20	843 0 0	20	..	..	..	4	12	2,22,300	41,050
15	Badolgachhi, ..	270	17	13	..	130	110	17	7	8	18	6	60	100	54	9223 17 1½	16	..	..	..	6	10	1,46,720	51,250
16	Lalbazar, ...	280	12	12	..	92	164	12	8	34	12	4	18	70	122	1055 0 0	25	4	12	2	6	10	2,93,100	53,100
17	Chintamon, ...	200	12	6	..	108	74	12	5	15	8	1	34	75	50	568 2 0	25	..	..	..	6	10	2,33,320	1,36,500
18	Howrah, ...	180	10	20	..	90	60	10	14	11	4	6	22	68	45	234 0 0	20	..	12	..	4	12	2,47,560	28,850
19	Nawabganj, ...	150	6	10	20	62	52	6	6	16	6	4	18	47	47	417 10 0	10	..	12	..	6	10	2,78,180	84,650
20	Ghoraghat, ...	140	5	4	18	71	42	5	2	12	4	2	10	70	35	619 10 6 3	11	1	10	1	4	12	2,56,400	63,800
21	Khyettal, ...	160	8	4	..	128	20	8	4	..	3	..	5	122	18	383 0 0	4	..	..	..	4	12	8,100	..
22	Dinajpúr, ...	4	1	..	..	..	3	1	..	..	1	..	..	..	2	16 0 0	5	..	6	..	6	10	2,35,530	2,00,500
	Totals	5374	353	381	38	2441	2161	353	261	221	305	120	529	1970	1615	12162 7 4 3	365	16	119	9	3	7	48,19,360	12,85,900

TABLE II.—*Abstract of an Estimate of the Annual Expenses of six Families of different ranks, in Dinajpúr.*

Heads of expense.	1st Class.			2nd Class.			3rd Class.			4th Class.			5th Class.			6th Class.		
	R.	*A.*	*P.*	*R.*	*A.*	*P.*	*R.*	*A.*	*P.*	*R.*	*A.*	*P.*	*R.*	*A.*	*P.*	*R.*	*A.*	*P.*
1 Lodging, ..	78	0	0	56	0	0	24	0	0	9	10	3	2	4	9½	0	7	0
2 Furniture,	118	11	10¼	40	13	7¾	16	7	3	5	2	9¾	1	3	3¾	0	10	0
3 Ornaments,	162	0	5¾	62	14	1	12	12	11¼	2	10	4¾	0	4	6¾	0	1	8
4 Clothing,..	210	0	0	72	0	0	37	8	0	17	12	0	3	6	0	2	6	0
5 Table, ...	334	13	0	174	0	0	128	2	9	66	0	0	30	0	0	16	10	3
6 Servants & Equipage,	286	13	0	60	0	0	15	0	0	0	12	0	0	8	0	0	8	0
7 Holidays, priests, and the like, ..	300	0	0	80	0	0	48	0	0	15	0	0	6	0	0	2	0	0
8 Stationery, and Instruction of Children,......	6	0	0	4	0	0	0	0	0	0	0	0	0	0	0	0	0	0
Total,..	1496	6	4	549	11	8¾	281	14	11¼	116	15	5½	43	10	8	22	10	11

TABLE III.—*An Estimate of the Population of Dinajpúr, and of the numbers contained in each class of its Inhabitants.*

Total, 30,00,000 { 21,00,000 Muhammedans.
  9,00,000 Hindûs.

{ 10,000 Brahmins.
  8,90,000 Sudras.

  { 4,40,000 Proper Bengalis.
    { 70,000 Pure Tribes, *(Suddhojati.)*
      3,70,000 Impure Tribes, *(Osuddhojati.)*
    1,50,000 Vile, *(Nich.)*
    2,20,000 Abominable, *(Ontyoj.)*
  4,50,000 Tribes not included among the Bengalis by Bollalsen.
    15,000 Tribes of Hindústan, about 3,000 pure, among these are the Síks and Oshoyals.
  4,35,000 Tribes of Eastern India, all impure.

Table IV.—*Estimate of the Manner in which the Occupied Lands of Dinajpúr are employed, and of the Value of the Produce at the Harvest Season.*

Manner of Occupation.		Extent in Bigahs.	Value in Rupees.
1 Cultivated for Grain of various kinds, ...		64,00,000	1,70,00,000
2 Occupied by Houses and Gardens, viz.		5,00,000	
Houses, ...	1,80,000		
Plantations, chiefly of Mangoes and Bambús,	1,40,000	....	9,50,000
Kitchen Gardens, ...	1,80,000	....	} 10,00,000
3 Vegetables for Kitchen cultivated in the fields, ...		1,50,000	
4 Plants for Thread or Ropes, ...		80,000	2,45,000
5 Plants yielding a saccharine juice (inspissated), ...		25,000	4,50,000
6 Plants for smoking or chewing, ...		16,000	1,87,500
7 Plants used for Dying, (chiefly, Indigo weed,)		15,000	37,500
8 Plants for feeding Silk Worms, (leaves,)		8,000	90,000
Total, exclusive of milk, (about 14,34,350)		71,94,000	1,99,60,000

Table V.—*An Estimate of the Extent and Value of the various Crops of Grain cultivated in the District of Dinajpúr.*

Extent in Bigahs.	Nature of Crop.	Value of the produce in Rs.
42,66,000	Winter rice, at $2\frac{9}{16}$ Rs.	1,09,31,625
6,40,000	Winter rice and summer rice, at $2\frac{13}{16}$ Rs.	18,00,000
2,56,000	Winter rice, 3 Rs.; pulse, ¾ R.	9,60,000
1,44,000	Summer rice, 2 Rs.; pulse, ¾ R.	3,96,000
5,76,000	Summer rice, 2 Rs.; Oil-seed, 2 Rs.	23,04,000
72,000	Summer rice, 2 Rs.; wheat or barley, 1¾ R.	2,70,000
38,000	Summer rice alone, 2 Rs.	76,000
13,000	Spring rice, at 1½ R.	19,500
64,000	Oil-seeds alone, at 2 Rs.	1,28,000
38,000	Oil-seeds, 1 R.; wheat or barley, ½ R.; pulse, ¾ R.	85,500
78,000	Pulse alone, ...	78,000
2,15,000	For seedling rice in stiff soils, producing nothing else, ..	
64,00,000	Total, Average R. 2¾, Total....	1,70,48,625

TABLE VI.—*Explaining the Cultivation*

Kind.	Labouring Season.	Number of Double ploughing.	Seed time.	Quantity of seed required for one bigah, in seers.	Season for Transplanting.	Number of smoothing with the *moyi*.	Number of weedings with the *bida*.
Fine winter rice as a single crop on high land,	12th April, 12th June,	7 or 8	12th April, 12th June,	15	13th June, 14th July,	3 or 4	..
Fine winter rice on high land, followed by summer rice,	15th Augt. 15th Mar.	3 or 4 6 or 7	13th June, 11th April,	15 20	15th Aug. 14th Sept.	2 or 3	..
Ordinary winter rice transplanted in low ground,	12th April, 12th June,	6 or 7	12th April, 12th May,	15	13th June, 14th July,	2 or 3	..
Coarse winter rice sown broad-cast, on low land of a free soil,	12th April, 12th May,	3 or 4	12th April, 12th May,	20	..	2	..
Coarse winter rice sown broad-cast, on low land of a stiff soil,	12th April, 12th May,	4 or 5	12th April, 12th May,	20	..	2	..
Coarse winter rice sown broad-cast, along with summer rice, on inundated land,	13th Jan. 12th April,	6 or 7	12th April, 13th May,	20	..	2 or 3	..
Summer rice sown broad-cast, by itself,	13th Jan. 11th April,	6 or 7	12th April, 12th May,	20	..	2 or 3	3 or 4
Summer rice transplanted,	12th Mar. 12th May,	6 or 7	13th May, 12th June,	15	13th June, 14th July,	2 or 3	..
Spring rice,	15th Oct. 12th Jan.	5 or 6	15th Oct. 13th Nov.	15	13th Jan. 10th Feb.	2 or 3	..
Wheat,	15th Sept. 14th Oct.	3 or 4	15th Oct. 13th Nov.	..	..	2	..
Barley,	15th Sept. 14th Oct.	3 or 4	15th Oct. 13th Nov.	..	..	2	..
Merua by itself,	13th May, 12th June,	4 or 5	13th May, 12th June,	..	..	2	..
Sorisha,	15th Oct. 13th Nov.	3 or 4	15th Oct. 13th Nov.	..	..	2	..
Turi,	15th Oct. 15th Nov.	3 or 4	15th Oct. 13th Nov..	..	..	2	..
Rayí,	15th Oct. 13th Nov.	3 or 4	15th Oct. 13th Nov.	..	..	1	..
Til,	13th June, 14th July,	6 or 7	13th June, 14th July,	..	..	2	..
Thakuri,	13th June, 14th Augt.	4 or 5	13th June, 14th Aug.	..	..	..	..
Oror,	13th May, 12th June,	3 or 4	13th May, 12th June,	..	..	1	..
Harimug,	11th Feb. 11th Mar.	5 or 6	11th Feb. 11th Mar.	..	..	2	..
Field Pease,	15th Sept. 14th Oct.	3 or 4	15th Oct. 13th Nov.	..	..	1	..
Chona,	15th Oct. 13th Nov.	3 or 4	15th Oct. 13th Nov.	..	..	1	..
Khesari,	14th Nov. 13th Dec.	1	15th Oct. 13th Nov.	..	..	..	..
Mosúr, or Lentils,	15th Sept. 13th Nov.	5 or 6	15th Oct. 13th Nov.	..	..	2	..

of Grain in the Dinajpúr District.

Number of weedings with the spud.	Harvest Season.	Average produce of one bigah, in seers.	Average No. of seers sold at harvest for one rupee.	Number of bigahs cultivated in this manner.	Total produce in Maunds.	Produce for consumption after deducting seed.	Total value.		
2	14th Nov. 12th Jan.	200	70	5,76,000	28,80,000	26,64,000	16,45,714	4	7
.	13th Jan. 14th Aug.	100W. 220 S.	90W. 120 S.	5,12,000	12,80,000 28,16,000	10,88,000 25,60,000	5,68,888 9,38,666	14 10	3 8
..	14th Dec. 27th Jan.	240	100	20,90,000	1,25,40,000	1,17,56,250	50,16,000	0	0
..	14th Dec. 12th Jan.	320	110	12,16,000	97,28,000	91,20,000	35,37,454	8	9
..	14th Dec. 12th Jan.	280	120	6,40,000	44,80,000	41,60,000	14,93,333	5	4
..	15th Aug. 13th Jan.	100W 180 S.	120	1,28,000	3,20,000 5,76,000	8,32,000	2,98,666	10	8
2or3	15th Aug. 14th Sept.	240	120	8,00,000	48,00,000	44,00,000	16,00,000	0	0
..	29th Aug. 29th Sept.	240	110	30,000	1,80,000	1,68,750	65,454	8	9
..	12th April, 12th May,	180	120	13,000	58,500	53,625	19,500	0	0
..	12th March, 11th April,	..	45	..	1,12,000	..	99,555	8	10⅔
..	12th March, 11th April,	..	60	..	68,000	..	45,333	5	4
..	15th Sept. 14th Oct.	..	120	..	9,000	..	3,000	0	0
..	13th Jan. 10th Feb.	..	56	..	11,20,000	..	8,00,000	0	0
..	13th Jan. 10th Feb.	..	54	..	6,75,000	..	5,00,000	0	0
..	13th Jan. 10th Feb.	..	56	..	16,800	..	12,000	0	0
2	13th Jan. 10th Feb.	..	40	..	6,000	..	6,000	0	0
..	15th Oct. 13th Nov.	..	80	..	1,00,000	..	50,000	0	0
..	11th Feb. 11th March,	..	48	..	48,000	..	40,000	0	0
..	13th May, 12th June,	..	54	..	43,000	..	31,851	13	7⅓
1	12th March, 11th April,	..	70	..	10,000	..	5,714	4	6
1	12th March, 11th April,	..	48	..	5,000	..	4,166	10	8
..	12th March, 11th April,	..	100	..	4,40,000	..	1,76,000	0	0
1	12th March, 11th April,	..	70	..	16,60,000	..	94,857	2	3
						Total, ..	1,70,52,157	12	3

Table VII.—*Containing the Produce of Ten Specimens of rough Rice, each measuring* 1728 *cubical inches, when carefully dried and cleaned by boiling.*

Description of the Rice.	Cubical inches of clean rice.	Weight in Ounces Avoirdupois.					
		Total of rough rice.	Total of clean rice.	Broken pieces of rice.	Bran.	Husks.	Total of the four last columns.
No. 1 Old winter rice of 2nd quality,	918	568½	410½	17½	41	107	576
2 Ditto ditto,	963	567	428	3	20½	118	570
3 Ditto ditto,	909	563	414	17	21	126	574
4 New ditto ditto,	1008	570½	449	..	24½	121	594½
5 Ditto ditto,	972	570½	435	..	23	119	577
6 Ditto ditto,	945	579	427	..	26½	117½	571
7 New summer rice,	967½	593	447½	..	20½	109	577
8 Ditto ditto,	967½	585	444	..	32	112½	588½
9 Ditto ditto,	931½	575	426½	..	25½	121	573
10 Ditto ditto,	981	586	444½	..	29½	115	589
Average,	956.25	575.75	432.6	12.5	26.4	116.6	579

No. 8.—*A Table explaining various Circumstances relative to the Ancient Estates (Pergunnahs), in the District of Dinajpúr.*

No.	Present Name of Pergunnah.	Name in Mr. Gladwin's Ayeen Akbery.	Sircar in which situated.	Thannas in which situated.	Mauzas' Number.	Actual size of Bigah.	Division of Land and usual rent of each kind.
					B. C. Ch.		
1	Haveli Panjra, ..	Havilly Pinjerah,	Panjra, ..	Birgunj, Rajarampúr, ..	156	83 Sekunderi cubits, Sq. feet, ... 20,500	Poli, 1½ R. Khyar, 14 Annas.
2	Vijoynogor, ..	Bijanagur, ..	Ditto, ..	Dinajpúr, Birgunj, Bongsihari, Pirgunj, Chintamon, Gonggarampúr, Rajarampúr, ..	405	80 Sekunderi cubits, Sq. feet, ... 19,041	Poli, 1½ R. Khyar, 14 Annas.
3	Nurpur, ..	..	Ditto, ..	Birgunj, Chintamon, Rajarampúr, ..	136	83 Sekunderi cubits, Sq. feet, ... 20,500	Poli, 1½ R. Khyar, 14 Annas.
4	Vihinogor, ..	Behenagur, ..	Ditto, ..	Pirgunj, Rajarampúr, Birgunj, ..	163	..	Probably the same with the two first.
5	Dayora, ..	Dewra, ..	Ditto, ..	Pirgunj, Chintamon, Rajarampúr, Howrah, Birgunj, ..	319	80 Sekunderi cubits, Sq. feet, ... 19,041	Average 14 Annas.
6	Solimabad, ..	Solimanabad, ..	Ditto, ..	Birgunj, Rajarampúr, ..	41	Probably the same with the preceding.	
7	Salvari, ..	Sidherbari, .	Ditto, ..	Birgunj, Thakurgram, Ranisongkol, Pirgunj, Hemtabad, ..	438	87 Sekunderi cubits, Sq. feet, ... 22,529	Nina, 1 R. avg. 14 As. Dangga, 9 As.
8	Dehotto, ..	Deyhut, ..	Tajpúr, ..	Thakurgram, Ranisongkol,	62	87 Sekunderi cubits, Sq. feet, ... 22,529	Nina, 1 R. Dangga, 12 Annas.
9	Borogang, ..	Bergong, ..	Ditto, ..	Ditto ditto, ..	36	83 Sekunderi cubits, Sq. feet, ... 20,500	Nina, 1½ R. Dangga, 9 Annas.
10	Mohoso, ..	Mhajoon, ..	Ditto, ..	Ranisongkol, Pirgunj, Kaliyagunj, Hemtabad,	166	87 Sekunderi cubits, Sq. feet, .. 22,529	Whole, 14 Annas.
11	Jhaportol, ..	Chupurtall, ..	Ditto, ..	Pirgunj, Kaliyagunj, Rajarampúr, ..	92	87 Sekunderi cubits, Sq. feet, ... 22,529	Poli, 1½ R. Khyar, 14 Annas.
12	Kismot Jhaportol,	..	Ditto, ..	Pirgunj, ..	34	Probably the same with the preceding.	
13	Mahinagur, ..	Mahynagur, ..	Jennutabad, ..	Kaliyagunj, Gonggarampúr, ..	33	87 Sekunderi cubits, Sq. feet, ... 22,529	Average, 14 Annas.

No. 8.—(Continued.)

No.	Present Name of Pergunnah.	Name in Mr. Gladwin's Ayeen Akbery.	Sirkar in which situated.	Thannas in which situated.	Mauzas' Number.	Actual size of Bigah.	Division of Land and usual rent of each kind.
					B. C. Ch.		
14	Sujunogor, ..	..	Tajpúr, ..	Kaliyagunj, Hemtabad, Bongsihari, ..	63	87 Sekunderi cubits, Sq. feet, ... 22,529	Whole, 10 Annas.
15	Dhonongjoy, ..	..	Jennutabad, ..	Kaliyagunj, Bongsihari, ..	197	84 Sekunderi cubits, Sq. feet, ... 20,927	Poli, Khyar, 1½ R. average 1 R.
16	Bazitpúr, ..	Baizeedpúr, ..	Panjra, ..	Birgunj, Kaliyagunj, Bongsihari, Rajarampúr	163	Probably the same.	
17	Maligang, ..	Maligang, ..	Jennutabad, ..	Bongsihari, Gonggarampúr, ..	168	84 Sekunderi cubits, Sq. feet, ... 20,927	Poli, Khyar, 1½ R. avg. 1 R. 12 As.
18	Modonawoti, ..	Mudnowty, ..	Ditto, ..	Ditto ditto, ..	51	84 Sekunderi cubits, Sq. feet, ... 20,927	Poli, Khyar, 1½ R. avg. 1 R. 12 As.
19	Sosvir, ..	Sassbur, ..	Panjra, ..	Bongsihari, Potiram, Gonggarampúr, Rajarampúr, ..	161		
20	Devikoth, ..	Dehykote, ..	Jennutabad, ..	Bongsihari, Gonggarampúr, ..	118½	83 Sekunderi cubits, Sq. feet, ... 20,500	Poli, Khyar, 1 R. avg. 1 R. 12 As.
21	Ajhor, ..	Ajore, ..	Ditto, ..	Jogodol, ..	157	87 Sekunderi cubits, Sq. feet, ... 22,529	Poli, Khyar, 2 Rs. avg. 1½ R. 14 As.
22	Phulvari, ..	Phoolwari, ..	Ghoraghat, ..	Nawabgunj, Chintamon, Howrah, ..	111	87 Sekunderi cubits, Sq. feet, ... 22,529	
23	Kordaho, ..	Kerdeha, ..	Barbukabad, ..	Jogodol, Potnitola, Chintamon, Potiram, Gonggarampúr,	414	81 Sekunderi cubits, Sq. feet, ... 22,529	Poli, Khyar, 1½ R. avg. 1 R. 14 As.
24	Mohasinghopúr, ..	..	..	Badolgachhi, Khyetlal, .	169 5 12½	87 Sekunderi cubits, Sq. feet, ... 22,529	Poli, Khyar, 2 Rs. 12 Annas.
25	Sakahar, ..	..	Ghoraghat, ..	Nawabgunj, ..	1		
26	Khorayil, ..	Khera, ..	Barbukabad, ..	Potiram, Gonggarampúr, ..	82		
27	Shahpul, ..	..	Panjra, ..	Rajarampúr, ..	1		
28	Batason, ..	..	Ghoraghat, ..	Howrah, ..	13		
29	Rajanogor, ..	..	Jennutabad, ..	Kaliyagunj, Bongsihari, Jogodol, Maldeh, Gonggarampúr, ..	605	84 Sekunderi cubits, Sq. feet, .. 20,927	Poli, Khyar, 2 R. avg. 1½ R. 12 As.

30	Sontosh, ..	..	Barbukabad, ..	Purusa, Potnitola, Badolgachhi, Lalbazar, Chintamon, Potiram, Gonggarampúr, ..	1,501 10 13	87 Sekunderi cubits, Sq. feet, .. 22,529	Poli, 2 R. Khyar, 12 Annas.
31	Sultanpúr, ..	Sultanpúr, ..	Panjra, ..	Lalbazar, Chintamon, Potiram, ..	172	Probably the same. ..	
32	Gilavari, ..	Keedabary, ..	Ditto, ..	Lalbazar, Nawabgunj, Chintamon, Potiram, Howrah, ..	456 2	87 Sekunderi cubits, Sq. feet, .. 22,529	Poli, 2 R. Khyar, 11 Annas.
33	Apaul, ..	Apole, ..	Ditto, ..	Lalbazar, Ghoraghat, Khyetlal, Nawabgunj, .	305	87 Sekunderi cubits, Sq. feet, .. 22,529	Garden, 3 R. Poli, 2 R. Khyar, 1 R.
34	Sorohoto, ..	Serhutta, ..	Ghoraghat, ..	Nawabgunj, ..	54 6	87 Sekunderi cubits, Sq. feet, .. 22,529	Poli, 2 R. Khyar, 1 R.
35	Khatta, ..	Kh 'tta, ..	Panjra, ..	Badolgachhi, Khyetlal, ..	71 10 10		
36	Khoraivari, ..	Gurrybary 9, Khyaabady 9,	Ghoraghat, ..	Nawabgunj, ..	30 4	Probably the same with No. 4. ..	
37	Chalun, ..	Haloon, ..	Panjra, ..	Potiram, Gonggarampúr, Rajarampúr, ..	31		
38	Shikarpúr, ..	Shikarpoor, ..	Barbukabad, ..	Jogodol, Maldeh, Purusa, .	225 7	80 Sekunderi cubits, Sq. feet, .. 19,041	1st, 2d, 3rd, 4th, 3 R. 2¼ 2 R. 1¼ R. This is in the Jahangirpúr parts.
39	Soguna, ..	..	Ditto, ..	Lalbazar, ..	270	87 Sekunderi cubits, Sq. feet, .. 22,529	Poli, 3 to 1 R. Khyar, 1 R. This is in the Dinajpúr parts.
40	Khanggor, ..	..	Ghoraghat, ..	Lalbazar, Chintamon, ..	125		
41	Sonkoyir, ..	..	Ditto, ..	Lalbazar, Ghoraghat, Nawabgunj, ..	30		
42	Khyetlal, ..	Gauttall, ..	Ditto, ..	Badolgachhi, Lalbazar, Khyettal, ..	40		
43	Bazidpúr Ghoraghat, ..	Baizeedpoor, ..	Ditto, ..	Khyetlal, Ghoraghat, ..	23		
44	Khastaluk, ..	Talook Kessay, ..	Ditto, ..	Lalbazar, Khyetlal, Ghoraghat, Nawabgunj, ..	184 6 10		
45	Bairi Ghoraghat, Bairi Jalal, ..	Berry Ghoraghat, ..	Ditto, ..	Ditto, ..	33		
46	KungjoGhoraghat, Kungjo Sakpal, . Kungjo, ...	..	Ditto, ..	Lalbazar, Ghoraghat, Nawabgunj, ..	172		

No. 8.—*(Continued.)*

No.	Present Name of Pergunnah.	Name in Mr. Gladwin's Ayeen Akbery.	Sircar in which situated.	Thannas in which situated.	Mauzas' Number.	Actual size of Bigah.	Division of Land and usual rent of each kind.
					B. C. Ch.		
47	Kholsi, ..	Khulsi, ..	Ghoraghat, ..	Ghoraghat, Nawabgunj,	97 3 16¼	In the part belonging to Dinajpúr, the Bigah is 87 Sekunderi cubits, Square feet, 22,529. In the part belonging to Bordhonkuthi, the Bigah of clay land is 48 guz, or square feet, 20,344; of land with a free soil 52 guz, or square feet, 23,937.	In the part belonging to Dinajpúr the land is divided into Poli-renting at, from 3 to 2 Rs. & into Khyar-renting from 1 R. to 14 As., average 1¼ R. In Bordhonkuthi the clay-lands are div'd. into, *Rice.* 1st, 2nd, 3rd, 4th, 2 R. 1 R. 8 A. 4 A. *Cotton.* 1st, 2nd 3rd, 4th, 3 R. 2¾ R. 2¼ R. 2 R. *Mulb.* 1st, 2nd, 1 R. 1¼ R. The lands of a free soil are divided into, *Rice.* 1st, 2nd, 3rd, 4th, 2 R. 1 R. 8 A. 4 A. *Sugar & Cotton.* 1st, 2nd, 3rd, 4th, 3 R. 2¼ R. 2 R. 1¼ R. *Mulberry.* 1st, 2nd, 2¼ R. 2 R.
48	Vohomonkundo, ..	..	Ditto, ..	Nawabgunj, ..	79		
49	Chorkuye, ..	..	Ditto, ..	Ditto, ..	25		
50	Belghat, ..	Bhaleghautty, ..	Ditto, ..	Ditto, ..	2		
51	Azimghur, ..	..	Ditto, ..	Ditto, ..	11		
52	Bamongor, ..	..	Ditto, ..	Ghoraghat, ..	23		
53	Serpúr,	Sheerpúr, Gowreybary, ..	Ditto, ..	Ditto, ..	25		
54	Vindhora, ..	Nimdhera, ..	Ditto, ..	Khyetlal, ..	18		
55	Islampúr, ..	..	Ditto, ..	Ditto, ..	1		
56	Abdulpúr ..	..	Ditto, ..	Purusa, Lalbazar, Khyetlal, Ghoraghat, ..	70		
57	Aligang, ..	Allgong, ..	Ditto, ..	Lalbazar, ..	8		
58	Uchayi, ..	Wutchy, ..	Ditto, ..	Khyetlal, ..	11		
59	Mulgang, ..	..	..	Khyetlal, Ghoraghat, ..	7		
60	Chatnogor, ..	..	Ditto, ..	Ditto, ..	150		
61	Poladosi, ..	..	Ditto, ..				
62	Lalvari Khalisa, ..	..	Ditto, ..	Howrah, ..	20	87 Sekunderi cubits, Sq. feet, .. 22,529	Poli, 1 R. Khyar, 1 R.
63	Maldwar, ..	..	Tajpúr,	Thakurgram, Ranisongkol, Pirgunj, Hemtabad,	92	85¼ cubits of 20 inches Sq. feet 20,181.	1st, 2nd, 3rd, 3th, 1 R. 12 A. 8 A. 4 A.
64	Kholora, ..	..	Ditto,	Ranisongkol, Pirgunj, Kaliyagunj, Hemtabad, ..	114		
65	Toppe Mothurapúr, ..	..	Ditto,	Ranisongkol, Kaliyagunj, Hemtabad, Bongsihari, .	68		
66	Delaworpúr, ..	Delawerpore, .	Ditto,	Ranisongkol, Hemtabad, Bongsihari, Pirgunj, ..	159	84 Common 1¼ cbts. Sq. feet, .. 15,861; 74 Do. do.. .. 12,321	Inundated, 8 annas, 4 annas, Dry, 12 annas. 8 annas.
67	Haveli Tajpúr, ..	Havelly Tajipoor,	Ditto,	Ranisongkol, Kaliyagunj, Hemtabad, Pirgunj, ..	106	Probably the same with 65.	

No.							
68	Bhuyihara, ..	..	Tajpúr,	Pirgunj, Kaliyagunj, Hemtabad, ..	75 14 0	84¼ Cubits of 20 In. Sq. feet, .. 20,181	Nina, Dangga. R. 1. 4. 9 annas.
69	Surahor Monkoyi,	..	Jennutabad,	Kaliyagunj, Bongsihari, Jogodol, Gonggarampúr,	94 4 0	Calcutta Measure, ..	1st, 2nd, 3rd. 1 R. 12 A. 8 A.
70	Kasimpúr, ..	..	Ditto,	Kaliyagunj, Bongsihari, Jogodol, Maldeh, ..	134	Probably the same, ..	1st, 2nd, 3rd, 4th, 8 A. 6 A. 4 A. 2 A. This rent is nominal: the leases which I saw, where the rent is mentioned as 2 As. made the amt. of charges 10 As. average 12 As.
71	Rokonpúr, ..	Rokenpoor, ..	Ghoraghat and Jennutabad, ..	Kaliyagunj, Bongsihari, Jogodol, Maldeh, Howrah,	162	80 Sekunderi cubits, Sq. feet, .. 19,041	
72	Amirabad, ..	..	Jennutabad, ..	Maldeh, ..	34	79 Sekunderi cubits, Sq. feet, .. 18,526	
73	Shajadpúr, ..	..	Barbukabad, ..	Badolgachhi, ..	3		
74	Andolgong, ..	Undelgong, ..	Ghoraghat, ..	Lalbazar, Khyetlal, Ghoraghat, Nawabgunj,	84	84 Common cubits, Sq. feet, .. 15,861	Highland. Lowland. 3 R. 1¾ R. 3 A. to 12 A.
75	Baishazari, .	..	..	Ranisongkol, Pirgunj, Kaliyagunj, Hemtabad, Bongsihari, Jogodol, Maldeh, Potnitola, Badolgachhi, Potiram, Gonggarampúr, Rajarampúr. ..	93		
76	Chhyehazri, ..	..	..	Bongsihari, Jogodol, Maldeh, ..	19	These four Pergunnahs are so scattered that no estimate could be given.	
77	Radhabollobhpúr,	..	..	Kaliyagunj, Bongsihari, Jogodol, Maldeh, Potnitola, Gonggarampúr, ..	56		
78	Kantonogor, ..	..	..	Kaliyagunj, Bongsihari, Jogodol, Purusa, Potnitola, Badolgachhi, Lalbazar, Khyetlal, Potiram, Gonggarampúr, ..	240		
79	Kakjol, ..	..	Jennutabad, ..	Maldeh, ..	17		
80	Mosida, ..	Mussdha, ..	Barbukabad,	Jogodol, Purusa, Potnitola, Badolgachhi, ..	270		Garden, Sugar, Cotton, 5 to 20 R. 3 to 2 R. 1½ to 1 R. Rice. 1 R. to 10 Annas.
81	Jahanggirpúr ..	..	Ditto,	Potnitola, Badolgachhi, Khyetlal, Potiram, ..	418 7 4½	80 Secunderi cubits, Sq. feet, .. 19,041	
82	Fothejungpúr, ..	..	Ditto,	Badolgachhi, Lalbazar, Khyetlal, ..	294 15 17		
83	Pustaul, ..	Busstole, ..	Ditto, ..	Purusa, Potnitola, ..	299 11 7		

No. 8.—(Continued.)

No.	Present Name of Pergunnah.	Name in Mr. Gladwin's Ayeen Akbery.	Sircar in which situated.	Thannas in which situated.	Mauzas' Number.	Actual size of Bigah.	Division of Land and usual rent of each kind.
					B. C Ch.		
84	Chaura, ..	Chowra, ..	Barbukabad, ..	Purusa, ..	73 13 1	The part belonging to Jahanggirpúr at the same rate.	
85	Beerbukpúr, ..	Barbukpúr, ..	Ghoraghat, ..	Lalbazar, ..	40		
86	Khorida Selvorish,	Silberies, ..	Bazuha, ..	Khyetlal, ..	4		
87	Khorida Barbukpúr, ..	..	..	Badolgachhi, ..	19 2		
88	Khorida Chhirabazee, ..	..	Barbukabad, ..	Khyetlal, ..	4		
89	Soruppúr, ..	..	Ghoraghat, ..	Howrah, ..	57	56 guz or yards, Sq. feet,.... 26,786,	Poli, 2 R. Khyar. $1\frac{5}{8}$ R.
90	Ambari, ..	..	Panjra, ..	Lalbazar, Rajarampúr, Howrah, ..	72		
91	Sabek Soruppúr, ..	..	..	Howrah, ..	12		
92	Bobonpúr, ..	Bamonpúr, ..	Ghoraghat, ..	Ghoraghat, ..	88		
93	Joytaluk, ..	..	Ditto, ..	Lalbazar, Khyetlal, Ghoraghat, ..	16		
94	Sultanpúr, Ghoraghat, ..	Sultanpúr, ..	..	Ghoraghat, ..	32		
95	Ghagra, ..	Gogohra, ..	Tajpúr, ..	Kaliagunj, ..	9		
96	Baror, ..	..	Ditto, ..	Thakurgram, Ranisongkol, Hemtabad, Pirgunj, ..	29		
97	Hatinda, ..	..	..	Hemtabad, ..	2		
98	Surjyopúr, ..	..	..	Thakurgram, ..	17		
				Total,..	12,162 7 4		

NOTE—The total as given here is correct by the manuscript, but it does not correspond with the summation of the items (12,129, 11, 12): probably some errors in the figures have crept into the copy of Dr. Buchanan's original tables, or the total may be expressed in Calcutta bigahs, while the mauzas are of various measures as explained in column 7.—ED.

	Gonggarampúr.		Rajarampúr.		Howra.		Total.	
xp.	Imp.	Exp.	Imp.	Exp.	Imp.	Exp.	Imp.	Exp.
0,000	..	1,60,000	..	3,00,000	..	1,50,000	..	31,79,600
..	..	..	..	..	..	..	..	80,000
..	4,000	..	3,000	..	2,000	..	15,000	..
..	..	..	..	..	..	..	..	14,200
..	..	..	..	..	..	..	..	40,500
..	1,000	..	500	..	1,000	..	45,500	..
..	100	..	..	..	50	..	3,100	..
190	..	..	..	..	..	60	..	4,070
...	..	..	..	..	..	..	..	12,000
...	..	..	..	..	..	..	..	81,400
...	..	..	..	..	..	..	..	4,700
...	200	..	..	..	..	..	44,800	21,000
...	..	..	..	..	..	..	6,500	6,800
...	50.000	..	75,000	..	15,000	..	6,80,000	..
...	7,500	..	18,750	..	3,800	..	1,49,750	..
...	..	..	..	..	..	..	100	..
...	..	..	..	..	..	..	9,200	..
...	..	..	..	..	..	..	1,500	..
...	..	..	..	..	..	..	6,000	..
...	500	..	1,000	..	..	..	29,300	..
...	..	..	..	..	..	..	3,700	..
...	..	..	..	..	..	..	14,900	..
...	..	..	..	..	..	..	23,000	600
...	..	..	..	..	..	..	9,000	..
...	..	..	..	..	..	..	16,000	..
...	..	..	..	..	..	..	1,700	..
...	500	..	..	..	..	..	3,000	..
500	..	200	..	400	..	200	..	7,050
0,000	7,000	6,000	12,000	8,000	..	4,000	51,000	1,29,600
300	..	200	..	2,600	..	..	..	12,200
...	..	..	..	..	..	..	..	360
..	4,000	..	..	..	5,000	..	1,06,500	4,000
..	..	..	..	..	..	21,300	..	57,300
5,000	..	..	..	..	2,000	2,000	39,000	1,20,000
..	..	..	..	..	..	..	3,000	..
..	..	..	..	..	..	..	..	3,50,000
..	..	..	..	..	..	..	1,000	..
..	..	..	..	..	..	..	10,000	..
..	..	..	..	..	..	..	1,500	..
..	..	..	..	..	..	..	2,500	..
300	..	..	..	7,500	..	..	..	35,550
5,000	..	..	..	..	..	24,000	..	2,76,000
5000	..	..	..	..	..	4,000	..	66,000
5,000	..	10,500	..	7,000	..	42,000	..	2,49,900
2,290	74,800	1,76,900	1,10,250	3,25,500	28,850	2,47,560	12,75,550	47,52,830

's original table. By a gross error of copying the total of exports was in the